W9-COZ-401

The First Hollywood Musicals:
A Critical Filmography of 171 Features,
1927 through 1932

The First Hollywood Musicals

A Critical Filmography of 171 Features, 1927 through 1932

Edwin M. Bradley

McFarland & Company, Inc., Publishers
Jefferson, North Carolina, and London

Frontispiece: **Daniel L. Haynes and Nina Mae McKinney starred in King Vidor's groundbreaking *Hallelujah!* (1929).**

British Library Cataloguing-in-Publication data are available

Library of Congress Cataloguing-in-Publication Data

Bradley, Edwin M., 1958–
    The first Hollywood musicals : a critical filmography of 171
features, 1927 through 1932 / by Edwin M. Bradley.
       p.   cm.
    Includes bibliographical references and index.
    ISBN 0-89950-945-2 (lib. bdg. : 50 # alk. paper) ∞
    1. Music films—United States—History and criticism. I. Title.
PN1995.9.M86B73   1996
791.43'6—dc20   96-11762
                                               CIP

Manufactured in the United States of America

McFarland & Company, Inc., Publishers
  Box 611, Jefferson, North Carolina 28640

For Bernice Claire, Dorothy Lee and Anita Page,
and Kathy, Andrew and James

TABLE OF CONTENTS

INTRODUCTION

All Talking! All Singing! All Dancing!

All Vernon Dent had to do was put his lips together—and blow. The comedy short on which the rotund veteran actor toiled in the spring of 1929 was one of those new-fangled talking pictures everyone was worrying about, but the request from director Mack Sennett to enter a scene whistling a few bars of something-or-other seemed simple enough for him. Dent drew from his memory bank a song he'd heard years before, and the take went smoothly. Then the film was sent to a laboratory for processing. Back came a missive demanding to know what Dent had whistled, and how much. Nobody seemed to remember, not even the actor himself, until Sennett had the finished film run in a projection room.

There, the "King of Comedy," a cinema pioneer whose Hollywood reputation was now in free fall, learned the awful truth: Dent had whistled more than 12 bars. The penny-pinched Sennett would have to pay a fee to a foresighted publishing house that had just slapped a new copyright on Dent's ditty in the probability of its use in the infant talkie medium. The alternative was to reshoot the scene, and that would cost a bit more than the $500 the perturbed Sennett would end up shelling out because of his trouper's taste in mood music. The title of the long-forgotten song is insignificant; so, even, is the humor in a master of slapstick having to endure such a figurative pratfall. But the incident, as obscure as it is, does illustrate the uncertainty and trepidation with which movie-makers approached one of the most tumultuous periods in the history of film—the transition from silence to sound.

Mack Sennett's venture was a two-reel exercise in low comedy, not a two-hour rehashing of a Broadway-based song extravaganza, but Sennett had lots of perplexed company. The birth of the Hollywood musical—which roughly paralleled the birth of the talking film—was troubled by growing pains: haste, waste, failed experiments, shortsightedness and just plain bad decision-making. Too bad, for in 1929 and 1930, the first two full years of the American sound movie, it was rightly determined that the same public fascinated by the novelty of filmed talk would be dazzled by the spectacle of filmed song and dance. The musical became the industry's most lucrative form—until the greedy studios almost killed the genre by glutting the market with too many films that looked and sounded like clones of each other. Some of the same marquees that trumpeted "All Talking! All Singing! All Dancing!" attractions were, months later, assuring customers that "This Is NOT a Musical." At the end of 1930, a critic could conclude a review of an operetta called *Viennese Nights* with this: "Plenty of good production all in acceptable color, direction beyond reproach, well assembled cast and everything, but it's a musical. Let's see."

That we have since seen the likes of Fred Astaire, Alice Faye and Judy Garland is proof that the musical did not die a-borning, but not until the darkest Depression days of 1933 did the genre freshen its approach. Darryl F. Zanuck's gamble in making *42nd Street*, and the anointing of Busby Berkeley to create its visual pyrotechnics, gave the form a needed shot in the arm. Within a year, the studios would be back to producing musicals by the score (no pun intended)—although they never again would churn them out quite as blindly as they had back in 1930.

So, beyond its prodigiousness, why should we care about the first wave of movie musicals? Why recall a bunch of hoary, failed antiques that nobody remembers? For one, they were not all failures. Some are films of surprising beauty and creativity; others are much less arty but retain a certain timeless charm. True, for every *Hallelujah!* or *The Love Parade* or *Sunnyside Up,* there are a few more in the lesser class of *The Lottery Bride, Howdy Broadway* or *Dangerous Nan McGrew.* But of the 1927–1932 crop, the 171 films examined in this book, even the worst is not without historical value. The musical-film clichés that we have come to expect, and often to take delight in, were being invented practically at the dawn of sound. Without *The Broadway Melody,* there would have been no *Singin' in the Rain.* If Walter Wanger had not talked the Marx Brothers into committing *The Cocoanuts* to celluloid, we might not have had *Duck Soup.* We also might never have captured on film Bing Crosby, Ethel Merman, Maurice Chevalier, Jeanette MacDonald, Ginger Rogers and Jimmy Durante, to name some of the more endearing performers who were either recruited by Hollywood during the advent of sound, or who received career boosts through exposure in early musicals.

As it sought, and attracted, all manner of talent, Hollywood in 1929 and 1930 became a giant tryout camp. Although many of the auditions did not click, some of those who tried and failed were at least interesting. Great performers such as John McCormack, Gertrude Lawrence, Sophie Tucker, Lawrence Tibbett, Jack Buchanan and Marilyn Miller were introduced to large segments of the American public as they sang before the unyielding camera and sweated under the demanding hot lights. Even John Wayne played one of his first significant roles in a musical. The challenge for the first makers of musicals was to create a form distinctive to the medium, a goal that seemed all too unreachable with the preponderance of films that were little more than replicas of stage shows. What worked before the footlights in front of an intimate theater audience did not always play to people sitting in the dark before a big screen. Painful lessons were learned, but rather than join the present-day snickerers at the quirks of the early talkies, we should be impressed at the amazing speed of the sound revolution. To watch *The Singing Fool* and *42nd Street* in the same sitting is to marvel at their lack of similarity beyond director (Lloyd Bacon) and studio (Warner Bros.), yet they were produced within less than five years of each other.

When I began this project, there was only one book that had dealt exclusively with the first fascinating years of the movie musical. But Miles Kreuger's *The Movie Musical from Vitaphone to 42nd Street,* published in 1975 and out of print at this writing, carries the subtitle *As Reported in a Great Fan Magazine;* it is primarily a compilation of articles from *Photoplay* magazine. *Photoplay* was indeed one of the more important of the movie magazines of the time, but its pages provide little critical discussion of the content of most of the films. The goal here is to provide a wider-ranging, multi-source examination.

That has required the viewing of as many of the films as possible. This was no easy task, considering that prints of many of them no longer exist, because of chemical deterioration, legal complications, or poor maintenance by uncaring owners. Fortunately, one of the better-kept film libraries is the MGM–United Artists archive, now owned by Ted Turner, which includes all of Metro-Goldwyn-Mayer's vintage product, plus most RKO properties and Warner Bros.' pre–1948 output. During the first two years of the Turner Network Television cable channel, Turner's people cracked open the vaults to screen some of the earliest talkies— many of them musicals. Those of us who were dedicated enough to stay up until—or stumble out of bed at—3 and 4 a.m. to view *A Lady's Morals* or *On with the Show!* got a rare treat. Those who were foresighted enough to commit them to their VCRs would consider themselves lucky that they had done so before the channel's repertoire became limited to macho Westerns, war sagas—and, as one of my film-buff friends groused, "basketball, *endless* basketball!" However, a new channel, Turner Classic Movies, lately has been offering the same vintage delights—and without commercials. Through television viewings, videocassettes and laser-discs, prints owned by private collectors, prints in archives and a handful of soundtracks sans video, I was able to see or hear all or part of about two-thirds of the films chosen for this book.

Not all of the 171 movies covered here are musicals in the strictest sense—if one uses a rather imprecise definition that has to do with the significance of the music to a film's story, its frequency within, and the importance of who is performing it. Still, I have intended to be as inclusive as possible, keeping in mind that in these embryonic days it was not precisely clear what a movie musical should be. There were no absolutes about integrating songs with story; indeed, there was a Broadway tradition of presenting musical numbers that stopped the story dead, mainly for comic relief, and often with performers who were otherwise barely seen or not seen at all!

Some of the films in this book, such as *The Great Gabbo* and *The Cock-Eyed World*, dared not to be included because of their number of songs, even if the songs had little to do with the plot. Others—such as *Roadhouse Nights*, a gangster drama with four song numbers by Helen Morgan and Jimmy Durante—I have counted because they spotlighted musical talent that was crucial to their appeal. There are only three songs, all quite incidental, in *Check and Double Check*, a comedy that brought radio's Amos 'n' Andy to the screen, but said numbers are performed by Duke Ellington and his orchestra, in their feature debut. Only one song is performed on camera in *Follow the Leader*, but the singer is Ethel Merman and the feature film is her first. In fact, there were scores of non-musicals from the early sound era that were graced with a song or two. This trend may have prompted the celebrated wit Dorothy Parker, hired by MGM to write dialogue for the 1929 version of the warhorse melodrama *Madame X*, to ask director Lionel Barrymore, "Why not jazz up the story, stick in a few hot numbers and call it *Mammy X*?"

One area left undercovered, for reasons of time and space, was that of the musical short subject. A historian will write, for example, that Rudy Vallee made his movie debut in *The Vagabond Lover* (1929) or that Ginger Rogers was introduced to filmgoers in *Young Man of Manhattan* (1930) when both actually made their debuts in shorts. While studios were churning out feature-length musicals, most were producing one- or two-reelers with music. There were the "Vitaphone Varieties" and "Broadway Brevities" series from Warner Bros., "Movietone" selections and "Colortone Revues" at MGM, "Christie Talking Plays" and "Screen Songs" from Paramount, and "Melody Comedies" at Pathé. An appendix in this book covers some ground, but the short subject remains a fertile field for cinema researchers.

The length of the entries depends on the significance of each film to the history of the genre—or, in some cases, on its legitimacy as a musical, but I have devoted extra space to some films that may have been underrated or too seldom discussed. Some of the very best early musicals, particularly those by Ernst Lubitsch and Rouben Mamoulian, have been analyzed strenuously, and despite my view that I have relatively little to add to the mass of critical commentary, I have devoted an appropriate amount of space to them. Frankly, I found myself drawn to the more obscure, especially the pretty-good obscure, which is why you'll find more on *The Dance of Life, It's a Great Life, Sweet Kitty Bellairs* and *Kiss Me Again* than you would in any other book. Or, for that matter, more on the likes of Harry Richman, Rosetta Duncan and even "Whispering" Jack Smith—entertainers captured fleetingly, if erratically, on film before various factors forced their return to more familiar mediums.

As to the credit listings, some explanation is necessary:

Premiere dates: Mainly the New York or Los Angeles opening of the film, whichever date was first. But some films never made it to either city, or opened ahead of time in smaller markets. I sought to use the earliest date I could find.

New York opening: The dates and performance totals of plays that were adapted into movies are all taken from Burns Mantle's "Best Plays" series.

Songs or **Songs/Musical Numbers:** My guideline was to list music (not just songs, but ballets and symphonic works) presented, vocally or instrumentally and at more than fragmental length, in a formal context of a "number," plus music informally performed by a major player at more than fragmental length. Some purely incidental music is included, but only if I knew it was written for the film discussed. These standards may not be as exact for movies that were unavailable for screening. I have also, when possible, included the performer(s) of every song. Most of this information was garnered from personal viewings and some more came from contemporary reviews; however, listings are incomplete for some movies, usually because they were not available for viewing. To verify song titles and writing credits, I relied greatly on copyright information compiled by the Library of Congress. This led to some titles listed differently than the norm. For example, we may know the song from *The Vagabond Lover* as "I Love You, Believe Me, I Love You," but it was copyrighted as "The Dream of My Heart." And "That's the Song of Paree," from *Love Me Tonight,* was copyrighted as "The Song of Paree." For many films, the cue sheets on file at the American Society of Composers, Authors and Publishers were crucial in establishing musical content. Although some from these early years are incomplete, most of the cue sheets list, in order, the title and composer of every piece of music heard in a film, and usually whether a song was performed vocally and if it was complete or partial. What the ASCAP sheets cannot reveal is the specific performer of the music and its relationship to the activity on screen. And the films themselves were not always foolproof. Some surviving prints are missing numbers that were in the original release—*Rio Rita, Say It with Songs* and *Be Yourself!* are three of many examples. Other films, such as Maurice Chevalier's early pictures for Paramount, were also released in foreign-language versions, sometimes with whole numbers added or subtracted. Reference books are rife with errors on song lists; even the wonderful new American Film Institute catalog for 1931 to 1940 repeats mistakes found in earlier sources. My hope is that you will find this to be the most thorough published source for listings of music in pre–1933 musicals.

Disc: These are the U.S.-issued 78 rpm records recorded in a studio in connection with the release of a film by whoever performed it in the film, or long-playing records of music taken directly from the movie soundtrack (marked "ST"). I have included bootleg LPs, as the interest in them among collectors is too significant to ignore.

Video: At a trickle, early musicals are being made available to the home video market, on VHS but also lately through laserdisc. The best series of laserdiscs is MGM-UA's "The Dawn of Sound" collection, on which are rarely seen feature films in complete or partial form (including surviving bits of the long-lost *The Rogue Song* and *Gold Diggers of Broadway*), as well as short subjects.

Also, a note on lost films: I have usually prefaced any labeling of a so-called "lost" film with words like "apparently" and "believed to be." Prints of films that are feared to be non-existent may be misfiled in studio vaults, in the possession of private collectors, or reposing in unknown foreign archives. Material is being found all the time. Still, for the interest of the reader, I have endeavored to point out the movies thought to be unavailable.

I would like to thank these performers of the era who were gracious enough to provide recollections directly to me: George Burns, Bernice Claire, Douglas Fairbanks Jr., Dorothy Lee, Maureen O'Sullivan, Anita Page, Marion Shilling and the late William Bakewell. Those who are old enough to have lived through the transition to sound, much less experienced it directly, are dwindling in number.

I traveled all over the country in researching this book, but my journeys were made fruitful by many helpful people. Worthy of special mention is Miles Kreuger and his Institute of the American Musical. Not only was Miles personally helpful to me with the identification of songs in films I had not yet been able to see or could not see, but it has been through his efforts that more than a few of the movies in this book are extant at all. He has aided archives in preserving what may be the only remaining prints of some films, and his accumulation of published and unpublished research on the formative years of the musical is incomparable. In 1971, for the New York Museum of Modern Art, he organized an unrivaled series of early movie musicals, "The Roots of the American Musical Film (1927-32)," that did more than anything else to bring these films to the attention of other historians and the general public.

On the West Coast, Stuart Galbraith examined archival material (production records, newspaper clippings, press books) that I could not view in person. He also provided much-needed moral support. On the East Coast, Bill Cappello found addresses of some hard-to-find actors and located death certificates for Everett Marshall, Zelma O'Neal and Ethelind Terry, plus a long-sought year of death for Charles Kaley. Roy Hemming, author-historian and longtime musicals aficionado, graciously critiqued some of this manuscript in progress. My editor friend Don Dahlstrom read over the entire work, providing helpful advice. Dennis Ferrara read some of the chapters with an eye on the discographies. David A. Berry, assistant manager of the ASCAP cue sheets section, made available photocopies of a large number of sheets. Other thank-yous go to the Margaret Herrick Library of the Academy of Motion Picture Arts and Sciences (Samuel A. Gill); the University of Southern California for its Warner Bros. and MGM collections (Ned Comstock); the New York Museum of Modern Art Department of Film (Charles Silver); the New York City Public Library at Lincoln Center for its Billy Rose Theatre Collection (Robert Taylor); the Wisconsin Center for Film and Theater Research (Harry Miller, Maxine Fleckner Ducey, Crystal Hyde); the University of California at Los Angeles Film and Television Archive (Robert Rosen, Lou Ellen Kramer, Charles Hopkins, Eric Aijala); the Library of Congress (James Cozart, Rosemary Haines); the Great Lakes Cinephile Society (Dennis Atkinson); The Vitaphone Project (Ron Hutchinson); Laurence Austin (William Austin's son); Randal Malone (Anita Page's publicist); Lynette Garlan (Bernice Claire's niece); Film Favorites (the source for most of the stills); plus Michael Schwibs, David Ragan, Joe Savage, Leo Willette, Alan Cooperman, Richard Barrack, Charles Ziarko, Louis Spitzler, Mark Schroeder, Steven Tompkins, Jason Almeida, the late Arthur Siegel, Berthe Schuchat, Kathy Dahlstrom, David Forsmark , David Larzelere, Gene Mierzejewski, and my aunt Mary Ann Bradley. Mike Riha and Cookie Wascha, my supervisors at *The Flint Journal*, where I am the entertainment editor and movie critic, permitted me to alter my work schedule to accomodate time to work on this project.

My in-laws, Walter and Lois Jones, provided lodging during my stay in Los Angeles. My parents, James and Linda Bradley, are the reasons for my being. And, of course, I cannot fail to thank my wife, Kathy, and my sons, Andrew and James. They have me back now.

Edwin M. Bradley
January 1, 1996

CHAPTER 1

1927–1928: *"Who the Hell Wants to Hear Actors Talk?"*

If you were one of the 6 million inhabitants of New York City on October 6, 1927, you were likely to spend some part of your day tuned to the world's most popular mode of mass entertainment. With the turn of a radio dial on this autumn Thursday, you could tune into the second game of the World Series between the hometown Yankees and the Pittsburgh Pirates, hear a lecture on federal law reform, listen to the latest update on the stock market or be uplifted by a sermon or a poetry recital. But more often than anything else, you could hear music—live and by all manner of performers. There were sopranos and baritones, classical violinists and pop piano plunkers, soloists and ensembles. Their names are mostly forgotten now, but they kept their listeners at home and diverted them from a rival, and formerly more powerful, medium—the motion picture.

The men who ran Hollywood grumbled about their upstart adversary, but radio was not above lending the movies some free publicity. At 8 p.m. on this October 6 in New York, station WRNY would broadcast highlights from the world premiere of a film called *The Jazz Singer*. There would be interviews with stage and screen celebrities arriving for the ballyhooed opening at the Warner Theatre, plus music played by an orchestra hired especially for the occasion. But had WRNY thought to interview the notables as they exited the house, its listeners would have been eagerly informed about the success of a dazzling experiment by one bold little studio—in a movie for which the curious soon would be lining up for blocks. The integration of music and dialogue into a few minutes of a feature-length film propelled a revolution of sound that was a direct response to

the popularity of radio. *The Jazz Singer,* billed by Warner Bros. Pictures as its "supreme triumph," also launched a revolution within a revolution, for although it was not the first talking picture (as legend would have it), it was the first movie musical. Within two years of its premiere, Hollywood would be filled with singers, dancers, composers and choreographers blanketing the market with all-talking, all-singing, all-dancing productions. Al Jolson predicted it, sort of: They ain't seen nothin' yet.

Actually, music had long been a part of the moviegoing experience. As far back as the 1890s, the primitive moving pictures displayed in penny arcades or peep shows were accompanied by phonographic arrangements. During the first decade of this century, piano players in nickelodeons pounded out songs direct from Tin Pan Alley to be played prior to a screening or even to be worked into the movie's action. Soon, films had their own formal scores (*The Birth of a Nation*, in 1915, was among the first), which were played by pianists, or, in big cities, by pit orchestras. If a film had no formal score, the musicians would improvise background themes appropriate to the mood and emotions on screen.

The beauty of the silent movie was that it truly was never silent. "There never was a silent film," noted Irving Thalberg, the great production chief at Metro-Goldwyn-Mayer.

> We'd finish a picture, show it in one of our projection rooms, and come out shattered. It would be awful. We'd have high hopes for the picture, work our hands off on it, and the result was always the same. Then we'd show it in a theater, with a girl down in the pit, pounding away at a piano, and there would be

all the difference in the world. Without that music, there wouldn't have been a movie industry at all.[1]

In the 1920s, theme songs became a convenient way to publicize film, star and tune at once. Song pluggers would prevail upon theater musicians to plug a song prior to a film's release, and the longer the movie remained in circulation, the longer its sheet music would sell. By 1928, the last full year of silent-film production, "Charmaine," from the World War I comedy *What Price Glory?*, and "Diane," from the romantic drama *Seventh Heaven*, each had sold nearly 1 million copies of sheet music and had contributed mightily to the box office successes of their speechless films for Fox Studios. "Ramona" plugged a middling romantic drama starring Delores Del Rio, who sang the delicate title theme, and helped it to a gross of more than $1.5 million. In many cases, theme songs were easily forgotten ditties designed solely to promote their films, which resulted in some ludicrous titling. *The Woman Disputed*, a 1928 Norma Talmadge weepie for United Artists, boasted "Woman Disputed I Love You." Almost as laughable was the title of the tune attached by Paramount to the college story *Varsity*: "My Varsity Girl, I'll Cling to You."

There were even "silent musicals"—adaptations of stage shows that often used the original songs as suggested accompaniment. As early as 1894, Thomas Edison's Kinetograph was capturing on film many artists then appearing in Broadway musicals; their performances were excerpted from the shows *A Gaiety Girl*, *The Passing Show*, *A Milk White Flag* and many others.[2] In 1926, Eddie Cantor made his feature-film debut in Paramount's loose adaptation of his Broadway hit *Kid Boots*, but it failed to sell. MGM, however, made a mint when it paired John Gilbert and Mae Murray with the exacting director Erich von Stroheim in *The Merry Widow* (1925), adapted from the Franz Lehár operetta. Even before Marilyn Miller transferred her New York success to a sound *Sally*, that musical comedy was made by First National in 1925 with the popular Colleen Moore in the title role. Two years before his *The Love Parade* became a seminal screen musical, Ernst Lubitsch directed Norma Shearer and Ramon Novarro in MGM's *The Student Prince in Old Heidelberg* (1927). The film was meant to

capitalize upon the Sigmund Romberg operetta *The Student Prince*, the longest-running Broadway musical of the 1920s, but was essentially a retelling of the 1902 play on which the operetta was based, with entirely new music as recommended accompaniment.

In the mid to late '20s, the silent cinema achieved some of its greatest artistic triumphs: *Sunrise*, an expressionistic drama directed by German import F. W. Murnau; *The Big Parade*, King Vidor's shattering antiwar saga with matinee idol John Gilbert in the role of his career; Frank Borzage's romantic *Seventh Heaven*, with Janet Gaynor and Charles Farrell; inventive feature-length comedies from Charlie Chaplin, Buster Keaton and Harold Lloyd. But attendance in movie houses fell as radio made inroads on their audience. Filmmakers tried gimmicks to bring back customers, including a primitive form of Technicolor and a widescreen format (Paramount used Magnascope for its big-budget action pictures *Old Ironsides* and *Wings*), but they were hardly worth the expense. Movies could do everything but talk, and they could do no more with music than use it as a kind of adjunct.

There was no foolproof way to synchronize dialogue and music with action, although it had been attempted almost continuously in American and European laboratories since before the turn of the century. Mostly, these were "sound-on-disc" formats, in which the sound was recorded on cylinder or flat-disc phonograph records and played to match the projected material. Because the records were easily damaged or worn, the synchronization was often imprecise. A more advanced system was developed around 1907 by the French inventor Eugene Lauste, a former employee of Thomas Edison. Lauste was the first to create a "sound-on-film" format, a combination of the visual images and a photographically recorded sound track on the same strip of celluloid. But, like so many pioneers in the development of this technology, he could not find a way to amplify the sound so it could be heard in a large theater.

Lauste's mentor, Edison, tried to meld picture and sound more than once, starting with his first publicly shown motion picture, accompanied by a phonograph record, at the 1893 Columbian Exposition in Chicago. But when he did so in 1913 with his new and improved

On a Manhattan movie set in 1926, a clumsy, soundproof booth kept camera noise from reaching the microphones—but restricted the camera's movement.

Kinetophone, his poorly recorded actors and singers sounded like foghorns. This happened all too frequently when the film was projected at the wrong speed. After a few weeks' "honeymoon" period from the fascinated viewers who watched these little productions between live acts in vaudeville houses, the lowering of the screen became a clear signal for boos and jeers.

"I can remember that we talked into a horn, and it was sort of elevated," the actress Viola Dana told historians Kevin Brownlow and David Gill in a 1970s interview for the *Hollywood* television series.

> My elder sister ... made one of them [Kinetophone films] and she played a little fairy queen. Here came this little, dainty thing, in a skirt and everything, pretty. And she was supposed to say, "I am the fairy queen" or something. And she came out saying [affecting a deep voice] "I AM THE FAIRY QUEEN" ... which was fantastic!

Although musical films as we know them could not be produced reliably, musical performers from the era were captured in short sound presentations. Beginning in 1904, Leon Gaumont (later to become a major producer of British films) used his Chronophone to make films of top British entertainers such as Harry Lauder and Vesta Tilley.[3] In 1908-09, J. A. Whitman's Cameraphone—the first American disc system to gain a degree of success—captured the likes of Blanche Ring, Anna Held, Eva Tanguay (singing "I Don't Care") and Stella Mayhew (in a "coon" song called "I Guess I'm Bad") for posterity, although the quality of their efforts varied widely. The Cameraphone studio was located above Daly's Theatre on Broadway, so it had convenient access to top stage talent. The lackluster synchronization of one of the programs prompted this comment from a reviewer for *Moving Picture World*: "Perhaps in the near future it will be properly

Mary Astor and John Barrymore share a tense moment during Warner Bros.' *Don Juan* (1926) — the first fully synchronized feature film.

adjusted so closely that the action of the pictures will be in perfect consonance with the words."[4]

It took the great director D. W. Griffith to become the first to insert a song into a feature-length film, although the experiment was hardly worth bragging about. For his 1921 drama *Dream Street,* a trilogy of moralistic tales based on the writings of Thomas Burke, Griffith had his leading man, Ralph Graves, record a love song that would be matched to an appropriate scene. The system used was the sound-on-disc Photokinema, developed by Orlando Kellum a decade before. Griffith's motives were less artistic than capitalistic. *Dream Street* had already begun its New York run to disappointing grosses, and Kellum's company suggested that the insertion of sound would be a potential attraction for the film. The director also recorded a prologue in which he explained "The Evolution of Motion Pictures." The revamped *Dream Street* was teamed with a group of Kellum-pro-

duced musical and dramatic short subjects and premiered at New York's new Town Hall center on May 1, 1921, five days after Graves sang his song at the Kellum studios.[5] However, the recording and synchronization were so clumsy that Griffith dropped the sound content from the picture after its run at the Town Hall.

Much more successful was the electronics pioneer Lee De Forest, who invented the audion amplifier tube and what became the modern sound track. He made his first talking picture (of himself) in 1921, and by 1923, his Phonofilm system made its theatrical debut with a program that accompanied Paramount's *Bella Donna,* Pola Negri's first American film. Operating out of a tiny studio in New York City, De Forest produced more than 1,000 short subjects by 1927. His product included sound dramas, newsreels, condensed adaptations of stage musicals, and numbers by early stage, radio, and vaudeville performers, among them Eddie Cantor, Sophie Tucker, Harry Richman,

George Jessel, Harry Lauder, Chic Sale and, in his famous recitation of "Casey at the Bat," DeWolf Hopper. But De Forest was no showman, and his lack of publicity savvy left him a failure at generating any kind of public appetite for talking movies.

That task was left to a minor studio on the West Coast. In 1925, the four siblings who ran the two-year-old Warner Bros. company—Harry, Jack, Sam and Albert—sought a new way to promote their stable of stars, the most bankable of which were a Shakespearean actor (John Barrymore) and a dog (Rin Tin Tin). So they bought a small Los Angeles radio station and rechristened it KFWB. They needed the publicity the station could provide because they had big deals in mind. Then they expanded their space by buying the old Vitagraph studios in Brooklyn, along with the defunct company's North American theater exchanges, and, for a recording facility, the deserted Manhattan Opera House. They established a partnership with Western Electric, a subsidary of the American Telephone and Telegraph Company, and Bell Telephone Laboratories to form, on April 20, 1926, the Vitaphone Corporation for the express purpose of continuing their experiments with sound.

Strange as it may seem now, the Warners were not aiming to introduce dialogue to movies; they simply wanted to furnish them with pre-recorded sound, which would save theater owners the cost of hiring live musicians. The brothers hailed from a small town (Youngstown, Ohio) and they had accumulated the funds to open their own studio by exhibiting other people's movies in fleabag theaters in tank towns. Possibly they realized the inequity in major-city moviegoers hearing symphony musicians with their movies while audiences in smaller markets were lucky to have any more than a single pianist. In any case, the brothers were firm about limiting their use of sound to background music. "Who the hell wants to hear actors talk?" was the reason offered by Harry Warner, the business-minded member of the clan.[6]

That question would remain unanswered only until August 6, 1926, the date of the premiere, in New York, of the first synchronized feature film, *Don Juan*, directed by Alan Crosland and starring John Barrymore. *Don Juan* offered a musical score, which was painstakingly composed by William Axt, David Mendoza and Major Edward Bowes, and sound effects, which were most conspicuously heard in Barrymore's climatic sword battle with the villainous Montagu Love. These noises were novel enough, but the first-night Warners Theatre audience was more impressed by the Vitaphone "prelude," which consisted of a short spoken introduction by a very stiff Will Hays, head of the Motion Picture Producers Association, and musical specialities by seven acts, all but one from the classical realm.

The 107-piece New York Philharmonic Orchestra, conducted by Henry Hadley, opened the musical program with the Overture from *Tannhäuser;* the youthful Metropolitan Opera star Marion Talley sang "Caro Nome" from *Rigoletto;* and violinist Mischa Elman played Dvořák's "Humoresque." A novelty number by pop guitarist Roy Smeck provided a needed break from the highbrow fare, then Efrem Zimbalist (violin) and Harold Bauer (piano) teamed for variations from Beethoven's "Kreutzer Sonata." Met star Giovanni Martinelli offered an impassioned "Vesti la giubba" from *I Pagliacci,* and, finally, Anna Case weighed in with "La Fiesta," with assistance from the Metropolitan Opera chorus, the Cansino Dancers (including Eduardo Cansino, the father of Rita Hayworth) and the full orchestra.

The numbers were staged with a minimum of complexity—the singers barely had to move—although some members of the press complained about the murky acoustics and the wooden delivery of Miss Talley. "Long shots—and good, long ones—were just invented for that girl," opined *Photoplay.*[7] Mostly, though, the papers ate up the musical stuff. *The New York Morning Telegraph* called it "perhaps the most brilliant motion picture premiere that was ever held." *The New York Times* declared the Vitaphone "a marvelous device … the future of this new contrivance is boundless."[8] As other theaters made themselves available to exhibit Vitaphone, the *Don Juan* program ran for nearly eight months, at a gross of nearly $800,000.

But "boundless" was hardly the word for the Vitaphone's future, for the system was fraught with peril. This was, after all, a sound-on-disc format. The wax records used were inclined to develop a surface hiss and, with loud noises, skip grooves, thus fouling up the synchronization. The arc lights used for filming had to be replaced, for their "sizzle" could be heard on the recordings. An even bigger drawback, however, was the noisy whirring of the hand-cranked camera, which forced its enclosure in a small, soundproof and practically immovable booth. This limited mobility of the camera, which had become so nimble in the silent cinema, made the sound film static and its players stationary.

But Vitaphone was new, and an intrigued public wanted more of it. So the Warners, flush with the success of *Don Juan* and Vitaphone, rushed out more shorts to accompany score-synchronized features. The second Vitaphone program, which opened the comedy *The Better 'Ole* in its premiere on October 5, 1926, was more popularly oriented in its repertoire; the warm reception for Roy Smeck's performance must have made an impact. It included baritone Reinald Werrenrath singing "The Long, Long Trail" and "The Heart of a Rose" and The Four Aristocrats warbling "jazzy songs and melodies." George Jessel presented a monologue and an Irving Berlin tune, and there were appearances by the comic brothers Eugene and Willie Howard and the singer Elsie Janis, but all of them were overshadowed by a blackface appearance by the most popular entertainer in the world. *Al Jolson in a Plantation Act* began with a brief monologue, then his forceful renditions of "April Showers," "When the Red, Red Robin Comes Bob, Bob, Bobbin' Along" and "Rock-a-Bye Your Baby with a Dixie Melody." The first-night audience was silent, commented a witness, "so keen was everybody to catch every word and note of the popular entertainer, and when each number was ended it was obvious that there was not a still pair of hands in the house."[9]

This Vitaphone program scored even more strongly than the first, and Warner Bros. moved to put out more. But the studio soon had good reason for uncertainty. None of its competitors—the "Big Five" of Paramount, MGM, Universal, First National and Producers' Distributing Corporation—were lining up to rent the Vitaphone system, for they had met secretly in December 1926 and agreed to hold off on sound, mainly because of the tremendous cost of retooling their facilities for it. However, the maverick among the majors, William Fox, announced a month later that his company was developing a competing sound-on-film format

called Movietone. This system was very similar to Phonofilm; in fact, its inventors, Theodore W. Case and Earl I. Sponable, had worked with De Forest. It was also much less cumbersome than Vitaphone, for there was no fiddling with the fallible wax records. Movietone made its public debut on January 21, 1927, at the Sam H. Harris Theatre in New York in a program of songs sung by Requel Meller that preceded Fox's big war comedy *What Price Glory?*

Harry Warner was forced to sell $4 million of his own bank stock to keep Warner Bros. solvent, and the brothers decided to take the gamble of Vitaphoning a feature-length film. The property chosen was *The Jazz Singer*, a play adapted by Samson Raphaelson from his short story "The Day of Atonement." Warner Bros. had purchased the rights to the play for $50,000 on June 4, 1926, for use as a silent feature for George Jessel, who was then starring in the play on Broadway. Jessel seemed to be a natural for the role of Jack Robin (né Jakie Rabinowitz), a cantor's son torn between the modern footlights and ancient familial traditions. Not only did he have the stage identification, he already had appeared in Vitaphone shorts. Although Jessel was signed by Warners in 1926 with *The Jazz Singer* in mind, he first appeared for the studio in what would be a profitable ethnic comedy, *Private Izzy Murphy*.

Yet, sometime between the end of 1926 and May 26, 1927, when Al Jolson signed on for *The Jazz Singer*, something happened to sour the studio on Jessel, or vice versa. The show-business trade paper *Variety* reported that Jessel had become upset over Warners' alteration of the play's ending, in which religion won out over showbiz, and its refusal to cast Jewish actors as Robin's parents.[10] Another story, supported by Jack L. Warner, later claimed that Jessel wanted an extra $10,000 that the brothers were willing to pay but not inclined to guarantee in writing.[11] The success of *Don Juan* had inspired Warner Bros. to decide to make *The Jazz Singer* as a synchronized film, and Jessel allegedly wanted the extra money for sound-related royalties. Also, Jolson—renowned as the "World's Greatest Entertainer"—was a bigger name than Jessel, and would be a better fit now that Warner Bros. was considering *The Jazz Singer* to be a prestige sound project.

Late in his life, retired from a career as a film producer and America's "Toastmaster

General," Jessel (1898–1981) told an interviewer:

> Harry Warner offered me $25,000 in cash and $75,000 in stock to do the picture. But he wouldn't ever put the deal on paper. ... Warner wouldn't do it because he and his brothers didn't have any money. ... One morning, Jolson got up early [he was sharing a hotel suite with Jessel] and he said, "You go back to sleep, kid. I'm going out to play golf." Instead, he went straight to the studio and signed the contract to do *The Jazz Singer*. I didn't even know that he'd been approached. ... When we talked about it, I said, "How did you get the picture?" (He said,) "I put up about a million dollars of my own money."[12]

Jolson was paid $75,000 in cash—a third of it as a down payment, and the rest in installments—to do *The Jazz Singer*. Sources differ as to whether he put up any of his own money, although the amount probably was much lower than the $1 million claimed by Jessel.[13]

If Jolson (1886–1950) comes off as the heavy in Jessel's story, it is no fluke. For all his fabulous talent—sometimes unfathomable to modern audiences who can't get past his blackface schtick—he was a cad. Vain in the extreme, he chafed at even the slightest hint of competition among his peers, as Jessel's tale indicates. Yet it was the heart on his sleeve that so endeared him to his public. Jolson could put across a song like no other because his audience knew it was backed by his heart and soul. In *The Jazz Singer*, Mary Dale, the actress whom Jack Robin loves, tells him (via title), "There are lots of jazz singers, but *you* have a tear in your voice." She might just as well been referring to the man playing that jazz singer; Jolson was a cantor's child himself, and author Raphaelson's admitted inspiration for writing "The Day of Atonement."[14] Jolson's self-evaluation was more direct: "I won't say that I'm the best singer in the world—I'll just say I sound better than anybody else."[15]

When he signed for what would be his first feature film, Jolson was pulling down a lofty $3,500 a week plus half the profits from his touring stage hit *Big Boy*. The motion picture was one medium he had not conquered. In 1924, D. W. Griffith had hired him to star in a silent film called *Mammy's Boy*, in which he was to play a lawyer who dons blackface to solve a murder. But early in filming, Jolson became disenchanted enough to quit the picture. Griffith sued him for breach of contract, but a judge awarded the director only $2,627.50. Ironically, the same week Jolson was in court trying to convince a jury that he was a poor movie subject, he was drawing raves for his appearance in the *Plantation* short.

THE JAZZ SINGER
(Warner Bros. production; premiered October 6, 1927)

Director: Alan Crosland. Producer: Darryl F. Zanuck. Scenario: Alfred A. Cohn. Based on the play *The Jazz Singer* by Samson Raphaelson (New York opening, September 14, 1925; 303 performances). Titles: Jack Jarmuth. Photography: Hal Mohr. Editor: Harold McCord. Sound: George R. Groves. Assistant Director: Gordon Hollingshead. Musical Director: Louis Silvers. Running Time: 89 minutes (part-talking version; also released as silent).

Cast: Al Jolson (Jakie Rabinowitz/Jack Robin), May McAvoy (Mary Dale), Warner Oland (Cantor Rabinowitz), Eugenie Besserer (Sara Rabinowitz), Bobby Gordon (Jakie at age 13), Otto Lederer (Moisha Yudelson), Cantor Josef Rosenblatt (himself), Richard Tucker (Harry Lee), Nat Carr (Levi), William Demarest (Buster Billings), Anders Randolph (Dillings), Will Walling (doctor), Roscoe Karns (agent), Myrna Loy, Audrey Ferris (chorus girls).

Songs: "Blue Skies" [sung by Jolson] (Irving Berlin); "Dirty Hands, Dirty Face" [Jolson] (Edgar Leslie, Grant Clarke, Al Jolson, James V. Monaco); "Mother (of Mine), I Still Have You" [Jolson] (Grant Clarke, Al Jolson, Louis Silvers); "My Gal Sal" [Gordon, dubbed] (Paul Dresser); "My Mammy" [Jolson] (Sam M. Lewis, Joe Young, Walter Donaldson); "Toot Toot Tootsie, Goodbye" [Jolson] (Gus Kahn, Ernie Erdman, Ted Fiorito, Dan Russo); "Waiting for the Robert E. Lee" [Gordon, dubbed] (L. Wolfe Gilbert, Lewis F. Muir); "Kol Nidre" [Oland, dubbed by Joseph Diskay; reprised by Jolson], "Yahrzeit" [Rosenblatt] (trad.)

Special Academy Award as "the outstanding pioneer talking picture," 1927-28. Academy Award Nominations: Best Adapted Screenplay (Alfred A. Cohn); Best Engineering Effects (Nugent Slaughter).

With the microphone close by, Al Jolson records "My Mammy" on the set of *The Jazz Singer*.

Disc: Brunswick 3696, Brunswick 3719 (Jolson/"Mother (of Mine), I Still Have You"/78); Brunswick 3790, Brunswick 3912 (Jolson/"Dirty Hands, Dirty Face"/"My Mammy"/78); Sountrak STK-102 (bootleg LP; ST).

Video: MGM-UA (cassette/laserdisc).

If Warner Bros. had not decided to boost it with seven popular songs (five sung by Al Jolson), a synchronized score and a couple of minutes of supposedly ad-libbed dialogue, *The Jazz Singer* would have been little different than the studio's 42 other 1927 releases. Its story of Old World vs. New World conflict had been played out in numerous other American pictures; the theme was an apt one in a nation bursting with generations of immigrants deciding whether to assimilate into society or hold fast to their origins.

Jakie Rabinowitz (Jolson) wants to pursue a showbiz career, but his father (Warner Oland) wants him to carry on the Orthodox Jewish family tradition as a cantor. The son leaves home, changes his name to Jack Robin and gets a career boost from the comely actress Mary Dale (May McAvoy). This means a return to New York for an important spot in a Broadway revue. He has a happy reunion with his mother (Eugenie Besserer) but is still rejected by his father. The Broadway opening is on the eve of Yom Kippur, and Jack leaves the troupe to sing the Kol Nidre for his seriously ill father. Father and son are reconciled on the former's deathbed, and Jack goes on to make a hit on stage.

The film's sentimentality is cloying. An introductory subtitle describes mama Rabinowitz thusly: "God made her a woman, and love made her a mother." Later, when the grown-up Jack learns that his new job will return him to the city of his birth, he exclaims, in a series of screaming titles of increasing size: "NEW YORK!" "BROADWAY!" "HOME!"

"MOTHER!" It is no wonder that critics of the time were lukewarm about *The Jazz Singer* aside from the technical achievements. "As presented with Vitaphone, it's a credit to everybody concerned," commented the *Variety* reviewer "Sid." But he also added: "… *The Jazz Singer* minus Vitaphone is something else again."[16] His was a significant observation because most of the country, with theaters not yet equipped to exhibit talking pictures, would have to see a concurrently released silent version. But the film retained interest everywhere, thanks almost entirely to the magnetism of its star.

The first musical number in *The Jazz Singer*, which comes almost at its very outset, features not Jolson but the young Bobby Gordon, who plays 13-year-old Jakie singing ragtime in a saloon. His snatches of "My Gal Sal" and "Waiting for the Robert E. Lee" are obviously lip-synched; Jolson is said to have supplied the voice, but it does not sound like his. The real history is made 18 minutes into the picture, as a 15-years-older Jack has just finished singing "Dirty Hands, Dirty Face" at Coffee Dan's nightclub in San Francisco.

To an applauding chorus of rattling silverware, Jolson's voice is heard saying this: "Wait a minute! Wait a minute! You ain't heard nothin' yet. Wait a minute, I tell ya, you ain't heard nothin'! You want to hear 'Toot Toot Tootsie'? All right, hold on, hold on. … (He turns to the band leader.) Lou, listen, play 'Toot Toot Tootsie,' three choruses, you understand. In the third chorus, I whistle. Now, give it to 'em hard and heavy. Go right ahead." And they do, although the audiences who saw the film in 1927 might have been too amazed by the dialogue to fully enjoy the tune that followed. The famous phrase "You ain't seen nothin' yet" was already a stage trademark of Jolson's, and legend asserts that he blurted it out in impulsive anticipation of the big number, that the dialogue was recorded only because the microphone was opened for the delivery of "Toot Toot Tootsie, Goodbye."

Jolson also is seen and heard performing "Blue Skies," "Mother (of Mine), I Still Have You" and, in the triumphant finale, "My Mammy." "Mother (of Mine), I Still Have You," the first song to be written expressly for a talkie, became a major pop hit of 1928, as did "My Mammy" and "Dirty Hands, Dirty Face"—all were propelled by the film's popularity. The ending was tacked on, for the play had

concluded with the father's death and Jack's rejection of show business. The famed Cantor Josef Rosenblatt appears as himself singing the traditional hymn "Yahrzeit" in a concert hall. The music was the intended novelty, but what really had filmgoers talking were the "ain't heard nothin' yet" sequence and a second, much lengthier dialogue passage when Jack and his mother are reunited. Besserer seems astonished as she offers one-word responses to Jolson's impromptu talk about her pink dress, their "move up in the Bronx" and his "kind of jazzy" voice-and-piano rendition of "Blue Skies." (The piano-playing was dubbed by Bert Fiske.) Jolson's speech is remarkably fresh and naturalistic, which makes it all the more plausible that it was spontaneous. However, according to studio records, the Jolson-Besserer scene was a retake. In the new scene, "Blue Skies" replaced the initially filmed "It All Depends on You," but the make-over may also have been intended to integrate written dialogue. At least one contemporary report stated that Warner Bros. was contemplating the experimental use of dialogue well before the film went into production.[17]

In any case, Jolson's moxie helped make the Warners' gamble very profitable. *The Jazz Singer* grossed $2.6 million worldwide ($1.97 million domestically) on an investment of less than $500,000—and spawned scores of imitators. At first, the only copycats were the Warners themselves, as for now William Fox was confining Movietone to short subjects and the odd synchronized score. Vitaphone shorts were being produced regularly—there were more than 400 within two years of *Don Juan*—and a program of 12 feature "talkies" was announced for 1928. The first of these—the mostly silent *Tenderloin*, *Glorious Betsy* and *The Lion and the Mouse*—had wretchedly primitive dialogue sequences. The camera was more movable than in 1926, but the actors' movements were still dictated by the position of the microphones, which had to be masqueraded by props such as lamps or potted plants.

Significantly, upon the arrival of the first all-talking feature, Warner Bros.' *Lights of New York* (July 8, 1928), all that *The New York Times* saw fit to laud was the film's one musical number, in which an obscure vaudevillian named Harry Downing, playing a nightclub master of ceremonies, sang "At Dawning" under a microphone disguised as a festoon. The song was

In *The Singing Fool*, Al Jolson sings the future hit "Sonny Boy" to a precocious Davey Lee.

preceded by a brief dance sequence, possibly the first in a talkie, in which under-rehearsed chorines dressed in pseudo-military garb march into the nightclub to the strains of "Stars and Stripes Forever."

Praise such as The Times' would become more common as critics and public, bored by reams of stilted dialogue, sought a tuneful novelty. But at this point, Warner Bros. could have Vitaphoned barnyard noises and made money. *Lights of New York,* a hastily filmed and atrociously acted gangster melodrama derided by *Variety* as "100 percent crude," grossed some $2 million.

THE SINGING FOOL
(Warner Bros.; September 19, 1928)

Director: Lloyd Bacon. Scenario: C. Graham Baker. Dialogue: Joseph Jackson. Story: Leslie S. Burrows [C. Graham Baker]. Titles: Joseph Jackson. Photography: Byron Haskin. Editor: Ralph Dawson, Harold McCord. Sound: George R. Groves. Assistant Director: Frank Shaw. Musical Director: Louis Silvers. Running Time: 101 minutes (part-talking version; also released as silent).

Cast: Al Jolson (Al Stone), Betty Bronson (Grace), Josephine Dunn (Molly Winton), Arthur Housman (Blackie Joe), Reed Howes (John Perry), Davey Lee (Sonny Boy), Edward Martindel (Louis Marcus), Robert Emmett O'Connor (Bill, the café owner), Helen Lynch (maid), Agnes Franey ("balloon" girl).

Songs [all by Jolson]: "Golden Gate" (Dave Dreyer, Al Jolson, George W. Meyer); "I'm Sittin' on Top of the World" (Sam M. Lewis, Joe Young, Ray Henderson); "It All Depends on You" (B. G. De Sylva, Lew Brown, Ray Henderson); "Keep Smiling at Trouble" (Al Jolson, B. G. De Sylva, Lewis Gensler); "Sonny Boy" (Al Jolson, B. G. De Sylva, Lew Brown, Ray

Henderson); "The Spaniard That Blighted My Life" (Billy Merson); "There's a Rainbow 'Round My Shoulder" (Al Jolson, Billy Rose, Dave Dreyer).

Disc: Brunswick 3879, Brunswick 4033 (Jolson/"Sonny Boy"/"There's a Rainbow 'Round My Shoulder"/78); Take Two 106 (bootleg LP; ST).

Video: MGM-UA (laserdisc).

As *Lights of New York* was making news, Hollywood's second silent-sound "hybrid" musical was in production at Warner Bros. *The Singing Fool* was thematically no more original than *The Jazz Singer*, but it also had Jolson, whose film career was already peaking. Warners' big publicity slogan was "You Ain't Seen Nothin' Yet—Till You Have Seen *The Singing Fool*."

This time, Jolson portrayed Al Stone, a New York speakeasy waiter whose golden voice is discovered when he entertains the house with "It All Depends on You" and "I'm Sittin' on Top of the World" with a big-name Broadway producer (Edward Martindel) in attendance. Al's good fortune is also a break for Molly Winton (Josephine Dunn), a club chanteuse who has been spurning his affections. She had haughtily practiced dance steps upon the crumpled sheet music for a ballad the lovesick Al had just written for her. "You've got as much business writing songs as a bowlegged girl has on a stepladder," she snaps in one of the film's many attempts at witty titling. But after fame beckons to Al, she suddenly becomes chummy, and the two marry and rise to Broadway stardom together.

Four years later, Al is a leading singer, comedian and songwriter, but his domestic life is in shambles, thanks to Molly's two-timing with her "friend" John Perry (Reed Howes). By the time Al realizes something is wrong, Molly secures a divorce, which separates him from his beloved little boy, Sonny (Davey Lee). "The heavy heart is not attuned to song," announces a glum transitional title. The parting ruins Al's initiative, halts his career, and pushes him into alcoholism. All that saves him is a return to his old haunt, Blackie Joe's, and Grace (Betty Bronson), the cigarette girl who has always carried a torch for him.

Al emerges from his drunken haze and puts his life back together, writing and per-

forming again, but then he's hit with the news that his long-estranged Sonny is critically ill. He rushes to the hospital, just in time to comfort the lad before his death from an unidentified malady. Al must perform in a big Broadway revue that night, and he barely makes it through a teary rendition of "Sonny Boy" before collapsing just as the curtain falls.[18] The stage manager apologizes to Al for forcing him to go on, but Al tells him not to worry. "I'm all right," he says, Grace at his side. "You know, I was a quitter once, but I know I'll never quit again. As long as there are people who will listen to me, I'm gonna keep on singing."

Unlike *The Jazz Singer*, the majority of *The Singing Fool*—66 of the film's 101 minutes—contains dialogue, music or sound effects. The clichéd story was merely a thread on which to hang seven songs delivered by Jolson, one of which ranked among the era's biggest hits. "Sonny Boy," written for the film by B. G. "Buddy" De Sylva, Lew Brown and Ray Henderson, became the first song to sell more than 1 million copies of sheet music; it sold 3 million in all. With three solid months atop the bestseller list, it helped make De Sylva, Brown and Henderson the first songwriters to make it big in the early talkie era. For *The Singing Fool*, they also contributed—either as a unit or separately with others—"I'm Sittin' on Top of the World," which Jolson had introduced in 1925; "It All Depends on You," from his 1925 stage success *Big Boy*; and that same year's "Keep Smiling at Trouble." Jolson co-wrote "Golden Gate" (in 1925) and "There's a Rainbow 'Round My Shoulder." He donned bullfighter's garb to sing "The Spaniard That Blighted My Life," but a copyright-infringement lawsuit brought by the song's composer, Billy Merson, forced the excision of the number from all prints of the film.[19]

"Sonny Boy," the film's theme song of sorts, is performed three times—as Al cuddles Sonny on Christmas Eve, then as the boy is dying, then again in the tense climax. The exceedingly mauldin song was allegedly written that way in jest. Irving Berlin, whose "Blue Skies" had been heard in *The Jazz Singer*, had written a song for Jolson to sing to Lee, but Jolson wasn't happy with it. He called cross-country to his friends De Sylva, Brown and Henderson, who were preparing a stage show in Atlantic City, and asked them to come up with a replacement. Four hours later, they called back with "Sonny

Boy," but there still would be some dickering over content.

"The music was great," Jolson would be quoted as saying ...

> but the words—I dunno. I couldn't feel 'em. It said, "Who's that behind my chair?" And the kid is on my knee, so how can he be behind my chair? I told 'em about it. I said, "Now, listen," I said, "I've been writin' songs and singin' em since I was a punk kid. B-b-b-boy, I know!" Last year I didn't know a thing about pictures. I just said, "Gentlemen," I said, "Here I am just like a li'l child, do with me as you will, 'cause this is a new racket to me." But this time I'm speaking up some.[20]

Ego aside, Jolson was at the top of his powers in *The Singing Fool*. The $150,000 Warner Bros. paid him to make it, and the $388,000 it took to produce the film, were drops in the hat next to the film's worldwide gross of $5.9 million. Its $3.8-million gross in this country set a box-office record that would not be surpassed until Walt Disney's *Snow White and the Seven Dwarfs* (1937). No wonder the critic and documentary filmmaker Pare Lorentz wrote of Jolson's dominating presence: "Obvious and tedious as the climax is, when the blackface comedian stands before the camera and sings 'Sonny Boy,' you know that the man is greater, somehow, than the situation, the story, or the movie."[21]

But to the public, Jolson could not upstage what it considered to be an even bigger sensation, 3½-year-old Davey Lee (b. 1924), who became the hottest child actor since Charlie Chaplin's *Kid*, Jackie Coogan. Lee's charming lisp and disarming cuteness made moviegoers want to pack him up and take him home. An unknown before this film (his father worked in the print shop at Paramount), Lee and his older

brother were taken by their mother to a casting call. Since the brother was to try out for the role, Davey was left to play on his own. As his mother and brother sat waiting in the casting office, Davey got to playing piggyback with Jolson, who insisted that the boy be cast. Jolson and Lee were teamed in a second musical, *Say It with Songs* (1929; Chapter 3), and Lee made a handful of films on his own before his parents, concerned about the abnormal attention he was getting, ended his career by packing him off to public school.

The overwhelming commercial success of *The Singing Fool* meant that sound was here to stay. A trade-publication commentator was not thought to be exaggerating when he claimed that *The Singing Fool* "will be to talking pictures what *The Birth of a Nation* has been to silent pictures."[22] Even before its debut, the other major Hollywood companies were clamoring to catch up with Warners and Fox. Facilities were being retooled overnight. Studios had to tear down their outdoor sets and replace them with indoor sound stages, and theater owners would have to wire their buildings for sound. At the beginning of 1928, only 157 out of some 20,000 movie theaters in the United States were able to exhibit sound pictures; by year's end, there would be more than 1,000. On May 15, 1928, MGM, Paramount and United Artists signed with Western Electric for the use of talkie equipment; other sound holdouts would join the fold soon.

Although the movie industry was too busy worrying about the future to dwell on the past, there were many who rued the lost artistry of the silent film. The writer R. F. Delderfield summed it up for them: "Something of the fragrance and mystery of the screen departed on the echoes of 'Sonny Boy.'"[23]

CHAPTER 2

1928–1929: *Fanny, Bessie and The Broadway Melody*

The men who ran America's movie companies in 1928 responded to the inevitability of sound much as many humans in positions of power have responded to great upheaval: They panicked. First, they decided they had to integrate sound into their pictures in any way possible, and as soon as possible. Then, they came to the very hasty conclusion that actors without experience in speaking dialogue—in other words, without stage training—were probably unfit to appear in a talking film. The first assertion sparked one of the strangest periods in the annals of moviemaking; the second may have been the biggest blunder of the sound revolution.

The quest to qualify something as a "sound" picture—all the better for the marquee—was not limited to films yet to be finished. A few that were already in circulation—for example, the Samuel Goldwyn romance *Two Lovers* and Universal's historical drama *The Man Who Laughs*—were pulled back and synchronized with a score and sound effects. After a profitable initial run in the spring of 1928, Paramount re-released its comedy *Abie's Irish Rose* at year's end with snatches of dialogue—and made millions more. As little as a few seconds of clumsy conversation was enough to advertise a film as "talking." Occasionally, a musical number or two was added as well, as with a pair of backstage dramas: *Hit of the Show* (September 23, 1928), a Joe E. Brown effort for FBO that had been released the previous July as a silent, and *Show Girl* (November 4, 1928), which starred Alice White, First National's answer to Clara Bow.

At least these films had the stage atmosphere to excuse their use of music. Not so with the likes of MGM's first dialogue film, the part-talkie *Alias Jimmy Valentine* (November 14, 1928), a crime melodrama about a reformed safecracker (William Haines) hunted by a suspicious police detective (Lionel Barrymore). At one point, Haines and Leila Hyams were found singing a clumsily inserted William Axt-David Mendoza composition, "Love Dreams." The *New York Times'* Mordaunt Hall sarcastically observed, "...One may be treated to the love theme song with a scene in which the affectionate couple ... are just visible through a wealth of apple blossoms."[1] An even funnier (but unintentionally so) musical moment occurred in *Tenderloin* (March 20, 1928), one of Warner Bros.' earliest part-talkies, when the gangster melodrama was halted in its tracks for a finale in which Conrad Nagel, George E. Stone and Pat Hartigan inexplicably sang "Sweet Adeline."

"Sound came in like gangbusters. Every picture had to have at least one sequence in sound," William Bakewell, then a juvenile lead under contract to First National, said in a 1992 interview with the author. His studio, soon to be incorporated into Warner Bros., didn't have enough equipment to "goat-gland" more than one film at a time, so the actors who were asked to talk had to do it on odd hours. "We worked from evening until dawn, Alice White and Louise Fazenda and I," recalled Bakewell of his work on the comedy *Hot Stuff* (May 5, 1929) in the fall of 1928. "We were tired and we would blow our lines, which made our director, Mervyn LeRoy, very cranky."[2]

It didn't help that the gentle intimacy between director and actors in silent films was gone. In silents, the director could instruct the actors extemporaneously as a scene was being shot or soothe them by having music played by live musicians or on a handy phonograph. Now, the set had to be silent once the cameras rolled, which left the performers figuratively naked. They would become distracted with having to direct their voices toward the hidden microphone placements. The come-lately sound technicians, who knew little about film technique, rapidly became the most influential people on the set. They insisted that actors' voices be clearly modulated, which often overruled the director's desire for a faster pace and greater emotional expression. A frustrating trait of many early talkies, especially for a modern viewer, is the agonizingly slow delivery of dialogue. This problem was not lost on '20s moviegoers, either—many of them clamored for a comeback by the silents.

Evelyn Brent, a Garboesque leading lady for Paramount, appeared in that studio's first all-talking film, *Interference* (November 16, 1928), for Roy Pomeroy, the studio effects expert turned director. As she told the film historian John Kobal in 1972:

> They had microphones all over the place … everybody would have one. And if you got up to walk toward the other people, you had to remember to stop talking before you left this mike and pick it up when you reached another one. Otherwise, your voice would go out and in. Then they would take you at the finish of the first scene that was shot, you'd go into the other room and they'd play it back. Scared the daylights out of me … when I heard my voice. I thought, "This is it." I sounded like this British singer Dame Clara Butt … with an enormous voice … that's how I sounded to myself. I didn't know at the time that they'd stepped the volume up. … They had boomed it up because of bad facilities in the studio, because it was experimental then.[3]

Anita Page, a rising young star at MGM as talkies arrived, told the author of an experience on the set of *Navy Blues* (December 20, 1929):

> I'll be honest with you: I loved silents. They were my favorite kind of pictures. But I loved the movies, and if the movies were going to move to talk, then I was going to like to talk. … Clarence Brown was directing me in this film and he wanted one tear to come down my one cheek. Try it sometime! I could cry buckets, that was all right, but one tear? That was the only time, I think, that I ever worried about anything I had to do. So, the next day I was sitting there pondering, and Polly Moran came by and I said, "Oh, Polly, how do you get only one tear down one cheek?" "Oh, it's easy," she said. "Turn your profile!" So, believe it or not, I got the one tear. And somebody opened a door, and an airplane flew over, and I had to do the whole thing over again. If it had been a silent film, the plane wouldn't have bothered anybody.[4]

Sound equipment was in such short supply that lesser studios had to borrow from the pacesetters, Warner Bros. and Fox. This occurred to rather amazing effect in August 1928, when Universal leased a Movietone sound truck from Fox, ostensibly for sound tests on the part-talkie musical *Show Boat* (Chapter 7). In nine days, Universal hastily added sound sequences to the feature films *Lonesome*, *The Last Warning* and *It Can Be Done*; made three short subjects— and produced an 88-minute romantic drama called *Melody of Love*. Directed by A. B. Heath, the studio's supervisor of sound projects, and produced for only $30,000, it was Universal's first 100 percent talkie feature. *Melody of Love*, released on October 10, 1928, also may have been the first all-talking movie musical. Reviews indicate that it contained multiple song interpolations, but the film is apparently lost and the existing evidence of its legitimacy as a musical is inconclusive.

The film, written by Robert Arch, starred Walter Pidgeon as a composer named Jack Clark who loses the use of his right arm in the World War. After many setbacks—including a jilting by his chorus-girl sweetheart (Jane Winton)—he is reunited with Madelon (Mildred Harris), a singer he'd met in France who has come to America to find her lost love. The joy of seeing Madelon somehow enables Jack to regain the use of his arm, and he sits down at the piano to sing the love song written for the woman of his dreams. Because *Melody of Love* is unavailable for viewing, there is no way to evaluate its musical content directly, although we know that both Pidgeon and Harris sang in it. The cue sheet held by ASCAP reveals that, of 21 different compositions within, four were heard more than once. However, there is no indication of which songs were performed vocally, nor can their significance to the story be divined. "My Sweetheart," a contemporary ballad written by the bandleader Gene Rodemich, was heard five times, three in its entirety. "Made-lon," a French love song of 1918 vintage, was heard all the way through twice. Most of the other tunes were battle standards of the "Over There" and "Hinky-Dinky Parlez-Vous" variety, and may have been used only incidentally. Unless *Melody of Love* resurfaces, historians will have to regard it, like *Show Girl* and *Hit of the Show*, as a drama with songs rather than a bona fide musical. Still, Walter Pidgeon displayed a surprisingly robust baritone that almost immediately would triple his weekly paycheck (from $750 to $2,500) and soon get him plenty of work in official musicals.

Pidgeon was fortunate that the quality of his voice was not ignored, for his relatively brief stage experience might otherwise have left him struggling for jobs. Those who did have legitimate-stage backgrounds—actors, directors, producers, writers—were flooding into Hollywood or to the studios' New York facilities. The pages of the trades filled with ads placed by legit, vaudeville and radio acts declaring themselves available for work in talkies. Capitalizing on the studios' assumption that movie actors needed crash courses in elocution, schools of dramatic and voice training sprang up with such rapidity that they required their own section in the Los Angeles phone book. Hundreds of performers from the East submitted to screen tests. Fox seemed the busiest in the new-talent search; it reportedly evaluated stage actors almost daily. The studio admitted, however, that only 5 percent of them were good enough to pass.[5]

Most of these tests were blind and under-cover, not just to defeat competitive offers but to protect the actors from threats of litigation by any concerns—theatrical producers, for example—to whom they were under contract. The tests cost from $100 to $250 to make, depending on the length of film used. For example, when the Metropolitan Opera singer Mary Lewis was granted a test by MGM in early 1929, she began by singing two songs from *The Merry Widow*, in which she had appeared in Paris, then had to recite a short speech from the operetta. When the technicians heard the playback of the test and noticed flaws in the recording on the wax disc, they asked Lewis to do the test over again.[6] Even when there was no vacancy for an aspirant, his or her footage was screened and filed in a studio vault. Maybe, just

maybe, it would be recalled and screened again when an appropriate part came up.

But the home-grown talent was fighting back. Vaudeville, which was dying a slow death from wounds inflicted by radio, got a transfusion when scores of silent-picture actors requested bookings to establish themselves with stage credentials before the talkie avalanche; these actors had given booking agents the chill months before. Hollywood-area playhouses such as the Community Players, the Lucerne Club and the Academy of Theatre Arts reported a big increase in participants, and so did West Coast radio shows. Reported *Variety*:

> Actors with speaking experience in the slimmest of minor parts are boldly recalling their stage training, and former legits who have been getting the go-by and the cold shoulder on the lot are now demanding that they be starred in the talkers. ... Directors are almost in the same boat. Those who graduated from the footlights to the Klieg lights are sitting on top of the world, while the others are waiting fearfully for the influx of stage directors.[7]

Feisty little Alice White, a Hollywood girl all the way, hardly tolerated the presence of the imports from the opposite coast, if one believes this statement to a fan magazine:

> They can go home as far as I'm concerned. They're too studied. Their voices are all wet; too cultured. They make you feel self-conscious, make you feel like you shouldn't say "ain't." ... What do you think my fans would say if they heard Alice White asking, "Ah you shuah, sah?" instead of piping up like they always expected, "Ain't you got the lowdown, kid."[8]

As it turned out, those artists and writers with movies-only experience were no less suitable for talkies than their stage counterparts, except in one key area: musical talent. Hollywood had no backlog of singers, dancers and choreographers; they had to be imported. So did songwriters. De Sylva, Brown and Henderson had already made a fortune from *The Singing Fool*. Their contemporaries—Irving Berlin, Walter Donaldson, Con Conrad, Gus Kahn, Richard Whiting and many others— began to come West, or go to work in the East, for the movies. They expected a financial windfall, and they were not disappointed. Typically, a songwriter would have to market a song to a performer or create it for a stage show, then hope the performer would keep it in his repertoire or that the show would enjoy a long run. Maybe it would sell as many as 30,000 copies in its first three months. But within a month of the release of a film, the average motion picture tune, if it had any commercial potential at all, would sell from 100,000 to 500,000 copies.[9] Moreover, composers were paid a regular salary by a studio—anywhere from $200 to $1,500 weekly, in addition to their royalties. Easy money.

And that being the case, the studios wanted more of it for themselves. Warner Bros., having not received a cent of the "Sonny Boy" royalties cache, in January 1929 bought the prestigious New York publishing company M. Witmark & Sons, one of the oldest in the business, for $900,000. This gave the studio the copyrights, and thus the future profits, to music by such notables as Victor Herbert, Sigmund Romberg and George M. Cohan. In August, Warners continued cutting its swath through Tin Pan Alley by absorbing the Harms Music Company for $8.5 million in a huge merger that also took in seven affiliated publishers, among them the young but thriving De Sylva, Brown and Henderson firm and the Jerome H. Remick Company, a New York fixture since 1905. By the end of the year, Warner Bros. controlled the majority of the governing board of the American Society of Composers, Authors and Publishers.

MGM and Paramount were also early starters in the quest for music. In September 1928, Metro obtained a controlling interest in the Robbins Music Corporation. Paramount created its own concern, Famous Music, in 1928; in the spring of '29 it bought out Spier and Coslow Inc., owned by songwriters Larry Spier and Sam Coslow, to fortify its catalog. Soon, all of the Hollywood majors would forge agreements with or buy out Tin Pan Alley firms.

MY MAN

(Warner Bros.; December 21, 1928)

Director: Archie Mayo. Scenario: Robert Lord. Dialogue: Joseph Jackson. Story: Mark Canfield [Darryl F. Zanuck]. Titles: Joseph Jackson, James A. Starr. Photography: Frank

Kesson. Editor: Owen Marks. Running Time: 99 minutes (part-talking version; also released as silent).

Cast: Fanny Brice (Fannie Brand), Guinn Williams (Joe Halsey), Edna Murphy (Edna Brand), André De Segurola (Landau), Richard Tucker (Waldo), Billy Seay (Sammy), Arthur Hoyt (Thorne), Ann Brody (Mrs. Schultz), Clarissa Selwynne (forelady).

Songs [all by Brice]: "I Was a Florodora Baby" (Harry Carroll, Ballard MacDonald); "I'd Rather Be Blue Over You Than Be Happy With Somebody Else" (Billy Rose, Fred Fisher); "If You Want the Rainbow, You Must Have the Rain" (Billy Rose, Mort Dixon, Oscar Levant); "I'm an Indian" (Blanche Merrill, Leo Edwards); "My Man" (Channing Pollock, Maurice Yvain); "Second-Hand Rose" (Grant Clarke, James F. Hanley).

Disc: RCA Victor 21168 (Brice/"My Man"/78); RCA Victor 21815 (Brice/"If You Want the Rainbow, You Must Have the Rain"/"I'd Rather Be Blue Over You ... "/78).

As solid as the outlook for composers was in the talkie surge, such was not the case for actors, as Warner Bros. found when it issued the third part-talking musical. The star of *My Man* was Fanny Brice (1891–1951), famed for her singing and dialect comedy in vaudeville and Broadway revues. She was the first of many stage stars to reach the hinterlands with a musical feature, and the largely negative response proved to be a portent of things to come.

Jolson had come from the stage too, but his popularity, especially from record sales, had been much broader even before *The Jazz Singer*. They'd at least heard of Jolson in Peoria and Sioux City, but Brice had less grass-roots support to fall back on. She looked and sounded too ethnic and, by conventional standards, seemed a little goofy. One can imagine a less sophisticated crowd, accustomed to demure females such as Lillian Gish and Janet Gaynor, being quite amazed by Brice. And when it played in smaller markets not yet wired for sound, *My Man* had little value, for no one would get to hear Fanny put across her "Mrs. Cohen at the Beach" comedy sketch and six of her best songs, among them "I Was a Florodora Baby," "I'm an Indian," "Second-Hand Rose" and, of course, the title song.

Even *Variety*, which generally praised the

For Warner Bros.' *My Man*, Fanny Brice committed many of her famous songs and comedy highlights to the big screen.

film, had to admit that "it doesn't lessen the fact that Miss Brice is a one-picture star. ... (Brice's) numbers all click because she is America's Beatrice Lillie, even if slightly Jewish. Both these women are subject to the same handicap, enough is enough. That's why each is more at home in a revue where they can come and go with their specialties than when playing a book."[10] Lillie, as we'll see later, tried talkies with no better results.

My Man, now considered a lost film, was named for Brice's most famous song, a torchy ballad adapted from the French tune "Mon Homme" that was immortalized by the singer in the 1921 Ziegfeld Follies. Appropriately, the film's story, penned by future mogul Darryl F. Zanuck under a *nom de plume,* was one of ill-fated love. Fannie Brand, owner of a theatrical costume shop, falls for a shop-window elastic exerciser (Guinn "Big Boy" Williams), only to lose him on the eve of their nuptials to her con-

niving little sister (Edna Murphy). Fannie makes it big on the stage, which creates a happy ending, but not before Brice has jerked wells of tears by singing the title song while decked out in her wedding dress.

There were five other songs, two with lyrics credited to Brice's future husband, Billy Rose (1899–1966). Rose, the famed producer and nightclub owner, was quite a character. After Brice had decided to appear in *My Man* for $25,000, Rose told her that her services were worth much more. "All right," said Fanny, "see if you can get me $50,000." Aware of the exposure the film would give his paramour, Rose went to Warner Bros. and demanded $250,000 for her. He got $125,000, an investment the studio would later regret.[11]

Brice appeared in only a handful of feature films, including one more starring musical, *Be Yourself!* (Chapter 8). She admitted that she never did get used to movies. "You have to be able to forget the camera," she said. "In the theater I was always at ease, but in pictures there was that camera following me around like a cop."[12] How many other performers accustomed to the intimacy of the proscenium stage must have had the same complaint!

THE BROADWAY MELODY
(MGM; February 1, 1929)

Director: Harry Beaumont. Producer: Laurence Weingarten. Scenario: Sarah Y. Mason. Dialogue: Norman Houston, James Gleason. Story: Edmund Goulding. Titles: Earl Baldwin. Photography: John Arnold. Editors: Sam S. Zimbalist, William Le Vanway. Sound: Douglas Shearer. Art Director: Cedric Gibbons. Costumes: David Cox. Dance Direction: George Cunningham. Running Time: 110 minutes (sound version; also released as silent). Technicolor sequence.

Cast: Anita Page (Queenie Mahoney), Bessie Love ("Hank" Mahoney), Charles King (Eddie Kerns), Jed Prouty (Uncle Jed), Kenneth Thomson (Jock Warriner), Eddie Kane (Francis Zanfield), Eddie Dillon (stage manager), Mary Doran (Flo), Emmett Beck (Babe Hatrick), Marshall Ruth (Stew), Drew Demarest (Turpe), James Burroughs (singer), Ray Cooke (bellhop), James Gleason (himself), Nacio Herb Brown (piano player at Gleason's), Earl Burtnett and His Los Angeles Biltmore Hotel Orchestra, The Biltmore Trio.

Songs: "The Boy Friend" [Love, Page], "Broadway Melody" [King, with Brown at piano; reprised by King, Love, Page], "Harmony Babies" [Love, Page], "Love Boat" [Burroughs], "The Wedding of the Painted Doll" [Burroughs, danced by chorus], "You Were Meant for Me" [King] (Arthur Freed, Nacio Herb Brown); "Truthful Parson Brown" [Biltmore Trio] (Willard Robison).

Academy Award: Best Picture, 1928-29.

Academy Award Nominations: Best Director (Harry Beaumont), Best Actress (Bessie Love).

Disc: RCA Victor 21964 (King/"Broadway Melody"/"The Wedding of the Painted Doll"/78); RCA Victor 21965 (King/"You Were Meant for Me"/78); Mark 56-11847 (bootleg LP; ST); Music Masters JJA-19802 (bootleg LP; ST); Radiola BMPB-1929 (bootleg LP; ST).

Video: MGM-UA (cassette/laserdisc).

As fewer silents and part-silents were being produced, the first all-talking, all-singing, all-dancing musical was inevitable. It turned out to be one of the more notable films of the transitional period—*The Broadway Melody*, which premiered at Grauman's Chinese Theatre in Hollywood on the first evening of February in 1929. For the debut of its first all-talkie, Metro-Goldwyn-Mayer spared no expense. It brought in no fewer than 14 singing and dancing acts to precede the screening. Once the audience was seated, George Gershwin was seen and heard playing "Rhapsody in Blue" with the Chinese Symphony Orchestra. Dimitri Tiomkin, the composer-conductor, directed a stage finale that featured the movie's stars descending a specially designed white staircase in elaborate, sequined costumes. The huge crowd welcomed the finished film with a standing ovation.[13]

The Broadway Melody would be the first talkie—and second film of any kind, after *Wings*—to win the Academy Award for Best Picture. But, most importantly, *The Broadway Melody* was the first movie musical in the true sense. For the first time, score and screenplay were written for the film, and the numbers were more or less integrated into the action, in at least one case directly advancing the plot. It was also the first musical seen by many moviegoers, for despite the popular success of *The Jazz Singer* and *The Singing Fool*, their part-talking versions were not available where theaters were not yet wired for sound.

The Broadway Melody, the story of a love triangle of two Midwestern sister-entertainers and a big-city song-and-dance man, was the product of many varied, sometimes unexpected talents. It grew out of the desire of MGM, the last of the major studios to make its first all-talkie, to break its silence after months of indecision. Neither Louis B. Mayer, the bottom line-oriented studio chief, nor Irving Thalberg, Metro's artistically minded head of production, believed that talkies were more than a fad—until too many competitors successfully exploited the new technology. MGM's first part-dialogue release, the crime drama *Alias Jimmy Valentine* (1928), was like many of the earliest

The title number from MGM's history-making *The Broadway Melody*: **Charles King at center, flanked by Anita Page (left) and Bessie Love.**

talkies: urban melodramas peppered with gangsters, guns and grit. Thalberg wanted something different.

While visiting New York in the summer of 1928, Thalberg met with Major Edward Bowes, the *Don Juan* composer who was now the executive manager of the Capitol Theatre, the largest first-run house in the massive Loew's theater chain, which was operated by the studio's parent company. Bowes complained about the trend toward melodrama and suggested that Thalberg make a light romantic film. Thalberg liked the idea and assigned Laurence Weingarten, his producer brother-in-law, to supervise the project. Said Weingarten: "Irving called me in and said ... it would have to be a hurry-up job, we thought we would do it with synchronized sound effects. But everybody was clamoring for 'all-talk.' So we switched to that. We asked Eddie Goulding to suggest something."[14]

Edmund Goulding (1891–1959), who concocted the story for *The Broadway Melody*, was a London-born director, screenwriter and composer best known for his urbane tastes and his sensitive handling of female talent. He would direct the all-star drama *Grand Hotel* for MGM, as well as some of Bette Davis' better vehicles at Warners (*Dark Victory, The Great Lie, The Old Maid*). By 1928, he had gained attention for directing MGM's Greta Garbo–John Gilbert hit *Love*, a version of Tolstoy's *Anna Karenina*, and for adapting and directing the backstage drama *Sally, Irene and Mary*, which boosted rising stars Joan Crawford, Constance Bennett and Sally O'Neil. His new story, dictated off the cuff to Thalberg, was said to be loosely modeled on the lives of the Duncan Sisters, the famed stage duo.

When *The Broadway Melody* began to receive critical acclaim, Goulding was rumored as having played an unusually strong role be-

hind the cameras, but in fact the directorial duties were handled by Harry Beaumont, a technically efficient studio craftsman whose credits
dated back to the mid 'teens. Sarah Y. Mason,
credited with shaping Goulding's story into a
working scenario, would win an Academy
Award for her adaptation (written with her husband, Victor Heerman) of *Little Women* (1933).
James Gleason, best known for a long career as
a character actor but more recognized at the
time as a playwright, and Norman Houston,
also a Broadway author, supplied the tangy,
timely dialogue. Their slang-filled speech rarely
contained a sentence that did not, according to
a *New York Times* critic, "contain a word or two
of Broadway's none too edifying parlance."[15]
But the most endearing contributions to *The
Broadway Melody* were made by the two men
who created all of its important music and the
three actors who sang most of it.

Thalberg and Weingarten considered several other songwriters, but the production chief
wanted the team of Nacio Herb Brown (1896–
1964) and Arthur Freed (1894–1973) to create
what would become a standard-filled score.
Though new to MGM, the duo had been col-
laborating off and on for nearly a decade.
Brown, a former Beverly Hills tailor-shop
owner, garnered a 1927 best-seller with a novelty piano rag, "The Doll Dance," and he was
just beginning to make it big as a composer
when given his first shot at the movies. Freed
began his show-business career as a song plugger and vaudeville actor, wrote a hit tune called
"I Cried for You" in 1923, and was directing
a stage musical in Hollywood when hired by
Metro as a staff lyricist. Brown and Freed would
become the first songwriting team whose primary reputations rested with the sound cinema.

The Duncans themselves were sought for
the sister roles, but the assignments went to
Anita Page, as the beautiful younger Mahoney
sister Queenie, and Bessie Love, as Hank, the
older pepperpot who runs the act. Page (b.
1910), a tallish blonde who turned 18 as filming
began, was an MGM contractee who had recently made waves as Joan Crawford's self-destructive buddy in the Beaumont-directed jazz-
baby drama *Our Dancing Daughters* (October 8,
1928). The film made Crawford a star, but it
initially did as much (or more) for Page, who
after only a handful of pictures was receiving

more fan letters than any other actress in Hollywood.[16]

Long retired from show business and
newly widowed after a 54-year marriage to a
Navy admiral, 82-year-old Anita Page recalled
her rise to stardom with delight in an interview
with the author:

> I have all the clippings that say that I stole the
> picture [*Our Dancing Daughters*] and that I
> should have been the star. ... Crawford did
> very well dancing the Charleston, as we all
> understand, but to me the Charleston isn't
> acting, the Charleston [laughing] is the
> Charleston. So that picture is the one that
> put *me* on the road to stardom.[17]

Bessie Love (1898–1986) was one of D. W.
Griffith's demure "child-woman" discoveries.
The director had reputedly changed the name
of the Texas-born actress from Juanita Horton,
and one of her first film appearances was in his
Intolerance (1915). Love was a reliable ingenue,
most notably for Paramount, during the early
'20s. She could even sing and dance a little, but
in the silent era, her performances to her own
ukelele accompaniment were limited to Hollywood house parties. By late in the decade, Love
had been out of demand for film roles because
she was said to lack Clara Bow's "it." In fact, she
was about to leave Hollywood, as she told John
Kobal years later:

> When the offer came from MGM I had just
> done a 16-week variety tour. I had a very
> clever agent who decided to try me for the
> stage during one of my down periods in films.
> I had had quite a few of those and instead of
> trying to get me parts in films, he thought it
> might be a good idea to take a different di-
> rection altogether, and do a musical comedy
> in New York. The variety tour was a testing
> ground for that. ... At about this time, some-
> body at MGM, Thalberg possibly, wanted me
> to do a test for *The Broadway Melody*. ...
> While I was against it, my agent wisely
> booked me into Grauman's Egyptian The-
> atre in Hollywood for a week, and they saw
> me there.[18]

More difficult to cast was the role of Eddie
Kerns, the cocky song-and-dance man, which
went to Charles King (1889–1944), a performer
with a long string of Broadway musical comedy
successes (*Hit the Deck!*, *Present Arms*, *Watch
Your Step*). King's wife was a first cousin to
George M. Cohan, and it was in Cohan's *The*

Yankee Prince that he gained his initial break in the legitimate theater. Because neither Page nor Love had much musical experience, King would be asked to handle most of the major vocal chores.

The male lead had been hired after a lengthy search. Louis B. Mayer, in New York on political business, was approached by Benny Thau, a booking agent for Loew's vaudeville circuit, who recommended the studio hire King. Mayer went to see King, who was just finishing up a road tour of *Hit the Deck!*, and was so delighted by his performance that he not only signed the actor but also Thau, who would go on to become a top administrator at MGM. "Charlie was great," was Anita Page's fond remembrance of King. "He was happy as a lark. He wasn't a bit uncomfortable doing his first picture, and that really came across on the screen. He was very well-liked. A little old for me, I'll tell you that, [but] he was a very happy man."[19]

From a technical standpoint, *The Broadway Melody* was quite primitive: Filmed in 26 days between September and November of 1928, it would appear plainly outdated inside of a year later. Many transitions between scenes were bridged by titles, and the actors' movements were still unduly shackled by camera and microphone placements. Director Beaumont partially solved the problems by placing the camera kiosk on wheels and moving the microphone around the set with the help of technicians dressed in stocking feet. In another sequence, most of a female chorus had to pad their shoes with adhesive tape to muffle the noise of their movements. Page recalled one of her stints before the camera:

> One time I was doing a scene in which I'm sitting down, and we'd hear this sort of "tap-tap-tap" as I was filing my nails, and the moment the scene would start, the tapping would start. Well, we went all around and looked under things and we still didn't know what it was. so we did it [the shot] once more, and this time I realized it was my foot tapping. Of course, we had to retake it all over again.[20]

Yet, the MGM brass knew quickly that something special was brewing. Page again:

> Irving Thalberg, or one of the other executives who was very important ... came over,

and kept coming over and coming over and watching the picture, and he was the one who felt this had great potential—I think in the beginning it was meant to be a special—but nobody knew at the time that it would be as great as it was[21]

The sound technology was improving even as shooting progressed, and reviewers noticed this in the finished film. "The talkies find new speed and freedom," *Photoplay* reported. "The microphone and its twin camera poke themselves into backstage corners, into dressing rooms, into rich parties, and hotel bedrooms."[22] Cinematographer John Arnold, praised *Variety*, "has moved his camera all over the place, constantly ranging from closeups, to mediums, to full length [shots]."[23]

The movie begins, in fact, with an aerial shot of New York City, accompanied by a snatch of "Give My Regards to Broadway." Abruptly, we are whisked into Gleason's, a fictional Tin Pan Alley publishing house filled with the typical creative cacophony of instruments and voices. Eddie Kerns, a singer-songwriter in the George M. Cohan-Eddie Dowling mold, is perfecting his newest song, which he has written for the newest Francis Zanfield revue. (Eddie's pianist is played by Nacio Herb Brown, and the owner of the place turns out to be James Gleason, playing himself.) The song is "Broadway Melody," with a rousing tune and hopeful lyrics that make for a snappy jam session. A comely singer asks Eddie if he'd let her and her partner "smack" his song over. His answer reveals his king-sized ego: "If you want a song, see Georgie Cohan. Heh, heh ... he writes good songs, too."

Eddie has summoned the Mahoney Sisters to the big town, unbeknownst to Zanfield, to smack over his song in the revue. His interests are more than professional, for he's practically engaged to Hank, who's been too busy touring Podunk towns with Queenie to think about matrimony. But Hank's dream is to end the duo's nomadic life, no more "cheap hotels and lobby comics, cooking our own food, washing our own clothes, (or) traveling in smelly day coaches." She doesn't expect her less ambitious kid sister to understand: "Honey, they were plenty smart when they made you beautiful."

Dialogue like that made Anita Page wince:

> In the beginning, I didn't like [*The Broadway Melody*]. I love good English, and I hated

Spunky vaudevillian "Hank" Mahoney (Bessie Love, left) learns the truth about her fiancé (Charles King) and her sister (Anita Page) in the pivotal scene of *The Broadway Melody*.

when [Queenie] had to say "Gee, ain't it elegant!" It used to just drive me up a wall … and of course, I was supposed to be a little on the dumb side….[24]

Actually, Queenie isn't such a dimwit. Zanfield (Eddie Kane) gives in to Eddie's urging and gives the Mahoneys a tryout. Not too impressively, they sing "Harmony Babies." But Hank's hot and bossy temper—she accuses the piano player of "crabbing" their act and then gets into a hair-pulling match with a mouthy chorine—motivates the producer to hire the younger sister only. Queenie has to take Zanfield aside and talk him into hiring them both, but without either telling Hank of her intercession. This is an important revelation about the character of Queenie, who spends much of the film protecting her sister's well-being instead of the expected opposite. Meanwhile, Eddie has overheard Queenie's plea to Zanfield, which adds to his growing affection for the younger sister.

The film moves ahead to a dress rehearsal for the revue. Eddie's song may have over-romanticized Broadway, but here realism reigns.

As bickering abounds amid the backstage hustle-bustle, Zanfield, surrounded by his coterie of "yes" men, assures financial backers that the show is solid. Eddie scolds the orchestra for being "heavy on the brass," the stereotypically effeminate costumer complains about Zanfield's color choice, and a self-impressed thespian wants more spotlight from the man in the rafters. Eddie soon launches into a longer version of "Broadway Melody," accompanied by the strutting Mahoneys and then by a line of slightly overweight chorus girls against a painted skyline. MGM chose a clip from this number to show at the outset of its musical compiliation *That's Entertainment!* (1974). Watching the full version reminds us that the cinema's long history of high steppers, velvet voices and splashy production numbers begins right here.

> Don't bring a frown to old Broadway,
> You've gotta clown on Broadway.
> Your troubles there are out of style,
> For Broadway always wears a smile.
> A million lights, they flicker there,
> A million hearts beat quicker there.

No skies are gray upon the Great White Way,
That's the Broadway melody!

There's more history to be made. Zanfield
decides to turn Queenie into a nearly nude
human masthead for a "Love Boat" chorus
number, which gives an eyeful to rich playboy
and Zanfield crony Jock Warriner (Kenneth
Thomson). He makes a play for Queenie, but
Hank and Eddie warn her about mixing with
his kind of company. Of course, we already
know the sulking Eddie isn't exactly being pa-
ternalistic. Alone with Queenie in the girls'
hotel room, he blurts out his feelings, and the
music swells to "You Were Meant for Me," the
first song in a movie musical to advance a plot.[25]
Eddie's "plaintive melody" seemingly fails to
win the girl, for she spurns the birthday party
Hank and Eddie put on for her in favor of a
more ritzy bash—and the gift of a diamond
bracelet—at Jock's. There, we see the Biltmore
Trio perform Willard Robison's "Truthful Parson Brown," a gospel-tinged pop hit of 1928
that is the only non–Brown and Freed song in
the film.

The plot mechinations are halted temporarily for a sequence filmed in two-strip
Technicolor—the first use of this primitive form
in a musical—featuring a couple of selections
from the Zanfield revue, which has become a
hit. One is a duet of "The Boy Friend," on
which Love and Page show off their less-than-
booming voices and dance a little. "I didn't
think I had a good singing voice, but I enjoyed
it," Page recalled.[26]

The other song, a pop ballet to "The Wedding of the Painted Doll," adds to the list of
Broadway Melody innovations. Like all of the
other numbers in the film, this one (sung by
James Burroughs) was recorded as the cameras
rolled, the musicians just out of range of the
lens. But upon viewing the rushes, Irving Thalberg was unhappy enough with the dancing to
order a retake. But the picture was already over
budget, and Douglas Shearer, head of MGM's
sound department—then practically a one-man
operation—suggested that the music already
suitably recorded could be played through loud-
speakers as the actors mimed to it.[27] The sound
disc was played back as the 60-member troupe
restaged the number. This practice of pre-
recording, although it would be modified some,
would become standard in Hollywood within a

year or two. Viewing the number today (it survives, at this writing, only in black and white),
it's hard to believe that it predated the Busby
Berkeley era by only four years: The camera is
stationary and the choreography is elementary.
But it was state of the art.

Now, the love plot is resolved. We have
been made to realize that Queenie actually loves
Eddie but is carrying on with Jock so that Hank
will end up with Eddie. The film's pivotal scene
is set in the Mahoneys' dressing room. After
Queenie threatens to go off with Warriner and
break up the act, the sisters tussle and the
younger knocks the elder to the floor. Eddie enters the room and the fray. "You can't do this!"
he barks at Queenie. "You can't get away with
it! I'll kill that guy just as sure as anything. I'll
make him suffer the same way he's making me
suffer!" Cut to an astonished Hank, who is beginning to get the picture. Queenie storms out.

The Broadway Melody may have been a
sound film, but here we are reminded of the
beauty of silence. For more than a minute, the
camera is on a shocked, muted Hank, whose
love life and professional well-being have just
been shattered. She seems to be wondering how
to react, and we wonder, too. Finally, she decides to get out the lash. For effect, she slaps the
crestfallen Eddie on the coat. "Say, what kind
of sap are you, anyway?" she snaps. "Are you
gonna let a john like that steal her away from
you because he's got a little more jack? … You
love her, don't you? Say, if I loved a girl like you
do Queenie, I'd go out and fight for her!" And
so on, until Eddie is inspired enough to do just
that.

Hank slams the door behind him and
buries her head in her hands. She sits down at
her dressing table and tries to remove her hair-
band, but her eyes are diverted to a photo of her
lost love. She tries to remove her makeup, but
all she can do is cry, softly and uncontrollably.
Finally, she fights the tears enough to phone
her agent (Jed Prouty) and arranges a new
booking—without sis. "She did everything she
could," Anita Page said of Love's emoting in
the pivotal scene. "She was an excellent actress."[28]

And of course, Eddie rescues Queenie, although he gets pushed around pretty badly
while doing so, and then marries her. As the
film ends, the newlyweds have returned from
their honeymoon, and Hank is headed off to

nowhere with her new partner, the mouthy Zanfield girl. We can't help but believe Hank would have made a better mate for Eddie.

In any case, Bessie Love's dressing-room emoting resurrected her career. Love earned an Academy Award nomination as best actress—she lost to Mary Pickford for *Coquette*—and MGM signed her and Charles King to five-year contracts. His pay was doubled to $2,000 weekly, and her $500-a-week free-lance rate ballooned to a guaranteed $3,000. And why not? *The Broadway Melody*, with a negative cost of $379,000, grossed $2.8 million in the United States, $4.8 million worldwide, and made a recorded profit of $1.6 million for MGM. Its title was used for a series of Metro musicals identified by year: 1936, 1938 and 1940. (The Edmund Goulding script was rewritten for the 1940 musical *Two Girls on Broadway*.) The title song became a hit for Charles King, the Ben Selvin Orchestra, and Nat Shilkret and the Victor Orchestra. Both Shilkret and Selvin guided "You Were Meant for Me" into the hit parade. "The Wedding of the Painted Doll" was successfully covered by both King and Earl Burtnett's Los Angeles Biltmore Hotel Orchestra, but Leo Reisman's orchestra made the biggest splash with it. Arthur Freed himself sang it, to Nacio Herb Brown's piano, in the 1929 MGM short *The Song Writers' Revue* (see Appendix II); part of that rendition was repeated in Metro's 1976 compilation film *That's Entertainment, Part 2*.

But what *The Broadway Melody* did best of all was to send the West Coast the reassuring message that it could beat the East Coast at its own game. The possibilities, *Variety* eagerly opined, "are what jolt the imagination. ... If the talker studios can top the production efforts of the stage and get the camera close enough to make the ensemble seem to be in the same theater, what's going to happen in Boston between a musical comedy stage at $4.40 and screen at 75 [cents]?"[29] Arthur James of *Motion Pictures Today* called *Broadway Melody* "the one thing needed to assure the world in general that sound pictures are no longer an experiment." For movie watchers as well as moviemakers, music seemed a happy alternative to the stilted talk that flowed in excess from so much carelessly made drivel. But would the future live up to its lofty potential?

CHAPTER 3

1929: *No Business Like Show Business*

As 1929 dawned, *Variety* reported that studio rosters listed 18 musical films either in production or scheduled for production, at a total cost of more than $9 million.[1] The astonishing success of *The Singing Fool* and *The Broadway Melody* made these potentially lucrative investments. Had more of the works-in-progress—or the films that followed them—been intended to build upon the earliest efforts, the Hollywood musical might have flourished even more than it did in the next few months. Instead, the studios mostly chose the path of least resistance: formula-bound variations on the same backstage stories. Of the 22 "official" musicals that premiered during the first seven months of '29, all but five offered plots directly or indirectly related to show business—meaning the legitimate stage, vaudeville, burlesque, nightclubs, the recording studio, radio or the movie industry itself.

Anita Page, Bessie Love and Charlie King may have turned heads with their snappy insider lingo, but the showbiz movie hardly began with them. During the '20s, there were successes such as *Ella Cinders*, *The Gold Diggers*, *The Last Command*, *Pretty Ladies*, *Show People*, *Sally, Irene and Mary* and even Charlie Chaplin's *The Circus*. Much of *Lights of New York*, the first 100 percent talkie, took place in a nightclub. And, of course, the three hybrid musicals released in 1927 and 1928—*The Jazz Singer*, *The Singing Fool* and *My Man*—all took place within the realm of entertainment. They would be imitated incessantly. After all, it was natural that people would like these films, for backstage plots allowed eager patrons to peer into private worlds of glamour, to live vicariously as a Hollywood leading man or a star-dom-seeking Broadway baby for an hour or two. Sound only added to the verisimilitude.

There were sociological implications as well. America's urban areas were growing with unprecedented speed, and rural people simultaneously became fascinated with, and fearful of, life in the big city. And, of course, big-city dwellers were always interested in themselves. The better backstage films responded to these attitudes. The critic Tom Shales has written:

> The established truth of the day was that Broadway was a wicked, worldly place where life was acted out with as much fervor and drama backstage as onstage. And that, further, it symbolized and epitomized real life; it was real life with the edges sharpened, the pulses quickened, the crises more critical, the vagaries of fate—and fame—even more relentless.[2]

There were also more practical reasons for the infant sound medium to embrace the backstager, which for purposes of this book is defined as a film set primarily in any branch of the entertainment world. With all that "new" talent for the studios to introduce to the moviegoing public, show business was a naturally comfortable milieu. The idea was to transfer to the big screen as much as possible of what made a performer attractive elsewhere. Harry Richman, for example, could be cast as a self-assured pop singer who headlines on Broadway, owns a fashionable nightclub on the side, and even manages to write a snappy song or two. Richman didn't go blind, but otherwise his Harry Raymond in *Puttin' on the Ritz* wasn't far from the truth, conceited strut and all. A radio and club crooner like Rudy Vallee could be introduced as essentially what people thought he was: a nice, young, "regular" guy whose sex appeal bloomed whenever he opened his mouth to sing suggestive songs like "I'm Just a Vagabond Lover." Sometimes the strategy worked. More often it did not, for it was one thing to ask Harry and Rudy to toss off their specialities in a one- or two-reeler, and quite another to make them sustain a 60- to 100-minute feature without turning to wood or stone.

The trend toward backstagers also made it easier to integrate music and plot. A performer's spontaneous burst into song was a long-accepted tradition in the theater, but Hollywood types seemed reluctant to go along with the fantasy. They worried about the large segment of the public that was unfettered by the playgoing experience. But a movie *about* a show could present its music naturally. You could just have someone walk up to a microphone or to the front of a stage and deliver the goods. No fuss.

So in the first full year of sound, there were a lot of ethnics forsaking family for fame, teary-voiced songsters with cheerleading Sonny Boys in tow, and a glut of two-acts whose spats over love and money imperiled their close harmony. Here are their stories.

LUCKY BOY

(Tiffany-Stahl; February 2, 1929)

Directors: Norman Taurog, Charles C. Wilson. Dialogue Director: Rudolph Flothow. Scenario: Isadore Bernstein. Dialogue: George Jessel. Story: Viola Brothers Shore. Titles: Harry Braxton, George Jessel. Photography: Harry Jackson, Frank Zucker. Editors: Desmond O'Brien, Russell Shields. Art Director: Harvey Libbert. Set Director: George Sawley. Musical Arrangements: Hugo Riesenfeld. Musical Director: Sasha Bunchuk. Running Time: 97 minutes (part-talking).

Cast: George Jessel (Georgie Jessel), Gwen Lee (Mrs. Ellis), Richard Tucker (Mr. Ellis), Gayne Whitman (Mr. Trent), Margaret Quimby (Eleanor), Rosa Rosanova (Momma Jessel), William H. Strauss (Poppa Jessel), Mary Doran (Becky), Patty and Fields, Joe Sevely (amateur-night acts), Charles Wilson, Glenda Farrell.

Songs: "Lucky Boy" [Jessel, chorus], "My Mother's Eyes" [Jessel, four times] (L. Wolfe Gilbert, Abel Baer); "In My Bouquet of Memories" [Jessel], "You're My Real Sweetheart" [Jessel] (Sam M. Lewis, Joe Young, Harry Akst); "Keep Sweeping the Cobwebs Off the Moon" [Jessel] (Sam M. Lewis, Joe Young, Oscar Levant); "My Blackbirds Are Bluebirds Now" [Jessel] (Irving Caesar, Cliff Friend).

Disc: RCA Victor 21852 (Jessel/"My Mother's Eyes"/78).

The fourth of Hollywood's five part-talking hybrid musicals was released the day after *The Broadway Melody*, but to much less acclaim. *Lucky Boy* was produced by Tiffany-Stahl, a small but ambitious independent company that was to its Poverty Row brethren what MGM and Paramount were to the majors. George Jessel, presumably still smarting over his *Jazz Singer* snub, starred, sang almost all of the songs, wrote the dialogue for the sound sequences, and penned the titles for the silent footage. Apparently, he was too busy to come up with a name for his character, who was called ... Georgie Jessel.

Lucky Boy was initially filmed as a silent called *The Ghetto*, but after talkies began to take hold, Tiffany-Stahl informed Jessel that the movie would not be released unless sound could be added to it.[3] Jessel was offered 25 percent of the potential profits to supervise the new scenes, but he asked for, and received, a flat fee of $20,000. Jessel filmed the talking and singing sequences in New York; he employed the National Theatre and a full company of actors for the final scene.

The cinematic Georgie, son of a jeweler from the Bronx, repeatedly fails to break into show business, and his conservative parents (Rosa Rosanova, William H. Strauss) are against the idea. "Singing and joking is no business—better fix the watches," declares his papa. Still, Georgie scrounges up enough money to rent a theater to put on his own show, "Georgie Jessel's Bronx Follies." To lend realism to this amateur-night sequence, Tiffany-Stahl hired a talent agent to track down the two worst acts he could find in New York, which turned out to be a singing sister duo billed as Patty and Fields and an alleged comic called Joe Sevely.[4] Georgie, whose comedy monologue and rendition of "My Mother's Eyes" are part of the festivities, tells the audience that it doesn't matter whether they like him or not, because in any case his mama is praying for him.

With this very uneven lineup, the show fails. Georgie reins in his humiliation and travels to San Francisco to build a successful career as a radio and nightclub singer. He also meets a lovely young woman (Margaret Quimby). His career is temporarily stalled when mama becomes ill, but by the climax, Georgie has achieved permanent stardom in a Broadway revue, watched his mother recover and obtained parental blessing for his upcoming marriage.

Although it was an obvious rip-off of *The Jazz Singer*, *Lucky Boy* was fairly well reviewed. *Exhibitors Herald-World* awkwardly described it as "highly spectacular" and *Time* magazine's critic actually preferred it to *The Broadway Melody*.[5] *Variety* editor-critic "Sime" Silverman chose to compare Jessel to his former rival: "Of course, admitting no person in the world today can sing a ballad or a pop like Al Jolson, don't doubt but that George Jessel can sing. On top of that Jessel is a finished actor, on the stage or screen."[6]

Lucky Boy made a healthy profit—perhaps causing its star to regret his decision not to take a percentage—but Jessel never liked it very much. Its only lasting contribution was its theme song (sung no fewer than four times), "My Mother's Eyes," which became Jessel's signature tune. Except for Universal's 1929 part-talkie *Show Boat* (Chapter 7), all of the legitimate Hollywood musicals released after *Lucky Boy* were all-talking and all-singing.

QUEEN OF THE NIGHT CLUBS

(Warner Bros.; March 16, 1929)

Director: Bryan Foy. Screenplay: Murray Roth, Addison Burkhart. Photography: Ed Du Par. Running Time: 60 minutes (sound version; also released as silent).

Cast: Texas Guinan (Tex Malone), John Davidson (Don Holland), Lila Lee (Bee Walters), Arthur Housman (Andy Quinlan), Eddie Foy Jr. (Eddie Parr), Jack Norworth (Phil Parr), George Raft (George Raft), Jimmie Phillips (Nick Martin), William B. Davidson (assistant district attorney), John Miljan (Grant), Lee Shumway (Crandall), James T. Mack (judge), Joe Depew (boy), Agnes Franey (flapper), Charlotte Merriam (girl).

Songs: "It's Tough to Be a Hostess on Old Broadway" [Guinan] (authorship undetermined); "Sincerely I Do" [Lee, chorus] (Benny Davis, Joe Burke); "Sweet Georgia Brown" [danced by Raft] (Ben Bernie, Maceo Pinkard, Kenneth Casey); "There Must Be a Silver Lining" (Dolly Morse, Walter Donaldson); "Twelfth Street Rag" (Euday L. Bowman).

No history of the Jazz Age is complete without a mention of Mary Louise Cecilia Guinan (1884?–1933), a brassy blonde known to New York partygoers and government revenooers as "Texas." Guinan, who really was born in Texas (Waco), starred in a handful of movie Westerns between 1918 and 1921 while billed as "the female Bill Hart." But her lasting fame came as a hostess in a series of Big Apple nightclubs, the recurrent padlockings of which provided publicity for her succeeding ventures. Despite her knack for snappy catch phrases such as "Hello, sucker!" and "Give this little girl a hand!", Guinan allegedly lived quietly with her mother in Greenwich Village.

Guinan's "sucker" tag could have described the few people who turned out to view her movie comeback, a semi-musical melodrama called *Queen of the Night Clubs*. There was a good deal more dancing than singing. Most of the hoofing was done by Eddie Foy Jr. (brother of the film's director, Bryan Foy) and George Raft, who was cast as a bandleader in his film debut. Raft (1895–1980) was trading on his billing as the "world's fastest Charleston dancer," and one reviewer was moved enough to call his footwork "rip-snorting."[7] Raft, a protégé of Guinan's, had worked with her in the notoriously salacious stage musical *Padlocks of 1927*. Jack Norworth (1879–1962), the vaudeville actor-singer-composer best known for writing "Shine On, Harvest Moon" and "Take Me Out to the Ball Game," appeared in *Queen of the Night Clubs* as Guinan's ex-lover.

Unimaginatively cast as a speakeasy owner named Tex Malone, Guinan sang at least one song, with the autobiographical lyric "it's tough to be a hostess in a Broadway cafe," with a throaty voice described by *The New York Times* as "more powerful than melodious."[8] Judging from the partial soundtrack that exists (the picture portion is lost), Guinan also must have had a hand in the dialogue. When Tex is asked if she understands English, she replies, "Yes, but I'm

Buddy Rogers fumes as Jack Oakie (right) and Skeets Gallagher attempt some *Close Harmony* with Nancy Carroll.

more familiar with Scotch." She also boasts that she knows her way downtown to the police inspector's office—"blind-folded."

Tex clears the Foy character of a murder charge; it turns out that he's her long-lost son. Ruth Chatterton would do that kind of thing better in *Madame X*, and *Queen of the Night Clubs*, primitive in audio and visual even by early–1929 standards, turned out to be a royal flop. After a cameo in *Glorifying the American Girl* later in '29, Guinan would appear in only one more film: *Broadway Thru a Keyhole*, a backstage musical in which she played a supporting role. It was released four days before her sudden death of an intestinal infection.

CLOSE HARMONY

(Paramount; March 21, 1929)

Directors: John Cromwell, A. Edward Sutherland. Scenario: Percy Heath. Dialogue:

John V. A. Weaver, Percy Heath. Story: Elsie Janis, Gene Markey. Photography: J. Roy Hunt. Editor: Tay Malarkey. Sound: Franklin Hansen. Running Time: 66 minutes.

Cast: Charles "Buddy" Rogers (Al West), Nancy Carroll (Marjorie Merwin), Harry Green (Max Mindil), Jack Oakie (Ben Barney), Richard "Skeets" Gallagher (Johnny Bay), Matty Roubert (Bert), Ricca Allen (Mrs. Prosser), Wade Boteler (Kelly), Baby Mack (Sybil), Oscar Smith (George Washington Brown), Greta Granstedt (Eva Larue), Gus Partos (Gustav), Jesse Stafford and His Orchestra, Jean Harlow.

Songs: "I Wanna Go Places and Do Things" [Carroll, chorus], "I'm All A-Twitter and All A-Twirl" [Rogers, band], "She's So, I Dunno" [Oakie, Gallagher] (Leo Robin, Richard A. Whiting); "Twelfth Street Rag" [Rogers, band] (Euday L. Bowman).

Disc: Music Masters JJA-19806 (bootleg LP; ST).

Nancy Carroll (1906–1965) was a feisty Irish redhead from New York. Charles "Buddy" Rogers (b. 1904) was an unassuming all-American boy-type from the heartland. Despite the disparity in their backgrounds, Paramount found them a pleasing screen team in *Abie's Irish Rose,* the adaptation of the popular stageplay that was made as a silent and then fortified with patches of talk to become one of the biggest money-makers of 1929. For the pair's first all-talking release, the studio saw fit to show off Carroll's talent for song and dance (she'd been a Broadway chorine) and Rogers' ability to lead a jazz band and play a few instruments (which he'd done at Kansas University).

Close Harmony proved to be another hit. It was one of those "give the kid a break" stories, he being the "kid" and she being his benefactor. Al West is the leader of a struggling band whose only listeners are the boarding-house neighbors they keep awake every night. When Al, three weeks shy in his rent, is apprehended by his landlady and the corner cop after he tries to sneak out one evening, who should be watching but the musical comedy star Marjorie Merwin. Immediately attracted to Al, she pays his debt and gets the band a week's tryout at the Babylon Theatre, the palatial movie house where she headlines the stage show. The Babylon's manager, Max Mindil (Harry Green, the Jewish dialect comic), grants Marge's request because he's got a crush on her and wants to make her happy.

Meanwhile, Al vows to Marge that he will ask for her hand once his salary rises to $1,000 a week. "Al West's Admirals" are a success, but when Al impulsively asks for a raise to the desired amount, the jealous Max cans him in favor of a Van and Schenck-type duo, Barney and Bay—played by Jack Oakie and Richard "Skeets" Gallagher, both in the first of their many musicals for Paramount.[9] The so-called "Kings of Harmony" are self-impressed boors who bicker constantly offstage and show off their pipes at the drop of a hat. They debut at the Babylon with a sprightly comedy song, "She's So, I Dunno."

Marge schemes to break up Barney and Bay so Al can get his job back, and her feigned romantic interest in both singers sparks a nightclub fight that leaves the pair physically battered and professionally estranged. Max, needing a fill-in act, wants to hire Al back for the

$1,000 he'd requested, but the bandleader turns down the opportunity because it was gained through deception. Marge admonishes Al: "You can't live on promise. You've got to show them something ... you're yellow!" Whereupon Al is angered enough to take the stage and whip his orchestra through "Twelfth Street Rag." He does only the singing at first, but when his trumpeter blows a wrong note, he grabs the instrument away from him and plays a few bars. When the drummer slips up, Al moves behind the skins. Ditto for the tuba and piano. This number was modeled on a stunt Rogers had used in a stage act. As Al and Marge retreat to a dressing room to make amends, the contrite Barney and Bay serenade them outside their door with "The Wedding March."

Close Harmony was the first film directed by John Cromwell, a Broadway recruit who shared behind-the-camera duties with Hollywood veteran Eddie Sutherland. Many early talkies, especially those at Paramount, paired directors so the stage-trained half could concentrate on handling dialogue. Leo Robin and Richard A. Whiting contributed three songs, the most salable being "I Want to Go Places and Do Things," performed by Carroll before a head-on camera that cuts off most of the chorus behind her (which includes an extra named Jean Harlow). "I'm All A-Twitter and All A-Twirl" is delivered in a nasal tenor by Rogers, backed by the band. As in their subsequent musical *The Dance of Life,* Cromwell and Sutherland exhibit some dexterity with the camera, twice using lengthy tracking shots that move the action from the dressing rooms to the Babylon stage area.

Photoplay was exaggerating when it declared that *Close Harmony* was "the last word in talking pictures," but the film survives as an entertaining programmer that does its best to belie its early sound origins.

SYNCOPATION
(RKO; April 6, 1929)

Director: Bert Glennon. Dialogue Directors: Bertram Harrison, James Seymour. Producer: Robert T. Kane. Executive Producer: Joseph I. Schnitzer. Adaptation: Frances Agnew. Dialogue: Gene Markey. Based on the novel *Stepping High* by Gene Markey (1929).

Bobby Watson and Barbara Bennett were the primary couple in RKO's *Syncopation*, but Morton Downey (not pictured) ended up with the real Barbara.

Titles: Paul S. Haschke. Photography: Dal Clawson, George Webber, Frank Landi. Editor: Edward Pfitzenmeier. Sound: Tommy Cumming. Assistant Directors: Basil Smith, Fred Uttal. Running Time: 83 minutes.

Cast: Fred Waring's Pennsylvanians (themselves), Barbara Bennett (Flo Sloane), Bobby Watson (Benny Darrel), Ian Hunter (Alexander Winston), Morton Downey (Lew Lewis), Osgood Perkins (Jake Hummel), Verree Teasdale (Rita), Dorothy Lee (Peggy), Mackenzie Ward (Sylvester Cunningham), Gania Zielenska, David Buttolph, The Melody Boys.

Songs/Musical Numbers: "Do [Do] Something" [Lee, Downey] (Bud Green, Sam H. Stept); "I'll Always Be in Love with You" [Waring's Pennsylvanians; reprised by Downey] (Herman Ruby, Bud Green, Sam H. Stept); "Jericho" [Downey, Melody Boys; reprised by Downey, then by Waring's Pennsylvanians] (Leo Robin, Richard Myers); "Mine Alone"

[Waring's Pennsylvanians, danced by Bennett, Watson] (Clifford Grey, Richard Myers); "Tin Pan Parade" [Waring's Pennsylvanians] (Haven Gillespie, Richard A. Whiting); "Ah! Sweet Mystery of Life" [Waring's Pennsylvanians, danced by Bennett, Watson] (Rida Johnson Young, Victor Herbert); "Blue Yada-Da-Do" [Waring's Pennsylvanians], "My Inspiration Is You" [Downey] (authorship undetermined); "Bell Song" from *Lakme* [Zielenska] (Leo Delibes).

Disc: RCA Victor 21860 (Downey/"I'll Always Be in Love with You"/"My Inspiration Is You"/78); RCA Victor 21870 (Waring and Pennsylvanians/"I'll Always Be in Love with You"/"Jericho"/78).

The Radio-Keith-Orpheum Corporation—the future home of Fred Astaire, Ginger Rogers, *King Kong* and *Citizen Kane*—began life in October 1928 after a series of complicated mergers that united the powerful Radio

Corporation of America (RCA), the Keith-Albee-Orpheum circuit of vaudeville houses and the Film Booking Offices studio (FBO). The union was forged by two of America's most famous businessmen—radio giant David Sarnoff, who headed RCA, and presidential-father-to-be Joseph P. Kennedy, who controlled FBO—and was a rare studio merger completed at a time when Hollywood insiders incorrectly envisioned a handful of "super-studios" that would exert tight control over the industry. Warner Bros.' union with First National also came off, but pairings of Fox with MGM and Paramount with Warners never passed the rumor stage.

Sarnoff, who took control of the new RKO, envisioned an alliance between radio (NBC, which was RCA's network) and the movies, which led to its releases being trade-named "Radio Pictures." The first Radio release was a nightclub story called *Syncopation,* a film originally produced under FBO auspices. It was the first movie recorded with RCA's Photophone sound system. Top billing went to the popular Fred Waring and His Pennsylvanians, but Waring (1900–1984) and the boys had little to do other than attract patrons into RKO theaters. The band appeared twice in the completed film, playing six numbers over about 20 of the 83 minutes. One of the songs, "Jericho," became a sizable hit.

The first-billed actors were Bobby Watson, a stage juvenile who would become best known for impersonating Adolf Hitler in '40s films, and Barbara Bennett, the younger sister of Constance and Joan. They played a husband-and-wife ballroom adagio team, Flo Sloane and Benny Darrel, who hook up with a New York revue. Their union is threatened by a handsome playboy (Ian Hunter), who woos the impressionable dancing wife while her husband hangs out with his unsophisticated Broadway buddies. The money man dazzles his target with orchids and discreet dinners, and even sets up Flo (by now demanding to be billed as "Florette") as the headliner in her own club. But his proposal that the two run off to Paris goes over the moral line. She's "not that kind of a girl," the jilted millionaire is told, and Flo returns to her hubby and her original name.

Syncopation is believed to be a lost film, but the surviving sound elements reveal its true star. Lew Lewis, Benny's singing and songwriting

sidekick, was played by film newcomer Morton Downey (1902–1985), a chubby tenor popularly known as "The Irish Nightingale." Actually, Downey hailed from Wallingford, Connecticut—but the nightingale tag took, especially when he caressed the song hit "I'll Always Be in Love with You" in *Syncopation.* When Downey isn't crooning one of his many numbers in the film, he is uttering the kind of eternally optimistic dialogue that would become a staple of showbiz talkies:

Watson (speaking soberly about his character's suddenly shaky marriage): "We've been so happy for three years..."

Downey (upbeat): "Boy, that's a record, too!"

Watson (ignoring him): "I'll always be in love with her!"

Downey (making what sounds like a slap of his head): "What a song title! There it is! 'I'll Always Be in Love with You.' Words and music by Lew Lewis!" (He sits down at the piano to tinker with the melody as his chum is left alone to ponder his marital future.)

Lew also spends much time fending off the advances of his Dumb Dora sweetheart, played by Dorothy Lee. The real Downey succumbed shortly after the film's release; he married Barbara Bennett. You can blame them for the acid-tongued TV talk-show host Morton Downey Jr.

Lee (b. 1911), a vivacious teenage actress-singer, had appeared with Waring and band in their Broadway hit show *Hello Yourself,* and when the musicians were signed to appear in *Syncopation* in New York, she came along. In 1993, still well remembered for the comedies she made with Bert Wheeler and Robert Woolsey, she recalled her first film leading man.

> Morton Downey was a really nice man and I liked him. ... (But) he was very difficult to work with. I was 17 or 18 ... and he knew that even though I was in show business, I didn't know all the four-letter words. And he used them continually. He tried to shock me, which he did. Then I finally got the message to just let it roll over my head. I was horrified, and I'd tell Fred Waring ... how shocked I was and he'd say, "Just don't pay any attention to it."[10]

Another famous father on hand was Osgood Perkins, who was three years away from siring Anthony. The elder Perkins was a highly esteemed stage actor, but even he, cast as a pushy vaudeville agent, must have had problems with Gene Markey's clichéd story and talk. His best film role would come opposite Paul Muni in *Scarface* (1932).

Audiences were undiscerning about *Syncopation*, which RKO backed with a huge radio-boosted publicity push. Fascinated by the musical novelty, viewers packed New York's Hippodrome Theatre and broke all the house box-office records in two weeks. This was despite the warning by Mordaunt Hall, the highbrow film critic of *The New York Times*, that prospective patrons "who want something more subtle or polished will hardly enjoy the ramifications of the narrative."[11] That means he didn't like it too much.

MOTHER'S BOY

(Pathé; April 15, 1929)

Director: Bradley Barker. Dialogue Director: James Seymour. Producer: Robert T. Kane. Screenplay: Gene Markey. Photography: Philip Tannura, Harry Stradling, Walter Strenge. Editor: Edward Pfitzenmeier. Sound: V. S. Ashdown, J. A. Delaney. Set Director: Clark Robinson. Running Time: 82 minutes.

Cast: Morton Downey (Tommy O'Day), Beryl Mercer (Katie O'Day), John T. Doyle (Mr. O'Day), Brian Donlevy (Harry O'Day), Helen Chandler (Rose Lyndon), Osgood Perkins (Jake Sturmberg), Lorin Raker (Joe Bush), Barbara Bennett (Beatrix Townleigh), Jennie Moskowitz (Mrs. Apfelbaum), Jacob Frank (Mr. Apfelbaum), Louis Sorin (Mr. Bumble), Robert Gleckler (Gus Le Grand), Tyrrell Davis (Duke of Pomplum), Allan Vincent (Dinslow), Leslie Stowe (evangelist), Ruth Hunt (singer), Ruthie Mahon, De Leon and Bibi (dancers).

Songs: "Come to Me" [Downey], "I'll Always Be Mother's Boy" [Downey, twice], "There'll Be You and I" [Downey, twice] (Bud Green, Sam H. Stept); "I Was Not So Particular" [Downey] (Jack Val, Bud Green, Sam H. Stept); "There's a Place in the Sun for You" [Downey] (Bud Green, Sammy Fain); "The World Is Yours and Mine" [Downey] (Bud Green, Sam H. Stept, James F. Hanley); "Irish Song" [Downey] (B. H. Downey); "Onward, Christian Soldiers" [Downey, chorus] (Sabine Baring-Gould, Arthur Sullivan); "Tango Cal-legita" [danced by De Leon and Bibi] (Don Pedro De Leon); "What's the Use of Repining?" [Downey] (trad.).

Disc: RCA Victor 21940 (Downey/"I'll Always Be Mother's Boy"/"There'll Be You and I"/78); RCA Victor 21958 (Downey/"There's a Place in the Sun for You"/"The World Is Yours and Mine"/78).

Mother's Boy premiered on the heels of *Syncopation*, but this time Morton Downey had star billing all to himself. Unfortunately, the prolific Gene Markey, having also knocked out the script for *Syncopation* and the story basis for *Close Harmony*, didn't have much left to give the earnest tenor in Pathé's wretched knock-off of *The Jazz Singer*.

Downey played Tommy O'Day, a lumpy grocery delivery boy who contends with his much handsomer brother (Brian Donlevy, at 30 already in need of a toupee) for the affections of their lovely young neighbor (Helen Chandler). Actually, Tommy has stronger yearnings for his cuddly Ma (Beryl Mercer), to whom he writes songs and calls by her first name. But his family ties are abruptly severed after he is framed by the caddish brother over the latter's brazen theft from the family piggybank.

At a mission for the down-and-out, Tommy's hymn-singing attracts the attention of an unemployed press agent (Lorin Raker), whose contacts bring the tenor to nightclub prominence. A gold-digging society lass helps Tommy gain a spot in a Broadway revue, but on the eve of the show's debut, he's told that his heartsick mama is near death. Of course, he ditches the show to sing "I'll Always Be Mother's Boy" at her bedside—and, of course, she recovers. So does sonny's career, thanks to the front-page human interest stories the wily PR man has fed to the papers. Tommy also wins the ingenue, the bad brother having confessed his frame-up in a letter written from South America.

Downey, as if to make his public forgive the scatterbrained plotting, sings early and often—nine songs, six with lyrics by Bud Green. Bradley Barker's creaky direction is from the *Lights of New York* school, but *Mother's Boy* at least boasts an interesting cast. Besides Donlevy, little more than a bit actor in his first talkie, and Chandler, the star-crossed leading lady of *Dracula* fame, there are two holdovers from

Morton Downey is encouraged by his "best girl" (Beryl Mercer) in Pathé's insipid *Mother's Boy*.

Syncopation: the inevitable Barbara Bennett (she's the femme fatale) and Osgood Perkins. Perkins is almost unrecognizable as an elderly, vaguely Middle European violinist who cheers Downey on with dialogue like "You must sing tonight as you have never sung before!"

"It is a pity," wrote *The New York Times* about *Mother's Boy*, "that there is not more fun and less jerking at the heart strings."[12] The crosstown *Post* was more direct in its summation of "a dull, uneventful and sentimental debauch."[13]

THE RAINBOW MAN

(Sono Art/Paramount; April 16, 1929)

Director: Fred Newmeyer. Producers: George W. Weeks, O. E. Goebel. Screenplay: George J. Crone. Adaptation: Frances Agnew. Dialogue: Frances Agnew, Eddie Dowling.

Story: Eddie Dowling. Photography: Jack McKenzie. Editor: J. R. Crone. Running Time: 96 minutes.

Cast: Eddie Dowling (Rainbow Ryan), Frankie Darro (Billy Ryan), Marian Nixon (Mary Lane), Sam Hardy (Doc Hardy), Lloyd Ingraham (Colonel Lane), George "Gabby" Hayes (Bill), The Rounders.

Songs: "Little Pal" [Dowling, Darro] (Eddie Dowling, James F. Hanley); "The Rainbow Man" [Rounders] (James F. Hanley); "Sleepy Valley" [Dowling, twice] (Andrew B. Sterling, James F. Hanley).

Filling up a page of the July 18, 1928, issue of *Variety* was an ad with these words: "Mr. Talking Picture Executive! Who Has Greater Personal Popularity? Who Has More Impressive Box-Office Records? Who Knows Better What the Public Wants—Than EDDIE DOWLING and His Associate James F. Hanley!" Few entertainers would have had the ego to place an ad like that, but few entertainers had as much moxie as Eddie Dowling.

Dowling (1894–1976) is largely forgotten today, but he was one of the most versatile talents of Broadway and vaudeville. An actor, director, producer, playwright and songwriter, he made his Broadway debut in 1917; five years later, *Sally, Irene and Mary* became the first of his many musical comedy hits. With Hanley, a composer of some renown, he'd written the score to the 1926 stage success *Honeymoon Lane*. Dowling had no pretentions about his audience—Irish and working class. His shows were moralistic, uncomplicated in plot and broadly sentimental. Critics sniped at his fervent Roman Catholicism and Democratic political leanings. (Dowling was a vocal supporter of New York Governor Al Smith in Smith's 1928 presidential run against Herbert Hoover.)

But now, like so many others, Dowling had caught the movie bug. Since few people west of, say, Schnectady knew him by name, it figured to be a challenge. He made a deal with Fox, but it fell through and he settled for the independent Sono Art company, for which he would star and write stories and music for dialogue pictures. The first of these, released by Paramount, was *The Rainbow Man,* an exceedingly maudlin comedy-drama recalling *The Singing Fool.*

Dowling played fast-talking minstrel man Rainbow Ryan, whose showbiz motto is "Bigger and better than ever!" On tour in vaudeville, Rainbow adopts Billy (Frankie Darro), the 6-year-old son of an acrobat friend (George Hayes, pre–"Gabby") who perished on the job. ("I'm getting out of the four-a-days at last!" exclaims the victim in one of his final gasps.) After hooking up with Doc Hardy's blackface troupe, Rainbow falls in love with a small-town beauty, Mary Lane (Marian Nixon, 1904–1983), whose conservative father disapproves of theater people. This, and Rainbow's abrupt discharge from the minstrel show, threatens to end their romance. Rainbow and Billy go to New York, but Mary follows him and discloses that the boy is the child of her long-deceased sister. Rainbow is prompted to blurt out a nervous, and lengthy, marriage proposal, but Mary doesn't need that much convincing.

Almost immediately, Old Man Lane (Lloyd Ingraham) shows up to remind Rainbow that he has no money and no job. Rainbow gallantly gives up his two loves, who return to the sticks. But Doc (Sam Hardy) saves the day by offering an apology to his old colleague. Rainbow is made a partner in the Hardy show, which happens to be headed for the Lanes' locale. At said performance, Rainbow interrupts his singing of "Sleepy Valley" to plead for a reconciliation with Mary, whom he has spotted in the audience. Mary replies that the theater is a terrible place to bring up the subject, but...

One of the film's three songs, "Little Pal," a duet for Dowling and the 11-year-old Darro, not only recalled "Sonny Boy" from *The Singing Fool,* it duplicated the title of the upcoming Al Jolson-Davey Lee-Warner Bros. follow-up, which was produced as *Little Pal* but necessarily released as *Say It with Songs.* The ballad "Sleepy Valley" became a prolific seller as covered by both Gus Arnheim's band and James Melton.

Dowling and his producers, O. E. Goebel and George W. Weeks, pulled out all the stops for the New York premiere of *The Rainbow Man.* They erected a flashing sign shaped like a phonograph disc on dark walls of tall buildings along 42nd Street east and west of Broadway. Dowling recruited his friend Al Smith to introduce the movie, on camera as well as from the live audience. In his own pre-curtain speech, the star told the first-nighters that he would continue to make "clean" pictures, which inspired the *Variety* reviewer to ask Dowling in print to make better movies than *The Rainbow Man* or "devote the rest of his life to national campaigning before clubs and societies."[14] The public did not share this view, for—surprise!— *The Rainbow Man* turned out to be a moderate hit.

INNOCENTS OF PARIS
(Paramount; April 26, 1929)

Director: Richard Wallace. Producer: Jesse L. Lasky. Adaptation and Dialogue: Ethel Doherty, Ernest Vajda. Based on the story "Flea Market" by Clarence Edward Andrews (1928). Titles: George Marion Jr. Photography: Charles Lang. Editor: George Arthur. Sound: Franklin Hansen. Art Director: Hans Dreier. Dance Direction: LeRoy Prinz, Fanchon and Marco. Running Time: 78 minutes (sound version; also released as silent).

"It" man Maurice Chevalier (right) easily outshone fellow actors Russell Simpson and Sylvia Beecher in Paramount's *Innocents of Paris*.

Cast: Maurice Chevalier (Maurice Marny), Sylvia Beecher (Louise Leval), Russell Simpson (Émile Leval), George Fawcett (Monsieur Marny), Mrs. George Fawcett [Percy Haswell] (Madame Marny), John Miljan (Monsieur Renard), Margaret Livingston (Madame Renard), David Durand (Jo-Jo), Jack Luden (Jules), Johnnie Morris (Sunshine, a musician).

Songs: "It's a Habit of Mine" [Chevalier], "Louise" [Chevalier], "On Top of the World, Alone" [Chevalier, three times], "Wait Till You See Ma Chérie" [nightclub band] (Leo Robin, Richard A. Whiting); "Dites-Moi, Ma Mère" [Chevalier] (Maurice Yvain); "Les Ananas" [French version of "Yes! We Have No Bananas"] [Chevalier] (original lyrics and music, Frank Silver, Irving Cohn); "Valentine" [Chevalier] (Albert Willemetz, Herbert Reynolds, Henri Christine).

Disc: RCA Victor 21918 (Chevalier/ "Louise"/"Wait Till You See Ma Chérie"/78);

RCA Victor 22007 (Chevalier/"It's a Habit of Mine"/"On Top of the World, Alone"/78); RCA Victor 22093 (Chevalier/"Les Ananas"/ "Valentine"/78); WRC SH 156 (bootleg LP; ST).

To consider *Innocents of Paris* is to marvel that it produced the first new superstar of the musical cinema. A banal, incongruous tale about a song-and-dance vagabond—a Parisian junk dealer—who befriends an orphaned little boy and then falls in love with the lad's upper-crust aunt, its story practically mirrored that of *The Rainbow Man*. But Eddie Dowling was no Maurice Chevalier; there was no one quite like Maurice Chevalier.

Before he made his American movie debut at age 40, Chevalier (1888–1972) was famous in his native France as a top-billed star of music halls. His appeal lay in his roguish manner, twinkling blue eyes and suggestive swagger, and what he lacked in voice he more than made up for in charm. Chevalier, whose only previous on-camera experience was in a dozen short French films, made a successful screen test for MGM in Paris in the summer of 1928, but negotiations on a contract fell through. Despite this, Metro production chief Irving Thalberg gifted the singer with a print of the test. When Jesse L. Lasky, Thalberg's counterpart at Paramount, offered a tryout of his own, Chevalier screened the MGM test for him and was signed.

Chevalier's journey to America was high-profile—thanks to Paramount, which filmed a short documentary, *Bonjour New York!*, during his first few days there, and then furnished the "French Al Jolson" and his singer-actress wife, Yvonne Vallee, with an elaborate, star-studded reception upon their arrival in Los Angeles after a five-day cross-country train ride. But upon being shown the lackluster script for *Innocents of Paris*, Chevalier threatened to return home. He became even more upset when Harry d'Abbadie d'Arrast, a director he respected, turned down an offer to helm the picture. Journeyman Richard Wallace got the assignment instead. Chevalier committed to the project only after Paramount agreed to include three songs—"Dites-Moi, Ma Mère," "Les Ananas" and "Valentine"—that Chevalier had popularized in his music-hall act.[15]

At the end of 1928, Paramount had only enough equipment to make two talkies at a time. Then a fire destroyed the studio's newly built soundstage, and *Innocents of Paris* had to be completed during the night shift, on makeshift sets that were heavily draped to keep out outside noise. (The fire interrupted the production of two other musicals, *Close Harmony* and *The Dance of Life*.) But Paramount took pains to make its new star comfortable, and a duplicate of his dressing room at the Parisianna music hall was built for use in the picture. An unexpected problem for Chevalier was the scene-stealing savvy of 6-year-old David Durand, cast as the orphan. Wrote Chevalier in his autobiography, *The Man in the Straw Hat*:

> In the course of the film the child was supposed to be overcome with grief at the memory of his mother. I had to put my arms around his neck and console him. Finally to distract him I put on a soldier costume and sang a song called "Dites-Moi, Ma Mère"

[Tell Me, Mother]. He was to stop crying, look at me in surprise, and then finally join me in singing and climb on my back shouting with joy. ... When we came to the part where I put my arm around his shoulder and spoke to him tenderly the cameras stopped and the director said we must do it over again. This happened twice and I finally asked what was wrong. ... The director explained that the child ... kept moving just far enough away from me so that I had to turn to speak to him and, whereas his whole face would show on the screen, only the back of my neck would be seen. I couldn't believe that an old veteran like me was being buffaloed by this small child.[16]

After Durand received a good talking-to from Richard Wallace, he and Chevalier did the scene over again, and the same thing happened. So there was another take:

> Once more we got to the spot where he was sobbing. I put my arm around his neck. And, as I spoke tender words in English to him, I clutched the neck of that little beast with all my strength and thus managed to get through the whole scene with at least my profile showing.[17]

Generally, however, Chevalier found the atmosphere agreeable, and the studio was so happy with the daily rushes that, by the end of the fourth week of production, it offered him a year's extension on his contract and a hefty raise. Chevalier jumped at the offer, thinking that the awful script would ensure the film's failure and prompt Paramount to buy out his pact. Imagine his astonishment when *Innocents of Paris* became a big hit!

Foremost among the picture's attractions was Chevalier's treatment of "Louise," one of four songs by composer Richard A. Whiting (1891–1938) and lyricist Leo Robin (1900–1984), in their first movie assignment. Chevalier's character, the junkman Maurice Marny, uses it to serenade the ingenue (Sylvia Beecher). The number was staged with little imagination—the star stands stiffly and sings while holding Beecher's hands as she sits on a fence in a park on a moonlit night. But his rendition lingered in enough minds, in and out of theaters, to turn it into a major seller. Actually, the film's theme song is another Robin-Whiting tune, "On Top of the World, Alone," which Chevalier's Marny sings three times as he rises to the verge of overnight stardom, then forsakes his new career for happiness with his sweetheart.

To ease the challenge of acquainting the Frenchman to American audiences, it was decided to begin the film with a brief, and rather elementary, prologue in which Chevalier (sounding ill at ease) introduces himself:

Ladies and gentlemen, before presenting my first international talking picture, I would suggest this: Our story is a story of Paris. All the characters portrayed in it are French. But don't be afraid (laughs)—we will play it in English. You will notice that one of the cast speaks with an accent. That would be me. (Laughs) But of course, I thought it was much better for me to struggle with your English than to make you struggle with my French. Because if I spoke French, you might misunderstand.

Chevalier makes his point with a short story about a comment he made to an American female dinner acquaintance who mistook it for a come-on.

Then the junkman's saga begins as he rescues poor little Jo-Jo from the Seine, into which the boy's mother has just thrown herself.[18] After cheering the lad up with "Dites-Moi, Ma Mère," Maurice returns him to his lovely aunt, Louise Leval (Beecher), and his embittered grandfather, Émile (Russell Simpson). The well-to-do Émile, whose meanness had prompted his older daughter's suicide, opposes his sheltered younger daughter's romance with a man of such lowly station.

But the self-billed "antique dealer" sings on the side, and his delivery of "Les Ananas" at the obscure Flea Market club catches the attention of the glamorous Madame Renard (Margaret Livingston) and her theater-manager husband (John Miljan). Maurice's career aspirations are furthered at an amateur talent show with a rendition of "Valentine," complete with "impressions" of various Frenchmen (a nervous nellie and a passionate patriot, for two) as they would sing it. The Renards sponsor the newcomer and arrange for his debut, as "The Mysterious Prince," at the prestigious Montmartre Casino. Madame Renard's flirting with Maurice makes Louise jealous, and she promises her father that since she won't be marrying Maurice, she cannot marry anyone.

Thinking the worst of the younger man,

Emile rushes to the theater and stalks his prospective son-in-law with a pistol. Louise, seeking to keep Maurice from an early demise, distracts him from arriving at the casino by having him arrested for attempted assault (on her). But Maurice talks the local gendarmes into letting him take the stage for his coming-out, while Jo-Jo, endowed by the screenwriters with a wisdom beyond his years, dresses down grandpa by telling him, "All you do is hate ... don't hate them any more." Maurice, thinking he's lost Louise, glumly sings "On Top of the World, Alone" in junkman garb, then shocks the enthralled audience with an announcement: "Now I go back to the streets. This is my first, and last, appearance." From the wings, Louise exhorts Maurice to appreciate the applause, and he summons her to the stage to share an embrace and to hear his reprise of "On Top of the World, Alone."

Not surprisingly, the skimpy, soapy plot of *Innocents of Paris* (which was also filmed in a French-language version, *La Chanson de Paris*) displeased many critics. *Variety*'s "Sid" was miffed enough to declare that "it is difficult to figure (Chevalier) in a successful American screen career."[19] *The New York Times* was somewhat more prescient: "Without Chevalier, this latest specimen of audible films would be a sad affair.... He is the whole show, and when he is off the screen the suspense consists of waiting until he reappears."[20] Truly, the Frenchman receives little help from his decidedly non-Gallic supporting cast, especially Simpson, better cast in movies as a hick type, and Beecher, who gives an inexpressive, insipid performance in her one-shot as a leading lady.

Chevalier, suddenly Paramount's most valuable commodity (next to Clara Bow), won a five-year contract from the studio and became the subject of another massive publicity campaign that touted him as the "It" man of the screen. He was soon to get better stories—and much better directors.

ON WITH THE SHOW!
(Warner Bros.; May 20, 1929)

Director: Alan Crosland. Producer: Darryl F. Zanuck. Scenario and Dialogue: Robert Lord. Based on the play *Shoestring* by Humphrey Pearson. Photography: Tony Gaudio.

Sally O'Neil and William Bakewell are dressed for success in Warner's all–Technicolor *On with the Show!*

Editor: Jack Killifer. Sound: Lewis Geib, Max Parker, F. N. Murphy, Victor Vance. Musical Director: Louis Silvers. Dance Direction: Larry Ceballos. Running Time: 103 minutes. Technicolor.

Cast: Betty Compson (Nita French), Louise Fazenda (Sarah Fogarty), Sally O'Neil (Kitty), Joe E. Brown (Joe Beaton), Purnell B. Pratt (Sam Bloom), Arthur Lake (Harold Astor), William Bakewell (Jimmy), Sam Hardy (Jerry Price), Wheeler Oakman (Bobby Wallace), Thomas Jefferson (Dad), Lee Moran (Pete), Harry Gribbon (Joe), Josephine Houston (Harold's fiancée), Henry Fink (father), Otto Hoffman (Bert), Ethel Waters (herself), Fairbanks Twins (Dorsey Twins), Mildred Carroll, Angelus Babe, Harmony Four Quartette, Four Covans.

Songs: "Am I Blue?" [Waters, Harmony Four], "Birmingham Bertha" [Waters, danced by Babe], "Don't It Mean a Thing to You?" [Houston, Lake; reprised by Houston], "In the Land of Let's Pretend" [Carroll, chorus], "Let Me Have My Dreams" [Compson, twice; then O'Neil, twice; all dubbed by Houston], "Lift the Juleps to Your Two Lips" [Fink, Houston, chorus, danced by Four Covans], "Welcome Home" [Fink, chorus] (Grant Clarke, Harry Akst).

Disc: Columbia 1837 (Waters/"Am I Blue?"/"Birmingham Bertha"/78).

Hardly satisfied with having made the first synchronized feature film, the first part-talking feature and the first all-talkie, Warner Bros. set out to produce the first all-talking, all-singing, all-dancing, *all-Technicolor* movie. But the studio might have picked a better item with which to splash its hues than the lackluster backstager *On with the Show!*

Two-strip Technicolor photography had appeared in the movies as early as 1917; it was an improvement over the practice of hand-tinting films frame by frame. The process really didn't catch on until two major releases, *The Ten Commandments* (1923) and *Ben-Hur* (1925), offered two-color sequences. Thereafter, color was employed more often, but primarily to provide an interlude to the action than to heighten its drama. Only occasionally was there an all-color feature film, the most notable being the Douglas Fairbanks swashbuckler *The Black Pirate* (1926). Even in the very late silent era, when Hollywood sought novelties with which to battle radio, the two-color system was not widely popular.

The process had far too many inconsistencies, for one. It could not provide "pure" hues — greens and certain shades of red looked fine, but solid reds, yellows and blues could not be produced naturally. Cameramen had to use an abnormal amount of light, supplemented by heaps of makeup on the actors, to achieve certain colors. William Bakewell, who acted in *On with the Show!*, remembered that "blue had a tendency to turn green on screen. I played an usher, and my blue uniform had green overtones. And the flesh tones came out pink!"[21]

Still, the fancy sets and costumes of the new musicals necessitated the expanded use of color. *The Broadway Melody* contained a memorable Technicolor section, and as *On with the Show!* was being filmed, color reels were being added to *Broadway* and *William Fox Movietone Follies of 1929*. But the Warner Bros. movie would be two-color for every one of its 103 minutes, an asset appreciated by a *Film Daily* critic when he saw the picture with an enthralled audience.

> The first tremor of excitement was created by a prosaic taxicab. It appeared to be yellow. When it sidled across the screen in the opening scene, horn screeching, the audience applauded. It was the color that did it.[22]

Watched in an age in which color is the norm instead of a novelty, *On with the Show!* reveals the liabilities identified by perceptive critics of 1929. It's talky, overly melodramatic and, like many Warners pictures of the time, needlessly plotty. Moreover, since the color negatives are long lost, this is now a landmark film that is without its landmark. Robert Lord's screenplay, based on an unpublished play by Humphrey Pearson about a theatrical troupe struggling to bring a musical comedy to the big time, abounds in unnecessary characters and complicating storylines. But the biggest disappointment is the uninventive presentation of the musical numbers. Director Alan Crosland, cameraman Tony Gaudio and dance director Larry Ceballos were hampered by technical limitations. The camera, still encased in its soundproof booth, had to be placed at some distance from the stage, where a total of 38 (according to the film's pressbook) hidden microphones aspired to catch the hackneyed dialogue. This resulted in almost constant long or medium shots that frustratingly cut off at the knees of the chorus members. With two notable exceptions, the poorly synchronized songs by Harry Akst and Grant Clarke are mediocre, although given the premise of the film, they may have been written that way on purpose.

The cast of *On with the Show!* contains no Jolsons or Chevaliers, which befits its concept as a *Grand Hotel*-type piece with multiple stories linked by time and place. Stuck in a tank town with the future of his show, *The Phantom Sweetheart*, in jeopardy, producer Jerry Price (Sam Hardy, ill at ease before King Mike) is besieged by financial woes. His actors have been forced to beg for their paychecks — especially Harold Astor (Arthur Lake), the whiny juvenile lead — and the props-and-scenery dealer (Purnell B. Pratt) now threatens to attach the box office. Although his girlfriend, Nita French (Betty Compson), is the leading lady, money man Bobby Wallace (Wheeler Oakman) has reneged on his backing. Only with the life savings of "Dad" (Thomas Jefferson, a descendant of the original), the kindly old stage doorman, has Jerry been able to keep the production going. Other key characters on hand are the show's soubrette (the delightful Louise Fazenda), whose only real talent is her risque giggle, and the troupe's usher and hat-check girl (William Bakewell and Sally O'Neil), who are both young and in love.

The film alternates between the off-stage theatrics and the on-stage performance of the show, which unfolds in real time and is visible enough so that we can easily follow its story. *The Phantom Sweetheart* is a vapid musical comedy about a young Southerner (Lake) who is enticed by a veiled, mysteriously reappearing beauty (Compson) on the eve of his wedding. The youth's requisite comic sidekick is played by a surprisingly unfunny Joe E. Brown, in the first of his many films for Warner Bros. One of the running gags is that the Lake and Brown characters are as acrimonious away from the footlights as they are chummy before them. The nadir of this production is a fantasy sequence set in "The Land of Let's Pretend," an excuse for high production values and low comedy:

Brown: "There's a mortal within our portal, who is guilty of the greatest offense in the Land of Let's Pretend."

Compson (as the queen of the land): "But there is no offense in the Land of Let's Pretend."

Brown: "Let's pretend there is!"

You get the idea. Meanwhile, a catfight breaks out off stage (just as the ingenue on stage declares, "How calm and peaceful the old plantation is at dusk!"); a bit actor passes out from hunger, forcing producer Jerry on stage for a few jittery moments; and the box office is robbed. Worst of all, Nita refuses to continue her performance without some ready cash. The quick-thinking usher recruits his ambitious sweetie to take the star's place—the character is veiled, remember—and *The Phantom Sweetheart* is catapulted from near-ruin to a Broadway destiny. The hat-check girl becomes a star, "Dad" is saved from prison, and Nita—who, we learn, is secretly married to Wallace—beats her unreliable hubby into a pulp.

"It would have been better if this film had no story and no sound, for it is like a clumsy person arrayed in Fifth Avenue finery," declared *The New York Times*.[23] Indeed, for all its splashy hues, *On with the Show!* grossed less than $200,000 in the United States. The film edged out of the red only on the strength of its foreign box office, according to studio financial records. It is best remembered today as the movie debut of the great Ethel Waters (1896–1977), albeit in two extraneous numbers, "Am I Blue?" and "Birmingham Bertha," that could be easily cut for screenings to less racially tolerant audiences. "Am I Blue?" became a huge hit, which was what Warners expected. Its composer, Harry Akst (1894–1963), had brought Waters to the studio especially to sing the spotlight song; she had popularized his earlier "Dinah." Waters recorded the most popular version of "Am I Blue?", but it was notably covered by Libby Holman, Annette Hanshaw and the Nat Shilkret, Ben Selvin and Tom Gerun orchestras. Waters was paid $5,000 for a guaranteed four weeks of work in what would be her only feature before 1934. There wasn't much opportunity in Hollywood for a black star with more energy than Stepin Fetchit.

For years, *On with the Show!* was considered to be a precursor to the more famous *42nd Street* (1933) because of their similarity in plot. The latter film was even called a remake of *On with the Show!* by some. But as the 1929 movie became available for reappraisal, it became apparent that the films' only major connections were their Warner Bros. origins and their resolutions—an acting newcomer saves a show. They don't even derive from the same source. As overrated as Ruby Keeler's climactic performance in *42nd Street* is, Sally O'Neil (1908–1968) does even less to merit instant stardom. She just stands there and mouths a few bars of "Let Me Have My Dreams" to an astonished Lake. That she sounds very familiar to Compson when we heard her sing the same song twice before is more than just a necessity for the actress-switch ploy, for it's the same voice! Josephine Houston dubbed the singing for both women.

"Voice-doubling" was not an uncommon practice in early talkies. The Hungarian tenor Joseph Diskay sang "Kol Nidre" for Warner Oland in *The Jazz Singer*. Richard Barthelmess and Gary Cooper already had been dubbed for songs in the non-musicals *Weary River* and *Wolf Song*, respectively. And that definitely wasn't Laura La Plante playing and singing "Deep River" in *Show Boat* (Chapter 7). Because post-synchronization was still rare, the real singer had to do his or her stuff before a microphone just out of camera range as the actor mouthing the words was being filmed. The actor, in turn, had to train his eyes on the singer to be able to move her or his lips in time to the voice. What makes the doubling in *On with the Show!* unusual is that the actress who plays the juvenile's fiancée in *The Phantom Sweetheart* is none other than Josephine Houston, which means that she's competing against herself, kind of, for the affections of Arthur Lake. In the flesh, Houston sings "Don't It Mean a Thing to You?" (with Lake) and "Lift the Juleps to Your Two Lips" (with Henry Fink and the *Phantom Sweetheart* chorus).

Of course, William Bakewell (1908–1993) knew all the time that the voice wasn't his sweetheart's. "Sally O'Neil was not a singer at all," he recalled to the author. "She had kind of a shanty Irish accent. But she was a sweet girl— we did three pictures together." *On with the Show!* may not have been one of their better teamings, but its large cast enabled Bakewell to enjoy himself.

> We worked at the old Vitagraph studio, which had a huge sound stage with a marvelous theater set, and that's where we spent long hours for weeks and weeks and weeks. Arthur Lake and I palled around a lot— we had done *Harold Teen* together—and we had more fun because there were lots of pretty girls.[24]

WILLIAM FOX MOVIE-TONE FOLLIES OF 1929

(Fox; May 25, 1929)

Directors: David Butler, Marcel Silver. Story: David Butler. Dialogue: William K. Wells. Photography: Charles Van Enger. Editor: Ralph Dietrich. Sound: Joseph E. Aiken. Costumes: Sophie Wachner, Alice O'Neill. Musical Director: Arthur Kay. Dance Direction: Archie Gottler, Fanchon and Marco. Running Time: 80 minutes. Multicolor sequence.

Cast: John Breeden (George Shelby), Lola Lane (Lila Beaumont), DeWitt Jennings (Jay Darrell), Sharon Lynn (Ann Foster), Arthur Stone (Al Leaton), Stepin Fetchit (Swifty), Warren Hymer (Martin), Archie Gottler (stage manager), Arthur Kay (orchestra leader), Mario Dominici (Le Maire), Vina Gale and Arthur Springer, Helen Hunt and Charles Huff, Harriet Griffith and John Griffith (adagio dancers), Evans and Weaver, Mitchell and Redman, Four Covans, Sam and Sam, Brown and Stevens, Jackie Cooper. Principals in Song and Dance Numbers: Sue Carol, Dixie Lee, David Percy, David Rollins, Frank Richardson, Melva Cornell, Paula Langlen, Carolynne Snowden, Jeanette Dancey, Bobby Burns, Henry M. Mollandin, Frank La Mont.

Songs: "Big City Blues" [Lane], "The Breakaway" [Carol, Dancey, chorus], "Legs," "Pearl of Old Japan" [danced as "underwater" ballet], "That's You, Baby" [Percy, Lynn, Carol, Rollins, Lee, Richardson, Burns, Cooper], "Walking with Susie" [Richardson, chorus], "Why Can't I Be Like You?" [Lee] (Sidney Mitchell, Archie Gottler, Con Conrad).

Also Known As: *Fox Movietone Follies of 1929*.

In many film histories, *William Fox Movietone Follies of 1929* (the copyrighted title) is included as one of the all-star revues churned out by the major studios with the advent of sound. Actually, it was not quite an "all-star" film—Fox's biggest names didn't appear until 1930's *Happy Days*—but was more a backstager with revue scenes tacked on. Still, it was a big deal for the studio, or else William Fox wouldn't have put his name on it.

As discussed earlier, Fox's studio had pioneered the Movietone sound-on-film system. After use in newsreels and shorts and for underscoring, sound effects, and dialogue scenes in a few otherwise-silent features, Movietone debuted as a feature-length talking format in the landmark Western *In Old Arizona* (December 25, 1928). The film, which brought Warner Baxter a Best Actor Academy Award as the Cisco Kid, demonstrated Movietone's superiority over the disc-based Vitaphone with an inventive use of sound and a surprising clarity of recording in the many outdoor scenes. But even before the premiere of *In Old Arizona*, chairman Fox had given the go-ahead for a big-budget musical, and *Movietone Follies* went into production in November of 1928.

The initial idea was to present *Movietone Follies* as a plotless revue, the first of a series (which explains the "1929" in the title). The company considered it something of an experiment, and the filming was shrouded in mystery. Each director on the lot was to helm a scene; each director would provide the story and gags, as well as select his personnel from the list of contract players. But this method proved too unwieldy. By March of 1929, it was decided to weave a love story throughout the film and supplement it with the musical numbers. By this time, the film's budget was already about $850,000.[25] A Frenchman named Marcel Silver was assigned to direct, but he soon was replaced by David Butler (1894–1979), a character actor who was just beginning a 40-year career as a director.

Silver began the project by filming a series of elaborate musical numbers, but nothing else, which—as Butler recalled nearly 50 years later—alarmed Fox production head Winfield Sheehan enough to put in a call for reinforcements.

Stepin Fetchit has an urgent message for the charming Sue Carol in *William Fox Movietone Follies of 1929.*

Buddy [De Sylva] phoned me and said, "We've got a meeting tonight at 8 o'clock in Sheehan's office." So we went in: De Sylva, Brown, Henderson and myself. Sheehan said, "You've got to save us. We've got 10 numbers. If we can get any kind of a story—Dave, you can direct it fast—we'll save some of this money that I've spent." We said we'd look at these numbers the next day, which we did. We sat down that night and the next day and came up with the story of the *Fox Follies of 1929.* ... I shot the story in five days and five nights. We used some of the numbers, but we threw out six of them.[26]

The biggest gamble Fox took with *Movietone Follies,* however, was not on film, but *in* the film. William Fox had envisioned the so-called "Grandeur" process for nearly two years; his company had spent $1.5 million on the lab research alone. The new film stock was 70 millimeters wide instead of 35. It was stereoscopic and could be used to shoot in color, but its principal advantage was that it offered space for a

wider sound track, which, it was thought, would permit better sound recording. Fox intended to exhibit the 70mm version only in large cities; the rest of the country would be shown the standard format. Both versions would contain a revue sequence in two-color Multicolor. However, beyond the preview stage, *Movietone Follies* was seen only in 35mm. The first real test of "Grandeur" would not come until *Happy Days* (Chapter 10).

Butler's slim *Movietone Follies* story concerned George Shelby, a well-to-do Southern lad who comes to the big city to dissuade his sweetheart, Lila Beaumont, from making a career on the wicked stage. These roles went to John Breeden (1904–1977), a film newcomer, and Lola Lane (1906–1981), the eldest of the three acting sisters who would go on to fame at Warner Bros. in the '30s. George decides to buy out the controlling interest in the revue in which his sweetie will appear. Then he fires her, but she claims he can't.

"Why not?" he asks firmly.

"Because Equity won't let you," she replies. "Who's he?" demands the unknowing country boy.

Lila not only stays, but when the temperamental leading lady (Sharon Lynn) balks at going on for opening night, she is pressed into duty. She's a big hit. So George sells the show back to the original producer at a hefty profit and goes back home to marry his suddenly unambitious fiancée. This "give the kid a break" theme beat the similarly scripted *On with the Show!* to its New York premiere by three days, but the Warner Bros. film actually debuted in Los Angeles five days earlier than *Follies* bowed in the East.

Comedy relief was provided by Stepin Fetchit, valued by Fox for his stereotypical portrayals of lazy, shiftless black men. For the sake of "cleverness," his character was named "Swifty." Featured in the color revue numbers were the youthful Sue Carol, Dixie Lee and David Rollins; tenor Frank Richardson; baritone David Percy; and the adagio dancers Harriet and John Griffith, but that was about the extent of the talent in *Movietone Follies*. Carol's "Breakaway" number proved to be the most popular in the film; the *Los Angeles Times* called it a "typical, head-topping, side-kicking, stepping specialty ... this mild marathon is likely to be taken up as a sequel to the Charleston."[27] Lola Lane introduced "Big City Blues," which was recorded by the George Olsen and Arnold Johnson orchestras.

A number called "That's You, Baby" marked the movie baptism of 7-year-old Jackie Cooper, whose mother worked as a secretary and rehearsals pianist for *Follies* songwriters Archie Gottler, Sidney Mitchell and Con Conrad. "Somebody got the bright idea that I should audition for that number as one of the kids who would sing it first," wrote Cooper in his autobiography, *Please Don't Shoot My Dog*:

> ...My mother knew the song, of course, so she taught it to me at home. ... But she didn't think it would be a good idea if ... whoever was doing the auditioning knew I was her son. So my grandmother was drafted to bring me in, and make believe she was my mother, and I was carefully coached to ignore my mother. When I got there, they told me, I was NOT—repeat NOT—to run over and hug and kiss my mother, as I would ordinarily have done, but to make believe I had never

> seen her before in my life. I guess they made it into a game—I could understand games. ... Of course, I had a head start because I knew the song so well—the others had just heard it that day—and maybe that helped. I was hired.[28]

William Fox Movietone Follies of 1929—which is thought to be lost but is rumored to exist in the hands of one or more private collectors—performed well in the sticks but lagged at big-city theaters. "The story is flimsy," opined *The Film Daily*, apparently taking the rural point of view, "but who said a good revue had to have anything further ... catchy music, plenty of pretty girls and keen limbs, snappy tempo, attractive sets, a dash of comedy. *Fox Movietone Follies* has 'em."[29]

BROADWAY
(Universal; May 27, 1929)

Director: Paul Fejos. Producer: Carl Laemmle Jr. Scenario: Edward T. Lowe, Jr., Charles Furthman. Dialogue: Edward T. Lowe, Jr. Based on the play by Philip Dunning and George Abbott (New York opening, September 16, 1926; 603 performances). Titles: Tom Reed. Photography: Hal Mohr. Photographic Effects: Frank H. Booth. Editors: Maurice Pivar, Robert Carlisle, Edward Cahn. Sound: C. Roy Hunter. Assistant Director: William J. Reiter. Art Directors: Charles D. Hall, Thomas F. O'Neill. Costumes: Johanna Mathieson. Dance Direction: Maurice L. Kusell. Synchronization and Score: Howard Jackson. Running Time: 105 minutes (sound version; also released as silent). Technicolor sequence.

Cast: Glenn Tryon (Roy Lane), Evelyn Brent (Pearl), Merna Kennedy (Billie Moore), Thomas Jackson (Dan McCorn), Robert Ellis (Steve Crandall), Otis Harlan (Andrew "Porky" Thompson), Paul Porcasi (Nick Verdis), Marion Lord (Lil Rice), Fritz Feld (Mose Levett), Leslie Fenton (Jim "Scar" Edwards), Arthur Housman (Dolph), George Davis (Joe the Waiter), Betty Francisco (Maizie), Edythe Flynn (Ruby), Florence Dudley (Ann), Ruby McCoy (Grace), George Ovey, Gus Arnheim and His Cocoanut Grove Ambassadors.

Songs: "Bounce a Little Ball at Your Baby" [Tryon, chorus], "Broadway" [Tryon, Kennedy, chorus], "The Chicken or the Egg" [Tryon,

In Universal's oft-imitated *Broadway*, gun moll Evelyn Brent points the Hollywood musical toward realism. Robert Ellis is the unwilling victim.

chorus], "Hittin' the Ceiling" [Tryon, chorus], "Hot Footin' It" [Arnheim band, danced by Tryon], "Sing a Little Love Song" [Tryon, Kennedy] (Sidney Mitchell, Archie Gottler, Con Conrad).

For a pet project of Carl Laemmle, Jr., the ambitious producer son of the studio head, Universal spent a cool $1 million to bring Philip Dunning and George Abbott's hit drama *Broadway* to the silver screen. Laemmle, Jr. commissioned a huge art-deco nightclub set—70 feet high and a city block wide—which replaced the intimate speakeasy of the play. Production numbers were set to six songs by Con Conrad, Archie Gottler and Sidney Mitchell. The quantity of music is enough to merit the inclusion of the film here, but the numbers have nothing to do with the storyline. *Broadway*, a saga of love and vice and death in a Manhattan nightclub, is rooted more in the gangster movie tradition than in the backstage musical.

But the place of *Broadway* in the history of the early sound film is neither in words nor music, thanks to the ingenuity of its director, Paul Fejos. Fejos (1897–1963) made movies in his native Hungary before coming to the United States to work as a bacteriologist for the Rockefeller Institute. In 1927 he directed *The Last Moment*, a striking experimental film with suicide as its theme, which led to his signing by Universal. His first Hollywood film was the part-talkie *Lonesome* (1928), a charming study of "little" people living in the big city that reminded many of King Vidor's more acclaimed *The Crowd*. Fejos' cameraman on *Broadway* was the estimable Hal Mohr, whose credits included *The Jazz Singer* and Erich von Stroheim's *The Wedding March*.

For *Broadway*, Fejos designed a crane that was to give Mohr's camera greater fluidity than was seen heretofore in a talking picture. The crane, which cost $75,000 to build, was able to travel from every conceivable angle at a speed of 600 feet a minute horizontally and 400 feet a minute vertically. This device was used most strikingly in the musical numbers, staged by Maurice Kusell and performed by Glenn Tryon—as Roy Lane, the resident song-and-dance expert at the Paradise Night Club—and his chorines. After they emerge from behind the curtain (which, in a nice effect, the camera pushes through instead of parting) and begin to sing, Mohr takes the camera airborne, revealing the individual work of the performers, then glides it around the club, as if to remind us that the happy music masks the real-life drama of the figures below. Typically, the performance visual yields to the backstage intrigue—with the music clearly heard in the background of the dialogue—then Fejos returns to the number as the song concludes. Despite the secondary nature of the music in *Broadway*, the plot is wrapped up before the final reel, an uninterrupted two-color Technicolor production number featuring the title song (which, unfortunately, is missing from the only American archival print of the film, at the Library of Congress).

With its tense dramatics and slangy dialogue, *Broadway* was a stage sensation, and even though the film version necessarily truncated the play, critics agreed that the movie retained the flavor of the original. One new touch in Universal's version was a striking opening, in which a barechested, devilish reveller mockingly splashes hooch over miniatures of the New York skyline even before the credits begin to roll. The moral corruption of its characters having been implied, the story begins with Roy dreaming of fame with his singing partner and best girl. "I can see our names in lights right now—Roy Lane ... and Company," he tells Billie Moore (Merna Kennedy). Billie is a good-hearted soul—"If I've ever seen a professional virgin, she's it," a jealous showgirl snaps—but her on-and off-stage partnership with Roy is imperiled by a slick bootlegger, Steve Crandall (Robert Ellis).

For both good and ill, Crandall is an unusually passionate crook, tenderly calling Billie his "little fella" then vowing that he'd "do murder for you." But it is Crandall's murder—by gunshot, and in the back—of rum-running rival "Scar" Edwards (Leslie Fenton) that signals his downfall. When the vigilant police detective Dan McCorn (Thomas E. Jackson) arrives to investigate, Crandall summons up all the bravado he can ("Should I have my pockets sewed up because there's a bull outside?"), but he's clearly spooked. Roy and Billie had witnessed the removal of Edwards' body from the Paradise, but Crandall has sworn Billie to secrecy and her false testimony temporarily clears him.

Roy, however, is not so easily silenced; he vows to kill Crandall if he harms Billie. Neither is Crandall's moll, Pearl (Evelyn Brent), who has been spying on Crandall as a dancer at the Paradise. Pearl confronts and then kills Crandall with a shot "through the old pump." The Paradise's hard-nosed proprietor, Nick Verdis (Paul Porcasi, reprising his stage role), attempts to make Roy a suspect. But McCorn wisely, if inaccurately, declares that Crandall has committed suicide, clearing Pearl and enabling Roy and Billie to answer a booking agent's call for shows, beams Roy, "in Chambersburg and Pottsville next week."

In *The New York Times*, Mordaunt Hall called the film "handsome entertainment, in which much of the drama of the original survives."[30] Jackson (1886–1967), who excelled in *Broadway* on Broadway, got most of the critical acclaim for the movie. His stone face and robotic, authoritative line-reading soon typecast him as a tough urban lawman in the likes of *Little Caesar* (1931) and *Mystery of the Wax Museum* (1933). Tryon (1894–1970), who would soon abandon his acting career to become a producer and screenwriter, also was praised, although Hall declared that Lee Tracy was a far better Roy Lane on the stage. Universal was pleased enough with the Tryon-Kennedy chemistry in *Broadway* that it teamed the pair in two more 1929 films, the comedies *Barnum Was Right* and *Skinner Steps Out*. Also getting good notices was Brent (1899–1975), a darkly attractive leading lady on loan from Paramount.

Broadway the play spawned all kinds of unacknowledged imitators, some of which attempted to steal the thunder of the film even before its release. There were *Broadway Nights*, *Broadway Babies* (see below) and *Broadway Bound ... Times Square*, *Backstage* and *Broadway or Bust*. The lifting was in a sequence here, an incident there, even a line. But, asserted one commentator, "all they could steal were stones from the mountain. The mountain itself remained."[31]

Sophie Tucker—"Last of the Red Hot Mammas"—made an inauspicious film debut in *Honky Tonk*.

HONKY TONK
(Warner Bros.; June 4, 1929)

Director: Lloyd Bacon. Adaptation: C. Graham Baker. Dialogue: Jack Yellen. Story: Leslie S. Burrows [C. Graham Baker]. Titles: De Leon Anthony. Photography: Ben Reynolds. Assistant Director: Frank Shaw. Dance Direction: Larry Ceballos. Running Time: 68 minutes (sound version; also released as silent).

Cast: Sophie Tucker (Sophie Leonard), Lila Lee (Beth), Audrey Ferris (Jean Gilmore), George Duryea [Tom Keene] (Freddie Gilmore), Mahlon Hamilton (Jim Blake), John T. Murray (café manager), Wilbur Mack.

Songs [all by Tucker]: "He's a Good Man to Have Around," "I Don't Want to Get Thin," "I'm Doing What I'm Doing for Love," "I'm Feathering a Nest for a Little Bluebird," [also Lee], "I'm the Last of the Red Hot Mammas," "Take Off Your Mask" (Jack Yellen, Milton Ager); "Some of These Days" (Shelton Brooks).

Disc: RCA Victor 21993 (Tucker/"I'm Doing What I'm Doing for Love"/"I'm Feathering a Nest for a Little Bluebird"/78); RCA Victor 21994 (Tucker/"He's a Good Man to Have Around"/"I'm the Last of the Red Hot Mammas"/78); RCA Victor 21995 (Tucker/"I Don't Want to Get Thin"/78); Take Two 104 (bootleg LP; ST).

In the studios' mad rush for new movie talent, it figured that an old hand like Sophie Tucker (1884–1966) would get the call. The 45-year-old "Last of the Red Hot Mammas" was wowing vaudeville audiences at home and abroad when Warner Bros. signed her for her first movie. Upon reading the script for *Honky Tonk*, however, Tucker threw up her hands in disgust. The endearingly earthy singer-comedienne was floored by the flowery language of her martyr-like character in the *Stella Dallas* knockoff, and by the indifference of studio executives at assigning her such a tear-jerking mediocrity.

"I found I was up against a blank wall," Tucker would write in her autobiography.

I could see they put me down as one of those temperamental vaudeville dames who was trying to teach the motion-picture industry how to run its own business. ... If only there had been a clause in the contract "script subject to approval." But there wasn't. I was in for it. I did manage to get the studio to send for Jack Yellen and get him and Milton Ager to write some numbers for me that would be more my kind of thing than what was in the script of *Honky Tonk*.[32]

The picture was made, and then a worried Tucker settled in to watch a preview at the Westlake Theatre in Los Angeles.

Yes, I looked very nice for a big woman.... But as scene after scene was played, I kept thinking—if only I had been properly rehearsed, if only I had had the chance to break that in, I would have played it and I would have sung that number so much better.[33]

Yellen and Ager, Tucker's favorite writers, penned six songs for her in *Honky Tonk*. Two of those tunes, "He's a Good Man to Have Around" and "I'm the Last of the Red Hot Mammas," became pop hits. Tucker's signature song, "Some of These Days," was also heard.

The unremarkable plot of the now-lost *Honky Tonk* told of one Sophie Leonard, a saloon singer whose Europe-educated daughter (Lila Lee, 1902–1973) is unaware of her mom's humble profession. When she learns the truth, the girl renounces her mother, but with the help of her rich but unexpectedly kind fiancé, the two women are reunited. Playing the fiancé was George Duryea (1898–1963), who would soon ditch his real name and become a cowboy star (also the miscast lead in King Vidor's *Our Daily Bread*) as Tom Keene. Reviewers were kind to Tucker, but they used adjectives like "simple" and "idiotic" to describe the rest. Richard Watts Jr. of *The New York Herald Tribune* put the film on his year's "10 worst" list.

Like Fanny Brice's *My Man*, this picture died in the hinterlands. Apparently, it made something of a splash abroad. Tucker, who didn't make another Hollywood film until 1938, for years got letters from fans all over the world praising her for *Honky Tonk*. She never could understand why.

BROADWAY BABIES
(First National; June 30, 1929)

Director: Mervyn LeRoy. Producer: Robert North. Adaptation: Monte Katterjohn. Dialogue: Monte Katterjohn, Humphrey Pearson. Based on the magazine story "Broadway Musketeers" by Jay Gelzer (1928). Titles: Paul Perez. Photography: Sol Polito, Alvin Knechtel. Editor: Frank Ware. Art Director: Jack Okey. Costumes: Max Rée. Running Time: 84 minutes (sound version; also released as silent).

Cast: Alice White (Delight Foster), Charles Delaney (Billy Buvanny), Fred Kohler (Percé Gessant), Tom Dugan (Scotty), Sally Eilers (Navarre King), Marion Byron (Florine Chandler), Bodil Rosing (Sarah), Jocelyn Lee (Blossom Royale), Louis Natheaux (Gus Brand), Maurice Black (Nick).

Songs [all by White, chorus]: "Broadway Baby Dolls," "Jig-Jig-Jigaloo" (Al Bryan, George W. Meyer); "Wishing and Waiting for Love" (Grant Clarke, Harry Akst).

The success of *Broadway* on stage and screen prompted many cinematic variations on the showbiz-and-gangsters theme. One was *Broadway Babies*, which used a trio of song-and-dance numbers to showcase its star, Alice White (1907–1983). White's voice was suitable for "singies" as well as talkies, but it was her petite vivaciousness that put her over.

Looking good didn't hurt. As *Broadway Babies* was being filmed, White became tangentially involved in a legal tussle with Mae Murray, the haughty falling star whose career had been on the skids since 1925's *The Merry Widow*. Murray's masseuse sued Murray after the actress fired her for allegedly calling Murray's husband, a bogus Russian prince named David Mdivani, a "bum." The masseuse summoned White into the courtroom as a living example of her art. And what art! Everybody, including the court, got a kick out of White's bare limbs—everybody except Murray, who lost her case and had to shell out $2,100 that she had supposedly borrowed from the masseuse.[34]

In the Mervyn LeRoy-directed *Broadway Babies*, White again shows off her gams as chorus-girl blondie Delight Foster, who teams with her clean-living roommates (Marion Byron, Sally Eilers) as the so-called "Broadway Musketeers." No gold-digging for them! Delight is working in a revue directed by her boyfriend (Charles Delaney), but her attentions are diverted by a French bootlegger from Detroit (twangy Western heavy Fred Kohler, who talks as if he's just wandered in from a cattle drive). The lovebirds are reunited only after the bootlegger is shot by hoods who have unsuccessfully tried to scam him at poker.

Broadway Babies is little remembered but very watchable. It moves fairly fast and its performers are peppy. Kohler (1889–1938) shines as a likable rogue. "It's all very obvious, but also entertaining," opined *The Film Daily*. "The White baby stare, talk and curves are there aplenty. Kohler, however, almost steals the picture and Tommy Dugan plays him a close second."[35] The film also uses sound creatively. A xylophone is heard during the poker-playing sequences, as the notes pound out a secret code devised to benefit the card sharks.

Also lending atmosphere to this little melodrama is the orchestral accompaniment heard throughout. Background scoring for dialogue films began not (as widely thought) with *King Kong* and Max Steiner, but with *The Lights of New York* and Vitaphone composer-conductors such as David Mendoza and Louis Silvers. Many of the earliest talkies, especially those made by Warner Bros., came complete with wall-to-wall, if rudimentary, background music, usually played into the film by an on-set orchestra as the cameras silently cranked.

This use of incidental music fell out of favor for a time, as reviewers and segments of the public complained about it. Some filmgoers beefed that it added to the cacaphony of soundtrack noise; others were confounded by the fact that music was playing from a source unseen or unmentioned on screen. At any rate, many early '30s films, even musicals, limited their instrumental scoring (as opposed to song scores) to the opening and closing credits.

MELODY LANE

(Universal; July 15, 1929)

Director: Robert F. Hill. Adaptation: J. G. Hawks, Robert F. Hill. Based on the play *The Understander* by Jo Swerling. Photography: Joseph Brotherton. Editor: Daniel Mandell. Running Time: 80 minutes (sound version; also released as silent).

Cast: Eddie Leonard (Des Dupree), Josephine Dunn (Delores Dupree), Rose Coe (Constance Dupree), George E. Stone (Danny Kay), Huntley Gordon (Juan Rinaldi), Jane La Verne (young Constance), Blanche Carter (nurse), Jake Kern (orchestra leader), Monte Carter (stage manager).

Songs [all by Leonard]: "The Boogy Man Is Here," "Here I Am," "There's Sugar Cane Around My Door" (Eddie Leonard, Jack Stern); "I'm on My Way," "(Roll Dem) Roly Boly Eyes" (Eddie Leonard); "Beautiful" (Eddie Leonard, Grace Stern, Jack Stern); "Ida! Sweet as Apple Cider" (Eddie Leonard, Eddie Munson); "The Song of the Islands" (Charles E. King).

In his book *The Encyclopedia of Vaudeville*, historian Anthony Slide calls Eddie Leonard (1883–1941) "the greatest of all minstrel men in vaudeville." From his boyhood in Virginia before the turn of the century, the publicity-savvy Leonard built his career with a graceful performing style that was as respectful of African-American traditions as any white in blackface could be. Even as vaudeville began its decline in the 1920s, Leonard remained a familiar and respected name.

But was he hearing footsteps? In 1928, Leonard used three pages of advertising in *Variety* to point out that he was as good a blackface man as Al Jolson. Somehow it was fitting that Leonard would begin his film career in yet another copy of Jolson's *The Singing Fool*—for Universal, the poor-man's Warner Bros. *Melody Lane* even had the same leading lady, Josephine Dunn. Not surprisingly, the lachrymose rip-off would rank as one of the most roundly panned of 1929 musicals.

Universal initially announced that its contract players Glenn Tryon and Laura La Plante would be teamed with Leonard in his first film, but although Leonard soon was left to star on his own, he retained high hopes for the project. As quoted in his Southern dialect for a Hollywood fan periodical, he was confident he could show movie actors a thing or two.

You picture people [would] make good in the talkies, only they don't want to study. They been used to havin' someone yell, "You hold 'er, Joe" and Joe holds her until they tell 'im not ter. The directors done the work of the silents. Now they [actors] got to work and they don't hanker to sit up all night studyin'.[36]

Presumably, Leonard lost sleep cramming for his *Melody Lane* test as a vaudeville hoofer who is partnered with his wife—until she walks out with their young daughter. Three years later, they meet again, she as a dramatic star, he as the prop man at the New York theater she's playing. The hoofer effects a reunion with his little girl, much to mommy's dismay, but when the moppet is seriously injured in a fall, it is Leonard who must sing her back to health. Fortunately, he is more successful at this than Jolson was with Davey Lee.

Leonard got to croon three of his standards—"Beautiful," "(Roll Dem) Roly Boly Eyes" (his theme song) and "Ida! Sweet as Apple Cider"—as well as three tunes he cowrote specifically for the film. But his bid for Hollywood stardom was as disastrous as any in the early sound period. At the New York premiere at the Globe Theatre, Leonard appeared in person to perform specialty songs as a prologue, but the reception to the picture was so negative that he became "ill" and canceled his future appearances there. He placed full-page trade ads quoting what positive reviews he could find, but there were too few of those.

Nearing 50 and with a specialty that was falling out of style, Leonard was not going to get a second chance in the movies. He appeared in only one more feature, Universal's Bing Crosby musical *If I Had My Way*, which was released the year before his death from natural causes in a New York hotel room. So his cinema legacy rests with what *Photoplay* called a "maudlin Pagliacci yarn ... about as dramatic and sophisticated as a monosyllabic nursery rhyme."[37]

SMILING IRISH EYES

(First National; July 23, 1929)

Director: William A. Seiter. Producer: John McCormick. Screenplay: Tom J. Geraghty. Photography: Sid Hickok, Henry Freulich. Editor: Al Hall. Art Director: Anton Grot. Assistant Director: James Dunne. Costumes: Edward Stevenson. Musical Director: Louis Silvers. Dance Direction: Larry Ceballos, Walter Wills, Carl McBride. Running Time: 90 minutes (sound version; also released as silent).

Cast: Colleen Moore (Kathleen O'Connor),

James Hall (Rory O'More), Robert Homans (Shamus O'Connor), Claude Gillingwater (Michael O'Connor), Tom O'Brien ("Black Barney" O'Toole), Robert Emmett O'Connor (Sir Timothy Tyrone), Aggie Herring (Grandmother O'More), Betty Francisco (Frankie West), Julanne Johnston (Goldie Devore), Edward Earle (George Prescott), Fred Kelsey (county fair manager), Barney Gilmore, Charles McHugh (county fair assistants), Madame Bosocki (fortune teller), George "Gabby" Hayes (taxi driver), Anne Schaefer (landlady), John Beck (Sir Timothy's butler), Oscar Apfel (Max North), Otto Lederer (Izzy Levi), William H. Strauss (Moe Levi), Dave Thursby (Scotch barker), Dan Crimmins (The Troublemaker).

Songs: "Old Killarney Fair," "Then I'll Ride Home with You" [Moore], "A Wee Bit o' Love" [Moore] (Herman Ruby, Norman Spencer); "Smiling Irish Eyes" [Moore, Hall; reprised by Hall, then by Moore, Hall] (Herman Ruby, Ray Perkins); "Come Back to Erin" [Moore] (Claribel).

You don't see Colleen Moore's movies on the Late, Late Show anymore, but she was once one of the most popular actresses in Hollywood. She made her film debut in 1917, but it wasn't until the early '20s that she achieved stardom as a jazz-baby heroine. Her light-hearted comedies had titles like *Flaming Youth* (the film that really put her over), *The Perfect Flapper* and *Flirting with Love*. Legions of fans copied her bobbed hairstyle. Moore (1900–1988) worked at First National, where her husband, John McCormick, was the head of production, ensuring that she always got good roles in profitable pictures. At the dawn of the sound era, she was—at $12,500 a week—the highest-paid movie actress in the world.

But in 1929, First National was integrated into Warner Bros. McCormick lost his power; an alcoholic, he was reduced to producing only those films in which his wife appeared. As the sound revolution raged, Colleen Moore turned 29 years old. Her speaking voice was adequate, but she knew she couldn't play flappers forever. Her bosses decided she needed voice training, which she got for a time from the Broadway star Constance Collier. But with her unsophisticated roles, Moore really didn't need the lah-de-dah stuff.

Her first talkie was a project that

McCormick had been able to pull her out of two years before. *Smiling Irish Eyes* was the insipid story of an Irish colleen whose sweetheart, a fiddle player and songwriter (played by James Hall), journeys to New York to pursue a song-and-dance career. When he fails to answer her letters, she borrows money to come after him, but she leaves America in a huff after she sees her man on stage singing "Smiling Irish Eyes" to a comely blonde. It takes some explaining on his part, but the two are reconciled in Ireland before they move to the States for good.

Not surprisingly, Moore was asked to sing (four songs) and dance. She recalled the experience in her autobiography, which was tellingly titled *Silent Star*:

> I could barely carry a tune. But in the early talkies, the star always had to sing, so in *Smiling Irish Eyes*, I sang—if I may call it that—"Come Back to Erin." Every morning I got up at 6 o'clock to go have a singing lesson. … But my best wasn't good enough, especially when it came to the high notes at the end of the song. The 100-piece orchestra did its best, too—trying to drown me out, I was so off-key. But my voice carried right through them. We finally hit on a way out. I was supposed to be singing to my lover across the sea in America, so when I came to the high notes at the end, I broke down, weeping.[38]

The film made money, but primarily on the basis of its star's reputation. Critics were polite to Moore, but they dismissed the rest as blarney, citing the predictable story, the obvious "fiddle faking" by Hall (1900–1940), and William A. Seiter's unimaginative direction. Wrote "Kann" in *The Film Daily*: "Several well-worn pigeon holes were invaded, the dust blown aside and aged formulas thrown blinking into the light. … The sum total was a story that wallowed unpardonably in saccharine through a long array of senile situations that passed out with horse cars."[39]

Smiling Irish Eyes did mark a technical first for Vitaphone, as it went outdoors for the Irish village scenes. The outdoor set was about 500 yards from the Warners' sound stages, and cables were laid to send the sound back to the studio. The results, apparently, were more than adequate. But we cannot judge for ourselves, for like Moore's second talkie musical, *Footlights and Fools* (see below), *Smiling Irish Eyes* is apparently a lost film.

STREET GIRL
(RKO; July 30, 1929)

Director: Wesley Ruggles. Producer: William LeBaron. Associate Producers: Luther Reed, Louis Sarecky. Adaptation and Dialogue: Jane Murfin. Based on the magazine story "The Viennese Charmer" by W. Carey Wonderly. Photography: Leo Tover. Editors: Ann McKnight, William Hamilton. Art Director: Max Ree. Costumes: Max Rée. Musical Director: Victor Baravalle. Dance Direction: Pearl Eaton. Running Time: 87 minutes.

Cast: Betty Compson (Freddie Joyzelle), John Harron (Mike Fall), Ned Sparks (Happy Winter), Jack Oakie (Joe Spring), Guy Buccola (Pete Summer), Joseph Cawthorn (Keppel), Ivan Lebedeff (Prince Nicholaus), Eddie Kane (Café Royale manager), Rolfe Sedan (Little Aregon patron), Doris Eaton and the Radio Pictures Beauty Chorus, Raymond Maurel and the Cimini Male Chorus, Gus Arnheim and His Cocoanut Grove Ambassadors [including Russ Columbo], June Clyde.

Songs: "Broken Up Tune" [Eaton, Beauty Chorus], "Lovable and Sweet" [Harron, Sparks, Oakie, Buccola, dubbed by Arnheim band, played or sung four times], "My Dream Memory" [Compson on violin with band; reprised by Maurel, Compson, then by Compson, band] (Sidney Clare, Oscar Levant).

Betty Compson's singing voice wasn't good enough to be heard in *On with the Show!*, but she could play the violin, and RKO used that talent to her advantage in *Street Girl*, the young studio's first "official" production and its biggest hit to date.

The film, directed by the capable Wesley Ruggles, centers on the rise from obscurity of a blonde Middle European violinist and a talented but unheralded jazz quartet who flourish after they join forces. This develops after little Fredericka "Freddie" Joyzelle, a destitute street musician, is saved from a masher by Mike Fall (John Harron), the pianist for the Four Seasons. He takes her back to the flat he shares with his professional partners, clarinetist Joe Spring (Jack Oakie), accordion player and guitarist Pete Summer (Guy Buccola) and fiddler "Happy" Winter (Ned Sparks, unhappy as ever). Freddie's poignant rendition of "My Dream Memory" makes her homesick for her homeland of Aregon but endears her to the boys. Well, maybe not to Happy. "Only 3 million dames in New York, and he picks one without a home!" he grumbles.

Denmother Freddie wrangles a well-paying gig for the band at Keppel's Little Aregon nightclub. Their theme song is "Lovable and Sweet." When Prince Nicholaus of Aregon (Ivan Lebedeff) shows up one night and gratefully bestows a kiss upon Freddie, she and the Seasons become well-known enough to get $3,000-a-week jobs in a better nitery. The jealous Mike quits the group, but the prince helps clear up the misunderstanding and reunites the couple.

Compson's charming performance, ersatz accent and all, made *Street Girl* another in a series of triumphs in a career-saving comeback for this veteran actress. Compson (1897–1974) had been a leading lady at Paramount before losing her contract and being relegated to lesser studios. But director George Fitzmaurice gave her a lift by casting her in the part-talkie circus melodrama *The Barker* (1928), for which Compson earned an Academy Award nomination for Best Actress and landed plenty of work in early talkies. For *Street Girl*, Compson's string music was her own, if one trusts the affidavit she signed to that effect on July 19, 1929. The document, reproduced in a fan magazine, recalled her days in vaudeville as "The Vagabond Violinist."[40] Gus Arnheim and His Cocoanut Grove Ambassadors, which at the time included future crooning phenom Russ Columbo on violin, dubbed for the Four Seasons.

Street Girl (working title: *The Viennese Charmer*) grossed more than $1 million for RKO, and we can understand why. Although the dialogue is too deliberately paced—the sound men at work, perhaps—the musical numbers are well photographed, especially the elaborate finale that features Pearl Eaton and the Radio Pictures Beauty Chorus in "Broken Up Tune." And Oakie, who overacted in so many of his musicals for Paramount, is held in restraint by director Ruggles, to whom the comic actor was under personal contract. The music for the three songs in *Street Girl* was written by future bon vivant Oscar Levant (1906–1972), who was teamed with Sidney Clare as RKO's house composing duo. The story was reused loosely for two more RKO musicals, *That Girl From Paris* (1937) and *Four Jacks and a Jill* (1942).

Before she ends up with a true-blue American guy, Betty Compson falls for a prince (Ivan Lebedeff) in RKO's *Street Girl*.

SAY IT WITH SONGS

(Warner Bros.; August 6, 1929)

Director: Lloyd Bacon. Screenplay: Harvey Gates. Dialogue: Joseph Jackson. Story: Darryl F. Zanuck, Harvey Gates. Photography: Lee Garmes. Sound: George R. Groves. Musical Director: Louis Silvers. Running Time: 93 minutes (sound version; also released as silent).

Cast: Al Jolson (Joe Lane), Davey Lee (Little Pal), Marian Nixon (Katherine Lane), Holmes Herbert (Dr. Robert Merrill), Kenneth Thomson (Arthur Phillips), Fred Kohler (Fred), Frank Campeau (officer), John Bowers (Dr. Burnes), Ernest Hilliard (radio station employee), Arthur Hoyt (Mr. Jones), Claude Payton (judge).

Songs [all by Jolson]: "I'm in Seventh Heaven," "Little Pal," "Used to You" (B. G. De Sylva, Lew Brown, Ray Henderson); "Why Can't You?" (Al Jolson, B. G. De Sylva, Lew Brown, Ray Henderson); "Back in Your Own Back Yard," "I'm Ka-razy for You" (Al Jolson, Billy Rose, Dave Dreyer); "Mem'ries of One Sweet Kiss" (Al Jolson, Dave Dreyer).

Disc: Brunswick 4400 (Jolson/"I'm in Seventh Heaven"/"Little Pal"/78); Brunswick 4401

(Jolson/"Used to You"/"Why Can't You?"/78); Brunswick 4402 (Jolson/"Mem'ries of One Sweet Kiss"/78); Subon 1234 (bootleg LP; ST). Video: MGM-UA (laserdisc).

When *Say It with Songs* premiered at the Warners Theatre in New York, the program included Will Hays' speech and Giovanni Martinelli's aria from the first Vitaphone prelude of exactly three years before. With nostalgia in the air, the audience settled back to watch the latest Al Jolson musical, hoping it would be as noteworthy as *The Jazz Singer*. They must have left the theater crestfallen. The reaction on the West Coast to *Say It with Songs* was unquestionably averse: The Warners Theatre in Los Angeles withdrew the film on 48 hours' notice. Reviewers on both coasts had very little to praise; *Photoplay* did not publish an opinion at all. In the critics' eyes, *Say It with Songs* was a monumental flop.

Why? Jolson was thought to be at his peak. And, as in the incredibly popular *The Singing Fool,* he was teamed with Davey Lee, who in the meantime had made a solo hit for Warner Bros. in the comedy *Sonny Boy,* and director Lloyd Bacon. The leading lady was the beautiful and talented Marian Nixon. De Sylva, Brown and Henderson contributed four of the film's seven songs, and one of theirs was "Little Pal," a surefire follow-up to "Sonny Boy" that did top the national sales list for more than a month. But a look at the film betrays the culprit: the depressing, unbearably maudlin plot, concocted by a writing team that included Darryl F. Zanuck. " ... It lapses into sentimentality that makes it somewhat tedious, except for the singing of Mr. Jolson," wrote *The New York Times.*[41] *Say It with Songs* grossed $1.7 million in the United States, mainly on the good will of its star's earlier triumphs, but it permanently harmed Al Jolson's film career.

Zanuck (1902–1979) was then general manager of Warner Bros.' West Coast studio. He had a hand in writing scores of films for the company before his departure in 1933 to found his own corporation, 20th Century. As a scenarist, he was more prolific than talented, although some of his inspirations turned into profitable movies. Zanuck, it was said, could ad-lib a story on the spot, and he could turn an unpromising film into a hit by reshaping the plotline and leaving its faults on the cutting-room floor. But such wholesale editing was more easily done with a silent picture, in which the titles could be reassembled to alter the effect. *Say It with Songs* (originally titled *Little Pal*) was a much tougher edit.

Jolson played Joe Lane, a happy-go-lucky radio singer-songwriter whose neglected but patient wife Kitty (Nixon) and darling little 4-year-old "Little Pal" (Lee) endure his social drinking and dice games with the boys. His boss (Kenneth Thomson, an even bigger cad here than in *The Broadway Melody*) puts the moves on Kitty, who rejects them and then reports the indiscretion to her husband. Joe, his temper boiling, knocks the boss to the ground with a punch during a street skirmish, and the poor fellow hits his head hard on the curbstone. Shortly thereafter, he expires. Joe is convicted of manslaughter, thanks to the innocent but damaging "testimony" of Little Pal from the courtroom gallery. "He used to be a prize-fighter!" the little boy chirps about his daddy, much to the delight of the persistent but unethical judge who eggs him on.

In prison, Joe misses his family terribly but allows Kitty to divorce him to preserve her dignity. Now working as a nurse, she falls for her employer, a big-shot surgeon (Holmes Herbert). Once paroled, Joe shows up at Little Pal's schoolyard to watch the boy. After a brief reunion, Al shambles off, but the lad follows him, waddling like a pint-sized Little Tramp—and gets hit by a truck. This calamity evokes great theatrics from Mistah Jolson. The boy will live, but his injured spine has cost him the use of his legs and the shock from the accident, his voice. Only Kitty's new man can save him, and the not-so-good doctor consents to do the operation for free—if Joe will just go away and leave everybody alone. Joe goes away to pray for his son's health.

The operation stirs the limbs, but Little Pal's voice returns only after he hears his dad sing (on a phonograph record) the song bearing his name. The Lanes reunite, and the film ends with Joe singing "I'm in Seventh Heaven" over the airwaves and then ordering the listening Kitty to make dinner. "Ham and eggs," he says mischievously, perhaps expecting a gasp from kosher filmgoers, " ... well, never mind the eggs." Interestingly, in the even more sappy last draft of Harvey Gates' screenplay, Joe "kidnaps" the boy from school and there is no final reconciliation; instead, Joe undergoes a religious conversion of sorts through the prayers that have brought Little Pal's recovery.[42]

Jolson does his best, and in those few moments when he's not on the verge of tears, he is his old, inimitable self. When Joe meets a displeased radio-show sponsor and is asked to come up with a new theme song along the banal lines of "I'm Going to Smother My Mother with Kisses When I Get Back to My Home in Tennessee," his title is a Yiddish in-joke: "I'll Smother My Father in Gedaemfte Rinderbrust When I Get Back to Odessa." (Pot roast, he means.) However, sound pictures were requiring a more naturalistic mode of acting than the breast-beating method that had been fine for silents, and even a presence as distinctive as Jolson's could be too overbearing. But would YOU dare tell Al Jolson that he was trying too hard?

Buffs will note the brief appearance of John Bowers as the surgeon who delivers to Joe the bad news about Little Pal after his accident. Bowers, a leading man of the late 'teens to mid '20s, in 1929 could find movie work only in this bit part and a larger supporting role in the Warner Bros. drama *Skin Deep*. Despondent over his lack of appeal in talkies, he became an alcoholic and committed suicide by drowning in 1936 at age 36. The circumstances of his death—Bowers was estranged from the actress Marguerite de la Motte—are alleged to have provided inspiration for the scene depicting the suicide of the down-and-out actor Norman Maine, portrayed by Fredric March in *A Star Is Born* (1937).

Surviving prints of *Say It with Songs* are without Jolson's performance of two songs, "Back in Your Own Back Yard" and "I'm Karazy for You," during the opening scenes at the radio station. Because of rights problems, the songs were deleted from the film when it was made available to television.

THE DANCE OF LIFE
(Paramount; August 16, 1929)

Directors: John Cromwell, A. Edward Sutherland. Associate Producer: David O. Selznick. Screenplay: Benjamin Glazer. Dialogue: George Manker Watters. Based on the play *Burlesque* by George Manker Watters and Arthur Hopkins (New York opening, September 1, 1927; 372 performances). Titles: Julian Johnson. Photography: J. Roy Hunt. Editor: George Nichols, Jr. Sound: Harry D. Mills. Dance Direction: Earl Lindsay. Running Time: 111 minutes (sound version; also released as silent). Technicolor sequence.

Cast: Hal Skelly (Ralph "Skid" Johnson), Nancy Carroll (Bonny Lee King), Dorothy Revier (Sylvia Marco), Ralph Theodore (Harvey Howell), Charles D. Brown (Lefty Miller), Al St. John (Bozo), May Boley (Gussie), Oscar Levant (Jerry Evans), Gladys Du Bois (Miss Sherman), Jimmie Quinn (Jimmy), James Farley (Champ), George Irving (minister), Fred Kelsey, Rolfe Sedan (actors), Gordona Bennett, Miss La Reno, Cora Beach Shumway, Charlotte Ogden, Kay Deslys, Magda Blom (Amazon chorus girls), Thelma McNeal (gilded girl, "Lady of India"), John Cromwell (doorkeeper), A. Edward Sutherland (theater attendant), Marjorie "Babe" Kane (singer).

Songs: "Flippity Flop" [Kane, chorus, danced by Skelly], "I Want to Cuddle Some Cuddlesome Baby" [Carroll], "The King of Jazzmania" [Boley, chorus, danced by Skelly], "Ladies of the Dance" [offscreen vocalist, danced by Skelly, chorus in Ziegfeld show], "The Mightiest Matador" [burlesque chorus], "True Blue Lou" [Skelly] (Sam Coslow, Leo Robin, Richard A. Whiting); "The Daughter of Rosie O'Grady" [Levant at piano, danced by Carroll, Skelly] (Monte Brice, Walter Donaldson); "In the Gloaming" [Carroll, with Levant at piano] (Annie Fortesque Harrison); "Old Folks at Home" [orchestra, danced by Carroll, Skelly] (Stephen Foster); "Sam, the Old Accordion Man" [Skelly, with Levant at piano] (Walter Donaldson).

Disc: Music Masters JJA-19806 (bootleg LP; ST).

Video: various public-domain distributors (cassette).

Joseph Harold "Hal" Skelly (1891–1934) was a tall, loose-limbed song-and-dance man whose career encompassed the legitimate stage, films, vaudeville, and even the circus. He was not famous enough in any one of those areas to merit inclusion in standard reference books, but there was one role with which he left an indelible memory. The character: Ralph "Skid" Johnson, a gifted but self-destructive stage

Nancy Carroll and Hal Skelly (center) hit the burlesque circuit in Paramount's underrated *The Dance of Life*.

comic. The play: *Burlesque,* a major hit of the 1927-28 Broadway season.

Burlesque was a backstage drama written by Arthur Hopkins and George Manker Watters about a husband-and-wife performing team and the price that success makes them pay. Paramount bought the property in 1928 and, after some delay, signed Skelly to reprise his role, retained Watters to adapt the story, and added songs by Sam Coslow, Leo Robin and Richard A. Whiting. The film was named *The Dance of Life,* a title taken from a totally unrelated book by the sexologist Havelock Ellis. It turned out to be one of the most highly regarded musicals of 1929, and, although rarely recalled by historians, has survived to demand appraisal as a standout early talkie. Made at a time when most movies taken from the stage were inferior imitations of the originals, *The Dance of Life,* directed by John Cromwell and A. Edward Sutherland, is bolstered by fine acting and enhanced by sound cinematic technique.

If this, probably the least known of three film adaptations of *Burlesque,* is remembered at all, it is not for who appears in it, but for who does not. On stage, Bonny King—the dancer who loves Skid despite of himself—was played by the 20-year-old Barbara Stanwyck, whose sensitive portrayal made her a New York "name." But for the film version, Paramount used its popular contractee Nancy Carroll. Cromwell, new to the studio after a successful New York stage career as an actor and director, wanted to hire Stanwyck along with the others from the Broadway cast—Skelly, Charles D. Brown, Ralph Theodore and 23-year-old Oscar Levant. Walter Wanger, manager of Paramount's East Coast studio, arranged with Hopkins, the producer of *Burlesque,* to send the stage company to the Long Island facility for a one-act screen test.

All of the actors came—except one. Levant claimed in his autobiography that Stanwyck's husband, the stage comedian Frank Fay, refused to let his wife do the film.[43] It would have been characteristic of Fay, an egomaniac with his own movie-star aspirations, to keep Stanwyck from Hollywood until he was summoned there himself. Officially, a commitment to the national tour of *Burlesque* kept Stanwyck away from the movie, and Paramount felt surer with Carroll anyway. Carroll's presence on the set made her the butt of much good-natured humor from the legit actors, but she gave the movie a needed boost at the box office. When Stanwyck did come West a few months later, it was for career-stunting claptrap such as *The Locked Door* (1929) and *Mexicali Rose* (1930).

The Dance of Life begins as Bonny and Skid meet in a railroad station in the middle of nowhere. She is an out-of-work dancer who has just failed a tryout with a small-time vaudeville troupe; he is a putty-nosed clown who has just been fired from that troupe for complaining that the girl wasn't given a chance. She spots a magazine ad calling for a lead comic and a specialty dancer. He doesn't have the ambition to ask for $100 a week in salary, but Bonny has seen Skid perform and she knows better. "You're good," she says. "Hey, you wouldn't kid me, lady?" he asks, starting an exchange that is repeated throughout the film. "I would if I could, mister, I would if I could" is her reply. They send off a telegram to the High Steppers Burlesque Company; she builds him up by adding the $100 request without his knowledge.

Lefty Miller (Charles D. Brown) hires the duo for his company, and during the next couple of seasons, Bonny and Skid fall in love and are married. But Skid's insecurity and recklessness—he thinks nothing of taking dangerous stage tumbles to get extra laughs—worry Bonny. So does the presence of a comely actress rival, Sylvia Marco (Dorothy Revier). Worst of all is Skid's increasing thirst for alcohol: He spends his wedding night partying with cronies as Bonny goes to bed alone. The nature of their relationship is best expressed in "True Blue Lou," a song written for the film that Skid declaims as part of his solo act:

He gave her nothing; she gave him all.
But when he had his back to the wall,
Who fought to save him, smiled and forgave him?
True Blue Lou.

Skid is summoned to New York to appear in the *Ziegfeld Follies*. Bonny talks him into going, although she'll be left behind and Sylvia has been cast in the same New York show. Immediately after saying a final farewell to Skid, Bonny is told that it's time to go on, and J. Roy Hunt's camera follows her forlorn, limp figure trudging through the theater from dressing room to stage. As she steps before the footlights, she instinctively perks up to the strains of "Old Folks at Home," Bonny and Skid's favorite dance duet. A close-up reveals the anguish on Bonny's face, then a medium shot places Bonny on the right and empty space on the left, emphasizing her loneliness. This was the kind of purely cinematic presentation that could not have been lifted from the stage show. In the film's one Technicolor sequence, set on Skid's first night at the *Follies,* he does an eccentric dance to "Ladies of the Dance" and "Flippity Flop." Afterward, he's escorted from the theater by his new "friends." "You own Broadway!" enthuses piano player Jerry Evans (Oscar Levant). Sylvia is there, too, distracting Skid from sending the optimistic telegram he's written to Bonny.

Weeks pass, and Bonny hears nothing from her husband. She's heard through the theatrical grapevine that Skid has made good, but also that Sylvia has re-entered the picture. With Lefty's show having closed, she goes to New York "to give him one last chance." She wires Skid to meet her at a given place and time, but when she arrives at Ziegfeld's theater, he's not there. Skid had received the wire but, not knowing who it was from, hadn't read it yet. Bonny is told she might find Skid at a certain speakeasy, where she asks the doorkeeper (director Cromwell in a bit) to locate her husband. As she looks inside, the subjective camera circles the floor, then zooms rapidly to one table just as Skid turns toward the camera. Sylvia peers out from behind him, and Bonny sees them kiss. Bonny runs away. She looks up at the giant *Follies* marquee, on which Skid has star billing, and decides he'll be happy without her. When Skid returns to the theater, he is given a note from Bonny stating her intention to file for divorce. In shock, he sits down in front of the mirror and, in a scene recalling Bessie Love's anguish in *The Broadway Melody*, wordlessly puts on his makeup. The show must go on.

Months later, Bonny visits New York as the

fiancée of Harvey Howell (Ralph Theodore), a wealthy Western cattle rancher who had been a devoted fan. As she entertains an old friend (May Boley) from the High Steppers, there is a knock at the door of her hotel suite. It's Skid, with Lefty and Jerry in tow. Skid and Bonny, whose divorce will become final in a few months, nervously exchange small talk, then Skid talks her into doing a soft-shoe together to "The Daughter of Rosie O'Grady." Harvey's entrance increases the tension. Skid becomes upset: "What are we celebrating, anyway, a wedding or a funeral? ... Why can't we do the wedding march?" He begins to act out a nuptial ceremony, dancing frantically to Jerry's accompaniment. Bonny is shattered. Harvey tells Skid to leave.

Skid drinks himself into a stupor and is fired by Ziegfeld. We see an item in *Variety* about him: "Couldn't stand success. Even the burlesque producers are ducking him." All except one. Lefty helps his fallen friend with handouts but won't hire him. However, when he must replace a comedian for a new show, he is forced to turn to Skid. The gamble fails, and Skid falls off the wagon, the show faces failure even before it opens. The desperate producer wires Bonny in Wyoming, where she's preparing for her wedding, and implores her to come East for a few days and guide Skid through the remaining rehearsals. She agrees, but she can only watch on opening night as Skid misses a cue, then collapses on stage to ruin a big production number. She vows to get him through the rest of the show. She joins Skid for his "Old Folks at Home" dance specialty. He stumbles, but she steadies him and asks if he can make it. "I can—if you stay," he replies. She'll stay.

Although *The Dance of Life* centers on the standard backstage cliché of the bickering duo act, it treats the story with realism and dignity. The scenes of backstage comraderie ring true, and they compare favorably to similar sequences in the more heralded *Applause* (see Chapter 9). Loyalty is a major theme: When times get tough for Skid, big-shots Sylvia and Jerry conveniently disappear, but Bonny and Lefty, untainted by success, are there for him. The atmosphere is enhanced by sensitive direction and Hunt's fluid camera. The "True Blue Lou" number is very effective, handled with just the right jauntiness by Skelly. The song was successfully covered by Ethel Waters and was re-

vived in the 1950s by Tony Bennett and Frank Sinatra.

The film has some of the typical drawbacks of 1929 cinema: The Technicolor number is unremarkably staged and filmed too often in long shot, and the performances of some of the supporting players (especially Theodore, horribly wooden, and minor comic Al "Fuzzy" St. John) are second-rate. But *The Dance of Life* is certainly better than the typical studio product of the time. Reviewers of '29 agreed. "It tops any talkie ever made! It's perfect!" crowed Regina Crewe in the *New York American*.[44] "A remarkably successful adaptation of a genuinely touching original," said Richard Watts, Jr., in the *Herald Tribune*.[45] In *The Times*, Mordaunt Hall complimented the creative camera work and called Skelly's performance "sincere and true."[46]

The Dance of Life was the first standout film in a long Hollywood career for Cromwell (1888–1979). He would become known as an "actor's director" with the likes of *Of Human Bondage* (1934), *The Prisoner of Zenda* (1937) and *Abe Lincoln in Illinois* (1940). Skelly's film future was far less lasting. Paramount handed him two routine assignments for 1930: *Behind the Makeup*, a non-musical backstager, and *Woman Trap*, a crime melodrama. His only other film of note was D. W. Griffith's unsuccessful finale, *The Struggle* (1931), in which Skelly drew favorable reviews for another performance as an alcoholic. Skelly returned to the stage as an actor and producer before his death in an auto accident in 1934.

Burlesque was a durable enough property to be made into a movie twice more. Paramount's *Swing High, Swing Low* (1937) was a semi-musical drama with Fred MacMurray and Carole Lombard. *When My Baby Smiles at Me*, a profitable 20th Century-Fox musical of 1948, starred Betty Grable and, as Skid, the Oscar-nominated Dan Dailey.

GOLD DIGGERS OF BROADWAY
(Warner Bros.; August 30, 1929)

Director: Roy Del Ruth. Scenario and Dialogue: Robert Lord. Based on the play *The Gold Diggers* by Avery Hopwood (New York opening, September 30, 1919; 282 performances). Titles: De Leon Anthony. Photography: Barney

Winnie Lightner (in hat, with Helen Foster) became an unlikely movie star after *Gold Diggers of Broadway*.

McGill, Ray Rennahan. Editor: William Holmes. Sound: George R. Groves. Assistant Director: Ross Lederman. Costumes: Earl Luick. Musical Director: Louis Silvers. Dance Direction: Larry Ceballos. Running Time: 92 minutes (sound version; also released as silent). Technicolor.

Cast: Nancy Welford (Jerry La Mar), Conway Tearle (Stephen Lee), Winnie Lightner (Mabel Munroe), Ann Pennington (Ann Collins), Lilyan Tashman (Eleanor), William Bakewell (Wally Saunders), Nick Lucas (Nick), Helen Foster (Violet Dayne), Albert Gran (Jim Blake), Gertrude Short (Topsy St. Clair), Neely Edwards (stage manager), Julia Swayne Gordon (Cissy Gray), Lee Moran (dance director), Armand Kaliz (Barney Barnett), Louise Beavers (Sadie).

Songs: "And Still They Fall in Love" [Lightner], "Blushing Bride" [Welford], "Go to Bed" [Lucas, twice], "In a Kitchenette" [Lucas], "Keeping the Wolf from the Door" [Lightner; reprised by dancers], "Mechanical Man" [Light-

ner], "Painting the Clouds with Sunshine" [Lucas, chorus, danced by Pennington; reprised by Lucas, then by company], "The Poison Kiss of That Spaniard" [band], "The Song of the Gold Diggers (Dig, You Little Diggers, Dig)" [Pennington, chorus; reprised by Welford, chorus, then by company], "Tip-Toe Thru the Tulips (with Me)" [Lucas; reprised by Lucas, chorus, then by dancers], "What Will I Do Without You?" [Lucas] (Al Dubin, Joe Burke).

Disc: Brunswick 4418 (Lucas/"Painting the Clouds with Sunshine"/"Tip-Toe Thru the Tulips (with Me)"/78).

Video: MGM-UA (laserdisc; excerpt only).

In 1923, the newly incorporated Warner Bros. studio allied with the showman David Belasco to produce a successful silent adaptation of the Avery Hopwood comedy *The Gold Diggers,* which Belasco had presented on Broadway. Hope Hampton and Louise Fazenda starred. When the studio revived the property six years later for a talkie, it was as *Gold Diggers of Broadway*, a lavish, all-Technicolor musical that would become one of 1929's biggest hits. It's a shame that only one reel of the film exists for evaluation, although for many years there was nothing at all.

Robert Lord tinkered with Hopwood's original by adding a stage show-within-a-show to provide an excuse for the sound film's many musical numbers, but the story still centered on a group of New York showgirls aiming for companionship, and more, from "gentlemen" of the moneyed set. The primary bachelorettes are Jerry La Mar (Nancy Welford), Mabel Munroe (Winnie Lightner) and Violet Dayne (Helen Foster), choristers in a Broadway-bound revue that's marooned in Newark. Perky, good-hearted Jerry makes romance look easy: She "tries to be a good fellow and likes it," says one of her contemporaries admiringly. The over-sized Mabel is fun-loving but love-starved. "I'm gettin' to the point that I don't care what kind of a man he is," she says of her dream lover, "as long as he has pants and an income." Her "super-dynamic" male is the "Mechanical Man" of which she sings.

Demure little Violet loves the equally chaste Wally Saunders (William Bakewell), but Wally's Boston Brahmin uncle, Stephen Lee (Conway Tearle), has come to town to object to the couple's marriage. Abetted by his suspicious attorney, Jim Blake (Albert Gran), the stuffy Stephen thinks all chorus girls are vamps. Alerted to Lee's impending arrival, Jerry, as a token of her friendship with Violet, decides to go after Mr. Lee with such fervor that the man will realize how sweet Jerry's roomie is in comparison. Mabel attempts to charm Blake as only she can: "The very moment I laid my two eyes on you, I knew you were my weakness."

In a nightclub, a singing and guitar-strumming member of the girls' troupe (Nick Lucas) performs "Painting the Clouds with Sunshine," after which Mabel dedicates "Keeping the Wolf from the Door" to her new sweetie. Jerry, meanwhile, is getting nowhere with Stephen; not only is he refusing to be shocked at her contrived flirting with others, he's secretly "having the time of my life." At a late-night party, Jerry decides to pull out all the stops for the slightly inebriated Bostonian: She "confesses" about her life of poverty and bad romances, of one husband who fell into the Grand Canyon, and an-

other who tried to set her afire for "being too cold." She tries to talk up Violet, but Stephen is less inclined to talk about his nephew's future than to "forgive" Jerry and admit his love for her. But in the same breath, he rejects her for his having been made to play the fool.

The next day, Jerry is glum, for she thinks she's not only gummed things up for Violet and Wally, but she realizes how much she truly cares for Stephen, who is to sail for Europe that evening. That's also the night of the show's big opening. During a dress rehearsal, the star, Ann Collins (Ann Pennington), is dealt a black eye during a backstage catfight, and Jerry is asked to go on in her place. As the former understudy waits in her dressing room minutes before the opening curtain, Stephen arrives to patch things up, not only to give his blessing for Violet and Wally's marriage but to himself propose to Jerry. The show begins with the movie's every-thing-but-the-kitchen-sink finale, performed by the now-blissful Jerry, scores of dancers in all styles and costumes, and what was billed as a "dazzling beauty chorus of 300."

Everything seemed to be right about *Gold Diggers of Broadway*. It grossed an impressive $2.5 million domestically and nearly $4 million worldwide. Critics lauded Roy Del Ruth's lively direction (the picture made *The Film Daily*'s top 10 for the year), and the choreography by Larry Ceballos was deemed much more cinematic than his claustrophobic work in *On with the Show!* Even the Technicolor, derided as overly gaudy in that earlier film, here was blessed, remarked *Photoplay*, with "startling beauty."[47] *Gold Diggers of Broadway* also marked the talkie-feature debuts of three talented performers from other realms of the entertainment world. Pennington (1892–1971) won stardom for her frenetic dancing in Ziegfeld shows; her film footwork, which showed off her famous "dimpled" knees, reportedly far eclipsed her emoting.

Lucas (1897–1982), a popular recording artist, achieved further prominence with his hitmaking renditions of Al Dubin and Joe Burke's "Painting the Clouds with Sunshine" and "Tip-Toe Thru the Tulips (with Me)." Recordings of the songs (by Lucas for Brunswick, and the Jean Goldkette orchestra for Victor), as well as the sheet music for them, placed among the year's biggest sellers. Disingenuously cast as "Nick" in the film, he sings no less than eight times, with no more transition from the plot than a "Hey, Nick, sing us another song" request from one of the bit players.

Lucas was spotted by a Warner Bros. talent scout during an appearance at the Orpheum Theatre in Los Angeles. As he told Anthony Slide many years later:

> After the show, this chap came backstage and asked me if I would be interested in making a picture. I said, "Why not?" So the next day I went up to the studios and Mr. [Darryl] Zanuck heard me and said, "Hire him." They had only one song written for me in [*Gold Diggers of Broadway*], "Painting the Clouds with Sunshine," and so the writers, Joe Burke and Al Dubin, were requested to write some more songs for me. And they wrote this song "Tip-Toe Thru the Tulips" and when Zanuck heard this song he turned it into a big production number. That's how I latched onto "Tip-Toe Thru the Tulips," which became synonymous with me.[48]

"Tulips" became a hit all over again when Tiny Tim revived it in the late '60s, and when the falsetto-voiced novelty artist got married before a national TV audience on *The Tonight Show* in 1969, Lucas sang the song during the ceremony.

But the most immediately significant development of *Gold Diggers of Broadway* was its elevation to fame of Lightner (1901–1971). "Somebody tossed the picture right into Winnie Lightner's lap, or else she stole it," wrote *Variety* editor "Sime" Silverman, who reviewed the film for his publication. "The talkers gain another comedienne and they haven't too many, so Winnie is set."[49] Stocky and hard-nosed, yet cheerfully endearing, Lightner had come up through the ranks in a vaudeville sister act, then was a featured solo for five seasons of *George White's Scandals*. She was called "The Song-a-Minute Girl" for the pace and power with which she put over her tunes. Except for a couple of short subjects, *Gold Diggers* was her very first movie.

William Bakewell's memories of *Gold Diggers of Broadway* were hazy late in his life, but he remembered Lightner as "a Martha Raye type. ... She could sing, too, but not in a romantic way. Her talent was comedy, broad comedy."[50] The Lightner gag most recalled by fans and reviewers of *Gold Diggers* was a product of chance. During filming, the comedienne lost her balance and fell heavily from her seat at a table right into the lap of the sizable Albert Gran. The incident was so amusing in the rushes that it was left in the film by director Del Ruth, who would marry Lightner in 1934.

Warner Bros. would immediately find other projects for Lightner, and Pennington would get steady work as a specialty dancer, but for Lucas *Gold Diggers of Broadway* was no springboard to a movie career. The swarthy singer appeared as himself in the Warners revue *The Show of Shows* (see Chapter 10) and was offered a multi-year contract by the studio, but he found other performance arenas more profitable. Lucas continued to appear in movie shorts, but did not turn up in another feature until 1951. That was the year Warners remade *Gold Diggers of Broadway* as *Painting the Clouds with Sunshine*, a weak effort that starred Virginia Mayo (in the Welford role) and Gene Nelson; the title song and "Tulips" were revived (sans Lucas). Of course, the Hopwood story also was spun off as the popular *Gold Diggers of 1933*—which had an entirely new batch of songs—which indirectly inspired that film's Berkeleyesque successors of 1935 and 1937.

Meanwhile, *Gold Diggers of Broadway*, last seen in its entirety in a 1939 re-release, came to be regarded as a lost film. The unofficial story goes that the original negative of the film languished in the Warners vaults for some time, but lacking a permanent melding of the sound, which existed only on disc, and picture. By the 1950s, when the studio began to locate its gems for sale to television, it found that the negative, which was the only available visual of the film, had become irreparably damaged. A special trailer made to promote the movie apparently did survive.

However, in the 1980s, footage of the closing color reel was donated by a private collector to the National Film Archive in London, which preserved it. The reel was included as supplementary material on one of MGM-UA Home Video's "Dawn of Sound" laserdisc packages. The surviving footage begins as the Tearle and Welford characters mend their disagreement. Then follows the climactic production number, which repeats the film's score in medley form. The picture portion of the video fragment disappears just before the end title, which is immediately preceded by Lightner's conclusion to a running joke: "I … I am … I … oh, darn it, I've forgotten that second line!"

In the last year, more of *Gold Diggers* has come to light. A large collection of American nitrate film located in Australia and returned in 1994 to this country was found to contain the sixth reel of the 1929 musical. It is said to include the "Tip-Toe Thru the Tulips" number. The UCLA Film and Television Archive was slated to handle the restoration of the footage to surviving sound elements.

THE GREAT GABBO

(James Cruze Inc./Sono Art-World Wide; September 12, 1929)

Director: James Cruze. Producers: Henry D. Meyer, Nat Cordish. Scenario and Dialogue: F. Hugh Herbert. Story: Ben Hecht. Photography: Ira H. Morgan. Sound: Helmer Bergman. Art Director: Robert E. Lee. Costumes: André-ani. Dance Direction: Maurice L. Kusell. Musical Director: Howard Jackson. Running Time: 96 minutes. Multicolor sequence.

Cast: Erich von Stroheim (Gabbo), Betty Compson (Mary), Donald Douglas (Frank), Marjorie "Babe" Kane (singer), Otto (himself, a dummy), John Frank Hamilton, Edna Gregory, Harry Ross, Biltmore Orchestra.

Songs: "The Ga-Ga Bird" [chorus], "I'm in Love with You" [orchestra in restaurant; reprised by Compson, Douglas, chorus, then by dancers, then by company], "The New Step" [Kane, chorus; reprised by company], "The Web of Love" [Compson, Douglas, chorus, twice] (Paul Titsworth, Lynn Cowan); "Every Now and Then" [Kane, Douglas, chorus; reprised by company], "I'm Laughing" [Otto-Stroheim, dubbed by Georgie Grande], "Icky" [Otto-Stroheim, dubbed by Grande] (Donald McNamee, King Zany).

Video: various public-domain distributors (cassette).

Erich von Stroheim, "The Man You Love to Hate," was one of the most talented movie directors of the 1920s. But his inability to work cooperatively with studio managers—specifically, in keeping his sophisticated, extravagant dramas within proscribed budgets—caused his unspoken blacklisting from work behind the camera. The last straw was *Queen Kelly*, an ill-fated collaboration with Gloria Swanson. Stroheim, as was his custom, shot the film at a snail's pace, and in January 1929, a frustrated Swanson prevailed upon her producer and paramour, Joseph P. Kennedy, to fire the director midway through production. The film, a decadent continental melodrama, was never finished as planned, and an effort to convert it into a part-talking operetta was short-lived.[51] In 1932, a truncated version patched together by Swanson was briefly released, and only in Europe.

The unemployed Stroheim (1885–1957) was signed as an actor for the title role of *The Great Gabbo* by director James Cruze, who was producing the independent release. Cruze himself was attempting to rejuvenate an accomplished career, which peaked with *The Covered Wagon* (1923) but began to slide downhill after the expensive flop *Old Ironsides* (1926). However, *The Great Gabbo*, a drama loosely based on an original story by Ben Hecht about the mental breakdown of a brilliant but egomanical ventriloquist, has become a "camp" favorite among modern film buffs. That it is an easy mark for unintentional laughs is due less to the sappy dramatic content than to the film's singing and dancing sequences, which lend show-business "atmosphere" but are otherwise entirely independent of the plot. Many straight dramas of the early talkie era were injected with music, but in this instance, the results are terribly awkward.

As the story begins, Gabbo is an underachieving vaudevillian who, on a cold night in Paterson, arrogantly forces his long-suffering gal pal, Mary (Betty Compson, Cruze's soon-to-be ex-wife), out of their household. She leaves with some sage advice for the selfish Gabbo: "We only take out of this life what we put into it." But she knows she will miss the kindness of Gabbo's wooden buddy, Otto, who is less a ventriloquist's dummy than a spokesman for his owner's repressed humanity. Two years later, Gabbo is featured on Broadway in the *Manhattan Revue*, which also includes singer-dancer Mary and her new partner, Frank (Don Douglas). Gabbo, taking Mary's advice to heart, attempts to win her back. But after a while she tells him the truth, that she and Frank are married. The revelation pushes Gabbo over the edge; he goes into a screaming tirade that ruins the show's finale. The suddenly jobless Gabbo punches Otto in the face and, at the end,

Erich von Stroheim, playing a crazed ventriloquist, tells Betty Compson to get lost at the start of the bizarre *The Great Gabbo*.

shuffles away from the theater as the letters spelling "THE GREAT GABBO" are removed from the marquee.

Stroheim is practically the only reason to see *The Great Gabbo,* and he doesn't disappoint in his talkie debut. He yells, preens, plots, huffs and leers, gets tender now and again, and even the Continental extravagance with which he orders a "romantic" catered dinner is a kick. Surprisingly, the film turned a profit and garnered many positive reviews, but in retrospect, it is betrayed by its sloppiness and shabby production values. Cruze didn't bother to retake Stroheim's periodic flubbing of his lines; one stumble comes during a tense scene at the climax. Even stranger, there is no attempt to account for the source of Otto's speech (dubbed, says Miles Kreuger, by Georgie Grande). Even when Otto's comments are directed to someone other than Gabbo, Stroheim does not move his mouth when the dummy "speaks," and Otto

even "talks" out loud at times when the ventriloquist is not maneuvering him. But there are some interesting touches, especially in snatches of sardonic, and possibly Stroheim-influenced, dialogue. In response to Compson's first-scene remark that this is their second anniversary together, Stroheim replies, "Two years too much. Flowers are for dead people." And a climactic montage that represents Gabbo's complete mental dissolution shows invention that could have been Stroheim's.

The Film Daily, for one, lauded *The Great Gabbo* for its "magnificent stage sets … and spectacular singing and dancing acts."[52] In retrospect, those numbers—which consume most of the second half of the film to complement the off-stage conflict—don't fare so well. Tunes such as "I'm in Love with You" and "Every Now and Then" are forgettable enough, but a strong contender for the hotly contested honor of Worst Production Number in an Early Talkie is the jaw-dropping "(When You're Caught in) the Web of Love." Compson and Douglas, dressed in spider garb, are mounted in the center of a giant web. They sing a couple of verses, then after a round of heavy applause from the extras hired to play the audience, she begins an apache dance on stage. He follows, jumping from web to floor with an embarrassing thud.

Douglas' character is stewing over Compson's innocent flirting with Stroheim, and he wants her to tell her ex-lover that she's got a new guy. Cruze alternates long shots of real dancers (the team of Myles and Kover) with contrived close-ups of the two actors. Right in the middle of this ludicrous ballet, Douglas, in close-up, mumbles that "we might as well settle this thing right now and save a lot of trouble." In front of thousands? A few delicate moves later (such concentration!), Compson picks up the conversation: "What do you mean, a lot of trouble?" On and on it goes.

An even more bizarre number, "The Ga-Ga Bird," was filmed for *The Great Gabbo* but is absent from the public-domain prints now in circulation, as well as (regrettably) the recent restoration of the film by the Library of Congress. James Cozart, who oversaw the restoration, believes that "The Ga-Ga Bird," and also maybe "The Web of Love," were filmed in color some time after the rest of the film was made, probably as a booster for the box office. (Although *Gabbo* survives only in black-and-white, its opening credits boast "Color Sequences by Multicolor.") *Variety* and *The New York Times*, reviewing the road-show version that premiered in New York, both mention one color scene but criticize its hues for poor quality. So, it's possible the color footage was excised for general release. "The Web of Love" survives; "The Ga-Ga Bird" has not, apparently. A glimpse of the number—dancers moving around in chicken suits—can be seen during the climactic montage. The restored print is missing the few seconds of accompanying music, but it can be heard on other prints. There is also a short sequence earlier of chorus girls removing what looks to be the same costumes; this was probably where "Ga-Ga Bird" was positioned in the film. For the sake of history—if not art—we hope this lost footage will be found.

Another interesting sidelight to *Gabbo:* An honest-to-goodness ventriloquist, Edgar Bergen, bought the rights to the film in 1943 for a possible remake. But we never did get to see Charlie McCarthy play Otto.

IS EVERYBODY HAPPY?
(Warner Bros.; October 19, 1929)

Director: Archie Mayo. Screenplay: Joseph Jackson, James A. Starr. Titles: De Leon Anthony. Photography: Ben Reynolds. Editor: Desmond O'Brien. Dance Direction: Larry Ceballos. Running Time: 78 minutes (sound version; also released as silent).

Cast: Ted Lewis (Ted Todd), Alice Day (Gail Wilson), Ann Pennington (Lena Schmitt), Lawrence Grant (Victor Molnar), Julia Swayne Gordon (Mrs. Molnar), Otto Hoffman (landlord), Purnell B. Pratt (Abrams), Eddie Kane (host).

Songs: "(I'm Blue for You) New Orleans" [Lewis; reprised by Lewis, band], "I'm the Medicine Man for the Blues" [Lewis, band, twice], "Samoa" [Pennington, chorus, twice], "Wouldn't It Be Wonderful?" [Lewis, band; reprised by Lewis] (Grant Clarke, Harry Akst); "In the Land of Jazz" [Lewis, band] (Ray Perkins, J. Keirn Brennan); "Start the Band" [Lewis, band] (Ted Lewis); "St. Louis Blues" [Lewis, band] (W. C. Handy); "Tiger Rag" [Lewis, band] (The Original Dixieland Jazz Band).

Disc: Columbia 1882 (Lewis/"I'm the Medicine Man for the Blues"/78); Columbia CB-5 (Lewis/"In the Land of Jazz"/78).

"Is everybody happy?" was the trademark question for bandleader-clarinetist-singer Ted Lewis (1891–1971) to his audiences. He always knew the answer. Lewis was known as "The High-Hatted Tragedian of Song" or, if you weren't partial to Paul Whiteman, "The King of Jazz." Among his hits were "Me and My Shadow," "The Sunny Side of the Street" and his theme song, "When My Baby Smiles at Me." He was brought to Hollywood by Warner Bros., which introduced him to the movies in yet another *Jazz Singer* clone.

In *Is Everybody Happy?* Lewis portrayed Ted Todd, the son of a once-famous Hungarian concertmaster. Ted is encouraged by his father (Lawrence Grant) to pursue a career as a violinist. But since our star is not the King of String, we can expect him to toss away his fiddle for a clarinet and sax, a decision that estranges

After passing his peak as a musician, band leader and occasional film actor Ted Lewis (1967 photograph) sought to stay active in show business until his death in 1971.

him from dad. Ted hits the big time and attracts the attention of two women, a dancer from back home in Budapest (Ann Pennington) and an all–American type (Alice Day). Patriotically, the latter wins out. At film's end, Ted and band serenade a beaming poppa, who has been won over by his son's triumphant appearance at his "office." Seems the old guy cleans the restrooms at Carnegie Hall.

Warner Bros. tried to make it easy for Lewis by supplementing original songs by staff tunesmiths—among them the future hit "I'm the Medicine Man for the Blues" by Grant Clarke and Harry Akst—with tunes he'd find more comfortable, such as "Tiger Rag" and "St. Louis Blues." ("Samoa" was sung and danced by Pennington in a Hawaiian-style number.) But Lewis wasn't much of an actor, and *Is Everybody Happy?*, which no longer exists for perusal, ap-

parently wasn't much of a picture. "Will not set the world on fire" was the succinct summation by *The Film Daily*.[53]

For Columbia in 1943, Lewis made another musical called *Is Everybody Happy?* This time, he played himself opposite Nan Wynn and the future Al Jolson, Larry Parks.

BROADWAY SCANDALS

(Columbia; October 28, 1929)

Director: George Archainbaud. Producer: Harry Cohn. Dialogue Directors: James Seymour, Rufus Le Maire. Scenario: Gladys Lehman. Dialogue: Norman Houston, Howard J. Green. Story: Howard J. Green. Photography: Harry Jackson. Editors: Leon Barsha, Ben Pivar. Sound: John Livadary, W. Hancock. Assistant Director: C. C. Coleman. Art Director:

Harrison Wiley. Running Time: 73 minutes (sound version; also released as silent).

Cast: Sally O'Neil (Mary), Jack Egan (Ted Howard), Carmel Myers (Valeska), Tom O'Brien (Bill Gray), J. Barney Sherry (Le Maire), John Hyams (Pringle), Charles Wilson (radio announcer), Doris Dawson (Bobby), Gordon [William "Wild Bill"] Elliott (George Holloway).

Songs: "Can You Read in My Eyes?" [Myers] (Sam Coslow); "Does an Elephant Love Peanuts?" [Egan, O'Neil] (James F. Hanley); "Kicking the Blues Away" (James F. Hanley, Dave Franklin); "Love's the Cause of All My Blues" [Egan] (Charles Daniels, Jo Trent); "Rhythm of the Tambourine" (Dave Franklin); "What Is Life Without Love?" [Egan] (Jack Stone, Fred Thompson, Dave Franklin); "Would I Love to Love You?" [Egan, Myers] (Sidney Clare, Dave Dreyer).

Before Frank Capra's films put it on the map, the Columbia Pictures Corporation was a ramshackle operation along Poverty Row, Hollywood's low-rent district in the area around Sunset Boulevard and Gower Street (hence the name "Gower Gulch"). Harry Cohn, who for 40 years would rule the studio he founded, presided with an abrasive tongue and a closed pocketbook. But unlike many other small-time operators, Cohn dished out enough dough to fund three musicals, all lost now, during the first full year of sound.

For the first, *Broadway Scandals,* Cohn hired the non-singer Sally O'Neil and teamed her with Jack Egan, a singing-and-dancing vaudeville emcee. They made two-thirds of a backstage romantic triangle that also included Carmel Myers, a declining silent star cast as a Broadway songstress exotically named Valeska. The real "scandal," reviewers complained, was the film's over-reliance on second-rate revue numbers at the expense of plot. Sam Coslow's "Can You Read in My Eyes?" made a small splash after being introduced by Myers, but neither it nor any of the other six songs (including one called "Does an Elephant Love Peanuts?") has survived. At last report, the sound discs for *Broadway Scandals* had been rediscovered, but there was no sign of the picture element.

The Song of Love, Columbia's next stab at a musical, at least had behind it the formidable talents of Belle Baker (1895–1957), a famed vaudeville singer, comedienne and recording artist. However, even the presence of "the female Al Jolson and the Sarah Bernhardt of song" hardly justified the studio's trade-ad declaration of "an event as important as the coming of sound." The hefty Baker had to slim down a bit for the big screen, but she won critical kudos as the long-suffering ex-actress wife of an alcoholic vaudevillian (Ralph Graves). With their young son (David Durand), they call themselves "The Three Musketeers," but viewers were made to realize something is amiss when, at a birthday celebration, the boy cuts his cake by separating the decorative figure of his father away from those of mother and son. This blatant attempt at symbolism was leavened by many Baker-delivered songs, a couple of which were cowritten by her husband, Maurice Abrahams. The blonde siren who nearly stole Graves' heart was played by Eunice Quedens, whom we know better as Eve Arden. Eunice/Eve had a much easier time in Hollywood than Baker, whose only other feature-film appearance was as a specialty act in the 1944 Republic musical *Atlantic City.*

Egan returned for *The Broadway Hoofer,* in which his costar was Marie Saxon, another legit thespian new to Hollywood. Saxon (1904–1941) played a Broadway star who goes slumming in a hick village and, incognito, gets hired for a third-rate burlesque revue managed by Egan. The comedienne Louise Fazenda was the only familiar name in the cast. Both Egan and Saxon would all but disappear from talkies after this so-called "musical drama that is different." Saxon's only other recorded feature-film credit was a minor role in the 1930 musical *Under Suspicion* (see Chapter 7).

Saxon, Egan and Baker certainly could have picked a better place to launch their film careers: In 1930, Columbia filmed a popular Broadway musical comedy, *Rain or Shine,* after draining the songs out of it. Cohn didn't take another full-speed spin at the genre until the popular *One Night of Love,* which accomplished for the grateful Grace Moore in 1934 what *The Song of Love* could not for Belle Baker in 1929.

FOOTLIGHTS AND FOOLS

(First National; November 4, 1929)

Director: William A. Seiter. Producer: John McCormick. Adaptation: Tom Geraghty.

In First National's *Footlights and Fools*, Colleen Moore progresses from the chorus to stage headliner.

Dialogue: Carey Wilson. Based on the magazine story by Katharine Brush (1929). Photography: Sid Hickox, Henry Freulich. Sound: Oliver Garretson. Dance Direction: Max Scheck. Running Time: 70 minutes. Technicolor sequences.

Cast: Colleen Moore (Betty Murphy/Fifi D'Auray), Raymond Hackett (Jimmy Willet), Fredric March (Gregory Pyne), Virginia Lee Corbin (Claire Floyd), Mickey Bennett (call boy), Edward Martindel (Chandler Cunningham), Adrienne D'Ambricourt (Jo), Frederick Howard (treasurer), Sidney Jarvis (stage manager), Cleve Moore (press agent), Andy Rice, Jr. (song plugger), Ben Hendricks, Jr. (stage doorman), Larry Banthim (Bud Burke).

Songs: "If I Can't Have You" [Moore], "Ophelia Will Fool You" [Rice], "Pilly Pom Pom Plee," "You Can't Believe My Eyes" (Al Bryan, George W. Meyer); "Wouldn't It Be Wonderful?" (Grant Clarke, Harry Akst).

Even before the release of Colleen Moore's first talkie, *Smiling Irish Eyes,* she and director William A. Seiter were at work on another backstage musical, *Footlights and Fools.* This one had Moore playing an unknown chorus girl who is transformed by an enterprising Broadway producer into a Parisian sensation. Five songs—plus dances created by Max Scheck, late of the Folies Bergére—provided breaks from the dramatic tension created by the love triangle in the story.

The former Betty Murphy, now named Fifi D'Auray, refuses to marry her longtime beau (Raymond Hackett) because he gambles too much. Instead, she turns to a gentlemanly millionaire (Fredric March, on loan from Paramount for his sixth film). The twist on this plot is that the richer man is the better human being, but Fifi/Betty decides in the end that she can do without either fellow. Audiences decided they could do without, too, despite *Motion Picture* magazine's forecast that "*Footlights and Fools* indicates a new career for [Moore] in more sophisticated pictures."[54]

Moore, 2-for-2 in talking clunkers, did not have her contract renewed by Warner Bros.–

First National. Her producer husband, John McCormick, unsuccessfully attempted to negotiate a deal with United Artists, and Moore remained off the screen until 1933. That year, she gained attention opposite Spencer Tracy in Fox's *The Power and the Glory*, but she followed that up with three quickies and then, at age 34, retired for good. The career of the '20s' most famous flapper had declined not because she couldn't act in talkies, but, as with John Gilbert, because her character type had gone out of style.

THE SONG OF LOVE

(Columbia; November 13, 1929)

Director: Erle C. Kenton. Producer: Harry Cohn. Story and Scenario: Howard J. Green, Henry McCarthy, Dorothy Howell. Dialogue: Dorothy Howell, Norman Houston. Photography: Joseph Walker. Editor: Gene Havlick. Sound: John Livadary, Harry Blanchard, Edward L. Bernds. Assistant Director: Sam Nelson. Running Time: 76 minutes (sound version; also released as silent).

Cast: Belle Baker (Anna Gibson), Ralph Graves (Tom Gibson), David Durand (Buddy Gibson), Eunice Quedens [Eve Arden] (Maizie), Arthur Housman (acrobat), Charles Wilson (traveling salesman).

Songs [all by Baker]: "I'm Somebody's Baby Now," "I'm Walking with the Moonbeams, Talking to the Stars" (Mack Gordon, Max Rich, Maurice Abrahams); "Atlas Is Itless" (Lew Brown); "I'll Still Go On Wanting You" (Bernie Grossman, Mickey Kippel, Arthur Sizemore, Maurice Alexander); "Take Everything but You" (Maurice Abrahams); "White Way Blues" (Mack Gordon, Max Rich, George D. Weist).

Disc: Brunswick 4558 (Baker/"I'm Walking with the Moonbeams, Talking to the Stars"/78); Brunswick 4624 (Baker/"I'll Still Go On Wanting You"/78).

Also Known As: *The Cradle of Jazz.*

For description, see the entry for *Broadway Scandals* (October 28, 1929).

RED HOT RHYTHM

(Pathé; November 23, 1929)

Director: Leo McCarey. Producer: William Conselman. Scenario and Dialogue: Earl Baldwin, Walter De Leon. Story: William Conselman, Leo McCarey. Photography: John J. Mescall. Sound: Charles O'Laughlin, Ben Winkler. Art Director: Edward Jewell. Set Director: Ted Dickson. Costumes: Gwen Wakeling. Running Time: 75 minutes (sound version; also released as silent). Technicolor sequences.

Cast: Alan Hale (Walter), Kathryn Crawford (Mary), Walter O'Keefe (Sam), Josephine Dunn (Claire), Anita Garvin (Mable), Ilka Chase (Mrs. Fioretta), Ernest Hilliard (Eddie Graham), Harry Bowen (Whiffle), James Clemmons (Singe).

Songs: "At Last I'm in Love" [Crawford], "My Idea of Heaven," "On the Night That Elmer Died," "Out of the Past," "Red Hot Rhythm" [Clemmons, chorus], "When You're Apart from Me" (Walter O'Keefe, Robert Emmett Dolan).

Red Hot Rhythm, a musical drama from the second-rank Pathé studio, gained a limited release in late 1929, but its only New York booking (one day) wasn't until September of 1930. To *Variety*, the Walter O'Keefe–Robert Emmett Dolan songs, two of which were spotlighted in Technicolor numbers, were "weak" and the dancing was "of no value."[55]

O'Keefe also appeared in the film as a New York music publisher, the "other man" for a nightclub singer (Kathryn Crawford) who actually loves a songwriter (Alan Hale, Sr.) who makes his living from stealing other people's tunes. The cheating composer himself has an interlude with a shady lady (Josephine Dunn) whom he hires as his secretary, but he returns to his sweetheart when he sees her sing "their" song, "At Last I'm in Love," at the aptly named Frivolity Club.

Despite its upbeat finish, most of the moviegoing public gave *Red Hot Rhythm* the ice-cold shoulder. All that apparently exists now of the film is a clip of the Technicolor title-song number. Singer and eccentric dancer James Clemmons, devilishly goateed as a character named "Singe," leads a chorus of girls who seem to be dressed as human flames.

THE VAGABOND LOVER

(RKO; November 26, 1929)

Director: Marshall Neilan. Producer: James A. Creelman. Associate Producer: Louis

Rudy Vallee 'fesses up in *The Vagabond Lover*; witnesses include (foreground, from left) Nella Walker, Sally Blane, Charles Sellon and Marie Dressler.

Serecky. Screenplay: James A. Creelman. Photography: Leo Tover. Editor: Arthur Roberts. Sound: John Tribby. Assistant Director: Wallace Fox. Art Director: Max Rée. Running Time: 65 minutes (sound version; also released as silent).

Cast: Rudy Vallee (Rudy Bronson), Sally Blane (Jean Whitehall), Marie Dressler (Mrs. Whitehall), Charles Sellon (Officer Tuttle), Norman Peck (Swiftie), Danny O'Shea (Sam), Eddie Nugent (Sport), Nella Walker (Mrs. Todhunter), Malcolm Waite (Ted Grant), Alan Roscoe (manager), The Connecticut Yankees.

Songs: "The Dream of My Heart"["I Love You, Believe Me, I Love You"] [Vallee, band, twice] (Ruby Cowan, Philip Bartholomae, Phil Boutelje); "Georgie Porgie" [children] (Louis Herscher, Harold Raymond, Nat Simon); "If You Were the Only Girl" [Vallee, band] (Clifford Grey, Nat D. Ayer); "I'll Be Reminded of You" [Vallee, band] (Edward Heyman, Ken Smith); "I'm Just a Vagabond Lover" [Vallee;

reprised as dance by chorus] (Rudy Vallee, Leon Zimmerman); "A Little Kiss Each Morning, a Little Kiss Each Night" [Vallee, band, four times] (Harry Woods); "Nobody's Sweetheart" [Vallee, band] (Gus Kahn, Ernie Erdman, Billy Meyers, Elmer Schoebel); "Sweetheart, We Need Each Other" [danced by chorus] (Joseph McCarthy, Harry Tierney).

Disc: RCA Victor 21967 (Vallee/"I'm Just a Vagabond Lover"/78); RCA Victor 22193 (Vallee/"A Little Kiss Each Morning..."/78); RCA Victor 22227 (Vallee/"If You Were the Only Girl"/"The Dream of My Heart"["I Love You, Believe Me, I Love You"]/78).

To radio listeners regularly mesmerized by Rudy Vallee's voice, it must have been strange to see the man prove as visually dull and unappealing as he was in his first full-length film. The atrocious *The Vagabond Lover* marked a clear regression in the sound cinema.

Hubert Prior Vallee (1901–1986) was one of

America's first singing idols. His soft, nasal tones, amplified by his trademark megaphone, made him the object of the affections of millions of women during the 1920s and '30s. A saxophonist as well as a singer, he made his first recording in 1921, but it was not until after his 1928 graduation from Yale that Vallee and his Connecticut Yankees caught on in nightclubs, radio and vaudeville. Vallee's rise to stardom was rapid; by early 1929 he'd appeared in two movie shorts, Paramount's *Radio Rhythm* and Warner Bros.' *Rudy Vallee and His Connecticut Yankees*. It was no wonder that the toddling RKO considered it a major coup to sign Vallee and company to make a feature.

In the film, named for Vallee's song "I'm Just a Vagabond Lover," the star plays a rube named Rudy Bronson, the leader of a small-town college band. Rudy proudly shows his bandmates his "brand-new, gold-plated, de-luxe Ted Grant saxophone," which he has just obtained by mail from his idol, a big-name musician. Rudy has learned to play through Grant's "jazz correspondence school," and he thinks that if the band visits the performer's Long Island estate, he'll be impressed enough to give them an audition. Instead, Grant (Malcolm Waite) gives them the gate, but after he departs, the boys prepare to break into the house. But as they are doing so, they are spotted by a neighbor, Mrs. Whitehall (Marie Dressler, 1869–1934) and her daughter Jean (Sally Blane, b. 1910). The Whitehalls summon a curmudgeonly cop (Charles Sellon), and to evade arrest, Rudy claims to be Grant. To prove his musical prowess, Rudy sings "The Dream of My Heart," which have a very pronounced effect on the suddenly smitten Jean.

Rudy wants to end the charade ASAP, but he's falling in love with Jean, and her mom wants to impress her friends by hiring the band for a big benefit musicale. The event is broadcast over a national radio hookup, and Rudy is exposed as an imposter. As the Keystone Kop is about to drag Rudy to jail, Grant—who has shown up just in time to hear Rudy sing "I'll Be Reminded of You"—hails the youngster as a great find. Rudy and Jean embrace to the closing strains of the film's theme song, "A Little Kiss Each Morning, a Little Kiss Each Night."

Later in life, long after he'd built a solid movie career as a fuddy-duddy character actor, Vallee was fond of telling people that *The Vagabond Lover* was shown only to captive audiences in prisons and comfort stations. The film made money and produced song hits in "I'm Just a Vagabond Lover" and "A Little Kiss Each Morning, a Little Kiss Each Night," but RKO saw no potential in Vallee as an actor and declined to exercise an option on a second film. The singer found no solace in the snide comments of a *Photoplay* writer:

> [Vallee] hero-worshipped a good deal in Hollywood, and got very little. The picture people have a way of looking down the nose at nice-looking boys from the East who go to Hollywood with a little too much publicity. And they gave Mr. Vallee the gentle and polite bird.[56]

Mr. Vallee might have fared better had he received some help from his director, Marshall Neilan. Neilan, once one of Hollywood's top helmsmen (he was Mary Pickford's personal favorite), was now a hopeless alcoholic. *The Vagabond Lover* was Neilan's third sound film, yet it is staged as poorly as a 1928 talkie. The mechanically recited dialogue is spaced by uncomfortably long pauses, ostensibly to help audiences digest the "unfamiliar" speech. Vallee's flat monotone is particularly awkward. The actors are constantly rooted to stationary locations. In one scene, Dressler enters the Grant house with an important announcement that has her noticeably excited, but she has to carefully walk across the room to a spot a couple of feet away from Vallee and Blane (because they're where the microphone is) before she can utter a word.

The Vagabond Lover helped to revive Dressler's faltering career, but she would be in much sturdier hands at MGM, where she would soon become one of the most beloved of stars. Vallee remained popular as a radio crooner, but he had to wait until 1934 for his next movie starring role, in *George White's Scandals*.

THE PAINTED ANGEL
(Warner Bros.; December 1, 1929)

Director: Millard Webb. Screenplay: Forrest Halsey. Based on the magazine story "Give the Little Girl a Hand" by Fannie Hurst (1929). Photography: John F. Seitz. Editor: Harold

Young. Running Time: 68 minutes (sound version; also released as silent).

Cast: Billie Dove (Mamie Hudler/Rodeo West), Edmund Lowe (Brood), George Mac-Farlane (Oldfield), Cissy Fitzgerald (Ma Hudler), J. Farrell MacDonald (Pa Hudler), Norman Selby (Jule), Nellie Bly Baker (Sippie), Will Stanton (Joe), Douglas Gerrard (Sir Harry), Shep Camp (Mac), Peter Higgins (singer), Red Stanley (dancer).

Songs: "A Bride Without a Groom," "Everybody's Darling," "Help Yourself to My Love," "Only the Girl," "That Thing" (Herman Ruby, M. K. Jerome).

Also Known As: *The Broadway Hostess.*

"Do you want to know the Truth about NIGHT CLUB HOSTESSES?" teased the ads for *The Painted Angel*, a drama with songs. Today's viewers probably never will, for the film may be lost. Directed by Millard Webb and based on a magazine story by Fannie Hurst, it marked the musical debut of the beautiful Billie Dove (b. 1900?), a former Ziegfeld showgirl who had been acting in movies since 1921.

Dove appeared as Mamie Hudler, a New Orleans saloon entertainer who escapes a checkered past by moving to New York to become "queen of the nightclubs." Edmund Lowe, on loan from Fox, costarred as Mamie's manager, a disabled violinist who carries a torch for Mamie until he finally blurts out his love for her. There were five Herman Ruby–M. K. Jerome songs, mostly sung by Dove, and plenty of dancing numbers. *The Film Daily* thought it prudent to mention that "several near-undressing scenes are jammed in quite obviously for the sexy."[57]

However, the reception for the film was mostly indifferent. Dove's elaborate wardrobe was praised more than her warbling. *Variety* commented that "Miss Dove has no singing voice, choosing to articulate and pout her way through."[58]

IT'S A GREAT LIFE
(MGM; December 6, 1929)

Director: Sam Wood. Scenario and Comedy Dialogue: Al Boasberg. Dialogue: Willard Mack. Story: Byron Morgan, Alfred Block. Photography: Peverell Marley. Editor: Frank

Sullivan. Sound: Douglas Shearer. Art Director: Cedric Gibbons. Costumes: David Cox. Dance Direction: Sammy Lee. Running Time: 94 minutes (sound version; also released as silent). Technicolor sequences.

Cast: Rosetta Duncan (Casey Hogan), Vivian Duncan (Babe Hogan), Lawrence Gray (James Dean), Jed Prouty (David Parker), Benny Rubin (Benny Friedman), Pat Harmon (policeman), Ann Dvorak.

Songs/Musical Numbers: "Fashion Show" [male singer], "Hoosier Hop" [Duncans, chorus], "I'm Following You" [Duncans; reprised by Duncans, then Gray, then Duncans], "I'm Sailing on a Sunbeam" [Gray, danced by chorus; reprised by Duncans], "It Must Be an Old Spanish Custom" [Duncans], "Smile, Smile, Smile, for Mandelbaum and Weil" [Duncans, store employees], "The Sun of a May Morning" [male singer], "Won't You Be My Lady Love?" [Gray; reprised by Vivian Duncan] (Ballard MacDonald, Dave Dreyer); "Let a Smile Be Your Umbrella (on a Rainy Day)" [off-camera male singer] (Irving Kahal, Francis Wheeler, Sammy Fain); "Tell Me Dirty Maiden" [parody of "Tell Me Pretty Maiden"] [Duncans] (original music and lyrics, Owen Hall, Thomas A. Barrett); "There's a Rainbow 'Round My Shoulder" [Duncans] (Al Jolson, Billy Rose, Dave Dreyer); "Ach Du Liebe Augustin" [Rosetta Duncan] (anon.).

Disc: RCA Victor 22269 (Duncans/ "Hoosier Hop"/"I'm Following You"/78); RCA Victor 22345 (Duncans/"It Must Be an Old Spanish Custom"/78).

Video: MGM-UA (laserdisc; excerpts only).

Also Known As: *Cotton and Silk* and *Imperfect Ladies.*

Had one of them not been in Europe at the time MGM was casting *The Broadway Melody*, it might have been Rosetta and Vivian Duncan and not Bessie Love and Anita Page who made movie-musical history. As a consolation prize, the studio cast the famed sister team in a musical comedy called *It's a Great Life*, which faltered at the box office and helped to cut short the Duncans' movie career. Too bad, for the film—a charming, high-spirited showcase for the duo—is hardly deserving of its fate.

It's a Great Life was the second feature film for Rosetta (1901–1959), the foghorn-voiced

Vivian (left) and Rosetta Duncan sing "I'm Following You," the best tune in their ill-fated talkie, *It's a Great Life*. Lawrence Gray is at the piano.

comedienne of the act, and Vivian (1899–1986), the taller, dumb-blonde half. The pair came to prominence in the cast of Gus Edwards' famous "Kiddies' Revue," then matured into first-rate vaudeville troupers who wrote much of their music and dialogue. By the mid '20s, the Duncan Sisters were headlining on Broadway—most notably as "Topsy and Eva," the characters from *Uncle Tom's Cabin*—and touring Europe; they were particularly popular in England. Walter Winchell supposedly paid them $1,000 a minute to sing on his radio show, and Charlotte Greenwood, herself a contender, called Rosetta Duncan "the greatest clown on the American stage." The sisters were inordinately close off screen as well as on. "We think alike and feel alike. We have never been apart except for two weeks," Rosetta told an interviewer as *It's a Great Life* was being filmed. " … I don't think we could ever live without each other."[59]

The Duncans' starring film debut, for United Artists in 1927, was *Topsy and Eva,* an adaptation of their famous stage routine. The picture was questionable as a silent since so much of the show's comedy was verbal, and director Del Lord ruined it by inserting some especially rude gags. Last-minute doctoring by D. W. Griffith could not save the $300,000 flop. The sisters were hoping for much better when they signed a three-picture, $160,000 contract with MGM in the spring of 1929. The project created for them, sprinkled with new songs by Ballard MacDonald and Dave Dreyer, had more than a passing resemblance to *The Broadway Melody*, but it was no pale imitation.

It's a Great Life begins with a funny gag that stems from a beat cop's suspicion about two women he sees dash from an apartment with a pocketbook in hand. He gives chase down a busy New York street, attracting a crowd and causing all manner of property destruction—only to realize, when a door is slammed in his face, that the "culprits" are two department-store employees who are a few minutes late for work. The store is Mandelbaum & Weil's, where Casey and Babe Hogan are tardy for their jobs in the sheet music section. The piano player there is one James Dean (Lawrence Gray), an amateur composer with big dreams but little talent. Songwriting's a snap, he says, "if you've got the gift." Jimmy and Babe—that's Vivian—are sweet on each other, but Casey—she's Rosetta—can't stand the guy.

Jimmy is placed in charge of the store's talent show, but backstage mishaps and stage-frightened performers (during the first of two Technicolor sequences) threaten to make it a flop. Babe, singing "Won't You Be My Lady Love?" to Jimmy's piano, freezes before the footlights, but Casey saves the show by walking on stage and ad-libbing Baby Snooks–type jokes. Unfortunately, Mr. Mandelbaum thinks such hijinks are disrespectful to the company, especially when Casey shows disrespect to the store's song, "Smile, Smile, Smile, for Mandelbaum and Weil." He fires Casey, Babe and Jimmy, but Jimmy's friend Benny Friedman (Benny Rubin), a theatrical agent, has seen the show and is impressed enough to hire the trio for a vaudeville tour.

We are then treated to a typical performance by "The Hogan Sisters with James Dean." The women sing the harmonious "I'm Following You" (their utter sincerity, and Rosetta's imitation of a jazz trombone, makes the number work); the catchy spoof "It Must Be an Old Spanish Custom," on which Casey dons Mexican garb to sing nonsense lyrics; and a risque *Florodora* takeoff ("Oh, tell me, painted oil can"). Their stuff goes over well, but the bickering between Casey and Jimmy reaches the boiling point one morning in Brooklyn, where she fires him from the act. "When I leave," his response goes, "my wife goes with me," and he pulls out a newly inked marriage license. Casey is left alone to be consoled by David Parker (Jed Prouty), her old friend from Mandelbaum & Weil's. David pops up from time to time intending to propose marriage, but his timing is always bad.

Casey can't pass muster as a single, and "Dean & Hogan" are even worse off. "We don't want two intermissions on the same bill," says a theater manager upon giving them an early notice. Babe, distraught over the estrangement from her sister, becomes deathly ill. Jimmy, who can't afford medical care for his wife, seeks out Casey—just as she's accepting David's long-delayed proposal. She decides to nix the marriage and nurse sis back to health.

In the Deans' junky flat, the delirious Babe tells Casey she's been imagining that the trio has finally made the big time, and the screen dissolves into a Technicolor dream sequence that opens with a tableau of a golden stage with golden rows of seating and segues into a series of flashy production numbers. The sisters do the "Hoosier Hop," first in modern semi-formal dress and then in farmer's outfits (Rosetta with beard and spectacles) before the company changes to college-style garb for the finish. A medley of reprised songs from the film follows, then Gray goes solo for "I'm Sailing on a Sunbeam." After the Duncans join in, eager choristers slide down giant "beams" of light. At this point, Babe's fever breaks, and Casey and Jimmy promise to reunite the trio and get along with each other. (The fashion show and "Hoosier Hop" color sequences from *It's a Great Life* were released on laserdisc as part of MGM's recent "The Dawn of Sound" series, and part of "Hoosier Hop" was glimpsed in the compilation film *That's Entertainment! III*.)

On paper, *It's a Great Life* is little different than a number of backstage musicals of the time; its love triangle is right out of *Broadway Melody* (except that, this time, a woman is fought over) and the climax echoes *Melody Lane* and even *The Singing Fool*. But the Duncans' vivaciousness—particularly Rosetta's comic talents—and Sam Wood's energetic direction justified comments like Mordaunt Hall's: "When they are ... backstage and before the footlights, these sisters naturally are in their element, and the fact that they are so familiar with the life of a stage performer is perhaps one reason why this production is so much more pleasing than the usual run of stage yarns."[60] A dissenting vote was cast by Bland Johansen of the New York Mirror: "Too long, too trite, too much Duncan ... if you're a Duncan addict, *It's a Great Life* is a good stiff dose of them."[61]

As *It's a Great Life* was being released, the Duncans were waiting to make an autobiographical film, but MGM canceled it after the disappointing returns on their first talkie. Then they were signed to appear in the all-star musical *The March of Time,* but that ill-fated picture was never released (see Chapter 10). This became an especially tumultuous period for the high-living sisters. In the summer of 1930, actor Rex Lease was ordered to stand trial for an alleged physical assault on Vivian Duncan, whose eye was blackened after a "mysterious" incident at a Fourth of July party given for her at Charles Farrell's home. Lease, a Poverty Row leading man, pleaded guilty to battery and was fined $50. A day after the court date, the girls' brother Harold gave Lease his own black eye at a Hollywood eatery. Before July was out, the Duncans would be sued by their business manager for lost wages; the claim was eventually dismissed. In late '30, the sisters announced their professional break-up, for Vivian was pregnant with a daughter by her new husband, actor Nils Asther.

Life imitated art for a time, as Rosetta attempted an unhappy solo act. But Vivian's marriage would be short-lived (Asther was a closet bisexual), and so would be the interruption of the act, although the sisters were now past their career peak. Their lives weren't always great, but that didn't keep the Duncans from trouping on.

GLORIFYING THE AMERICAN GIRL
(Paramount; December 7, 1929)

Director: Millard Webb. Producer: Florenz Ziegfeld. Revue Director: John Harkrider. Story: J. P. McEvoy, Millard Webb. Photography: George Folsey. Editor: Barney Rogan. Sound: Ernest T. Zatorsky. Musical Director: Frank Tours. Dance Direction: Ted Shawn. Running Time: 87 minutes. Technicolor sequences.

Cast: Mary Eaton (Gloria Hughes), Edward Crandall (Buddy Moore), Olive Shea (Barbara), Dan Healy (Miller), Kaye Renard (Mooney), Sarah Edwards (Mrs. Hughes), Edward J. Le Saint (Pop Morgan), Bull Montana (store patron), Johnny Weissmuller (Adonis figure in chorus), Claudia Dell (chorine). As Themselves: Eddie Cantor, Helen Morgan, Rudy Vallee, Florenz Ziegfeld, Billie Burke [Mrs. Florenz Ziegfeld], Adolph Zukor, Otto Kahn, Mayor and Mrs. Jimmy Walker, Ring Lardner, Noah Beery, Texas Guinan, Norman Brokenshire.

Songs: "Changes" [danced by Eaton, Healy], "Sam, the Old Accordion Man" [danced by Eaton, Healy], "There Must Be Somebody Waiting for Me in Loveland" [danced by Eaton; reprise sung by Eaton, chorus] (Walter Donaldson); "Blue Skies" [band in acrobatic display], "A Pretty Girl Is Like a Melody" [Ziegfeld medley] (Irving Berlin); "Sally, Won't You Come Back?" [Ziegfeld medley], "Tulip Time" [Ziegfeld medley] (Gene Buck, Dave Stamper); "Baby Face" [Eaton] (Benny Davis, Harry Akst); "Die Lorelei" [chorus] (Friedrich Glicher, F. H. Heine); "Fountain of the Acqua Paola" [danced by chorus] (Charles T. Griffes); "Heimer's" [band and chorus, to tune of "Bye Bye Blackbird"] (original lyrics and music, Mort Dixon, Ray Henderson); "Hot Feet" [Eaton, Healy] (Dorothy Fields, Jimmy McHugh); "I'll Be There" [Eaton, Crandall] (Lou Davis, J. Fred Coots, Larry Spier); "I'm Just a Vagabond Lover" [Vallee] (Rudy Vallee, Leon Zimmerman); "No Foolin'" [Ziegfeld medley; reprised by Eaton] (Gene Buck, Irving Caesar, Rudolf Friml, James F. Hanley); "Spooning with the Girl You Love" [Healy, Renard] (Dan Healy); "What Wouldn't I Do for That Man?" [Morgan] (E. Y. Harburg, Jay Gorney).

Disc: RCA Victor 21967 (Vallee/"I'm Just a Vagabond Lover"/78); RCA Victor 22149 (Morgan/"What Wouldn't I Do for That Man?"/78); Trisklog 4 (bootleg LP; ST).

Video: Various public-domain distributors (cassette).

"There is nothing the matter with the talkies. They are mechanically perfect. The trouble is with the dumb stars who are making them. Someone has got to teach Hollywood how to use the instrument. I don't believe there is anyone out there who knows anything about it. There are others out there besides Al Jolson, but you have to get them from the stage."[62]

Such was the pronouncement from Broadway's greatest showman, Florenz Ziegfeld (1867–1932), in the spring of 1929. Ziegfeld, of course, knew next to nothing about making motion pictures—a fact that *Photoplay,* from which this quote is excerpted, had no hesitation about emphasizing. But at a time when the vast majority of Hollywood musicals were inferior copies of the best New York product, the thought of the impresario using the resources of

Ziegfeld girl Mary Eaton made an unsuccessful bid for movie stardom in Paramount's *Glorifying the American Girl*.

a movie studio to mount one of his typically extravagant, talent-laden productions—particularly one of his famous girlie revues—was downright tantalizing. It also seemed a bit unrealistic, for how could a control freak such as Ziegfeld adapt to the regimented studio system?

Not very well, it turned out. Only a few months after *The Jazz Singer*, Ziegfeld and Paramount announced that a film version of the showman's *Follies* would be produced in the fall of 1928. But *Glorifying the American Girl*, with a title derived from the slogan originated by Ziegfeld for his 1922 revue, was hampered by repeated delays. The studio was uncertain over the future of sound, no one could come up with a suitable script, and Ziegfeld's distraction with other projects made him reluctant to contribute time and money. Shooting didn't begin at Paramount's Astoria, New York, facility until the end of April in 1929. By then, it had been decided to complement the revue numbers with a story (by Millard Webb and *Follies* comedy specialist J. P. McEvoy) about the rise to fame of a "typical" Ziegfeld girl.

One of Ziegfeld's brightest stars, singer-dancer Mary Eaton (1901–1948), was enlisted to head the cast. She had just appeared with the Marx Brothers in Paramount's *The Cocoanuts* and her identification with Ziegfeld dated back to the 1920 *Follies*, for which she successfully replaced Marilyn Miller as the featured aesthetic dancer.[63] In *Glorifying the American Girl*, Eaton was directed by Webb, whom she had just married (the two had met on the set of *The Cocoanuts*). The boast in the opening credits that the film was made "under the personal supervision of Florenz Ziegfeld" was little more than studio publicity, although the filmmakers more or less succeeded in capturing the "look" of his shows.

Glorifying the American Girl begins with a short prologue: a chorus of 75 Ziegfeldians parades across a giant map of the United States, then, to a medley of *Follies* song hits, we see various images of womanhood—at home, on the job, in church—alternated with shots of *Follies* girls elaborately garbed by Ziegfeld associate John Harkrider. The story begins as Gloria Hughes, who works in the sheet-music section of a department store, dreams of breaking into show business. Like the Hogan sisters in *It's a Great Life,* she is "discovered" singing and dancing at an employee get-together. A fast-talking vaudevillian (Dan Healy) hires her as the female half of a song-and-dance team called "Mooney and Miller." Miller averages a Mooney a month, but an unsuspecting Gloria—pushed into the job by her ambitious mother (Sarah Edwards)—decides to leave behind her clean-cut but dull sweetie, Buddy (Edward Crandall), and their best friend, Barbara (Olive Shea), for life on the road.

Gloria sees through her sleazy partner, but only after he forces her to sign a contract awarding him half of any future earnings. Buddy falls in love with Barbara, who has curried the young man's favor by being hit by a truck. One night in Chicago, Gloria is spotted by a Ziegfeld scout and is hired as a single for the showman's new revue, *Glorifying the American Girl.* (The hearing-impaired director of the revue, Pop Morgan, is modeled upon Ziegfeld's real-life collaborator Julian Mitchell.) On opening night, Gloria's toe dancing will make her the toast of Broadway, but her joy is tempered by the news of Buddy and Barbara's nuptials. Gloria falls into mama's arms—"What will I do now?" she sobs. At the end of the "Garden of Love" Technicolor finale, in which she leads the feathered-and-sequined chorus in Walter Donaldson's "There Must Be Somebody Waiting for Me in Loveland," Gloria sadly accepts the adoring applause. Her stardom is hollow.

The downbeat ending gives the dull, trite tale more novelty than it deserves. What does give *Glorifying the American Girl* some historical significance is the pre-"show" festivities. As the first-nighters file into the theater, radio announcer Norman Brokenshire (as himself) alerts his listeners of the presence of celebrities who are shown arriving in very brief clips. Ziegfeld biographer Charles Higham has written that the VIP shots were staged in a mock-up of the Ziegfeld Theatre lobby,[64] but they look slapdash enough to have been filmed during an actual premiere. Ziegfeld wanders by with his wife, the actress Billie Burke. New York Mayor Jimmy Walker strides in. A smiling

Texas Guinan mouths a wisecrack to the silent camera. Also glimpsed are Paramount chief Adolph Zukor, financier Otto Kahn, actor Noah Beery and writer Ring Lardner.

The on-stage cameos, filmed on a massive replica of the New Amsterdam Theatre, are a good deal lengthier. Between Eaton's two dance numbers, Rudy Vallee croons "I'm Just a Vagabond Lover" and Helen Morgan, typically presented in a black dress atop a white piano against a black background, sings "What Wouldn't I Do for That Man?" Also preserved is Eddie Cantor's famous "Cheap Charlie" tailor-shop comedy skit, which had originated in the 1922 Broadway show *Make It Snappy.* However, its draggy 12 minutes seem like twice that. According to Brian Taves, biographer of the director Robert Florey, the Morgan and Cantor performances were taken from shorts supervised by Florey at Astoria.[65] They were added to *Glorifying the American Girl* late in the going to give the foundering production publicity and extra marquee value.

Glorifying the American Girl was released six months after most of it was completed, and it shows. The sound recording is very poor; dialogue is dubbed in for the frequent bits of stock footage. For example, as the hands of a theatergoer are shown opening a playbill that will introduce "I'm Just a Vagabond Lover," we hear "voices" excitedly whispering "Rudy Vallee! Rudy Vallee!"—but "they" sound suspiciously like one voice hastily filling in the silence.

Had it been made on the West Coast—where sound technology was improving by the day, and where more experienced actors would have replaced the no-name cast—*Glorifying the American Girl* might not have been the costly flop that it was.

THE BROADWAY HOOFER
(Columbia; December 15, 1929)

Director: George Archainbaud. Producer: Harry Cohn. Dialogue Director: James Seymour. Screenplay: Gladys Lehman. Photography: Joseph Walker. Editor: Maurice Wright. Sound: John Livadary, Harry Blanchard. Assistant Director: David Selman. Art Director: Harrison Wiley. Dance Direction: Jack

Cunningham. Running Time: 65 minutes (sound version; also released as silent).

Cast: Marie Saxon (Adele), Jack Egan (Bobby), Louise Fazenda (Jane Brown), Howard Hickman (Larry), Ernest Hilliard (Morton), Gertrude Short (Annabelle), Eileen Percy (Dolly), Charlotte Merriam (Mazie), Fred Mackeye (Billy), Billy Franey (baggage man).

Songs: "Hawaiian Love Song" (Ballard MacDonald, Dave Franklin); "I Live to Love Only You" (Mack Gordon, Max Rich); "Mediterranean Moon" (Buddy Valentine, Robert A. King, Ted Fiorito); "Oh! So Sweet" (George Waggner, Abner Silver).

For description, see the entry for *Broadway Scandals* (October 28, 1929).

POINTED HEELS
(Paramount; December 21, 1929)

Director: A. Edward Sutherland. Dialogue Director: Percy Ivins. Adaptation and Dialogue: Florence Ryerson, John V. A. Weaver. Based on the magazine story by Charles Brackett (1928). Photography: Allen Siegler. Editor: Jane Loring. Sound: Harry M. Lindgren. Running Time: 62 minutes (sound version; also released as silent). Technicolor sequence.

Cast: William Powell (Robert Courtland), Fay Wray (Lora Nixon), Helen Kane (Dot Nixon), Richard "Skeets" Gallagher (Dash Nixon), Phillips Holmes (Donald Ogden), Eugene Pallette (Joe Clark), Adrienne Doré (Kay Wilcox), Albertina Rasch Ballet.

Songs/Musical Numbers: "Ain'tcha?" [Kane, twice] (Mack Gordon, Max Rich); "I Have to Have You" [Holmes; reprised twice by Kane, Gallagher] (Leo Robin, Richard A. Whiting); "Pointed Heels Ballet" [Rasch girls] (Dimitri Tiomkin).

Disc: RCA Victor 22192 (Kane/"Ain'tcha"/ "I Have to Have You"/78).

William Powell was not a singer, but the first movie in which he achieved top billing was a backstage musical comedy-drama, *Pointed Heels.* In the fortieth film of a Hollywood career heretofore dominated by heavy-type roles, Powell (1892–1984) portrayed a Broadway producer who plays guardian angel to a troubled

young couple played by Fay Wray (b. 1907) and Phillips Holmes (1907–1942).

This millionaire producer, Robert Courtland, definitely has a yen for chorus girl Lora Nixon, but she loves Donald Ogden, a sensitive socialite whose only goal in life is to write a "jazz" symphony à la Gershwin. Donald's family disowns him when he marries Lora, and the two are forced into a shabby apartment, where she works to support his songwriting dream. Making a bad situation worse is the meddling of Lora's brother and sister-in-law (Skeets Gallagher and Helen Kane), a bickering low comedy team billed as "Dot and Dash."

Courtland, still torching, gives both couples a break by using their talents in a show that will star the Nixons and spotlight Donald's new pop song. He talks Lora into leaving Donald "for his own good" and invites her to his mansion to make whoopee, but he has a change of heart and tucks the tipsy Lora into a separate bed. Donald, thinking his wife has dumped him for Courtland, makes plans to sail abroad, but when the show makes a big splash, Courtland effects a happy reunion of the husband and wife. At the end, he tells a confidante, "For the first time in my life, I've seen it … love."

Based on a "College Humor" magazine story by Charles Brackett (his first film credit in a long association with Paramount), *Pointed Heels* contains only two songs, plus a Technicolor ballet sequence choreographed by Albertina Rasch.[66] Kane does most of the singing, predictably turning Holmes'—actually Whiting and Robin's—"I Have to Have You" into a variation on her trademark "boop-boop-a-doop." She and Gallagher, actors best sampled in small doses, amusingly lend their characters a new meaning of the word "unsophisticated." A. Edward Sutherland directs briskly for slightly over an hour, and multiple-exposure camera work by Allen Siegler depicts the tense disorder of a Broadway opening night.

Pointed Heels was a rare musical venture for Wray, whose role was initially intended for Mary Eaton and then Esther Ralston. The future paramour of King Kong wrote in her autobiography, *On the Other Hand,* that her infatuation with Powell's smooth sophistication made the experience bearable.

I learned a few [dance] steps, used the same false eyelashes I had worn as the gangster's moll in *Thunderbolt*, felt thoroughly miscast, happy only to be working with William Powell. He had grace, style, wit and technique. ... He was Olympian in the sense that he seemed to have achieved an elegant arrogance. When I see photos of him in splendid profile, I think of how he told me he achieved a taut chin line: "I start a swallow but do not finish it."[67]

BLAZE O' GLORY

(Sono Art; December 30, 1929)

Director: Renaud Hoffman, George J. Crone. Producers: O. E. Goebel, George W. Weeks. Scenario and Dialogue: Henry McCarty. Adaptation: Renaud Hoffman. Based on the magazine story "The Long Shot" by Thomas Alexander Boyd (1925). Photography: Harry Jackson. Editor: Arthur Huffsmith. Sound: Ben Harper. Running Time: 78 minutes.

Cast: Eddie Dowling (Eddie Williams), Betty Compson (Helen Williams), Frankie Darro (Jean Williams), Henry B. Walthall (Burke), William B. Davidson (district attorney), Ferdinand Schumann-Heink (Carl Hummel), Eddie Conrad (Abie), Frank Sabini (Tony), Broderick O'Farrell, The Rounders.

Songs: "Doughboy's Lullaby" [Dowling, soldiers; reprised twice by Dowling], "Put a Little Salt on the Bluebird's Tail Before It Flies Away" [Dowling, chorus] (Eddie Dowling, James Brockman, James F. Hanley); "Welcome Home" [chorus; reprised numerous times by Dowling, soldiers] (Ballard MacDonald, James F. Hanley); "Wrapped in a Red, Red Rose" [Dowling, twice] (Eddie Dowling, Joseph McCarthy, James F. Hanley); "Bon Soir M'sieu" [Conrad] (Eddie Conrad).

After the success of *The Rainbow Man*, Eddie Dowling was certain that he knew what the public wanted. Unfortunately, he put whatever it was into a depressing musical melodrama, Sono Art's *Blaze o' Glory*, which unlike his first film did not have the benefit of a major-studio release.

Dowling (singing four songs, three with his own lyrics) played Eddie Williams, a former Broadway star who has become embittered and unemployed after returning from the Great War. He shoots to death his old battle buddy (Ferdinand Schumann-Heink) after finding his so-called friend carrying on with his wife (Betty Compson). All this is related in flashback during a trial at which Eddie inexplicably will be declared innocent.

At a draggy 78 minutes, *Blaze o' Glory* was severely panned by the press. *Variety*'s summation was particularly vicious ("sugared for tears to the point of nausea ... the hokiest kind of melodrama").[68] After some editing and a request from the producers for a second review, the trade paper shot the film down again ("all the cutting ... cannot change the theme and dialogue").[69] There was also a Spanish version, *Sombras de Gloria*, released on February 1, 1930. Directed by Andrew L. Stone and starring singer-actor José Bohr (1901–1994), it was also a casualty of *Variety*'s poison pen.

Sono Art announced two more Dowling pictures for 1930, but only one was made, and it wasn't released until 1931. Dowling's third, and final, feature was an adaptation of his *Honeymoon Lane*, but with the stage score trimmed to one song. There would be future blazes of glory for Eddie Dowling—but on the Broadway stage, not the Hollywood set.

CHAPTER 4

1929–1930: *"Some Laughs, Some Songs, and Even a Little Acting"*

While much of the Hollywood elite lost sleep over the inevitability of Vitaphone, show people on the opposite coast reveled in the happiest and most fruitful period in the history of the Broadway stage. This "golden age," which began as the '20s neared their halfway point, was marked both by remarkable quantity and quality. During the 1927-28 season alone, the Great White Way welcomed a record 270 plays, among them *Strange Interlude, Burlesque, The Royal Family* and *Paris Bound.* Included in the season's unsurpassed crop of 51 musicals were *Good News, The Five O'Clock Girl, A Connecticut Yankee, Rosalie, Present Arms* and *Funny Face.* An unheard-of total of 11 productions premiered on December 26, 1927. The next night, only two opened, but one of those, *Show Boat,* was to forever change the shape of American musical theater. This astounding output gave Hollywood producers plenty of grist for the movie mill once sound provided the impetus for them to grind out their own versions.

Show Boat was advertised as a musical comedy, but its unconventional libretto and score tilted it toward operetta or, more accurately, an entirely new form of musical play. The other book musicals of the period had no such identity crisis, for the majority were rooted either in the tradition of the romantic operetta or in the newer, hipper genre of musical comedy. In contrast to the lush, middle European-influenced stories and music presented in operettas, musical comedies were brassy, pop-oriented and vaudeville-influenced. The flimsy, frivolous plots churned out by quipsters like Guy Bolton, P. G. Wodehouse and William Anthony McGuire were mainly excuses for which to showcase melodies created by Jerome Kern, Vincent Youmans, George Gershwin, Richard Rodgers, Bert Kalmar and others. Just as the books were highly bound by formula, so, by now, was the music, which adhered strictly to the 32-bar AABA pattern. This could be either a blessing or a curse, depending on one's attitude, but some of the best lyricists—Cole Porter, Harry Ruby, Ira Gershwin, Lorenz Hart—met the creative challenge by constantly finding inventive ways to turn an eight-bar phrase.

You could spot a musical comedy from a mile away—even by its title. There would be a short, catchy phrase (*Hit the Deck!, Top Speed, Hold Everything*) or a one-word tribute to a central character, usually female (*Sally, Sunny, Rosalie*). There would be slumming playboys, modern Cinderellas, pleasure-mad collegians, or idle-rich resort vacationers with colorful, self-descriptive handles: Dick Trevor, Sadi La Salle, T. Boggs Johns, Lord Raybrook and "Peachy" Robinson. There was little doubt about who would end up with whom, or without whom. Yet, like the grade-B Western or the programmer horror film, the golden-age musical comedy still has plenty of adherents in buffdom, and it's due in no small part to this fidelity to formula. In the 1950s, Sandy Wilson cannily satirized the conventions of the form in his stage hit *The Boy Friend,* but the real thing was much more interesting.

Given the overwhelming supremacy of score over libretto in the typical '20s Broadway musical comedy or operetta, it would have made some sense for adapting moviemakers to tinker with the plots while respecting the music. In fact, exactly the opposite happened. Studio minds eliminated all or most of the original tunes of many scores and replaced them with new, and usually inferior, songs written by in-house staffers. A typical adapted movie song score contained only two or three originals, usually those most identifiable with the stageplay—for example, "Look for the Silver Lining" from *Sally*, or "Give My Regards to Broadway" from *Little Johnny Jones*.

This meddling should have been no surprise. From day one of the sound revolution, Hollywood was motivated by profit. Now that the major studios owned or were allied with some of the nation's largest publishing houses, they were more inclined to create their own musical properties than to pay hefty royalties for originals that would bring others profit. Commentators of the day tended to explain away the artistic facelifting by asserting that the public had grown tired of the stage standards, but few of them allowed that the heightened sheet-music sales and radio airplay were making a mint for the companies whose works were being critiqued. This way of thinking by the studios also might explain the casting of contract actors—say, Joe E. Brown or Buddy Rogers—over better qualified but more expensive players who'd appeared in the stage versions of musicals adapted for Hollywood.

Then again … film was an entirely different medium than the stage, with new demands and freedoms and constraints. The typical Broadway musical production ran for two and a half to three hours, varied from 15 to 25 songs or so, and had its content arranged to facilitate costume or set changes, as well as an intermission. Conversely, few films at the dawn of sound ran more than an hour and a half, and there was no need for concessions to live performance. Something had to give, and most often it was the music. Also, the cinema demanded a stronger reliance on visuals. Filmmakers were challenged to "open up" stagebound material by trimming lengthy dialogue sections, working the obstinate camera creatively, and even moving appropriate scenes to outdoor locations. But too few 1929-30 musicals even tried; too many of them were merely photographed clones of live theater, right down to their 10-minute intermissions. The first stage-to-film transfers hardly looked as if they'd left New York. Certainly this may have stemmed from the desire to bring Broadway to the hinterlands, warts and all, and in retrospect, we are happy to have surviving documents of a Broadway that no longer is. But for audiences who were accustomed to the visual feasts of the late silent period, these films were often perceived as artistically deficient.

Although the cinema had not fully capitalized on its advantages over the stage, the popularity of sound—and the rush for talent that resulted—was killing the legitimate theater. So was the stock market crash. The Broadway that spawned more than 50 original musicals in 1927-28 could muster no more than 32 in 1929-30, and four fewer than that a season later. Many of its theaters were converted into movie houses. The empire builders—Florenz Ziegfeld, Charles Dillingham, Arthur Hammerstein, the Shuberts—went bust. The very best productions of the 1930s would be as good as they ever were, but even as the Depression eased, musical theater would remain in the doldrums throughout the decade. As early as the middle of 1930, *Variety* was compelled to admit: "New York has degenerated into an ordinary key city. … There's nothing Broadway can offer the out-of-towner [that he] can't get right on his own main or side street."[1]

In this chapter, we'll discuss the films based on Broadway musical comedies and straight plays, as well as a few adapted from other sources (books, magazine stories, other films, et al.). Musical comedies written expressly for the screen, as well as college-themed shows and certain backstagers, are contained elsewhere.

THE COCOANUTS
(Paramount; May 24, 1929)

Directors: Robert Florey, Joseph Santley. Producers: Walter Wanger, Monta Bell. Screenplay: Morris Ryskind. Based on the musical play, book by George S. Kaufman, lyrics and music by Irving Berlin (New York opening, December 8, 1925; 373 performances). Photography: George Folsey. Editor: Barney Rogan. Musical Director: Frank Tours. Running Time: 96 minutes.

Cast: Groucho Marx (Hammer), Harpo Marx (Harpo), Chico Marx (Chico), Zeppo Marx (Jamison), Mary Eaton (Polly Potter), Oscar Shaw (Bob Adams), Kay Francis (Penelope), Margaret Dumont (Mrs. Potter), Cyril Ring (Harvey Yates), Basil Ruysdael

(Hennessey), Sylvan Lee (bell captain), Barton MacLane (man in bathing suit), Alan K. Foster Girls, Gamby-Hall Girls (dancing bellhops).

Songs/Musical Numbers: "The Bellhops" [bellhop chorus], "Florida by the Sea" [chorus], "Monkey-Doodle-Doo" [Eaton, chorus], "When My Dreams Come True" [Eaton, Shaw; reprised by Harpo on harp, then sung by Eaton] (Irving Berlin); "The Tale of a Shirt" [Ruysdael, chorus] (Berlin; lyrics set to "Toreador Song" from Bizet's *Carmen*); "Gypsy Love Song" [Chico on piano] (Harry B. Smith, Victor Herbert); ballet music from *The Music Box Revue* [dancers] (Frank Tours).

Disc: MCA MUP-395 (Marx Brothers/LP; ST); Sandy Hook 2059 (bootleg LP; ST); Soundtrak STK-108 (bootleg LP; ST).

Video: MCA-Universal (cassette/laserdisc).

Groucho Marx first brought his painted-on moustache — and Margaret Dumont — to the screen in *The Cocoanuts*.

"We were four young guys, full of hell," Zeppo Marx said years after he and three of his brothers showed Broadway how much hell they had. The Four Marx Brothers — as the erstwhile vaudeville team of Groucho, Harpo, Chico and Zeppo was billed — took New York by storm in 1924 with their rambunctious antics in a nearly plotless music-and-comedy revue called *I'll Say She Is!* Nobody had seen anything quite like their unpredictable, nonsensical clowning, which was made a little different each night by the brothers' yen for spontaneity. Harpo (1888–1964) was the wordless, leering pixie who romped in a red wig and rumpled hat. Groucho (1890–1977) was the punning cynic with the greasepainted mustache and omni-present wisecrack. Chico (1886–1961) was the heavily accented Italian con artist/piano player, in stark contrast to Zeppo (1901–1979), the bland, clean-cut straight man confined mainly to romantic relief.

After the success of *I'll Say She Is!*, the brothers signed with producer Sam Harris for his next show, *The Cocoanuts*, with libretto by George S. Kaufman and music by Irving Berlin. Kaufman's book made fun of the then-raging Florida land boom, in which thousands were gypped into buying swampland real estate. Groucho, doing the swindling as the savvy entrepreneur of a resort hotel, drew most of the inevitable raves. The only person not so en-amored with the brothers was their costar, Margaret Dumont (1889–1965), whose patience was tested in trying to keep up with their nightly departures from the script. *The Cocoanuts* opened in New York at the end of 1925, to an enthusiastic public response.

Three years later, the Marxes were starring in their third Broadway success, *Animal Crackers,* at which time Paramount hired these very verbal (save for Harpo, of course) comics for the talkies. The studio bought the rights to *The Cocoanuts* and the services of the brothers for $100,000, and shooting began in late 1928 at Paramount's facility in Astoria, N.Y. The filming, done early each day so the Marxes could appear on stage each evening in *Animal Crackers,* was frought with problems. The crude recording equipment broke down constantly, the restless brothers never reported for work on time, and, worst of all, neither codirectors Robert Florey and Joseph Santley nor producer Monta Bell were in tune with the Marxes' peculiar brand of humor.

Wrote Groucho in his autobiography, *Groucho and Me*:

> I was called into a conference and informed that I would have to discard the black, painted mustache. When I asked why, they explained, "Well, nobody's ever worn a black, painted mustache on the screen. The audience isn't accustomed to anything as phony as that and just won't believe it." "The audience doesn't believe us anyhow," I answered. "All they do is laugh at us and, after all, isn't that what we're getting paid for?"[2]

Groucho got to keep the ersatz mustache, but that didn't put an end to the squabbling. The camera operators complained that they couldn't keep the Marxes in frame; their ad-libs made them liable to ignore their marks, a habit that is quite apparent in the finished film. At one point—and this shows how confounded moviemakers were by sound—Santley insisted that when music started to play over a dialogue sequence, the motion picture audience had to be shown where it came from. Since *The Cocoanuts* was filmed before pre-recording became commonplace, this would require photographing the on-set musicians. Instead, Santley dressed a bunch of actors up to sit in a bandstand and look like an orchestra. They sat around and got

paid for a day's work, but the director never bothered to film them.[3]

The final result was little more than a filmed play. The story was basically the same as it was on stage: While Groucho, as the hotel manager Hammer, schemes to sell off his real estate and hold off the hotel's creditors, Chico and Harpo get tangled up in a scheme by two villains (Cyril Ring and, in her second film, Kay Francis) to steal the jewels of a wealthy widow (Margaret Dumont) and pin the crime on the would-be architect fiancé (Oscar Shaw) of the widow's daughter (Mary Eaton) so the male villain can have the girl for himself. The progress of this plot took a back seat to the comedy, although maybe not as much as it should have.

The major problem with *The Cocoanuts,* besides its technical sloppiness, is that it cannot decide whether to be a conventional musical comedy or a Marxian laff riot. There are only five Berlin songs—four from the stage show and one, the cloying theme song "When My Dreams Come True," written for the picture— to clutter the clowning.[4] Yet the Marxes seem sluggish in their routines. Some remain quite funny, especially the famous "Why a Duck?" banter between Groucho and Chico and the former's flirting with the hefty Dumont ("I'll meet you tonight under the moon. Oh, I can see you now—you and the moon ... you wear a necktie so I'll know you"). But one yearns for more r.p.m.

The worst concession to convention occurs at the very end, as Eaton, who has been reunited with Shaw, reprises "When My Dreams Come True." Florey cuts away first to the villains, shown heading for the hoosegow, then to the Marxes, who grin stupidly and wave to the camera, seemingly unaware that they have been made secondary players in their own picture. At the fadeout, we are back to Shaw and Eaton (as a background chorine spoils their clinch by glaring at the camera). Shaw and Eaton, a popular love team on Broadway, show very little on screen. Eaton dances adequately but is poorly photographed. Shaw (1891–1967) tries gamely to keep up with the Marxes—at one point, he must openly cue Chico, who is spouting ad-libs instead of the lines he's forgotten—but he comes off as a little swarmy and makes no impression with his tenor. Maybe, surmised one critic, it was the reproduction: "Mary Eaton and Oscar Shaw ... sound like people singing on an old phonograph needle with a blunt needle."[5] Neither Shaw nor Eaton would make it in talkies, although Paramount gave her another chance with the unsuccessful *Glorifying the American Girl* (see Chapter 3) and Shaw would return to the studio in 1940 to play a supporting role in the Bing Crosby musical *Rhythm on the River*.

The importance of *The Cocoanuts* in movie-musical history is in its brief use of an overhead camera during one of its production numbers. Although Busby Berkeley, in *Whoopee!* (1930), was the first filmmaker to use overhead photography *extensively* in a dance sequence, the credit for its first documented use must go to Robert Florey (1900–1979). As he told Marx chronicler Richard Anobile, the Frenchman knew what he had in mind when he requested the vertical view, which lasted only a few seconds during a ballet number.

I had done shots like that in little avant-garde films I produced years earlier. You see something and get a feeling about how you'd like to photograph it. As I watched the chorus girls rehearse I noticed that in one dance they formed a circle of petals around the base of a fountain. I was interested in the movement and asked Joe Ruttenberg, one of my cameramen, that I'd like to try to shoot the scene straight down. We installed a camera on top of the studio and mounted it with a wide-angle lens. It was quite a job getting the camera up there so to make it easier we shot the scene silent and added the sound later. Other shots were achieved by placing the camera in a pit around the stage and shooting through the legs of the dancers with a long lens.[6]

The number, in which the ballet dancers were grouped in the kind of kaleidoscope pattern Berkeley liked so well, drew a noticeable reaction from audiences. "The sequence proved so engaging that it elicited plaudits from many in the jammed theater," *The Times'* Mordaunt Hall wrote after the picture's New York premiere.[7]

There are a few other interesting musical moments. Florey shot the opening credits sequence, in which a chorus line dances to an instrumental of "Monkey-Doodle-Doo," in negative form. A production number featuring the same otherwise-forgettable song features some multiple-angle cinematography, although Eaton's lower legs tend to disappear during long shots.

"The Tale of a Shirt," in which Berlin's lyrics are amusingly set to the "Toreador Song" from *Carmen*, is delivered with punch by Basil Ruysdael, portraying the hotel detective. Ruysdael, a prominent singer and teacher of opera, and Dumont were the only non-Marxes held over from the Broadway cast. This would be Ruysdael's only screen appearance prior to 1949, after which he would become a fairly busy film character actor.

Even with its faults, *The Cocoanuts* became a big hit. It grossed some $2 million, to the very mixed feelings of the Marxes, who hated the film so much that they reportedly wanted to buy up the negative and destroy it. As poorly paced as the brothers' comedy seems now, the film did a lot of repeat business. Patrons were coming back to see it two and three times just to pick up all the fast talking!

THE COCK-EYED WORLD
(Fox; August 3, 1929)

Director: Raoul Walsh. Scenario: Raoul Walsh. Dialogue: William K. Wells. Based on the unpublished play *Tropical Twins* by Laurence Stallings and Maxwell Anderson. Titles: Wilbur Morse, Jr. Photography: Arthur Edeson. Editor: Jack Dennis. Sound: Edmund H. Hansen. Assistant Director: Archibald Buchanan. Art Direction: David Hall, Ben Carré. Running Time: 115 minutes (sound version; also released as silent).

Cast: Victor McLaglen (Top Sergeant Flagg), Edmund Lowe (Sgt. Harry Quirt), Lily Damita (Elenita), El Brendel (Olson), Leila Karnelly (Olga), Bobby Burns (Connors), Jeanette Dagna (Katinka), Jean Bary (Fanny), Joe Brown (Brownie), Stuart Erwin (Buckley), Ivan Linow (Sanovich), Solidad Jiminez (innkeeper), Albert Dresden (O'Sullivan), Joe Rochay (Jacobs), Warren Hymer (scout), U. S. Naval Barracks Orchestra, Kamerko Balalaika Orchestra, Jose Arias Spanish Troubadors, Aqua Caliente Marimba Band.

Songs: "Elenita" [Damita], "So Dear to Me" [Burns], "So Long" [soldiers] (Sidney Mitchell, Archie Gottler, Con Conrad); "The Marine's Hymn" [military band] (Henry C. Davis; based on music by Jacques Offenbach); "Palolo" [danced by Brendel, girl] (Charles E. King); "Semper Fidelis" [soldiers] (John Philip

Sousa); "That's Glorianna" [soldiers] (Sidney Clare, Lew Pollack); "You're the Cream in My Coffee" [orchestra in restaurant] (B. G. De Sylva, Lew Brown, Ray Henderson); "La Hamaca," "Korobushka," "Laughing Polka" (trad.); "The Wishing Song" [Brendel] (authorship undetermined). Instrumental Medley by Barracks Band: "Over There" (George M. Cohan); "The Rose of No Man's Land" (James Caddigan, James Brennan); "K-K-K-Katy" (Geoffrey O'Hara); "Mademoiselle from Armentières"["Hinky Dinky Parlez Vous"] (authorship uncertain).

In 1926, Fox Studios teamed its stars Victor McLaglen (1883–1959) and Edmund Lowe (1890–1971) with director Raoul Walsh in an adaptation of the Laurence Stallings–Maxwell Anderson stage hit *What Price Glory?*—and made a mint with its raucous comedy about two battling Marines of the Great War. Three years later, *The Cock-Eyed World*, a sequel based on the unpublished Stallings-Anderson play *Tropical Twins*, was just as boisterous and about as profitable.

This time, Flagg (McLaglen) and Quirt (Lowe) have postwar duty in a wide variety of locales. There's a woman in every port: a fiery Russian (Leila Karnelly) in Vladivostok, a fun-loving flapper (Jean Bary) in New York City, and a hoydenish tease (Lily Damita) in Nicaragua. The hijinks with Damita, who received equal billing with the male stars, take up the second half of the overlong, episodic film.

Fox sought to attract audiences by mixing music into the comedy of *The Cock-Eyed World*, and on such rests the film's arguable claim as a musical. The song interludes are mostly brief and, except for one number, are performed by secondary players, notably comic El Brendel and youthful tenor Bobby Burns, or supplementary musicians. Burns (not the "Bazooka Bob" Burns of '30s fame) does a nice job with the tender ballad "So Dear to Me," one of three songs written for the film by Sidney Mitchell, Archie Gottler and Con Conrad. The other two were "Elenita," delivered by Damita, and a marching song, "So Long," sung by what were billed as "600 lusty leathernecks" filmed aboard the U.S.S. *Henderson* in San Francisco Bay. Most of the other tunes are interpolated battle standards or scene-setting international melodies.

The Cock-Eyed World is full of the robust "Sez You! Sez Me!" banter that made its predecessor so popular (McLaglen: "I can trace me ancestors back to George the Third!" Lowe: "Yeah, well, I can trace mine back to July the Fourth!"). *The Film Daily* put the picture on its annual "10 best" list, but some critics complained that the sequel captured the flavor but not the spirit of *What Price Glory?* The spoken dialogue, even if too plentiful, gives a more earthy dimension to the comedy. Brendel, accompanied by a tropical miss, tells McLaglen he's brought him "the lay of the land." (He's referring to a map, not the miss.) Later, the he-man stars argue over the parentage of Damita's child. The raunch created a minor stir, but that hardly dented the film's ample box office, said to exceed $2 million.

WHY LEAVE HOME?
(Fox; August 25, 1929)

Director: Raymond Cannon. Associate Producer: Malcolm Stuart Boylan. Adaptation: Robert S. Carr. Dialogue: Walter Catlett. Based on the play *Cradle Snatchers* by Russell G. Medcraft and Norma Mitchell (New York opening, September 7, 1925; 478 performances). Photography: Daniel Clark. Editor: Jack Murray. Sound: Frank Mackenzie. Assistant Director: Clark Murray. Running Time: 70 minutes.

Cast: Sue Carol (Mary), Nick Stuart (Dick), Dixie Lee (Billie), Jean Bary (Jackie), Richard Keene (José), David Rollins (Oscar), Jed Prouty (George), Walter Catlett (Elmer), Gordon De Main (Roy), Ilka Chase (Ethel), Dot Farley (Susan), Laura Hamilton (Maude).

Songs: "Doing the Boom-Boom," "Look What You've Done to Me" [Carol], "Maudita," "Old Soldiers Never Die" (Sidney Mitchell, Archie Gottler, Con Conrad).

Alternate Title: *Imagine My Embarrassment.*

The movie musical comedy *Why Leave Home?* began life as *Cradle Snatchers*, a long-running Broadway straight comedy from 1925 and a Fox silent of 1927. As the plot centered on the love lives of a trio of chorus girls—played by Sue Carol, Dixie Lee and Jean Bary—it seemed logical for the studio to add to the talkie version four songs by Sidney Mitchell, Archie Gottler and Con Conrad, as well as an elabo-

In Warners' *So Long Letty*, Patsy Ruth Miller and Bert Roach played a mismatched "trial" couple.

rate nightclub set with an orchestra platform that spiraled high into the air.

The racy story concerned three chorines who book dates with three older married men (Walter Catlett, Jed Prouty, Gordon De Main) but are diverted into going out with a trio of fraternity boys (Nick Stuart, Richard Keene, David Rollins). Later, the wives (Ilka Chase, Dot Farley, Norma Hamilton) of the three philanderers, who have been misled into believing that their husbands have gone duck-hunting, engage the college hunks as paid escorts and are then taught how to do the black-bottom. They head to the nearest road house to find the showgirls paired up with the husbands. Confusion ensued in what one critic saw as a "noisy, dull relic."[8]

Sue Carol capped the slapstick climax by serenading real-life sweetie Nick Stuart atop the orchestra platform with "Look What You've Done to Me," and she made the biggest overall impression among the cast. Petite and viva-cious, Carol (1906–1982) was one of moviedom's most popular young actresses. Fox saw her as its own "It" girl, and she played Bow-style flappers in picture after picture. She supposedly was the inspiration for the popular song "Sweet Sue."

Films such as *Why Leave Home?*, which came just after Carol's much-praised singing stint in *William Fox Movietone Follies of 1929* (see Chapter 3), kept her in demand. It helped that her sudden marriage to Nick Stuart was being kept secret. Carol's stardom would last until the very early '30s, after which she became a top talent agent and found marital bliss with Alan Ladd.

SO LONG LETTY
(Warner Bros.; October 16, 1929)

Director: Lloyd Bacon. Adaptation and Dialogue: Robert Lord, Arthur Caesar. Based on the musical play *So Long, Letty*, book by

Elmer Harris and Oliver Morosco, lyrics and music by Earl Carroll (New York opening, October 23, 1916; 96 performances). Titles: De Leon Anthony. Photography: James Van Trees. Editor: Jack Killifer. Musical Director: Louis Silvers. Running Time: 64 minutes (sound version; also released as silent).

Cast: Charlotte Greenwood (Letty Robbins), Claude Gillingwater (Claude Davis), Grant Withers (Harry Miller), Patsy Ruth Miller (Grace Miller), Bert Roach (Tommy Robbins), Marion Byron (Ruth Davis), Helen Foster (Sally Davis), Hallam Cooley (Clarence de Brie), Harry Gribbon (Joe Casey), Lloyd Ingraham (judge), Jack Grey (police sergeant).

Songs: "Clowning" [Greenwood, Roach, Withers], "My Beauty Shop" [Greenwood], "My Strongest Weakness Is You" [Greenwood], "One Sweet Little Yes" [Withers, Byron] (Grant Clarke, Harry Akst); "So Long, Letty" [Roach; reprised by Greenwood, Roach, Withers, Miller, Gillingwater, Byron, Foster, Cooley, Gribbon] (Earl Carroll).

Video: MGM-UA (laserdisc; excerpts only).

In the 1914 stage musical comedy *Pretty Mrs. Smith,* the gangling comedienne Charlotte Greenwood (1890–1978) used her loose limbs and boundless energy to steal the show from leading lady Fritzi Scheff and gain fast stardom. Producer-librettist Oliver Morosco was so delighted with Greenwood that he headlined her in a 1915 follow-up, *So Long, Letty,* which thrived on the West Coast and on the road despite a relatively short stint on Broadway. Greenwood's high-kicking character of Letitia Proudfoot was so popular that she spawned a series of "Letty" shows, among them *Linger Longer, Letty* (1919), *Let 'Er Go, Letty* (1921) and *Letty Pepper* (1922). In 1929, Warner Bros. paid $30,000 to Greenwood, whose movie experience was limited to scattered appearances in silents, to star in a talkie version of *So Long Letty* (no comma). Save for the title song, the original Earl Carroll score was replaced by material by Grant Clarke and Harry Akst.

In the Robert Lord–Arthur Caesar script, Greenwood was named Letty Robbins. The self-proclaimed "Queen of the Beauty Parlor" at the resorty Ardmore Beach Hotel, she scouts for business by visiting some new guests, ketchup-and-tomato king Claude Davis

(Claude Gillingwater) and his two comely granddaughters (Marion Byron, Helen Foster). But the grumpy old man finds "that tall creature" abominable. What he doesn't know, because he's new in town, is that she's married to his own nephew, Tommy (Bert Roach).

Tommy, fed up with Letty's poor housekeeping and tasteless cooking, knows his rich uncle is coming for a visit and fears Letty will make a bad impression, inheritance-wise. Meanwhile, his next-door neighbor, Harry Miller (Grant Withers), is bored with his homebody spouse, Grace (Patsy Ruth Miller). The husbands propose to their wives that they switch partners for a week; the women agree but conspire to teach a lesson by making trouble. Sure enough, within days Grace has made Tommy sick of good food and Letty's energy has worn Harry to a frazzle. The moralistic uncle invades a boozy party hosted by Letty and Harry, but the police show up and everyone is arrested. Before a forgiving judge, Letty admits the entire charade, and the financially generous Mr. Davis changes his mind about her. He invites her to join him and his granddaughters on a yearlong world cruise, but Letty can't bring herself to part with her Tommy.

The climactic party provides an excuse for four of the six musical numbers. Greenwood sings "My Strongest Weakness Is You" and joins Withers and Roach for "Clowning." Withers and Byron duet for "One Sweet Little Yes," and Roach sings the title song. Besides a reprise by the cast of "So Long, Letty" in the finale, the only other number is Greenwood's introductory rendition of "My Beauty Shop," in which Letty explains to the dumbfounded Davises that the husbands of her customers don't know their wives when she gets through with 'em. Many sources list "Am I Blue?" and "Let Me Have My Dreams," two Clarke-Akst hits from *On with the Show!* (see Chapter 3), as part of the *So Long Letty* score, but although Greenwood informally sings a few bars of the first, both songs are otherwise limited to underscoring.

So Long Letty is fast-paced and lively, although the premise was considered old hat even at the time of its release. The picture was not a big box-office hit, and the reviews were middling. Rightfully, Greenwood emerged with the highest praise: "Picture fans who never had the pleasure of seeing and hearing the lanky and limber Charlotte Greenwood are pretty sure to

Peppery Irene Bordoni meets her match in *Paris*, in which she reprised her Broadway starring role.

get a heap of enjoyment out of seeing her cavort," wrote *The Film Daily*.[9] But the screen wasn't quite big enough for Greenwood's expansive presence, and she would find her biggest movie successes as a middle-aged character comedienne.

PARIS

(First National; November 7, 1929)

Director-Producer: Clarence Badger. Producer: Robert North. Adaptation: Hope Loring. Based on the musical play, book by Martin Brown, lyrics and music by Cole Porter and others (New York opening, October 8, 1928; 195 performances). Photography: Sol Polito. Editor: Edward Schroeder. Dance Direction: Larry Ceballos. Running Time: 97 minutes (sound version; also released as silent). Technicolor sequences.

Cast: Irene Bordoni (Vivienne Rolland), Jack Buchanan (Guy Pennell), Louise Closser Hale (Cora Sabbot), Jason Robards (Andrew Sabbot), ZaSu Pitts (Harriet), Margaret Fielding (Brenda Kaley).

Songs: "Crystal Girl" [chorus, twice], "I'm a Little Negative Looking for a Positive" [Buchanan], "I Wonder What Is Really on His Mind" [Bordoni], "Miss Wonderful" [Buchanan, chorus; reprised by chorus], "My Lover, Master of My Heart" [Bordoni], "Paris" [Bordoni, chorus, twice], "Somebody Mighty Like You" [Bordoni, Buchanan] (Al Bryan, Eddie Ward); "Among My Souvenirs" [Bordoni] (Edgar Leslie, Horatio Nicholls); "Don't Look at Me That Way" [Bordoni, twice] (Cole Porter); "The Land of Going-to-Be" [Bordoni, Buchanan; reprised by Bordoni] (E. Ray Goetz, Walter Kallo).

Disc: Columbia 1983 (Bordoni/"I Wonder What Is Really on His Mind"/"My Lover, Master of My Heart"/78).

Cole Porter's sparkling, sophisticated music should have been introduced to American moviegoers in *Paris,* the screen version of Martin Brown's comedy about a New England matron who goes to France to break up her son's engagement to a Gallic singer-actress. Chief among Porter's delights was the mischievous "Let's Do It," which couched its provocative passions in allusions to the behaviors of animals, insects and fish.[10] But Warner Bros.–First National chose to replace almost all of the stage score with less memorable compositions by Al Bryan and Eddie Ward.

Whether any original songs remained is subject to debate. Most sources say no; the film is lost, and the cue sheet on file at ASCAP is inconclusive. But the author did hear a soundtrack to the French release, which was silent except for the musical numbers (in both French and English). On it are two songs, each performed twice, from the stage show: Porter's "Don't Look at Me That Way" and E. Ray Goetz and Walter Kallo's "The Land of Going-to-Be." These may also have been heard in the American version.

Warners did recruit Irene Bordoni to recreate her stage role as the French chanteuse in *Paris*. The Corsican-born Bordoni (1895–1953) had been performing in the United States since 1912; before that, she had starred on the Paris stage. Diminutive, chic and at times fiery, she had wide, expressive eyes and a quaint but charming accent that made her alluring in a mildly naughty kind of way. She was married to Goetz, the stage producer who had collaborated on some of the minor tunes in the original *Paris*. For the movie version, plus one number in the studio revue *The Show of Shows*, Warners paid Bordoni $10,000 a week, though she came to Hollywood—with tons of clothes, a secretary, a chauffeur and two maids—looking like she didn't need a cent of it.

Bordoni was undoubtedly the main attraction of *Paris*—her voice and manner were generally praised—but mentioned nearly as much in the reviews was Louise Closser Hale, reprising her Broadway role as the Yankee mom, Cora Sabbot. In the course of the movie, Hale transforms Cora from a grouchy puritan into a giddy schoolgirl with a scandalous crush on revue singer Guy Pennell (Jack Buchanan, a leading British stage actor in his first American film). After she gets her hair bobbed, Cora and Guy even announce their engagement, but their alliance is merely part of a plan to wrest Cora's son Andrew (Jason Robards) from Vivienne Rolland (Bordoni), whom Guy

covets. Fortunately for good taste, the plan works.

Buchanan (1891–1957) drew mixed reviews in his talkie debut, with critics noticing his acting flair but faulting him for a lack of sex appeal—a flaw that would become even more apparent in Ernst Lubitsch's *Monte Carlo* a year later. Buchanan later complained that he thought the film was made too hastily.[11] Director Clarence Badger was no expert at musicals, though he did try to spice this already bubbling brew with two color production numbers, which cluttered nearly one-third of the picture with extraneous singers and dancers. At least one reviewer called the Technicolor footage "blurred," which was not an uncommon complaint about the fledgling technology.

Bordoni came West with the intention of fulfilling her two Warners assignments, then returning to Broadway for a show, and then going back to Hollywood for more movie work. She turned out not to need the return ticket to Los Angeles. Bordoni simply wasn't widely known enough to give *Paris* the necessary box-office oomph, and she was a little too unconventional for most of America. The same moviegoing public that was charmed by Chevalier's Gallic impishness couldn't seem to accept a woman behaving in the same sexy fashion. Bordoni made a strong comeback on Broadway in *Louisiana Purchase* (1940). One of her last roles, before her death from cancer, was Bloody Mary in the first national tour of *South Pacific*.

LITTLE JOHNNY JONES
(First National; November 17, 1929)

Director: Mervyn LeRoy. Adaptation: Adelaide Heilbron, Eddie Buzzell. Based on the musical play, with book, lyrics and music by George M. Cohan (New York opening, November 7, 1904; 52 performances). Photography: Faxon Dean. Editor: Frank Ware. Running Time: 73 minutes.

Cast: Eddie Buzzell (Johnny Jones), Alice Day (Mary Baker), Edna Murphy (Vivian Dale), Robert Edeson (Ed Baker), Wheeler Oakman (George Wyman), Raymond Turner (Carbon), Donald Reed (Ramon Lopez).

Songs: "Give My Regards to Broadway," "Yankee Doodle Boy" (George M. Cohan); "Go Find Somebody to Love" (Herb Magidson,

Michael H. Cleary); "My Paradise" (Herb Magidson, James Cavanaugh, Michael H. Cleary); "Painting the Clouds with Sunshine" (Al Dubin, Joe Burke); "She Was Kicked on the Head by a Butterfly" (Herb Magidson, Ned Washington, Michael H. Cleary); "Straight, Place and Show" (Herman Ruby, M. K. Jerome).

The first (1904) of George M. Cohan's many stage hits, *Little Johnny Jones* initially came to the big screen in 1924 as a Warner Bros. silent. When the talkies came along, young Mervyn LeRoy (who had acted in a minor role in the previous film) was assigned to direct the patriotic, if passé, story of a singing small-town jockey who regains his sweetheart's love by going to England and winning the Epsom Derby.

To play the lead role originated by Cohan in the First National release, Warners hired Eddie Buzzell (1897–1985), a pint-sized comic singer and dancer from the stage. Buzzell also cowrote the screenplay. Alice Day, a First National contractee, drew the assignment as Johnny Jones' fickle love interest. Wheeler Oakman, cast as the villainous gambler, was a much-in-demand heavy since he glowered through the first all-talkie, *Lights of New York* (1928). Predictably, Cohan's music was excluded, except for two unimpeachable standards, "Give My Regards to Broadway" and "Yankee Doodle Boy." Among the new tunes, none of which you'll hear being whistled any time soon, was something called "She Was Kicked on the Head by a Butterfly."

Buzzell acquitted himself well, showing a flair for comedy and, when called for, pathos. If it hadn't been for his performance and the Cohan songs, *Photoplay* noted, "this would have been just another race track yarn."[12] But as Edward Buzzell, he would find more lasting movie employment as a director, with credits that woud include the Marx Brothers comedies *At the Circus* (1939) and *Go West* (1940), and the Esther Williams musical *Neptune's Daughter* (1949). The age and paucity of its material kept *Little Johnny Jones* from being nothing more than a lightweight diversion.

SALLY
(First National; December 23, 1929)

Director: John Francis Dillon. Adaptation and Dialogue: Waldemar Young. Based on the musical play, book by Guy Bolton, lyrics by P. G. Wodehouse and Clifford Grey, music by Jerome Kern (New York opening, December 21, 1920; 570 performances). Photography: Dev Jennings, C. Edgar Schoenbaum. Editor: Le Roy Stone. Art Director: Jack Okey. Costumes: Edward Stevenson. Musical Director: Leo Forbstein. Dance Direction: Larry Ceballos. Running Time: 100 minutes (sound version; also released as silent). Technicolor.

Cast: Marilyn Miller (Sally Bowling Green), Alexander Gray (Blair Farell), Joe E. Brown (Connie), T. Roy Barnes (Otis Hooper), Pert Kelton (Rosie), Ford Sterling ("Pops" Shendorff), Maude Turner Gordon (Mrs. Ten Brock), Nora Lane (Marcia), E. J. Ratcliffe (John Farell), Jack Duffy (The Old Roué), Ethel Stone (cutie), Albertina Rasch Ballet.

Songs: "All I Want to Do-Do-Do Is Dance" [Miller], "If I'm Dreaming, Don't Wake Me Up (Too Soon)" [Miller, Gray, twice] (Al Dubin, Joe Burke); "Sally" [Gray, chorus; then danced by Miller, Rasch girls], "Wild Rose" [Miller, chorus; then danced by Miller, Rasch girls] (Clifford Grey, Jerome Kern); "Look for the Silver Lining" [Gray, Miller] (B. G. De Sylva, Jerome Kern).

Academy Award Nomination: Best Interior Decoration (Jack Okey, 1929–30).

Disc: Take Two 104 (bootleg LP; ST).

Video: MGM-UA (laserdisc).

In Marilyn Miller's short life, no triumph was more glorious than *Sally*. Miller was at the peak of her meteoric Broadway career when the Florenz Ziegfeld production debuted on December 21, 1920, at the New Amsterdam Theatre. After one performance, the final ovation was said to be so great that it became impossible for the star to leave the stage. Finally, she exited by dashing down an aisle, but the appreciative crowd followed her out the door for a time, then returned to its seats and continued to applaud.[13] The show ran a lofty 570 performances and crowned Miller as the queen of musical comedy.

It had been quite a journey for Miller (1898–1936). Born Marilynn Reynolds in

Marilyn Miller's masquerade in *Sally* has been exposed; pictured from left are Maude Turner Gordon, Joe E. Brown, Miller, Ford Sterling and T. Roy Barnes.

Evansville, Indiana, she toured with her vaudevillian parents as early as age 5, then traveled the world for nearly a decade in a family act called the Five Columbians. She was "discovered" not by Ziegfeld, but by his rival producer Lee Shubert, while she danced in a London nightclub. A vital, petite blonde with exquisitely graceful movements that made one forget her underpowered singing voice, she took her first Broadway bow in a Shubert revue, *The Passing Show of 1914*. Ziegfeld fell in love with her from afar, and he cast her in a major role in his 1918 *Follies*.

Sally had all the tools of a smash hit: a fine score by Jerome Kern (with various lyricists), lovely ballet music by Victor Herbert, and a sturdy libretto by Guy Bolton. Fortunately, most of those assets would also be found in the initial sound film adaptation of the play, produced in two-color Technicolor by Warner Bros.-First National in 1929. (First National had starred Colleen Moore in a 1925 silent ver-

sion.) Kern's contribution was trimmed to three songs: "Sally," "Wild Rose" and the ever-popular "Look for the Silver Lining." The well-liked "The Church 'Round the Corner" was an unfortunate omission, but new selections by Al Dubin and Joe Burke fit in adequately and scenarist Waldemar Young left the libretto pretty much intact.

Best of all, Miller was asked to repeat her role as an orphaned café hostess who dances her way to Broadway fame. Her star had continued to shine throughout the '20s, despite two short-lived marriages (one ended by divorce, one by death) and a stormy professional relationship with Ziegfeld. "Now the screen has robbed the stage of its most prized possession!" boasted the trade ads, which did not mention that it took $100,000 of Warners' money to execute the "theft." Miller, said to be a strong personal favorite of Jack Warner, got to select the leading man—Alexander Gray, a young baritone who had appeared in *Sally* on tour. Gray had starred briefly on Broadway in *The Desert Song*—he replaced male lead Robert Halliday when the latter underwent a throat operation in mid–1927—and then headed the national company of the operetta.

Miller soon proved that she was not to be trifled with. The $100,000 she was being paid for *Sally* was to be for 10 weeks of work, according to the agreement forged with Warners-First National before production began in the spring of 1929, and for each week she was required to work beyond the 10, she was to be given $16,000, or about $2,800 per day. Came the extra day with no money in sight, and Miller walked off the set and out of the studio. The studio quickly realized that it would be much more expensive to reshoot the film without its star than to dish out the extra money, and so Miller returned, somewhat richer. The studio covered up the tiff by sending out stories that Miller had an abcessed tooth or a sprained ankle. The new movie star also chafed at doing press interviews and publicity poses, and she was especially bothered by the long hours that brought restrictions on her social life.[14]

In *Sally,* the moneyed young Blair Farell (Farquar on the stage), is in love with Sally Bowling Green, so named because she was found, as a waif, on the steps of a home with that telephone exchange. He has watched her charm the apathetic patrons of the popular restaurant where she waitresses. She falls for him, too, but she doesn't know that Blair's father has arranged his son's match with the wealthy Marcia Ten Brock (Nora Lane). When Sally, an aspiring dancer, tries to impress the pompous talent agent Otis Hemingway Hooper (T. Roy Barnes), she accidentally dumps a plate of spaghetti on him and finds herself out of a job. But not for long, as "Pops" Shendorff (Ford Sterling), the owner of the Elmtree Inn, hires her as a hostess. One of Sally's coworkers is Connie (Joe E. Brown), an exiled grand duke who keeps his identity a secret from everyone but his exasperated boss, from whom the duke extracts nights off at will.

The romance between Sally and Blair blossoms ("If I'm Dreaming, Don't Wake Me Up [Too Soon]"). She still feels the pain of a loveless upbringing, but he encourages her to "Look for the Silver Lining," to pursue her dreams despite life's drawbacks. He talks Pops into letting Sally perform for the Elmtree patrons, and she

displays her athletic footwork in "All I Want to Do-Do-Do Is Dance." Hooper is impressed enough to hire Sally to impersonate a no-show Russian dancer he has booked for the Ten Brocks' prestigious garden party. As "Madame Noskerova," Sally delights the wealthy guests. When told that she looks "as innocent as a primrose," she responds with a fiery interpretation of "(I'm Just a) Wild Rose," as a phalanx of tuxedoed males follows along.

Sally is exposed when Pops shows up with the police and accuses Hooper of kidnapping. This humiliation, coupled with the announcement of Blair and Marcia's engagement, drives her into seclusion. Declares a title card: "When the glittering raiment of Noskerova was left behind—so was a heart—." But Hooper and his girlfriend Rosie (Pert Kelton) track Sally down to offer an invitation to perform in the *Ziegfeld Follies.* The first-nighters' enthusiastic reception to her dancing in the "ballet of butterflies" makes Sally the toast of New York, and all that is left is a reunion with, and then marriage to, her Blair.

Under the direction of John Francis Dillon, and with choreography by Larry Ceballos, *Sally* was endowed, asserted its trade ads, with as many resources as Warners could give it: "150 beauties in the largest indoor scene ever photographed in color ... 36 Albertina Rasch girls who toedance more perfectly than other choruses can clog ... and an orchestra of 110." Jack Okey's set decoration was nominated for an Academy Award. His elaborate sunken garden layout was one of the heaviest-lighted sets employed up to then in Hollywood. It occupied an entire stage and, for the filming in color, required 1,500 lamps pulling 24,000 amps. Additional generators had to be installed to handle all the juice.

Unlike so many of the earliest musicals, *Sally* was well received both critically and commercially. *The New York Times*' Mordaunt Hall, for example, called the film "still another example of the extraordinary progress achieved in screen material," then put it on his "10 best" list for the year.[15] *The Film Daily* declared *Sally* "a screen tonic for the most exacting picture audience ... filled with those necessary box office elements."[16] Even commentators who were more restrained in their praise lauded Miller for her lively performance. It hardly seemed to matter that at 31, she was a little old for the part. Of her three films—the others were *Sunny* (1930) and *Her Majesty, Love* (1931)—this is the only one in which she comes close to projecting the effervesence that marked her stage work. She exhibits a fine flair for comedy without sacrificing the sympathetic nature of her role, and, as that unprescient talent scout said of Fred Astaire, she can dance a little, too. Alexander Gray proves surprisingly spirited, at least in comparison to his overly mannered later performances.

Some reviewers took the film to task for its so-so comedy, a drawback that is even more apparent upon watching *Sally* 60 years later. Joe E. Brown seems a shade too mild to be the secret duke, especially when one envisions the more blustery Leon Errol playing the role on stage and in the Colleen Moore silent. Brown's lengthy comic interlude with professional drunk Jack Duffy, playing a clumsy restaurant patron, is terribly labored. The earthy young comedienne Pert Kelton is wasted, with much more dialogue going to T. Roy Barnes, who inherited Walter Catlett's Broadway role and turns in a one-note, sourpuss performance.[17]

However, *Sally* was an excellent example of what Hollywood could do with the musical if it mixed the ingredients properly. For decades, the film was considered lost, but it resurfaced in 1990 in a black-and-white print duped from a two-strip Technicolor print that apparently has since decomposed. MGM-UA Home Video brought out the film in 1993 as part of its "Dawn of Sound" laserdisc series, and it now includes a recently discovered color fragment that gives an added kick to the "Wild Rose" number.

HIT THE DECK!

(RKO; December 25, 1929)

Director: Luther Reed. Producer: William LeBaron. Adaptation: Luther Reed. Based on the musical play, book by Herbert Fields, lyrics by Leo Robin and Clifford Grey, music by Vincent Youmans (New York opening, April 25, 1927; 352 performances). Photography: Robert Kurrle. Photographic Effects: Lloyd Knechtel. Editor: William Hamilton. Sound: Hugh McDowell. Art Director: Max Rée. Assistant Director: Frederick Fleck. Costumes: Max Rée. Musical Director: Victor Baravalle. Dance Direction: Pearl Eaton. Running Time: 93 minutes. Technicolor sequences.

Cast: Jack Oakie (Bilge), Polly Walker (Looloo), Roger Gray (Mat), Franker Woods (Bat), Harry Sweet (Bunny), Marguerita Padula (Lavinia), June Clyde (Toddy), Wallace MacDonald (Lieutenant Allen), George Ovey (Clarence), Ethel Clayton (Mrs. Payne), Nate Slott (Dan), Andy Clark (Dinty), Dell Henderson (Admiral), Charles Sullivan (Lieutenant Jim Smith), Grady Sutton.

Songs: "An Armful of You," "Hallelujah" [Padula, chorus], "Harbor of My Heart," "Join the Navy" [Oakie, chorus], "Nothing Could Be Sweeter," "Sometimes I'm Happy" [Oakie, Walker] (Clifford Grey, Leo Robin, Vincent Youmans); "Keepin' Myself for You" [Oakie, Walker] (Sidney Clare, Vincent Youmans).

Heady from his success with *No! No! Nanette!* (1925), which became one of Broadway's top-grossing musicals of the '20s, Vincent Youmans expanded his creative role in *Hit the Deck!*, which came to New York in 1927. Youmans (1898–1946) not only wrote the music, but also functioned as coproducer (with Lew Fields) in what would be his last great hit on the stage. *Hit the Deck!* told the nautical tale about a coffee-shop proprietress who falls for a reluctant sailor and then chases him halfway around the world. Louise Groody and Charles King originated the roles, and two standards—the rousing chorus song "Hallelujah" and the cheery duet "Sometimes I'm Happy"—emerged from the score. Herbert Fields based his book on Hubert Osborne's 1922 stage comedy *Shore Leave*, which had inspired a 1925 Richard Barthelmess feature of the same name and would spawn the 1936 Fred Astaire–Ginger Rogers musical *Follow the Fleet*.

Having already paid a sizable $85,000 for the film rights to *Rio Rita* (see Chapter 7), RKO sought to add to its musical stable by acquiring *Hit the Deck!* in February of 1929 for a price estimated at more than $100,000. The casting of Jack Oakie (1903–1978) in King's role as Bilge Smith was considered something of a coup for Radio. Oakie was on loan from Paramount, where a breakneck workload was molding him into one of America's hottest film funsters. His singing was spirited at best, but the new studio figured that his boisterous personality would sell the picture. It would have to, for his leading lady was a newcomer to films. Polly Walker was a discovery of George M. Cohan, who had showcased her in *Billie,* his Broadway musical-comedy swan song of 1928.

Youmans, with lyricist Sidney Clare, wrote one new song, the hitbound "Keepin' Myself for You," to go with selected holdovers. Luther Reed, who had adapted and directed *Rio Rita,* did the same for *Hit the Deck!* Two actors who played gobs in the original stage cast—Roger Gray and Franker Woods—did likewise for the film. Radio built an exact replica of the deck of a battleship that was roomy enough for 300 players. It was constructed after the technical staff had spent several days at a Navy base in San Diego. Because RKO's silent stages were being converted into sound stages, shooting had to be done at night. In his posthumously published memoir, Oakie recalled that "for realism, the property men burned smoke pots to simulate a bit of fog, so that the stationary battleship would appear to be sitting in some moving water."[18] When the company ran out of the regular fuel for the smoke pots one night and substituted a laxative, the smell forced much of the company to the washrooms.

Another drawback, not surprisingly, was the sound recording, which periodically was hindered by the grinding noises of the camera, Oakie remembered.

> The … noises were being recorded right along with my singing. "Well, get some more blankets! Wrap it up!" Luther Reed ordered. The camera was already practically buried in blankets to try to muffle its sounds. By 3 o'clock in the morning, the [live] musicians were becoming too cold and their instruments too wet to play, and I began having real trouble with that good old Southern California cold night dew. Every time I opened my mouth to sing "Sometimes I'm Happy," I covered [Polly Walker's] face with my steaming breath.[19]

Reviewers described *Hit the Deck!*—which premiered in Los Angeles on Christmas Day of 1929—as a plodding, unimaginative copy of the stage show. "The comedy is vague, and the story [is] straggling," noted *Motion Picture* magazine.[20] Oakie wasn't convincing enough as a primary vocalist, Reed's dialogue was deemed too theatrical, and the big "Hallelujah" number, performed on stage by a group of gobs, was "awkwardly dragged in" (*Variety*) as a chorus of

black revivalists headed by chubby white actress Marguerita Padula in blackface.[21] A half-hour Technicolor sequence that included the intended socko finale of "Keepin' Myself for You" was not enough.

Hit the Deck! made money, but perhaps not as much as RKO expected, given the resources devoted to it. The company later sold the property to MGM, whose 1955 remake (Vic Damone, Jane Powell, Debbie Reynolds) would be an improvement musically, if in no other fashion. The first *Hit the Deck!* is believed to be a lost film, although a silent theatrical trailer exists in private hands.

NO, NO, NANETTE
(First National; January 3, 1930)

Director: Clarence Badger. Producer: Ned Marin. Adaptation: Howard Emmett Rogers. Dialogue: Beatrice Van. Based on the musical play *No! No! Nanette!,* book by Otto Harbach and Frank Mandel, lyrics by Irving Caesar, music by Vincent Youmans (New York opening, September 16, 1925; 321 performances). Photography: Sol Polito. Editor: Frank Mandel.

Costars from the stage, Bernice Claire and Alexander Gray were recruited to headline First National's version of *No, No, Nanette.*

Sound: Hal Brumbaugh. Dance Direction: Larry Ceballos. Running Time: 98 minutes (sound version; also released as silent). Technicolor sequences.

Cast: Bernice Claire (Nanette), Alexander Gray (Tom Trainor), Lucien Littlefield (Jimmy Smith), Louise Fazenda (Sue Smith), Lilyan Tashman (Lucille), Bert Roach (Bill Early), ZaSu Pitts (Pauline), Mildred Harris (Betty), Henry Stockbridge (Brady), Jocelyn Lee (Flora).

Songs: "The Dance of the Wooden Shoes," "Dancing on Mars" (Herb Magidson, Ned Washington, Michael H. Cleary); "As Long as I'm with You" (Grant Clarke, Harry Akst); "I Want to Be Happy" (Irving Caesar, Vincent Youmans); "King of the Air" (Al Bryan, Eddie Ward); "Were You Just Pretending?" (Herman Ruby, M. K. Jerome).

The 1925-26 stage smash *No! No! Nanette!* came to the screen (sans exclamation points) as the '30s began, although without most of the Vincent Youmans score. Only "I Want to Be Happy" made a full transition from Broadway; the famed "Tea for Two" was limited to instrumental use in an opening scene. (ASCAP's cue sheet—relied on here because the film is believed to be lost—lists neither the Irving Caesar–Youmans version of the title song nor a composition of the same name copyrighted for the film by Al Bryan and Eddie Ward.) Warners–First National did lavish nearly half of the movie with Technicolor, then depended on the charm of a new romantic team to put it over. Soon, appreciative audiences were saying "Yes, yes" to a new hit.

The stars of *No, No, Nanette*, cast in the roles originated by Jack Barker and Louise Groody, were practically untested in Hollywood. Alexander Gray (1902–1976), a handsome baritone from Pennsylvania, had debuted in a specialty in Warner Bros.' all-star revue *The Show of Shows* and as Marilyn Miller's leading man in *Sally*. Both films were released just ahead of *No, No, Nanette*. Bernice Claire (b. 1909), a petite soprano from California, was making her debut in features. She was billed as "The Screen's Youngest Prima Donna." Gray and Claire had known each other for some time, although the circumstances were not always the best. The two were starring in the road company of *The Desert Song* when, in January

of 1929, his wife was killed and her brother seriously injured in an auto accident. The victims had been driving through Ohio on their way to visit the *Desert Song* troupe in Chicago.

When Gray was asked by Warner Bros. to appear in *Sally*, he had to make a screen test, but he didn't want to work alone. In an interview with the author in 1993, Claire—her communication skills limited by failing health—recalled what happened next:

> He needed someone to do the test with him. So we did a duet from *The Desert Song* and the producers took a look at it and said, "We want him, but we also want the girl for *No, No, Nanette*." I've lived a charmed life ... had the Midas touch. ... He [Gray] was a very personable man, and kind. Really a gentleman.[22]

Nanette is a vivacious young woman who wants to sing and dance on Broadway in a show newly written by her fiancé, Tom Trainor. She asks for backing from her ward, wealthy Bible publisher Jimmy Smith (Lucien Littlefield, in the part played by Charles Winninger on stage), who responds with a kind heart and an open wallet, although he neglects to tell his stingy spouse (Louise Fazenda) about his participation. Smith innocently also pays the bills for two chorus girls (Mildred Harris and Jocelyn Lee), news that prompts Mrs. Smith to have her hubby shadowed by detectives. When the show opens in Atlantic City, all of the aforementioned characters, plus Smith's blundering lawyer and his wife (Bert Roach and Lilyan Tashman), encounter each other and sort out the complications.

The cast was not generally considered a match for the Broadway roster, but what it lacked in seasoned talent it made up for in spirit and verve. Larry Ceballos' choreography in the color scenes of the play within the play, and Clarence Badger's comic-friendly direction, were oft-praised, and the new songs had some staying power. Gushed *Photoplay*: "First National has learned a stupendous secret. ... It has discovered that these girl-and-music things need laughs! ... The little Claire girl is pretty, and sings like a birdie. Entertainment plus!"[23]

No, No, Nanette returned to the screen in 1940 in an RKO release that starred Anna Neagle, then England's leading film star, with a watered-down score that at least included a full "Tea for Two" and the original title song.

THE GOLDEN CALF
(Fox; March 16, 1930)

Director: Millard Webb. Associate Producer: Ned Marin. Stage Director: Frank Merlin. Adaptation: Marion Orth. Dialogue: Harold Atteridge. Based on the magazine story by Aaron Davis (1926). Assistant Director: R. L. Hough. Photography: Lucien Andriot. Editor: Alexander Troffey. Sound: Donald Flick. Costumes: Sophie Wachner. Dance Direction: Earl Lindsay. Running Time: 69 minutes.

Cast: Jack Mulhall (Philip Homer), Sue Carol (Marybelle Cobb), El Brendel (Knute Olson), Marjorie White (Alice), Richard Keene (Tommy), Paul Page (Edwards), Walter Catlett (master of ceremonies), Ilka Chase (comedienne).

Songs: "Can I Help It If I'm in Love with You?" "I'm Tellin' the World About You," "Maybe, Someday," "A Picture No Artist Can Paint," "You Gotta Be Modernistic" (Cliff Friend, James V. Monaco).

Also Known As: *Her Golden Calf.*

Marybelle Cobb, the plain, old-fashioned girl at the center of *The Golden Calf,* could have been whom Dorothy Parker had in mind when she coined that phrase about boys not making passes at girls who wear glasses. Marybelle (Sue Carol) is a secretary secretly in love with her boss, commercial illustrator Philip Homer (Jack Mulhall), yet she's content to tromp around in soda-bottle goggles, long skirts and no makeup. What happens when she suddenly gets serious about her looks was the premise of this peppy but implausible tale.

The Golden Calf, now believed to be a lost film, was adapted from the *Liberty* magazine story of the same name and refers to the shapely part of Marybelle's anatomy that could earn her a plum job as a model in a hosiery manufacturer's ad. Because Philip has the company's account, it's doubly important that the rest of the girl be as appealing as her lower limbs, so Marybelle ditches the specs, cakes on the makeup and transforms herself into a beauty. Philip is such a dimwit that he can't even recognize her. Marybelle gets both the job and her man anyway.

Carol put across a pair of Cliff Friend–James Monaco songs with her customary charm. The secondary couple, Richard Keene

(1890–1971) and perennial best pal Marjorie White, teamed on three of the five songs, the flimsy excuse for the numbers being the in-house talent show staged by the ad artists. "For purposes of amusement, there are dancing girls who cavort on glossy floors and run up and down staircases," warned *The New York Times.*[24] But with White, Keene, Walter Catlett (1889–1960) and the ever-present El Brendel in its cast, *The Golden Calf* was a musical comedy with an distinct emphasis on the comedy.

HOLD EVERYTHING
(Warner Bros.; March 20, 1930)

Director: Roy Del Ruth. Screenplay: Robert Lord. Based on the musical play, book by John McGowan and B. G. De Sylva, lyrics by De Sylva and Lew Brown, music by Ray Henderson (New York opening, October 10, 1928; 413 performances). Photography: Dev Jennings. Editor: William Holmes. Sound: Glenn E. Rominger. Running Time: 78 minutes (sound version; also released as silent). Technicolor.

Cast: Joe E. Brown (Gink Schiner), Winnie Lightner (Toots Breen), Georges Carpentier (Georges La Verne), Sally O'Neil (Sue Burke), Edmund Breese (Pop O'Keefe), Bert Roach (Nosey Bartlett), Dorothy Revier (Norine Lloyd), Jack Curtis (Murph Levy), Tony Stabeneau (Bob Morgan), Lew Harvey (Dan Larkin), Jimmie Quinn (The Kicker), Harriette Lake [Ann Sothern], Abe Lyman and His Band.

Songs/Musical Numbers: "Isn't This a Cock-Eyed World?" [Lightner], "Physically Fit" [Lightner], "Sing a Little Theme Song" [Carpentier, O'Neil, chorus], "Take It on the Chin" [Lightner, chorus], "When the Little Red Roses Get the Blues for You" [male chorus, twice; reprised by Lyman band] (Al Dubin, Joe Burke); "To Know You Is to Love You" [Carpentier, O'Neil, chorus; reprised by Carpentier, O'Neil], "You're the Cream in My Coffee" [Carpentier, O'Neil, chorus] (B. G. De Sylva, Lew Brown, Ray Henderson). Closing Medley [Brown, Carpentier, Lightner, O'Neil]: "All Alone Together," "The Girls We Remember," "Physically Fit" [reprise], "When the Little Red Roses Get the Blues for You" [reprise] (Dubin, Burke); "Don't Hold Everything" (De Sylva, Brown, Henderson).

Hold Everything, a spoof of the prizefight game, was one of New York's biggest hits of 1928-29, running for a solid year. It made a Broadway star out of Bert Lahr, a veteran vaudeville and burlesque trouper whose performance as punch-drunk pugilist Gink Schiner was filled with facial contortions, crossed eyes and "gnong-gnong-gnong" exclamations—gags that the comic had been doing for years. The big hit in the De Sylva–Brown–Henderson score was "You're the Cream in My Coffee," sung by the romantic lead, Jack Whiting, to his costar, Ona Munson. It was one of only three songs retained for the Warner Bros. screen version; seven new tunes were written by Al Dubin (1891-1945) and Joe Burke (1884-1950).

Warner Bros. sought Lahr for the movie; the comic signed a three-picture contract with Warners and made Vitaphone shorts until the pact was canceled because of his commitment to touring with the stage show.[25] Joe E. Brown (1892-1973) was thus handed his most important movie role to date. He shared prominence in ads with the white-hot Winnie Lightner, cast as his girlfriend, Toots. An odd piece of casting was Georges Carpentier, the French champion boxer, in Whiting's role of a lovesick heavyweight title contender. To explain Carpentier's thick accent, the name of the character was changed from "Sunny Jim" Brooks to Georges La Verne. Carpentier (1894-1975) was being groomed by Warners as a Chevalier clone, albeit without the latter's voice and charm, which didn't leave much else.

Georges' preparations for a title fight are distracted by a society miss (Dorothy Revier, typecast as the "other woman") who seeks to alienate his affections from his childhood sweetheart, Sue Burke (Sally O'Neil). Gink is to fight on the undercard, but Toots is miffed over his flirting with various pretties. The manager of Georges' opponent attempts to have the fight fixed in his man's favor; the Frenchman is slipped a Mickey Finn during a party, but Gink saves the day by switching that drink with his own. Both men win their fights—and their girls.

Warner Bros. had enough faith in *Hold Everything* to use it to open its new Warners Theatre on Broadway, and the film was very favorably reviewed. Director Roy Del Ruth maintained a swift pace, and Robert Lord's script wisely kept the Carpentier-O'Neil twosome off screen as much as possible. He couldn't sing,

and she probably didn't, judging by the difference between Sue's singing and speaking voices on the surviving soundtrack of the apparently lost film. But most of the plaudits went to Brown, who (judging by the audio) chose to mimic—or was made to mimic—Lahr's delivery. He wasn't helped by the dialogue, none of which was tailored to Brown's own personality. Lahr's typical shouting, repetitive style—in lines such as "Now you're talkin' … NOW you're talkin'"—made Brown come off as a second-rate imitator.

"Brown must have seen *Hold Everything* on the stage 18 times to lift as minutely as he screens here," opined *Variety*. "It's practically a cinch that this picture is going to ruin Lahr's golf for the summer."[26] Indeed, a couple of weeks later, the trade bible published a nasty letter from Lahr, who declared that Brown had "lifted my original business, mannerisms, methods, and unique phrases, which I have been identified with for years."[27]

Brown needn't have fretted, for disputes among comedians over material were common. One critic (*Variety*'s, again) even noted in rebuttal that Lahr's routines were suspiciously like that of Solly Ward, a stage comic Lahr had seen nearly a decade before, and that Ward had lifted *his* material from an even older funnyman named Sam Bernard. The fuss died in a hurry.

HIGH SOCIETY BLUES
(Fox; March 23, 1930)

Director: David Butler. Associate Producer: Al Rockett. Adaptation and Dialogue: Howard J. Green. Based on the magazine story "Those High Society Blues" by Dana Burnet (1925). Photography: Charles Van Enger. Editor: Irene Morra. Sound: Joseph E. Aiken. Assistant Director: Ad Schaumer. Costumes: Sophie Wachner. Running Time: 90 minutes.

Cast: Janet Gaynor (Eleanor Divine), Charles Farrell (Eddie Granger), William Collier, Sr. (Horace Divine), Hedda Hopper (Clara Divine), Joyce Compton (Pearl Granger), Lucien Littlefield (Eli Granger), Louise Fazenda (Mrs. Granger), Brandon Hurst (Jowles), Gregory Gaye (Count Prunier).

Songs: "Eleanor (The Song That I Sing in My Dreams)" [Farrell, Gaynor, chorus], "High Society Blues" [Farrell], "I'm in the Market for

You" [Farrell; reprised by radio singer, then by band at party], "Just Like in a Story Book" [Gaynor; reprised three times by Gaynor, Farrell] (Joseph McCarthy, James F. Hanley).

After a highly successful all-talkie debut in *Sunnyside Up* (see Chapter 5), the popular duo of Janet Gaynor and Charles Farrell appeared in a similarly themed musical-comedy-romance, *High Society Blues*, based on a *Saturday Evening Post* story. It made good money, as did all the couple's films, but it was a comedown from *Sunnyside Up*.

In *Sunnyside Up*, also directed by David Butler, Gaynor played a poor shopgirl to Farrell's society man. Here, it's her family who has the pedigree. Her parents, the Divines (William Collier, Sr., Hedda Hopper), are from old money in Scarsdale; his mom and dad, the Grangers (Lucien Littlefield, Louise Fazenda), are newly wealthy bumpkins from Iowa. The conflict begins when the two clans find themselves neighbors, which severely tests the budding relationship between the young-adult children.

Her snooty mother wants Eleanor Divine (Gaynor) to be married off to a foreign nobleman (Gregory Gaye), but she's falling for Eddie Granger (Farrell), the Jethro Bodine of this silly mix of *Romeo and Juliet* and *The Beverly Hillbillies*. (When the family arrives in New York to view their new, gargantuan mansion, Eddie cries, "This means we can take in a lot of boarders!") He'd like to while his life away as a ukelele-playing "troubador," but the new girl he loves inspires him to aim higher. When their fathers go to war on Wall Street, the hero and heroine effect their own merger by eloping.

Eddie acquaints himself with Eleanor by giving her uke lessons, and these provide Gaynor and Farrell with ample opportunities to sing four now-forgotten songs by James F. Hanley and Joseph McCarthy. Most notable are "Just Like in a Storybook," which is supposed to depict Eleanor's dream romance, and "I'm in the Market for You," which became a hit for George Olsen and His Orchestra. Eddie's own fantasy is revealed—with necessary help for the reedy-voiced Farrell from a backing chorus—in "Eleanor (the Song That I Sing in My Dreams)."

High Society Blues had precious little to recommend it beyond its stars. "Some laughs, some songs, and even a little acting," was the so-what summation of *Photoplay*, which pretty much echoed the conventional wisdom.[28]

The film was mediocre enough, in fact, to motivate Gaynor to walk off the Fox lot for seven months. The Oscar-winning actress did not want to appear in a second musical—or third, if she were counting her appearance in the Fox revue *Happy Days* (see Chapter 10)—because she feared that the casting would harm her career. In 1932, she was quoted thusly:

I hated *High Society Blues*, which followed immediately after [*Sunnyside Up*] and promised to be only the forerunner of others like it. It looked as though an attempt were being made to establish me as a musical comedy actress. And I'm not! I love doing a musical show now and then, but I know perfectly well that I can't sing, that I don't really belong in that sort of film. ... I'd saved my money and I felt that I might just as well get out of films then and there with my screen reputation intact.[29]

Having made her point for more than $40,000 in lost salary, Gaynor returned to Fox in late 1930 to film, again with Farrell, the romantic melodrama *The Man Who Came Back*. She had avoided being cast in *Just Imagine*, the De Sylva–Brown–Henderson team's inferior encore to *Sunnyside Up*. But she also lost a probable starring role in the prestigious (and non-musical) fantasy *Liliom*, in which a miscast Farrell played opposite stage import Rose Hobart.

HONEY

(Paramount; March 29, 1930)

Director: Wesley Ruggles. Screenplay: Herman J. Mankiewicz. Based on the play *Come Out of the Kitchen* by Alice Duer Miller and A. E. Thomas. Photography: Henry Gerrard. Sound: Harry M. Lindgren. Dance Direction: David Bennett. Running Time: 73 minutes.

Cast: Nancy Carroll (Olivia Dangerfield), Stanley Smith (Burton Crane), Skeets Gallagher (Charles Dangerfield), Lillian Roth (Cora Falkner), Harry Green (J. William Burnstein), Mitzi Green (Doris), ZaSu Pitts (Mayme), Jobyna Howland (Mrs. Falkner), Charles Sellon (Randolph Weeks).

Songs: "I Don't Need Atmosphere to Fall in Love" [Carroll, Smith; reprised by Roth,

Gallagher], "In My Little Hope Chest" [Carroll, three times], "Let's Be Domestic" [Roth, Gallagher], "Sing You Sinners" [Roth, M. Green, black vocalist] (Sam Coslow, W. Franke Harling).

Disc: Caliban 6018 (bootleg LP: ST).

In 1916, the Alice Duer Miller novel *Come Out of the Kitchen* was adapted by A. E. Thomas into a successful stage vehicle for the young Ruth Chatterton. In 1919, the play was made into a Paramount silent film that starred Marguerite Clark. The play became a Broadway musical comedy (book by Anne Caldwell, songs by Caldwell and Harold Levey) called *The Magnolia Lady,* which starred Chatterton again but ran only six weeks. In 1930, Herman J. Mankiewicz reworked the story, W. Franke Harling and Sam Coslow added new songs, and—voilà!—Paramount had what it called a "musical farce" for its most popular star, Nancy Carroll.

The tale had a new title, *Honey,* but the same old premise. Olivia and Charles Dangerfield (Carroll and Skeets Gallagher), two young-adult siblings from a suddenly impoverished Virginia family, are forced to lease the family mansion to a cranky New York widow (Jobyna Howland). Unfortunately, of the three servants they've hired for the occasion, only the crybaby maid (ZaSu Pitts) shows up, so Olivia and Charles must impersonate the absentees. Accompanying the new tenant, Mrs. Falkner, are her fun-loving daughter, Cora (Lillian Roth); Cora's nice-guy fiancé, Burton Crane (Stanley Smith), and kibitzing detective J. William Burnstein (Harry Green).

Cora almost immediately falls for the "butler," despite his broad English "accent" and exaggerated gait, and they sing a bouncy duet called "Let's Be Domestic." Olivia and Burton gravitate toward each other; their theme, "In My Little Hope Chest," is a ballad. The private eye and the maid want to pair up, too. All this is unknown to Mrs. Falkner, until the maid's nosy daughter (nine-year-old Mitzi Green) pops up throughout, yelling "I know a secret! I know a secret!" and bribing the battleaxe for the inside dope. The Dangerfields' duplicity is revealed, but love wins out.

Honey, considered light and breezy in its day, hasn't held up well. Wesley Ruggles' direction is sluggish, particularly during the overly talky first couple of reels. Once the characters are established, the film becomes a little livelier, but Carroll (affecting an Irish brogue as "Jane Ellen") and romantic counterpart Smith suffer from a lack of mutual chemistry. The supporting actors fare better; Gallagher (1891–1955) is at ease in a role he had played on stage in *The Magnolia Lady,* and Mitzi Green's precocious clowning in her second film established her as the '30s' first child star. She would be billed in vaudeville as "The I-Know-a-Secret Girl."

The film's best asset by far is the fourth-billed Lillian Roth, cast as the spunky soubrette. Dressed in a slinky strapless gown, she belts out the film's big song hit, Harling and Coslow's "Sing You Sinners," backed by a chorus of go-to-meetin' black plantation workers who celebrate a yearly jubilee. Earlier, she and Gallagher cavort in "Let's Be Domestic," which begins with fairly innocuous lyrics about washing the windows and mowing the lawn and then segues into the more suggestive, with the pair practically prostrate over a loveseat—although with feet on the floor all the while.

At 19, Roth (1910–1980) was already a veteran performer, having appeared on stage, and in at least one silent film, during her first decade of life. During the '20s, she alternated between Broadway, vaudeville and nightclubs, popularizing such songs as "Ain't She Sweet," "When the Red, Red Robin Comes Bob-Bob-Bobbin' Along" and "I'd Climb the Highest Mountain." Paramount signed her to a seven-year contract in 1929, and she made her musical-feature debut in her most remembered screen role, as the saucy maid Lulu in *The Love Parade* (see Chapter 9). Roth's career would soon be ruined by her heavy drinking, hot temper and bad marriages, then be revived for a while in the 1950s with the publishing of the best-selling autobiography *I'll Cry Tomorrow.* But in 1930, Roth was living high and looking great, and in no film was she presented more pleasingly than *Honey.*

In his autobiography, Sam Coslow (1902–1982) wrote that the young Bing Crosby nearly was cast in Smith's role in *Honey.* Coslow also asserted that, as the end of shooting neared on *Honey,* director Ruggles complained to Coslow that the film lacked a socko production number. A couple of days later, out of curiosity, Coslow and some friends attended a Sunday evening revival meeting. Of the frenzied

Paramount's *Honey* was a musical reworking of the comic play *Come Out of the Kitchen*.

chanting, singing and stamping of feet, Coslow wrote, "I don't know whether it was all that uplifting, but it was certainly great entertainment."[30]

This experience gave Coslow the germ of an idea, and his lyrics quickly joined Harling's tune for "Sing You Sinners," which became Coslow's biggest movie hit to date and a favorite of swing bands and nightclub singers for decades to come.

THE CUCKOOS
(RKO; April 8, 1930)

Director: Paul Sloane. Producer: William LeBaron. Associate Producer: Louis Sarecky. Adaptation: Cyrus Wood. Additional Material: Roscoe [Fatty] Arbuckle. Based on the musical play *The Ramblers,* book by Guy Bolton, Bert Kalmar and Harry Ruby, lyrics by Kalmar, music by Ruby (New York opening, September 20, 1926; 289 performances). Photography:

Nicholas Musuraca. Editor: Arthur Roberts. Sound: John Tribby. Art Director: Max Rée. Costumes: Max Rée. Musical Director: Victor Baravalle. Dance Direction: Pearl Eaton. Running Time: 97 minutes. Technicolor sequences.

Cast: Bert Wheeler (Sparrow), Robert Woolsey (Professor Cunningham), June Clyde (Ruth Furst), Hugh Trevor (Billy Shannon), Jobyna Howland (Fannie Furst), Dorothy Lee (Anita), Ivan Lebedeff (The Baron), Marguerita Padula (Gypsy Queen), Mitchell Lewis (Julius, the Gypsy King), Raymond Maurel (gypsy singer), Harry Semels, Bob Kortman (gypsies), Hector V. Sarno (tamale vendor), Kalla Pasha (cowboy).

Songs/Musical Numbers: "All Alone Monday" [Clyde, Trevor], "Caballero Number" [chorus], "California Skies" [chorus], "Goodbye" [Wheeler, Woolsey, Howland, chorus], "I Love You So Much" [Wheeler, Lee; reprised by chorus, then by Wheeler, then by Wheeler, Lee, chorus], "I'm a Gypsy" [Woolsey], "Oh! How We Love Our Alma Mater" [Wheeler,

In RKO's *The Cuckoos*, June Clyde, Hugh Trevor, Bert Wheeler and Robert Woolsey look as if danger is ahead.

Woolsey], "Tomorrow Never Comes" [Maurel, chorus], "Wherever You Are" [Clyde, Trevor, chorus; reprised by Clyde, Trevor] (Bert Kalmar, Harry Ruby); "Dancing the Devil Away" [Padula, chorus, danced by Lee] (Bert Kalmar, Harry Ruby, Otto Harbach).

With nearly 300 Broadway performances, *The Ramblers* was the biggest musical comedy hit yet for the team of lyricist Bert Kalmar (1884–1947) and composer Harry Ruby (1895–1974). The native New Yorkers specialized in lightweight songs with humorous, often silly, wordplay, and by this time (the 1926-27 season), they'd been writing them together for a decade. They were already known for hits like "Who's Sorry Now?" but *The Ramblers* was their real breakthrough. A score highlighted by "All Alone Monday," a popular duet for Jack Whiting and Marie Saxon, boosted the Kalmar-Ruby–Guy Bolton libretto about two traveling fortune tellers who become entangled with a

movie company filming in Tijuana. The show made marquee-toppers out of the duo of Bobby Clark and Paul McCullough, whose vaudeville-based lunacy overcame the mixed reviews.

For the part-color movie version, retitled *The Cuckoos*, RKO enlisted its hot comedy team of Bert Wheeler (1895–1968) and Robert Woolsey (1889–1938). The bubbly, baby-faced Wheeler and the caustic, bespectacled Woolsey had worked separately for years in vaudeville and on Broadway—with Wheeler by far the bigger name—until Florenz Ziegfeld teamed them in *Rio Rita*. They made their film debut in RKO's hit version of that show (see Chapter 7), and the company decided that the funnymen should have more to do. For *The Cuckoos*, pixieish Dorothy Lee returned as their partner in tomfoolery. The romantic leads were June Clyde, lately of *Tanned Legs* (see Chapter 5), and Hugh Trevor, a colorless juve whose aunt happened to be the wife of RKO production chief William LeBaron.

Cyrus Wood's script altered the locale from a movie set to a gypsy camp near the California resort where Professor Cunningham (Woolsey) and his assistant, Sparrow (Wheeler), are stranded. Sparrow loves an American girl (Lee) who lives with a band of gypsies, although he is threatened by a romantic rival, the tough-guy leader of the pack (Mitchell Lewis). Meanwhile, a swarmy baron (Ivan Lebedeff) covets lovely heiress Ruth Furst (Clyde), who instead loves clean-cut aviator Billy Shannon (Trevor). And the professor seduces Ruth's matronly aunt (Jobyna Howland) upon learning of her $6 million fortune. She wonders: "Will you love me til I die?" He replies: "Well, that depends on how long you live."

Ruth rejects the baron's proposal of marriage in favor of a "secret" engagement bid by Billy. In league with the gypsy chieftain, the baron has the ingénue kidnapped and taken into Mexico, but the flier and fortune-tellers set out to rescue her. At a seedy hotel, Sparrow dresses in drag to entice the he-man gypsies into a knock on the head by the club-wielding professor. The distraction gives Billy time to reclaim Ruth, and the four escape to the States in a Technicolor climax described by *The New York Times* as "a fantastic flight in an airplane."[31]

Paul Sloane's direction is uninspiring, but *The Cuckoos* is a technical improvement over the static *Rio Rita*, and it too made good money for RKO. Clyde and Trevor are paired for the duet on "All Alone Monday," the title of which refers to the dearth of other assignations in their respective date books. Hefty Marguerita Padula, who led the big "Hallelujah" number in RKO's *Hit the Deck!* here contributes "Dancing the Devil Away" as netherworldly gypsies gyrate to ward off evil spirits in a Technicolor fantasy sequence. (The song was taken from *Lucky*, a short-lived Kalmar-Ruby show of 1927.) Wheeler and Woolsey joke and soft-shoe through "Oh! How We Love Our Alma Mammy," their tribute to their days of majoring in women at Vassar.

Better still are two new Kalmar-Ruby songs, "I'm a Gypsy" and "I Love You So Much." The fortune-hunting Woolsey, strumming a guitar caballero-style, sings the first to Aunt Fannie. With the lyrical promise that they'll stay together as long as her money holds out, the odd couple are distinctly reminiscent of Marx (Groucho) and Dumont. "I Love You So Much," which became a hit, is charmingly introduced by Wheeler and Lee as they meet under an apple tree, where her character has been exiled for cavorting with an American. They begin to sing (the camera moves to a pair of lovebirds perched in the branches above), then he grabs an apple and attempts to kiss her. She indicates that she won't smooch until he gives her a bite of his apple. He is inspired to fetch a bushelful, and a shot of their amorous feast fades to a shot of an empty basket and two people nearly passed out from doing something (you guess) too much.

The gluttony wasn't the only hazard faced by Dorothy Lee during the filming of *The Cuckoos*:

> I've been kidnapped by the gypsies, and [one of them throws] knives at me. In the picture, the knives actually come through the back [of the platform]. Well—and this was crazy because I was the biggest tomboy in the picture business—at lunch hour one day, the director was walking by, and the knife thrower was *really* throwing knives at me. Paul Sloane almost had a stroke. He said, "Don't you ever do anything crazy like that again!" ... No one in their right mind would stand up and let them throw a knife right by your ear. I tell you, it's a wonder anybody survived living near me, because I wasn't afraid of anything.[32]

Interestingly, *Variety* editor "Sime" Silverman, who reviewed *The Cuckoos* for the trade paper, declared that Wheeler and Woolsey were so good during their separate stints in the film that they should be split up and starred on their own. RKO later gave each man his own solo shot, but neither could make it alone.

Dorothy Lee, who appeared with the duo in 13 of their 21 feature films, summed up the qualities that helped make Bert and Bob click on stage and screen—if not off.

> Bert was always happy and wonderful, and Woolsey was always caustic. I got along with both of 'em, but they used to fight a lot. Woolsey was always trying to put Bert down, and, after all, Bert was a star before Woolsey was. ... Woolsey was just a caustic guy and Bert was always the happy-go-lucky guy. It was just their dispositions.[33]

An interesting side note on *The Cuckoos:* The blacklisted silent comic Roscoe "Fatty" Arbuckle worked as a gag writer during filming in

January and February of 1930. Arbuckle, whose career as a star had ended with the 1921 Virginia Rappe scandal and three ensuing trials, also contributed to the Wheeler and Woolsey comedy *Half Shot at Sunrise* (1930). He was a particular favorite of Bert Wheeler, who later remembered: "We had another director, but Arbuckle worked on all our scenes ... and he wasn't even getting billed for it. ... [He] was really a clever man, and one of the sweetest men I've ever known in my life."[34] Arbuckle, having never regained his lost stature in Hollywood, died of heart disease in 1933.

SPRING IS HERE
(First National; April 13, 1930)

Director: John Francis Dillon. Adaptation: James A. Starr. Based on the musical play, book by Owen Davis, lyrics by Lorenz Hart, music by Richard Rodgers (New York opening, March 11, 1929; 104 performances). Photography: Lee Garmes. Running Time: 68 minutes.

Cast: Lawrence Gray (Steve Alden), Alexander Gray (Terry Clayton), Bernice Claire (Betty Braley), Ford Sterling (Peter Braley), Louise Fazenda (Emily Braley), Inez Courtney (Mary Jane Braley), Frank Albertson (Stacy Hayden), Natalie Moorhead (Rita Conway), Gretchen Thomas (Maude Osgood), Wilson Benge (butler), The Brox Sisters.

Songs: "Bad Baby" [Courtney], "Cryin' for the Carolines" [Brox Sisters], "Have a Little Faith in Me" [Alexander Gray, Claire], "How Shall I Tell?" [Claire], "What's the Big Idea?" [Albertson, Courtney] (Sam M. Lewis, Joe Young, Harry Warren); "Spring Is Here (in Person)" [Albertson, Courtney], "With a Song in My Heart" [Lawrence Gray, Claire; reprised by Alexander Gray, Claire], "Yours Sincerely" [Claire, Alexander Gray] (Lorenz Hart, Richard Rodgers).

Disc: Music Masters JJA-19766 (bootleg LP; ST).

Video: MGM-UA (laserdisc; excerpts only).

Spring Is Here was a modestly successful Richard Rodgers–Lorenz Hart Broadway musical of 1929, but as a film of 1930 it was merely modest. The First National production was hardly seen upon its release. As we began research on this book, we wondered why neither *The New York Times* nor *Variety* published a review of *Spring Is Here*, for only three other major-studio films discussed in this volume (*A Song of Kentucky, Oh! Sailor, Behave!* and *They Learned About Women*) were similarly ignored. A check of *Variety*'s weekly national theater grosses revealed that *Spring Is Here* was given a "gala" world premiere—but not in New York or Los Angeles. In Toledo, Ohio.

Then the film went to, in order, Boston (where exhibitors reported the box office as "fair"), Los Angeles ("light"), Minneapolis ("didn't click"), Denver (no report), Chicago ("[no] name draw"), San Francisco ("below average"), Baltimore ("did little"), and even London ("light" again). In none of these cities did it run longer than a week. We could find no evidence of a New York run. First National may not have had enough faith in the film to expose it to the more discerning Great White Way.

"But why?" we wondered. *Photoplay*'s critic, who probably saw *Spring Is Here* in a studio preview, described it as excellent entertainment. The cast included Bernice Claire and Alexander Gray of *No, No, Nanette*, Lawrence Gray of *Marianne* and *It's a Great Life*, and peppy comediennes Louise Fazenda (1895–1962) and Inez Courtney (1908–1975). There was one of Rodgers and Hart's better early ballads, "With a Song in My Heart," and two new hits, "Cryin' for the Carolines" and "Have a Little Faith in Me," written for the screen by Sam M. Lewis (1885–1959), Joe Young (1889–1939), and Hollywood newcomer Harry Warren (1893–1981). In fact, *Spring Is Here* marked the first time that music by Rodgers, Hart or Warren was heard in a feature film.

Then we tracked down the picture—and our mind cleared, for *Spring Is Here* is an idiotic musical comedy populated by idiot characters. In a genre filled with light-hearted stories, this one about sex-minded rich youth and their dunderheaded parents can only be described as light-headed. The blame may well lie with the original librettist, Owen Davis, a Pulitzer Prize–winning playwright writing his first musical comedy. After two of his works had been transformed by others into hit Broadway musicals (*Whoopee!* and *Lady Fingers*), Davis adapted his unsuccessful play *Shotgun Wedding* into *Spring Is Here*. His story leaves one wondering where the laughs were misplaced,

James A. Starr's uncinematic screenplay is lousy with bad dialogue, and John Francis Dillon's direction leaves his players practically paralytic.

Spring Is Here begins as the blustering Peter Braley (Ford Sterling), head of a wealthy Long Island household, berates his fun-loving daughter Betty (Bernice Claire) for staying out until 5 a.m. He also disapproves of her new boyfriend, the brash and mysterious Steve Alden (Lawrence Gray, on loan from MGM), although the patient Emily Braley (Louise Fazenda) pleads with her husband to lay off a little. Dad would rather see Betty with Terry Clayton (Alexander Gray), a good-natured but shy neighbor lad. Terry finds it hard to flirt, but he gets up the courage to sing to Betty the heartfelt "Yours Sincerely."

Claire and Alexander Gray then engage in a lesson right out of the Judy Garland–Mickey Rooney School of Cinematic Lovemaking:

He: "I'm no fool. You liked me pretty well until you met that Steve Alden last night."

She (looking away and smiling fondly): "Why shouldn't I like him? He's smart and up to date. He gives me a real thrill!"

He: "Well, I can give you a real thrill, too!"

She (turning toward him): "Jerry!"

He (taking her in his arms): "I..."

She: "Ohhh...!"

He: "I..."

She (awaiting his kiss): "Ohhh...!"

He (letting her go): "Oh, gee! I just get all tangled up when you're around!"

Betty's teen sister, Mary Jane (Courtney, reprising her Broadway role), decides Terry needs help, so she advises him to make her jealous by flirting with other women. This Terry does—but to anyone in a skirt. At a party hosted by the Braleys, he takes on a couple of the family's more comely but very grown-up acquaintances, which prompts the husband of one to threaten to come to blows. Both Grays get to sing "With a Song in My Heart," but Betty decides she still prefers Lawrence's tinny tenor to Alex's somber baritone. ("With a Song in My Heart" later became identified with Jane Froman, who sang it better than anyone here.)

Later, mama Emily tries to give Terry yet another lesson in amour, only to have Terry turn on her in a passionate fury:

He: "You're wonderful! ... All night long, all I could think of was that tender look in your beautiful eyes."

She (swooning): "Well...!"

He: "Mother!"

She: "Not mother ... Emily!"

He: "Emily!"

Then—eeewwwww!—he gives her a soul kiss. Actually, Terry's just practicing for Betty. Steve shows up to propose marriage, and she seems agreeable. Night passes. Steve returns during breakfast to present a letter of introduction to papa Braley, who readily accedes, as he too-belatedly realizes that Steve is the son of one of his oldest friends. Peter knocks on Betty's bedroom door to tell her the good news. She emerges ... with Terry right behind. After the usual suggestive byplay, we discover that Betty and Terry had run off and gotten married during the night. We know this for sure because the suddenly confident Terry snaps at Betty as if she's some kind of servant. They reprise "With a Song in My Heart." The end.

What impressions are left? Claire and Alexander Gray are miscast. Lawrence Gray is wasted. Ford Sterling's ver-r-r-r-y broad comedy strips the picture of any class to which it might have aspired. What keeps *Spring Is Here* out of the category of really, really awful early musicals is its listenable score. (Eight of its nine song numbers can be seen and heard on an MGM-UA "Dawn of Sound" laserdisc.) First National retained three Rodgers and Hart songs, including "Spring Is Here (in Person)," which is not to be confused with the composers' "Spring Is Here" from the 1942 film *I Married an Angel*. Of the new material, "Cryin' for the Carolines" fares best. Often heard as a ballad, the song is given a jazzy rendition by the Brox Sisters, appearing as entertainers at the Braleys' party. The Fred Waring, Guy Lombardo and Ben Bernie orchestras cut discs of the song, as did Ruth Etting.

The Broxes—Lorayne, Bobbe (a.k.a. Dagmar) and Patricia—were popular recording artists who appeared in Ziegfeld revues and other Broadway productions (*The Cocoanuts*), as well as three early talkie features, *The Hollywood Revue of 1929*, *King of Jazz* and *Spring Is Here*. But not even this reliable trio could give life to a turkey like *Spring Is Here*.

THE BIG POND

(Paramount; May 3, 1930)

Director: Hobart Henley. Producer: Monta Bell. Stage Director: Bertram Harrison. Scenario: Robert Presnell, Garrett Fort. Dialogue: Preston Sturges. Based on the play by George Middleton and A. E. Thomas (New York opening, August 21, 1928; 47 performances). Photography: George Folsey. Editor: Emma Hill. Sound: Ernest F. Zatorsky. Musical Arrangements: John W. Green. Running Time: 79 minutes.

Cast: Maurice Chevalier (Pierre Mirande), Claudette Colbert (Barbara Billings), George Barbier (Mr. Billings), Marion Ballou (Mrs. Billings), Andrée Corday (Toinette), Frank Lyon (Ronnie), Nat Pendleton (Pat O'Day), Elaine Koch (Jennie).

Songs: "Mia Cara" [offscreen tenor], "You Brought a New Kind of Love to Me" [Chevalier; reprised by Chevalier, Colbert, then by Chevalier twice] (Sammy Fain, Irving Kahal, Pierre Norman); "Come Little Leaves" [Koch] (Margaret Osgood); "Livin' in the Sunlight, Lovin' in the Moonlight" [Chevalier] (Al Sherman, Al Lewis); "This Is My Lucky Day" [Chevalier] (B. G. De Sylva, Lew Brown, Ray Henderson).

Academy Award Nomination: Best Actor (Maurice Chevalier, 1929-30).

Disc: RCA Victor 22045 (Chevalier/ "Livin' in the Sunlight, Lovin' in the Moonlight"/"You Brought a New Kind of Love to Me"/78); RCA Victor 22415 (Chevalier/"You Brought a New Kind of Love to Me" in French/ 78); WRC SH 156 (bootleg LP; ST).

Those who perceive the early years of Maurice Chevalier's American film career as a charmed flight from one incomparable Ernst Lubitsch (or Rouben Mamoulian) musical to another ought to dive into *The Big Pond*, the Frenchman's third Hollywood feature. As shown by *Innocents of Paris* (see Chapter 3), Chevalier could triumph under the guidance of lesser craftsmen, even in subpar material, but routine pictures like *The Big Pond* and *Playboy of Paris*, both produced in 1930, did little to stretch his talents.

The Big Pond was adapted from the non-musical play of the same name by George Middleton and A. E. Thomas, but Paramount added a handful of songs—only two of which were sung all the way through in the English-language version—to the tale of an impoverished Frenchman and his entree into a snooty American family. In the first five minutes, filmgoers were introduced to what would become one of Chevalier's greatest hits, "You Brought a New Kind of Love to Me," sung by Pierre Mirande to Barbara Billings (Claudette Colbert) as they sit in a Venetian gondola, he as the guide and she as the tourist. They fall in love, but Barbara's suitor Ronnie (Frank Lyon) and suspicious father (George Barbier) think Pierre's a fortune hunter.

Ronnie and Mr. Billings scheme to offer Pierre a job in the Billings' New York chewing-gum factory, then intend to discourage him by working him to a frazzle. Indeed, the foreigner's work assignments are menial and his scant salary forces him into a dingy boarding house. Ronnie pretends to befriend Pierre, even to the extent of taking lovemaking tips from him. But fate intervenes for Pierre when the foreman's secret stash of liquor spills on a supply of newly produced gum. Pierre is blamed for the incident and then fired, but he chances to taste a stick of the ruined commodity. An idea! He sells Billings on manufacturing liquor-flavored chews (with artificial alcohol, of course), and the resulting success lifts Pierre into the white-collar ranks.

The inspired Pierre decides to set "New Kind of Love" to lyrics for an advertisement about "a brand-new chew with an old-time kick." Barbara, disgusted with Pierre's new money madness and his exploitation of "their" song, jilts him for Ronnie, but Pierre kidnaps her and heads for their honeymoon on a speedboat. "This is one lesson in love I forgot to teach Ronnie," quips Pierre at the fadeout. Barbara is quick to agree.

The Big Pond, directed by Hobart Henley, is no better than programmer fare, but it is no drudge to sit through. Chevalier delivers his expected zesty performance—his other big song is "Livin' in the Sunlight, Lovin' in the Moonlight"—and he received an Academy Award nomination for his acting in this film as well as for *The Love Parade*. Colbert (b. 1905) is less impressive in a clichéd rich-miss part. The talk in *The Big Pond* is sharply written. Preston Sturges, a young playwright who would go on to better things at Paramount, took the

Ole Olsen and Chic Johnson (with Lotti Loder) brought their vaudeville antics to film with Warner Bros.' *Oh! Sailor, Behave!*

dialogue credit, although he did more than that. Not only did he rewrite most of the dialogue, he made fundamental alterations in the plot and characterization.[35] He played up the love triangle of the play in a way that it resembled his Broadway hit *Strictly Dishonorable,* made the chewing-gum magnate the first of his befuddled business tycoons (as in his '40s classics *The Lady Eve* and *The Palm Beach Story*), and filled *The Big Pond* with typically caustic comic lines such as Barbier's about Venice being a "sewer."

"This is a pleasant change from the costume things. Still another slant on the fascinating Parisian," commented *Photoplay,* referring to the star's first modern-dress talkie.[36] A French-language version, *La Grande Mare,* was filmed simultaneously, also with Chevalier and Colbert, who would reunite (with Barbier) in another year for Lubitsch's *The Smiling Lieutenant* (see Chapter 11).

OH! SAILOR, BEHAVE!
(Warner Bros.; July 16, 1930)

Director: Archie Mayo. Adaptation and Dialogue: Joseph Jackson. Additional Dialogue: Sid Silvers. Based on the play *See Naples and Die* by Elmer Rice (New York opening, September 24, 1929; 62 performances). Photography: Dev Jennings. Sound: Clare A. Riggs. Running Time: 90 minutes.

Cast: Irene Delroy (Nanette Dodge), Charles King (Charlie Carroll), Ole Olsen (Simon), Chic Johnson (Peter), Lowell Sherman (Prince Kasloff), Vivien Oakland (Kunegundi), Noah Beery (Romanian general), Lotti Loder (Louisa), Charles Judels (deMedici), Elsie Bartlett (Mitzi), Lawrence Grant (von Klaus), Gino Corrado (Stephan), Hallam Cooley.

Songs: "Highway to Heaven" [King, Delroy, Judels, Olsen, Johnson, Loder, chorus; reprised by King, Delroy, chorus], "Leave a Little Smile" [King, Oakland, twice], "When Love

Comes in the Moonlight" [King, Delroy, Olsen, Johnson, chorus; reprised by King, Delroy], "Which One Do You Love?" [Olsen, Johnson] (Al Dubin, Joe Burke); "The Laughing Song" [Olsen, Johnson, Judels] (Ole Olsen, Chic Johnson).

Disc: Brunswick 4840 (King/"Highway to Heaven"/"When Love Comes in the Moonlight"/78); Brunswick 4849 (King/"Leave a Little Smile"/78).

Oh! Sailor, Behave!—a reworking of the Elmer Rice stage comedy *See Naples and Die*—was given a scant release by Warner Bros. after some months' delay. It went unreviewed by *Variety*, *The New York Times* and *The Film Daily*. Charles King, the *Broadway Melody* star on loan from MGM, and Irene Delroy, a stage actress in her film debut, were the romantic leads, but as was so often the case, the real stars were the comics. When the studio became nervous about releasing a musical with no major names, it recruited the duo of Ole Olsen (1892–1965) and Chic Johnson (1891–1962), billed as "America's Funniest Clowns," to fill out the picture with comedy sequences unrelated to the plot.

The "Funniest Clowns" allegation stemmed from Olsen and Johnson's many seasons of vaudeville headlining. Their antics of sight gags and bad puns have not worn well, and even their best routine in *Oh! Sailor, Behave!* would be objectionable by '90s standards. Assigned to find a wooden-legged man who has robbed the Navy storehouse in Venice, the two sailors man a street corner and aim a pea-shooter at the lower limbs of passers-by. The idea is that if one of them fails to jump, he is the culprit!

The needlessly complicated plot concerns an American newspaper reporter who falls for a young heiress and then must rescue her from a kidnapper. The heavy is a Russian prince (Lowell Sherman) with whom the heroine's sister (Elise Bartlett) has had an ill-fated affair. A local siren (Vivien Oakland) goes for the hero in a big way, and she almost marries the guy before he comes to his senses and shoots the nasty nobleman. Meanwhile, Olsen and Johnson ride through the canals of Venice on a pair of water-bicycles. Al Dubin and Joe Burke wrote the score, except for "The Laughing Song," which was composed for the film by Olsen and Johnson themselves.

Oh! Sailor, Behave! was silly enough to pro-

voke this response from *Photoplay*: "A few more like this, and song writers and song birds will be going back to Broadway."[37]

QUEEN HIGH
(Paramount; August 8, 1930)

Director: Fred Newmeyer. Producers: Frank Mandel, Laurence Schwab. Adaptation: Frank Mandel. Based on the musical play, book by Laurence Schwab and B. G. De Sylva, lyrics by De Sylva and others, music by Lewis Gensler and others (New York opening, September 8, 1926; 378 performances). Photography: William Steiner. Editor: Barney Rogan. Sound: C. A. Tuthill. Musical Arrangements: John W. Green. Running Time: 75 minutes.

Cast: Stanley Smith (Dick Johns), Ginger Rogers (Polly Rockwell), Charles Ruggles (T. Boggs Johns), Frank Morgan (George Nettleton), Helen Carrington (Mrs. Nettleton), Theresa Maxwell Conover (Mrs. Rockwell), Betty Garde (Florence Cole), Nina Olivette (Coddles), Rudy Cameron (Cyrus Vanderholt), Tom Brown (Jimmy).

Songs: "Brother! Just Laugh It Off!" [Rogers, Morgan] (E. Y. Harburg, Arthur Schwartz, Ralph Rainger); "I Love a Girl in My Own Peculiar Way" [Ruggles] (E. Y. Harburg, Henry Souvain); "I'm Afraid of You" [Smith, Rogers] (Edward Eliscu, Arthur Schwartz, Ralph Rainger); "Seems to Me" [Smith, Rogers] (Dick Howard, Ralph Rainger).

During the lengthy Broadway run of *Queen High* (1926), patrons exited the Ambassador Theatre whistling the popular B. G. De Sylva-Lewis Gensler song "Cross My Heart" or chortling over the genial comedy of Charles Ruggles. Ruggles earned most of the kudos for his role as T. Boggs Johns, part-owner of a garter and novelty business, who bickers with his partner, George Nettleton (Frank McIntyre), so heatedly that the two agree to play a winner-take-all game of draw poker. The victor will gain control of the business for a year; the loser will become a butler in the household of the winner. Laurence Schwab's libretto was based on Edward H. Peple's straight play *A Pair of Sixes*.

When Paramount decided to film the stage musical in 1930—under the supervision of the

Broadway producers, Schwab and Frank Mandel—it was a given to cast Ruggles, who was already under contract to the studio. Another good choice was made in casting the Nettleton part—Frank Morgan (1890–1949), a reliable stage comic who was just breaking into talkies. The pair's rapid-fire patter was the chief asset of the film, which is best known for being the movie-musical debut of 19-year-old Ginger Rogers. Rogers and Stanley Smith carry on a secret romance as, respectively, Nettleton's niece and Johns' nephew. The lovers sing two Ralph Rainger songs, "I'm Afraid of You" and "Seems to Me," and Rogers teams with Morgan for "Brother! Just Laugh It Off!" None of the stage score was retained; these were songs written for the film.

Rogers (1911–1995) was at a level of show-business experience that belied her age. Starting in the mid–'20s, she toured in vaudeville in a singing-and-dancing trio called "Ginger and Her Redheads," and by 1928 she was earning $350 a week as half of an act that included her first husband, Jack Pepper. Her Broadway debut came in *Top Speed*, which opened at the end of 1929, and the experience earned her a screen test with Paramount. Rogers began her screen career in a handful of short subjects, then was cast as a flapper in *Young Man of Manhattan* (1930), a comedy-drama in which she popularized the catch phrase "Cigarette me, big boy" and sang a number called "I've Got It, but It Don't Do Me No Good."

Queen High was Rogers' second feature—its filming at Paramount's Astoria facility on Long Island allowed her to continue on stage in *Top Speed*—and she did not go unnoticed. "Miss Rogers does quite nicely by her role," said *The New York Times*, which for the stingy Mordaunt Hall was expressive enough.[38] The stagy film earned decent notices, and with a pair of potent comics as the primary draws, Rogers would have to wait a couple more years for parts that were more than the standard window-dressing.

TOP SPEED

(First National; August 15, 1930)

Director: Mervyn LeRoy. Adaptation and Dialogue: Humphrey Bolton, Henry McCarty. Based on the musical play, book by Guy Bolton,

Bert Kalmar and Harry Ruby, lyrics by Kalmar, music by Ruby (New York opening, December 25, 1929; 102 performances). Photography: Sid Hickox. Editor: Harold Young. Sound: Earl Sitar. Running Time: 73 minutes.

Cast: Joe E. Brown (Elmer Peters), Bernice Claire (Virginia Rollins), Jack Whiting (Jerry Brooks), Frank McHugh (Tad Jordan), Laura Lee (Babs Green), Rita Flynn (Daisy), Edwin Maxwell (J. W. Rollins), Wade Boteler (sheriff), Edmund Breese (Spencer Colgate), Cyril Ring (Vincent Colgate), Billy Bletcher (Ipps), Al Hill (Briggs).

Songs: "As Long as I Have You and You Have Me" [Claire, Whiting], "If You Were a Traveling Salesman and I Were a Chambermaid" [Brown, Lee], "Knock Knees" [Brown, Lee, chorus], "Looking for the Lovelight in the Dark" [Claire, Whiting, chorus] (Al Dubin, Joe Burke).

Ginger Rogers was on the wrong side of the country when the show that gave her an early lift in New York was being filmed out in Hollywood. No matter, for *Top Speed* the movie was purely a comedy showcase for the fast-rising Joe E. Brown. The Kalmar-Ruby score was entirely replaced by new songs by Al Dubin and Joe Burke, and there would be only one ensemble dance.

Brown plays Elmer Peters, a young bond clerk on a weekend vacation with his office buddy Jerry Brooks (Jack Whiting). The two go fishing, but Elmer's undersized catches in the government hatchery catch the eye of the local sheriff. The boys evade the lawman and take a room at the posh Lackawanna Lodge, where Elmer's habitual lying has everyone believing he and Jerry are big-shot financiers. By chance, they rescue two rich lasses, Virginia Rollins (Bernice Claire, taking the role originated by Irene Delroy) and Babs Green (Laura Lee, in Rogers' stage part), after a minor auto mishap.

Virginia and Jerry become attracted ("Looking for the Lovelight in the Dark"). Her father owns one of the two entries in the big speedboat race, and she hopes that Jerry, built up by Elmer into an expert boatsman, can help. Babs thinks she has too much money to land a good-hearted husband, and she asks Elmer to imagine life "If You Were a Traveling Salesman and I Were a Chambermaid." Virginia's father (Edwin Maxwell) fires his underachieving pilot, who's been paid off to throw the race, and hires Jerry in his place. Jerry accepts a $30,000 bribe from Rollins' major opponent (Edmund Breese) to go in the tank himself, but he wins the contest in a thrilling finish and then announces that he only pretended to take the money, which Elmer has bet on Rollins' boat. Elmer and Jerry, let off by the pesky sheriff, are cheered as heroes.

At a shade over 70 minutes, *Top Speed* is fast-paced fun. The climactic boat race, well staged by director Mervyn LeRoy, does not disappoint, as Brown and Frank McHugh drive under water, climb over buoys, and remove much of their engine in a fruitless attempt to stop their craft. Brown and Lee make an athletic couple as they join the chorus for a hip dance to "Knock Knees" and do a duet of eccentric steps for "Traveling Salesman." Another funny, and definitely pre–Code, gag has Brown hiding under a bed of a hotel room as the female guests prepare to undress. Both the Brown-and-McHugh portion of the boat race and Brown's bedroom antics—the latter sequence also appearing in the stageplay—were added to the screenplay late in the going, possibly to give Brown more footage or to punch up the comedy in general. Marine daredevil Brown proved all too human off screen; he missed a few days of shooting after he dived head-first into a too-shallow pool.

Whiting (1901–1961), McHugh (1899–1981) and Lee were all stage actors appearing in their first feature. McHugh, who plays the inebriated inventor of an inflatable suit, was beginning an alliance with Warner Bros. that would last into the '40s. Compared to her three compatriots, Bernice Claire was a relative film veteran, but she was already being wasted. Her surprisingly small part, to judge from the TV print the author viewed, seemed to have been trimmed down along the way. As Claire tells Whiting how inseparable they are, as the music swells for what should be "As Long as I Have You and You Have Me," but just as she opens her mouth to sing, there's an abrupt jump to another scene. Unfortunately, Miss Claire wouldn't be opening her mouth before the cameras for much longer.

ANIMAL CRACKERS
(Paramount; August 29, 1930)

Director: Victor Heerman. Adaptation: Morris Ryskind. Continuity: Pierre Collings. Based on the musical play, book by George S. Kaufman and Morris Ryskind, lyrics by Bert Kalmar, music by Harry Ruby (New York opening, October 23, 1928; 191 performances). Photography: George Folsey. Editor: Barney Rogan. Sound: Ernest F. Zatorsky. Musical Arrangements: John W. Green. Running Time: 92 minutes.

Cast: Groucho Marx (Captain Jeffrey Spaulding), Harpo Marx (The Professor), Chico Marx (Emanuel Ravelli), Zeppo Marx (Horatio Jamison), Lillian Roth (Arabella Rittenhouse), Margaret Dumont (Mrs. Rittenhouse), Louis Sorin (Roscoe Chandler), Hal Thompson (John Parker), Margaret Irving (Mrs. Whitehead), Kathryn Reece (Grace Carpenter), Robert Greig (Hives), Edward Metcalf (Hennessey), The Music Masters (six footmen).

Songs: "Hooray for Captain Spaulding" [Groucho, Zeppo, chorus], "Why Am I So Romantic?" [Roth, Thompson; reprised by Harpo on harp] (Bert Kalmar, Harry Ruby); "My Old Kentucky Home" [Groucho, Chico, Zeppo] (Stephen Foster); "Silver Threads Among the Gold" [Chico on piano] (Eben E. Rexford, Hart P. Danks); "Some of These Days" [Harpo on piano] (Shelton Brooks).

Disc: Decca 5405 (Marx Brothers/LP; ST); MCA MUP-395 (Marx Brothers/LP; ST).

Video: MCA-Universal (cassette/laserdisc).

When the movie version of *The Cocoanuts* premiered at the Rialto Theatre in New York on May 24, 1929, the Marx Brothers weren't around to see it (considering their alleged antipathy to the film, they might not have wanted to anyway). They were a couple of blocks away, at the 44th Street Theatre, performing live in *Animal Crackers*. And when the siblings' first film became such a big hit, it was inevitable that Paramount would attempt to duplicate its success with *Animal Crackers*.

This was another George S. Kaufman satire, this time on high society and this time with music by Kalmar and Ruby. Morrie

To Louis Sorin's chagrin, Harpo and Chico Marx are planning a horseshoes-and-piano duet in
Animal Crackers.

Ryskind, Kaufman's collaborator on the book, wrote the screenplay. *Animal Crackers* the film is similar to *The Cocoanuts* the film in that it wants to show off the unconventional Marxes while following musical comedy convention. It is, without Robert Florey's adventuresome camera, even more static than the 1929 film, although sound technology had improved remarkably in the interim. And for all of its fondly remembered humor, the picture bogs down terribly in its second half, especially during a series of sketches that are too long by half.

Still, the film does profit by its lack of musical interludes. There are only two formal singing numbers. "Why Am I So Romantic?" is delivered by Hal Thompson, here from the stage show, and Lillian Roth, who was allegedly assigned her thankless ingénue role as an off-camera punishment for hotheadedness. She walks through the picture with a disdainful smirk. Roth termed the atmosphere during

filming, which was burdened by the Marxes' off-camera tardiness and on-camera ad-libs, as "one step removed from a circus."[39] One probably apocryphal story had tight-fisted director Victor Heerman chaining the four brothers into specially constructed cells on the sound stage to keep them at hand.[40]

The other full-length song in *Animal Crackers* is the one remembered more than any other in a Marx Brothers film. "Hooray for Captain Spaulding" introduces Groucho's most famous character, a breezy African explorer whose return to the States is being celebrated with a party at the palatial Long Island home of Mrs. Rittenhouse (Margaret Dumont). Jeffrey Spaulding makes his much-awaited entrance preceded by his aide, Horatio Jamison (Zeppo), who sings to the gathering that the big-game hunter will camp there only if the women are warm and the men old. Then Spaulding himself is carried in on a bamboo and tiger-skin hammock carried by a quartet of African warriors. The lyrics are typical of the whimsical style of Kalmar, especially when Jamison reminds the crowd of Spaulding's strong morality and the explorer responds by admitting that he really doesn't mind a strong drink or a dirty joke, as long they're furnished by somebody else.

After the first 20 minutes, Jeff is already romancing the dowager with, "Mrs. Ritten-house, ever since I met you, I've swept you off my feet." She fends him off, presumably more concerned about the rare painting that an art connoisseur (Louis Sorin, repeating his stage role) will exhibit in her home. It is around that picture that this picture revolves. Mrs. Ritten-house's daughter Arabella (Roth), who wants her struggling-artist boyfriend, John Parker (Thompson), to impress the art patron, schemes to switch the real painting with a copy made by her guy. She enlists itinerant musicians Ravelli (Chico) and "The Professor" (Harpo) to do the dirty work. Confusing matters is Mrs. Ritten-house's jealous chum (Margaret Irving, from the stage cast), who recruits the Rittenhouses' butler (Robert Greig) to switch the painting with a replica made by *her* daughter (Kathryn Reece). On a stormy night, the paintings are jumbled. The forgery is exposed at the unveil-ing the next day, and the lengthy attempt to lo-cate the culprit chews up the film's lackluster second half. John is about to be arrested, but the art expert is impressed enough with his work to offer him a lucrative commission. Harpo ends the lunacy by putting everyone to sleep with knockout spray.

Despite all the ad-libbing, the Kaufman-Ryskind dialogue shows some sparkle. Groucho spoofs the "asides" of Eugene O'Neill's then-popular *Strange Interlude* during a sarcastically amorous conversation with the two society ma-trons. His hyper-literary utterances are gradu-ally replaced by inanities: "This would be a bet-ter world for children if the parents had to eat the spinach," he declaims as Margaret Irving, out of focus in the background, fails to stifle a grin. Later, Harpo stages a nonsensical physi-cal attack on poor Dumont, then he and Chico talk her and Irving into a surrealistic game of bridge. Harpo tosses aside the cards he won't deal to himself, and the boys' stash of aces of spades gives them an insurmountable advan-tage. And, of course, there is Groucho's famous description of his African adventures: "One morning, I shot an elephant in my pajamas. How he got into my pajamas, I don't know."

On the minus side is Chico's deadly-dull wordplay summation of the stolen-painting mystery. First, he announces to Groucho that because he's deduced that the painting was in the house, the thief must be in the house, and so all they have to do is ask everyone in the house if he is the thief. The byplay ranges far beyond the boundaries of the plot, which isn't necessarily a bad idea, but by the time Chico decides that a left-handed moth must be the culprit, you're reminded of Groucho's quip in *Horse Feathers* (see Chapter 12): "I've got to stay here, but there's no reason why you folks shouldn't go out into the lobby while this thing blows over." Or, in this modern age, why we shouldn't press the VCR fast-forward button.

Still, *Animal Crackers* was another solid hit for Paramount—the biggest for the studio dur-ing 1930—and this time, even the Marxes were able to stomach the finished product. For Marx fanatics of later years, this film was frustratingly out of circulation because of a legal tie-up with the George S. Kaufman estate. But it re-emerged in the early 1970s to be avidly scruti-nized in theaters and then, in the decades to follow, on home video.

BIG BOY
(Warner Bros.; September 5, 1930)

Director: Alan Crosland. Adaptation and Dialogue: Perry Vekroff, William K. Wells, Rex Taylor. Based on the musical play, book by Harold Atteridge, lyrics by B. G. De Sylva, music by James F. Hanley and Joseph Meyer (New York opening, January 7, 1925; 48 per-formances). Photography: Hal Mohr. Editor: Ralph Dawson. Sound: Hal Brumbaugh. Run-ning Time: 68 minutes.

Cast: Al Jolson (Gus), Claudia Dell (Annabel Bedford), Louise Closser Hale (Mrs. Bedford), Lloyd Hughes (Jack Bedford), Eddie Phillips (Coley Reed), Lew Harvey (Doc Wilbur), Franklin Batie (Jim), Noah Beery (Sheriff John Bagby), John Harron (Joe War-ren), Colin Campbell (Steve Leslie), Tom Wil-son (Tucker), Eddie Kane (diner), The Monroe Jubilee Singers.

Songs: "Liza Lee" [Jolson], "Tomorrow Is

Another Day" [Jolson, three times] (Bud Green, Sam H. Stept); "Hooray for Baby and Me" [Jolson], "Little Sunshine" [Jolson] (Sidney Mitchell, Archie Gottler, George W. Meyer); "Dixie" [Monroe Jubilee Singers] (Daniel Decatur Emmett); "All God's Children Got Shoes" [Jolson, Jubilee Singers], "Go Down, Moses" [Jolson, Jubilee Singers] (trad.).

Disc: A Jay 3749 (bootleg LP; ST).
Video: MGM-UA (laserdisc).

His movie career suddenly faltering after the disastrous *Say It with Songs* (see Chapter 3), Al Jolson made two more flops in 1930. *Mammy* (see Chapter 5), which was released first, at least had Irving Berlin's influence and some well-staged minstrel-show numbers. *Big Boy*, based on Jolson's stage hit of 1925 but with none of its music, had little to beef up a severely dated story. It was one of the last mainstream Hollywood films in which a black central character was played by a white actor (RKO's *Check and Double Check*, with two whites as Amos 'n' Andy, debuted weeks later). *Big Boy* would be Jolson's final movie under his Warner Bros. contract before what he expected to be a more fruitful alliance with his friend Joseph M. Schenck and United Artists.

At least Jolson isn't packed off to prison or shown as a drunken derelict, as he had been in his three previous films. In *Big Boy*, directed by Alan Crosland, Jolson is the happy-go-lucky Gus, a loyal stable boy and jockey for a Kentucky horse-racing clan. Typically, his unsophisticated way with the language is made sport of by his employers. Retained from the play was this exchange between a trainer (Franklin Batie, from the Broadway cast) and Gus over the stable boy's aches and pains inflicted by a stubborn steed:

Jolson: "You know what I think is wrong with me?"
Batie: "No, what?"
Jolson: "I think I've got inferno complications. Inferno means the lower regions."
Batie: "No, you mean *internal* complications."
Jolson: "The lower regions? Brother, that's where I've got 'em!"

Unfortunately, Gus is discharged from the farm for tampering with the titular animal, the family's Derby hopeful. Actually, Gus has done no such thing, but he's been framed by crooks (Eddie Phillips, Lew Harvey) who are blackmailing the Bedford family's dissolute young heir (Lloyd Hughes) and who intend the replacement jockey (Colin Campbell) to lose on purpose. Gus finds work as a waiter in a swank Lexington eatery, and it is there, on the eve of the big race, that he uncovers the race-throwing plot. He then rides Big Boy to victory.

En route, we find Jolson singing "Little Sunshine" to his favorite foal, and there is a lengthy Reconstruction Era flashback in which Gus's grandfather saves a lovely Bedford miss (Claudia Dell, as the grandmother of her modern-dress counterpart) from a racist bully (Noah Beery). This kind of melodrama was considered heavy-handed in 1870, much less 1930. A more lasting contribution of *Big Boy* is the introduction of Bud Green and Sammy Stept's "Tomorrow Is Another Day" by Jolson when the 19th Century Gus, on the eve of a duel with the bully, recalls an optimistic song taught him by his "mammy."

It's somewhat diverting anyway, but *Big Boy* would be worth watching just to marvel at the finale. As Gus steps up to a microphone in the Kentucky Derby winner's circle, there's a fadeout to the real, Caucasian Jolson, who stands upon a stage surrounded by the other cast members, who stand silent as statues or chess pawns. Jolson tells the on-screen audience that he hopes they enjoyed the picture, then is asked to sing a song. One of the actors suggests the over-exposed "Sonny Boy," a request that causes the patrons to jeer and threaten to walk out. (An in-joke?) Jolson quiets the mob with a reprise of "Tomorrow Is Another Day."

This bizarre final sequence was added for the final draft of the screenplay by original scripter Rex Taylor.[41] Nervous Warners executives may have thought it prudent to add such a scene to a film in which a black character cracks numerous jokes at whites' expense—just to remind the customers that it was only their pal Jolie all along. *Big Boy* "isn't any special artistic triumph for Jolson," wrote *Variety*, "but it will please the Jolson following."[42]

LOVE IN THE ROUGH
(MGM; September 6, 1930)

Director: Charles F. Reisner. Adaptation: Sarah Y. Mason. Dialogue: Joe Farnham,

Robert E. Hopkins. Based on the play *Spring Fever* by Vincent Lawrence (New York opening, August 3, 1925; 56 performances). Photography: Henry Sharp. Editor: Basil Wrangell. Sound: Douglas Shearer. Art Director: Cedric Gibbons. Costumes: David Cox. Dance Direction: Sammy Lee. Running Time: 82 minutes.

Cast: Robert Montgomery (Jack Kelly), Dorothy Jordan (Marilyn Crawford), Benny Rubin (Benny Lipitowicz), J. C. Nugent (Dave Waters), Dorothy McNulty [Penny Singleton] (Virgie Wilson), Tyrrell Davis (Sidney Tewksbury), Allan Lane (Harry Johnson), Catherine Moylan (Martha), Harry Burns (gardener), Edwards Davis (Mr. Crawford), Roscoe Ates (proprietor), Clarence H. Wilson (Brown), George Chandler (taxi driver), Ray Cooke (bellhop), The Biltmore Trio, Ann Dvorak.

Songs: "Go Home and Tell Your Mother" [Montgomery, Jordan; reprised by Biltmore Trio], "I'm Doing That Thing" [Jordan, Biltmore Trio], "I'm Learning a Lot from You" [Montgomery, Jordan, Rubin, McNulty], "One More Waltz" [Biltmore Trio] (Dorothy Fields, Jimmy McHugh).

A taciturn Georgian named Bobby Jones made 1930 a red-letter year for golf by winning all four legs of the sport's "Grand Slam"—the U.S. Open, Masters, British Open and British Amateur tournaments. Jones would parlay his feat into a contract to make a popular series of instructional Vitaphone shorts, but it would take real actors to bring the pastime to life on the screen. Hence, two golf-themed musicals— MGM's *Love in the Rough* and Paramount's *Follow Thru*, released within a week of each other—marked a year in which the song cycle made sport of just about everything else.

Love in the Rough was a remake of a 1927 MGM silent called *Spring Fever*, which starred William Haines and Joan Crawford and which was in turn an adaptation of a stage comedy by Vincent Lawrence. The sound version, infused with songs by Dorothy Fields and Jimmy McHugh, tells the same basic story. Department store clerk Jack Kelly (Robert Montgomery) is good enough on the links to be invited by his lessons-hungry boss (J. C. Nugent) to set up shop for two weeks at an exclusive country club. There, posing as a wealthy shipping executive, he meets rich and pretty Marilyn Crawford (Dorothy Jordan). The two fall in love and then elope, but on their first night together Jack owns up to his modest background and walks out in shame.

Jack plays for the prestigious club championship the next day, and falls behind against Marilyn's stuffy ex-boyfriend (future cowboy star Allan Lane, then without his "Rocky" moniker). Marilyn, who has stayed away from the course, is visited by her angry father, the wheat king. Dad (Edwards Davis) is certain his new son-in-law is a fortune-hunter, but when Marilyn tells him of Jack's current whereabouts, Mr. Crawford's mood brightens: "Why didn't you TELL me he was a golfer?" Dad and daughter head off to the 18th green and root Jack on to a comeback victory.

Love in the Rough is merely a programmer, and although the musical numbers are nothing special, Montgomery and Jordan's underpowered but charming duet on "Go Home and Tell Your Mother (That She Certainly Did a Wonderful Job on You)" is a highlight. A caddy with a harmonica is conveniently nearby to provide accompaniment for this future hit song, as well as for the sprightly "I'm Learning a Lot from You," a double duet for the leads and secondary couple Benny Rubin (clowning as Montgomery's caddy) and Dorothy McNulty (the future Penny Singleton of *Blondie* fame). The Biltmore Trio, practically a fixture in early MGM musicals, backs Jordan in a song-and-dance number, "I'm Doing That Thing," and sings "Go Home and Tell Your Mother" and "One More Waltz" during a party scene.

FOLLOW THRU
(Paramount; September 12, 1930)

Directors: Laurence Schwab, Lloyd Corrigan. Producers: Laurence Schwab, Frank Mandel. Screenplay: Laurence Schwab, Lloyd Corrigan. Based on the musical play, book by Laurence Schwab and B. G. De Sylva, lyrics by De Sylva and Lew Brown, music by Ray Henderson (New York opening, January 9, 1929; 403 performances). Photography: Henry Gerrard, Charles Boyle. Editor: Alyson Shaffer. Sound: Harry M. Lindgren. Dance Direction: David Bennett. Running Time: 93 minutes. Technicolor.

Cast: Charles "Buddy" Rogers (Jerry Downs), Nancy Carroll (Lora Moore), Zelma

O'Neal (Angie Howard), Jack Haley (Jack Martin), Eugene Pallette (J. C. Effingham), Thelma Todd (Ruth Van Horn), Claude King (Mac Moore), Kathryn Givney (Mrs. Bascomb), Margaret Lee (Babs Bascomb), Don Tomkins (Dinty Moore), Albert Gran (Martin Bascomb), Sidney Bracey (Watson), George Olsen and His Orchestra.

Songs: "Button Up Your Overcoat" [O'Neal, Haley], "I Want to Be Bad" [O'Neal, chorus, Olsen band; reprised by Carroll], "Then I'll Have Time for You" [Lee, Tomkins] (B. G. De Sylva, Lew Brown, Ray Henderson); "It Must Be You" [Carroll, Rogers; reprised by Haley, O'Neal] (Edward Eliscu, Manning Sherwin); "A Peach of a Pair" [Carroll, Rogers, twice; then by Rogers, then by Carroll, Rogers] (George Marion, Jr., Richard A. Whiting).

Premiering less than a week after *Love in the Rough* was another golf-themed musical comedy, the all–Technicolor *Follow Thru*, based on the Broadway hit of 1929. Charles "Buddy" Rogers and Nancy Carroll were paired once again, but in other personnel the film adhered to its stage roots. Comedy leads Jack Haley and Zelma O'Neal were summoned to Paramount's Long Island complex to reprise their Broadway roles, as was a second comic duo, a teen couple played by Don Tomkins and Margaret Lee. Laurence Schwab and Frank Mandel produced the film as they had the stage show, and Schwab, co-librettist of the play, shared directorial and screenplay credit with erstwhile actor Lloyd Corrigan.

Not surprisingly, three of the five songs in the film were holdovers from the De Sylva-Brown-Henderson stage score—including the standard "Button Up Your Overcoat," sung now, as then, by Haley and O'Neal. Richard Rodgers and Lorenz Hart wrote four songs— "Because We're Young," "I'm Hard to Please," "It Never Happened Before" and "Softer Than a Kitten"—that were copyrighted for the film but were not used. No new Rodgers-Hart material would be heard in any motion picture until 1931's *The Hot Heiress* (see Chapter 11).

Like *Love in the Rough*, *Follow Thru* is climaxed by a big match on the links, this one pitting the good-hearted Lora Moore (Carroll) against the vampy Ruth Van Horn (Thelma Todd) for the women's championship of the Mission Country Club. Lora has more than a

trophy in mind, for Ruth has attempted to steal the affections of her man, Jerry Downs (Rogers), hailed as the "best golf pro in the West." Meanwhile, Jerry is giving lessons to his pal Jack Martin (Haley), the girl-shy chain-store heir who conquers his fears of romance when perky Angie Howard (O'Neal) attracts him with her mysterious "love perfume." There are numerous complications—one of which compels Jerry and girdle-company czar J. C. "Effie" Effingham (Eugene Pallette) to sneak into the women's locker room at the club and then depart in drag. But a double wedding seems afoot at the fade.

Haley and O'Neal steal the film right out from under the prettier faces. Without Haley's wit, said *The New York Times*, "it would be just so many scenes of Miss Carroll looking lovingly into the romantic eyes of Charles Rogers."[43] Haley (1899–1979) had kicked around vaudeville for years, both as a light-comic single and as half of a two-act. His role here allowed him to repeat Jack's hilarious "involuntary" twitch of head and eyebrows that besieges him when in the presence of a pretty girl. The stage version of *Follow Thru* made Haley a big name, and the movie version began his Hollywood career, although he did not make another film until *Sitting Pretty* in 1933.[44] Of course, he's best remembered as the Tin Man in *The Wizard of Oz*.

Zelma O'Neal (1903–1989) was a doll-faced soubrette who had clowned and sung ("The Varsity Drag") her way to notoriety in *Good News*, Broadway's college-musical hit of 1927-28. The pairing of her and Carroll clashed with Hollywood's unwritten limit of only one redhead per film. Carroll's hair photographed red, but O'Neal's didn't—until she mischievously dyed it just the right shade. A viewing of the film, from a beautiful UCLA color print preserved from the two-color camera negative, reveals dark red on both women.

Despite the presence of the stage songs, *Follow Thru* relies more on two new Richard Whiting melodies—"A Peach of a Pair," performed four times by Rogers or Carroll, and "It Must Be You," done twice by Haley and O'Neal. "Then I'll Have Time for You," from the stage, is a duet for Tomkins and Lee. The most extravagant number in the film is "I Want to Be Bad," a fantasy sequence very similar to De Sylva, Brown and Henderson's "Turn On

"When I look at a girl – she makes me feel so——" 1258-122

Girl-shy Jack Haley used his comical twitch of the head to upstage star Buddy Rogers in Paramount's adaptation of *Follow Thru*.

the Heat" from *Sunnyside Up* (see Chapter 5). The number benefits greatly from camera tricks that would have been impossible to match on the stage. Set as the entertainment of a masquerade party, the sequence begins as O'Neal "materializes" out of flame, sings to the accompaniment of George Olsen's orchestra, and then is made to disappear by a troupe of "devil" chorines. Scantily dressed singing "angels" appear next, but a bolt of lightning transforms their garb to crimson, sprouts horns from their heads, and raises a coat of smoke around them. Rays of "fire" spurt from the band members' own horns. A little girl sitting in a "cloud" summons O'Neal, who puts out the conflagration with a celestial fire extinguisher. The halos reappear, but O'Neal, deciding she's got to be bad after all, points her hose at the angels and envelops them in smoke.

Some reviewers sniped at the film's too-close resemblance to the stage production. But *Follow Thru* salvaged par at the box office, thanks to the duo of Rogers and Carroll.

LEATHERNECKING
(RKO; September 12, 1930)

Director: Eddie Cline. Producer: William LeBaron. Associate Producer: Louis Sarecky. Continuity: Jane Murfin. Adaptation: Alfred Jackson. Based on the musical play *Present Arms*, book by Herbert Fields, lyrics by Lorenz Hart, music by Richard Rodgers (New York opening, April 26, 1928; 155 performances). Titles: John Krafft. Photography: J. Roy Hunt. Photographic Effects: Lloyd Knechtel. Editors: Ann McKnight, George Marsh. Sound: John Tribby. Assistant Director: Frederick Fleck. Art Director: Max Rée. Costumes: Max Rée. Musical Director: Victor Baravalle. Dance Direction: Pearl Eaton. Running Time: 80 minutes. Technicolor sequences.

Cast: Irene Dunne (Delphine Witherspoon), Ken Murray (Frank Derryberry), Eddie Foy, Jr. (Chick Evans), Louise Fazenda (Hortense Mossback), Ned Sparks (Sparks), Lilyan Tashman (Edna Stevens), Benny Rubin (Stein),

Fred Santley (Douglas Atwell), Rita Le Roy (Moulika), William von Brincken (Baron von Richter), Carl Gerrard (colonel), Werther Weidler, Wolfgang Weidler (Richter's sons), Claude King, George Chandler, John Tiller's "Sunshine" Girls.

Songs: "A Kiss for Cinderella," "You Took Advantage of Me" (Lorenz Hart, Richard Rodgers); "All My Life," "Shake It Off and Smile" (Sidney Clare, Oscar Levant).

The screen version of Rodgers and Hart's *Present Arms* is most recalled today for its introduction of one of the decade's top film stars. Irene Dunne (1898–1990) had been appearing in Broadway musicals since 1922, but her big break came in mid–1929 when she was brought in to replace Norma Terris as Magnolia for the first national tour of *Show Boat*. She was with the troupe throughout the following fall and spring, and when the tour played in Baltimore in March 1930, RKO scouts spotted her and then quickly placed her under contract.

In *Leathernecking*, Dunne took the role of Delphine Witherspoon, a Honolulu high-society lass who becomes the object of the affections of Marine Buck Private Chick Evans (Eddie Foy, Jr., a comedian oddly cast in the role originated by Charles King). In order to improve his social standing, Chick has stolen the uniform and Distinguished Service Medal of his captain. Although Chick's ruse is exposed, he stops at nothing to win Delphine, even arranging to fake the wreck of a yacht on which both are to sail. Instead, the two, and the rest of their party, become marooned on a desert island. Because of his resulting heroism, Chick is allowed to keep the pilfered uniform—and the rank that goes with it. He also gets his girl.

From all indications, RKO used only two Rodgers and Hart songs, "A Kiss for Cinderella" and the standard "You Took Advantage of Me." Others, which had little to do with the actual goings-on, were newly written by Sidney Clare and Oscar Levant. The song list above is somewhat speculative, because the film is lost and there is no cue sheet on file at ASCAP. The pressbook lists three more songs, "Careless Kisses," "Evening Star" and "Nice and So Particular," apparently credited to Benny Davis and Harry Akst, but the continuity script of the opening credits shows only the Rodgers-Hart and Clare-Levant duos.

In any case, the comedy definitely took a front seat to the music, as such mirthmakers as Ken Murray, Louise Fazenda, Benny Rubin, Ned Sparks and Lilyan Tashman filled out the cast, and director Eddie Cline was known for his way with a punch line. The studio even decorated the final two reels in Technicolor. But none of it brought in the expected audience, and reviewers balked especially at the romantic pairing of the eccentric Foy with the more sophisticated Dunne.

Dunne would do better with her next assignment, the Western epic *Cimarron* (1931), for which Richard Dix requested Dunne as his leading lady. The film won the Oscar for Best Picture, earned Dunne a Best Actress nomination and firmly established her in Hollywood.

WHOOPEE!
(Samuel Goldwyn/United Artists; September 30, 1930)

Director: Thornton Freeland. Producers: Samuel Goldwyn, Florenz Ziegfeld. Scenario: William Conselman. Based on the musical play, book by William Anthony McGuire, lyrics by Gus Kahn, music by Walter Donaldson (New York opening, December 4, 1928; 379 performances). Photography: Lee Garmes, Ray Rennahan, Gregg Toland. Editor: Stuart Heisler. Sound: Oscar Lagerstrom. Assistant Director: H. B. Humberstone. Art Director: Richard Day. Costumes: John Harkrider. Musical Director: Alfred Newman. Dance Direction: Busby Berkeley. Running Time: 94 minutes. Technicolor.

Cast: Eddie Cantor (Henry Williams), Eleanor Hunt (Sally Morgan), Paul Gregory (Wanenis), John Rutherford (Sheriff Bob Wells), Ethel Shutta (Mary Custer), Spencer Charters (Jerome Underwood), Chief Caupolican (Black Eagle), Albert Hackett (Chester Underwood), William H. Philbrick (Andy McNabb), Walter Law (Judd Morgan), Marilyn Morgan [Marian Marsh] (Harriett Underwood), Lou Scha-Enya (Indian maiden), The Goldwyn Girls [including Betty Grable, Virginia Bruce, Claire Dodd], George Olsen and His Orchestra.

Songs: "Cowboys" [Grable, chorus], "A Girl Friend of a Boy Friend of Mine" [Cantor], "Makin' Whoopee" [Cantor], "My Baby Just

Eddie Cantor finds the ideal recipe for comedy in *Whoopee!*—the only collaboration between producing giants Samuel Goldwyn and Florenz Ziegfeld.

Cares for Me" [Cantor], "The Song of the Setting Sun" [Chief Caupolican, Goldwyn Girls], "Stetson" [Shutta, chorus], "Today's the Day" [chorus] (Gus Kahn, Walter Donaldson); "I'll Still Belong to You" [Gregory] (Edward Eliscu, Nacio Herb Brown).

Academy Award Nomination: Best Interior Decoration (Richard Day, 1930-31).

Disc: Meet Patti PRW-1930 (bootleg LP); Take Two 104 (bootleg LP; ST).

Video: Goldwyn/HBO (cassette/laserdisc).

Florenz Ziegfeld's mercurial economic fortunes were temporarily placed on the upswing with the smash hit of the 1928-29 Broadway season. *Whoopee!* was boosted by a catchy score by Walter Donaldson and Gus Kahn, dazzling sets by Joseph Urban, sparkling costumes by John Harkrider (with the usual bevy of beauties to fill them), and a wisecrack-filled libretto by old pro William Anthony McGuire. McGuire based his book on *The Nervous Wreck*, the Owen

Davis play about a shy hypochrondriac and his encounters with cowboys, Indians, and chorus girls in Arizona. But of all these assets, the greatest was the star: Eddie Cantor, the brightest in Ziegfeld's populous galaxy of stars. *Whoopee!* could have run well beyond its total of 379 New York performances, but when Ziegfeld hit hard times, he had to close the expensive production and sell its rights to the movie people.

Fortunately for posterity's sake, Ziegfeld allied himself corporately, in the spring of 1929, with one of the few West Coasters who could do his show justice. Samuel Goldwyn, known to fancy himself as "The Ziegfeld of the Pacific," had been seeking just this kind of extravagant production for his first foray into musicals. As the chiefs of the Z and G Corporation, Ziegfeld and Goldwyn would share the producer's credit for *Whoopee!* and *Kid Boots* (which was never filmed as a talkie), although Ziegfeld must have questioned from the first how he would fare in this potential battle of egos. Goldwyn had the deep pockets Ziegfeld needed—and fast, for the latter would be virtually wiped out in the collapse of the stock market. Predictably, the two men argued constantly during the production of *Whoopee!* Eventually, Ziegfeld was barred from the set, being relegated to little more than a very expensive "adviser" and publicity device.

Most of the Broadway cast came West to make the all–Technicolor film, with the notable exception of Ruth Etting, whose song specialties were independent of the plot anyway. Three of the stage songs were retained—although not Etting's "Love Me or Leave Me"—and Goldwyn commissioned Donaldson (1893–1947) and Kahn (1886–1941) to write four more, among them "A Girl Friend of a Boy Friend of Mine" and the rousing "My Baby Just Cares for Me." Ethel Shutta (1897–1976) was brought in to repeat her comedy role as the hypochondriac's amorous nurse, and the ingénue part was filled, after a lengthy and highly publicized search, by Eleanor Hunt, a chorine in the original show.[45] Cantor (1892–1964) was engaged to reprise his role as the singing-and-joking Henry Williams for $100,000 and 10 percent of the profits.[46] It was a hefty sum for someone whose feature-film career consisted of two silents—*Kid Boots* (1926), adapted from his stage success, and *Special Delivery* (1927), both for Paramount—and a specialty number in that studio's 1929 talkie *Glorifying the American Girl* (see Chapter 3). The eye-rolling clown's penchant for ad-libbed Yiddish jokes, so popular among big-city Jewish theatergoers, raised questions about his salability to the mostly Gentile national movie audience.

Not to worry. Before departing for California, Cantor asked Goldwyn if he would hire Busby Berkeley (1895–1976) as the film's dance director—a suggestion that would do much to give *Whoopee!* a place in movie-musical history. Berkeley, born William Enos, was one of Broadway's leading choreographers, with credits that included *Present Arms* (in which he also was the lead comic), *A Connecticut Yankee, Good Boy* and *Rainbow*. Already, he was playing around with the inventive, kaleidoscopic dance formations that would make him a Hollywood pioneer. Berkeley went West on a train with Cantor and *Whoopee!*'s adaptor and director, respectively William Counselman and Thornton Freeland. As they endured the five-day trip in the early spring of 1930, they talked about how

the stage play could be opened up for the big screen. Recalled Cantor:

> Counselman and Freeland knew so exactly what they were doing that the entire movie was shot in 36 days [actually 43]. They explained points of movie technique to me. Certain scenes had to be condensed, the choreography had to be changed completely. Present a line of 32 girls on the stage and you have something highly effective. Present the same line on the screen and the camera has to move so far back the girls become inch-high midgets.[47]

Goldwyn had some location filming done in Arizona, but that footage appears to be limited to the opening credits and end title. Most of the rest is little more than a filmed play—albeit a very visually attractive one, thanks to the Technicolor and Richard Day's splashy, Oscar-nominated art direction. The main plot centers on a love triangle that has two men in love with young Sally Morgan (Hunt)—Wanenis (Paul Gregory), a young man of Indian background who has been her sweetheart since childhood, and Bob Wells (John Rutherford), the local sheriff. Wanenis returns from an educational sojourn just as Sally and Bob are about to be married. The pining Wanenis sings "I'll Still Belong to You" to Sally, who realizes he is her true love. Unwilling to go through with her wedding to Bob, Sally asks the sickly, bespectacled Henry Williams to spirit her away in his broken-down Ford. She hopes to rendezvous with Wanenis, but she leaves behind a note that misleads Bob and his deputies into thinking that Henry is her intended. Henry's battleaxe nurse, Miss Custer, isn't too pleased, either, for she's got a crush on her woman-fearing patient.

Henry and Sally run out of gas in the middle of nowhere, where they encounter the wealthy but perpetually nervous Jerome Underwood (Spencer Charters), whom they "rob" to get the needed petrol. They seek refuge at a nearby ranch, only to discover that it's Underwood's, but the owner fails to recognize Henry and delights in comparing surgical scars with his new pal. The deputies arrive, but Henry disguises himself in blackface (a convenient stove explosion alibis Cantor's trademark appearance) to sing a very spirited "My Baby Just Cares for Me." Goldwyn biographer A. Scott Berg calls this "one of the most spontaneously joyous moments ever preserved on film,"[48] although it helps that Sheriff Bob has a gun to Henry's stomach, placed there so this so-called stranger can prove his claim that he's a "singing cook."

Henry tricks his way out of a primitive lie-detector test devised by Underwood's college-boy son (Albert Hackett, the future screenwriter), then he escapes with Sally to the local Indian reservation, where he gets sick on the peace pipe offered by Chief Black Eagle (Chief Caupolican). Wanenis, believing that his racial background makes a pairing with Sally impossible, is seriously considering marriage to the chief's plain-jane daughter. At the climax, an unfortunate nod to social convention, Black Eagle resolves the love plot by announcing that Wanenis isn't a redskin after all, which sends Sally into the young man's arms and provokes Henry into succumbing to Miss Custer. Cantor reprises "My Baby Just Cares for Me," then sends everybody home with a spoken "That's all there is."

Whoopee! made Eddie Cantor a movie star, which may baffle modern audiences who can't cotton to his dated brand of comedy. His Henry has no brains or sex appeal to speak of, yet his energy is absolutely infectious, and audiences were charmed, more or less, by the star's knowingly incongruous references to his Jewishness. ("An Indian in a Hebrew school?" is Henry's answer to Wanenis' statement that he's been educated "in your schools.") And besides, Cantor's way with a song is remarkable. He can explode into something like the up-tempo "My Baby Just Cares for Me," yet treat "Makin' Whoopee," the show's most enduring hit, with the breezy understatement it requires. "One never tires of Mr. Cantor," wrote *The New York Times'* Mordaunt Hall, who did not suffer fools gladly. "Even during those periods of respite, in which the charming showgirls go through their drills and dances, one looks forward to another chance to chuckle and giggle at the ludicrous conduct of the 'nervous wreck.'"[49]

The singing and clowning, and the estimable performers behind them, were mainly what enabled *Whoopee!* to become a critical hit, but it is Berkeley's multi-angled dance magic that lingers with the modern viewer. Berkeley has been accused of copying many of Ziegfeld's concepts,[50] and certainly he must have been influenced by the showman's style. But Berkeley had the added challenge of playing to the camera, and he made the camera take his craft

to new heights. He was given free rein by Goldwyn, and his touch is evident right from the opening number, "Cowboys."

The first note is sung by a very young Betty Grable in her first recognizable appearance in a film. At 16, already having been in the choruses of Fox's *Let's Go Places, Happy Days* and *New Movietone Follies of 1930*, Grable was found dutifully practicing routines by herself on the set of *Whoopee!* Here, this cowgirl lassoes an amorous cowhand before the unit forms a dancing triangle—all the easier for the camera to include the whole group—then Berkeley goes overhead for a circular kaleidoscopic effect using the chorus' members hats. This seems to be the first extended use of the overhead technique, although it was employed briefly and awkwardly in a handful of earlier films, starting with *The Cocoanuts*. The number is capped by one of those snake-like effects achieved by the well-timed ducking of the dancers' heads.

The next production number, "Today's the Day," is more conventional, although filled with the femininity Berkeley so enjoyed, as the soon-to-be-named Goldwyn Girls, adorned in wedding finery, celebrate on the morning of Sally and Bob's soon-to-be squelched nuptials. "Stetson," somewhat later, is much more interesting. Shutta kicks off the number with a shimmy-style dance, then Berkeley seeks to bring his faceless choristers some identity. He lines up the Stetsons along a ledge, as the females pop up, one by one, to plop the hats on their heads as the camera pans the row. Then, he places the women in a straight line, dips the hats over their faces, and has them hop toward the camera. Each of them adjusts her hat to reveal her face as the spotlight hits it. The chorus-line close-ups were a musical film first, this only a year and a half after the claustrophobic choreography of *On with the Show!*

The last dance number, "Song of the Setting Sun," sung by Chief Caupolican, takes place on the reservation and is right out of the Ziegfeld Follies. The Goldwyn Girls prance around in headdresses and scanty Indian costumes, occasionally gathering for an kaleidoscopic overhead shot. Other dancers show up on horseback for a fashion show-style parade, then the whole group forms an old-fashioned tableau similar to the one seen at the end of *Glorifying the American Girl*, but it looks better here.

Unlike most filmmakers of the time, Berkeley chose to use a single camera, which prompted a more meticulous planning of his complicated numbers. He explained it like this:

> The art director of *Whoopee!*, Richard Day, … gave me a piece of advice that helped me greatly. "Buzz, they try to make a big secret out of that little box, but it's no mystery at all. All you have to remember is that the camera has only one eye, not two. You can see a lot with two eyes but hold a hand over one and it cuts your area of vision." This was very simple advice, but it made all the difference. I started planning my numbers with one eye in mind. … My idea was to plan every shot and edit in the camera.[51]

The innovations brought Berkeley acclaim, if not immediate work, for musicals were fading despite entries such as *Whoopee!* Goldwyn spent $1.3 million on the production, but got more than $1.5 million back. He picked up the option on Cantor's contract, and the star prepared for a second musical, *The Kid from Spain*. The remaining member of this estimable creative foursome did not fare as well as the others. Florenz Ziegfeld never had another Broadway hit, and financial and health problems continued to dog him. He died, of complications from pleurisy, in 1932. The source material for *Whoopee!* was readapted by Goldwyn in 1944 as *Up in Arms*, which introduced Danny Kaye to the big screen.

Whoopee! survives as a cinematic document of Ziegfeld's uniquely colorful brand of entertainment, but for a long time after its only re-release (in 1933) it was believed that no prints of it existed. Finally, a print with German subtitles turned up in Czechoslovakia, where it had lingered since the conquering Russians confiscated it from a Berlin archive at the end of World War II. The print was exhibited in New York and Los Angeles in 1971. With interest in the film revived, the Samuel Goldwyn Co. struck a brand-new print from the original negative after two years of restoration. *Whoopee!* has since found a whole new audience on cable television and in videotape and laserdisc releases.

HEADS UP

(Paramount; October 10, 1930)

Director: Victor Schertzinger. Screenplay: John McGowan, Jack Kirkland. Continuity: Louis Stevens. Based on the musical play *Heads Up!*, book by John McGowan and Paul Gerard Smith, lyrics by Lorenz Hart, music by Richard Rodgers (New York opening, November 11, 1929; 144 performances). Photography: William Steiner. Dance Direction: Georgie Hale. Running Time: 76 minutes.

Cast: Charles ["Buddy"] Rogers (Jack Mason), Victor Moore (Skippy Dugan), Helen Kane (Betty Trumbull), Margaret Breen (Mary Trumbull), Helen Carrington (Mrs. Trumbull), Gene Gowing (Rex Cutting), Billy Taylor (Georgie Martin), Harry Shannon (Captain Denny), C. Anthony Hughes (Larry White), John Hamilton (Captain Whitney), Stanley Jessup (naval officer), Preston Foster (Blake).

Songs: "My Man Is on the Make" [Kane, Taylor], "A Ship Without a Sail" [Rogers, chorus] (Lorenz Hart, Richard Rodgers); "If I Knew You Better" [Rogers, Breen; reprised by Kane], "Readin', Ritin', Rhythm" [Kane, chorus, danced by Rogers, Breen] (Don Hartman, Victor Schertzinger).

Disc: RCA Victor 22475 (Kane/"My Man Is on the Make"/78); RCA Victor 22520 (Kane/"If I Knew You Better"/"Readin', Ritin', Rhythm"/78); Music Masters JJA-19766 (bootleg LP; ST).

"GARBO TALKS!" was the marquee boast for MGM's *Anna Christie* in 1930. Maybe Paramount should have taken a cue by promoting *Heads Up* with "BUDDY SMOKES!"

Such a revelation would have jibed with the studio's attempt to revise Buddy Rogers' straight-arrow image—the company, claiming his fans wanted it that way, was now billing him only by his real name of Charles. And, after the musical comedy *Heads Up*, all fans and critics could talk about was the star's brief dalliance with a cigarette. "It wasn't so long ago," recalled a *Variety* commentator, "that directors were having a tough time getting Rogers to strike a match in front of the lens. … Rogers apparently wants to be the model youth if it kills him—and it eventually and probably will."[52]

The minor controversy obscured the tepid reception for the rest of the film, and in retrospect, *Heads Up* offers little to separate it from the rest of Paramount's often mediocre musical output of 1930. The story, adapted by John McGowan from his modest Broadway success, concerns a Coast Guard ensign who falls for a young socialite (Margaret Breen) and then must expose a bootleg racket from within her family's luxury yacht. The family honor is saved when it's revealed that the socialite's previous beau (Gene Gowing), in league with the yacht's captain (Harry Shannon), is the party running the rum, although the affair isn't settled until after the principals are boatwrecked on a deserted island.

Victor Moore (1876–1962) repeated his stage role as "Skippy" Dugan, the yacht's comic cook, an amateur inventor who automates his kitchen so thoroughly that he has practically nothing to do but whine. Moore did that very effectively in a show-business career that encompassed movies, vaudeville and the legit stage for more than a half century. More comedy is provided by Helen Kane, who lost 15 pounds for what would be her final role in a feature film. She may have realized that her cutesy schtick was growing stale, for she utters her "boop-a-doop" phrase only twice in 76 minutes. Kane, in a professor's spectacles and tassled hat and gown, leads a nifty Georgie Hale–staged dance number to "Readin', Ritin', Rhythm," a song added by director-composer Victor Schertzinger to complement what remained from the original Rodgers and Hart score. She also sings Rodgers and Hart's "My Man Is on the Make" and a solo reprise of the Schertzinger love duet "If I Knew You Better."

The Broadway show is best remembered for the ballad "A Ship Without a Sail," a seaman's lament sung by the hero after he's ordered to undertake the assignment that he believes will betray his lady love. In the film, the music swells as the uniformed Rogers walks to the end of a pier in the moonlight. He takes a drag or two on his Marlboro—which is what got everyone a-twitter—then croons gamely, but weakly, through the first verse before being rescued by a chorus of lonely seafarers aboard a ghostly derelict ship. The song is good and the staging is effective enough, but Rogers hasn't enough voice to put it over. Jack Whiting sang it better in the New York version.

Breen, who sings ("If I Knew You Better," with Rogers) and dances pleasingly, was one of three New York performers who made the short trip to Paramount's Astoria studio for their talkie baptisms. The others were Gowing and Billy Taylor, a colorless comic who played Kane's boyfriend. Their chances for future film

roles were blunted when musicals went out of favor right after *Heads Up.*

PLAYBOY OF PARIS
(Paramount; October 31, 1930)

Director: Ludwig Berger. Scenario: Vincent Lawrence. Adaptation: Percy Heath. Based on the musical play *Le Petit Café* [*The Little Café*] by Tristan Bernard (1912). Photography: Henry Gerrard. Editor: Merrill White. Sound: M. M. Paggi. Running Time: 82 minutes.

Cast: Maurice Chevalier (Albert Loriflan), Frances Dee (Yvonne), O. P. Heggie (Philbert), Stuart Erwin (Paul Michel), Eugene Pallette (Pierre Bourdin), Dorothy Christy (Berengère), Cecil Cunningham (Hedwige), Tyler Brooke (Cadeaux), Frank Elliott (Mr. Jabert), William B. Davidson (Mr. Bannock), Erin La Bissoniere (Jacqueline), Charles Giblyn (Gastonet), Frederick Lee (Plouvier), Edmund Breese (General de Karodek), Olaf Hytten (doctor), Edward Lynch (nightclub manager), Guy Oliver (street cleaner), William O'Brien (waiter), Sidney Bracey (irate diner).

Songs: "In the Heart of Old Paree" [Chevalier], "It's a Great Life If You Don't Weaken" [Chevalier], "My Ideal" [Chevalier; reprised by band at skating rink], "Yvonne's Song" [Cunningham] (Leo Robin, Richard A. Whiting, Newell Chase).

Disc: RCA Victor 22542 (Chevalier/"It's a Great Life If You Don't Weaken"/"My Ideal"/78); RCA Victor 22549 (Chevalier/ above songs in French/78).

Maurice Chevalier's immense charm put across the so-so *The Big Pond* earlier in the year, but he didn't fare nearly as well with the modest comedy-with-songs *Playboy of Paris*. It was based on the 1912 French stage farce *Le Petit Café*, which in 1919 became a film starring the comedian Max Linder. The Paramount version was weakly directed by German émigré Ludwig Berger, albeit with a reliance on closeups unusual for an early talkie.

Chevalier appears as Albert Loriflan, a waiter at a Paris café who is about to come into a large inheritance from a distant relative. Unfortunately, his boss (O. P. Heggie) learns of the windfall ahead of time from a shyster lawyer (Tyler Brooke), and they connive to place an unknowing Albert under a 20-year contract, confident that the waiter will award the café owner a hefty settlement to get out of the deal. No way. Albert defiantly remains a waiter by day as he enjoys his expensive nightlife. The story ends with a duel that is interrupted by the café owner's beautiful but heretofore icy daughter (Frances Dee, in her first important film role), who admits her love for a receptive Albert.

Playboy of Paris contains a funny sequence in which Chevalier lovingly samples the contents of a wine cellar as if they were contestants in a beauty pageant, but its pace is leaden and the star is clumsily paired with miscast sidekicks (Stuart Erwin, Eugene Pallette). Chevalier's fans also may have been disappointed at his singing of only two complete songs, "It's a Great Life If You Don't Weaken" and "In the Heart of Old Paree," in the American release. The future hit "My Ideal," also by Leo Robin, Richard Whiting and Newell Chase, is heard only as background music in the English-language version, except for a refrain blurted out by the drunken Chevalier in the wine cellar. The song received fuller exposure in the better-reviewed French-language version, *Le Petit Café*, in which Chevalier's wife, actress-singer Yvonne Vallee, took the role played by Dee. "Yvonne's Song" is sung by Cecil Cunningham, who plays Chevalier's old girlfriend, but it turns out to be little more than background to a dialogue sequence in a nightclub.

Dee, a 22-year-old former extra, supposedly was a discovery of Chevalier's. After her screen test was rejected by Berger—Paramount was seeking a new face to play the female lead in *Playboy of Paris*—the director was sitting in the studio commissary with Chevalier when the Frenchman pointed to Dee and said she "was just the girl for the part."[53] Dee (b. 1907) would become one of Hollywood's most beautiful leading ladies of the 1930s and '40s.

SUNNY

(First National; November 9, 1930)

Director: William A. Seiter. Adaptation: Humphrey Pearson, Henry McCarty. Dialogue: Humphrey Pearson. Based on the musical play, book and lyrics by Otto Harbach and Oscar Hammerstein II, music by Jerome Kern (New York opening, September 22, 1925; 517 performances). Photography: Ernest Haller. Editor: Le Roy Stone. Musical Director: Erno Rapée. Dance Direction: Theodore Kosloff. Running Time: 77 minutes.

Cast: Marilyn Miller (Sunny Peters), Lawrence Gray (Tom Warren), Joe Donahue (Jim Deming), O. P. Heggie (Mr. Peters), Inez Courtney (Weenie), Barbara Bedford (Marcia Manners), Mackenzie Ward (Wendel-Wendel), Judith Vosselli (Sue), Clyde Cook (Sam), Harry Allen (barker), William B. Davidson (first officer), Ben Hendricks, Jr. (second officer).

Songs/Musical Numbers: "The Hunt Dance" [danced by Miller], "I Was Alone" [Miller, twice], "When We Get Our Divorce" [danced by Miller, Donahue], "Who?" [Gray, Miller] (Otto Harbach, Oscar Hammerstein II, Jerome Kern); "Oh! Didn't He Ramble" [Gray, men] (Bob Cole, J. Rosamond Johnson).

Marilyn Miller again, her per-picture take doubled to $200,000 by a grateful Jack Warner after *Sally* was on its way to becoming First National's top grosser of 1930. *Sunny* was adapted from another of her Ziegfeld productions, this one having marked the first teaming of Jerome Kern and Oscar Hammerstein II. The 1925 show lasted more than 500 performances on the strength of great Kern–Hammerstein–Harbach songs—the best was "Who?" There was also a first-rate supporting cast in Jack Donahue, Cliff "Ukelele Ike" Edwards, Joseph Cawthorn, Pert Kelton and the dance duo of Clifton Webb and Mary Hay. The studio hoped the movie version would match the success of the original—but it never came close. Bad timing, perhaps?

Sunny lacks the color and spectacle of the stage production, and there isn't nearly enough music. Because the commercial climate for musicals in general had cooled considerably by late 1930, the trend was to de-emphasize the "musical" in musical comedy. Thus, although she has three dance numbers, Miller sings only two songs in *Sunny*. "Who?" is an intimate duet with her hand-picked leading man, Lawrence Gray. The downbeat "I Was Alone," written for the film by Kern, Hammerstein and Harbach, is twice blurted out awkwardly by the star in lieu of sensible transitions from story. Music from the stage—mainly "Sunny," "Two Little Bluebirds" and "D'Ye Love Me?"—is relegated to underscoring, albeit heard frequently.

For even more of Warners' money than in *Sally*, Marilyn Miller repeated her boyish stage role as *Sunny*.

The disuse of the music only highlights the deficiencies of Hammerstein and Harbach's overwritten book, compressed into 77 minutes of celluloid by scripters Humphrey Pearson and Henry McCarty. And the movie's supporting cast can't match the Broadway lineup. Joe Donahue, a gangling Irish dancer, was Miller's choice to replace his brother Jack, whom he had understudied on the stage, in the comic lead. Jack Donahue would die suddenly from a heart ailment a month before the film's release.

The movie tells the story of Sunny Peters, a horseback rider for a circus in England. She has been pledged by her father (O. P. Heggie) to marry the fuddy-duddy big-top owner, Wendel-Wendel (Mackenzie Ward)—who, she is reminded by dad, was so well liked by his father "that he named him twice." But a chance reunion with Tom Warren (Gray), an American she had known when his Army unit was stationed in England during the war, rekindles old feelings. Those feelings become apparent in "Who?" the hit song best remembered for the lyrical use of its title, which begins the refrain with a single note held for 2 1/4 measures. Hammerstein's selection of the word was truly inspired, for few others would have been ex-

pressive enough to sustain such a lengthy melodic phrase.

Tom is also smitten, but he, too, is promised to another, Marcia Manners (Barbara Bedford). Unwilling to marry a man she does not love, or to be apart from the one she does, Sunny stows away on the ocean liner on which Tom and his old war buddies are returning home. She dresses as a boy to escape detection, but she is caught ("I Was Alone") and faces deportation to England. Instead, to obtain a U. S. passport, Sunny marries Tom's best friend, Jim Deming (Donahue). The marriage is in name only, as the two agree to divorce upon landing. After the shipboard vows are said, best man Tom astonishes the onlookers by kissing the bride, while the groom smooches his wallet-sized photo of his real love, the pert but dim-bulbed Weenie (Inez Courtney).

Jim operates a thriving gymnasium resort, which gives Miller and Donahue a perfect excuse to do a tap routine to a section of Kern's "When We Get Our Divorce." The unlikely couple must bide their time before a decree can be granted. But the unexpected arrival of Weenie and Wendel-Wendel confuses matters, as the trumped-up divorce decree, which now comes to light, makes Jim out to be a brute. Tom turns against Sunny, and even her feigning of a horse-riding injury does not recapture his love. At a ball during which she performs "The Hunt Dance," Sunny and Tom are reunited just as she prepares to return to England for a very unwilling marriage to Wendel-Wendel.

First National spent a bundle on the production—a cavernous wedding set, the gym layout, an ornate ballroom for the climactic dance—and *The Film Daily*, for example, considered the result "very well adapted to the screen."[54] But one comes away wondering why Marilyn Miller was worth so much expense. The petite charm that made her so appealing on the stage simply did not transfer sufficiently to the big screen, although she came closest, in three attempts, with her first, *Sally*. By this time, she was a little past her prime, her singing voice was thin, she read her lines in a flat tone, and she was hampered by what Ethan Mordden calls "a crazy grin and, for a dancer, some bizarre ideas on posture."[55] As a costly property in a fading genre, her movie-star days were numbered.

Even Ed Wynn is speechless at the happy reunion of Stanley Smith and Ginger Rogers in *Follow the Leader*.

Sunny was remade in 1941 by RKO with the British star Anna Neagle opposite Ray Bolger. Four songs from the original score were used.

FOLLOW THE LEADER
(Paramount; December 5, 1930)

Director: Norman Taurog. Dialogue Director: Albert Parker. Adaptation: Gertrude Purcell, Sid Silvers. Based on the musical play *Manhattan Mary*, book by William K. Wells and George White, lyrics by B. G. De Sylva and Lew Brown, music by Ray Henderson (New York opening, September 26, 1927; 264 performances). Photography: Larry Williams. Editor: Barney Rogan. Sound: Ernest F. Zatorsky. Running Time: 76 minutes.

Cast: Ed Wynn (Crickets), Ginger Rogers (Mary Brennan), Stanley Smith (Jimmy Moore), Lou Holtz (Sam Platz), Lida Kane (Ma Brennan), Ethel Merman (Helen King). Bobby Watson (George White), Donald Kirke (R. C. Black), William Halligan (Bob Sterling), Preston Foster (Two-Gun Terry), Holly Hall (Fritzie Devere), James C. Morton (Mickie).

Songs: "Broadway, the Heart of the World" [offscreen chorus] (B. G. De Sylva, Lew Brown, Ray Henderson); "Satan's Holiday" [Merman] (Irving Kahal, Sammy Fain).

Disc: Encore 101 (LP; ST).

This comedy with songs was heralded as the feature-film debut of the popular vaudeville star Ed Wynn, upon whose Broadway hit *Manhattan Mary*, a George White musical comedy production with a De Sylva–Brown–Henderson score, this film was based. Nowadays, however, buffs recall *Follow the Leader* as the debut of one of the greatest singers of her era, Ethel Merman.

Actually, Ethel Agnes Zimmermann (1909–1984) had appeared on celluloid once before, wearing jungle garb and singing a comedy song called "Sockety-Sock" in a 1930 Vitaphone short, *The Cave Club*. The long-forgotten film was the only tangible result of a six-month, $125-a-week Warner Bros. contract, which she signed after being spotted singing in a New York nitery. After getting out of the pact, she adopted her new professional name and performed in clubs and vaudeville when she wasn't working as a secretary. Broadway producer Vinton Freedley hired Merman as a rhythm singer for the new Gershwin musical *Girl Crazy,* and there she made her first splash with a typically exultant rendition of "I Got Rhythm," in which she attracted attention by holding a high C for 16 measures of the chorus. During her daylight hours, she began to make movies at Astoria for Paramount—the first of them being *Follow the Leader,* in which she was a last-minute replacement for Ruth Etting.

In sharp contrast to her Broadway debut. Merman made little impression in a film that is all Wynn's. "The Perfect Fool" (1886–1966), whom Jack Benny called "the world's greatest comedian," brought his familiar giggling-idiot persona to his role as Crickets, a would-be acrobat and inventor who aspires to ditch his job as a restaurant waiter and go for the big time. Crickets gets his chance when he gets mixed up with a New York neighborhood gang after inadvertently knocking a rival tough unconscious. Wynn's scene with the gangster (a young Preston Foster) includes the legendary old-groaner gag in which the bully barks to the waiter, "I'm so hungry I could eat a horse!"—to which the waiter, after marching in with such an animal in tow, replies, "Do you use ketchup or mustard?"

Made leader of the gang, Crickets is obliged to find his employer's daughter (Ginger Rogers, daylighting from her ingénue role in *Girl Crazy*) a job in George White's *Scandals.* With help from a dopey press agent (dialect comic Lou Holtz, reprising his stage role in his screen debut), Crickets blunders his way to success, and young Mary Brennan is hired as the understudy to the star of White's upcoming production. The star is Helen King (Merman), whom we first see on the eve of the show's premiere, entertaining a nightclub crowd with "Satan's Holiday," the only song number in the film.[56]

Even as Helen sings, Crickets is hatching his plan to kidnap her so that Mary will get her big break. After a false start, he goes to Helen's apartment and gags and ties her to a chair, then, in a typical Wynn gag, he determines how much chloroform to give his victim by experimenting on himself. Mary is a big hit that night, but her acknowledgment of Helen's stardom compels her to accept a berth in the Folies Bergère. Months later, Crickets reunites Mary, who has returned from Paris, with her estranged saxman boyfriend (Stanley Smith). For all we know, poor Helen may still be trying to writhe her way out of bondage.

Follow the Leader, shorn of almost all the music of its Broadway predecessor, received tepid reviews and appealed little to anyone who hadn't acquired a taste for Ed Wynn. Lou Holtz lost his, for he claimed that Wynn had ordered the deletion of most of his scenes.[57] Merman didn't escape the reviewers' quibbling: "Faulty makeup marked down her true appearance," declared *Variety*, "and recording didn't carry her voice naturally."[58] The unsuccessful first stab at movies seemed to portend the balance of Merman's cinema career, in which she was often wasted in secondary parts and deprived of reprising stage glories. There certainly was no glory in the way she was presented in *Follow the Leader.*

CHAPTER 5

1929–1930: *If I Had a Talking Picture of You…*

Broadway's formula for musical comedy seemed simple enough to duplicate, but at first, Hollywood scenario writers didn't fall all over each other putting it to use. The earliest musicals written for the screen—the likes of *Lucky Boy, Mother's Boy* and *The Rainbow Man*—drew their inspiration less from the lighthearted fun of *Sally* and *No! No! Nanette!* than the maudlin melodramatics of *The Jazz Singer* and *The Singing Fool.* As 1929 turned into 1930, the glut of weepy backstagers had abated some in favor of light comedies, and there would be nearly as many original stories, comedic or dramatic, as those taken from other sources.

Helping to ease this change was Fox's hugely successful original musical *Sunnyside Up*, which premiered in October of 1929 and entered general release by Christmas.[1] Not only did the film have the potent star power of Janet Gaynor and Charles Farrell behind it, but there also was a very hummable score by B. G. "Buddy" De Sylva, Lew Brown and Ray Henderson and surprisingly inventive direction by David Butler. These assets made filmgoers forget that its familiar Cinderella story, also supplied by De Sylva, Brown and Henderson, was no more original than the love-triangle plot of *The Broadway Melody. Sunnyside Up* grossed an impressive $3 million.

The Hollywood money men were finding that fresh material for scenarios was, like the movies' self-generated songs, pleasingly cost-effective. As the studios sought to satisfy the seemingly endless demand for stories for dialogue pictures, the rights to existing works were inflated wildly. Observed *Variety* in September 1929: "Past history shows that in a number of cases after fabulous sums were paid out for the rights to plays and novels, it became necessary to reconstruct the entire story and give it a new box office title, thus losing the original value the studio set out to obtain."[2]

In this chapter, we'll cover 1929-30 musicals written expressly for the screen—mainly musical comedies—that cannot be categorized as backstagers, college stories or operettas.

MARIANNE

(Cosmopolitan Productions/MGM; August 24, 1929)

Director: Robert Z. Leonard. Story and Screenplay: Dale Van Every. Dialogue: Laurence Stallings, Gladys Unger. Titles: Joe Farnham. Photography: Oliver Marsh. Editor: Basil Wrangell. Sound: Douglas Shearer. Art Director: Cedric Gibbons. Costumes: Adrian. Running Time: 112 minutes (sound version; also released as silent).

Cast: Marion Davies (Marianne), Lawrence Gray (Stagg), George Baxter (André), Cliff Edwards (Soapy), Benny Rubin (Sam), Scott Kolk (Lieutenant Frane), Robert Edeson (general), Emil Chautard (Père Joseph), Oscar Apfel (major), Victor Potel. Roles cast differently in silent version: Oscar Shaw (Stagg), Robert Castle (André), Robert Ames (Soapy), Mack Swain (general).

Songs: "Believe Me You Should Know That Girl from Noo Chateau" [Rubin], "Marianne" [Baxter, in French; reprised by Gray, in English], "Oo, La, La, La, La" [Davies, soldiers], "When I See My Sugar, I Get a Lump in My Throat" [Edwards, soldiers] (Roy Turk, Fred E. Ahlert); "Hang On to Me" [Edwards],

As *Marianne*, Marion Davies must choose between two soldiers: an American (Lawrence Gray, left) and a Frenchman (George Baxter).

"Just You, Just Me" [Davies, Gray; reprised by Edwards, Gray] (Raymond Klages, Jesse Greer); "Blondy" [soldiers] (Arthur Freed, Nacio Herb Brown); "Louise" [Davies] (Leo Robin, Richard A. Whiting); "Le Regiment de Sambre et Meuse" [French soldiers] (George Harris, Jr., Robert Planquette); "Where Do We Go from Here?" [soldiers] (Howard Johnson, Percy Wenrich).

Disc: Columbia 1907 (Edwards/"Hang On to Me"/"Just You, Just Me"/78); Music Masters JJA-19802 (bootleg LP; ST).

An even earlier original musical than *Sunnyside Up* was Metro-Goldwyn-Mayer's *Marianne*, a World War I romance that premiered in Los Angeles on August 24, 1929. (*Sunnyside Up* debuted in New York in early October, two weeks before *Marianne* opened there.) *Marianne* was an original not only in the literal sense, its story having been written from scratch by Dale Van Every (dialogue by Laurence Stallings and Gladys Unger), but also in that it was free of

some of the usual trappings of musical comedy. Experience counted. Van Every had been a driver for the U. S. Ambulance Corps during the war, and Stallings was the ex-soldier author of *What Price Glory?* and *The Big Parade*. For *Marianne*, the stock ingénue was replaced by a feisty French maiden, whose town has been gutted by the occupying, post–Armistice American soldiers who attempt to befriend her. The male lead was a doughboy from New Jersey doing his bit for his Uncle Sam. There were no high-stepping dancers to halt this love affair in its tracks. And how many properties could boast a pig as a major story component?

The porcine is claimed as a pet by Marianne (Marion Davies), who grudgingly consents to cook it for the commanding officers. But Private Stagg (Lawrence Gray), jealous of a smooth-talking lieutenant (Scott Kolk) whom he thinks has a yen for the girl, swipes the main course for the enjoyment of the enlisted men, including his two best buddies (Cliff "Uke-lele Ike" Edwards and Benny Rubin).[3] The transgression lands him in the stockade, but only until Marianne, dressed as a male French officer, intercedes on his behalf. This leads to a suggestive sequence in the back seat of an Army car. Stagg, not fooled by the uniform and upper-lip adornment of his new "friend," grabs her knee ("You young officers are soft … don't ya take no exercise?"), plies her with a nauseating cigar, then rips off her fake moustache and lands a passionate smooch.

The romance has one major complication: Marianne has sworn to be faithful to her childhood suitor (George Baxter), a soldier who now returns home blinded. Marianne and Stagg must part, but when the blind man comprehends the strength of their love, he steps aside by entering the priesthood (no kidding), and Marianne is free to join her sweetheart in New York.[4]

Marianne was lukewarmly received, and, at just under two hours, it suffers from the typical laggard pace of early talkies. Still, it remains quite enjoyable, mainly because of the performance of its star. This was the kind of role at which Davies (1897–1961) excelled, and she would have done more light comedy had it not been for the interference of William Randolph Hearst, who wanted his mistress to be the next Sarah Bernhardt. (*Marianne,* like most of Davies' films, was produced by Davies and Hearst's Cosmopolitan Productions.) But maybe Hearst was lightening up a little, for this film apparently ended the publisher's unwritten ban against Davies kissing her leading men on screen.[5]

In her first starring talkie—she'd sung one song in MGM's *Hollywood Revue of 1929*— Davies shows no sign of her potentially career-threatening stutter. She capably handles a French accent, dances a little and even sings a verse, in a duet with Gray, of Raymond Klages and Jesse Greer's bright "Just You, Just Me." (The song became a disc hit for Cliff Edwards, who also sang it in the film.) Better yet, Davies does amusing imitations of Maurice Chevalier (singing "Louise") and—happy, W. R.?—Sarah Bernhardt. Robert Z. Leonard's direction is above average, and there is some first-rate battle footage that looks to have lifted from *The Big Parade.*

The Film Daily said of *Marianne:* "Marion Davies is trouping all the way, and how. She looks as appealing as ever, and has a pip of a love story to put over that carries a strong human punch at the close. Surefire with the femmes … good everywhere."[6]

SUNNYSIDE UP
(Fox; October 3, 1929)

Director: David Butler. Adaptation: David Butler. Story and Dialogue: B. G. De Sylva, Lew Brown, Ray Henderson. Photography: Ernest Palmer, John Schmitz. Editor: Irene Morra. Sound: Joseph E. Aiken. Art Director: Harry Oliver. Assistant Director: Ad Schaumer. Costumes: Sophie Wachner. Musical Directors: Arthur Kay, Howard Jackson. Dance Direction: Seymour Felix. Running Time: 115 minutes. Multicolor sequence.

Cast: Janet Gaynor (Molly Carr), Charles Farrell (Jack Cromwell), El Brendel (Eric Swenson), Marjorie White (Bee Nichols), Frank Richardson (Eddie Rafferty), Sharon Lynn (Jane Worth), Mary Forbes (Mrs. Cromwell), Joe Brown (Joe Vitto), Alan Paull (Raoul), Peter Gawthorne (Lake), Ivan Linow (unsmiling man), Jackie Cooper (little boy), Mary Gordon (grocery patron).

Songs: "If I Had a Talking Picture of You" [Gaynor, Farrell; reprised by children, then by Gaynor, Farrell], "I'm a Dreamer, Aren't We All?" [Gaynor, three times], "It's Great to Be Necked" [White], "Sunnyside Up" [Gaynor, partygoers; reprised by White, Richardson], "Turn On the Heat" [Lynn, Richardson, danced by chorus], "You Find the Time, I'll Find the Place" [Lynn], "You've Got Me Pickin' Petals Off of Daisies" [Gaynor] (B. G. De Sylva, Lew Brown, Ray Henderson).

The sometimes earthy nature of the talk in *Marianne* contrasted with the more homey chatter of *Sunnyside Up,* the first full-length talkie for "America's Favorite Lovebirds," the squeaky-clean Janet Gaynor (1906–1984) and Charles Farrell (1901–1990). For such, Fox decided to spare no expense, luring the songs-and-scenario team of B. G. "Buddy" De Sylva (1895–1950), Lew Brown (1893–1958) and Ray Henderson (1896–1970). The trio passed up several other screen and stage offers for Fox's sweetheart deal: $150,000 in advance for the book, score and lyrics for this film, plus profits on royalties on all songs written for the studio's

The principal cast of Fox's *Sunnyside Up*: **(back row, from left) Sharon Lynn, Frank Richardson, El Brendel, Marjorie White and (front) Charles Farrell and Janet Gaynor.**

productions.[7] Further, the writers for said productions were to be supplied by De Sylva, Brown and Henderson's publishing company, which would own all the song copyrights.

Although Gaynor and Farrell had both already appeared in two films with dialogue sequences (*Street Angel* and *Lucky Star*), rumors strangely circulated that they could not talk adequately; this was especially the case with Gaynor.[8] Her voice was slight and a little breathy, his mildly high-pitched and New England-accented, but they were not at odds with the perception of them as just folks. The Fox management agreed and, in April 1929, declared that both were suitable for talkies. The *Sunnyside Up* supporting cast included the erstwhile vaudevillian El Brendel (1890–1964), who had proved his talkie mettle as the foil of *The Cock-Eyed World*, and Marjorie White (1908–1935), a spunky stage comedienne from Broadway and, before that, Canada. Frank Richard-

son (1898–1962) was a glib tenor from the nightclub circuit. Director David Butler, a supporting actor in Gaynor and Farrell's 1927 hit *Seventh Heaven*, had cut his teeth musically on *William Fox Movietone Follies of 1929*.

The love plot was as simple as a Gaynor-Farrell romance required. Molly Carr (Gaynor) is a New York department-store clerk who lives in an East Side tenement with her bubbly pal Bee Nichols (White). She and a platonic friend, grocer Eric Swenson (Brendel), attend a Fourth of July celebration with Bea and her boyfriend, Eddie Rafferty (Richardson), the kind of aspiring songwriter who thinks every corny phrase he hears is a great idea for a tune. In an effective crane shot that opens the film, Butler allows Ernest Palmer to pan his camera around Molly's neighborhood on the holiday afternoon. To the strains of "Sidewalks of New York," children play ball in the street ... a disapproving wife snatches away her husband's copy of the *Police Gazette* … a mother uses a mixing bowl to give her young son a quick haircut … a woman relaxing on her doorstep with her brood is offered the "Birth Control Review" by a stern-looking reformer, who earns the reply, "This is a fine time to be tellin' me!" In *Sunnyside Up*, the poor are energetic but mainly satisfied to be without, while the moneyed characters are weak, strait-jacketed by customs and convention.

Molly, vaguely unhappy with her life, moons over a newspaper photo of a handsome young man whose engagement has been announced. She tells Bee that "there's a song that expresses my feelings exactly," then overcomes the weak transition by charmingly introducing "I'm a Dreamer, Aren't We All?" to her own zither accompaniment. (The original intent was for a small orchestra to back Gaynor, but her delivery was so soft that a zither had to be used.) Her dream man, the wistful melody goes, is ideal, if he were only real. Actually, he's over in Southampton, playing the piano as his fiancée, Jane (Sharon Lynn, 1904–1963), belts out "You Find the Time, I'll Find the Place." Jane finds time to flirt with a handsome party guest, which prompts the jealous and slightly intoxicated Jack Cromwell (Farrell) to jump into his car and dash into the city. On Molly's block, he nearly hits a little girl, and, dazed, wanders into Molly's flat. To her astonishment, she realizes that he's the man in her newspaper clipping!

Molly would like to chat, but first she has to entertain her neighbors for the Fourth of July block party. With Jack watching, she sings "Sunnyside Up," a cheery ode to optimism. Gaynor dances pleasingly, too, borrowing the top hat and cane of the local undertaker. The deficiencies in her voice are compensated for by her energy. This was the kind of number that immediately endeared her to a moviegoing public unsure if her charm would carry over to the talking medium. A comic bit is also part of the block-party sequence, as a lad played by the young Jackie Cooper gets up to recite "Under the Spreading Chestnut Tree" but runs off to the bathroom in mid-verse.

Jack is won over by Molly's song, so to be close to her, he offers to put her up in the empty home next door to his, and, so she can perform in the rich folks' annual charity show, plans to pass her off as a visitor from Detroit society.

Eric, Bee and Eddie can come along as Molly's butler, maid and chauffeur, respectively. For a while the ruse works, but at a reception given for Molly by Jack's mother (Mary Forbes), a butler overhears an innocent remark by Bee and then starts spreading the word that Molly is being "kept" by Jack.

Soon it's time for the charity show. It begins as the picture transforms from black-and-white to Multicolor for what has been called "the first purely cinematic" production number, "Turn On the Heat."[9] Sharon Lynn, bundled up Eskimo-like in a heavy fur parka against an Arctic tableau, declares that the passions of dancing feet will dissolve the ice and snow. With "Northern lights" flashing in the background, a chorus of 36 females emerges from "igloos" and gyrates suggestively to the refrain. Frank Richardson, standing in the wings, adds his own suggestive verse. Meanwhile, the girls shuck their coats in rhythm from the center of the formation outward, revealing scanty summer outfits. Palm trees suddenly emerge from the ground, steam rises, then smoke and fire, as the bizarre dance continues. Finally, the tropical "island" goes up in flames as the dancers dive into the water that surrounds the stage.

This spectacular sequence was choreographed by Seymour Felix, Fox's resident dance whiz, who utilized a mammoth water tank with an innovative heavy glass top on which the dancers performed.[10] Today, the number remains the highlight of *Sunnyside Up*, but in 1929, it was positively astounding. "The staging of 'Turn On the Heat' is the greatest thing the talking movies have yet achieved in the line of musical comedy," wrote Bland Johaneson of the *New York Daily Mirror*.[11] Gushed the editor of *Variety*, "Sime" Silverman: "Seymour Felix has surpassed himself. It was the talk of Broadway immediately.… If they get this number right in the sticks, the natives will arrange to sleep in the theater."[12] This risqué display was jarring next to the more bland tone of the rest of the picture, but this testified more to the acknowledged songwriting versatility of De Sylva, Brown and Henderson than to any flaw in their story.

In an interview two years before his death in 1979, David Butler recalled the filming of the "Turn On the Heat" number:

> We shot that at night on the back lot right where the Century Plaza Hotel stands now.

There was a moat in front of the stage, where the girls dove into the water. Our camera was on a float, and the boom went way up in the air from there. The water curtain was under the stage, with 59 plumbers. I'd give a signal for it to come down and to go up with a cue light. ... First the igloos melted, and they pulled those down. That was canvas with ice on it. We had holes right next to the igloos where the trees came up. Then we had special effects where the fire started. We worked hard on that number. But it was worth it. It's pretty good now, even. It had an idea to it, and I think that's probably what made it.[13]

Butler remembered that the idea for "Turn On the Heat" came from Buddy De Sylva. Given the fire-and-ice motif, it's very possible that De Sylva may have been thinking about the similarly themed "I Want to Be Bad" number from his stage musical *Follow Thru*, which had opened on Broadway in January of 1929. When that number was duplicated in the 1930 movie version of *Follow Thru* (see Chapter 4), some filmgoers might have thought "I Want to Be Bad" was inspired by "Turn On the Heat."

Gaynor and Farrell follow the big splash with the more conventional love duet of "If I Had a Talking Picture of You," for which they are joined by a cadre of children adorned in wedding garb. Jack now knows that he must marry Molly, not Jane. Meanwhile, the gossip about Jack and Molly's alliance has been passed to Mrs. Cromwell, who orders the young woman to leave. Distraught, she gamely performs "I'm a Dreamer"—a subjective shot shows the tears in her eyes obscuring her view of the audience—but once off the stage she collapses, and her friends take her back to New York.

The next morning, Jack wonders why Molly left so abruptly and, while gazing at a photograph of her, promises that he will win her for good. Her "reply," which animates the image in the photo, is "You've Got Me Pickin' Petals Off of Daisies." Back in their apartment, Bee tries to cheer Molly up with a comic rendition of "It's Great to Be Necked," sung as "It's Great to Be Necht on a Braw Brecht Moonlicht Necht" in parody of the Scottish singer Harry Lauder. Molly not only fails to get the joke, but she spurns Jack when he shows up begging for another chance Bee wants to know why she's kicked him out. "He asked me to marry him,"

Molly sniffles. "Well, what the hell are you crying about?" snaps the soubrette, using some of the profanity that was a surprisingly casual part of the nascent sound cinema. Then Molly realizes that she's left her diary in the rented home in Southampton and, fearing that Jack will find it, rushes for a train. Bee, Eric and Eddie follow in the Swede's jalopy. Fortunately, it is Mrs. Cromwell, not Jack, who finds the book. Realizing that Molly's intentions toward Jack are honorable, she blesses their marriage.

Sunnyside Up may seem archaic even to the most forgiving film historians—especially ones who notice the shadow of a microphone, dangling from a boom, that travels with Brendel, White and Richardson during their footage in Eric's moving car. But, along with films like *Applause*, *The Love Parade* and *The Dance of Life*, this picture nudged the musical toward the cinematic freedom it eventually would capture. One commentator claimed *Sunnyside Up* was "among the year's leaders in finding out how sound and action can combine on the screen in a special form of its own."[14] In a poll sponsored by the *Chicago Tribune* and the *New York Daily News*, the film was cited as the most enjoyable production of 1929.[15] It grossed more than $2 million.

Despite some snickers about how much Gaynor and Farrell sounded alike, they helped to make "Sunnyside Up," "I'm a Dreamer, Aren't We All?" and "If I Had a Talking Picture of You" solid song hits. The latter two were covered by Paul Whiteman and His orchestra, among others, and "Turn On the Heat" was further popularized on disc by Earl Burtnett and His Biltmore Hotel Orchestra. Many critics raved over the antics of the diminutive (4 foot 10½) White, who would spend the next two years as a Fox regular and then work on and off in pictures before her death in an auto accident. But studio executives, anxious over the reception accorded their high-profile stars in the sound medium, had to smile widest over comments like those of Richard Watts, Jr., in the *New York Herald Tribune*: "Miss Gaynor's voice reveals a baby treble that is hardly as poetic as we had hoped for, but it is not long before its unaffected honesty recaptures all of her pantomimic charm. ... [It] is an enormous asset to any motion picture."[16]

Gaynor and Farrell could now safely proceed with their careers as sound-era stars. "We were lucky with that picture," recalled David Butler.

> Janet Gaynor had a lot of guts, that girl, to sing. She had never sung in her life before. ... [Farrell] had never sung before either. But I think the fact that sound was just coming in—I think we could get away with things like that. I think a lot of people got away with it.[17]

A SONG OF KENTUCKY

(Fox; November 10, 1929)

Director: Lewis Seiler. Associate Producer: Chandler Sprague. Scenario and Dialogue: Frederick Hazlitt Brennan. Story: Sidney Mitchell, Archie Gottler, Con Conrad. Photography: Charles G. Clarke. Editor: Carl Carruth. Sound: Frank MacKenzie. Assistant Director: Horace Hough. Art Director: William Darling. Costumes: Sophie Wachner. Running Time: 81 minutes.

Cast: Joseph Wagstaff (Jerry Reavis), Lois Moran (Lee Coleman), Dorothy Burgess (Nancy Morgan), Douglas Gilmore (Kane Pitcairn), Herman Bing (Jake Kleinschmidt), Hedda Hopper (Mrs. Coleman), Edwards Davis (Mr. Coleman), Bert Woodruff (Steve).

Songs/Musical Numbers: "A Night of Happiness" [Wagstaff], "Rhapsody" [Wagstaff on piano, orchestra], "Sitting by the Window" [Wagstaff] (Sidney Mitchell, Archie Gottler, Con Conrad).

For this romantic drama promoted as an "All-Talking Musical Movietone," Fox secured the services of Joseph Wagstaff (b. 1905?), a stage juvenile best known as the male lead in *Billie* (1928), the last of George M. Cohan's Broadway musical comedies. In the now-lost *A Song of Kentucky*, he was a successful songwriter who falls for a society beauty (Lois Moran) who has a promising colt entered in the Kentucky Derby. Dorothy Burgess, typecast after her important role in Fox's early all-talking hit *In Old Arizona*, was the "other woman." Douglas Gilmore, a dependable heavy of the period, was her partner in connivery.

The book, lyrics and music were contributed by the prolific Con Conrad, Sidney Mitchell and Archie Gottler. The trio not only furnished two songs for Wagstaff to sing and

play piano to, but also wrote a modern symphony called "Rhapsody" for him to play during a climactic concert. Moran's character has been estranged from Wagstaff after her colt has inexplicably lost the Derby, and she is about to marry Gilmore. But she hears the symphony and is reminded of the love she and the composer still share, and they happily reunite. The 11-minute sequence aimed the camera almost entirely on Moran in what the film's pressbook boasted was "the longest closeup ever made in all-talking motion pictures."

Director Lewis Seiler provided atmosphere for the big race in *A Song of Kentucky* by filming the real Kentucky Derby at Louisville's Churchill Downs in May of 1929. *The Film Daily* declared *A Song of Kentucky* "modest on plot, but built up with a musical background and skillful direction to the point of a soaking human interest wallop."[18]

THE BATTLE OF PARIS

(Paramount; November 30, 1929)

Director: Robert Florey. Screenplay: Gene Markey. Photography: George Folsey. Editor: Emma Hill. Sound: Edward Schebbehar. Running Time: 71 minutes.

Cast: Gertrude Lawrence (Georgie), Charles Ruggles (Zizi), Walter Petrie (Tony), Gladys Du Bois (Suzanne), Arthur Treacher (Harry), Joe King (Jack).

Songs: "Here Comes the Band Wagon" [Lawrence], "They All Fall in Love" [Lawrence, chorus] (Cole Porter); "What Makes My Baby Blue?" [Lawrence, men], "When I Am Housekeeping for You" [Lawrence, twice] (Dick Howard, Jay Gorney); "The Boys with the Little Red Drum" [men] (Gibson, Field); "Give Me the Moonlight, Give Me the Girl" [Ruggles, men] (Lew Brown, Albert Von Tilzer); "It's a Long Way to Tipperary" [Lawrence, chorus] (Jack Judge, Harry Williams); "Madelon" [men] (Louis Bousquet, Alfred Bryan, Camille Robert); "Mademoiselle from Armentières" ("Hinky Dinky Parlez Vous") [chorus, danced by Lawrence] (authorship uncertain); "Sous les Pontsch Paris" [Lawrence] (Jean Rodor, Vincent Scotto).

Disc: Box Office (number undetermined; bootleg LP; ST); Music Masters JJA-19767 (bootleg LP; ST).

The great British revue star Gertrude Lawrence (1898–1952) had one of her few stage disasters to thank for the pleasure of her first feature-film appearance. *Treasure Girl*, a musical comedy with a George and Ira Gershwin score, closed in early 1929 after only two months on Broadway, and Lawrence hung around New York hoping another job offer would come around before her return to London. The call came, not from a theatrical producer, but from Paramount, for a film called *The Gay Lady* to be made in Astoria on Long Island. Prior to release, the title was changed to *The Battle of Paris*, although a new name couldn't save what was labeled by one critic as practically a "floperetta."[19]

The Battle of Paris, poorly written by Gene Markey and indifferently directed by Robert Florey, was a musical comedy about a Paris nightclub singer who becomes the partner of a pickpocket (Charlie Ruggles) and then falls in love with one of his victims (Walter Petrie). She remains true to her beau, an American artist, despite his infidelity and the intrusion of the World War. Its filming, which had to be done almost entirely on the night shift because of the busy production schedule at Astoria, was marred by Florey's near walkout over the lackluster assignment. The director called the scenario "afflicted ... ridiculous ... stupid,"[20] and he "made the film the best I knew how but without any particular enthusiasm."[21] According to Florey, Lawrence didn't have much interest in the project, either, for when he asked her what she thought of the screenplay, he found that she had paid little attention to it, favoring instead the score and period costumes.[22]

The highlights indeed were in the music, for two of the four new songs—"Here Comes the Band Wagon" and "They All Fall in Love"—were the first written by Cole Porter for the big screen. The latter, reminiscent of its author's mischievous "Let's Do It," is sung by a mugging Lawrence in a cabaret conveniently filled with a chorus of Yank soldiers. But *Variety* called *The Battle of Paris* "perhaps the poorest picture to come out of a major studio this season and a terrible break for Gertrude Lawrence."[23]

Lawrence returned to Broadway for a triumphant performance in the Viennese comedy *Candle-Light*. She made only seven feature films in her remaining 23 years.

TANNED LEGS
(RKO; November 30, 1929)

Director: Marshall Neilan. Producer: William LeBaron. Associate Producer: Louis Serecky. Screenplay: Tom Geraghty. Story: George Hull. Photography: Leo Tover. Editor: Archie Marshek. Sound: John Tribby. Assistant Director: Ray McCarey. Art Director: Max Rée. Costumes: Max Rée. Dance Direction: Doris Eaton. Running Time: 68 minutes.

Cast: June Clyde (Peggy Reynolds), Arthur Lake (Bill), Sally Blane (Janet Reynolds), Allen Kearns (Roger), Nella Walker (Mrs. Reynolds), Albert Gran (Mr. Reynolds), Edmund Burns (Clinton Darrow), Dorothy Revier (Mrs. Lyons-King), Ann Pennington (Tootie), Lincoln Stedman (Pudgy), Helen Kaiser, Kay English (hosiery models), Doris Eaton and the Radio Pictures Beauty Chorus, Grady Sutton.

Songs: "Come On In" [Clyde, Eaton girls], "Love to Take a Lesson from You" [danced by chorus], "Tanned Legs" [Clyde, Pennington, chorus], "With You—With Me" [Clyde, Lake; reprised by Kearns, then by Clyde], "You're Responsible" [Pennington, Kearns; reprised as dance by Pennington] (Sidney Clare, Oscar Levant).

"Funny how sensible people do a lot of things at a summer resort that they wouldn't dream of doing at home," says an anonymous spectator to the inanities of *Tanned Legs*, a half-baked tale of the infidelities of the idle rich.

Top-billed June Clyde (1910?–1987) was a vaudeville and musical comedy trouper who reputedly was selected for the film because of her lovely legs. She was touted by RKO as "the Luckiest Girl in Hollywood." Clyde played pretty, prudish Peggy Reynolds, who is embarrassed at the way her father (Alfred Gran) is carrying on with a young widow (Dorothy Revier) and at the dalliance of her mother (Nella Walker) with a dapper artist (Allen Kearns). The artist's flapper girlfriend (Ann Pennington) isn't thrilled about this, either. Peggy's own sweetie (Arthur Lake) is no help, for his self-possessed response to Little Miss Fix-It's complaints about her folks is this: "Never mind them ... will you marry me?"

The musical numbers are, plot-wise, rehearsals for the resort population's important "orphans' benefit." But that climactic bash, and this mediocre little picture, end up in a mess as Peggy is accidentally shot by her sister (Sally Blane, in a role initially intended for Marceline Day), who had intended her bullet for a crumb (Edmund Burns) who is blackmailing her over some incriminating love letters. Peggy, afflicted merely with a flesh wound, finds the strength to berate her parents for their childish carryings-on.

The Oscar Levant–Sidney Clare songs are mediocre, although there is peppy dancing by Pennington and Clyde, plus the rare film appearance of Kearns (1895–1956), a popular Broadway leading man (*Funny Face, Girl Crazy*) whose character turns out to be the hero. "The whole," frowned *The New York Times* at director Marshall Neilan's sorry effort, "is unimaginatively directed, being very much like the senior play at high school, with sound."[24]

LUCKY IN LOVE
(Pathé; December 13, 1929)

Director: Kenneth Webb. Dialogue Director: James Seymour. Producer: Robert T. Kane. Screenplay: Gene Markey. Photography: Philip Tannura, Harry Stradling. Editor: Edward Pfitzenmeier. Sound: V. S. Ashdown, J. A. Delaney. Art Director: Clark Robinson. Musical Director: Sacha Bunchuk. Running Time: 76 minutes.

Cast: Morton Downey (Michael O'More), Betty Lawford (Lady Mary Cardigan), Colin Keith-Johnston (Captain Brian Fitzroy), Halliwell Hobbes (Earl of Balkerry), J. M. Kerrigan (Connors), Edward McNamara (Tim O'More), Richard Taber (Paddy), Mary Murray (Kate), Mackenzie Ward (Cyril), Louis Sorin (Abe Feinberg), Sonia Karlov (Lulu Bellew), Tyrrell Davis (Potts), Elizabeth Murray (landlady).

Songs [all by Downey]: "For the Likes o' You and Me," "Love Is a Dreamer," "When They Sing 'The Wearin' of the Green' in Syncopated Blues" (Bud Green, Sam H. Stept).

Disc: RCA Victor 22048 (Downey/"Love Is a Dreamer"/"When They Sing 'The Wearin' of the Green'..."/78).

The stocky, round-faced tenor Morton Downey hardly looked like a movie idol, which didn't prevent RKO from casting him in *Syncopation* and Pathé doing the same for *Mother's*

Boy (see Chapter 3). Downey's third musical was *Lucky in Love*, another sentimental comedy-drama. It contained only three songs but at least avoided the habitual backstage setting.

Downey played an American youth who works as a stable boy for an impoverished earl in Ireland. After nearly killing a rakish rival for the affections of the earl's lovely daughter (Betty Lawford), the lad flees to the United States to make a career with a prosperous department store. On these shores, he encounters his lost love, who had left Ireland to escape the villain. When the hero is dispatched to the Emerald Isle on business, the lovers cross the ocean to get married on familiar soil. The reviews were unenthusiastic: "This mawkish effusion ... amateurishly performed ... features Morton Downey, whose deplorable performance should be the despair of any audience," wrote *The New York Times*.[25]

The first three of Downey's pictures were filmed in New York, but after he made *Lucky in Love*, Pathé asked the singer to come West for more movie work. But Downey preferred to live on the East Coast, where he was making more than $4,000 a week in nightclubs and radio shows. Not wanting to give up that income, Downey asked to be released from his contract.[26] Aside from a bit as "Freddie the Tenor" in the 1930 Paramount non-musical *The Devil's Holiday*, Downey made only one more feature-film appearance, singing a song in Universal's Olsen-and-Johnson musical horror comedy *Ghost Catchers* (1944).

HOT FOR PARIS
(Fox; December 22, 1929)

Director: Raoul Walsh. Adaptation and Continuity: Charles J. McGuirk. Dialogue: William K. Wells. Story: Raoul Walsh. Photography: Charles Van Enger. Editor: Jack Dennis. Sound: George Leverett. Assistant Director: Archibald Buchanan. Art Direction: David Hall, Ben Carré. Costumes: Sophie Wachner. Running Time: 71 minutes (sound version; also released as silent).

Cast: Victor McLaglen (John Patrick Duke), Fifi D'Orsay (Fifi Dupré), El Brendel (Axel Olson), Polly Moran (Polly), Lennox Pawle (Mr. Pratt), August Tollaire (Papa Gouset), George Fawcett (ship's captain),

Frank Albertson lends an ear to the melodies of "Whispering" Jack Smith in *The Big Party*.

Charles Judels (Charlot Gouset), Yola D'Avril (Babette Dupré), Eddie Dillon (ship's cook), Rosita Marstini (Fifi's mother), Agostino Borgato (Fifi's father), Anita Murray (Mimi), Dave Vallos (Monsieur Furrier), Raoul Paoli (Raoul).

Songs: "Cuckoo Song" [Brendel], "If You Want to See Paree" [D'Orsay], "I'm the Duke of Kak-i-ak" [McLaglen], "Sing Your Little Folk Song," "Sweet Nothings of Love" [D'Orsay, twice] (Edgar Leslie, Walter Donaldson).

To cap its busy musical year, Fox reunited the director, costar and chief clown of *The Cock-Eyed World*—Raoul Walsh, Victor McLaglen and El Brendel, respectively—and put them in a similar tale of raw and rowdy overseas adventure.

In the now-lost *Hot for Paris*, McLaglen played John Patrick Duke, a roughneck first mate on a windjammer plying its trade between Sydney and Havre. He wins a cool million on a French horse race, but unknowingly thwarts the efforts of the lottery officials to inform him of his good fortune. He thinks the gendarmes

are after him for one of his frequent barroom brawls during his last stop at Havre. Brendel played his seafaring pal. Vaudeville import Fifi D'Orsay, who recently had impressed moviegoers in Will Rogers' *They Had to See Paris* (1929), was the woman who seduces Duke. He tells her that he's "a bit of driftwood on the sea of life"; she calls him her "Beeg Boy."

D'Orsay sang two of the five Walter Donaldson–Edgar Leslie songs. One of the others, "I'm the Duke of Kak-i-ak," was handed to McLaglen for what was an unremarkable debut as a jazz singer. *Hot for Paris* was lauded as a "riotous, colorful comedy" by *Motion Picture* magazine,[27] but its grosses paled next to those of *What Price Glory?* and *The Cock-Eyed World*.

THE BIG PARTY
(Fox; February 23, 1930)

Director: John Blystone. Screenplay: Harlan Thompson. Photography: George Schneiderman. Editor: Edwin Robbins. Sound: W. W.

Lindsay. Assistant Director: Jasper Blystone. Art Director: Jack Schulte. Costumes: Sophie Wachner. Running Time: 60 minutes (sound version; also released as silent).

Cast: Sue Carol (Flo Jenkins), Dixie Lee (Kitty Collins), Frank Albertson (Jack Hunter), Walter Catlett (Mr. Goldfarb), Richard Keene (Eddie Perkins), "Whispering" Jack Smith (Billy Greer), Douglas Gilmore (Allen Weatherby), Charles Judels (Dupuy), Ilka Chase (Mrs. Dupuy), Elizabeth Patterson (Mrs. Goldfarb), Dorothy Brown (Virginia Gates).

Songs [all by Lee or Smith]: "Bluer Than Blue Over You" (Harlan Thompson, William Kernell); "Good for Nothing but Love" (William Kernell); "I'm Climbing Up a Rainbow" (Harry Pease, Edward G. Nelson); "Nobody Knows but Rosie, but Oh! What Rosie Knows" (Joseph McCarthy, James F. Hanley).

Dixie Lee's roles were secondary to those of her friend Sue Carol in *Why Leave Home?* and *William Fox Movietone Follies of 1929*, but when Fox put the two women in *The Big Party*, a minor farce about gold-digging shopgirls, the lower-profile actress stole the show. "They hand it to her on a red-hot platter," exalted *Photoplay*.[28]

Lee (1911–1952), a vivacious blonde, appeared as Kitty Collins, a singing department-store clerk who is canned for insulting a customer. With the help of Flo Jenkins (Carol), she gets a job at a ritzy gown shop owned by two bickering fools (Walter Catlett, Charles Judels) who are constantly in trouble with their wives for their flirtations with young women. Kitty's dealings with an amorous and moneyed buyer (Douglas Gilmore) put furrows in the brow of her boyfriend (Frank Albertson), but in the end, the heroine gives up her truncated life of luxury for simpler pleasures.

Lee, who would give up her career in the early '30s after marrying Bing Crosby, presented three songs in the film. Two more were presented by baritone "Whispering" Jack Smith (1899–1950). Smith earned his nickname with an intimate half-singing, half-speaking style that was necessitated by vocal injuries incurred by an exploding gas shell during World War I service. By the mid–1920s he was a nightclub sensation, with a following in Europe as large as in the United States. His biggest hit was "Me and My Shadow" (1927). *The Big Party* gave

Smith his first part in a feature film. Tall and slim but lacking in matinee-idol looks, he was sniped at by critics for not photographing well.

The top-billed Sue Carol had an embarrassingly paltry part, as Fox had stopped boosting her as a box-office attraction. After her contract with the studio lapsed, she enjoyed a minor comeback with RKO (see *Check and Double Check*), but soon she would be promoting the acting talents of others, as an influential Hollywood agent, instead of using her own.

SONG O' MY HEART
(Fox; March 11, 1930)

Director: Frank Borzage. Continuity: Sonya Levien. Story and Dialogue: Tom Barry. Photography: Chester Lyons, Al Brick. Grandeur Camera: J. O. Taylor. Editor: Margaret V. Clancey. Sound: George P. Costello. Assistant Director: Lewis Borzage. Art Director: Harry Oliver. Costumes: Sophie Wachner. Running Time: 85 minutes (sound version; also released as silent).

Cast: John McCormack (Sean O'Carolan), Alice Joyce (Mary Lenehan), Maureen O'Sullivan (Eileen Lenehan), Tommy Clifford (Tad Lenehan), J. M. Kerrigan (Peter Conlon), John Garrick (Fergus O'Donnell), Edwin Schneider (Vincent Glennon), J. Farrell MacDonald (Dan Rafferty), Effie Ellsler (Mona), Emily Fitzroy (Elizabeth Kennedy), André De Segurola (Guido), Edward Martindel (Dennis Fullerton).

Songs [all by McCormack]: "A Fairy Story by the Fire" (Angela Campbell-MacInnes, Oscar Merikanto); "I Feel You Near Me" (Joseph McCarthy, James F. Hanley); "I Hear You Calling Me" (Harold Herford, Charles Marshall); "Ireland, Mother Ireland" (P. J. O'Reilly, Raymond Loughborough); "Just for Today" (Sybil F. Partridge, Blanche Ebert Seaver); "Little Boy Blue" (Eugene Field, Ethelbert Nevin); "Luoghi Sereni e Cari" (Stefano Donaudy); "A Pair of Blue Eyes" (William Kernell); "Plaisir d'Amour" (J. P. Claris de Florian, Giovanni Martini); "The Rose of Tralee" (Charles W. Glover, C. Mordaunt Spencer); "Then You'll Remember Me" (Alfred Bunn, Michael William Balfe); "All Mein Gedanken," "Kitty, My Love, Will You Marry Me?" "The Magpie's Nest" (trad.).

Fox's *Song o' My Heart* was ballyhooed as the talkie debut of the great singer John McCormack, but it also brought the lovely Maureen O'Sullivan to the big screen.

Disc: McCormack 5-2707/8 (privately pressed LP).

When one of the world's greatest concert singers consented to make his first film, it was not without the yield of a sizable chunk of William Fox's money. In the spring of 1929, after some urging from studio production chief Winfield Sheehan, the famed Irish tenor John McCormack signed with Fox to make a picture for which he'd be paid an unheard-of (at least for a newcomer to Hollywood) $500,000 for 10 weeks' work.

McCormack (1884–1945) was 45 years old when the filming of *Song o' My Heart* began in the fall of 1929. Tall and handsome, with a full head of wavy brown hair, he cut an imposing figure, although he was a good deal weightier than in his prime and his voice was thought by some to have lost some of its luster. But McCormack still had the power to thrill audi-

ences, and Fox considered it a major coup to land him, even at the high cost. The studio heavily promoted the film, which was shown in some theaters in 70mm. A Fox-concocted poll in *Photoplay* was headlined "Help John Mc-Cormack Select His Movietone Songs," although only one of the 24 songs on the published ballot made it into the picture, and that was the singer's most-loved melody, "I Hear You Calling Me."

Scripters Tom Barry and Sonya Levien turned in a rather conventional romantic story, but one that was considered well suited to the new star and his sentimentalist (*Seventh Heaven*) director, Frank Borzage. Sean O'Caro-lan, a music teacher in a quaint Irish village, long ago gave up a singing career because his heart was broken by his only sweetheart (Alice Joyce). Mary Lenehan had forsaken Sean to marry a much wealthier man, but he has left her by the time she returns to the village with her two children, teen-age daughter Eileen (Maureen O'Sullivan) and younger son Tad (Tommy Clifford). They live in the unhappy home of their cold-hearted spinster aunt (Emily Fitzroy). Filled with unspoken regret over her rejection of Sean, Mary is stirred when she hears him sing "Just for Today" and, later, "The Rose of Tralee." Sean is called to the United States to reactivate his career with a concert tour, but as he performs before an enthusiastic packed house in New York, the profoundly heartsick Mary dies back in Ireland, leaving Sean a letter asking him to care for her children. Eileen tells off the bossy aunt, and Sean encourages her marriage to the struggling architect (John Garrick) she loves. Sean triumphantly returns to his concert tour with little Tad in his charge.

After hiring McCormack, Fox and Borzage went to Ireland to seek out homegrown talent and extras; they came away with the 18-year-old O'Sullivan and 11-year-old Clifford. At a party at the Plaza Restaurant in Dublin, Borzage spotted future star O'Sullivan (b. 1911) sitting at an adjoining table. Although she had almost no previous acting experience, and had only just finished school, O'Sullivan and her fresh-faced beauty appealed so to Borzage that he immediately asked her to test for the film. She was a little intimidated—"well, naturally"—about being cast opposite a world-famous singer in her first movie, O'Sullivan recalled in a letter to the author: "But I was so happy and excited, that I did not dwell on that aspect of things. ... Mr. McCormack became my closest friend—he and his wonderful wife, Lily, and their children, Gwen and Cyril."[29]

Other than a couple of exteriors—including a scene filmed at McCormack's own Moore Abbey in which Sean sings "A Fairy Story by the Fire" to a group of children—*Song o' My Heart* was shot on a Fox soundstage. McCormack greatly enjoyed his time in Hollywood. A thatched cottage was built on the Fox lot as a dressing room, he enjoyed many rounds of tennis and golf, and he and his wife, Lily, quickly became a part of the social scene. The McCormacks even bought land on which to construct a small, custom-made house, which they named "San Patrizio." McCormack's one trouble was adapting himself to the script, for he disliked playing love scenes and would force their deletion. "I had to do too much lovemaking for too

many years in opera" was his simple reasoning.[30]

Happily for him, McCormack got to do much more singing than emoting in *Song o' My Heart*. He performed 14 songs, six of them during the lengthy "New York" concert sequence filmed in the Los Angeles Philharmonic Auditorium in May of 1929. Before 800 very willing extras who were paid $15 a head by Fox to listen, McCormack sang "Luoghi Sereni e Cari," "Little Boy Blue," "Plaisir d'Amour," "All Mein Gedanken," "Ireland, Mother Ireland" and, as an encore, "I Hear You Calling Me"—all while holding (for comfort's sake) his little booklet of lyrics. His longtime accompanist, Edwin Schneider, sat at the piano. Only three songs were written for the film. "A Pair of Blue Eyes" and "I Feel You Near Me" made the final cut; the title song, penned by Joseph McCarthy and James F. Hanley, was one of a handful of songs recorded but then deleted.

The reaction to *Song o' My Heart* was almost totally favorable. It opened in New York on March 11, 1930, to this enthusiastic response from *The Times'* Mordaunt Hall:

> Never has an audible film been recorded as flawlessly as this feature. The tone is subdued throughout, and when Mr. McCormack ... sings, a reason is offered for the melody. The story is charming and sensitive. ... The comedy is gentle and natural, really Irish. ... Considering that the hero of this adventure is no longer in his youth, it is a narrative suitable and adroitly handled. ... All the players do their share to make it a huge success. It is something from which a reporter bounds with glee to write about....[31]

Even the critic from *Motion Picture*, a magazine tailored for the more plebeian film fan, had nice things to say—in spite of himself.

> This expensive and much publicized John McCormack picture is charming. I hope you get the tone of surprise in which this comment is made. One had expected it to be soppy. One thought that John would be continually taking little children on his knee and singing them whimsical ditties. ... The thing has been handled deftly and with good taste. McCormack is at his best and the recording is the finest we have heard.[32]

Song o' My Heart, viewed nowadays, is tough sledding at times. The dialogue is delivered with frustrating slowness, even for an early–1930 release, and the ethnic comedy relief supplied by J. Farrell MacDonald and J. M. Kerrigan, as two bickering village curmudgeons, is beneath caricature. But McCormack is used well. He has little to do but sing, but his acting, kept to a minimum, does not disgrace him. Happily, the film does not fall into the trap of placing its non-romantic star into touchy "mush" scenes. Sean and Mary share a genuine fondness, even if their relationship is beyond repair, and as much as a viewer's sentimental side might long for a reunion, the drama carries a more realistic tone because there is none. There also is some imagination in the staging of the music. Early in the film, as Sean sings "Just for Today" in the choirloft of a church, the scene shifts outdoors as Mary walks alongside the building and hears Sean's voice, now slightly muffled as if coming from a distance. The variance in sound was supposedly McCormack's idea, accomplished despite the objections of the Fox engineers.[33] During the concert rendition of "Little Boy Blue," the static long shots of McCormack are punctuated periodically by a telling of the story suggested in the song, that of a little lad whose adventures with his toy soldiers and dog are interrupted by his passing. The final shot shows the playthings moored in cobwebs.

Song o' My Heart was enough of a hit that Fox wanted to make a second movie with McCormack. But the singer was now asking for $650,000, and negotiations broke off.[34] McCormack appeared in only one other film, singing three songs in an extended cameo as himself in *Wings of the Morning* (1937), a British romantic drama in Technicolor that starred Henry Fonda and Annabella.

Supposedly "lost" for decades, *Song o' My Heart* came to light in two versions. The John McCormack Society of Greater Kansas City spent 15 years trying to track down a print, and finally, with help from the historian Miles Kreuger, one was unearthed from the Fox vaults and restored for two sold-out screenings at the New York City Museum of Modern Art in 1971. A curious hybrid, the print was silent and subtitled except for the musical sequences, snatches of dialogue and an instrumental score. Although the subtitles were in English, this version may have been intended for theaters with foreign audiences. A complete dialogue print eventually surfaced. The author viewed

both versions for this book and, although some accounts indicate that McCormack's concert-hall renderings of "Plaisir d'Amour" and "All Mein Gedanken" are only in the hybrid version, the music is the same in each. However, there may be alternate prints out there somewhere.

MONTANA MOON
(MGM; March 20, 1930)

Director: Malcolm St. Clair. Story and Continuity: Sylvia Thalberg, Frank Butler. Dialogue: Joe Farnham. Photography: William Daniels. Editors: Carl L. Pierson, Leslie F. Wilder. Sound: Douglas Shearer, Paul Neal. Art Director: Cedric Gibbons. Costumes: Adrian. Running Time: 88 minutes (sound version; also released as silent).

Cast: Joan Crawford (Joan Prescott), John Mack Brown (Larry Carrigan), Dorothy Sebastian (Elizabeth Prescott), Ricardo Cortez (Jeffrey Pelham), Benny Rubin ("The Doctor"), Cliff Edwards (Froggy), Karl Dane (Hank), Lloyd Ingraham (Mr. Prescott).

Songs: "Happy Cowboy" [ranch hands, twice], "The Moon Is Low" [Brown; reprised by Crawford, then by Edwards and ranch hands, then by Edwards] (Arthur Freed, Nacio Herb Brown); "Montana Call" [Crawford, ranch hands], "Trailin' in Old Montan'" [Edwards, Rubin, partygoers; reprised by Edwards, Rubin, ranch hands] (Clifford Grey, Herbert Stothart).

Disc: Columbia 2169-D (Edwards/"The Moon Is Low"/78); Curtain Calls 100/23 (bootleg LP; ST).

A romantic comedy? A drama? A Western? A musical? *Montana Moon* was some of each, but what it wasn't was very good. Despite the drawing power of Joan Crawford—and for music lovers, four songs—the Mal St. Clair–directed film disappointed at the box office.

A viewing prompts one to blame the no-chemistry teaming of Crawford (1906–1977) with Johnny Mack Brown (1904–1974)—here billed as "John," for MGM was pushing him as a conventional leading man despite his thick Alabama accent. She's Joan Prescott, an impulsive socialite educated in the East; he's Larry Carrigan, an aw-shucks hand on her daddy's Montana ranch. Despite his observation that they're as different as "velvet and cactus," the two get married after the first half hour, which leaves plenty of time for Joan to enjoy a fling—and a mean tango—with her city-slicker ex-lover (Ricardo Cortez). He has been hanging around pretending to romance Joan's square sister (Dorothy Sebastian). Meanwhile, Benny Rubin (as a gabby dentist), Cliff Edwards (with uke), and the declining Karl Dane make mirth and music. At the end, the estranged Joan prepares to return to New York, but Larry wins her back by "holding up" her train. The one hit song to emerge from the film was "The Moon Is Low." It is sung at different times by Brown, Crawford and Edwards, but it was recorded by George Olsen and His Orchestra.

Crawford's flapper image needed an overhaul, and soon she would enter her "I vant to be Garbo" phase. She doesn't sing too well here and is not pleasingly photographed by the usually reliable William Daniels. "Taking it all in all," noted Mordaunt Hall of *The New York Times*, "the most pleasing features of this production are Miss Crawford's camel's-hair coat and her jodhpur riding outfit."[35]

DANGEROUS NAN MCGREW

(Paramount; June 20, 1930)

Director: Malcolm St. Clair. Screenplay: Paul Gerard Smith, Pierre Collings. Story: Charles Beahan, Garrett Fort. Photography: George Folsey. Editor: Helene Turner. Sound: Edwin Schabbehar, C. A. Tuthill. Running Time: 70 minutes.

Cast: Helen Kane (Nan McGrew), Victor Moore (Doc Foster), James Hall (Bob Dawes), Stuart Erwin (Eustace Macy), Frank Morgan (Muldoon), Roberta Robinson (Clara Benson), Louise Closser Hale (Mrs. Benson), Allan Forrest (Godfrey Crofton), John Hamilton (Grant), Robert Milash (sheriff).

Songs: "Dangerous Nan McGrew" [Kane], "I. O. U. (I Owe You)" [Kane, twice; reprised by band] (Don Hartman, Al Goodhart); "Aw! C'mon, Watta Ya Got to Lose?" [Kane] (Leo Robin, Richard A. Whiting).

Disc: RCA Victor 22407 (Kane/"Dangerous Nan McGrew"/"I. O. U. [I Owe You]"/78).

Previously a second lead, Helen Kane was top-lined by Paramount in the mediocre comedy with songs *Dangerous Nan McGrew*. It was the kind of flop that was fast sinking the movie career of "The Boop-Boop-a-Doop Girl"—and driving audiences away from all musicals.

Nan is the star of a medicine show owned by her traveling companion, Doc Foster (Victor Moore). In the Canadian Northwest, they get mixed up with Muldoon (Frank Morgan), a bank robber turned killer for whom a $10,000 bounty has been offered. At the climactic carnival, for which both Doc and Muldoon come dressed as Buster Brown(!), Doc and Nan thwart the villains' plan. They unmask Mr. Big as the suitor (Allan Forrest) of the ingénue (Roberta Robinson), who is reunited with her mountie lover (James Hall). Doc claims the reward and Dangerous Nan ends up in the arms of a rich boob (Stuart Erwin, 1903–1967) who has spent the entire movie carrying around a saxophone he can hardly play. One of the three songs is the title number, in which Kane tries to convince us she is so tough that she picks her teeth with a carving knife, among other unsavory habits.

Dangerous Nan McGrew was the first talkie for Moore, one of Broadway's greatest comedians, but the screenplay by Paul Gerard Smith and Pierre Collings paints his character as a bumbling, helpless fool who is as artificial as the unconvincing "wintry" sets that surround him. Moore would fare better in *Heads Up*, his only other film during this period.

The Film Daily was being overly kind to *Dangerous Nan McGrew* by calling it an "only fairly diverting comedy."[36] If you failed to catch this one on the Late, Late Show, you didn't miss a thing.

PARDON MY GUN

(Pathé; June 29, 1930)

Director: Robert De Lacy. Producer: E. B. Derr. Scenario and Dialogue: Hugh Cummings. Story: Betty Scott. Photography: Edward Snyder. Editor: Fred Allen. Sound: Ben Winkler, Homer Ackerman. Musical Director: Josiah Zuro. Running Time: 62 minutes.

Cast: Sally Starr (Mary Martin), George Duryea [Tom Keene] (Ted Duncan), Mona Ray (Peggy Martin), Lee Moran (Jeff), Robert Edeson (Pa Martin), Frank MacFarlane (Hank), Tom MacFarlane (Tom), Harry Woods

(Cooper), Stompie ("Lightnin'"), Lew Meehan (Denver), Ethan Laidlaw (Tex), Harry Watson, Al "Rubberlegs" Norman, Ida May Chadwick, Abe Lyman and His Band.

Songs/Musical Numbers: "A Cottage for Sale" [Lyman band] (Larry Conley, Willard Robison); "Cowboy Song" [cowhands' band] (Monty Collins, Henry Sullivan); "Deep Down South" [Ray; reprised by Lyman band, then danced by Stompie]; "Goodnight Ladies" [barn dancers] (Harry Williams, Egbert Van Alstyne); "Man from the South" [Lyman band] (Rube Bloom, Harry Woods); "Milenberg Joys" [Lyman band, danced by Norman] (Leon Rappolo, Paul Mares, Ferdinand "Jelly Roll" Morton); "Moanin' for You" [Lyman band, danced by Chadwick] (Edmund Goulding, Dan Daugherty); "St. Louis Blues" [danced by Stompie] (W. C. Handy); "Twelfth Street Rag" [Lyman band] (Euday L. Bowman); medley of "Home on the Range" and "Polly Wolly Doodle" [Frank MacFarlane] (both trad.).

Movie-music historians generally are disinclined to document musical "B" Westerns. Maybe it's because there are so many of those films to chronicle, or because their songs are so often detached from their plots. *Pardon My Gun,* a comic oater from Pathé, is an early example of the musical "B." None of its 10 numbers are integrated into the story, but a barn dance sequence in which all but two are presented makes up nearly half of the hourlong film. The volume of music merits this modest programmer mention here.

The barn dance is mainly a showcase for Abe Lyman and his band, who play six songs. Most notable is a rendition of "Twelfth Street Rag," which shows off the solo talents of various members, starting with Lyman himself on the drums. Al "Rubberlegs" Norman and Ida Mae Chadwick dance comically to "Milenberg Joys" and "Moanin' for You," respectively. "A Cottage for Sale" is sung by the band's vocalist, Phil Neely. The only two main cast members to sing are Mona Ray, a diminutive comedienne, and young Frank MacFarlane, who yodels to his own banjo. Frank and real-life twin brother Tom display their trick riding and roping skills later in the film.

The thin plot is climaxed by a thrilling relay race between the ranches of the virtuous Martin family, whose steed is ridden by hand-some cowhand Ted Duncan (George Duryea), and their villainous neighbor (Harry Woods). Duncan wins the race, and thereby the hand of comely Mary Martin (top-billed Sally Starr). Duryea (1898–1963) would change his name to Tom Keene shortly after *Pardon My Gun* and enjoy a few years as a "B" Western headliner, primarily for RKO.

LOVE AMONG THE MILLIONAIRES
(Paramount; July 5, 1930)

Director: Frank Tuttle. Adaptation: Grover Jones, William Conselman. Dialogue: Herman J. Mankiewicz. Story: Kenne Thompson. Photography: Allen Siegler. Sound: M. M. Paggi. Running Time: 75 minutes.

Cast: Clara Bow (Pepper Whipple), Stanley Smith (Jerry Hamilton), Skeets Gallagher (Boots McGee), Stuart Erwin (Clicker Watson), Mitzi Green (Penelope Whipple), Charles Sellon (Pop Whipple), Theodore von Eltz (Jordan), Claude King (Mr. Hamilton), Barbara Bennett (Virginia Hamilton).

Songs: "Believe It or Not, I've Found My Man" [Bow, Smith], "Don't Be a Meanie" [Green, Gallagher, Erwin], "Love Among the Millionaires" [Bow, Smith; reprised by Gallagher, Erwin], "Rarin' to Go" [Bow; reprised by Green], "That's Worth While Waiting For" [Bow] (L. Wolfe Gilbert, Abel Baer).

After her triumphant rendition of "True to the Navy" in *Paramount on Parade* (see Chapter 10), Clara Bow was assigned by Paramount to her only full-length appearance in a musical. Despite snide talk about her mike fright and Brooklyn foghorn, Bow (1905–1965) was still a very popular, and very bankable, performer. But in order to halt the gradual career decline that had already set in, she needed films that would enhance her star status, not merely exploit it. Instead, she was handed formula-bound, innocuous junk like *Love Among the Millionaires.*

Its story is the typical variation on "Cinderella," its songs are forgettable, and the supporting comics are annoying. Bow plays Pepper Whipple, a waitress at her father's café, which is a favorite hangout of nearby railroadmen. The only rivals for her affections are telegrapher

A rich railroad heir (Stanley Smith) petitions his dad (Claude King) for permission to marry a lowly waitress (Clara Bow) in Paramount's *Love Among the Millionaires*.

Clicker Watson (Stuart Erwin) and railroad detective Boots McGee (Skeets Gallagher), who are both so stupid that they have each purchased half of the same automobile. Fortunately, Pepper falls for intelligent and handsome brakeman Jerry Hamilton (Stanley Smith), who is hiding his pedigree as the son of the railroad company president. Jerry soon reveals his secret and the two become engaged. Jerry brings Pepper to the family mansion, but the senior Hamilton's displeasure over the pairing prompts her to play a mean drunk at a society party so that Jerry will be embarrassed enough to end their relationship. But he sees through her ruse, and the budding friendship of her father (Charles Sellon) and his father (Claude King) allows Pepper to realize that she belongs with Jerry.

Little Mitzi Green (1920–1969), who plays Bow's sister, gives the film some life with a rendition of "Rarin' to Go" that sounds vaguely like an imitation of Bow, but the star herself does not emerge unscathed. She seems fairly comfortable with the dialogue, and her voice lacks the rough edge apparent in her earliest talkies (*The Wild Party, Dangerous Curves, The Saturday Night Kid*). But her singing voice is only passable, although she goes at her four songs with an energy that belies her deficiencies in tone and range.

But what really does fail Bow in *Love Among the Millionaires* is her casting as a patently virtuous woman. Not only was the role a sharp contrast to the rowdy flapper types that had made Bow popular, it was patently unconvincing to a public that was hearing constant rumors about her hyperactive off-screen sex life. Commented *Variety*'s "Sime" Silverman: "It will call for a lot of faith from the Clara Bow admirers to accept her in this kind of a part, the sweet wishy washy thing, after the bum publicity she's been getting. Either Paramount might chop off that kind of publicity or give Miss Bow roles that will fit it much more happily."[37]

LET'S GO NATIVE

(Paramount; August 16, 1930)

Director: Leo McCarey. Scenario and Dialogue: George Marion Jr., Percy Heath. Photography: Victor Milner. Montages: Slavko Vorkapich. Editor: Merrill White. Sound: Harry D. Mills. Dance Direction: David Bennett. Running Time: 75 minutes.

Cast: Jack Oakie (Voltaire McGinnis), Jeanette MacDonald (Joan Wood), Skeets Gallagher (Jerry, the island king), James Hall (Wally Wendell), William Austin (Basil Pistol), Kay Francis (Constance Cooke), David Newell (Chief Officer Williams), Charles Sellon (Grandpa Wendell), Eugene Pallette (Deputy Sheriff "Careful" Cuthbert), Rafael Storm (Argentine), Virginia Bruce (Grandpa Wendell's secretary), Pat Harmon (policeman), Charlie Hall, Earl Askam, Harry Bernard (movers), E. H. Calvert, Grady Sutton (diners), John Elliott (captain), Oscar Smith (cook), The King's Men [voices only], Iris Adrian.

Songs: "I've Gotta Yen for You" [Oakie, Francis], "It Seems to Be Spring" [MacDonald, Hall], "Joe Jazz" [Oakie, danced by chorus], "Let's Go Native" [The King's Men; reprised by Oakie, Austin, band, danced by chorus], "My Mad Moment" [MacDonald, Hall, The King's Men] (George Marion, Jr., Richard A. Whiting).

Let's Go Native, a bizarre mix of *The Admirable Crichton* and *Gilligan's Island,* concerns a group of not-so-kindred souls shipwrecked on a tropical island where a mug from Brooklyn lords it over a bevy of beautiful women. The film touted in trade ads as "more fun than a circus" boasted a typical Paramount cast of 1930: overworked comedians Jack Oakie and Skeets Gallagher, bland juveniles James Hall and David Newell, "other woman" Kay Francis, silly-ass William Austin, rotund Eugene Pallette and grumpy codger Charles Sellon. One half expects Helen Kane to show up; instead, a miscast Jeanette MacDonald does her best to appear comfortable amid all the crazy inanity. Could the talented Leo McCarey really have directed this "ludicrous audible-film hodgepodge"?[38]

Poor Jeanette plays Joan Wood, a costumer who loses her shop because all of her money is tied up in a Buenos Aires–bound musical revue.

She is in love with Wally Wendell (Hall), who has been disinherited by his soap-czar grandfather because he won't marry the daughter (Francis) of a business rival. Joan, bound for South America via steamship to escape her creditors, secures Wally employment on the same craft, but he ends up in the hold stoking coal with his friend Basil (Austin) and taxi driver Voltaire McGinnis (Oakie). A storm capsizes the ship and, in a miraculous coincidence, propels the movie's five principals to the isle ruled by Jerry, a glib ex–New Yorker (Gallagher). Jerry has educated the "natives" in Brooklynese and discovered a wealth of "ersters" boasting giant-sized pearls. There's plenty of oil, too. "It was one of the Virgin Islands—but it drifted," is the monarch's wry explanation of his heaven on earth.

The picture is two-thirds over by the time trying-too-hard scripters George Marion, Jr. and Percy Heath begin to explore the tropical aspects of the story, and the characters' stay on the island is cut short when Wally's grandpa (Sellon) shows up. Joan has bought the island from Jerry in exchange for her theatrical costumes, which delights the old man enough to consent to her marriage to Wally. Joan then sells the island to the old man for $1 million, but a sudden earthquake jars the island, which soon disappears below the ocean. By this time, the cast has scurried to safety (and assignments in better movies).

Let's Go Native contains the sort of forced hipness that dates this musical comedy much more badly than any so-called "camp" operetta. Perceived as a mini-time capsule, this very broad film is periodically fun to watch. The jokey Richard Whiting–George Marion, Jr. songs are OK, but they're inadequately presented. The title number, sung by Oakie and Austin, is capably backed by an unbilled jazz band and danced to by a couple of dozen shapely islanders. But an over-directed shipboard number, "Joe Jazz," culminates in a dizzying array of unnecessary intercuts of Oakie and chorus girls. Even worse is "It Seems to Be Spring," a "dress rehearsal" sequence in which footage of real livestock and costumed frolicing "bears" alternates with MacDonald-and-Hall love stuff before the two actors are shown frozen into human snowmen. Maybe they should have stayed that way.

In Cecil B. DeMille's astounding *Madame Satan*, Kay Johnson (right) sees Lillian Roth as an obstacle to marital happiness with Reginald Denny.

MADAM SATAN

(MGM; September 20, 1930)

Director-Producer: Cecil B. DeMille. Screenplay: Jeanie Macpherson. Dialogue: Gladys Unger, Elsie Janis. Photography: Harold Rosson. Editor: Anne Bauchens. Sound: Douglas Shearer, J. K. Brock. Assistant Directors: Mitchell Leisen, Cullen Tate. Art Directors: Cedric Gibbons, Mitchell Leisen. Costumes: Adrian. Dance Direction: Le Roy Prinz. Running Time: 116 minutes.

Cast: Kay Johnson (Angela Brooks), Reginald Denny (Bob Brooks), Lillian Roth (Trixie), Roland Young (Jimmy Wade), Elsa Peterson (Martha), Boyd Irwin (captain), Wallace MacDonald (first mate), Wilfred Lucas (Roman senator), Tyler Brooke (Romeo), Albert Conti (empire officer), Lotus Thompson (Eve), Vera Marsh (Call of the Wild), Martha Sleeper (fish girl), Doris McMahon (Water), Marie Valli (Confusion), Julanne Johnston (Miss Conning Tower), Earl Askam (pirate), Betty Francisco (Little Rolls Riding Hood), Ynez Seabury (Babo), Countess De Liguoro (Spain), Katherine Irving (Spider Girl), Aileen Ransom (Victory), Theodore Kosloff (Electricity), Jack King (Herman), Edward Prinz (Biff), Katherine DeMille (King Henry's wife), Maine Geary, Allan Lane, Kenneth Gibson, Youcca Troubetzkoy, Henry Stockbridge, June Nash, Mary Carlisle, Mary McAllister, Dorothy Dehn, Louis Natheaux, Ella Hall, Edwards Davis, Kasha Haroldi, Natalie Visart, Vera Gordon, Natalie Storm, Elvira Lucianti, Marguerita Swope, Dorothy Vernon, Lorimer Johnson, John Byron, Abe Lyman and His Band.

Songs/Musical Numbers: "All I Know Is You Are in My Arms" [Denny, Johnson], "Auction Scene" ("The Girl Auction") [Young, partygoers], "Live and Love Today" [Peterson], "Low Down" [Roth, King, Prinz] (Elsie Janis,

Jack King); "The Cat Walk" [partygoers], "Meet Madam" [Johnson, partygoers; reprised by Johnson at piano], "This Is Love" [Johnson at piano], "We're Going Somewhere" [partygoers] (Clifford Grey, Herbert Stothart); "Ballet Mechanique" [danced by Kosloff, chorus] (Herbert Stothart); "It Ain't Gonna Rain No Mo'" [Denny, Young] (Wendell Hall); "May Heaven Forgive Thee" [excerpt from opera *Martha*] [Johnson] (Friedrich Flotow); "Where Do We Go from Here?" [Lyman band] (Howard Johnson, Percy Wenrich).

Video: MGM-UA (cassette/laserdisc).

"Don't try to believe it," was *Photoplay*'s perplexed introduction to its review of Cecil B. DeMille's second talkie—and only musical.[39] DeMille's films were nothing if not audacious, but *Madam Satan* marked a new high in moxie for the flashy, hit-making director. He transformed Jeanie Macpherson's risqué story about an upper-class love triangle into what *The Film Daily* called "a typical DeMille orgy of spectacular settings and costumes with 'hot' lines that kill it for the family trade."[40] But this is exactly what has made this excessive but fascinating film at all watchable more than six decades later.

DeMille (1881–1959), who helped put Paramount on the map during 15 profitable years there, was lured to MGM in 1928 after a short, unsuccessful stint with Pathé. His first release for the studio was his initial sound film, *Dynamite* (1929). It was a bizarre melodrama in which a rich miss (Kay Johnson) marries a condemned coal miner (Charles Bickford) on death row in order to satisfy the terms of her inheritance, then is stunned to learn that his sentence has been commuted. It was 2¼ hours of turgid soap opera, yet racy and luxurious in the DeMille style. It proved disappointing at the paybox, despite the insertion of a popular song, "How Am I to Know?" with a Dorothy Parker lyric sung by a then-unknown Russ Columbo to his own guitar. The future star crooner played a prisoner who witnesses the death-row nuptials.

For DeMille's follow-up, Louis B. Mayer suggested that he make a musical, for the director's penchant for overproduced climaxes would fit in well with the genre. The concoction of three female writers—Macpherson (DeMille's regular collaborator), Elsie Janis, and Gladys Unger—found a dull, underappreciated socialite, Angela Brooks (a miscast Kay Johnson, 1904–1975), barely tolerating the extramarital affairs of her handsome husband, Bob (Reginald Denny). His distraction this time is Trixie, a tough-talking showgirl (Lillian Roth); their hijinks are abetted by Bob's drinking buddy, Jimmy Wade (Roland Young). Confronted by Angela with evidence of the duplicity, Jimmy claims that the mystery woman is his new wife. Unconvinced, Angela follows Jimmy to Trixie's flat, where she is rehearsing her act. Bob shows up there, too, and the principals play a round of musical beds before Angela's suspicions about her hubby are finally confirmed. They separate.

Angela, shamed by Trixie's insult that she is a "typical boring wife," decides to respond with a vengeance, and the picture careens from *Guardsman*-style pre–Code light comedy to outrageous farce. At an elaborate masquerade party hosted by Jimmy aboard a giant dirigible, Angela appears as the mysterious, French-accented "Madam Satan," in a tight-fitting, backless black costume with a frontal flame design that barely covers her breasts, a limb-revealing split skirt, and little sequined horns in the widow's peak-shaped cowl. Bob and Jimmy haven't a clue who this exotic creature is, although Trixie, dressed as "Miss Golden Pheasant," catches on fairly easily. Too late, for the alluring guest wins the highest bid of $3,000 from Bob (dressed as "H.E.-Man") in an ostentatious "girl auction." Trixie attempts to win Bob back with a hot rendition of Jack King and Elsie Janis' "Low Down." Bob, who is now led to believe that Madam is Jimmy's girl, becomes irked at her. "You've had your laugh; now I'm going to have mine," he says. Madam complies by removing her mask—to her husband's utter amazement. "All right, laugh!" is her dare.

Just then, a storm begins to rage, and the dirigible, struck by lightning, breaks from its moorings. With just one available parachute between the two women, Trixie is no profile in courage: "I don't want your husband—I want a parachute!" Angela makes her promise to stay away from Bob, should they all survive. *Madam Satan* spends most of the last quarter of its 116 minutes showing the various outlandishly costumed guests floating through the air en route to a comically appropriate destination on the ground. A fat man falls upon a vagrant on a park bench. A multi-armed Burmese goddess interrupts a group of drunken blacks playing craps. Trixie—the "pheasant," remember?—is momentarily caught on top of a weathervane, then falls through a glass skylight into a Turkish steam bath where there are plenty of men to make her forget Bob. Jimmy plops into the lion's den of a nearby zoo. Angela, who gets a parachute after all, ends up in the back seat of a convertible peopled by two young neckers. Bob, forced to jump without a chute at the last possible moment, splashes into the Central Park reservoir. An unbelievable newspaper account of the catastrophe announces that "all are safe." Bob comes away with a broken arm—but mended fidelity.

DeMille's production boasted no fewer than 46 credited players, not to mention Abe Lyman and his band. Most of the actors—as well as Adrian's delectable costumes and Cedric Gibbons and Mitchell Leisen's lavish sets—were found during the spectacular number devised by Le Roy Prinz that begins the dirigible party.[41] As they walk up the stairs to the craft, the guests sing the obvious "We're Going Somewhere," a mediocre Herbert Stothart-Clifford Grey collaboration. Then they find a handy dance floor for gyrations to a Stothart-Gray song called "The Cat Walk," in which a quartet of black-costumed "tabbies" leads the procession. Suddenly, an alarm sounds and a helmeted, metallic-looking convoy marches in, chugging to a musical beat as of a single throbbing machine. "That's the spirit of modern power!" cries one onlooker. Replies another: "You mean, the power of modern spirit!" An imposing figure—played by the Russian dancer turned choreographer Theodore Kosloff—materializes from thin air to the gasps of the guests; he's the Spirit of Electricity. Metal "currents" emitting from his arms and head, he leads an imaginative modern "Ballet Mechanique." As if there's not enough symbolism, DeMille cuts from the dancing to a shot of the massive engines running the dirigible. Later, the display is weakly explained as a ploy by Jimmy to advertise his oil company.

DeMille was his usual autocratic self during filming, as related by Roth in her autobiography, *I'll Cry Tomorrow.* For Trixie's climactic jump from the dirigible, DeMille called upon the actress to leap 200 feet from a narrow ledge; despite her pleas for a double, he made her do

it five times. Then, for her crashing entrance into the steam bath, she was supposed to plunge through a large sheet of realistic-looking candy glass.

> Again I protested. … DeMille said nothing. Instead, he strode over to a pane of candy glass leaning against the wall, lifted it high over his head like a platter, and brought it down hard on his skull. The glass smashed and shattered all about him. "If it didn't hurt my old bald head," he said caustically, walking away dripping splintered glass, "it won't hurt your young back end." I jumped on schedule.[42]

A potentially tragic incident was averted during an intermission in the filming of the Zeppelin dance sequence. Natalie Visart, a bit player who would go on to become DeMille's chief costume designer, saw her fancy taffeta dress ignite when it caught on the wires from an open electrical box. She stood in horror, affixed to the spot, before dance director Le Roy Prinz rushed over and put out the flames just before they reached the final layer of skirt covering Visart's flesh.[43]

DeMille's enthusiasm over the project didn't pay off financially: *Madam Satan* returned less than three-quarters of its $980,000 production budget. Of its eight new songs—five by King and Janis, the others by Stothart and Grey—none have lasted. The reviews were respectful, praising the actors generally but treating the production with a certain backhandedness. Said *Motion Picture* magazine, for example: "You will be dazzled, dazed, amused or bemused, according to your DeMille reaction, but you won't be bored! That isn't the way this director puts it over—he shoots the works or nothing."[44] After one more MGM film, an uninspired rehash of his early success *The Squaw Man*, DeMille would be shooting the works back at Paramount.

In his autobiography, DeMille wrote this about *Madam Satan*: "The characters burst into song at frequent intervals. None of their bursts have perturbed the dreams of the young Messrs. Gershwin, Hammerstein, Hart, Rodgers, or any of the others who have delighted so many, including me, with *good* musicals."[45]

CHECK AND DOUBLE CHECK
(RKO; October 3, 1930)

Director: Melville Brown. Producer: William LeBaron. Associate Producer: Bertram Millhauser. Adaptation: J. Walter Ruben. Story: Bert Kalmar, Harry Ruby. Photography: William Marshall. Editor: Claude Berkeley. Sound: George Ellis. Assistant Director: Fred Tyler. Art Director: Max Rée. Costumes: Max Rée. Running Time: 85 minutes.

Cast: Freeman F. Gosden (Amos), Charles J. Correll (Andy), Sue Carol (Jean Blair), Charles Norton (Richard Williams), Ralf Harolde (Ralph Crawford), Edward Martindel (John Blair), Irene Rich (Mrs. Blair), Rita La Roy (Elinor Crawford), Russell Powell (Kingfish), Duke Ellington and His Cotton Club Orchestra (themselves), The Rhythm Boys [Al Rinker, Harry Barris, Bing Crosby] [voices only].

Songs: "Old Man Blues" [Ellington band], "Ring Dem Bells" [Ellington band] (Duke Ellington, Irving Mills); "Three Little Words" [Ellington band, sung by Rhythm Boys] (Bert Kalmar, Harry Ruby).

Disc: RCA Victor 22528 (Ellington and orchestra with Rhythm Boys/"Ring Dem Bells"/"Three Little Words"/78).

Video: Turner (cassette).

Check and Double Check, the only film to star the popular radio duo of Amos 'n' Andy (white actors Freeman F. Gosden and Charles J. Correll), is included here only because of the brief but significant appearance of Duke Ellington and His Cotton Club Orchestra. The band is on screen for no more than 10 minutes, but the stint helped greatly in building the budding national celebrity of Ellington (1899–1974), whose film career to this point consisted of a 1929 two-reeler called *Black and Tan*.

The orchestra appears as the ensemble hired to play at the birthday party of the ingénue (Sue Carol), but it shows up two hours late, thanks to dimwitted taxi drivers Amos and Andy. The band plays a Bert Kalmar–Harry Ruby number, "Three Little Words," and two of Ellington's own compositions, "Ring Dem Bells" and "Old Man Blues." "Three Little Words" is introduced by the Rhythm Boys (Bing Crosby, Al Rinker and Harry Barris),

who are heard but not seen. Two light-skinned members of Ellington's unit, clarinetist Barney Bigard and trombonist Juan Tizol, were made up in blackface, lest anyone erroneously believe that the band was integrated.[46]

The rest of *Check and Double Check* concerns the quest of Amos and Andy to locate the deed to a "haunted" mansion owned by the family of a young man (Charles Norton) who needs the document to cinch his marriage to Carol's character. RKO figured it had a coup when it signed the radio comics, who had turned down offers from Warner Bros. and Paramount to take $250,000 plus 50 percent of the net profit,[47] but Gosden (1899–1982) and Correll (1890–1972) irked studio publicists by refusing to be photographed without their makeup and by keeping mum about their personal lives. Because of Southern strictures against mixing of the races, the Ellington orchestra's presence in the picture could not be exploited there. The talented musicians attracted so many listeners during rehearsals that work on the RKO lot all but ceased whenever they got cooking on a number.

Fueled by a massive publicity push—it included the marketing of an "Amos 'n' Andy Candy Bar"—*Check and Double Check* became one of the year's biggest moneymakers. But RKO soon realized that the stars' sole appeal was as a "freak" attraction, that audiences showed up merely for the novelty of seeing them once. Hence, there would be no need for another Amos 'n' Andy movie—a sentiment that has grown stronger with the years.

But "Three Little Words" had more lasting appeal than the movie in which it was introduced. "Everybody predicted the song would lay an egg," Ruby recalled. "It was nearly dropped from the movie. But it was an overnight hit."[48] The song provided the title of Kalmar and Ruby's screen biography, produced by MGM in 1950 with Fred Astaire and Red Skelton as the writing team.

JUST IMAGINE
(Fox; October 10, 1930)

Director: David Butler. Associate Producers: B. G. De Sylva, Lew Brown, Ray Henderson. Continuity: David Butler. Story and Dialogue: B. G. De Sylva, Lew Brown, Ray

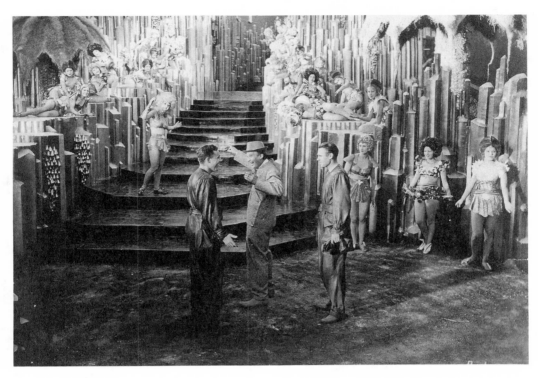

Just Imagine offered Academy Award–nominated sets in a story of a trip to Mars by three Earthlings (from left, Frank Albertson, El Brendel and John Garrick).

Henderson. Photography: Ernest Palmer. Editor: Irene Morra. Sound: Joseph E. Aiken. Assistant Director: Ad Schaumer. Art Direction: Stephen Goosson, Ralph Hammeras. Costumes: Sophie Wachner, Dorothy Tree, Alice O'Neill. Musical Director: Arthur Kay. Dance Direction: Seymour Felix. Running Time: 108 minutes.

Cast: El Brendel (Single O), Maureen O'Sullivan (LN-18), John Garrick (J-21), Marjorie White (D-6), Frank Albertson (RT-42), Hobart Bosworth (Z-4), Kenneth Thomson (MT-3), Wilfred Lucas (X-10), Mischa Auer (B-36), Joseph Girard (Commander), Sidney de Gray (AK-44), Joyzelle [Joyner] (Loo Loo/Boo Boo), Ivan Linow (Loko/Boko), George Irving (judge), Vera Lewis (census taker), Robert Keith, Fox Movietone Male Chorus, Abe Lyman and His Band.

Songs: "Drinking Song" [Garrick, Movietone Chorus], "I Am the Words, You Are the Melody" [Garrick, O'Sullivan; reprised by Garrick, chorus, then by O'Sullivan], "Monkey Business" [danced by chorus], "Never, Never Wed" [White], "Never Swat a Fly" [Albertson, White], "The Romance of Elmer Stremingway" [Brendel], "There's Something About an Old-Fashioned Girl" [Garrick] (B. G. De Sylva, Lew Brown, Ray Henderson); "Dance of Victory and Dance of Sacrifice" [danced by chorus] (Ray Henderson).

Academy Award Nomination: Best Interior Decoration (Stephen Goosson and Ralph Hammeras, 1930-31).

The folks at Fox were so giddy over the box-office returns for *Sunnyside Up* that they reunited the brains behind that film—songsters-scripters De Sylva, Brown and Henderson; director David Butler; and dance whiz Seymour Felix—and merely asked them to produce another smash musical comedy. By now, the confident studio was billing De Sylva, Brown and Henderson as "the three wise men of entertainment." But the *Sunnyside Up* actors handed them were not Charles Farrell and the AWOL Janet Gaynor (see Chapter 4), but El Brendel and Marjorie White, which ought to have prompted someone to wave a red flag right away. So should the bizarre choice of premise that made *Just Imagine* the first science-fiction musical.[49]

What Fox didn't have to dole out for pricey thespians, it put into technical wizardry. In a brief prologue, an offscreen narrator uses a series of comic vignettes to remind the audience of the sweeping changes in technology between 1880 and 1930, then asks, "Just imagine ... 1980!" Thus, the main story begins with shots of a gleaming New York techno-skyline in which giant skyscrapers vie for space with miniature airplanes traveling in multiple lanes and vertical levels (the effect is reminiscent of the cityscape in *Metropolis,* the German sci-fi epic of 1926). This society is so "advanced" that people are referred to by numbers, not by names, and the Orwellian government decides who marries whom.

This is a particular problem for young aviator J-21 (John Garrick), for his request to marry the beautiful LN-18 (Maureen O'Sullivan) has been denied in favor of wealthy newspaper publishing heir MT-3 (Kenneth Thomson). O'Sullivan loves Garrick, not Thomson, so it's her problem, too. The arranged marriage is to take place within four months, during which the flyer can bolster his image enough to request an appeal. The moping Garrick and his chatty best pal, RT-42 (Frank Albertson), attend an event at which a man (Brendel) killed by lightning in 1930 is revived by scientists and then left to his own devices. Taking pity on the fellow, Garrick and Albertson decide that he can room with them.

As the boys show the transplanted Swede (whose new monicker, Single 0, befits his IQ) his brave new world, *Just Imagine* offers most of its better moments. De Sylva, Brown and Henderson anticipate such contraptions as automatic doors, reversible clothing, vending-machine eateries, meals by pill, heated hair-driers and television-style phones—one of the last enables Albertson to catch his bubbly sweetheart (Marjorie White) in her skivvies. Many of these gadgets would become staples of science-fiction cinema. There even is a machine used by a couple to spit out a sex-selected newborn baby. Some of the humor is not so advanced: Upon learning that all of the airplane manufacturers have presumably Jewish surnames, Brendel exclaims, "Looks like somebody got even with

Henry Ford!" And, given their creation of the marriage edict, the authors hadn't a clue about the growth of feminism. But the overall presentation remains highly watchable.

The cook's tour provides only a temporary lift for the lovesick Garrick. As the young man contemplates suicide—"What good are words without a melody?" he tearfully sings—he is approached by an aide (Mischa Auer) to a famous scientist (Hobart Bosworth) who is seeking a brave soul to pilot his newly developed rocketship to Mars. Garrick, eyeing his ticket to success, immediately accepts the job, and the ever-loyal Albertson decides to go along for the ride. At an eve-of-the-launch party, the aerospace cadets toast the explorers' health in the "Drinking Song," although we have previously been told that Prohibition is still in force. Albertson and White sing the comical "Never Swat a Fly" (and prance around the stage with swatters), then Brendel performs a one-man mini-musical about "The Romance of Elmer Stremingway." He soon will stow away to join his friends in space.

Sadly, once the trio lands on the Red Planet, the semi-intelligent science fiction angle of *Just Imagine* degenerates into contrived silliness. The Earthlings stumble onto a strange tribe of mute, frizzy-haired Amazons ruled by the eccentric Queen Loo Loo (Joyzelle Joyner, dressed in what was asserted to be the first movie costume made solely of mica). Alleged comedy is provided by the monarch's effeminate muscleman aide (Ivan Linow), who takes a fancy to Brendel. ("She's not the queen ... *he* is!" replies the astonished Swede.) However, everyone on Mars has an evil twin, and the adventurers are abducted by a band of the bad halves. They witness an erotic native ritual, as gyrating dancers surround an enormous Martian idol with glowing eyes and moving arms; the filmmakers must have been intended this as a topper to the "Turn On the Heat" number in *Sunnyside Up.* Finally, our heroes escape to their ship for the trip home.

Garrick arrives just in time for the hearing in which his appeal for O'Sullivan's hand is being considered. Thomson asks that his rival provide proof that he actually has been to Mars, which Brendel provides by presenting Linow's evil alter ego, who in the confusion of the departure had ended up aboard ship. Garrick and O'Sullivan are united, and Brendel meets his stooped and bewhiskered son in a "Sonny Boy" takeoff (De Sylva–Brown–Henderson, remember?) at the fade.

Just Imagine was no *Sunnyside Up* at the box office, thanks in part to its out-of-this-world cost of production and public distaste for musicals (it didn't enter general release until the end of 1930). It did turn a small profit, mainly on the novelty factor. The miniature New York set, which took five months to build, ate up $250,000 alone, according to Fox. It helped designers Ralph Hammeras and Stephen Goosson earn an Academy Award nomination for "interior decoration." However, Fox made money from the set for years by selling its footage for use in Flash Gordon and Buck Rogers–type serials. Kenneth Strickfaden's electrical effects in the impressively constructed Art Deco laboratory were also highly praised. Wrote O'Sullivan in a letter to the author: "I thought the predictions in *Just Imagine* would come true closer to when they did—50 years hence."[50]

Just Imagine also was one of the first films to utilize back projection. In one notable example, O'Sullivan, who has just learned that Garrick is flying to Mars, is shown in the foreground running toward the enormous rocketship in a tardy attempt to stop him. "She had to make a long run for this place, and I had her fall down and trip," director Butler recalled about his coaching of O'Sullivan.

> Everybody is wondering whether she's going to catch him or not. She would run and fall down and get up and run again. We did this three or four times. Her knees were bleeding. I said to her, "Maureen, we'd better stop." "No, no," she said. "I *feel* the scene. I want to do it."[51]

The inexperienced cast tries hard, but Garrick (b. 1902) is too stiff, there's not nearly enough of O'Sullivan or White, and any film with the dismally unfunny El Brendel as the nominal star is doomed from the start. Worse, the score fails to linger, although the tender ballad "I Am the Words, You Are the Melody," a minor hit in 1930, probably deserved better. It's presented three times, most memorably as Garrick gazes through a Martian telescope to watch O'Sullivan, her head superimposed over the Earth, tearfully speak the lyrics. But *Time* magazine's commentator reflected the general reaction when he called *Just Imagine* the "fantasies of a tired vaudeville booking agent. ... In 1980 ... musical comedies will still be full of jokes that have been doing service for years, songs will not have improved, heroines will be coy and leading men pompous."[52]

On the heels of the *Just Imagine* setback, the De Sylva–Brown–Henderson troika—which had been contracted to Fox for two more years—moved to United Artists to write and produce films for Joseph Schenck. The composers' partnership dissolved with the sale of their publishing house to Warner Bros. and only one film, *Indiscreet* (1931), a romantic drama with two songs sung by Gloria Swanson. The bottom had dropped out of the market for tuneful frivolity.

ARE YOU THERE?
(Fox; November 30, 1930)

Director: Hamilton MacFadden. Story and Dialogue: Harlan Thompson. Photography: Joseph Valentine. Editor: Al De Gaetano. Sound: W. W. Lindsay. Assistant Director: Sam Wurtzel. Art Directors: Stephen Goosson, Duncan Cramer. Costumes: Sophie Wachner. Musical Director: Arthur Kay. Dance Direction: Edward Dolly. Choral Direction: Frank Tresselt. Running Time: 60 minutes.

Cast: Beatrice Lillie (Shirley Travis), John Garrick (Lord Geoffry Brent), Olga Baclanova (Countess Helenka), George Grossmith (Duke of St. Pancras), Jillian Sand (Barbara Blythe), Lloyd Hamilton (hostler), Roger Davis (barber), Gustav von Seyffertitz, Nicholas Soussanin, Richard Alexander, Henry Victor (international crooks), Paula Langlen (page), Bo Peep Karlin, Adele Cutler, Mary Carr, Lorraine Bond, Lucile Miller, Catherine Brown, Marbeth Wright, Bee Stephens (ensemble dancers), The Fox-Movietone Augmented Chorus.

Songs: "Bagdad Daddies" [Lillie], "Lady Detectives" [Lillie, Langlen, chorus], "Queen of the Hunt Am I" [Lillie, Langlen, chorus] (Grace Henry, Morris Hamilton).

Beatrice Lillie (1898–1989) was considered "The Funniest Woman in the World," but when it came to breaking into Hollywood she might as well have been just off the train from Peoria. The Canadian-born pixie made her feature-film debut in 1926, but the MGM comedy titled *Exit Smiling* didn't make much of an impression. In 1929, she appeared with the Warner Bros. stock company in *The Show of Shows,* in which she performed in two comedy sketches—one of which, "Beatrice Lillie and Her Boy Friends," was cut from the film prior to release. When Warners released the deleted sketch as a short subject, Lillie sued the studio for breach of contract and $50,000, claiming that by presenting her as a one-reeler comic, the company had "presented … [her] to the world as a cheap and inconsequential performer."[53]

In 1930, Lillie took another stab at Hollywood, although, as she wrote in her autobiography, "once again, it was a movie that stabbed me."[54] The timing of *Are You There?*, a musical farce, was definitely not in its star's favor, for in the fall of 1930 just about any film with music was considered a box-office gamble. Fox not only dropped three of the six songs from the final release print, it initially exhibited *Are You There?* only in Canada and England. The film didn't make it to this country—and scantily, at that—until the summer of 1931, when nobody cared. Fortunately, unlike so many early talkies, *Are You There?* has survived. Even in its truncated version—which reposes at the New York Museum of Modern Art after being rescued from the Fox vaults—it plays quite favorably.

Director Hamilton MacFadden and scripter Harlan Thompson allowed Lillie a goodly share of her deadpan expressions, raised eyebrows, and flute-like voice inflections as Shirley Travis, an intrepid London private detective. The opening of the film is particularly impressive. Shirley is doing well enough to afford a lavish, futuristic private office (art-deco sets by Steven Goosson, an Oscar nominee for *Just Imagine,* and Duncan Cramer). There is a TV-type monitor with which Shirley can check on comings and goings, and a revolving door-seat with which she can whisk in clients from the lobby. Shirley and six of her pupils show off their disguises—Napoleon, George Arliss, a Chinaman—in a clever dance routine, "Lady Detectives." Shirley then answers a round of telephone calls requesting her services. "That's much too pure," she tells one caller, "I only take immoral cases."

Lord Geoffry Brent (John Garrick) visits, asking Shirley if she will help him and his fiancée, Barbara Blythe (Jillian Sand), wrest his father, the Duke of St. Pancras (George Grossmith), from the money-grubbing clutches of the Russian Countess Helenka (Olga Baclanova). Geoffrey fears for the family estate, and rightly so, for the bogus Helenka is secretly part of a gang of international crooks planning a holdup at the duke's estate. The leader of said gang (Gustav von Seyffertitz) happens to be perched with his minions on Shirley's roof, and he tosses a bomb inside. When the smoke clears, Shirley and Geoffry surrealistically continue their conversation as if nothing has happened, and she agrees to visit the estate in the guise of Lady Diana Drummond, a famous big-game hunter and equestrian.

At a party in her honor, "Diana" makes a dramatic entrance, preceded by an ostrich and a gorilla. The duke, a passionate huntsman himself, takes her into his study to talk shop. She brags about killing a huge tiger in Africa.

"I suppose you used a 40-40 on the tiger," says the duke, referring to the kind of rifle.

"Nooo, nooo," Diana replies, "a 50-50."

"I haven't heard of a 50-50.…"

"Well, you see, it's like this: It's 50-50 if you get the tiger or the tiger gets a-youuu."

The crooks know that the visitor isn't the real Diana, so they plot to get her involved in the upcoming big fox hunt. Shirley needs a lesson in horsemanship—and fast. In the stables, she finds a hostler (Lloyd Hamilton, a well-known silent comic now fading and grown paunchy) who professes to know nothing about horses but is eager to help anyway. After an overnight lesson, Shirley is asked to lead the hunt atop a balky steed named Bullet. She is soon thrown from the horse, but as she rests against a tree, the exhausted fox jumps into her lap. The rest of the hunting party intervenes, and "Diana" is lauded for her skill at catching the fox with her bare hands. Giddily, she sings "Queen of the Hunt Am I" as the other hunters dance and sing along, though only Lillie fools with the high notes in her own inimitable way.

Geoffry continues to work on his dad about transferring his affections from Helenka to Lady Diana, but the duke suddenly decides that he will propose marriage to the countess at a party that night. Geoffry decides that he must make love himself to the Russian so as to create a scandal that will keep the duke away from her forever. He sneaks into Helenka's bedroom, but Shirley heads him off. Disguised as a Cockney nurse, she gives Helenka a violent "massage" as she looks around for evidence that would implicate the countess. The male crooks kidnap Shirley and, to keep her from the party, hold her captive at their hideout, but the hostler follows on a motorcycle, and his unintentional gunshot into the villains' lair enables Shirley to escape.

At the party, Shirley, posing as an acrobat, leads the entertainment with a "Bagdad Daddies" number set in an Arabian harem. She is tossed around onstage—so passionately that you're supposed to know it's fake—by a pair of big, bare-chested "harem attendants." The thieves have planned their holdup at the end of the song, but Shirley confuses them by jazzing the tune up a bit. The signal is made to begin the holdup, but the hostler and the gorilla knock cold two of the baddies and dump them on the stage. Helenka and her cohorts are exposed, the temporarily estranged Geoffry and Barbara are reunited, and the duke decides that Diana/Shirley is his marital choice after all.

The largely foreign cast was mostly at sea with American moviemaking technique. In her autobiography *Every Other Inch a Lady,* Lillie recalled that Grossmith, a British actor, producer and playwright for nearly 40 years, "wandered around the studios, elevating his celebrated eyebrows in horror, complaining, 'My dear fellow, it is not *done.* It is just not *done* like that, I assure you.'"[55] Some of the few who bothered to review *Are You There?* certainly agreed. *Variety* dismissed the film "made so long ago it's too bad Fox could not have forgotten it forever ... it looks and sounds as if made in England."[56] But *Exhibitors Herald-World* rightly considered Lillie "smart-looking, clever and mirth-provoking. ... Her personality and grace are registered superbly upon the screen."[57]

In hindsight, though, *Are You There?* might have been even more interesting with its full complement of songs. One of the deleted numbers, a choral-and-dance presentation of the Russian folk song "Advice to Lovers," is seen for only a few seconds prior to the "Bagdad Daddies" finale. Also filmed, then cut, were "It Must Be the Iron in the Spinach," with which the captive Lillie annoys her kidnappers, and "You Can Always Count on Me," a romantic ballad sung by Garrick to Sand. The absence of the latter helps to explain Sand's surprisingly brief time on screen.

Even so, *Are You There?* needs little apology for its amusing, and sometimes inventive, showcasing of an unusual star performer too infrequently captured on the silver screen. It deserved to be seen by more people in 1930 and '31, and it's a pity it's not in circulation today.

CHAPTER 6

1929–1930: *Hail to the Victors*

Only about 1 million Americans were enrolled in college at the end of the '20s, but you wouldn't have known it by the prominence of the campus experience in the nation's popular culture. The sweatered, hip-flasked Joe Colleges and flat-breasted, short-haired flappers depicted in the lively drawings of John Held, Jr., in *Life*, *Judge* and other magazines became vivid metaphors for the postwar nation—swaggering, exuberant, full of itself. With The War to End All Wars an increasingly distant memory, many Americans—particularly the members of the youthful "Lost" generation—figured it was time to embrace more self-fulfilling pursuits at the expense of the old moral order ... Prohibition, be damned. This societal revolution was certainly not limited to the colleges, but on few other fronts did the likes of petting parties, drinking binges, automotive joyrides and body-to-body dances hold a higher profile.

The yearning for physical freedom that complemented the boldness in thought was being played out on college football fields nationwide (the pro game had a negligible following at this point). Spectator sports in general were rocketing in popularity, but to the mostly moneyed youth in higher-learning institutions, football touched a nerve. It was fast, lively, hard-hitting, more instinctive and less cerebral than baseball, golf, or tennis. If Babe Ruth was the most revered athlete of the Golden Age of Sport, his football counterpart Harold "Red" Grange was the most explosive.

From the day in 1924 when he ran and passed the University of Illinois team to six touchdowns against the mighty U. of Michigan, Grange grabbed the national spotlight as if *he* were the defensive behemoth and not the slippery halfback. He rendered the country's cozier ballfields obsolete because they couldn't

handle the crowds, and he inspired a rise in radio sales so his enraptured fandom could monitor his exploits and those of contemporaries such as Ernie Nevers, Bronko Nagurski and the great Notre Dame coach Knute Rockne. As Grange's fame ballooned, a sportswriter had the temerity to tell the Illinois coach, Bob Zuppke, that all "The Galloping Ghost" could do was run with a pigskin. "Yeah," Zuppke sneered, "and all Galli-Curci can do is sing."

But could Galli-Curci sing "Hail to the Victors"? In his book *From Scarface to Scarlett: American Films in the 1930s,* film historian Roger Dooley explains the special relationship between popular music and collegiate chic:

> Thanks to the leading jazz orchestras of the day (many of which looked and sounded collegiate), like Rudy Vallee and his Connecticut Yankees and Fred Waring and his Pennsylvanians, as well as theater organ recitals, vaudeville, band concerts and radio programs, college medleys ... were almost as popular as those from the Gay '90s. Children learned all the "fight" songs: "On, Wisconsin," "Cheer, Cheer for Old Notre Dame," "Anchors Aweigh," "On, Good Old Army Team," while their elders, most of whom had never gone to college, listened appreciatively to wistful glee club numbers like "The Whiffenpoof Song" and "The Sweetheart of Sigma Chi" or more rousing ones like "The Maine Stein Song."...[1]

Even before they had music, the movies were eager to capitalize upon the hubbub. Most films about college life were in a distinctly lighthearted vein, emphasizing the extra-curricular over the academic; their deans, presidents and professors were all uptight killjoys. Some of Hollywood's top comedians took at least one campus course—most famously Harold Lloyd, the nerd turned football hero in *The Freshman* (1924). Buster Keaton enrolled in *College* in 1927. The Marx Brothers would get a turn in *Horse Feathers* (1932; see Chapter 12).

The coming of sound, and the musical possibilities that it brought, only fueled the hunger for collegiate stories. Even those early college talkies that weren't overtly musical—films like *College Love, College Lovers, The Sophomore, The Wild Party* and *The Time, the Place, and the Girl*—saw fit to include a song or two. But the real influence behind the college movie musical was not a film, but a Broadway musical comedy. Theater historian Gerald Bordman describes *Good News* (1927) as "probably the quintessential musical comedy of the 'era of wonderful nonsense.'"[2] It was the first musical for the prolific team of B. G. "Buddy" De Sylva, Lew Brown and Ray Henderson. As would become their custom, Henderson specialized in the music and the other two on the lyrics. Their sprightly score, which included the standards "The Varsity Drag" and "The Best Things in Life Are Free," was more thoroughly collegiate than anything that had come before. So was everything else. Ushers wearing college jerseys escorted the customers to their seats, and, just before every curtain, the members of George Olsen's orchestra donned campus sweaters and shouted football cheers as they ran down the aisles on their way to the pit.

The De Sylva–Laurence Schwab book suited the music perfectly. The story is set at football-mad Tait College, where star athlete Tom Marlowe (John Price Jones) is threatened with suspension from the team if he cannot pass his astronomy exam. With the Big Game against archrival Colton approaching, the plain and modest Connie Lane (Mary Lawlor) is brought in to tutor him into passing, and she falls for him although he is to be engaged to Patricia Bingham (Shirley Vernon). Meanwhile, Tom's teammate and friend Bobby Randall (Gus Shy) makes a play for the school vamp, Babe O'Day (Inez Courtney). In the game, Tom fumbles at a crucial moment, but Bobby recovers the ball, enabling Tait to win. Tom affirms his love for Connie, and with "The Best Things in Life Are Free" reminds her that no material barriers can block the way to their happiness.

Its youthful exuberance enabled *Good News* to rack up 551 performances in New York and many more on tour. A star was born in doll-faced Zelma O'Neal, whose speaking role was minor but whose animated singing and dancing of "The Varsity Drag" and the title number brought an irresistible delight. But *Good News* did not come to the screen until 1930, three years after its Broadway opening, a delay that enabled a handful of similarly plotted college musicals to steal a march. Most would adhere to the same formula, which centered around a Big Man on Campus whose path to gridiron glory would be stalled by forces internal (a character flaw) or external (a high-falutin' educator attempting to make an example). Of course, there would be a woman to straighten him out, usually on the eve of the climactic on-field showdown, which would fill the stands with hooch-guzzling undergrads who cared more about the numbers on the scoreboard than the scores on their next exam.

Of brainpower, there was little. We quote the typically single-minded pigskin coach in a Tiffany entry called *Sunny Skies*: "This college could turn out a whole regiment of Phi Betas, and who would know about it? But let us turn out just one All-American fullback, and the whole country will sit up and take notice." It would, too.

WORDS AND MUSIC
(Fox; August 18, 1929)

Director: James Tinling. Production Executive: Chandler Sprague. Stage Director: Frank Merlin. Dialogue: Andrew Bennison. Story: Frederick H. Brennan, Jack McEdwards. Photography: Charles G. Clarke, Charles Van Enger, Don Anderson. Editor: Ralph Dixon. Sound: Donald Flick, Joseph E. Aiken. Assistant Director: William Tinling. Costumes: Sophie Wachner. Musical Director: Arthur Kay. Dance Direction: Edward Royce. Running Time: 60 minutes (sound version; also released as silent).

Cast: Lois Moran (Mary Brown), David Percy (Phil Denning), Helen Twelvetrees (Dorothy Bracey), William Orlamond (Pop Evans), Elizabeth Patterson (Dean Crockett), Duke Morrison [John Wayne] (Pete Donahue), Ward Bond (Ward), Richard Keene (singer), Frank Albertson (Skeet Mulroy), Tom Patricola (Hannibal), Bubbles Crowell (Bubbles), The

As Duke Morrison, John Wayne got early billing (opposite Lois Moran) in Fox's long-lost *Words and Music*.

Biltmore Quartet, Dorothy Ward, The Collier Sisters, Harriet and John Griffith, Vina Gale and Arthur Springer, Helen Hunt and Charles Huff (adagio dancers), Dorothy Jordan, Helen Parrish, Jack Wade, Frances Dee, Paula Langlen, Paul Power.

Songs/Musical Numbers: "Beauty Waltz," "The Hunting Song" [Moran, Percy, chorus], "Take a Little Tip" (Harlan Thompson, Dave Stamper); "Shadows" (Sidney Mitchell, Archie Gottler, Con Conrad); "Spice Dance" (Dave Stamper); "Steppin' Along" [Keene] (William Kernell); "Too Wonderful for Words" [Patricola, chorus] (Paul Gerard Smith, Dave Stamper).

After the filming of *William Fox Movietone Follies of 1929* (see Chapter 3) was completed, somebody realized that there was far too much material at hand for one picture. Something had to go; actually, that would be someone—Lois Moran. Her musical numbers were deleted,

then a new story was created around them. (According to U. S. copyright records, the songs "Shadows," "Take a Little Tip" and "Hunting Song" were initially entered for use in *Movietone Follies of 1929*.) The hastily released end product, set at a college but refreshingly free of football, was the thinly plotted and hastily released *Words and Music*.

Moran (1908–1990) played Mary Brown, a college beauty whose singing and dancing talents are fought over by fraternity brothers Phil Denning (David Percy) and Pete Donahue (Duke Morrison), who are each staging numbers for the school's annual musical revue. She would prefer to help good-hearted Phil win the $1,500 prize for the best original number, but she is blackmailed by the campus hussy (Helen Twelvetrees) into working for Pete. Mary ends up leading the chorus for each impresario, but she gives her all for the boy she loves, and he wins the prize.

The boy, regrettably, was David Percy and not Duke Morrison, whom we all know better by the name bestowed upon him shortly after: John Wayne. In *Words and Music*, Wayne was just another fresh face in a large contingent of screen newcomers—Helen Twelvetrees, Richard Keene, Frank Albertson and Tom Patricola, who would all soon find quick work at Fox while the man who would become the most famous of movie heroes languished in bit roles. Wayne got billing (sixth) for the first time, but the career advance was only temporary, and soon he would be back doing cameos in two programmers, *Cheer Up and Smile* (elsewhere in this chapter) and *Rough Romance*. Wayne's longtime friend, Ward Bond, had a bit role in *Words and Music*. He, too, would enjoy better days.

In 1930, Fox—and director Raoul Walsh—attempted to make Wayne a leading man with the expensive Western *The Big Trail*, but the film flopped and the studio dropped him early in '31. A couple of years later, Wayne was cast as a singing cowboy in a "B" oater. His singing voice was dubbed, of course.

HOWDY BROADWAY
(Rayart; October 16, 1929)

Director-Screenplay: Charles J. Hunt. Photography: Frank Zucker, George Weber. Editor: J. S. Harrington. Sound: J. G. Byers, Mark Asch. Art Director: Charles Nasca. Dance Direction: Jack J. Clark. Running Time: 48 minutes (or 7 reels).

Cast: Tommy Christian and His Collegians (themselves), Ellalee Ruby (Lulu), Lucy Ames (Betty), Johnny Kane (Speedy), Jack J. Clark (producer/tap dancer), Diana Mullen, Daisy Dean, Art Barnett, Ted Kieth, Mona Soltis, James Parrish, Mart Britt.

Songs: "I Want You to Know I Love You" [Ames; reprised by Ames, band], "You're Gonna Be Blue" [Ames, Christian] (Art Terker, Tommy Christian); "Atta Boy! (Old Pal, Old Sock, Old Kid, Old Thing, Old Gold, Old Baby)" [unidentified singer] (Billy Moll, Tommy Christian); "Gazoozalum Gazoo" [Ruby, band] (Val Trainor, Tommy Christian); "Howdy Broadway" [chorus; reprised by band, unidentified singer] (Billy Moll, Benjamin Blanc); "Sophomore Strut" (Henri Berchman,

Wesley Ryan, Bob Causer); "Gypsy Love," "Somebody's Sweetheart—Not Mine" [band, male singer] (authorship undetermined).

The most obscure film is this book is *Howdy Broadway*. Distributed by the independent Rayart company, it was made to capitalize on the modest following of bandleader-saxophonist-composer Tommy Christian and his band, the Collegians. Christian was a Southerner, and it's likely this film was distributed primarily in that region on a states-rights basis. Rayart, which had specialized in serials during the silent era, went under soon after the coming of sound, but its founder, W. Ray Johnston, would establish Monogram Pictures in the early '30s.

Information on *Howdy Broadway* is very sparse. The entry in the 1921-30 American Film Institute catalog is incomplete, with data gained exclusively from Rayart's application for a New York State exhibiting license (the date listed with the credits above is the date on which this license was granted). Research uncovered no reviews by any of the standard film publications. In fact, the author was not even certain that *Howdy Broadway* ever actually existed—until a private collector made available a print of the film. The AFI book lists the film's length at seven reels; the viewed print was only 48 minutes long, but lacked a couple of the eight songs cited in the New York license application.

Despite the implication of its title, *Howdy Broadway* is actually a college film; only the last few minutes are set in New York. The hero, Tommy Christian in art and life, is a champion rower for Burdette U. who leads a snappy little dance band when he's not racing, studying or pitching woo to his sweetheart, Betty (Lucy Ames). The college widow, Lulu (Ellalee Ruby), talks Tommy and band into performing at a speakeasy so she can dance with a Broadway producer in attendance. The police raid the joint, but gallant Tommy manages to spirit everyone out the back door before he's left to face the cops. Tommy is expelled from school, and Betty, thinking her man is in love with Lulu, jilts him. Tommy decides to try his luck as a Broadway music man, and his band boys eagerly follow. On the Collegians' opening night at a popular club, Betty unexpectedly shows up with a reconciling rendition of "I Want You to Know I Love You," and the jubilant lovers dash out to get married.

Apparently no one asked Christian to make another picture, and 48 minutes are enough to reveal his flat diction and colorless screen presence. The acting styles in *Howdy Broadway* vary from wooden to histrionic, and the production values are shabby. Part of one number is shot with the back of the head of the singer toward the camera. During a duet to "You're Gonna Be Blue," Christian, declaiming lyrics previously sung by Ames, garbles a line and then repeats it as if no one would notice. Given the presumably small audience for this film, perhaps nobody did.

SWEETIE
(Paramount; October 25, 1929)

Director: Frank Tuttle. Scenario and Dialogue: George Marion, Jr., Lloyd Corrigan. Titles: George Marion, Jr. Photography: Alfred Gilks. Editor: Verna Willis. Sound: Eugene Merritt. Dance Direction: Earl Lindsay. Musical Director: Nathaniel Finston. Running Time: 95 minutes (sound version; also released as silent).

Cast: Nancy Carroll (Barbara Pell), Helen Kane (Helen Fry), Stanley Smith (Biff Bentley), Jack Oakie (Tap-Tap Thompson), William Austin (Percy "Pussy" Willow), Stuart Erwin (Axel Bronstrup), Wallace MacDonald (Coach Bill Barrington), Charles Sellon (Dr. Oglethorpe), Aileen Manning (Miss Twill), Joe Depew (Freddie Fry), The King's Men.

Songs: "Alma Mammy" [Oakie; reprised twice by students], "Bear Down Pelham" [football players; reprised twice by students and once by The King's Men], "I Think You'll Like It" [Kane], "My Sweeter Than Sweet" [Carroll; reprised by Smith, chorus, then twice by The King's Men], "The Prep Step" [Kane; danced by Oakie, chorus] (George Marion, Jr., Richard A. Whiting); "He's So Unusual" [Kane] (Al Lewis, Al Sherman, Abner Silver).

Disc: RCA Victor 22080 (Kane/"He's So Unusual"/78); Caliban 6018 (bootleg LP; ST).

The first college musical film to make a splash was *Sweetie*, a jaunty entry by the studio that was well known for pictures about flaming youth, what with Clara Bow, Nancy Carroll, Gary Cooper and Buddy Rogers in the fold.[3] This time, Paramount's little Nancy was the

headliner in the oft-recycled tale about a showgirl who inherits a men's school and nearly ruins it for spite.

The fellow she is miffed at is Biff Bentley (Stanley Smith), who has chosen to pass up his elopement with Barbara Pell (Carroll) and remain at dear old Pelham College in hopes of quarterbacking its team to a victory over hated rival Oglethorpe.[4] But after Barbara—who had changed her surname from Pelham—is informed that she is the new queen of the campus, she quits her New York stage career and, with actor chum Tap-Tap Williams (Jack Oakie), sets out for her domain in rural North Carolina.

The student body takes a shine to Barbara, and Tap-Tap, who finds he prefers college life to the theater, leads a band of partygoers in an energetic Al Jolson takeoff called "Alma Mammy." But Barb is determined to short-circuit her ex-boyfriend's gridiron dreams. On the week of the Oglethorpe game, she hits the footballers with an impromptu English exam—which prompts the team to worry over the eligibility of bonehead lineman Axel Bronstrup (Stuart Erwin). Axel passes the test; the QB doesn't. Barbara then threatens to sell her school to Old Man Oglethorpe (Charles Sellon), but she finally comes to her senses, grants Biff a successful repeat exam, and joins in the hurrahs as his last-second touchdown run wins the Big Game. Next, Mr. Bentley will write a few songs for the school's annual musical comedy.

A catchy score by Richard Whiting and George Marion, Jr., survives as the highlight of a dopey but engaging film that *Variety* called "a brooch of pearls inlaid in dried spinach."[5] Paramount must have known it had the goods, for three of the six songs are plugged relentlessly. The ballad "My Sweeter Than Sweet" is heard in some form no less than six times. The fight song "Bear Down Pelham" is played at least four times. "Alma Mammy" is given three hearings—the last by a stadium cheering section decked out in blackface. Oakie had been performing a Jolson takeoff at Hollywood parties, and Whiting and Marion wrote the song to give him the opportunity to do such a number on screen.

But the big hit was a non–Whiting and Marion tune heard only once: "He's So Unusual," written by Al Sherman, Al Lewis and Abner Silver. It is introduced by Helen Kane,

Jack Oakie ("Alma Mammy") and Helen Kane ("He's So Unusual") provided collegiate hilarity to the Paramount hit *Sweetie*.

who, as Helen Fry, a pupil at Pelham's neighboring Miss Twill's School for Girls, is complaining about her weak-sheikin' Axel's inclination to play ball rather than play around. "As a picture of college life, [*Sweetie*] is further from the truth than most of its predecessors," noted *Motion Picture News*. "But it doesn't pretend to be realistic. It kids its own theme—and broadly."[6]

Kane (1903–1966) cemented her popularity with this, her second film. Like so many troupers of her era, she began in vaudeville, then progressed to Broadway revues and musical comedies. Her debut in her home city came in the short-lived 1927 Marx Brothers show *A Night in Spain*. The chubby redhead attracted a good deal of attention in her appearances with the Paul Ash Orchestra, then made a great sensation in Kalmar and Ruby's *Good Boy* (1928) when she sang "I Wanna Be Loved by You" to her future husband (from 1939), Dan Healy. Its

suggestive "boop-boop-a-doop" lyric, which originated as an ad-lib by the singer, became her trademark. (Strictly fictional is the account in the 1950 Kalmar-Ruby film biography, *Three Little Words*, that the songwriters—played by Fred Astaire and Red Skelton—discovered Kane squeaking out this song on a Bronx sidewalk, athough Debbie Reynolds is dubbed by the real Kane.) Paramount signed Kane and introduced her to movies in a song number, "Do Something," in the 1929 comedy non-musical *Nothing but the Truth*.

Kane was an unlikely star by today's standards, but her chubbiness gave her a sensual appeal that was in vogue in the '20s. *Time* magazine eagerly reported that young males in Eastern colleges voted Kane as their favorite actress,[7] which was a strange honor considering that she did not so much act out a role than envelop it with her childlike, Bronx-inflected voice and semi-salacious catch phrases.

Filmgoers would tire rapidly of Kane—she appeared in only six features—but her influence survives in the animated persona of Betty Boop, for which the actress was the unofficial inspiration.

A final word: As Helen gripes about Axel's apathy in song, Stu Erwin sits high atop a ladder installing a set for Pelham's upcoming musical show (written, you'll remember, by Mr. Biff). When she finishes, the crowd that has gathered around her stares, as one, up at the big bruiser—who, jolted, responds by falling through a nearby window. That the onlookers respond to poor Axel with giggles and not screams is right in keeping with the rest of *Sweetie*.

SO THIS IS COLLEGE
(MGM; November 8, 1929)

Director: Sam Wood. Screenplay: Al Boasberg, Delmer Daves. Dialogue: Joe Farnham, Al Boasberg. Titles: Joe Farnham. Photography: Leonard Smith. Editors: Frank Sullivan, Leslie F. Wilder. Sound: Douglas Shearer. Art Director: Cedric Gibbons. Costumes: Henrietta Frazer. Running Time: 95 minutes (sound version; also released as silent).

Cast: Elliott Nugent (Eddie), Robert Montgomery (Biff), Cliff Edwards (Windy), Sally Starr (Babs), Phyllis Crane (Betty), Dorothy Dehn (Jane), Max Davidson (Moe), Ann Brody (Momma), Oscar Rudolph (Freshie), Gene Stone (Stupid), Polly Moran (Polly), Lee Shumway (Coach), Joel McCrea (Bruce), Delmer Daves, Ward Bond (USC players), Ray Cooke, Ann Dvorak (students).

Songs: "College Days" [Edwards, students], "Until the End" [students, twice] (Al Boasberg, Martin Broones); "Campus Capers" [Starr, Edwards] (Martin Broones); "I Don't Want Your Kisses If I Can't Have Your Love" [Montgomery, reprised by Nugent, then by Montgomery, then by Stone] (Fred Fisher, Martin Broones); "Sophomore Prom" [Edwards] (Raymond Klages, Jesse Greer); "Fight On" [students] (Milo Sweet, Glen Grant); "The Farmer in the Dell" [Montgomery, Nugent] (trad.).

Disc: Columbia 1980-D (Edwards/"Sophomore Prom"/78).

As Fox had broken in some of its young talent in *Words and Music*, MGM did the same with three stage imports in *So This Is College*. Robert Montgomery (1904–1981) had built his acting résumé with such Broadway credits as *Dawn* (1924), *The Garden of Eden* (1927) and *Possession* (1928). Elliott Nugent (1899–1980) was a playwright as well as an actor—his writing partner was his father, the esteemed author-performer J. C. Nugent—and had appeared in a couple of silents. He would become a director of note. Sally Starr (b. 1910) was a petite graduate of *George White's Scandals* who was brought to MGM by the impresario Gus Edwards. Edwards landed the chubby Clara Bow look-alike the job in *So This Is College* by introducing her to its director, Sam Wood.

Wood had been scouting for youthful faces to appear in his film (titled *College Life* and then *Happy Days* prior to release). Al Boasberg, Joe Farnham and future director Delmer Daves scripted a conventional comedy romance set at the University of Southern California. Montgomery and Nugent play Trojan football stars Biff and Eddie (no last names cited), frat brothers who casually trade girls "like we share neckties." But Babs Baxter (Starr)—"a sugar baby who certainly draws the flies"—drives them apart before the boys realize that no woman is worth ruining their friendship. Biff and Eddie come to this realization in the nick of time—midway through a losing effort in the big game against Stanford. Perfectly positioned next to a window inside the Trojans' locker room, they overhear Babs pledging her love to a strapping young man (uncredited newcomer Joel McCrea) who, we learn, is her fiancé. After the action restarts, Eddie scores an important touchdown but injures his foot, and Biff is called upon to kick the winning field goal in the final seconds of a 9-7 victory. For this sequence, Wood spliced footage from the real USC-Stanford contest of 1928, along with microphoned sound effects of same, into close-ups of the fictional heroics.

Reviewers found the football action convincing, and the same went for the key musical number, featuring the film's one durable song, Fred Fisher and Martin Broones' "I Don't Want Your Kisses If I Can't Have Your Love." A look at the sequence in the recently unearthed film elicits a markedly different reaction. Nugent sits at a piano and, with his head turned slightly away from the camera, begins to sing to Starr, but the smooth tenor that croons the lyrics is in stark contrast to the plaintive voice that speaks them alternately (when the camera provides a full face shot). Oddly, Nugent is allowed to use his own pipes when he joins in on a couple of less formal numbers later on. Fortunately, most of the singing in *So This Is College* was left to Cliff Edwards, cast as a rather overage college boy.

Montgomery's own tenor is too shaky to be anyone else's, and he was quoted by a fan magazine as saying that no task in Hollywood had been tougher.

> I have had to learn to fence and now I am in training and taking boxing lessons. ... But the worst thing I have had to do yet was sing. I had never sang before in my life and I haven't had any lessons, but they said I had to try it, so I did. It sounded a lot better than I ever thought it would when I heard it on the playback. Gee! Life is funny. Imagine me singing for publication, as it were![8]

So This Is College put Montgomery on the road to stardom, and MGM was satisfied enough with his crooning to place him in two more early musicals, *Free and Easy* and *Love in the Rough*. But the actor found his niche in more substantial assignments—fortunately for him, and us.

THE FORWARD PASS
(First National; November 10, 1929)

Director: Eddie Cline. Scenario, Dialogue and Titles: Howard Emmett Rogers. Story: Harvey Gates. Photography: Arthur Todd. Editor: Ralph Holt. Running Time: 78 minutes (sound version; also released as silent).

Cast: Douglas Fairbanks, Jr. (Marty Reid), Loretta Young (Patsy Carlyle), Guinn Williams ("Honey" Smith), Marion Byron (Mazie), Phyllis Crane (Dot), Bert Rome (Coach Wilson), Lane Chandler (Assistant Coach Kane), Allan Lane (Ed Kirby), Floyd Shackleford (trainer), University of Southern California Football Team.

Songs: "H'lo Baby," "Huddlin'," "I Gotta Have You," "One Minute of Heaven," "Onward Sanford," "Up an' at 'Em" (Herb Magidson, Ned Washington, Michael H. Cleary).

The inclination of the studios to push their non-singing stars into musicals continued with *The Forward Pass,* the only genre film to showcase Douglas Fairbanks, Jr., and Loretta Young. This, the second of six pairings of the likable young romantic duo, was a typically profitable entry.

Both Fairbanks (b. 1909) and Young (b. 1913) had made seamless transitions to sound. Fairbanks had passed his key test with an acclaimed performance in the 1928 First National part-talkie *The Barker,* which won him a year's contract from the company with options for four more years. The actor took in stride the task of adapting himself to sound. "I'd been on the stage and had no particular fear of speaking," Fairbanks told the author in 1992. "I'd been to drama school as well. So it didn't bother me particularly. ... I probably welcomed it."[9]

Most of his early sound films were undistinguished. Instead of the programmers to which he was assigned, Fairbanks recalled,

> I was more ambitious to do quality things—more serious pictures, or if it was a comedy, a higher class of comedy like a Noël Coward or an Oscar Wilde. ... [But not] these sort of routine things like racing cars and crooks across the border, and slick melodramas and newspaper stories.[10]

He might have added "college comedies" to that list, but Fairbanks eagerly looked forward to appearing in *The Forward Pass,* in which he would play a star quarterback accused of cowardice. For one, Fairbanks was an avid fan of the University of Southern California football team; he watched its practices and socialized with the athletes, who were hired as extras for the film. Another reason for his lack of reserve was that he would not be required to sing: "I wasn't a musical comedy character, so they wouldn't have cast me in the part in the first place had singing been a requirement."[11] Young was not so fortunate, for she had to sing one of the six songs, although a backing male chorus made the task easier on her contralto.

The central character in *The Forward Pass* is Marty Reid, the star signal-caller at Sanford College. Marty is so incensed by cheap shots from opposing tacklers that he threatens to quit the sport. His coach asks campus vamp Patsy Carlyle (Young) to keep Marty's mind off the perceived slights, but shortly after Marty catches wind of the scheme, he becomes distracted enough to fumble during a key game. Smart-mouthed split end Ed Kirby (Allan "Rocky" Lane), also a rival for Patsy, calls Marty "yellow" and the two tangle in the locker room at halftime. Forced to make up, they combine on a forward pass that wins the day. Marty and Patsy are reunited. Guinn "Big Boy" Williams provided comedy relief as a hulking lineman named Cecil who tries to convince everybody that he would rather be called "Honey."

Fairbanks recounted his experience with the real-life football players who stood on the other side of the line during the game sequences.

> Most of them were nice fellows who were unimpressed by movie people. When the cameraman began to shoot, the players thought it great fun to rush through my so-called protective linemen and, instead of letting me run with the ball or pass as rehearsed, to crash into me ... pile up on top of me, and then apologize. The director, Eddie Cline, was in on their joke and thought it fun too. So did everyone, except me. It was summer, it was hot, and I was not prepared for such rough going. But I knew if I so much as cried, "Ouch!" I'd never hear—or feel—the end of it. They knocked me right on my backside![12]

The experience wasn't Fairbanks' last with a Southern Cal football player. John Wayne, a former tackle for the Trojans, was a struggling contract actor at Warner Bros. in the early '30s when Fairbanks, then starring in *The Life of Jimmy Dolan*, arranged for Wayne to get a one-line part as a fight trainer. For the job, Wayne secured for Fairbanks a pair of 50-yard-line seats for—of course—a USC game.

SUNNY SKIES
(Tiffany; May 12, 1930)

Director: Norman Taurog. Additional Direction: Ralph De Lacy. Scenario: Earl Snell. Dialogue: George Cleveland. Story: A. P. Younger. Photography: Arthur Reeves. Editor: Clarence Kolster. Sound: John Buddy Myers. Musical Director: Al Short. Running Time: 72 minutes.

Cast: Benny Rubin (Benny Krantz), Marceline Day (Mary Norris), Rex Lease (Jim Grant), Marjorie "Babe" Kane (Doris Hill), Harry Lee (Papa Krantz), Greta Granstedt (college widow), Wesley Barry (Stubble), Robert Randall [Robert Livingston] (Dave Randall), James Wilcox (Smith).

Songs: "Must Be Love" [Lease; reprised by band at party, danced by Rubin, Kane; reprised in song by Kane], "So Long" [students], "Sunny Days" [students], "Wanna Find a Boy" [Kane, students], "You for Me" [Lease, Rubin, chorus] (Will Jason, Val Burton); "The Laugh Song" [Rubin] (Benny Rubin, Will Jason, Val Burton).

Disc: Brunswick 4798 (Rubin/"The Laugh Song"/78).

At MGM, Benny Rubin was just another featured clown, but at little Tiffany (formerly Tiffany-Stahl) he was a star. When the dialect comedian wasn't playing supporting roles in the likes of *Marianne* and *It's a Great Life,* he was taking top billing in the smaller studio's *Hot Curves,* a baseball comedy, and *Sunny Skies,* which was generally considered the worst of the 1929-30 crop of college football musicals.

Rubin (1899–1986) probably deserved a better break than he got in movies—after the late '30s, the industry's unwritten ban on dialect humor exiled him to small roles—for he was quite a versatile performer. Trained in vaudeville and burlesque, he could sing in an array of accents (complete with malaprops and wordplays such as "I would never cut off my nose to spite my race"), dance with a nimble flair, present convincing impressions, and even play the trombone. What he could not do, however, was carry a movie as second-rate as *Sunny Skies.*

By now, most of the comic variations on the wronged-athlete-makes-good plot had been used up, so the story by A. P. Younger threw in a heavy dose of pathos to complicate the mirth. Rubin was quite a sports fan—he played a baseball player in *They Learned About Women,* and his sprawling Encino, California, ranch contained its own ball diamond—but here he was merely the best chum of an egotistical college fullback played by Rex Lease, the Buddy Rogers of the quickies.

Brawny Jim Grant and nerdy Benny Krantz, freshmen at Standtech, find instant companionship in, respectively, the wholesome Mary Norris (Marceline Day, far too demure) and bubbly Doris Hill (Marjorie "Babe" Kane,

Marjorie "Babe" Kane gives Benny Rubin a twirl in Tiffany's lackluster *Sunny Skies*.

a younger, thinner Helen clone). Doris declares her intentions in song: "Wanna Find a Boy." Jim serenades his lady love with "Must Be Love" and "You for Me"; Lease's baritone is passable but appears to be dubbed. These dialogue and song sequences are disappointingly primitive for a mid-1930 release; Tiffany seemed not to have made much technical progress since George Jessel and *Lucky Boy*. The transitions into the songs are clumsy, too. At one point, Lease is giving Rubin pointers on lovemaking, then the music swells as a chorus from out of nowhere sings "You for Me," which inspires Lease to say forget it, just watch me sing. Besides his alleged way with a song, Grant also packs a mean right hand, which he uses to floor his teammate and major rival for Mary, breaking the latter's leg. Grant already has flunked off the squad, and the double setback hastens the fallen hero's departure for home.

The following year, Grant returns to Standtech to room with Benny, who has ma-

tured into a woman-chasing, drunken fool like everyone else on campus. Jim works his way back into good favor on the football field, but when an inebriated Benny high-steps it out of a window, Jim must choose between giving his severely injured pal a blood transfusion or scoring touchdowns for Alma Mater. Jim does both, redeeming himself with a life-saving pint and a game-winning dash, the latter ending with a flourish as the weakened youth collapses in the end zone.

"You can almost bear it," opined *Photoplay*, "until Benny Rubin starts getting pathetic and his pal gives him a blood transfusion. Then you've just got to get away from it all."[13] Done.

CHEER UP AND SMILE
(Fox; July 22, 1930)

Director: Sidney Lanfield. Associate Producer: Al Rockett. Adaptation and Dialogue:

Howard J. Green. Based on the magazine story "If I Was Alone with You" by Richard Connell (1929). Photography: Joseph Valentine. Editor: Ralph Dietrich. Sound: Al Bruzlin. Assistant Director: Ewing Scott. Running Time: 62 minutes.

Cast: Dixie Lee (Margie), Arthur Lake (Eddie Fripp), Olga Baclanova (Yvonne), "Whispering" Jack Smith (himself), Johnny Arthur (Andy), Charles Judels (Pierre), John Darrow (Tom), Sumner Getchell (Paul), Franklin Pangborn (professor), Buddy Messenger (Donald), John Wayne (student), J. Carrol Naish.

Songs: "The Scamp of the Campus," "The Shindig," "When You Look in My Eyes," "Where Can You Be?" [Smith], "You May Not Like It (but It's a Great Idea)" [Smith] (Raymond Klages, Jesse Greer).

Disc: RCA Victor 22443 (Smith/"You May Not Like It [but It's a Great Idea]"/"Where Can You Be?"/78).

No football in this one, just a story about a campus kid who pledges a fraternity and ends up a singing sensation on the radio—which was probably more of a stretch for Arthur Lake (1905–1986) than for Stanley Smith when he dashed the length of the field in *Sweetie*. But at 62 minutes, *Cheer Up and Smile* was at least over in a hurry.

Lake's character, one Eddie Fripp, is required by his fraternity to kick the first man he meets, who turns out to be an irate professor, and kiss the first female, who turns out to be a complete stranger. For the kick, the fellow is suspended from school; for the kiss, he is estranged from his girlfriend (first-billed Dixie Lee). Before the two are reunited, Eddie will go to work in a New York nightclub and attract the owner's flirtatious wife (a wasted Olga Baclanova), then take the place of a radio singer ("Whispering" Jack Smith, playing himself) when the singer is knocked unconscious during a holdup, then become an overnight hit despite, or perhaps because of, his unsteady voice.

Of the five Jesse Greer–Raymond Klages songs, "Where Can You Be?" was cited as the best. It and "You May Not Like It (but It's a Great Idea)" were sung in the film and subsequently recorded by Smith. But "Whispering" Jack flamed out on this, his third stab at motion pictures; the others were *The Big Party* (see

Chapter 5) and *Happy Days* (see Chapter 10). Smith was initially announced as the star of *Cheer Up and Smile* under its original title of *Alone with You*, which was touted by Fox as its first "radio romance."

The college scenes in *Cheer Up and Smile* were filmed on the campus of the University of Southern California. John Wayne, still hanging around the Fox lot, played a bit as one of Lake's fraternity cohorts. His appearance survives through the archive at UCLA, which holds a preserved print of the film.

GOOD NEWS
(MGM; August 23, 1930)

Directors: Nick Grinde, Edgar J. MacGregor. Screenplay: Frances Marion. Dialogue: Joe Farnham. Based on the musical play, book by Laurence Schwab and B. G. De Sylva, lyrics by De Sylva and Lew Brown, music by Ray Henderson (New York opening, September 6, 1927; 551 performances). Photography: Percy Hilburn. Editor: William Le Vanway. Sound: Douglas Shearer, Russell Franks. Art Director: Cedric Gibbons. Costumes: David Cox. Dance Direction: Sammy Lee. Running Time: approx. 88 minutes. Technicolor sequence.

Cast: Mary Lawlor (Connie Lane), Stanley Smith (Tom Marlowe), Bessie Love (Babe O'Day), Cliff Edwards (Kearney), Gus Shy (Bobby Randall), Lola Lane (Patricia Bingham), Thomas Jackson (coach), Delmer Daves (Beef Saunders), Billy Taft (freshman), Frank McGlynn (Professor "Comical Charlie" Kenyon), Dorothy McNulty [Penny Singleton] (Flo), Helyn Virgil, Vera Marsh (girls), Harry Earles (midget), Buster Crabbe (student with pipe), Ann Dvorak, Al "Rubberlegs" Norman, Abe Lyman and His Band.

Songs: "The Best Things in Life Are Free" [Smith], "Good News" [McNulty, chorus], "He's a Ladies' Man" [Shy; reprised by chorus], "Students Are We" [Lyman band; danced by chorus], "Tait Song" [students], "The Varsity Drag" [McNulty, chorus] (B. G. De Sylva, Lew Brown, Ray Henderson); "Football" [Smith, players; reprised by company], "If You're Not Kissing Me" [Smith, Lawlor] (Arthur Freed, Nacio Herb Brown); "Gee, but I'd Like to Make You Happy" [Shy, Love, twice], (Larry Shay, George Ward, Reggie Montgomery); "I Feel

Stanley Smith and Mary Lawlor get hitched in the now-lost Technicolor finale of MGM's *Good News*.

Pessimistic" [Edwards] (George Waggner, J. Russel Robinson); "Sweet Adeline" [players] (Richard H. Gerard, Harry Armstrong).

Disc: Music Masters JJA-19802 (bootleg LP; ST).

Video: MGM-UA (laserdisc; excerpts only).

It was bad enough that, as the film version of a hit Broadway show, *Good News* would have to face the inevitable comparisons to the original, but Metro's tardiness in bringing it to the screen led musical-wearied audiences to regard it as old hat.

Seeking to infuse the film with some originality, MGM supplemented the De Sylva-Brown-Henderson score with new material by the Arthur Freed–Nacio Herb Brown team and others. In fact, early publicity boasted that *Good News* would have no fewer than 15 songs.[14] But when the studio became nervous over the increasing public snubbing of musicals, some al-

ready filmed numbers were discarded. The stage originals "That's How You Know We're Co-eds" and "Lucky in Love" were snipped, as was the duet encore of "The Best Things in Life Are Free." Freed and Brown added "Football," a rah-rah song, and "If You're Not Kissing Me," a romantic duet. The bluesy "I Feel Pessimistic," was cowritten by George Waggner, best known as the director-producer of the 1941 horror classic *The Wolf Man*.

Mary Lawlor (b. 1911), the female romantic lead, was retained from the stage show, but not Zelma O'Neal, who was aligned with Paramount. Dorothy McNulty (the future Penny Singleton, b. 1908), who had played the soubrette in the Chicago company, was brought in for the secondary comic role. The vamp part was assigned to one of Metro's own, Bessie Love. Stanley Smith (1903–1971), a discovery from the Los Angeles legit stage who'd made his movie name with *Sweetie*, got to be a football hero again. He replaced the originally announced Charles Kaley. The Eddie Bracken look-alike Gus Shy (1894–1945) repeated his sidekick role from Broadway, and additional comedy was contributed by Cliff Edwards, cast as the Tait College team's singing trainer.

Sharing directorial duties were Nick Grinde, an MGM contractee whose career was spent mostly in "B" films, and Edgar McGregor, who had staged the Broadway production. In an interesting account to *The New York Times*, McGregor outlined the perceived differences between supervising a stage show and directing a motion picture.

> Everything you do on the stage must be "cheated" to your audience. ... We constantly have to keep figuring the mechanics with which to move the actors here and there about the stage to meet these demands. In producing the same play for the screen, however, you are free of all audience hampering and never need be bothered with juggling your players all around to keep them facing the audience. Here, your camera is your audience and you move it anywhere you choose....[15]

McGregor also noted the advantages that camera closeups lent to comedy sequences.

> For instance ... we show Bessie Love hiding under a bed with a huge cream cake. A fat man sits down suddenly on the bed and, plop! Her face is buried in the sticky mess. On the stage it would be impossible to take the audience under that bed and watch the action. All we had to do, however, was put the camera on a low tripod and shove it under the bed, just as if we moved our entire audience under the bed to watch Bessie's discomforture.[16]

Modern audiences may now have the chance to watch said discomforture, as *Good News* has re-emerged from obscurity. The film was kept out of circulation by MGM for decades because of the studio's 1947 remake, and it was not revived for television because it was missing the latter half of its final reel, a Technicolor production number reprising the song "Football" at a "jazz wedding" between star halfback Tom Marlowe (Smith) and his unlikely tutor (Lawlor). In 1990, with Penny Singleton in attendance, the incomplete version was screened at the Society for Cinephiles national convention in Hollywood. In 1993, most of the surviving musical numbers were released

on laserdisc for MGM-UA's "Dawn of Sound" series. In May 1994, with the missing footage replaced by stills, the reconstructed film was aired on the Turner Classic Movies cable channel. *Good News* is revealed to be a lively little feature, slowed by lengthy comic sequences (mainly antics by the severely overage Gus Shy) but highlighted by some well-filmed song-and-dance.

The "Varsity Drag" number, choreographed by Sammy Lee, is most delightful. The vivacious Flo (McNulty), sitting at the head of her Latin class with the professor away for a few minutes, asks her schoolmates, "Why don't they teach us something here that'll be of some good? ... We'll make Tait famous for 'The Varsity Drag'!" Her classmates push away their desks and chairs to create a dance floor, and the peppy blonde begins her breathtaking display of speed-singing and rubberlegged acrobatics. (Future star Ann Dvorak is easily recognized in the front row of the chorus.) During the refrain of the hotter-than-hot and newer-than-new melody, the routine segues into a series of imaginative sight gags—a map unspools to reveal a couple necking underneath, a trio of animated Roman soldiers dances atop a blackboard, the floor begins to smoke (as a superimposed thermometer shoots toward its top), and a temporarily exhausted McNulty is carted off in a wheelchair. And, as in the early Berkeley showcases for Warners, there's even a midget (Harry Earles, of *Freaks* and *The Unholy Three*). Complete with beanie, he climbs out of a wastebasket to join the fun!

The number winds down as the professor is about to return to the classroom, and the furniture is quickly returned to its usual positions. The prof, who tells his charges he's "delighted at your concentration," resumes the class by asking Flo what Caesar said upon his return from his first campaign. The dizzy dame grins, replying: "Down on your heads, and up on your toes!"

"Gee, but I'd Like to Make You Happy" is performed twice as an amusing song-and-dance duet for Shy and Love. The first rendition emphasizes the double meaning of the lyric "make you," as the bashful Bobby can only get that far in his titular declaration to his Babe. The reprise is sung after Bobby has "safely" promised to marry Babe if he wins the big game (he thinks he's not supposed to play), so now they can sing about their future together. McNulty, assisted by novelty dancer Al "Rubberlegs" Norman, leads the chorus again in a passable presentation of "Good News." Although *Good News* is hardly barren of music, there are signs of pre-release cutting. The "If You're Not Kissing Me" (Smith, Lawlor) and "I Feel Pessimistic" (Edwards) numbers, for example, both appear to be cut off in mid-note. A big disappointment is that the one surviving rendition of "The Best Things in Life Are Free," sung by Smith to Lawlor on the eve of Tait's showdown with rival Colton, lasts less than a minute.

After she watched *Good News* at the 1990 Cinecon, Penny Singleton had this to say about her first feature:

> I think you all deserve medals for sitting through that. The characters were supposed to have been representative of the college boys and girls of that era. But, looking at it today, I don't know. ... Actually, the movie version differed quite a bit from the Broadway rendition ... and I remember there was some talk at MGM that perhaps assigning Nick Grinde as director was a mistake. ... Nick had never done a musical film before, and he tended to give more emphasis to the story than to the songs and dances.[17]

After *Good News* and *Love in the Rough* (see Chapter 4), McNulty/Singleton returned to Broadway and her stage career, not to return to films for six years, and then with a new name and hairdo. "The first time I came to Hollywood, I really wasn't very interested in motion pictures. I was used to the theater and live audiences, and like most young people I thought I knew what was good for me," she said in 1990.[18]

Despite the care taken by the filmmakers, *Good News* couldn't counter the prevailing opinion that it was just another football story. Trimmed to less than 90 minutes, the film seemed little more than a programmer, although *Variety*'s "Bige" called the film "too fast, too peppy, too entertaining to flop."[19] Commented *Photoplay*: "This one, like the pardon from the governor, came too late. *Good News* has been stolen so many times that it's no longer news. But it is done in a sprightly manner, and if you haven't seen the Varsity Drag so often that you're bored, you'll love it."[20] Fairly or not, the 1930 *Good News* will always be in the shadow of the more popular remake, in which

Charles Walters directed June Allyson and Peter Lawford through their campus love affair.

MAYBE IT'S LOVE
(Warner Bros.; October 4, 1930)

Director: William Wellman. Screenplay and Dialogue: Joseph Jackson. Story: Mark Canfield [Darryl F. Zanuck]. Photography: Robert Kurrle. Editor: Edward McDermott. Costumes: Earl Luick. Musical Directors: Erno Rapée, Louis Silvers. Running Time: 71 minutes.

Cast: Joan Bennett (Nan Sheffield), Joe E. Brown (Speed Hanson), James Hall (Tommy Nelson), Laura Lee (Betty), Anders Randolph (Mr. Nelson), Sumner Getchell (Whiskers), George Irving (President Sheffield), George Bickel (trustee), Howard Jones (Coach Bob Brown). The All-Americans [colleges in brackets]: Bill Banker [Tulane], George Gibson [Minnesota], Howard Harpster [Carnegie Tech], Kenneth Haycraft [Minnesota], Ray Montgomery [Pittsburgh], Tim Moynihan [Notre Dame], Otto Pommerening [Michigan], Russell Saunders [Southern California], Wear Schoonover [Arkansas], Paul Scull [Pennsylvania], Elmer "Red" Sleight [Purdue].

Songs: "The All-American" [Hall, Bennett, players], "Keep It Up for Upton" [students; reprised by players, then by students, band], "Maybe It's Love" [Bennett; reprised by students, then by Hall, then on phonograph record, then by Hall, players] (Sidney Mitchell, Archie Gottler, George W. Meyer).

Warner Bros.' intended draw for *Maybe It's Love* was neither the starring trio of Joan Bennett, Joe E. Brown and James Hall, nor the undistinguished story and dialogue that came courtesy of Darryl F. "Mark Canfield" Zanuck and Joseph Jackson. Nor was the attraction musical, for the mere three songs were only so-so. No, the gimmick for this football romance was the presence of the 1930 All-America team, although the honest-to-goodness athletes who made up this eleven were actually members of the '28 and '29 units.

The plot has Brown's Speed Hanson, a standout player for tiny Upton College, conspiring with Bennett's Nan Sheffield, the bookish daughter of the school president, to attract the nation's best stars. This is to placate the impatient college trustees, which will oust the president if Upton loses for the 13th straight autumn to its archrival, Parsons. Nan discards her spectacles and sounds her siren's song, "Maybe It's Love," during a string of "chance" meetings with the athletes (who must have been every bit as uncomfortable before a camera as they appear to be). Also bolstering the squad is stuck-up rich kid Tommy Nelson (Hall), who disregards his father's wishes and follows Nan to Upton.

The players expose Nan's ruse on the night before the big game, but they forgive her and take the field against Parsons. Although they are supposed to have the best players in the country, the Uptons don't prevail until Tommy dashes for a last-second touchdown. Speed, shorn of his starting position, is forced to view most of the action from a locked stadium cellar with Tommy's fuming father (Anders Randolph).

Laura Lee, Brown's paramour in *Top Speed* (see Chapter 4), is allotted less than a minute on screen as Speed's girl. But a look at the orig-

inal screenplay reveals two Brown-Lee song-and-dance numbers, "I Love to Do It" and a reprise of "The All-American."[21] They either were filmed and then removed, or were deleted before shooting. Between them, romancers Bennett and Hall are asked to sing the theme song, "Maybe It's Love," three of the four times it's heard. On the final go-around, the All-Americans (allegedly) join in the singing, forming an impromptu chorus-line huddle captured in an overhead camera shot with Bennett in the middle, swaying her arms like a conductor and patting her boys on their oversized heads. It's the closest thing to a dance number in what survives of the picture.

No, *Maybe It's Love* (retitled *Eleven Men and a Girl* for television showings) is not about music, it's about football—right down to the Upton coach, the famed Howard Jones of the University of Southern California. Perhaps the funniest moment in the mediocre film comes when Jones takes a long look at goofball Brown, who is doing distracting windsprints in front of the bench, and barks, "Will somebody take care of this maniac?"

CHAPTER 7

1929–1930: *You Will Remember Vienna*

The operetta began to go out of fashion 60 years ago, although the kind of melodious and stylized entertainment represented by the form has survived in the likes of *The Phantom of the Opera*, *Les Misérables* and *Miss Saigon*—those blockbuster "musical plays" heavily attended on '80s and '90s Broadway. When many casual theatergoers think of operetta now, it is with a little derision, for what comes to mind is the old-fashioned, sentimental "camp" that was parodied so savagely in *Little Mary Sunshine*, a singing-mountie spoof written in the 1950s that, unfortunately, is revived more today than many of the shows that it targets.

Of course, not all "little operas" were sentimental stories or were set in mythological locales, and even those that were hardly deserve such a bad rap. Some of the very best operettas were written during the Golden Age of American musical theater, and they stack up pretty well against their musical comedy counterparts, which were generally more hip at the time but now may seem just as dated. Instead, the passage of years has endowed many of the better operettas with a fairytale quality that gives them a timeless feel.

Early in this century, the fledgling American operetta was being influenced more by the romantic Middle European model than by the droll British "comic opera" (best known in the works of Gilbert and Sullivan) or by the racier, more satirical French "opera comique." The major force behind early operetta in this country—the Irish-born composer Victor Herbert (1856–1924)—was trained in Germany, and the two composers who dominated the form in the '20s—Rudolf Friml (1879–1972) and Sigmund Romberg (1887–1951) hailed from Bohemia and Hungary, respectively. When Hollywood sought to bring operettas to the screen, it often

would be with music penned by one of those three. But among all the European-style operettas, there were also examples with French (*The Love Parade*, discussed in Chapter 9, and others) and English (*Sweet Kitty Bellairs*) influences.

There was also a new strain of operetta that was more uniquely American, both in music and libretto. Jerome Kern and Oscar Hammerstein II's *Show Boat*, which premiered in Washington, D.C., on November 15, 1927, and which opened on Broadway the following December 27, is cited variously as the first truly "American" operetta or as the first "musical play." It was set in America, its characters were American (and spoke as if they were), and its score adroitly mixed traditional, Europe-derived melodic styles with uniquely American idioms: jazz, blues and spirituals. More tellingly, *Show Boat* had a social conscience; its story, based on the Edna Ferber novel, dealt in an "adult" manner with themes of miscegenation, marital infidelity, alcoholism and the exploitation of the working class. Unfortunately, Hollywood failed to do justice to the Ferber novel when it was adapted for the screen in 1929. *Rio Rita*, another distinctly American operetta, received better treatment when it was made into a talkie a few months later.

But most early film operettas stiffed commercially, for the less sophisticated majority of the filmgoing public did not warm to them. Romantic escapism of the Valentino-Novarro school may have been popular in silents, but talkie audiences wanted more realism. Even as Hollywood, spurred by the success of a few early examples (*The Desert Song*, *Rio Rita*) began to churn out operettas more regularly, exhibitors dreaded having to book them. The public became so wary that when Universal re-

released its 1925 melodrama *The Phantom of the Opera* in 1930 with dialogue sequences, some would-be patrons stayed away because they thought the "Opera" in the title meant the film was a musical.

"Operettas are the hardest of all types of pictures to be sold now," read a *Variety* item in July 1930, "with exhibs claimed sidestepping them if at all possible. One important indie in the east who declares the best of the operettas were duds for him, shelved one that he booked rather than take a chance on playing it."[1]

SHOW BOAT
(Universal; March 16, 1929)

Director: Harry Pollard. Director of Prologue: A. B. Heath. Continuity: Charles Kenyon. Dialogue: Harry Pollard, Tom Reed. Story Supervision: Edward J. Montagne. Based on the novel by Edna Ferber (1926), with songs from the musical play with book and lyrics by Oscar Hammerstein II and music by Jerome Kern (New York opening, December 27, 1927; 572 performances). Titles: Tom Reed. Photography: Gilbert Warrenton. Editors: Maurice Pivar, Daniel Mandell, Edward Cahn. Sound: C. Roy Hunter. Assistant Director: Robert Ross. Art Direction: Charles D. Hall, Joseph C. Wright. Costumes: Johanna Mathieson. Synchronization and Score: Joseph Cherniavsky. Running Time (minus 18-minute prologue): 109 or 126 minutes (part-talking version), 114 minutes (silent version).

Cast: Laura La Plante (Magnolia Hawks), Joseph Schildkraut (Gaylord Ravenal), Otis Harlan (Captain Andy Hawks), Emily Fitzroy (Parthenia Hawks), Alma Rubens (Julie Dozier), Elise Bartlett (Ellie), Jack McDonald (Windy), Jane La Verne (Magnolia as a child/ Kim Ravenal), Neely Edwards (Schultzy), Theodore Lorch (Frank), Stepin Fetchit (Joe), Gertrude Howard (Queenie), George Chesebro (Steve), Harry Holden (Means), Blanche Craig (Mrs. Means), Grace Cunard (utility woman), Max Asher (utility man), Scott Mattraw (butcher), Joe Mills (old tragedian), Richard Coleman (Negro boss), James V. Ayres (drum major), Ralph Yearsley (The Killer), Jim Coleman (stagehand), Carl Herlinger (wheelsman), Tom McGuire (policeman). As Themselves in Prologue: Helen Morgan, Jules Bledsoe, Aunt Jemima [Tess Gardella], The Jubilee Singers, Carl Laemmle, Florenz Ziegfeld, Otis Harlan.

Songs in Main Story: "Can't Help Lovin' Dat Man" [La Plante, dubbed by Eva Olivotti], "Ol' Man River" [La Plante, dubbed by Olivotti] (Oscar Hammerstein II, Jerome Kern); "Coon, Coon, Coon" [La Plante, dubbed by Olivotti] (Gene Jefferson, Leo Friedmann); "Down South" (Sigmund Spaeth, William H. Middleton); "Here Comes That Show Boat" (Billy Rose, Maceo Pinkard); "The Lonesome Road" [Bledsoe, offscreen] (Gene Austin, Nathaniel Shilkret); "Love Sings a Song in My Heart" (Clarence J. Marks, Joseph Cherniavsky); "Deep River" [La Plante, dubbed by Olivotti], "I've Got Shoes" [La Plante, dubbed by Olivotti] (trad.).

Songs in Prologue: "Can't Help Lovin' Dat Man" [Morgan, Jubilee Singers], "C'mon, Folks" [Gardella, Jubilee Singers], "Hey, Feller!" [Gardella, Jubilee Singers], "Ol' Man River" [Bledsoe, Jubilee Singers] (Oscar Hammerstein II, Jerome Kern); "Bill" [Morgan] (P. G. Wodehouse, Oscar Hammerstein II, Jerome Kern).

Video: MGM-UA (laserdisc).

We include the first, part-talking film version of *Show Boat* in this chapter only by technicality. Its direct basis was in the original Edna Ferber dramatic novel, not the operetta-like stage show with which it has only a tenuous relationship. The story of why *Show Boat*—now known less as a literary classic than as the most famous musical of the American theater's Golden Era—turned out so strangely on its first cinematic interpretation begins with a look at the man behind the project.

Carl Laemmle, the eccentric czar of Universal Pictures, had been one of the first major movie tycoons to set up shop in Hollywood, but by the mid '20s his company had a decidedly second-rate posture. Unlike its larger competitors, Universal lacked the massive first-run theater chains with which to blanket its product; instead, its lifeblood was in the smaller, independently owned neighborhood, small-town and rural subsequent-run houses. Its fare leaned primarily to unpretentious "program" material— Westerns, melodramas, knockabout comedies— that larger studios utilized as filler. In the months following *The Jazz Singer*, Universal was slow to react to the inevitability of sound. Only the largest movie houses—few of which

Laura La Plante and Joseph Schildkraut played the ill-fated couple of Magnolia and Gaylord in Universal's part-talkie version of *Show Boat*.

showed Universal product—could afford to be wired for the new sound technology. So when Laemmle, in the summer of 1928, took out trade ads proclaiming his company as the steadfast "friend of the exhibitor," it was a gesture of self-interest, not altruism.

When Laemmle bought the screen rights to *Show Boat* for $65,000 in October 1926, it was in order to adapt Ferber's two-month-old book, not the stage musical based on the book, which then was barely in the talking stages.[2] Of course, the film would be made as a silent. Laemmle intended *Show Boat* as one of his first-rank "Jewel" productions, a costly adaptation of a prestigious literary work, like Universal's recent *Uncle Tom's Cabin*. Laemmle even hired the director of *Uncle Tom's Cabin*, Harry Pollard, to direct Ferber's sweeping story of life on the Mississippi.

Filming began in July of 1928 with Laura La Plante (b. 1904) and Joseph Schildkraut (1895–1964) in the lead roles—Magnolia Hawks, the star of her family's river-going Cot-

ton Palace (named the Cotton Blossom in the novel), and her love interest, the dashing but reckless gambler Gaylord Ravenal. La Plante was Universal's top female star, best known for her portrayal of the heroine in the popular horror thriller *The Cat and the Canary* (1927). Schildkraut had been in Hollywood since 1921, when he played Lillian Gish's nobleman beau in D. W. Griffith's *Orphans of the Storm*, but was better known as the son of the great German actor Rudolph Schildkraut. (Joseph's wife, Elise Bartlett, was cast in a secondary role.) Production was completed by October, but by then, Jolson's *The Singing Fool* was on its way to a record gross, and it became desirable to infuse *Show Boat* with some dialogue and music. Complicating this further was the tremendous popularity of the stage *Show Boat*, for the memorable music of the Broadway show would be inevitably associated with any subsequent version of the property.

Universal hastily added about 40 minutes of dialogue and singing to its film. The musical numbers, supervised by Joseph Cherniavsky, contained traditional black spirituals and a handful of pop tunes to lend Old South atmosphere (one of the latter, "The Lonesome Road," became a top seller). But clearly this would not do. On January 17, 1929, after months of negotiations, the studio purchased the rights to the theatrical version for $100,000 and a share of the net profits.[3] It was too late, and too costly, to do more than graft a couple of the Kern-Hammerstein songs onto the finished film. "Ol' Man River" replaced "Carry Me Back to Old Virginny" during a scene in which Magnolia sings river songs in a cabaret, and "Can't Help Lovin' Dat Man" supplanted "After the Ball" for a concert sequence in which Magnolia is watched by her estranged husband in the audience at a Broadway theater. Other themes from the stage score were used as background music.

Less than a week after his acquisition of the stage rights, Laemmle had filmed an 18-minute prologue of musical highlights from the stage production. There were selections sung by Helen Morgan ("Bill" and "Can't Help Lovin' Dat Man"), Jules Bledsoe ("Ol' Man River") and Tess "Aunt Jemima" Gardella ("C'mon, Folks" and "Hey, Feller!"). The prologue was introduced by Florenz Ziegfeld, the producer of the play, and Laemmle himself. Otis Harlan, Captain Andy Hawks in the main story, appeared as the master of ceremonies.[4]

To reviewers, the prologue looked pretty good compared to what they found to be an overlong, stilted melding of musical comedy and melodrama in the main story. The reviews were mixed, and the grosses could not match the lofty cost of production. Richard Watts, Jr., of the *New York Herald Tribune*, for example, called the film "a long, tedious and only occasionally attractive exhibit."[5] Although some commentators felt the role of Magnolia called for more than La Plante's range could give it, her effort was mainly applauded. (Her singing and banjo-playing were both dubbed, the former by Eva Olivotti.) Schildkraut's theatrical posturing was thought off-putting, and so was Emily Fitzroy's overdone matriarch Parthy Ann Hawks. Harlan hardly had a chance to give life to Captain Andy Hawks, for Charles Kenyon's screenplay had him drowned less than halfway through. (Andy dies at a midpoint of the book as well, but fans of the stageplay, and the sub-

sequent movie versions, are accustomed to seeing him stay on longer.)

"Kann" of *The Film Daily* declared the film "an orgy in footage ... practically every major sequence is drawn out ... to the point of fatigue. Several sequences, on the other hand, are splendid and the ending, beautiful. ... Pollard had an opportunity to make a memorable picture, but he didn't."[6] Laemmle responded to the criticism about the length by cutting the part-sound version from 126 to 109 minutes for general release. The tentative sound recording came in for additional knocks.

The most amazing casting was that of the drawling Stepin Fetchit as Joe, the proud black laborer played by Jules Bledsoe in the first Broadway production and by Paul Robeson on the London stage and in the 1936 film remake. The only principal to be completely unscathed critically was Alma Rubens, who played the ill-fated mulatto singer Julie Dozier (Julie La Verne in the play), but the actress would not be able to enjoy the praise. A heroin addict, Rubens suffered a nervous breakdown as the *Show Boat* filming ended, attempted suicide a month later and was committed to a mental hospital. She died in 1931. The film ignored the controversial miscegenation subplot of Ferber's novel by removing Julie from the show boat because of her firing by Parthy (the tall, angular Fitzroy as a rather monstrous presence) for her calming influence over the young Magnolia.

The 1929 *Show Boat* went unseen for decades, as the property was remade by Universal seven years later and then by MGM in 1951. Before making its version, Metro acquired the rights to the novel and assumed ownership of the two Universal films. In time, the '29 film was feared lost. The picture portion was found, but not without some effort. The search was prompted by Miles Kreuger, author of the book *Show Boat: The Story of a Classic American Musical.* Kreuger wanted to show all three *Show Boats* in a tribute he was organizing for the New York Museum of Modern Art on the 50th anniversary (December 27, 1977) of the Broadway opening of *Show Boat.* An incomplete negative for the picture portion to the part-talkie version was located at MGM, but it lacked the opening and closing sequences. Then, a complete negative of the *silent* version, with Danish intertitles, was found in the Danish Film Archives. A complete version could now be printed, but which—the silent silent or the silent part-talkie? Kreuger recommended the latter, so viewers could see how the musical numbers were staged for the hybrid edition, and the film was shown with its successors on the anniversary.[7]

Excerpts of the first *Show Boat* re-emerged in 1990 on a laserdisc produced by the Voyager Company, for its "Criterion Collection" series in cooperation with MGM-UA, as a supplement to the complete 1936 version. This footage was from the hybrid edition, so there was no speech, although Tess Gardella was seen and heard singing "C'mon, Folks" from the prologue.[8] However, in 1995 MGM-UA released a mainly complete version of the '29 feature (sans prologue) in a laserdisc package with the two later films. This 106-minute print, telecast on the Turner Classic Movies cable channel, was restored by Turner Entertainment Co. According to Turner preservationist Richard P. May, playback discs for about half of the film were found at the Library of Congress, and most of the remainder of the movie was covered by duplicating sections of the original music. In the reels that originally had talk and singing, subtitles were used where sound could not be recovered. The "new" *Show Boat* contains 13 minutes of dialogue, but the only singing that survives is a few seconds of La Plante's "Coon, Coon, Coon" and an off-screen rendition of "The Lonesome Road" by Jules Bledsoe as Magnolia and Gaylord are reunited on the Cotton Palace at the climax.

Although Laemmle's failure to keep up with the times blunted his first attempt at *Show Boat*, his son Carl, Jr., redeemed him by producing the superlative 1936 film—which featured Irene Dunne, Allan Jones, Paul Robeson and 1927 stage originals Helen Morgan and Charles Winninger. Ironically, its exorbitant cost helped cause the Laemmles to lose their cherished studio. By then, Universal had found an enduring niche, but it would be with monsters and not with musicals.

THE DESERT SONG
(Warner Bros.; April 8, 1929)

Director: Roy Del Ruth. Scenario and Dialogue: Harvey Gates. Based on the operetta, book by Laurence Schwab, Frank Mandel, Otto Harbach and Oscar Hammerstein II, lyrics by Harbach and Hammerstein, music by Sigmund Romberg (New York opening, November 30, 1926; 471 performances). Photography: Barney McGill. Editor: Ralph Dawson. Sound: George R. Groves. Costumes: Earl Luick. Running Time: 121 minutes. Technicolor sequences.

Cast: John Boles (Pierre Birabeau/The Red Shadow), Louise Fazenda (Susan), Myrna Loy (Azuri), Carlotta King (Margot Bonvalet), Johnny Arthur (Benny Kidd), Edward Martindel (General Birabeau), John Miljan (Captain Fontaine), Jack Pratt (Pasha), Otto Hoffman (Hasse), Robert E. Guzman (Sid El Kar), Marie Wells (Clementina), Del Elliott (rebel).

Songs: "The Desert Song" ("Blue Heaven") [Boles, King, twice], "French Military Marching Song" [King, soldiers, girls], "Let Love Go" [Pratt], "Love's Dear Yearning" [Boles], "My Little Castagnette" [Wells, girls], "One Alone" [Boles, men, twice; reprised by Boles, King], "One Flower Grows Alone in Your Garden" [Guzman, Pratt, men], "Pigeon Song" [Guzman, chorus], "The Riff Song" ("Ho!") [Boles, men], "Romance" [King], "Song of the Brass Key" [Wells, Guzman, girls] (Otto Harbach, Oscar Hammerstein II, Sigmund Romberg); "The Sabre Song" [King], "Then You Will Know" [Boles, King] (Frank Mandel, Otto Harbach, Oscar Hammerstein II, Sigmund Romberg).

In 1925 and '26, a band of Moroccan fighters called the Riffs mounted a fearless rebellion against the stern rule of the French protectorate. The world's newspapers were full of the exploits of Abdel Krim, a native chieftain who battled the French and Spanish before being forced into surrender and exile. The front-page accounts of this latter-day Robin Hood inspired the creation of *The Desert Song*, one of the most beloved of American operettas.

The original Broadway production received poor reviews, but the popularity of Sigmund Romberg's lush score (lyrics by Oscar Hammerstein II and Otto Harbach) enabled it to rack up nearly 500 performances. Strong sheet-music sales for three tunes—the rousing "Riff Song" and two moving love ballads, "One Alone" and the title song, also known as "Blue Heaven"—created a potent word of mouth that overcame the critical darts. Robert Halliday starred as the "Red Shadow," the mysterious

The fair Margot (Carlotta King) dares to find out the secret of the mysterious "Red Shadow" (John Boles) in Warner Bros.' *The Desert Song*.

leader of a tribe of Riff horsemen, and Vivienne Segal originated the female lead of Margot Bonvalet, the young French woman who is attracted to the masked marauder.

Warner Bros., which racked up so many "firsts" in the domain of sound films, gained a couple more with its 1929 part-color production of *The Desert Song*. It was the screen's initial all-talking, all-singing, all-dancing operetta, and was the first Broadway musical adaptation of the sound era. The studio purchased the screen rights to the property from its authors (Frank Mandel and Laurence Schwab, coproducers of the stage show, and Harbach, Romberg and Hammerstein) for $65,000 on May 4, 1928.[9] This was two months before the debut of Warners' landmark all-talking *Lights of New York*. But a snag over territorial theatrical rights threatened to hold up the deal, which stipulated that the film could not be released before April 1, 1929. One Lillian Albertson, who owned the West Coast rights, filed suit against Warner Bros., Schwab and Mandel, charging that a talking film version would be an infringement on her potential profits. A federal court set an important precedent by ruling in favor of the producers and picture makers.[10]

The production, which cost nearly $400,000, was further delayed, until early October, while a leading lady was being sought. Carlotta King (b. 1900?), a radio and concert-hall soprano who had spent three seasons on the Keith-Orpheum vaudeville circuit, was finally signed, allegedly after Jack Warner himself heard her on the studio-owned station KFWB. The male lead was John Boles (1895–1969), a handsome Texan with an eclectic background that included college (University of Texas at Austin) pre-med studies, a wartime stint in Army Intelligence and classical voice training in Paris. A discovery of Gloria Swanson, he lately had been reduced to playing leads in crime melodramas (*The Last Warning, Scandal*) for Universal. But Boles had some stage experience, and when sound came in, it revitalized his career. His rich baritone would be one of the prime assets of *The Desert Song*. The supporting cast included Louise Fazenda, one of Warners' top comediennes; Johnny Arthur, a whiny-voiced comic actor; and, as an exotic native dancer named Azuri, the young Myrna Loy (1905–1993), who had worked her way up to third billing.

Loy had been under contract to Warners for four years and nearly 30 films, a handful of which she had talked in, but she was dismayed to find that she would have to test for her *Desert Song* role. "It was a tough test," she wrote in her autobiography,

> I not only had to dance and talk but create my own dialect as well. … I was left on my own to determine how a North African native spoke. Having studied a little French in school, I used that as a base to create an incredible accent. For years afterward, friends would approach me with a strange look and mimic one of my lines, "Vere ees Pierrre?"[11]

Loy was nervous about taking the role—she felt that Warners production chief Darryl Zanuck didn't have enough confidence in her. But she did just fine—maybe too well. *The Desert Song* helped typecast Loy for several years as an exotic non-American.

"Vitaphone sings 'The Desert Song' with all its Original Stage Enchantment … Love's heart beat set to the golden notes of the most famous music play of our generation," claimed ads for the film. Yet in its souvenir program, Warners took pains to separate its version from the original: "Where the desert scenes in the stage production were painted drops, the same scenes in the film version were photographed in the heart of the Great American Desert, with the sweep of undulating sandhills and sandy ridges comparable to the wastes of the great Sahara itself." Although the book and score were shortened, the mildly illogical story was left mostly intact, thanks to scripter Harvey Gates and director Roy Del Ruth.

Behind the Red Shadow's mask is Pierre Birabeau, who sympathizes with the Riffs because of their unfair treatment by the French. He submerges all clues to his secret identity by pretending he is weak and simple-minded in the presence of his father (Edward Martindel), the commander of the occupying French forces, and Margot (King), the woman he pines for. Margot is engaged to be married to Captain Fontaine (John Miljan), who is determined to quell the Riff uprising by capturing the Red Shadow; his affections are sidetracked by the devious Azuri. Secondary to the main plot are Benny Kidd (Arthur), a cowardly newspaper reporter, and his loyal secretary, Susan (Fazenda). Her motto: "If you're going to let a man dictate to you, you might as well marry him."

Pierre, as the Red Shadow, shows up at the French fortress to court Margot with a melody—the famed "Desert Song"—but her reluctance to follow him into the desert forces him to abduct her to the desert palace of the powerful Ali Ben Ali (Jack Pratt). She tells her bemused kidnapper that her true love is Pierre, but in "The Sabre Song," she holds up the Red Shadow's weapon and realizes that the mysterious masked man owns her heart. General Birabeau shows up and challenges the Red Shadow to a duel; the masked one naturally refuses. By custom, for this presumed act of cowardice, the Red Shadow is forced into desert exile and certain death. Azuri reveals the charade to the heartbroken elder Birabeau by telling him that "a Christian will not fight his father." (In the play, the verb was "kill.") Fontaine returns from the desert and announces the death of the Red Shadow at the hands of Pierre, who walks in holding the chieftain's mask and costume. Margot is saddened by the news, but when the two are alone he dons his trophies as she realizes that Pierre and the Red Shadow are one and the same.

Considering the time at which it was filmed (shooting began on October 8, 1928), it seems futile to fault *The Desert Song* for its acute staginess. At this point, it seemed more crucial just to get the sound to register correctly than to provide cinematic nuance. *The Desert Song* is precisely what it was intended to be: a faithful transcription of a first-class Broadway show—right down to the 10-minute intermission announced by a title halfway through. Subtitles are used frequently, mainly to bridge scenes or introduce characters. They could also be conveniently transitional, as when Benny blunders into the Riff camp by falling off his horse and down a sand dune. We see him—in a long shot that was obviously filmed outdoors—tumbling through the sand, before a title appears to announce "Benny Kidd—society reporter for the *Paris Herald*—in Morocco for his health." This is followed by a medium shot—clearly taken on the soundstage—in which our man reaches the end of his fall, practically at the feet of the "Orientals."

Despite its uncinematic quality, *The Desert Song* was a hit, grossing $1.5 in the United States and $3 million worldwide. It inspired Warner Bros. to commission Romberg and Hammerstein to write one original operetta per year. The press was mostly favorable. *Photoplay* considered the film "pictorially beautiful and interesting to music lovers."[12] Both *The New York Times* and *The Film Daily* pointed out the unintentional laughs in the screenplay, but even Richard Watts, Jr., who had savaged the stage version, had to admit to his *Herald Tribune* readers that the movie was "an interesting experiment ... for all its obvious defects, a highly creditable bit of cinema reporting."[13]

Boles' singing is dynamic; his dramatic technique is less accomplished. Leading lady King hardly registers at all. Her voice tends toward the affected (although she capably sings the rousing "French Military Marching Song"), she is poorly photographed, and her acting isn't particularly convincing. One wishes that Vivienne Segal, the first Margot, or Bernice Claire, who played the role on Broadway and on tour, would have been given the chance here. Claire's livelier interpretation survives in a 1932 Vitaphone short, *The Red Shadow*, in which she and Alexander Gray, who played opposite her on the stage, present excerpts from the stage show. King never made another feature film. She was signed by MGM and at one point was announced to star in an adaptation of *Rose-Marie*, but after serving out the first five months of her yearlong contract without a nibble, she returned to vaudeville.

The Desert Song was remade twice, both times by Warner Bros. Dennis Morgan and Irene Manning starred in a 1943 film that was modernized so as to pit the Riffs against the Nazis in 1939. The version most familiar to modern audiences was produced in 1953 with Gordon MacRae and Kathryn Grayson, although the "Red Shadow" appellation became a casualty of the Cold War. The endurance of *The Desert Song*, which continues to be revived on the stage, may be summed up by a wry comment by John Boles years after he hung up his mask and cape: "No matter how well you might have played Hamlet at one time, they still remember you for the way you sang 'One Alone' from *The Desert Song*."[14]

MARRIED IN HOLLYWOOD
(Fox; September 21, 1929)

Director: Marcel Silver. Adaptation and Dialogue: Harlan Thompson. Based on the operettas *Married in Hollywood* by Leopold Jacobson and Bruno Hardt-Warden (1928), and *Ein Waltzertraum* by Oscar Straus (1907). Photography: Charles Van Enger, Sol Halperin. Editor: Dorothy Spencer. Sound: George Leverett. Assistant Directors: Virgil Hart, Sid Bower. Costumes: Sophie Wachner, Alice O'Neill. Dance Direction: Edward Royce. Running Time: 110 minutes. Multicolor sequence.

Cast: J. Harold Murray (Prince Nicholai), Norma Terris (Mary Lou Hopkins/Mitzi Hofman), Walter Catlett (Joe Glitner), Irene Palasty (Annushka), Lennox Pawle (King Alexander), Tom Patricola (Mahai), Evelyn Hall (Queen Louise), John Garrick (stage prince), Douglas Gilmore (Adjutant Octavian), Gloria Grey (Charlotte), Jack Stambaugh (Captain Jacobi), Bert Sprotte (Herr von Herzen), Lelia Karnelly (Frau von Herzen), Herman Bing (German director), Paul Ralli (Namari), Donald Gallaher (movie director), Carey Harrison, Roy Seegar (detectives).

Songs: "Deep in Love," "A Man ... a Maid" (Harlan Thompson, Oscar Straus), "Dance Away the Night," "Peasant Love Song" (Harlan Thompson, Dave Stamper); "Bridal Chorus," "National Anthem" (Arthur Kay).

The backstage and operetta genres were mixed in what was misleadingly billed as the first operetta written for the screen. Actually, *Married in Hollywood* was partially based on a 1928 light opera of the same name written by Leopold Jacobson and Bruno Hardt-Warden, and two of its six songs were adapted from *Ein Waltzertraum*, a 1907 work by Oscar Straus. But it was the first Viennese operetta made into a sound picture, and the first non-revue musical with a Hollywood setting.

Its stars were two Broadway imports best

known for their roles in Ziegfeld blockbusters. J. Harold Murray (1891–1940), a handsome baritone, played Jim in the original cast of *Rio Rita*. Norma Terris (1902–1989), a statuesque soprano, was the first Magnolia in *Show Boat*. In *Married in Hollywood*, he played a Balkan prince named Nicholai; she was Mary Lou Hopkins, an American singer who encounters the prince while on tour with an operetta company in Vienna.

Nicky wants to renounce his station and marry the girl. His mother (Evelyn Hall) is so opposed that she has her son locked up, and Mary Lou sadly returns to America. On the ship home, however, she gives a concert that wows a motion picture producer (Walter Catlett) who signs her to a contract. The renamed Mitzi Hofman becomes a Hollywood star, and her first film is such a great success that she is allowed to write the screenplay for her second. Lovesick, she concocts a story not unlike her own, except that it will end with her stabbing the prince in the back as he heads down the aisle with someone else. But there is no need for such melodramatics, for among the extras hired for the film is her beloved Nicky. A revolt has forced him from his homeland, and he can now marry the woman he loves.

All that exists now of *Married in Hollywood* is a 12-minute fragment, preserved at UCLA, from the final Multicolor reel. The footage originated with Norma Terris, who made it a gift to the historian Miles Kreuger. *Married in Hollywood*, according to Kreuger, contains the first dream sequence in a movie musical, as well as the first use of a split screen in a talkie. There is no music sung at the climax, an oddity for an operetta.

Fox reportedly spent about $750,000 making *Married in Hollywood*. The film earned some good reviews—*The New York Times* thought it "adroitly interspersed with joviality and extremely clever photographic embellishments,"[15] and Catlett, Tom Patricola, and Irene Palasty were praised for their comic acting. But this was the kind of picture that died in the sticks.

RIO RITA
(RKO; October 6, 1929)

Director: Luther Reed. Producer: William LeBaron. Scenario: Luther Reed. Dialogue: Russell Mack. Based on the operetta, book by Guy Bolton and Fred Thompson, lyrics by Joseph McCarthy, music by Harry Tierney (New York opening, February 2, 1927; 494 performances). Photography: Robert Kurrle, Lloyd Knechtel. Editor: William Hamilton. Sound: Hugh McDowell. Art Director: Max Rée. Costumes: Max Rée. Musical Director: Victor Baravalle. Chorus Master: Pietro Cimini. Dance Direction: Pearl Eaton. Running Time: 135 minutes. Technicolor sequences.

Cast: Bebe Daniels (Rita Ferguson), John Boles (Captain Jim Stewart), Don Alvarado (Roberto Ferguson), Bert Wheeler (Chick Bean), Robert Woolsey (Ed Lovett), Dorothy Lee (Dolly), Georges Renevant (General Ravenoff), Helen Kaiser (Katie Bean), Tiny Sandford (Davalos), Nick De Ruiz (Paroné), Sam Nelson (McGinn), Fred Burns (Wilkins), Eva Rosita (Carmen), Sam Blum (café proprietor), Fred Scott (singing ranger), Benny Corbett, Tom Smith, Bud Osborne, Bud McClure, Hank Bell (rangers), Blue Washington (bank robber), Richard Alexander (Gonzales), Charles Stevens (José), Pearl Eaton and the RKO Pictures Beauty Chorus, Pietro Cimini Grand Chorus, Robert Livingston.

Songs/Musical Numbers: "Are You There?" [Lee, Wheeler, chorus], "Beneath the Silken Shawl" [Rosita], "The Charro Dance" [dancers], "Espanola" [Woolsey, Rosita], "If You're in Love, You'll Waltz" [Boles], "I'm Out on the Loose Tonight" [Wheeler, chorus], "The Kinkajou" [Lee, chorus], "Little Jumping Bean" [band at saloon], "Over the Boundary Line" [Scott, chorus], "Poor Fool" [Daniels], "The Ranger's Song" [Boles, Scott, chorus], "Rio Rita" [Daniels, Boles; reprised by Daniels, chorus], "The River Song (River of My Dreams)" [Daniels], "Siesta Time" [chorus], "Sweetheart" [Daniels], "Sweetheart, We Need Each Other" [Lee, Wheeler; reprised by Wheeler, Woolsey, Lee, Kaiser], "You're Always in My Arms, but Only in My Dreams" [Boles, Daniels; reprised by company] (Joseph McCarthy, Harry Tierney).

Disc: RCA Victor 22132 (Daniels/"You're Always in My Arms, but Only in My Dreams"/ "If You're in Love, You'll Waltz"/78).

The fledgling RKO took quite a gamble in sparing no expense on *Rio Rita*. In December 1928, the studio bought the rights to Florenz

Bebe Daniels (with John Boles) resuscitated her career with a fine lead performance in RKO's *Rio Rita*.

Ziegfeld's Broadway hit for a lofty $85,000, then spent $675,000 to produce it. But what an investment! The movie grossed $2.4 million, brought the company much-needed prestige, and jump-started the stalled career of one of Hollywood's top stars.

Rio Rita, an exotic romance set in a Mexican border town, lasted nearly 500 performances on the stage and was the plum production picked to open the palatial Ziegfeld Theatre. The book and songs were reminiscent of *Rose-Marie* or *Naughty Marietta,* but the show was known as much for its handsome sets, costumes, and dances as anything, and it became the biggest success of the 1926-27 season. It also unveiled a popular comic duo in Bert Wheeler and Robert Woolsey, whose contributions were valued enough by RKO to be transferred to the movie version. John Boles, a hot property after *The Desert Song,* was borrowed from Universal to play the romantic lead role originated by J. Harold Murray.

For Boles' female counterpart, RKO considered it something of a coup to have the services of Bebe Daniels (1901–1971). But after 19 years in pictures, the last decade or so as a first-rank star, her fortunes were on the downswing. Angered over Paramount's failure to pick up her contract option, she bought out the 10 months remaining in the pact and allied herself with RKO because William LeBaron, a former Paramount producer, was the production chief there. When she heard that the studio was to make *Rio Rita,* she went to LeBaron and asked for the title role.

"He was completely taken aback by this," Daniels told John Kobal in 1969,

> "But you can't sing," he said. [I said,] "How do you know I can't? Try me." I had been taking singing lessons for several years. I had the same voice teacher as Jeanette MacDonald … Grace Newell. They were pleased with the test, and I got the part. I wasn't afraid of sound. I knew I could talk.[16]

LeBaron suddenly recalled hearing Daniels' soprano in an impromptu duo with Bessie Love at a recent party, and after exacting from Daniels her promise that she would take a sizable salary cut and work instead for a percentage of the gross, he decided to sign her on.[17]

Also cast was 18-year-old Dorothy Lee, in what would be the first of many teamings with Wheeler and Woolsey. The vivacious actress had not appeared in the stage *Rio Rita*—she'd sung and danced in the Broadway show *Hello Yourself* and in the New York–filmed RKO musical *Syncopation* (see Chapter 3). As she told the author, her participation in the movie was mainly due to the influence of Bert Wheeler.

> Bert Wheeler was starring in *Rio Rita* in New York. He saw me in *Syncopation* and he said, "I've got to find that little girl." They [Wheeler and Woolsey] had just been signed for [the film] *Rio Rita*. Bert was talking to a young man in a bar where all the actors went, and the young man said, "I do a big song with her in *Hello Yourself*." So immediately—Bert was a big star then—he went over to see me. … When I was through with *Hello Yourself*, I came back to Hollywood and began doing the Wheeler and Woolsey things. … Bert was very short and I'm 5 feet; he was about 5-4. He thought I was cute or something. … Of course, we were all cute when we were young.[18]

The Guy Bolton–Fred Thompson libretto—adapted for the movie by its director, Luther Reed—and the Harry Tierney score were more or less adhered to, and the film retained the original musical director, Victor Baravalle. But among six new songs Tierney and lyricist Joseph McCarthy wrote for the finished film was the love ballad "You're Always in My Arms, but Only in My Dreams," which emerged as one of the top hits of the year. The *Rio Rita* seen today is the truncated general release version, trimmed by at least a half hour from the 2½-hour road-show print, with five numbers absent—"The Kinkajou," "If You're in Love, You'll Waltz," "Espanola," "Are You There?" and Daniels' reprise of "You're Always in My Arms."[19]

Boles and Daniels sing "You're Always in My Arms" to each other soon after they meet. He is Jim Stewart, a captain in the Texas Rangers who is working incognito south of the border tracking down a notorious Mexican bandit called the Kinkajou. She is Rita Ferguson, the lovely sister of Roberto (Don Alvarado), a young man rumored to be the elusive badman. She is also a prospective romantic conquest of the powerful and wealthy General Ravenoff (Georges Renevant), who operates a floating gambling resort on the Mexican side of the Rio Grande. Totally independent of this main story is a subplot concerning Chick Bean (Wheeler) and his shyster attorney Ed Lovett (Woolsey); Chick is attempting to obtain a Mexican divorce so he can marry the impatient Dolly (Lee). "My Chickie always stops in the best hotels," she brags. "Yes, and I've got the towels to prove it!" he adds.

At a party at Ravenoff's villa—where he boasts "the most beautiful women in Mexico"—the general tells Rita of her new suitor's true identity. Rita agrees to Jim's pleas that she trust him, but later Ravenoff provides proof that Jim is specifically after her brother. She is heartbroken ("Poor Fool"). Jim answers in song ("Rio Rita"), and although Rita tells him off, she aids his escape when Ravenoff's men attempt to shoot him. Meanwhile, Chick and Dolly marry, but then he learns that a bigamy charge will face him once he returns to the United States; the U. S. government will not accept his divorce.

The final third of the film is in two-strip Technicolor. On the general's barge, the first Mrs. Bean (Helen Kaiser) shows up with the news that she's just inherited $3 million from a rich uncle. ("In other words, you're the has-Bean," cracks the suddenly amorous Lovett.) Rita prepares for her wedding to Ravenoff, but Jim, who is in hiding, patches things up with the would-be bride. As Rita diverts Ravenoff, Jim frees the barge, allowing it to float over to the American side—and the Rangers' jurisdiction. The captain clears Roberto and unmasks Ravenoff as the Kinkajou. Rita appears in her wedding dress, but a new groom will step in.

Under the laissez-faire direction of Reed, *Rio Rita* shows little invention in filmatic terms; in this respect it is no worse than *The Desert Song*, but because it was shot six months or so later it has more to answer for. Close-ups are infrequent; the actors' movements are fitful. Robert Kurrle and Lloyd Knechtel's cameras were still couped up in the soundproof booth, but that cannot completely explain their immovability. At one point, we see Daniels, back to camera, talking and gesturing to an off-camera Boles (he's in hiding on the barge); when she leans around a corner to be closer to him, we don't see anything above her midriff, but the camera doesn't budge.

The lack of invention may be explained by the film's hectic shooting schedule of 24 days (June 26 to July 20, 1929). Some exteriors were shot on location, which created synchronization problems because they had to be filmed silent with sound added later. Otherwise, it was all direct recording, and the microphones didn't always pick up the right sounds. The sounds of certain costume fabrics were magnified; even the hand fans used by Rita had to be created with noise-proof material. Daniels to Kobal: "Watching the results of a day's shooting, we thought that a humming bird had got into my mike; whenever I opened my mouth out came this hum. Since I was no good at synchronizing my voice to the movement of my lips, we had to re-shoot the scene."[20]

Another problem was that the Technicolor scenes had to be shot at night. RKO didn't have its own color camera, so it had to borrow one from Warner Bros. Of course, it was available only when Warners was closed. Said Dorothy Lee: "We would have to go to work at 6 o'clock at night and work through 6 a.m., then Warners would take the camera back."[21]

At least the music was good. Most of the Broadway score showcases the love duo, but there are two amusing songs by the comedians. Wheeler leads a ladies' chorus number in "I'm Out on the Loose Tonight," Chick's lament over his botched-up marital affairs. There is a brief overhead camera shot as the girls form a five-pointed star; Wheeler sits in the middle twirling like a top. The number ends as Wheeler wanders into a tête-à-tête between Boles and Daniels; Boles throws the little man out of the villa, and Wheeler dances away with his pants falling down. (In the version of the film that exists today, this is Boles' only contact with either of the lead comics.)

"Sweetheart, We Need Each Other," written by Tierney and McCarthy for the film, is performed twice. The first time, Lee sings to Wheeler and he replies in kind; they follow with some acrobatics and she ends up carrying him in her arms. The reprise, which is in Technicolor, is sung as Wheeler, Woolsey, Lee and

Kaiser sit on the rail of the barge, with the boys in the middle. As they sing, looking straight ahead, Wheeler and Woolsey begin to hit each other playfully, but the slaps get increasingly rougher. Just as the boys "make up" and start to kiss(!), they lose their balance and fall backward into the river. Almost as an afterthought, the two women do, too. We don't see any of them again until the final chorus.

Dorothy Lee on the "Sweetheart" numbers:

> They were two of the few numbers in which our voices didn't sound so terrible. Because, as you know, when they first started with *Rio Rita* ... our voices were up so high. All the ladies sounded like *this* [affects a high pitch]. [The color number] was taken at *four o'clock in the morning*, and it was K-O-L-D! It was on an open set. Oh, we almost froze to death. We had to fall in the water twice. After we fell in the first time, they said, "We want it again." Then you had to go get your hair dry, have to get on a whole new costume. Oh, boy! Those were the tough days! ... We had to do the thing right over again because Warners needed the camera.[22]

The strongly positive response to *Rio Rita* compensated for its troubled production. "In practically every respect it is the finest of the screen musicals. ... [The] music is ingratiating, warm and vivid," declared *Photoplay*, which heaped most of its praise upon Daniels: "Her voice, untrained as it is, has a rich quality which an experienced prima donna might well envy. Her performance is colorful and she appears lovelier than she has for years."[23] Said "Sime" of *Variety*: "Mr. Boles has a peculiar personality voice on the screen that never tires."[24] Richard Watts, Jr., chose to dwell on Wheeler and Woolsey: "[They] now compose an admirable team of low, but rather hilarious, comics. ... [To them,] the chief value of the work belongs."[25] *The Film Daily* named the film to its Top 10 list for 1929.

Rio Rita was remade 13 years after RKO's big splash, but by then Radio had sold the property to MGM for an Abbott and Costello vehicle. John Carroll and Kathryn Grayson were reduced to second leads. The updated wartime plot was enhanced by only two tunes—"Rio Rita" and "The Ranger's Song"—from the original; the rest were replaced by new songs by Harold Arlen and E. Y. Harburg.

DEVIL-MAY-CARE
(MGM; December 22, 1929)

Director: Sidney Franklin. Stage Director: J. Clifford Brooke. Scenario: Hans Kräly. Dialogue: Zelda Sears. Adaptation: Richard Schayer. Based on the play *La Bataille de Dames, ou un Duel en Amour* by Augustine Eugène Scribe and Ernest Legouvé. Photography: Merritt B. Gerstad. Editor: Conrad A. Nervig. Sound: Douglas Shearer, Ralph Shugart. Art Director: Cedric Gibbons. Costumes: Adrian. Ballet Music: Dimitri Tiomkin. Dance Direction: Albertina Rasch. Running Time: 88 minutes. Technicolor sequence.

Cast: Ramon Novarro (Armand de Treville), Dorothy Jordan (Léonie), Marion Harris (Louise), John Miljan (de Grignon), William Humphrey (Napoleon), George Davis (groom), Clifford Bruce (Gaston), George Chandler (soldier), Lionel Belmore (landlord).

Songs: "Bon Jour, Louie" [Novarro, soldiers], "Charming" [Novarro; reprised by Novarro, Jordan], "If He Cared" [Harris; reprised by Jordan], "March of the Old Guard" [Novarro, soldiers], "The Shepherd's Serenade" [Novarro, three times], "Why Waste Your Charms?" [Harris] (Clifford Grey, Herbert Stothart).

Mexican-born Ramon Novarro (1899–1968), a Latin lover in the Rudolph Valentino tradition, first opened his mouth to sing on-camera in the otherwise silent 1929 drama *The Pagan*. It was a South Seas tale in which the exposure of most of Novarro's torso greatly enhanced the response to his rendition of "The Pagan Love Song," a smash for composer Nacio Herb Brown, lyricist Arthur Freed and the MGM coffers. It didn't hurt that Novarro had—for a movie star, anyway—a finely tuned tenor, which the mercurial actor lost no time in putting to greater use. Even before *The Pagan* was unleashed, he had signed a contract with Metro in which he would alternate between opera and films.

The opera part would never really pan out, but Novarro took his new vocation very seriously.

> The motion pictures have been a sideline with me. I like them very much ... and now all the more because they have a voice. Yet since I can remember, I have wanted to be a singer. That has been my real life. All these years I have never given up studying, here with Louis Gravure, the great Metropolitan tenor; and on trips to Europe, anywhere I was, every moment I could spare.[26]

For Novarro's all-talking debut, Metro appropriately chose a romantic operetta, *Devil-May-Care*, adapted from an 1851 French play but with an original score by Herbert Stothart, in one of his first assignments at Metro. Stothart would head the MGM music department until his death in 1949. The female leads were both new to Hollywood. Dorothy Jordan (1908–1988) had played supporting roles on Broadway and in two talkies, the Fox thriller *Black Magic* and the Pickford-Fairbanks-Shakespeare comedy *The Taming of the Shrew*. Marion Harris (1906–1944) was a New York revue star and radio singer. The not-inappropriate working title of *Devil-May-Care* was *The Battle of the Ladies*.

Devil-May-Care, ably directed by Sidney Franklin, is an account of Armand de Treville, a daring young Bonapartist who is brought before a firing squad after his idol is banished to Elba. The officer in charge, de Grignon (John Miljan), makes the mistake of granting the victim his last request. Armand asks to direct his own execution, and his first order to the company is "About face!"—so that he can take leave while everyone's back is turned. He dashes into the boudoir of the lovely Léonie (Jordan), who responds by betraying the intruder to his Royalist pursuers. But they cannot keep up with his young legs, and he disappears into the countryside.

Disguised as a footman, Armand takes refuge in the country estate of Countess Louise (Harris), whose friendship with—and unrequited love for—the fugitive supersedes her loyalty to King Louis XVIII. Léonie, who happens to be Louise's cousin, shows up as a house guest, and Armand sets out to win her heart. Louise, who fails to recognize Armand, responds favorably—especially after he climbs up her balcony to sing the soothing "Shepherd's Serenade"—but she's confused about her love for a mere servant. The pompous de Grignon enters the picture as an aspiring suitor to Léonie, and after he finally gets around to recognizing Armand, the latter's identity is exposed to Léonie, who rejects him. Eventually, Napoleon is returned to power, and Armand, restored to his

Ramon Novarro has Dorothy Jordan right where he wants her in MGM's early operetta *Devil-May-Care*.

captain's rank, sneaks into de Grignon's house and makes off with his ultimately agreeable sweetheart.

Stothart's pleasingly varied score includes a romantic theme song in "The Shepherd's Serenade" (performed three times); the light, bouncy "Charming"; "Bon Jour, Louie," Armand's comic savaging of the unpopular king; and a stirring "March of the Old Guard" to inspire Armand and his comrades. There is also a brief Technicolor ballet, with the Albertina Rasch troupe dancing to an instrumental by Dimitri Tiomkin, set in the gardens of Grenoble. Harris, stiff in a thankless third-wheel role, sings two songs, only one ("If He Cared") in full. Despite having a standout singing voice, she didn't photograph too pleasingly—the camera brings out her slightly oversized nose—and it's not difficult to understand why she didn't make another film. But Novarro and Jordan make a pleasant team, her demure nature nicely complementing his flair for light comedy. In strong support is Miljan, whose de Grignon is ridiculously self-possessed. "Tell me," he asks Louise, "how did [Léonie] accept my proposal? Tremble and turn pale." "No, I can't say that she did," says the countess. "What magnificent self-

control!" replies the impressed military man. "Even to you she would not show her matronly trepidation!"

The musical highlight of *Devil-May-Care* is "Charming," which the smitten Armand, on the morning after Léonie's arrival at the countess's castle, sings admiringly as he cleans the girl's shoes. Novarro begins the love song as he sits before a row of shoes in a courtyard. After a few bars, the camera moves backward to reveal the kitchen, where the other servants complain about what an odd fellow Armand is. As Novarro continues, Merritt Gerstad's camera, in a precursor of sorts to the more famous "Isn't It Romantic?" number in *Love Me Tonight*, follows the sound of the song as it wafts up the side of the mansion into Jordan's room. Léonie is sitting up in bed, smiling and obviously listening intently. As the tune is completed, she comes to the window to gaze at him.

Novarro effectively wields a sword and rides a horse in his first talkie test, which was declared a success. "All around me, women were swooning at every note—both spoken and sung," wrote one attentive critic. "Furthermore, Ramon is the only movie actor I know of who can wear a butler's uniform and still not look like a butler."[27]

CAMEO KIRBY
(Fox; January 12, 1930)

Director: Irving Cummings. Screenplay: Marion Orth. Based on the play by Booth Tarkington and Harry Leon Wilson (New York opening, December 20, 1909; 24 performances). Photography: L. William O'Connell, George Eastman. Editor: Alex Troffey. Sound: Joseph E. Aiken. Assistant Director: Charles Woolstenhulme. Costumes: Sophie Wachner. Running Time: 55 minutes.

Cast: J. Harold Murray (Cameo Kirby), Norma Terris (Adele Randall), Douglas Gilmore (Jack Moreau), Robert Edeson (Colonel Randall), Myrna Loy (Lea), Charles Morton (Anatole), Stepin Fetchit (Croup), George MacFarlane (George), John Hyams (Larkin Bunce), Madame Daumery (Claire Devezac), Beulah Hall Jones (Poulette).

Songs: "After a Million Dreams" [Murray], "Home Is Heaven—Heaven Is Home" [Murray], "Romance" [Murray] (Edgar Leslie, Walter

Donaldson); "I'm a Peaceful Man" [Fetchit, Morton], "The Tankard and the Bowl" [Murray] (Ed Brady, Fred Strauss); "Look at That Mulatto" (M. Monroe); "Old-Fashioned Waltz" (George Lipschultz).

For their encore to *Married in Hollywood,* J. Harold Murray and Norma Terris were cast in a musical version of the Booth Tarkington melodrama set in 1850 New Orleans. This was the third film go-around of the famous 1909 play, Dustin Farnum and John Gilbert respectively having starred in the others as the riverboat gambler unjustly accused of murdering the woman he loves. Myrna Loy also showed up, this time as the crafty Creole mistress of the swindling heavy played by Douglas Gilmore.

There were seven songs, including the standout "Romance," written by Edgar Leslie and Walter Donaldson and sung by Murray. Inexplicably, Terris wasn't called upon to sing at all, and she was judged to be lacking the verve she'd shown in her first movie. Before *Cameo Kirby* was released, she'd been given her return ticket to New York. But Stepin Fetchit was handed a tune, the comic "I'm a Peaceful Man," which he delivered with his unintelligible drawl.

Even at a mere 55 minutes, the film was considered draggy and dull, especially with this kind of dialogue: "Corey? Why that's Kirby, Cameo Kirby, the man who slew and robbed your father, Miss Randall." She'll find out later that Daddy shot himself before honest Cameo could forgive his gambling debt. Complained *Time* magazine: "Its unintentional absurdities make it one of the most hilarious burlesques of Mississippi River fiction ever written."[28]

THE ROGUE SONG
(MGM; January 28, 1930)

Director: Lionel Barrymore. Screenplay: Frances Marion, John Colton. "Suggested" by: Wells Root. Based on the operetta *Gypsy Love* by Franz Lehár, A. M. Willner and Robert Bodansky (1910). Photography: Percy Hilburn, C. Edgar Schoenbaum. Editor: Margaret Booth. Sound: Douglas Shearer, Paul Neal. Assistant Director: Charles Dorian. Art Director: Cedric Gibbons. Costumes: Adrian. Ballet Music: Dimitri Tiomkin. Dance Direction: Albertina Rasch. Running Time: 115 minutes. Technicolor.

Cast: Lawrence Tibbett (Yegor), Catherine Dale Owen (Princess Vera), Stan Laurel (Ali-Bek), Oliver Hardy (Murza-Bek), Nance O'Neil (Princess Alexandra), Judith Vosselli (Countess Tatiana), Ulrich Haupt (Prince Sergei), Elsa Alsen (Yegor's mother), Florence Lake (Nadja), Lionel Belmore (Ossman), Wallace MacDonald (Hassan), Kate Price (Petrovna), Burr McIntosh (Count Peter), H. A. Morgan (Frolov), James Bradbury, Jr. (Azamat), Harry Bernard (guard), Albertina Rasch Ballet.

Songs [all by Tibbett]: "The Lash," "The Narrative," "Once in the Georgian Hills," "The Rogue Song," "When I'm Looking at You" (Clifford Grey, Herbert Stothart); "Love Comes Like a Bird on the Wing," "The White Dove" (Clifford Grey, Franz Lehár).

Academy Award Nomination: Best Actor (Lawrence Tibbett, 1929-30).

Disc: RCA Victor 1446 (Tibbett/"The Rogue Song"/"The Narrative"/78); RCA Victor 1447 (Tibbett/"When I'm Looking at You"/"The White Dove"/78); Pelican 2019 (LP; ST).

Lawrence Tibbett tries to budge an obstinate Catherine Dale Owen in his first movie, MGM's much acclaimed *The Rogue Song.*

Video: MGM-UA (laserdisc; excerpt only).

Metro-Goldwyn-Mayer advertised *The Rogue Song* as "The Greatest Operetta Ever Produced"—and why not, for it introduced to filmgoers one the brightest young stars of the Metropolitan Opera. But Lawrence Tibbett (1896–1960) was no typical baritone. He was homegrown—a native Californian—in an era when the top grand-opera performers were from Europe. He was physically attractive—tall (6–1½) and slim. He was a surprisingly capable actor, vigorous and engaging. And he wasn't too uppity to branch out into more popular media—the stage, radio, records ... and the movies.

Tibbett turned down an offer from Mack Sennett to make a sound short in favor of a contract with MGM that he signed in the summer of 1929. Some of Tibbett's loftier friends balked at this move. But, according to his autobiography, Tibbett sought a film career because he "owed a good many thousands of dollars to friends who had financed my career, and here was a chance to pay back every dollar."[29] Metro made Tibbett grow a moustache, put a permanent wave in his hair, and pasted back his sizable ears with glue and tape. Studio personnel immediately realized that they hadn't heard a voice quite like his. During sound tests, Tibbett was instructed to "croon" into the microphone. Indignant, he shot back that he could not croon, that he had to sing in full or not at all. The engineers had to experiment with moving the microphone various distances away from Tibbett before his sound could record properly—at 15 feet away.[30] Esther Ralston, who co-starred with Tibbett in the 1931 musical *The Prodigal* (see Chapter 11), also recalled Tibbett's impressive delivery.

> On the way over to the set, he would start warming up. Electricians would come down from their work, people would stand in the street to listen, and he was just warming up before doing a scene. He was simply incredible—and marvelous to work with.[31]

Such a prodigious talent merited a film to match. For Metro's first all–Technicolor talkie, filmed between August 3 and October 17, 1929, Frances Marion and John Colton wrote a scenario suggested by the 1910 Franz Lehár operetta *Gypsy Love*. Some of the Lehár music was used, but the balance of the score—including the showcase song, "When I'm Looking at You"—was penned by Herbert Stothart with lyrics by Clifford Grey. The yet-to-be-famous Dimitri Tiomkin provided incidental ballet music choreographed by his wife, Albertina Rasch. Actor-turned-director Lionel Barrymore had received good notices for his helming of the tear-jerker *Madame X* (1929).

Tibbett was cast as Yegor, a dashing Robin Hood–type bandit leader who defies the ruling Cossacks in the Carpathian Mountains of Czarist Russia. His name means "son of a hundred kings," and his motto is "No good man dies in bed." At a friendly inn, Yegor becomes attracted to the beautiful Princess Vera (Catherine Dale Owen), who is herself captivated by his singing of "Love Comes Like a Bird on the Wing." Yegor has spurned the advances of Vera's traveling companion, Countess Tatiana (Judith Vosselli), who vengefully responds by betraying the bandit to the Cossacks. Yegor escapes with Vera's help, but her brother, the Cossack commander Prince Sergei (Ulrich Haupt), kidnaps and violates Yegor's sister Nadja (Florence Lake), who is humiliated into suicide.

Yegor goes to the royals' palace, where he strangles Sergei to death and then kidnaps Vera, taking her to his mountain fortress, where he sings of his enduring love in "When I'm Looking at You." Still upset over her brother's demise, Vera works on the affections of Hassan (Wallace MacDonald), Yegor's second-in-command, in order to turn him against his chief. However, Vera is won over for good when, on a stormy night, Yegor takes the princess into his tent. ...

Too late, for Hassan now betrays Yegor to the Cossacks. In the city of Kars, the bandit is captured and then flogged mercilessly, but he fights off the pain and sings "The Lash" to confirm his love for Vera. Afterward, she consoles him in his cell, but it will be their farewell. Yegor, thought dead by his men, rides off into the mountains, knowing that he will never forget his forbidden lover.

The plot was classy enough for its star, but even before shooting was completed, Metro production chief Irving Thalberg thought the film needed some humor to lighten it up. So he asked Hal Roach, whose small but capable comedy studio released its films through

MGM, if Metro could borrow Stan Laurel and Oliver Hardy, Roach's top stars, to provide comic relief. Roach replied that if Thalberg had some funny gags for the pair, he'd consider the request.

As Roach told author Randy Skretvedt, Thalberg summoned him a couple of weeks later and, surrounded by a group of "yes" men, proposed that Laurel and Hardy play Tibbett's coachmen.

> Now, before I can open my mouth, these guys say, "Mr. Thalberg, how did you *think* of that *marvelous* idea? Oh, hell, Roach, that's gonna make it! That's just the thing!" All of them, like a chorus! Thalberg always had to have a big chorus. So, when this thing quiets down, I says, "Uh, wait a minute. What's funny about a coachman?" And they said, "Oh, well, Laurel and Hardy—." I said, "Laurel and Hardy are two comedians. Now tell me what they're gonna do that's funny." Thalberg says, "Can't you make them funny?" I said, "Maybe I can, but *you're* supposed to."[32]

Roach, uncredited, wrote and directed (between September 27 and October 17) eight incidental scenes featuring the comics, who ended up portraying members of Yegor's gang. In one lengthy sequence, Ali-Bek (Laurel) emits a strange buzzing sound as he eats a fly-covered piece of cheese. In another, Murza-Bek (Hardy) loses his shirt after he allows Ali-Bek to give him a disastrous shave. Although their characters were secondary, Laurel (1890–1965) and Hardy (1892–1957) were given top billing in smaller markets where Tibbett was not well known. In fact, wrote the singer,

> any conceit that I might have had regarding my box office value as a movie star was quickly eliminated when, passing through a small Western town on a train, I saw on a theater canopy "Laurel and Hardy in *The Rogue Song.*"[33]

The tinkering proved just right for *The Rogue Song*, which was warmly received by both fans and reviewers, although its high ($646,000) production cost led to a $109,000 overall loss for MGM. Even before the film's debut in Los Angeles, that city's *Times* devoted the entire front page of its Sunday "Preview" section to the film debut of its favorite son, who nine years before had been making $50 a week as a soloist between films in Sid Grauman's the-

ater. A few weeks later, on January 22, 1930, the newspaper trumpeted MGM's signing of the singer to a long-term contract. Tibbett was nominated for an Academy Award as best actor, and his recording of the title song and "The White Dove" became a good seller. He also received the lion's share of praise from *The New York Times'* Mordaunt Hall:

> When his voice swells from the screen, one forgets not only the trite lines and the farcical antics, but also that the singer himself is not on the stage. Never before have a singer's efforts on the screen been applauded so genuinely. … [Tibbett] is like a singing Fairbanks, who does not attempt Mr. Fairbanks' sleight of foot.[34]

"Here is a picture," chimed in *Photoplay's* reviewer. "Lusty as a north wind, wild as a virgin forest. … [The music] is more stupendous … than anything musical that has been filmed."[35] *Variety's* man was a little less impressed, noting Owen's lack of zest, Barrymore's lazy direction and the dearth of sophistication in the dialogue.[36]

Unfortunately, precious little of *The Rogue Song*—2½ minutes out of 115—exists for appraisal in this country. In 1956, when MGM examined its archives in preparation of selling its library to television, it discovered that the negative and prints of the film had either disintegrated or been destroyed. Primarily because of Laurel and Hardy's participation—and their rare appearance in a color film—historians rabidly sought the picture for years. The soundtrack discs were recovered, and excerpts (mostly music) were released on a Pelican Records album in 1980. Two years later, a clip finally turned up in the hands of a private collector in New Hampshire. It was preserved by the American Film Institute and released as part of MGM-UA Home Video's "Dawn of Sound" laserdisc series. (Recently, there has been an unconfirmed report of the existence of a complete *Rogue Song* reel, this consisting mainly of Tibbett footage, in an archive in Prague.)

The "Dawn of Sound" clip shows Tibbett's Yegor as he admonishes Owen's princess about her toying with the affections of his subordinate; then, as a storm begins to rage, he carries her into his tent. But most of the footage contains a Laurel and Hardy routine in which the boys' tent is blown away in the storm. They seek shelter in a dark cave, only to encounter—off camera—an angry bear. "Where'd you get that fur coat?" a suspicious Hardy is heard asking his partner before a ferocious roar solves the mystery. All we see is the cave entrance, but we can imagine what's happening inside.

Alas, a greater mystery remains: Will *The Rogue Song* ever be seen again in its entirety?

THE VAGABOND KING
(Paramount; February 18, 1930)

Director: Ludwig Berger. Adaptation and Dialogue: Herman J. Mankiewicz. Based on the operetta, book by William H. Post, lyrics by Brian Hooker, music by Rudolf Friml (New York opening, September 21, 1925; 511 performances), which was based on the play *If I Were King* by J. H. McCarthy (New York opening, October 14, 1901; 56 performances) Photography: Henry Gerrard, Ray Rennahan. Editor: Merrill White. Sound: Franklin Hansen. Art Director: Hans Dreier. Costumes: Travis Banton. Color Consultant: Natalie Kalmus. Running Time: 104 minutes. Technicolor.

Cast: Dennis King (François Villon),

Jeanette MacDonald and Dennis King were heavily made up for the two-strip Technicolor camera in Paramount's *The Vagabond King*.

Jeanette MacDonald (Katherine de Vaucelles), O. P. Heggie (King Louis XI), Lillian Roth (Huguette), Warner Oland (Thibault), Lawford Davidson (Tristan), Arthur Stone (Oliver the Barber), Thomas Ricketts (astrologer), Christian J. Frank (executioner), Gene Wolff (priest).

Songs: "Huguette Waltz" [Roth], "Love Me Tonight" [MacDonald, King], "Nocturne" [chorus], "Only a Rose" [MacDonald, King], "Some Day" [MacDonald; reprised by male chorus], "Song of the Vagabonds" [King, chorus, twice] (Brian Hooker, Rudolf Friml); "If I Were King" [King], "King Louie" [King; reprised by chorus], "Mary, Queen of Heaven" [chorus] (Leo Robin, Sam Coslow, Newell Chase); "Death March" [Wolff], "What France Needs" [King, chorus] (Leo Robin, Newell Chase).

Academy Award Nomination: Best Interior Decoration (Hans Dreier, 1929–30).

Disc: RCA Victor 19897 (King/"Song of the Vagabonds"/78); RCA Victor 22263 (King/"If I Were King"/78); Vertigo 2002 (bootleg LP; ST).

On the heels of his most successful operetta, *Rose-Marie*, Rudolf Friml composed the music for *The Vagabond King*, which, like its predecessor, ran for more than 500 Broadway performances. The 1925 production also boasted leading man Dennis King (1897–1971), a handsome Englishman whose Mountie Jim in *Rose-Marie* made a musical star out of the heretofore dramatic actor. King knew that an ability to sing would add greatly to his bankability as a performer, and he had taken lessons to bolster his light baritone long before he was signed to play Jim.

Friml's full-bodied score and King's swashbuckling performance as the 15th century French poet-scoundrel François Villon propelled the stage version of *The Vagabond King*, an adaptation of the Justin Huntly McCarthy play *If I Were King*. The tale of Villon had been filmed by Fox in 1920 (with William Farnum) and by Art Cinema through United Artists in 1927 (with John Barrymore as *The Beloved Rogue*), but by 1930, a version with songs seemed like a natural for the screen. Paramount, which made *The Vagabond King* its first all-Technicolor musical, complemented six songs from the original score with new material by

Sam Coslow, Newell Chase and Leo Robin. King's leading lady in his first film was Jeanette MacDonald, fresh from her successful debut in *The Love Parade*, as Katherine de Vaucelles, the beautiful niece of King Louis XI.

Cast in the pivotal secondary role as Huguette, the ill-fated streetwalker who loves Villon, was 19-year-old Lillian Roth, who had supported MacDonald in *The Love Parade*. Paramount reportedly tested more than 100 actresses for the part before studio head Jesse Lasky asked Roth to try out before the stern German director Ludwig Berger, who presumed that she wouldn't have the necessary zest. Worse, the morning of the test, Roth awoke with a fever of 101 degrees. Wrote the actress in her 1954 autobiography, *I'll Cry Tomorrow*:

A hand stuck a script in my face. "This is a death scene," said Mr. Berger. "Let's see you die." That was exactly what I wanted to do. Dennis King's stand-in took me in his arms, I recited my lines in a sepulchral voice, closed my eyes slowly, and died. "Wunderbar!" Mr. Berger threw his arms around me and kissed me. The role of Huguette was mine. I was the new dramatic find of the year.[37]

The Vagabond King begins as the Burgundians—supporters of the traitorious Duke of Burgundy—surround Paris and the people are revolting against the weak Louis for failing to protect them. The peasant leader Villon is little more than a petty thief, but he is distracted from that vocation when he rescues Katherine from a murder attempt. He falls in love with her, and when she sings of the imaginary man who will win her heart ("Some Day"), he responds with a musical version of his famous poem, "If I Were King."

Meanwhile, King Louis (O. P. Heggie, in a much-praised performance) is told by his astrologer that a vagabond will save his throne and redeem Paris. In disguise, the monarch goes to the Tavern of the Vagabonds, where he finds Villon mocking him in song ("What France Needs Is a King"). "That man must hang!" snarls the monarch to his henchman Tristan (Lawford Davidson). Villon tells the disguised king that he himself would make a better leader than Louis, then he fires up the tavern crowd with "Song of the Vagabonds." Thibault (Warner Oland), the king's grand marshal, en-

ters with plans to arrest Villon, but he is run through by the peasant leader's sword. The king reveals his true identity and orders the imprisonment of the rogue. Then, as a strange punishment, he decides to make Villon his new grand marshal. As Villon sleeps, Louis has his courtiers clean up the peasant leader and cut off his scraggly beard.

Louis forces Villon to pass judgment on his fellow vagabonds, who don't recognize him—not even Huguette can place the face of "Count de Montcorbier." Louis impulsively decides to grant Villon his wish of being king— but for only seven days, after which he will be hanged. Katherine pleads for Villon's life, and he promises her that he will be the savior that Paris needs. "Only a Rose" is her musical reply, for that is all she will give him as a token of his loyalty. But Katherine is won over after the poet repels a Burgundian messenger asking the surrender of Rome. "When we who drink are dry, when we who glow are frozen, when we who eat are hungry, our answer to rebellious Burgundy will be the same … the drawn sword!" Villon cries to the unwelcome visitor.

Thibault, who had faked his death, organizes a vagabond attack upon the palace during a masquerade ball to "save" Villon and kill the king. Accompanying him is Huguette, who sadly awaits Villon's return ("Huguette Waltz," sung by Roth as a torch song). Villon dresses as the king to protect him, and when Thibault attempts to kill "Louis" with a knife, Huguette intervenes and is instead stabbed to death. Villon responds by killing Thibault—again. Villon and Katherine duet with "Love Me Tonight." The next day, his last as king, Villon leads a fruitful attack on the Burgundians, and when it is time for him to face the gallows, Katherine offers her life for his. Louis relents, and the lovers are saved to the strains of "Only a Rose."

The Vagabond King— "easily the most effectively staged and directed operetta yet produced for the talking screen," crowed the fan magazine *Motion Picture*[38]—drew many strong reviews, if not overwhelming box office. However, some commentators criticized the awkward transitions between realism and romanticism in Herman J. Mankiewicz's screenplay; others, Jeanette MacDonald's surprisingly chilly performance. A viewing of the film (UCLA holds the only known color print) reveals two greater problems: Berger's unimaginative, static direction and King's affected, unbearably hammy acting. King makes no effort to tone down his emoting for the cameras, as opposed to a live house, and Berger fails to rein him in. Every utterance is broad—complete with rolling r's, and every gesture is exaggerated. He is a poor-man's John Barrymore—Barrymore, that is, as recalled in his final, overplaying years as an actor.

There is no real warmth between King and MacDonald, who even in their duets seem not to be singing to each other. MacDonald hated her role, which was reduced in the editing process, and she wrote to her manager, Bob Ritchie: "In view of the fact that my part has been cut to nothing ... I wish to be taken off the billing—so I can sneak thru the picture. ... [When] King sees how much of him has been cut he'll have pups ... ."[39] The height of King's egotism comes during MacDonald's solo of "Only a Rose," when the actor thrusts his hands (which awkwardly grasp for the flower MacDonald is holding) and the edge of his profile in and out of camera view. No wonder MacDonald liked to call the number "Only a Nose."

Paramount remade the source story in 1938 as a non-musical, *If I Were King,* with Ronald Colman and Frances Dee. The operetta was trotted out, also by Paramount, in 1956 with Kathryn Grayson, Rita Moreno, and the Maltese tenor Oreste. Some of the original score was retained, but even new songs by Friml and Johnny Burke couldn't keep that *Vagabond King* from being crowned a dated flop.

SONG OF THE WEST
(Warner Bros.; February 27, 1930)

Director: Ray Enright. Scenario and Dialogue: Harvey Thew. Based on the musical play *Rainbow,* book by Laurence Stallings and Oscar Hammerstein II, lyrics by Hammerstein, music by Vincent Youmans (New York opening, November 21, 1928; 29 performances). Photography: Dev Jennings. Editor: George Marks. Sound: Glenn E. Rominger. Running Time: 82 minutes. Technicolor.

Cast: John Boles (Stanton), Vivienne Segal (Virginia), Joe E. Brown (Hasty), Marie Wells (Lotta), Sam Hardy (Davolo), Marion Byron (Penny), Eddie Gribbon (Sergeant Major), Edward Martindel (Colonel), Rudolph Cameron (Singleton).

Songs: "The Bride Was Dressed in White" [Brown], "Hay-Straw," "I Like You as You Are," "The One Girl" [Boles] (Oscar Hammerstein II, Vincent Youmans); "West Wind" [Boles] (J. Russel Robinson, Vincent Youmans); "Come Back to Me" [Boles, Segal] (Grant Clarke, Harry Akst); "Kingdom Coming" (Henry Clay Work).

Disc: RCA Victor 22229 (Boles/"The One Girl"/"West Wind"/78).

One of the more interesting flops of Broadway's Golden Age was *Rainbow,* which opened at the end of 1928. The "romantic musical play" was compared to *Show Boat*—indeed, one of its two librettists was Oscar Hammerstein II—for its serious mood, its mid–19th century setting, and its infusion of native jazz and folk styles with traditionally operatic melodies. The Vincent Youmans score included the torchy "I Want a Man," which brought early acclaim to its singer, Libby Holman, and the comic "The Bride Was Dressed in White," performed memorably by Charles Ruggles. The dances were staged by Busby Berkeley. But *Rainbow* was beset by money problems from the beginning and closed after 29 performances, despite kudos from some critics who thought the show was ahead of its time.

Nobody, however, considered *Song of the West,* Warner Bros.' 1930 all-color adaptation of *Rainbow,* to be advanced for *its* time. In fact, it was behind its time already. Filmed by Warners in the spring of 1929 as *Rainbow,* the film was shelved by the studio for nearly a year. No wonder reviewers considered it colorless, uninspired, awkwardly written and poorly recorded, although the romantic leads were the battle-tested John Boles—this was supposed to have been his follow-up to *The Desert Song*—and the talented Broadway import Vivienne Segal.

Boles was cast as the young Army scout who kills an officer (Sam Hardy) in self-defense and escapes West to California for the Gold Rush. He opens a gambling hall in San Francisco and falls in love with the daughter (Segal) of his former commander. After an unfortunate "reunion" with some of his old military buddies, the scout is given the option of being deported or re-enlisting as a private. He re-ups, but his girl still loves him anyway.

Joe E. Brown, in the Ruggles role as Boles' doomed muleteer sidekick, was praised for his singing of "The Bride Was Dressed in White," one of four songs held over from the stage show. There was one new Youmans song, "West Wind," with lyrics not by Hammerstein but by J. Russel Robinson, and the new duet "Come Back to Me," penned by Warners staffers Grant Clarke and Harry Akst. "Ambitious but dull," was the representative summation of *Photoplay*.[40] *Song of the West* apparently no longer exists for viewing.

CAPTAIN OF THE GUARD
(Universal; March 29, 1930)

Directors: John S. Robertson, Paul Fejos. Dialogue and Titles: George Manker Watters. Screenplay: Arthur Ripley. Story: Houston Branch. Photography: Gilbert Warrenton, Hal Mohr. Editor: Milton Carruth. Sound: C. Roy Hunter. Running Time: 83 minutes (sound version; also released as silent).

Cast: Laura La Plante (Marie Marnay), John Boles (Rouget de l'Isle), Sam De Grasse (Bazin), James Marcus (Marnay), Lionel Belmore (Colonel of Hussars), Stuart Holmes (Louis XVI), Evelyn Hall (Marie Antoinette), Claude Fleming (magistrate), Murdock MacQuarrie (Pierre), Richard Cramer (Danton), Harry Burkhardt (Materoun), Otis Harlan (Jacques), George Hackathorne (Robespierre), DeWitt Jennings (priest), Harry Cording (Le Bruin), Ervin Renard (lieutenant).

Songs: "For You" [Boles], "Maids on Parade," "You ... You Alone" [Boles] (William Francis Dugan, Heinz Roemheld); "La Marseillaise" [Boles] (Claude Joseph Rouget de l'Isle); "Song of the Sword" (Houston Branch, Charles Wakefield Cadman).

Disc: RCA Victor 22373 (Boles/"For You"/"You ... You Alone"/78).

Having watched its contract player John Boles make money for competing studios with his booming voice, Universal got wise and cast him in one of its infrequent musicals. *Captain of the Guard* was a historical drama with a handful of songs, but the history was faulty. This alleged account of the French Revolution, and of the writing of the famous song "La Marseillaise," was so carelessly written that an opening credit was inserted to apologize for its many factual inaccuracies.

Captain of the Guard boasted two stars—with Laura La Plante joining Boles—and the film had a like number of directors, cinematographers, and titles. Production began as *La Marseillaise* with Paul (*Broadway*) Fejos in the director's chair. But Fejos would be replaced by John S. Robertson, who received sole screen credit, despite trade ads as late as one month before the film's release that listed the older title and Fejos only as director. Fejos was lucky to escape with his life from what would be his last English-language film. In October of 1929, he escaped serious injury after he fell 88 feet from a scaffolding, from where he had been shouting instructions for a mob scene. Fejos was initially thought to have a broken neck, but it turned out that he was merely suffering from shock.

For the record, the plot—which echoed both *The Desert Song* and *Song of the Flame*—went like this: Innkeeper's daughter Marie Marnay falls in love with Rouget de l'Isle, her singing teacher who is a captain of the king's guard. When Marie's father is killed by a soldier, she joins the revolutionaries and becomes a notorious figure known as "The Torch." The villainous Bazin, Marie's former paramour, has her and Rouget arrested. Queen Antoinette orders Rouget's release so he can sing his song "La Marseillaise" for the king, but then the young man renounces the crown and goes to Marseilles, where he organizes an army to begin the revolution. After the army marches on Paris, the lovers are reunited.

All that was deemed worthy of praise in *Captain of the Guard* was its score, by William Francis Dugan and Heinz Roemheld. Boles' recording of "For You" became a top seller. *The New York Times* knocked the dialogue and the lack of French flavor in the "ambitious but ... heavy-handed audible film."[41] *Captain of the Guard* was soon forgotten.

SONG OF THE FLAME
(First National; April 19, 1930)

Director: Alan Crosland. Adaptation and Dialogue: Gordon Rigby. Based on the operetta, book and lyrics by Oscar Hammerstein II and Otto Harbach, music by George Gershwin and Herbert Stothart (New York opening,

December 30, 1925; 219 performances). Photography: Lee Garmes. Editor: Al Hall. Sound: George R. Groves. Assistant Director: Ben Silvey. Art Director: Anton Grot. Costumes: Edward Stevenson. Musical Director: Leo Forbstein. Choral Direction: Ernest Grooney, Norman Spencer. Dance Direction: Jack Haskell. Running Time: 70 minutes. Technicolor.

Cast: Alexander Gray (Prince Volodya), Bernice Claire (Anuita, "The Flame"), Noah Beery (Konstantin), Alice Gentle (Natasha), Bert Roach (Nicholas), Inez Courtney (Grusha), Shep Camp (officer), Ivan Linow (henchman), Janina Smolinska (dancer).

Songs: "The Goose Hangs High" [Courtney; reprised by Claire, Gray, chorus], "Liberty Song" [Gentle, three times], "Passing Fancy" [Gentle], "Petrograd" [Gray, chorus] (Grant Clarke, Harry Akst, Eddie Ward); "The Cossack Love Song" [Gray, Claire, twice], "Song of the Flame" [Claire, chorus, three times], "Wander Away" [Gentle] (Oscar Hammerstein II, Otto Harbach, George Gershwin, Herbert Stothart); "One Little Drink" [Beery, chorus; reprised by Beery] (Grant Clarke, Harry Akst); "When Love Calls" [Gray, Claire] (Eddie Ward). Chorus Numbers: "Prayer" (Peter Ilich Tchaikovsky); "Berieza," "Grechanivi," "Schtchedryck" (trad.).

Academy Award Nomination: Best Sound Recording (George R. Groves, 1929-30).

Disc: Brunswick 4828 (Beery/"One Little Drink"/78).

A rare foray by George Gershwin into operetta—although it was advertised as a "romantic opera" when it debuted on Broadway in 1925—Song of the Flame came to movie theaters in 1930 courtesy of Warner Bros.–First National. The studio spent handsomely to reproduce the modestly successful Otto Harbach–Oscar Hammerstein II play about the Russian Revolution, but crammed the proceedings into 70 minutes and jettisoned all but three songs from the Gershwin–Herbert Stothart score. Among the holdovers were the rousing title song and the main romantic duet, "The Cossack Love Song" (also known as "Don't Forget Me").

In their second film pairing—the first was No, No, Nanette (see Chapter 4)—Bernice Claire and Alexander Gray starred as the fiery Russian rebel and the Cossack prince who attempts to tame her. Their adventures got the all–Technicolor treatment. "Gigantic scenes in gorgeous color vivify its sweeping drama," First National boasted in its trade ads. "Thundering choruses set your senses tingling. A sumptuous revel with scores of sinuous dancing girls exposes the pleasures of nobility on the brink of doom!"

Claire played the lovely Anuita, who is of royal blood but who, as "The Flame," sort of a Russian Joan of Arc, sings the "Song of the Flame" to incite the peasants into revolt against the Czarist government. Her fellow conspirator, Konstantin (Noah Beery), covets the young woman, to the chagrin of the jealous Natasha (Alice Gentle, a Metropolitan Opera star in her first feature film). Prince Voloyda vows to capture "The Flame," but the rebels, led by the ruthless Konstantin, overthrow the czar and plunge the country into chaos. In her native village in Poland, Anuita and the prince fall in love, and when he is captured by Konstantin's troops and faces execution, she secures his freedom by pledging to be Konstantin's mistress. Instead, Anuita is sent to prison, where Voloyda attempts to rescue her. Konstantin is arrested as a traitor and shot between notes of his reprise of "One Little Drink" (his last wish before the firing squad). The lovers are reunited with a reprise of "The Goose Hangs High."

Song of the Flame was one movie in which the sum of its parts was considered better than the whole. "Comic-opera bolshevists are silly," asserted Photoplay.[42] Gray and Claire earned kudos for their pleasant voices and restrained acting, although some considered Gray's "restraint" overly wooden. Claire earned a "Good Deed" citation from Film Daily. Gentle (1889–1958), who lost a lot of weight for her role, was considered a better singer than actress, but Beery pleasantly surprised many with his powerful voice. He sang "One Little Drink," Time magazine noted, in a basso "two notes lower than any ever recorded."[43]

The filming of Song of the Flame was marred by the death of a cast member. Shep Camp, who played a military officer, died on November 20, 1929, two days after suffering internal injuries incurred from a fall from a horse during shooting at the Warner ranch. Camp, a stage actor and composer appearing in only his third movie, was 47 years old.

Song of the Flame is apparently a lost film,

although some sound elements exist in private hands. An abridged version that does survive is the 1934 Vitaphone short *The Flame Song*, with Claire and J. Harold Murray. Its songs include "One Little Drink," "Song of the Flame," "When Love Calls" and "The Cossack Love Song." Greek Evans, Konstantin in the original New York cast, reprises that role in the two-reel "Broadway Brevity."

IN GAY MADRID
(MGM; May 17, 1930)

Director: Robert Z. Leonard. Continuity-Dialogue: Bess Meredyth, Salisbury Field, Edwin Justus Mayer. Based on the novel *La Casa de la Troya* by Alejandro Perez Lugin (1915). Photography: Oliver Marsh. Editor: William S. Gray. Sound: Douglas Shearer, Ralph Shugart. Art Director: Cedric Gibbons. Costumes: Adrian. Running Time: 80 minutes.

Cast: Ramon Novarro (Ricardo de Castelar), Dorothy Jordan (Carmina Rivas), Lottice Howell (La Goyita), Claude King (Marqués de Castelar), Eugenie Besserer (Doña Generosa), William V. Mong (Mr. Rivas), Beryl Mercer (Doña Concha), Nanci Price (Jacinta), Herbert Clark (Octavio), David Scott (Ernesto Rivas), George Chandler (Enríque), Bruce Coleman (Corpulento), Nicholas Caruso (Carlos), John Miljan (Armata, the matador).

Songs: "Dark Night" [Novarro], "Let Me Give You Love" [Howell], "Santiago" [Novarro, students] (Clifford Grey, Xavier Cugat, Herbert Stothart); "Into My Heart" [Novarro, twice], "Smile, Comrades!" [Novarro, students] (Roy Turk, Fred E. Ahlert).

Ramon Novarro and Dorothy Jordan made such a good team in *Devil-May-Care* (1929) that MGM gave them another operetta assignment. *In Gay Madrid* was misleadingly titled, however, for only the first 10 minutes or so take place there.

The remainder is set in the more sedate Spanish city of Santiago, which is where the playboy Ricardo de Castelar is sent by his irate father (Claude King) after one too many nights on the town. The young man is to continue his law school studies while living in the student boarding quarters, The House of Troy, where the residents spout distinctly American quips

Ramon Novarro woos Mexican maiden Dorothy Jordan in the second of their three operettas together, *In Gay Madrid*.

like "And how!" and "Real fun." (*The House of Troy* was the film's working title.) In the closest thing this film has to a production number, they march around outside singing the school song, "Santiago."

Ricardo also is greeted by the offspring of Mr. Rivas, his father's longtime friend. Rivas' teenage son, Ernesto (David Scott), befriends the city slicker, but his pretty older sister, Carmina, thinks the visitor is a jerk. He thinks she's a prig. (Ah, true love!) Time passes, and the romance slowly blossoms. But Carmina's jilted suitor (Herbert Clark) scuttles her and Ricardo's impending nuptials by reporting (truthfully, but …) that Goyita (Lottice Howell), a worldly nightclub singer and old chum of Ricardo's, is holed up in the guy's room. Carmina is heartbroken, and Ernesto feels so betrayed that he challenges Ricardo to a duel. Ricardo fires into the air, but he is seriously wounded by Ernesto's bullet. Carmina pours her heart out in begging for her beloved's recovery, and after he does mend, they are married.

In Gay Madrid, based on a Spanish novel of 1915, is light on song, but the music is used wisely. One of the more amusing moments has

Novarro secretly serenading the sweetheart of a chubby frat brother, Cyrano-style. When Jordan appears in an adjoining window, Novarro absentmindedly walks away from his hiding place and sings "Into My Heart" to her instead, leaving his fat friend to stew. Later, Novarro, perched on a balcony next to Jordan's bedroom, presents to her the lovely ballad "Dark Night," for which the Cuban bandleader Xavier Cugat teamed with composer Herbert Stothart and lyricist Clifford Grey.

Novarro, perhaps too mild-mannered to be totally convincing as a man-about-town, underplays with an often sarcastic charm that compensates for the lack of power in his speaking and singing voice. These faults would contribute to his gradual career downturn as talkies took hold. Faring less well is the poorly photographed Lottice Howell, a stage actress who made a brief stab at movies. *The New York Times* rightly called *In Gay Madrid* "excellent light entertainment ... interesting, amusing and enjoyable."[44]

BRIDE OF THE REGIMENT

(First National; May 21, 1930)

Director: John Francis Dillon. Associate Producer: Robert North. Screenplay: Humphrey Pearson. Adaptation and Dialogue: Ray Harris. Based on the operettas *Die Frau im Hermelin* by Rudolph Schanzer and Ernst Welisch and *The Lady in Ermine*, book by Frederick Lonsdale, lyrics by Cyrus Wood and Harry Graham, music by Al Goodman, Jean Gilbert and Sigmund Romberg (New York opening, October 2, 1922; 238 performances). Photography: Dev Jennings, C. Edgar Schoenbaum. Editor: Le Roy Stone. Sound: Hal Brumbaugh. Dance Direction: Jack Haskell. Running Time: 79 minutes. Technicolor.

Cast: Vivienne Segal (Countess Anna-Marie), Allan Prior (Count Adrian Beltrami), Walter Pidgeon (Colonel Vultow), Louise Fazenda (Teresa), Myrna Loy (Sophie), Lupino Lane (Sprotti), Ford Sterling (Tangy), Harry Cording (Sergeant Dostal), Claude Fleming (Captain Stogan), Herbert Clark (The Prince).

Songs: "Broken-Hearted Lover" [Prior], "Dream Away" [Pidgeon, Segal], "In a Gypsy Camp" [dancers], "Shrimp's Dance" [danced by Lane], "Soldier Song" [soldiers; reprised by Pidgeon, soldiers], "You Still Retain That Girlish Figure" [Lane, Fazenda] (Al Bryan, Eddie Ward); "When Hearts Are Young (in Springtime)" [Pidgeon, chorus] (Cyrus Wood, Al Goodman, Sigmund Romberg).

Warner Bros.–First National was pouring out all–Technicolor musicals in 1930—it made no fewer than nine of the 14 released that year. Like most of the others, *Bride of the Regiment* was based on a stage show—*The Lady in Ermine*, imported from Vienna for a successful New York run in 1922 and '23. However, the score for the film was almost entirely new, created by staff writers Al Bryan and Eddie Ward. Other than bits of underscoring, there was one holdover from the 1922 show: the standard "When Hearts Are Young (in Springtime)."

Vivienne Segal, who had failed to make much of an impression in *Song of the West*, showed little here as a newly married Italian countess who is used by the swashbuckling leader (Walter Pidgeon, 1897–1984) of the occupying Austrians to get to her husband (Allan Prior, the Australian tenor), who heads the aristocratic insurgents. Segal (1897–1992) was a major Broadway star. Her greatest triumph came as Margot in *The Desert Song*, in which she replaced the intended female lead just before opening night. She appeared in two Vitaphone shorts in 1927, singing selections from *Maytime* and *Mlle. Modiste*, respectively. Warner Bros. signed Segal in 1929 to a five-picture contract at $2,000 weekly, but the first phase of her Hollywood career consisted of four unremarkable films: *Song of the West, Bride of the Regiment, Golden Dawn* and *Viennese Nights*. She would return in 1934 to support Jeanette MacDonald and Ramon Novarro in MGM's version of *The Cat and the Fiddle*. Segal's stage career would receive a major boost when she played Vera in the 1940 and 1952 productions of Rodgers and Hart's *Pal Joey*.

Bride of the Regiment, now a lost film, differed from most movie operettas in that its singing and dancing were almost entirely incidental to the plot, and that it relied heavily on comedy, provided by Lupino Lane, Ford Sterling and Louise Fazenda. Prior, like Segal, was from Broadway, where his credits included the failed Vincent Youmans shows *Great Day* and *Rainbow*. But he got to sing only one song,

"Broken-Hearted Lover," in this film. Segal's own only number was a duet with Pidgeon, "Dream Away." Myrna Loy, bleached blonde for yet another thankless role, led a smouldering dance number, this one on top of a long dinner table surrounded by Austrian officers and their ladies. She played a dancer named Sophie who is the love interest of a bumbling ballet master portrayed by Lane.

The direction of John Francis Dillon did nothing to disturb the film's leaden tone, and the box office was tepid. "It seems," wrote Mordaunt Hall in *The New York Times*, "as though the actors were enjoying this film so much they did not care whether audiences found it entertaining or not."[45]

WOMEN EVERYWHERE
(Fox; June 1, 1930)

Director: Alexander Korda. Associate Producer: Ned Marin. Scenario and Dialogue: Harlan Thompson, Lajos Biró. Story: George Grossmith, Zoltan Korda. Photography: Ernest Palmer. Editor: Harold Schuster. Sound: Arthur L. von Kirbach. Assistant Director: Ned Marin. Art Director: William Darling. Costumes: Sophie Wachner. Running Time: 82 minutes.

Cast: J. Harold Murray (Charles Jackson), Fifi D'Orsay (Lili La Fleur), George Grossmith (Aristide Brown), Clyde Cook (Sam Jones), Ralph Kellard (Michel Kopulos), Rose Dione (Zephyrine), Walter McGrail (Lieutenant of Legionnaires).

Songs: "Beware of Love" [Murray], "Bon Jour," "Good Time Fifi" [D'Orsay], "Marching Song," "One Day He'll Come Along," "Where Is Honky Tonky Town?" "Women Everywhere" [Murray] (William Kernell); "All the Family" (George Grossmith, William Kernell); "Smile, Legionnaire" (Charles Wakefield Cadman, William Kernell).

An original romantic drama with music by William Kernell, *Women Everywhere* teamed J. Harold Murray (*Married in Hollywood, Cameo Kirby*) with a new leading lady, Fifi D'Orsay, and a new locale, North Africa, where he played a Moroccan gunrunner who becomes infatuated with a French cabaret singer.

Charlie Jackson is sought by the French authorities, and to keep him out of trouble, his gal, Lili La Fleur, disguises him as a singer, a masquerade that gives the baritone an excuse to perform "Beware of Love." Pursued by a quartermaster (Ralph Kellard) with the tenacity of Javert, Charlie dons the uniform of a dead Legionnaire, a move that forces him into the desert to battle the Arabs. But the hero returns home, body and voice intact, to his Lili.

Women Everywhere, which carried the improbable working title of *Hell's Belles*, was directed by the future producer Alexander Korda. *Variety* called it "one of those gems occasionally found in the herd of program pictures,"[46] but it did nothing for Murray's faltering movie career and is so completely forgotten now that most musical-film reference books don't even bother to list it.

GOLDEN DAWN
(Warner Bros.; June 14, 1930)

Director: Ray Enright. Screenplay and Dialogue: Walter Anthony. Based on the operetta, book and lyrics by Oscar Hammerstein II and Otto Harbach, music by Emmerich Kalman and Herbert Stothart (New York opening, November 30, 1927; 184 performances). Photography: Dev Jennings, Frank Good. Sound: Glenn E. Rominger. Musical Director: Louis Silvers. Dance Direction: Larry Ceballos. Running Time: 81 minutes. Technicolor.

Cast: Walter Woolf (Tom Allen), Vivienne Segal (Dawn), Noah Beery (Shep Keyes), Alice Gentle (Mooda), Lupino Lane (Pigeon), Marion Byron (Johanna), Dick Henderson (Duke), Lee Moran (Blink), Nigel De Brulier (Hasmali), Otto Matieson (Captain Eric), Nena Quartero (maid-in-waiting), Sojin (piper), Julanne Johnston (Sister Hedwig), Nick de Ruiz (Napoli), Edward Martindel (Colonel Judson), Frank Dunn (Anzac), Carlie Taylor (British officer).

Songs: "Here in the Dark" [Woolf], "Little Girl, Little Girl (Mooda's Appeal)" [Gentle], "Mulunghu Thabu" [natives], "My Bwanna" [Segal, twice], "We Two" [Byron, Henderson; reprised by Henderson], "The Whip" [Beery, twice] (Oscar Hammerstein II, Otto Harbach, Emmerich Kalman, Herbert Stothart); "Africa Smiles No More" [Gentle], "In a Jungle Bungalow" [Lane, men] (Grant

The vicious Shep Keyes (Noah Beery) has the hero (Tom Allen) collared in Warner Bros.' unbelievable *Golden Dawn*; **the title character (Vivienne Segal) frets at left.**

Clarke, Harry Akst); "Dawn" [Woolf; reprised by company] (Robert Stolz, Herbert Stothart); "It's a Long Way to Tipperary" [Woolf, men] (Jack Judge, Harry Williams); "You Know the Type—a Tiger" [Byron, Moran] (Walter O'Keefe, Robert Emmett Dolan).

Disc: Brunswick 4828 (Beery/"The Whip"/78).

Video: MGM-UA (laserdisc).

By the summer of 1930, the glut of operettas was beginning to tire the public, and entries as bad as *Golden Dawn* were killing whatever appeal was left. The concept of Caucasian actors playing it straight in blackface was still culturally acceptable, but racial incongruity was only one of the problems of this Viennese-style operetta set in East Africa. Despite nearly 200 performances, *Golden Dawn* was considered a disappointment in New York, considering that it had been selected to open the new Hammer-

stein Theatre (named for the first Oscar) in 1927. The play may be better known now for the early appearance of Cary Grant in a minor role, his first part on Broadway. When the property was made into a movie, it had even less going for it.

Vivienne Segal was the prime victim, suffering through her third movie bust in a role designed for a woman half her 33 years. She plays Dawn—"Golden" because of her blonde hair, a rare trait among the African natives. Could it be that she's white? Well, yes, but her tribespeople don't seem to believe so. To them, she's worthy enough to be sacrificed to the great god Mulunghu. This predicament hardly seems to faze her dark-skinned mother, Mooda (Alice Gentle), who runs a canteen for the occupying German forces of the Great War. "Africa Smiles No More," she sings. Captain Tom Allen (Walter Woolf), an English planter turned prisoner of war, describes his love for Dawn in "Dawn" and "Here in the Dark," but he is powerless to save her. Shep Keyes (Noah Beery, 1884–1946), the bald and bulky black overseer in league with the Germans, is jealous of their love. He sings "The Whip" (popularly called "The Whip Song") as he struts around the camp with an incongruous Southern accent, a chip on his shoulder, and a whip on his hip.

Shep claims to the camp commander (Otto Matiesen) that Tom has tried to "steal" Dawn from the natives, and the boss, not wanting to interfere in the tribal rituals, sends Tom back to England in an exchange of prisoners. A year later, after the British have reclaimed control of East Africa, Tom returns, determined to prove that Dawn is white so she will be released to the Brits. Just as he's about to confront Mooda—whom, we learn, is not really Dawn's mother—she is stabbed in a Mombasa dive by a drunken white trader who happens to be Dawn's father. (Her real mother is long dead.) A severe drought spurs the native chief (Nigel De Brulier) to begin the sacrifice. Shep's jealous lover (Nena Quartero) reveals the truth about Dawn, and it is the heartless heavy who is killed instead. A sudden downpour saves the heroine, who leaves with Tom on a ship headed for civilization.

Even in 1930, *Golden Dawn* was panned for its absurd story, lackluster songs and blurry Technicolor photography. "Sometimes the natives are washed in pink," complained the *New York Times*.[47] Another beef was the abundance of song compressed into the 81-minute film—although now one watches it begging for even more musical relief from the second-rate dramatics. The film bombed at the box office, too.

In retrospect, the most enjoyable moments are those intentionally comic. The humorous subplot has the pint-sized surgeon's daughter Johanna (4-foot, 11-inch Marion "Peanuts" Byron) fought over by a Mutt-and-Jeff pair. One suitor is a tall, skinny American named Blink (Lee Moran); the other is a short, balding, monocled Englishman called "The Duke" (Dick Henderson). Byron gets a song with each. To "You Know the Type—a Tiger," she and Moran demonstrate their love by slapping, kicking and choking each other. "We Two" makes a charming duet for Byron and Henderson. He was a droll British comic who made a handful of American films (his trademark line

was "Joke over!"). Much later, Henderson (1891–1958) reprises the tune in self-pity, as the Moran and Byron characters have married. This time, he's sitting at the soiled table of the Mombasa saloon, his new "date" the drunken, dissipated Mooda. The reliable Lupino Lane contributes a pleasing novelty dance to "In a Jungle Bungalow," one of three songs written for the film to complement seven from the stage.

Segal looks fetching in shoulder-length hair, but one can't get past the age and bad-material factors. "I was just a guinea pig for Technicolor. ... You felt like an ass, but what could you do? It was my livelihood," the actress told Anthony Slide in 1972 about her participation.[48] Woolf (1899–1984), a longtime Broadway leading man in musicals and non-musicals, is stiff enough as an actor to make Nelson Eddy look like Errol Flynn.

But Woolf's singing in *Golden Dawn* in no way justified the personal embarrassment he endured after he filed a $60,000 breach-of-contract lawsuit against Warner Bros., which had reneged on the final two pictures of his three-year, three-film contract. When the case came before the New York Supreme Court in 1932, the studio alleged that Woolf's singing voice was unsuitable for sound films, that his flatting of high notes during duets made Vivienne Segal's soprano ineffectual, and that his vocal range was too limited to be that of a baritone. At one point, Woolf had to admit that he could not read printed music. A settlement was reached just before Woolf was to be made to prove the quality of his voice by singing in the courtroom. Woolf returned to Hollywood shortly thereafter as a Fox contractee, but the studio changed his name to Walter Woolf King. And, although he was now playing more heavies than heroes, he did sing again before the camera, in the Marx Brothers musical comedy *A Night at the Opera* (1935)—as a tenor—and the Laurel and Hardy vehicle *Swiss Miss* (1938).

ONE MAD KISS
(Fox; July 13, 1930)

Directors: Marcel Silver, James Tinling. Stage Director: Frank Merlin. Adaptation and Dialogue: Dudley Nichols. Story: Adolf Paul. Photography: Charles Van Enger, Ross Fisher. Editor: Louis Loeffler. Sound: George Leverett.

Assistant Director: Virgil Hart. Dance Direction: Juan Duval. Running Time: 64 minutes.

Cast: José Mojica (José Savedra), Mona Maris (Rosario), Antonio Moreno (Don Estrada), Tom Patricola (Paco).

Songs: "Oh! Where Are You, My Imaginary Dream Girl?" "One Mad Kiss"["Un Béso Loco"] (José Mojica, Troy Sanders); "I Am Free," "In My Arms" (William Kernell); "Behind the Mask" (Joseph McCarthy, James F. Hanley); "Once in a While" (Clare Kummer, Cecil Arnold, Dave Stamper); "Only One" (Clare Kummer, José Mojica, Dave Stamper). Additional Songs for Spanish Version: "Florero Espanole," "Gitana" (Jarge Del Moral, Jose Mojica, Troy Sanders); "Fiesta Song" (José Mojica, William Kernell).

"Is he the new Valentino, who will sing his way into millions of hearts?" was the urgent question posed by *Photoplay* in a glowing profile of a Latin lad named José Mojica. Mojica was 30 years old, a Mexican-born engineering student turned tenor for the Chicago Opera Company. He had just signed a contract with Fox to make musical dramas, and all that was required of him was lasting stardom. "I am no saint," he confessed to his giddy interviewer. "Ramon Novarro … is a good boy. But I—I am not so good."[49]

Mojica was referring to his temperament, but he could have been referring to his acting in his first talking picture, *One Mad Kiss*, which reposed on Fox's shelf for some time before being given a hesitant and unfruitful release. The studio may have intended it as an experimental production for foreign markets, for a Spanish-language version contained additional music composed by Mojica himself. Marcel Silver or James Tinling (credit sources are in dispute) directed Dudley Nichols' over-familiar script about a Spanish Robin Hood who fights the government and fights off the ladies. Mona Maris was the female lead; Antonio Moreno, the villain. Fox proudly noted that the cast represented seven countries by birth or descent— Mexico, Argentina, Italy, Spain, France, Ireland, and Prussia.

After the failure of *One Mad Kiss*, Mojica (1899–1974) returned to Mexico to make movies, and—proving, perhaps, that he was better than he'd claimed to be in 1930—he eventually entered the priesthood.

DIXIANA
(RKO; July 22, 1930)

Director: Luther Reed. Producer: William LeBaron. Adaptation: Luther Reed. Story and Dialogue: Harry Tierney, Anne Caldwell. Photography: J. Roy Hunt, Lloyd Knechtel. Editor: William Hamilton. Sound: Hugh McDowell. Assistant Director: Frederick Fleck. Musical Director: Victor Baravalle. Orchestrations: Max Steiner. Art Director: Max Rée. Costumes: Max Rée. Dance Direction: Pearl Eaton. Running Time: 100 minutes. Technicolor sequence.

Cast: Bebe Daniels (Dixiana), Everett Marshall (Carl Van Horn), Bert Wheeler (Peewee), Robert Woolsey (Ginger), Joseph Cawthorn (Cornelius Van Horn), Jobyna Howland (Mrs. Van Horn), Dorothy Lee (Nanny), Ralf Harolde (Royal Montague), Edward Chandler (Blondell), Raymond Maurel (Cayetano), Bill "Bojangles" Robinson (specialty dancer), Bruce Covington (company porter), George Herman (contortionist), Eugene Jackson (Cupid), Robert Livingston.

Songs/Musical Numbers: "Cayetano's Prologue" [Daniels, chorus], "Contortionist Waltz," "Creole Number" [chorus], "Guiding Star" [Daniels, Marshall], "Here's to the Old Days, Good Bye Old Pals" [Marshall, men], "A Lady Loved a Soldier" [Woolsey, girls], "Mr. and Mrs. Sippi" [Marshall; reprised as dance by Robinson], "My One Ambition Is You" [Wheeler, Lee], "A Tear, a Kiss, a Smile" [Daniels, Marshall] (Anne Caldwell, Harry Tierney); "Dixiana" [Daniels, chorus; reprised by company] (Benny Davis, Harry Tierney).

Disc: RCA Victor 22471 (Marshall/"Here's to the Old Days, Good Bye Old Pals"/"Mr. and Mrs. Sippi"/78).

After the success of *Rio Rita* and *The Cuckoos*, RKO made plans to put Bert Wheeler and Robert Woolsey into an expensive version of Victor Herbert's *Babes in Toyland*. But production was called off in favor of a project that was considered much safer. *Dixiana* reunited the new comedy stars (and Dorothy Lee) with *Rio Rita* leading lady Bebe Daniels, director-writer Luther Reed, composer Harry Tierney and much of the support personnel. There was also Jobyna Howland, who had been so amusing in *The Cuckoos*. But instead of another high-grosser, Radio came away with a $300,000 loser,

Grand opera's Everett Marshall (left) played the troubled hero of RKO's *Dixiana*, with heroine Bebe Daniels and heavy Ralf Harolde.

or, as Miss Lee recalled it to the author, "a real dog."[50]

It would be easy to blame the new leading man. Everett Marshall, a tall, moustached baritone from the Metropolitan Opera—and before that, Cincinnati. He seemed exceedingly uncomfortable as Carl Van Horn, the scion of a wealthy 1840s Louisiana family. His love for a vivacious circus performer sets the Tierney-Anne Caldwell story in motion. Dixiana (Daniels), a singer and dancer, accepts Carl's marriage proposal and accompanies him—along with her trouping buddies Peewee and Ginger (Wheeler and Woolsey)—to the family plantation.

Carl's jovial father (Joseph Cawthorn) approves of the relationship, and at a ball in her honor, the lovers show their affection in song ("A Tear, a Kiss, a Smile"). But Peewee inadvertently reveals the secret of Dixiana's circus background, and the imperious Mrs. Van Horn

(Howland) orders the young woman to leave the premises. Dixiana, Peewee and Ginger attempt to get their jobs back, but the circus owner is ordered by Royal Montague (Ralf Harolde), a powerful New Orleans gambler, to reject them. Montague, who hates Carl and covets Dixiana, hires the trio for his gaming house; his intention is to attract Carl to the club, deplete his finances at cards and then dispatch him in a "fixed" duel.

On the eve of the annual celebration, Dixiana is to be crowned Queen of the Mardi Gras, thanks to Montague's influence. Carl turns up at the gambling house and is cheated out of his wealth by Montague and Dixiana. ("You're wonderful when you want revenge," the villain purrs to the fallen heroine.) When Dixiana realizes what Montague's intent is, she turns against him and tries to reconcile with Carl, but he will have no part of it. An angered Montague kidnaps Dixiana, but Carl intervenes and challenges his enemy to a duel. Montague had killed Carl's uncle in a duel years before by "forgetting" to load the victim's gun, and he attempts to do the same here. But Dixiana steals Carl's Mardi Gras costume and shows up for the duel in his place. She exposes the crook, and Carl's singing of "Guiding Star" signals that his love for Dixiana is revived.

Daniels told John Kobal that she didn't want to appear in *Dixiana*, that she'd wanted to make *Carmen* with John Boles instead, and that Marshall was "disastrous" and "looked dreadful when he sang."[51] True, Marshall grimaces through many of his songs and seems to spend the entire film looking away from the camera, his chin locked against his neck. But Dorothy Lee defends the foundering newcomer:

> They were so mean to Everett Marshall, and that made us [actors] all mad because he was such a nice guy. But … when he'd sing, he'd have to expand his lungs and [would] have to have elastic in the back of his vest and all. They had such a terrible time photographing him because he'd make such a face when he'd sing. He was a singer, not an actor. I don't think they did him justice. … He didn't get the treatment he should have. If you're a Metropolitan Opera singer [at that time], you don't know anything about acting. He probably stepped in too fast; he probably should've had private lessons in acting. Somebody should have been hired to show him how to do a scene, because he didn't know how to face the camera.[52]

As Nanny, a belle fought over by both of her comedy chums, Lee ends up, as usual, with Wheeler. They sweetly sing and dance to "My One Ambition Is You," which Lee considers her favorite number in all her films. Lee and Wheeler usually were left to work out the mechanics of their dance duos, this one taking place on a spiral stairway. Near the end of the song, they step down and do a little parody of a ballroom dance. Woolsey, hidden behind some nearby curtains, kicks both of them in the rear, and each dancer admonishes the other for landing the blow. Lee slaps Wheeler, Wheeler pushes Lee down, and her hooped skirt falls off to reveal lace pantaloons. Then the two smile, join hands and skip away as the music ends.

Having to remove her skirt away from the camera was the toughest part of the number, "That was a terrible job to do," Lee remembers,

"because … I had to get my hands behind my back and unhook my skirt so that when I fell over, my skirt would come off and stay on the floor. It's a wonder I didn't break my wrist."[53]

The rest of the Tierney-Caldwell score is not as accomplished, although "Mr. and Mrs. Sippi," sung by Marshall over the opening credits, is a better-than-average mammy song. During the Technicolor Mardi Gras finale, Bill "Bojangles" Robinson tap-dances to it in his movie debut. But the music and Marshall aren't the only problems with *Dixiana*. This time the Wheeler-and-Woolsey schtick is overlong and labored; the tired main gag is over a silly game in which one of them gets a kick in the pants when challenged to pick up three cigars without saying "Ouch!" Howland is barely seen after the first half hour or so, and the Yiddish-inflected Joseph Cawthorn is totally miscast as a Southern patriarch. The excuse for Cornelius Van Horn's accent is that he's a "Pennsylvania Dutch" transplant, but at one point, he calls his much-taller son a "schlemiel."

Harolde seems to relish his Snidely Whiplash role, and a similar observation prompted this response from *Variety*: "He had the idea. If the script had been thrown wholly into a satirical vein, it might have had a chance."[54] No wonder *Dixiana* lasted only one week at the RKO Globe Theatre in New York after a ballyhooed premiere there.

Just before the release of *Dixiana*, Marshall and Daniels were slated to costar, under Reed's direction, in *Heart of the Rockies*, an operetta that was aborted after musicals began to lose their appeal. Marshall (1900–1965) returned to New York, where he fared better on stage and in radio. His only other feature film, *I Live for Love* (1935), was an unsuccessful Warner Bros. programmer directed by Busby Berkeley. In 1939, Marshall filed for bankruptcy. Throughout the '40s, he toured in second-rate mountings of vintage operettas like *Blossom Time* and *The Student Prince*, sometimes paired with Ann Pennington, another forgotten star fallen on hard times. He was retired, a resident of Carmel, California, when he suffered a fatal heart attack, a happening too obscure to be noticed by the obituary writers from the likes of *Variety* and *The New York Times*.

Dixiana was shown on television for years without its closing Technicolor reels, which had deteriorated over time. But the UCLA Film and Television Archive took the color portion from the original camera negatives in the late 1980s and restored the film, which has since been shown frequently on cable TV. The complete movie accents the lavish sets by Max Rée and the luscious color photography by J. Roy Hunt, but those assets can't obscure its faults.

SWEET KITTY BELLAIRS
(Warner Bros.; August 9, 1930)

Director: Alfred E. Green. Screenplay and Dialogue: J. Grubb Alexander. Adaptation: Herman Harrison. Based on the play by David Belasco (New York opening, December 9, 1903; 206 performances) and the novel *The Bath Comedy* by Agnes and Egerton Castle (1900). Photography: James Van Trees, Frank Good. Editor: Owen Marks. Sound: George R. Groves. Musical Directors: Louis Silvers, Erno Rapée. Running Time: 63 minutes. Technicolor.

Cast: Ernest Torrence (Sir Jasper Standish), Perry Askam (Captain O'Hara), Walter Pidgeon (Lord Verney), Claudia Dell (Sweet Kitty Bellairs), June Collyer (Lady Julia Standish), Lionel Belmore (Colonel Villiers), Arthur Edmund Carewe (Captain Spicer), Douglas Gerrard (Tom Stafford), Tom Ricketts (rheumatic old man), Flora Finch (gossip), Christiane Yves (Lydia), Edgar Norton (Lord Markham), Bertram Jones (Verney's valet), Albert Hart (innkeeper), Tina Marshall (Megrim), Geoffrey McDonell (Lord Northmore), Rolfe Sedan (Alphonse).

Songs: "Drunk Song" [Torrence, Belmore, Norton], "Duelling Song" [Torrence, Askam, Norton, Belmore, Gerrard, others], "Highwayman Song" [Askam; reprised by Dell, then twice by Askam], "My Love, I'll Be Waiting for You" [Pidgeon; reprised by Dell, Pidgeon], "Peggy's Leg" [Pidgeon, Torrence, Askam, Belmore, Norton, Carewe, Gerrard], "Pump Room Song" [Dell, chorus], "Song of the Town of Bath" [chorus], "Tally Ho" [Dell, Pidgeon, Belmore, chorus], "You, I Love But You" [Dell, twice; reprised by Dell, Pidgeon] (Walter O'Keefe, Robert Emmett Dolan).

One of the little-seen delights of the early musicals period, the charming *Sweet Kitty Bellairs* is based on the David Belasco play of the same name, itself taken from the 1900 novel *The Bath Comedy*. Its cleverness and wit, both in dialogue and song, mark a welcome departure from the heavily sentimental Viennese-style operetta. This all–Technicolor ballad opera/farce retains the flavor of 18th-century England, when "men wore powdered wigs and fought duels and women's ankles were hidden beneath a maze of garments."[55] In this locale, a swipe at the shape of another's lower limb was grounds for man-to-man combat.

Warner Bros. chose the title role to introduce its ingénue Claudia Dell (1910–1977), a tall, blonde former Ziegfeld girl who hailed from a moneyed San Antonio family. After playing Marilyn Miller's starring part in *Rosalie* in London, Dell was signed to a five-year Warners contract. Her Kitty is a noted flirt of her day—hence the "Sweet." She is traveling from London to Bath by coach for a summer visit to her friends Sir Jasper and Lady Julia Standish. She and the other passengers—handsome Lord Verney (Walter Pidgeon) and gouty Colonel Villiers (Lionel Belmore)—introduce themselves with the rousing song "Tally Ho." Kitty quips that, despite her 30 or 40 affairs, she has lost none of her virtue. Suddenly, the coach is halted by a masked bandit. But the flamboyant highwayman is so taken with Kitty that he offers to return his loot to the passengers in exchange for a kiss from her. He kisses her, she insults him, he kisses her again, and she slaps him. She looks down at her ring, on which strands of the rogue's red hair have come off. "Consider yourself well kissed," grins the thief as he rides off, sans bounty, singing the "Highwayman Song."

Kitty and friends arrive at their stop, as townspeople sing the "Song of the Town of Bath," the lyrics of which describe their varying occupations. At a ball, Kitty reveals to the young Captain O'Hara (Perry Askam, 1898–1961) that she harbors a fascination for the mysterious bandit who kissed her. But she is also attracted to the shy Lord Verney. The feeling is mutual, as Verney tells Villiers that he will express his love to Kitty by writing her a poem; the colonel has a good laugh. Back at the Standishes, Kitty receives a love letter from the highwayman accompanied by a lock of his hair. She, too, sings the "Highwayman Song."

The mousy Lady Julia (June Collyer) asks Kitty how she can recapture the affections of her husband. Kitty tells her to invent an imaginary lover to make Sir Jasper (top-billed Ernest Torrence) jealous. Sir Jasper arrives, his buddies Villiers and Lord Markham (Edgar Norton) sending him off with a drunken tune ("Drunk Song"). The inebriated Sir Jasper, upon hearing his much-younger's wife stated "hints" about her "lover," becomes angry. Just then, Lord Verney knocks on their door, and Sir Jasper thinks he's Julia's paramour. He wants to challenge Verney to a duel, but for honor's sake, must observe the proper etiquette—the "code"—of the period. "The calf of your leg, it displeases me!" Jasper sneers. Verney is amused, but the foppish busybody Captain Spicer (Arthur Edmund Carewe) hastens to remind him that he's been "insulted." Verney and Sir Jasper are obligated to arrange a duel.

In the baths, Spicer and the townspeople gossip over the impending battle ("Pump Room Song"). Kitty overhears and is alarmed. While preparing for the duel, Sir Jasper finds the letter written to Kitty by the highwayman and thinks it's intended for Julia. As Villiers has red hair, Jasper insults him by implying that *he* might be Julia's swain. "Your leg looks like sausage!" is Villiers' reply. Jasper now challenges him to a duel, but their bout turns into a comedy of errors that produces no accurate pistol shots. But "honor" has been preserved.

Still, Jasper is stuck with having to duel Verney, although he's having second thoughts ("Duelling Song"). He, O'Hara, Markham, Villiers and others decide to go to Verney's home the night before the duel to mend the rift. Meanwhile, Kitty, chaperoned by Julia, arrives at Verney's hoping to talk him out of the showdown. Pining for Kitty but not realizing she's right there (because she's wearing a mask), Verney sings "My Love, I'll Be Waiting for You." Kitty's reply is "You, I Love But You." Verney now hears something familiar in his visitor's voice, but suddenly he has company. Sir Jasper and his friends come in; Kitty and Julia hide away. The men make amends, and sing the comic ditty "Peggy's Leg," but Jasper spies a loose slipper and is certain it's Julia's. Kitty, now unmasked, emerges to don the footwear herself. Verney, to protect the woman's honor (but actually because he truly loves her), announces that he and Kitty are to be married. Satisfied, Jasper and his party leave, as Verney and Kitty begin to argue over his true intentions. But

O'Hara emerges from behind a nearby curtain, having overheard the conversation. He vows to Verney that he will take Kitty away from him.

Later, on a balcony at the Standish house, Kitty reprises "You, I Love But You," but then she hears another familiar song. The singing highwayman reappears to carry her off in a coach. "You're a bigger thief than I am," he tells her, referring to all the male hearts she's broken. She demands to know his name. He gallantly takes off his mask … he's Captain O'Hara. "Oh, it's you—" is Kitty's disappointed response. But the coach is stopped by another masked marauder. He challenges O'Hara to a battle of swords, then wins it easily. A removal of his mask reveals the face of Lord Verney. Still the gentleman, O'Hara offers the couple the coach for their trip to London to a church. "Take it as your wedding gift!" he exclaims. As they ride off, Kitty and Verney sing another duet of "My Love, I'll Be Waiting for You" and "You, I Love But You."

Even a fan-oriented magazine like *Motion Picture* had to admit that *Sweet Kitty Bellairs* was "colorful as an old English print … a grateful event in a month of grimly realistic pictures,"[56] but a viewing public much more interested in underworld melodramas and backstage exposes could not warm to this unusual little picture. A shame, for Alfred E. Green's direction and J. Grubb Alexander's screenplay are brisk and spirited. The actors, especially the canny Scot Torrence, seem to be having a grand time, although baritone Askam, a West Coast operetta headliner, is the only real singer in the cast. The *Variety* reviewer "Rush" declared that Walter Pidgeon "is one of the very few actors who can wear pink satin knickerbockers and silk stockings and still look human."[57]

The film constantly pokes fun at the customs of the story's period, and the comic highlights concern the laughable extent to which maledom adheres to its ludicrous "code" of honor. When Colonel Villiers, lame from gout, shows up for his duel with Sir Jasper in a carriage, his opponent demands one of his own. As they square off in their contraptions, the colonel stumbles and gets off a wild shot. Jasper, not wishing to harm his friend but aiming to save face, "accidentally" shoots into the ground. Then all the gathered gentlemen congratulate each other for satisfying the conditions of their code.

Composer Robert Emmett Dolan and lyricist Walter O'Keefe—the latter would be more famous for his updating of the 1868 song "The Man on the Flying Trapeze"—contributed the clever score. It complements the story instead of bumping into it or stopping it cold. Even the two ultra-romantic duet pieces are appealingly fashioned. "Peggy's Leg," presented as a common ditty of the period, tells of a pretty young woman whose pretty leg turns out to be made of wood. Best of all is the "Duelling Song," which Jasper, Villiers and their seconds sung in a pub after their bout of inept gentlemanship.

Let's live and have our fling,
… What's the use of fighting duels?
Aren't we all a lot of fools?
I crack you,
Why crack you,
Instead, let's crack a quart of wine.

Although *Sweet Kitty Bellairs* was not an influential or historically significant musical, it did demonstrate the still-potent ability of the fading genre to entertain.

CALL OF THE FLESH
(MGM; August 16, 1930)

Director: Charles Brabin. Dialogue: John Colton. Story: Dorothy Farnum. Photography: Merritt B. Gerstad. Editor: Conrad A. Nervig. Sound: Douglas Shearer, Ralph Shugart. Art Director: Cedric Gibbons. Costumes: David Cox. Dance Direction: Eduardo Cansino. Running Time: 100 minutes. Technicolor sequence.

Cast: Ramon Novarro (Juan), Dorothy Jordan (Maria), Ernest Torrence (Esteban), Nance O'Neil (Mother Superior), Renée Adorée (Lola), Mathilde Comont (La Rumbarita), Russell Hopton (Enríque).

Songs [all by Novarro]: "Just for Today," "Not Quite Good Enough for Me" (Clifford Grey, Herbert Stothart); "Lonely" (Clifford Grey, Ramon Novarro, Herbert Stothart). Operatic Excerpts: "Ah! Fuyez, douce image," from *Manon* (Jules Massenet); "Cavatina," from *L'Elisir d'Amore* (Gaetano Donizetti); "Questa o quella," from *Rigoletto* (Giuseppe Verdi).

Disc: Stanyan 10055 (Novarro/LP; ST).

The third Ramon Novarro–Dorothy Jordan musical was their third operetta, this one set partially in the world of grand opera. *Call of the Flesh* (titled *The Singer of Seville* prior to release) was the slowly paced story about the unexpected love of Juan, a vain Spanish cantina singer, and Maria, a pretty young novice from the local convent. The pairing is greeted with alarm by Juan's jealous partner, Lola (Renée Adorée), and his opera-hungry vocal teacher, Esteban (Ernest Torrence, fighting to mute his Scottish burr), as well as the girl's pious soldier brother, Enríque (Russell Hopton).

Juan, Maria and Esteban go to Madrid for Juan's long-awaited audition for the opera; the verdict is that his voice is suitable but that he has "no heart or soul." Still, Esteban uses his influence, as a once-famous opera performer, to pay for a high-profile debut performance for Juan. The lovers become engaged, but Lola and Enríque intervene, and Juan is convinced by Enríque that he should give Maria up for her sake, and for the Church. In a well-acted sequence filmed in Technicolor, Juan sadly rejects Maria by pretending to make love to Lola.

Juan reluctantly goes on for his big night at the opera, but his heartbreak has given his singing the power it had lacked. His impassioned performance of the "Ah! Fuyez, douce image" excerpt from *Manon* earns great acclaim, even as he collapses at its climax. In his torment, Juan loses the will to live, and a contrite Lola goes to the convent and pleads with the Mother Superior to let Maria go. But as Maria has not taken her final vows, she is free to leave—which she does, bringing about a happy ending.

Call of the Flesh is hampered by a predictable denouement, slack pacing (blame director Charles Brabin) and three forgettable songs (by Herbert Stothart and Clifford Grey), but it's lifted by some good acting. In dialogue and song, Novarro adequately progresses from cavalier sinner to lovesick saint, but he was already beginning to fade as a box-office attraction. Jordan effectively projects the required innocence for her role, and Adorée and Torrence are capable in support. The same cannot be said for the miscast Hopton, who utters his lines in the monotone of a big-city gangster—the kind of role he would be more comfortable in during his two decades in Hollywood.

The "other woman" role would be the last

for Renée Adorée, who had debuted so memorably opposite John Gilbert in *The Big Parade*. The French actress, afflicted with tuberculosis, finished work on *Call of the Flesh* against the advice of her physicians. (She appears emaciated and haggard on screen.) She was rushed to a sanitorium in Arizona, where she spent much of the next two years confined to bed. In the spring of 1933, Adorée was released in order to begin a comeback, but her energy would not allow it. She was a patient in a California health resort when she died on October 5, 1933, six days after her 35th birthday.

Call of the Flesh was also produced in a Spanish-language version titled *La Sevillana*.

A LADY'S MORALS
(MGM; November 7, 1930)

Director: Sidney Franklin. Scenario: Hans Kräly, Claudine West. Dialogue: John Meehan, Arthur Richman. Story: Dorothy Farnum. Photography: George Barnes. Editor: Margaret Booth. Sound: Douglas Shearer, J. K. Brock. Art Director: Cedric Gibbons. Costumes: Adrian. Dance Direction: Sammy Lee. Running Time: 86 minutes.

Cast: Grace Moore (Jenny Lind), Reginald Denny (Paul Brandt), Wallace Beery (P. T. Barnum), Gus Shy (Olaf), Jobyna Howland (Josephine), Gilbert Emery (Broughm), George F. Marion (innkeeper), Paul Porcasi (Maretti), Judith Vosselli (Rosatti), Giovanni Martino (Zergo), Bodil Rosing (innkeeper's wife), Joan Standing (Louise), Mavis Villiers (Selma), Karl Dane (Swede in theater), Rolfe Sedan (Italian hairdresser).

Songs: "It Is Destiny" [Moore, twice], "Student's Song" [students] (Clifford Grey, Oscar Straus); "Lovely Hour" [Moore, twice] (Carrie Jacobs Bond); "Oh, Why?" [Moore] (Arthur Freed, Harry Woods, Herbert Stothart); "Swedish Pastorale" [Swedish villagers] (Howard Johnson, Herbert Stothart). Operatic Excerpts [Moore, chorus]: "Casta Diva," from *Norma* (Vincenzo Bellini), and "Rataplan," from *The Daughter of the Regiment* (Gaetano Donizetti).

Even before the encouraging reception to Lawrence Tibbett and *The Rogue Song*, MGM was inspired to recruit a second Metropolitan Opera standout. She was Grace Moore (1901–1947), a vivacious blonde soprano who had emerged from a Tennessee mining town to make the big time. Moore appeared successfully in Broadway musicals—in Irving Berlin's *Music Box Revue of 1924* she introduced "What'll I Do?"—but her goal was to make the grade at the Met, which she did in 1928 (as Mimi in *La Bohème*) to begin nearly two decades there. MGM ballyhooed Moore's signing in January 1930 by bringing her West in a private railroad car, and then venting her considerable charm upon the Hollywood press corps at a lavish, all-day "meet the star" party.

Hollywood, Moore would write years later, "was a strange, strange world,"[58] made even more curious by the choice for Moore's debut film, a biography of Jenny Lind, the world-famous "Swedish Nightingale" of nearly a century previous. The highly fictionalized story, written by Dorothy Farnum and fleshed out by a quartet of MGM staffers, attempted to add ginger to the real life of the notoriously priggish singer. After the project was announced, the studio was assailed with letters from members of the Society for Jenny Lind, which pleaded that their idol be cast in the best possible light. They needn't have worried, for *A Lady's Morals* (which initially carried the equally irrelevant title of *The Soul Kiss*) is every bit as chaste as its subject was alleged to be.

At a rural inn in the late 1840s, Jenny Lind and her traveling companion (Jobyna Howland) encounter the talented but cocky composer Paul Brandt (Reginald Denny). The inn is full, and Paul reluctantly relinquishes his room after insultingly kidding Jenny about her well-known chastity. The next morning, as a gesture of thanks, she consents to sing his newly composed song, "It Is Destiny." When she is finished, he takes her in his arms and kisses her. She slaps him. He replies that their meeting is no accident, that he has been following her for quite some time: "I fell in love with you the moment I saw you. … The gods have brought us together. We cannot throw their blessings back at them."

They part, but Jenny finds that she cannot forget the ingratitating young man. When she sings Donizetti's *The Daughter of the Regiment*, he appears on stage next to her as one of the soldiers. He crashes her dressing room to reserve dinner for two. Still, Jenny is not won over. In

Rome, she captures a skeptical audience with Bellini's *Norma*; foolishly permitted to perform a taxing encore, she loses her voice in mid-song. A fight breaks out in the gallery; Paul, defending Jenny's honor, is hit over the head with a bottle. The blow impairs his sight, which begins to disappear. However, Paul's concern is not for himself, but for Jenny. He convinces his uncle, a famous maestro, to work with Jenny on restoring her voice, but he hides his impending blindness from her. The cured Jenny finds out anyway, and her realization of Paul's selflessness stirs her love for him.

Jenny helps Paul to get the best medical treatment, but his eyes fail to respond. He cannot bear to tell her. At her secluded villa, Jenny tells him that she has dismissed her servants, that they are finally alone. "I have accepted your invitation," she says. "You haven't forgotten it, have you?" She kisses Paul's hand and he sheds a tear; she thinks it's out of gratitude. "I have a surprise for you," she says, and she departs. Paul follows her voice to the next room, where she is singing "It Is Destiny" to her own piano accompaniment. The music continues into "Lovely Hour" as the camera cuts to a despondent Paul at a waterfront watching ships sail off into the night. Despite his love for Jenny, he has decided to leave her. He departs for New York, where he becomes a wandering musician—and totally blind.

Now it is 1850, and the night of Jenny's long-awaited American debut, at the Castle Garden in New York as sponsored by the great P. T. Barnum (Wallace Beery, in a glorified cameo). Paul's American friend Olaf (Gus Shy), an immigrant from Sweden, encourages him to go hear Jenny perform, but he refuses. Olaf breaks into Jenny's dressing room and attempts to drop off a composition written by his gentleman friend. He is whisked away, but Jenny realizes that the mystery composer is her old flame. After her victorious performance of "Lovely Hour," she has the local police to track down Olaf, and then Paul, whom she will now never let go.

Despite its well-worn and sentimental story, *A Lady's Morals* earned solid notices from big-city critics. *The New York Times*, while conceding its "half-truths and fiction" and poor sound recording, called it "charming ... directed with intelligence and care."[59] *Variety* praised Moore as "an actress of an indescribable charm

with the added appeal of a voice ... with a human quality that gives it remarkable appeal."[60] The public did not respond in kind, however, and the film, which cost $600,000 to produce, came in at a loss of nearly $300,000. Maybe too many viewers saw Moore as did Julia Shawell of the *New York Graphic*: "She is attractive, but in that cold, unimpressive manner of Catherine Dale Owen or Kay Johnson."[61] The film's lack of success intensified the volatile relationship between Moore and MGM chief Irving Thalberg, who thought the mildly stout singer needed to lose weight. Faring better than *A Lady's Morals* was its French-language version, released in Europe under the title *Jenny Lind*.

A Lady's Morals was a disappointment in its time, but it survives quite nicely. The opera sequences are much lengthier than anything before seen on celluloid, and Moore handles them as well as the intimate theme song, "Lovely Hour" (written for the film by Carrie Jacobs Bond, the composer of "A Perfect Day"). Her acting is merely adequate, although Moore's own harsher analysis was that "one would have to travel far to find such comparable cardboard effects."[62] Denny (1891–1967), whose career as a light comedy actor was temporarily stymied when sound exposed his English accent, plays the suitor with polish and surprising likability. Sidney Franklin's direction is sensitive, especially in the romantic moments, which do not lapse into pure sentimentality. The comedy is unintrusive, with Shy's role held down and Beery given only a couple of minutes of his folksy Barnum. ("Howdy, Count!" he exclaims to a stuffy oldster who has come to visit Jenny in New York.) Beery would get to do more with the showman in 20th Century's 1934 biography *The Mighty Barnum*, in which Virginia Bruce played Jenny Lind.

Buffs may be surprised to note the uncredited appearance in *A Lady's Morals* of the Danish comedian Karl Dane, in whose filmographies this film is absent. The tall, gangly Dane rose to character stardom in a supporting role in *The Big Parade* and then in a series of slapstick comedies with George K. Arthur, but by 1930, his thick accent was killing his career. In five other feature-film appearances that year, he gained featured billing based on name value, but his screen time and dialogue were limited. Here, he's a vocal Swedish spectator at Jenny's

Rome concert who gets into a fight while defending his countrywoman's ability. It was Dane's final speaking role in a feature film. In 1931, he made shorts with Arthur for RKO. In 1932, he attempted to launch a vaudeville act that was panned by *Variety* as "15 minutes of dud gags ... in Swede dialect."[63] The only film work he could get thereafter was a role opposite Bela Lugosi in the low-budget 1933 Mascot serial *The Whispering Shadow*. Reduced to operating a hot-dog stand, Dane shot himself to death in 1934. He was 47 years old.

VIENNESE NIGHTS
(Warner Bros.; November 26, 1930)

Director: Alan Crosland. Screenplay: Oscar Hammerstein II, Sigmund Romberg. Photography: James Van Trees. Editor: Hal McLaren. Sound: George R. Groves. Musical Direction: Louis Silvers. Dance Direction: Jack Haskell. Running Time: 105 minutes. Technicolor.

Cast: Alexander Gray (Otto Stirner), Vivienne Segal (Elsa Hofner), Jean Hersholt (Mr. Hocher), Walter Pidgeon (Franz von Renner), Louise Fazenda (Gretl Kruger), Alice Day (Barbara), Bert Roach (Gus Sascher), June Purcell (Mary), Lothar Meyring (Baron von Renner), Milton Douglas (Bill Jones), Virginia Sale (Emma Stirner), Freddie Burke Frederick (Otto Jr.), Bela Lugosi (Count von Ratz), Los Angeles Symphony Orchestra.

Songs/Musical Numbers: "Goodbye My Love" [Gray, Segal, Roach, chorus], "Here We Are" [Segal, Pidgeon, Gray; reprised by Pidgeon, chorus, then by radio singers], "I Bring a Love Song" [Gray, Segal; reprised by Gray, then by Segal, then by Segal, orchestra, then by Gray, Segal], "I'm Bringing You Bad News" [Douglas], "I'm Lonely" [Purcell], "Oli, Oli, Oli" [chorus], "Otto's Dilemma" ("The Crazy Walk"), "Poem Symphonic" [orchestra], "Pretty Gypsy" [Pidgeon, Segal, chorus], "The Regimental March" [band, chorus], "When You Have No Man to Love" [Segal, Fazenda, women], "You Will Remember Vienna" [Gray, Pidgeon, Roach, Meyring; reprised by Segal, chorus, then by Gray] (Oscar Hammerstein II, Sigmund Romberg).

The Desert Song having secured them a Hollywood contract, Sigmund Romberg and

Oscar Hammerstein II set out to write the first of four original operettas they were to create for Warner Bros.–First National over a two-year period. Their booty was $100,000 apiece per film against 25 percent of the profits.[64] But by the time *Viennese Nights* was ready for release, the public apathy for musicals—and especially romantic operettas—put it at risk before it had a chance to gain a following.

Variety liked the film, but in an almost apologetic way:

> If this pretty and clean musical romance ... does not get over, it will settle any question at present as to whether the theatre-going public wants musical talkers. ... Plenty of good production all in acceptable color, direction beyond reproach, well-assembled cast and everything, but it's a musical. Let's see.[65]

With that kind of backhanded encouragement, it's no wonder *Viennese Nights* joined the growing ranks of failed musicals.

Romberg and Hammerstein could not have expected the fate that befell their first original film musical. Hammerstein (1895–1960), who preferred to supervise the production of his own stage works, worked closely with director Alan Crosland, who had already helmed many musicals for Warners. Despite the extravagant production values, shooting proceeded smoothly and lasted only 24 days in March and April of 1930.

Former President Calvin Coolidge visited the set on a day on which no major sequences were to be shot, but for the benefit of the dignitary, the cast was quickly assembled to re-enact a scene previously filmed. The scene took place in a café where the actors drank steins of beer—near beer, of course, this being Prohibition—but a couple of them were partaking from a smuggled-in case of the real brew. The habitually grumpy Coolidge asked Crosland what the actors were drinking.

> "Beer," replied Crosland.
> "Near beer?"
> "Of course, Mr. Coolidge. Near beer."
> The former president said he would like some and Crosland told an assistant to bring Mr. Coolidge a glass of beer. When he returned, Mr. Coolidge took a large draft and remarked, "Best near beer I ever tasted."
> Crosland investigated. "Oscar," he whispered. "They made a mistake. They gave him the real stuff."[66]

Walter Pidgeon woos Vivienne Segal away from the hapless Alexander Gray in Romberg and Hammerstein's disappointing *Viennese Nights*.

One of the culprits may have been Walter Pidgeon, a native of Canada, where there was no beer ban. Pidgeon was on the downside of his musically inspired comeback, and he was cast here as an infrequently-singing heavy. There were plenty of more experienced baritones in Hollywood now; one of them was the blond-wigged Alexander Gray, playing the romantic lead opposite Vivienne Segal. Segal was on the fourth (and last) operetta of her disastrous Warners–First National contract; the studio was already trying to farm her out after the first two films, *Song of the West* and *Bride of the Regiment*. Her failure in movies was attributable to both a lack of quality in her material and an offbeat beauty (high cheekbones and a slightly oversized nose) that did not always photograph favorably.

At the outset of *Viennese Nights*—a sentimental love-through-the-ages tale similar to *Bitter Sweet* or *Smilin' Through*—Elsa Hofner (Segal) is a Vienna shopgirl who falls in love with Otto Stirner (Gray), a sensitive music student and would-be composer serving a hitch in

the Austrian Army in 1879. Also in uniform are Otto's best friends from childhood: Franz von Renner (Pidgeon), a baron's son who has become a lieutenant, and Gus Sascher (Bert Roach), the rotund comedian of the trio. Otto breaks regulations by failing to wear his Army dress on a night out at a café; Franz, drinking there with the other officers, disciplines him and then claims his sweetheart ("Here We Are"). Elsa's ambitious father (Jean Hersholt) sabotages her romance with Otto by lying about her feelings for each man. A dejected Otto, drinking himself into a haze ("Otto's Dilemma"), grabs a prostitute off the street and makes a scene in front of Elsa and Franz at a restaurant. Saddened and shocked, Elsa reluctantly consents to marry the baron.

The scene shifts to 1890 in New York, where Otto is now working as a violinist for a Broadway orchestra. He has married a nagging shrew (Virginia Sale) who cares nothing about music; they have a young son. One night, he spots Elsa in a balcony box. (The bit players sitting with Segal in the box are Dorothy

Hammerstein, the lyricist's wife, and Bela Lugosi, a few months away from immortality as Count Dracula. Lugosi, unbilled as the Austrian ambassador to America, is on screen scarcely over a minute.) Elsa is wealthy but stranded in a loveless marriage to the womanizing Franz. Giddy with delight, Otto and Elsa seek solitude at a nearby park, where they decide to resume their romance, proper or not. But the baroness, upon learning of Otto's devotion to his little son, changes her mind and returns to Europe.

Forty more years pass. Otto is long dead. Elsa is a frail, crotchety widow with a granddaughter (Alice Day) who has fallen in love with a young American composer (Gray again, with his natural dark hair). The disapproving dowager has not met the young man, but upon hearing his tone poem—adapted from Otto's old melody "I Bring a Love Song"—she realizes that he is Otto's grandson! Overwhelmed, Elsa asks to be left alone at the very park bench where she and Otto pledged devotion to each other 40 years before. She sees him singing to her in a vision—then dies as the spirits of the reunited lovers embrace.

Viennese Nights is every bit as turgid as it sounds, unfortunately. Romberg's score is not his best, but it does have the grand "You Will Remember Vienna," a fond recollection of love lost and found. "Here We Are," billed as an Austrian "folk tune" with Hammerstein's deftly simple lyrics, serves as clever romantic byplay between the flirting Franz and the resistant Elsa. The less said about the other songs, the better, but the real failure of the film is in a libretto that is cornball even for an operetta. Otto is such a dolt, one has to strain to root for him. Most of his troubles—his impulsive decision to go out sans army uniform, the drunken spectacle that drives Elsa into Franz's arms, his marriage to someone completely unsuitable for him—are self-imposed. Gray's whiny characterization makes him even less appealing. Segal—who considered this her favorite film—is much better, although she is saddled with this kind of dialogue:

Roach (having heard the grandson's music for the first time): "How Otto would have loved to be alive today!"

Segal (with dramatic finality): "Otto WAS alive today!"

Viennese Nights was a hit in England, running for over a year in London's West End, but its reception domestically prompted Jack Warner to propose the cancellation of the Romberg-Hammerstein contract after two films. (*Children of Dreams*, released in mid–1931, already had been produced.) The two songwriters each took East a $100,000 settlement. "The most money I ever got for not making two pictures," Hammerstein would say.

Viennese Nights has been restored to its original two-strip Technicolor form by the UCLA Film and Television Archive from the only surviving color nitrate print.

THE LOTTERY BRIDE
(Art Cinema/United Artists; November 28, 1930)

Director: Paul L. Stein. Executive Producer: Joseph M. Schenck. Producers: Arthur Hammerstein, John W. Considine, Jr. Continuity and Dialogue: Howard Emmett Rogers. Adaptation: Horace Jackson. Based on the story "Bride 66" by Herbert Stothart. Photography: Ray June. Editor: Robert J. Kern. Sound: P. P. Reed, Frank Maher. Art Direction: William Cameron Menzies, Park French. Costumes: Alice O'Neill. Musical Arrangements: Hugo Riesenfeld. Running Time: 80 minutes. Technicolor sequence.

Cast: Jeanette MacDonald (Jenny Swanson), John Garrick (Chris Svenson), Joe E. Brown (Hoke Curtis), ZaSu Pitts (Hilda), Robert Chisholm (Olaf Svenson), Joseph Macaulay (Alberto), Harry Gribbon (Boris), Carroll Nye (Nels Swanson).

Songs: "Come Drink to the Girl That You Love" [chorus], "High and Low" [chorus, twice], "I'll Follow the Trail" [Chisholm], "My Northern Light" [Garrick, MacDonald], "Napoli" [Macaulay], "Round She Whirls" [chorus], "Shoulder to Shoulder" [Garrick, Chisholm, chorus], "Two Strong Men" [Gribbon, Brown], "You're an Angel" [Chisholm], "Yubla" [MacDonald] (J. Keirn Brennan, Rudolf Friml).

While Oscar Hammerstein II was misfiring on *Viennese Nights*, his producer brother Arthur was preparing an even worse musical for Joseph M. Schenck's Art Cinema company. *The Lottery Bride* had some estimable names behind it: Hammerstein, whose Broadway credits included *Rose-Marie* and *Song of the Flame*; Rudolf Friml, whose score was his first written for a movie; Herbert Stothart, on whose original story the film was based; William Cameron Menzies, the Oscar-winning art director; supporting comics Joe E. Brown and ZaSu Pitts; and the star, Jeanette MacDonald. But Jeanette was allowed only one solo in suffering through her one and only film appearance as an ex-convict. That should tell you how bad *The Lottery Bride* turned out. It's hardly worth enduring for two decent songs sung by one supporting player.

MacDonald, between early tenures at Paramount and Fox, had the title role of Jenny Swanson, a pigtailed Norwegian miss. She is loved by Chris Svenson (John Garrick), who affectionately calls her "My Northern Light" in song. With her brother Nels, she enters a marathon dance contest arranged by American bandleader Hoke Curtis (Brown) at an Oslo café owned by Hilda (Pitts). Jenny has done so because Nels needs money to replace what he's embezzled from his bank to pay off gambling debts to the aviator Alberto (Joseph Macaulay). As the contest nears an end after 84 hours, the police show up. A misunderstanding drives Chris away from Jenny, who then helps Nels escape—an act that will send her to prison for two months.

After her release, Jenny goes with Hoke and Hilda to the far north as a prospective "picture bride," chosen by the turn of a roulette wheel ("Round She Whirls") by one of the coal miners there. The lucky winner happens to be Olaf, the strapping, bearded older brother of Chris. (Actually, Chris, who has joined his sibling in the mines, draws the winning ticket, but he foolishly gives it to Olaf without looking at the woman's photograph.) Chris and Jenny, miffed at each other, keep secret their former relationship, which causes great tension in the household. Finally, the crestfallen Chris departs, having joined the crew of an Arctic Circle–bound dirigible piloted by Alberto. Olaf, now realizing the truth about Jenny and his brother, sings the mournful "I'll Follow the Trail." The dirigible crashes in the frozen wilderness; Olaf, leading a search party, rescues Chris and Alberto. In the Technicolor finale, an icebreaker shows up to take the trio home. With the presumed blessing of Olaf, who has not yet married Jenny, she and Chris are reunited for good. In the night sky, the northern lights flash their approval.

Thanks in part to Paul L. Stein's glacial direction, neither the drama nor the comedy in *The Lottery Bride* work very well. The only reason to enjoy the film today is for the only American feature-film appearance by the Australian-English baritone Robert Chisholm (1898–1960). Chisholm plays the spurned Olaf with understated honesty, and he sings the daylights out of "You're an Angel" and "I'll Follow the Trail." In the former, Olaf expresses his everlasting love for Jenny; he reduces her to tears and compels Chris to walk out of their lives. "I'll Follow the Trail" follows Jenny's histrionics at the departure of Chris on the dirigible. She has fainted; he has picked her up and carried her home, only to see that she has been clutching an old photograph of herself and Chris. The song is Olaf's determination that he will live alone, without a woman who cannot love him.

Chisholm's most conspicuous Broadway credit to this point was the blackfaced Shep in Hammerstein's *Golden Dawn*; in 1934, he would play Macheath in the first American production of Kurt Weill's *Threepenny Opera*. The failure of *The Lottery Bride* was the second major disappointment in a row for Chisholm, Hammerstein, Friml, Macaulay, scripter Howard Emmett Rogers and lyricist J. Keirn Brennan. They had just seen their $200,000 Broadway operetta, *Luana*, sink after 21 performances. *Luana* (based on Richard Walton Tully's play *The Bird of Paradise*) may have been a victim of the apathy toward movie musicals, for it originally was written for the screen and then adapted into a stageplay after filming was scrapped. Hammerstein had been signed by Schenck to make four musicals, but after *The Lottery Bride* no more would be required. Arthur Hammerstein would declare bankruptcy in 1931.

NEW MOON
(MGM; December 23, 1930)

Director: Jack Conway. Scenario: Sylvia Thalberg, Frank Butler. Dialogue: Cyril Hume. Based on the operetta *The New Moon*, book by Oscar Hammerstein II, Frank Mandel and Laurence Schwab, lyrics by Hammerstein,

Roland Young (left) looks on as opera luminaries Grace Moore and Lawrence Tibbett celebrate their quickie marriage in MGM's unsuccessful *New Moon*.

music by Sigmund Romberg (New York opening, September 19, 1928; 509 performances). Photography: Oliver T. Marsh. Editor: Margaret Booth. Sound: Douglas Shearer. Art Director: Cedric Gibbons. Costumes: Adrian. Running Time: 78 minutes.

Cast: Lawrence Tibbett (Lieutenant Michael Petroff), Grace Moore (Princess Tanya Strogoff), Adolphe Menjou (Governor Boris Brusiloff), Roland Young (Count Igor Strogoff), Gus Shy (Potkin), Emily Fitzroy (Countess Anastia Strogoff), Nena Quartero (Vadda), Tyler Brooke (man on ship).

Songs: "Lover, Come Back to Me" [Tibbett; reprised by Moore, then by Tibbett, Moore], "One Kiss" [Moore], "Stout-Hearted Men" [Tibbett, soldiers], "Wanting You" [Tibbett, Moore] (Oscar Hammerstein II, Sigmund Romberg); "The Farmer's Daughter" [Tibbett, twice; reprised by Moore], "What Is Your Price, Madame?" [Tibbett] (Clifford Grey, Herbert Stothart); "Barinia" [gypsies], "Bright Moonshine" [gypsies] (trad.).

Disc: RCA Victor 1506 (Tibbett/"Lover, Come Back to Me"/"Wanting You"/78); Pelican 2020 (LP); Radiola BMPB-1929 (bootleg LP; ST).

Lawrence Tibbett, who had made a strong first impression with *The Rogue Song*, and Grace Moore, who had not with *A Lady's Morals*, were paired in what MGM presumed to be an unbeatable teaming of operatic luminaries. Trade ads boasted of "the most amazing combination of world famous stars ever brought to the screen ... in the year's towering talkie achievement." The property chosen was one of Broadway's most successful recent shows, blessed with a sumptuous Sigmund Romberg score.[67] But *The New Moon* was practically the last of the old-fashioned Viennese-style romantic operettas that was able to flourish on the Great White Way, and it marked the final success for the Romberg–Oscar Hammerstein II team. Of course, the movie people had no way of seeing that as an omen.

Possibly because of the familiarity of the play, MGM production chief Irving Thalberg chose to alter the setting of *New Moon*—the article was dropped from the title—from late 18th-century France and Louisiana to early 20th-century Russia. (The movie's French roots might explain why MGM, seeking to avert confusion with its 1940 remake, carelessly renamed the '30 version *Parisian Belle* when it was sold to television. Surviving prints still carry the alternate title.) Courtesy of Frank Butler and Sylvia Thalberg, Ernest's screenwriting sister, the French aristocrat-revolutionary and shipowner's daughter became a Russian lieutenant and princess. Metro-Goldwyn-Mayer announced it had studied the film market in the world's English-speaking nations and decided to include as few songs in *New Moon* as possible.[68] Only four of the Romberg-Hammerstein songs were held over, and Metro's prolific house duo of Herbert Stothart and Clifford Grey provided new numbers.

The MGM brass continued to carp about Moore's weight, which had increased since her arrival in Hollywood, and there were reports of discord between the temperamental diva and her costar. But in her 1944 autobiography, Moore said that she and Tibbett developed a lasting friendship during filming, and that they enjoyed cutting up on the set.

> Larry is a great character actor and one of the most gallant men in the world, and I am not averse to what is called the tender passion myself, but something would happen to us when we were thrown into one another's arms, trilling and tra-la-ing about how I love you. It seemed all too funny, and giggles would emerge instead of passionate gurgles. *New Moon* is one of those pageants of war and blood and flossy romance, whereas Larry and I belonged in a rough-and-tumble singing version of *The Guardsman*.[69]

On a day when a menthol spray was used to duplicate heavy fog, the stars lost their voices and were forced to play their amorous scenes silently, with menthol tears streaming down their made-up faces. On other occasions, the combined power of their voices blew out the primitive sound recording machines. The production perils proved too much for director Jack Conway, who became ill during filming. He was replaced by an uncredited Sam Wood.

At least one of the two leads is on screen for all but a minute or two of *New Moon*. Tibbett is Lieutenant Michael Petroff, a skirt-chasing soldier who, while sailing East on the ship the *New Moon*, is stopped dead in his tracks by the beauty of Princess Tanya Strogoff (Moore). She's smitten, too. They sing "Wanting You" (a duet dominated by Moore's soprano), but she is promised to the governor of the province where Michael is being sent. Tanya's on-shore reunion with Governor Boris Brusiloff (Adolphe Menjou, 1890–1963) sends Michael to the nearest tavern, where he despairingly sings "Lover, Come Back to Me." He then decides to crash a ball Boris is giving in honor of the Princess. Tanya's seeming loyalty to the governor angers Michael, who angrily insults her honor with "What Is Your Price, Madame?"—a Stothart original.

Boris announces his engagement to Tanya, then exiles Michael to what figures to be certain death: the distant garrison at Fort Darvaz, where the enlisted men have the bad habit of murdering their commanding officers. Accompanied by her sympathetic uncle (Roland Young), the princess follows Michael into nowhere, just as the opposing Tourkamens are about to attack. On the eve of battle, Michael and Tanya are married, and he leads his "Stout-Hearted Men" in a surprise maneuver against the enemy the next morning. Boris shows up at the fort with reinforcements, but Michael is feared dead. Tanya mournfully sings "Lover, Come Back to Me" from the wall of the fort—and an unscathed Michael is heard responding in the distance.

New Moon generally received good reviews—*Variety* called it "music-drama of the first rate"[70]—but, as with nearly all musicals by now, it performed modestly with the paying public. Audiences simply would not accept a plump Grace Moore as a romantic figure, and neither she nor Tibbett were exactly riveting thespians. There also was a feeling that the picture had come too late, that too many swashbuckling, high-stepping musical romances had erased what novelty the film had besides the teaming of its two stars. A year earlier, perhaps, and *New Moon* might have been sensational. The film does have much to recommend it: The Moore-Tibbett pairing is historically important, Menjou's performance is solid, the 78-minute narrative has little fat, and the music is wonderful—especially "Lover, Come Back to

Me," perhaps Romberg's most beautiful melody.

Metro-Goldwyn-Mayer allowed Moore's contract to lapse after this film. When she triumphantly returned to Hollywood with Columbia's surprise hit *One Night of Love* (1934), it would be with much less of the poundage she'd carried at Metro. *New Moon* would prove more financially successful in 1940 with the voices of Jeanette MacDonald and Nelson Eddy, whose lovers were rightly moved back to North America for a version that was more opulent—but a good deal less interesting.

ONE HEAVENLY NIGHT
(Samuel Goldwyn/United Artists; December 24, 1930)

Director: George Fitzmaurice. Producer: Samuel Goldwyn. Executive Producer: Arthur Hornblow, Jr. Adaptation: Sidney Howard. Story: Louis Bromfield. Photography: George Barnes, Gregg Toland. Editor: Stuart Heisler. Sound: Frank Grenzback. Art Director: Richard Day. Musical Director: Frank Tours. Running Time: 82 minutes.

Cast: Evelyn Laye (Lilli), John Boles (Count Mirko Tibor), Leon Errol (Otto), Lilyan Tashman (Fritzi Yajos), Hugh Cameron (Janos), Marian Lord (Liska), Lionel Belmore (Zagon), George Bickel (Papa Lorenc), Vince Barnett (Egon), Henry Victor (Almady), Henry Kolker (police chief), Luis Alberni (violinist).

Songs: "Goodnight Serenade" [Boles, Laye], "Heavenly Night" [Boles, Laye], "I Belong to Everybody" [Tashman, chorus; reprised by Laye] (Edward Eliscu, Nacio Herb Brown); "Along the Road of Dreams" [Laye], "My Heart Is Beating" [Boles, Laye] (Clifford Grey, Bruno Granichstadten).

Disc: Music Masters JJA-19802 (bootleg LP).

One Heavenly Night (initially reviewed as *The Queen of Scandal*) was the only true operetta ever produced by Samuel Goldwyn. Besides *Whoopee!* it was his only attempt to cash in on the first wave of movie musicals. Goldwyn's trump card was Evelyn Laye (1900–1996), the alluring English musical comedy star whom the producer had watched perform during a trip to London. Laye had just debuted on Broadway

in Florenz Ziegfeld's ill-fated production of Noël Coward's *Bitter Sweet*. But *One Heavenly Night* had to be an even worse disappointment for Laye, and not just because she was losing her actor husband, Sonnie Hale, to British musical star Jessie Matthews at the time of filming. The picture was lambasted in the press and lost more than $300,000, Goldwyn's biggest dud since entering the movies.[71]

Sidney Howard, a Goldwyn favorite, adapted the Cinderella story written by another Pulitzer Prize winner, Louis Bromfield. A virginal Budapest flower girl (Laye) poses as a tarty cabaret singer (Lilyan Tashman) so the latter, pinched by the police after a particularly naughty escapade, can avoid serving her sentence at the rural château of a handsome count (John Boles, on loan yet again from Universal). The count and the flower girl fall in love, and not even the vengeful intervention of the real singer can stop the romance. There were five songs, the only highlight being the lusty "I Belong to Everybody," sung by Tashman and reprised briefly by the mimicking Laye.

One Heavenly Night survives as a dull, talky relic, too light on music and too heavy on comic "interludes" by Leon Errol, cast as Laye's drunken café-owner chum. Most reviewers praised the star, but nothing else, and even Bromfield saw fit to repudiate the final product. His original story, which he claimed had been altered by Goldwyn and director George Fitzmaurice, had Laye playing the sexier Tashman role. "To me, it is as interesting as so much dishwater," Bromfield said of the film in a letter published in *Variety*.[72] There were no published rebuttals.

UNDER SUSPICION
(Fox; December 26, 1930)

Director: A. F. Erickson. Screenplay: Tom Barry. Photography: George Schneiderman, Arthur Todd. Editor: Edwin Robbins. Art Director: William Darling. Sound: Albert W. Protzman. Costumes: Sophie Wachner. Running Time: 63 minutes.

Cast: J. Harold Murray (John Smith [Sir Robert Macklin]), Lois Moran (Alice Freil), J. M. Kerrigan (Doyle), Marie Saxon (Suzanne), Lumsden Hare (Freil), George Brent (Inspector Turner), Erwin Connolly (Darby), Rhoda

Cross (Marie), Vera Gerald (Ellen), Herbert Bunston (Major Manners).

Songs: "'Round My Kingdom's Door," "Sas-katch-a-widja-go-way-on-on!" "When You Don't Know What to Do with It," "Whisper to the Whisp'ring Pines" (Joseph McCarthy, James F. Hanley).

After three failed operettas, Fox starred J. Harold Murray in a fourth operetta-type film and then bought out his contract two months before the public had a chance to see the doomed little programmer. In New York City, *Under Suspicion* sneaked for one week into Brooklyn's Fox Theatre, where it was ignored by *The Times* and most of the other dailies. Murray, having already played an exotic prince, a genteel gambler and a French legionnaire in films, completed the he-man gamut in a story of a Canadian Mountie doing good deeds in the Rockies. "The only time the hero does not sing is when he is sliding down a cliff for a rescue," complained *Variety*'s music-weary commentator.[73]

Lois Moran, the leading lady, got to show off plenty of fancy clothes, but she was merely waiting out her contract and looking ahead to stage work. The outdoor cinematography by George Schneiderman—some of which was achieved at Jasper National Park in Alberta—was deemed good enough to suggest a travelogue. But *Under Suspicion* (titled *Tonight and You* prior to release) really matters only in retrospect, for buried somewhere in the cast list was future star George Brent, a former Dubliner making his film debut.

Brent plays a Mountie inspector who is jealous of the love that new recruit "John Smith" (Murray) has for the lovely Alice (Moran). Because Smith is believed to be using a pseudonym to hide a serious blot on his Great War record, the inspector threatens to reveal the so-called secret to his rival's English family. After completing a couple of dangerous solo rescue missions, the second of which saves Alice's father (Lumsden Hare) from a forest fire, Smith is found to be innocent of any past wrongdoing. He also admits that his real name is *Sir* Robert Macklin—to which Alice will add a "Mrs." when she marries him.

Murray returned to the stage once Hollywood rejected him. In 1940, virtually retired from show business as a gentleman brewer in upstate Connecticut, he died of a kidney ailment at age 49.

KISS ME AGAIN
(First National; January 7, 1931)

Director: William A. Seiter. Producer: Robert North. Screenplay: Julian Josephson, Paul Perez. Based on the operetta *Mlle. Modiste,* book and lyrics by Henry Blossom, music by Victor Herbert (New York opening, December 25, 1905; 202 performances). Photography: Al Gilks, Lee Garmes. Editor: Pete Fritch. Art Director: Anton Grot. Musical Directors: Leo Forbstein, Ermo Rapeé. Dance Direction: Larry Ceballos. Running Time: 74 minutes. Technicolor.

Cast: Bernice Claire (Mademoiselle Fifi), Walter Pidgeon (Captain Paul de St. Cyr), Edward Everett Horton (René La Motte), Claude Gillingwater (Count de St. Cyr), Frank McHugh (François), Judith Vosselli (Madame Cecile), June Collyer (Marie de Villafranche), Albert Gran (General de Villafranche), Lionel Belmore (café owner), Sisters "G" (dancers).

Songs/Musical Numbers: "Ah! But in Dreams So Fair" [Claire], "Alas! To Part, How Great the Sorrow" [Pidgeon], "I Want What I Want When I Want It" [Gillingwater], "If I Were on the Stage" [Claire], "Kiss Me Again" [Claire, Pidgeon, chorus; reprised by Claire, then by company], "The Mascot of the Troop" [Claire, soldiers; reprised by company] (Henry Blossom, Victor Herbert); "Clothes Parade" [models], "A Make Believe Ladies Man" [McHugh] (Al Bryan, Eddie Ward). Ballet Medley [Sisters "G", chorus]: "Pan Americana" (Herbert); "If I Were on the Stage" (Blossom, Herbert); "Air de Ballet" (Herbert); "The Time, the Place, and the Girl" (Blossom, Herbert); reprise of "Pan Americana"; reprise of "The Mascot of the Troop"; "Al Fresco" (Herbert).

Kiss Me Again, yet another all–Technicolor operetta from Warner Bros.–First National, premiered in New York during the first week of 1931, although it had been filmed in March 1930 and reviewed in the trades during the summer under the title *The Toast of the Legion.* The decision to delay its release may have been due to the generally hostile public reception to musicals—and, despite favorable reviews, *Kiss Me*

Bernice Claire and Walter Pidgeon steal a kiss before scores of onlookers at the close of First National's charming *Kiss Me Again*, adapted from Victor Herbert's *Mlle. Modiste*.

Again faded from view almost immediately. Too bad, for the first sound version of Victor Herbert and Henry Blossom's famous *Mlle. Modiste* has many of the qualities that were lacking in too many of its market-killing predecessors.[74]

A re-evaluation of *Kiss Me Again* reveals smooth direction by William A. Seiter, a manageable running time of 74 minutes, stingy but clever employment of the Herbert songs and Blossom libretto, attractive sets by Anton Grot, a capable cast—and the sizable charm of Bernice Claire. Claire's appealing acting and lively singing bring a surprising freshness to the lead role made famous a quarter-century earlier by Fritzi Scheff. "This girl has not been heard in finer voice than in this film ... she sings warmly and delightfully," commented *Variety*.[75] But *Kiss Me Again*—named for the great waltz hit of the Herbert operetta—was the last of the six films the petite actress made for Warners–First National during her yearlong Hollywood stint.[76] By the time *Kiss Me Again* made it to public

view, Claire was working out her contract in vaudeville with sometime partner Alexander Gray.

The plot, shorn of a few extraneous characters from the stageplay, was the familiar Cinderella story of Fifi, a Paris shopgirl who loves a titled Legionnaire, Captain Paul de St. Cyr (Walter Pidgeon). Paul's gouty count father (Claude Gillingwater) has instead matched the young man with Marie (June Collyer), the daughter of the elder de St. Cyr's longtime friend, General de Villafranche (Albert Gran). Marie, meanwhile, actually loves Paul's best friend, René La Motte (Edward Everett Horton). Fifi pledges her love for Paul with the lovely "Kiss Me Again," backed by an eavesdropping chorus of coworkers from the dress shop owned by Madame Cecile (Judith Vosselli). Fifi's soprano indicates the promise of an operatic career for which she is scraping to pay for singing lessons. "I want to amount to something, be somebody," she says.

Count de St. Cyr enters the salon to buy a gift for Paul to give to Marie, and Fifi, who waits on him, learns about Paul's intended future. Paul explains the situation to Fifi and the two make plans to elope, but dad overhears and visits Fifi's flat with the intent of buying her off. Convinced by the count that Paul's honor is at stake, she accepts $30,000 and then breaks up with the man she loves, her feigned laugh belying her sorrow as she plays a mocking "Kiss Me Again" on the piano. At a café weeks later, Fifi—fetching in a soldier's cap, drum set and short skirt—sends the fighting men off to battle with a rousing rendition of "The Mascot of the Troop," but she just misses making connections with Paul, who is searching for her.

A few years pass. Paul has served in Algiers. Fifi, renamed Madame Bellini, has used the count's money to fund a blossoming career. Unaware of her past, the elder de St. Cyr invites Fifi to perform at a ball celebrating the return of his son's regiment. She accepts, offering to spurn a lucrative gig to do this one for nothing. At the party, she sings "If I Were on the Stage" and then "Kiss Me Again," which jogs the rusty memories of Paul and his father. Backstage, Paul makes up with Fifi, but the count intercedes. "You promised me you would give him up," he tells Fifi. Replies Paul: "But *I* haven't given her up—and I don't intend to. From now on, it's our happiness that I'm going to worry about—not yours, father!" Impressed by Paul's spunk, the count consents to their marriage. The legionnaires rejoice, reprising "The Mascot of the Troop" and "Kiss Me Again."

Only four complete Herbert songs are sung in *Kiss Me Again*—there is other material written by Warner Bros. staffers—but primary and secondary themes from the stage original are heard constantly through effective underscoring by the Vitaphone Orchestra. Among these are "The Time, the Place, and the Girl," "Hats Make the Woman," "Love Me, Love My Dog" and "When the Cat's Away." Other Herbert compositions, some not from *Mlle. Modiste*, are heard during a ballet at the climactic ball. Pidgeon hasn't much to do but look soldierly, as he's allowed only a brief solo of "Alas! To Part, How Great the Sorrow." His character's vocal of "The Time, the Place, and the Girl" is listed among the numbers in production records, but it did not make the final release print. Gillingwater's comic rendition of "I Want What I Want When I Want It," the Count's demand that he get real meals instead of a bland antigout diet, is nicely done. Gillingwater appeared in the original 1905 production of *Mlle. Modiste* as an American millionaire who funds Fifi's career; this character was eliminated for the screen version. Frank McHugh, an annoying low comic in so many Warner Bros. movies, scores here as the clumsy ex-husband of the dressmaker; he solos on a new comedy song, "A Make Believe Ladies Man," which seems out of place in a Victor Herbert operetta. Horton and Collyer are a suitable secondary couple.

Kiss Me Again quietly completed the once-noisy cycle of 1929-30 musical films. It would be two months before another musical (*The Hot Heiress*) was released. Only three more operettas—Ernst Lubitsch's fine *The Smiling Lieutenant* and two Lawrence Tibbett starrers— would come out during 1931. Maybe there should have been fewer musicals in the first place—but more of them ought to have matched the quality of *Kiss Me Again*.

CHAPTER 8

1930: *There's a Tear for Every Smile in Hollywood*

The deluge of backstage musicals during 1929 slowed to a steady stream in 1930. The studios saw less of a need to rely on show-business clichés, and other types of musicals—operettas, for example—were attempted more frequently. There was less apprehension over introducing songs without the "easy" locales of Broadway shows or nightclubs. And for their part, moviegoers were tiring of repeated trouper-makes-good kinds of stories.

In November 1929, *Variety* was cognizant enough of the backstager overkill that it published a list of "ingredients for backstage talkers ... what writers of scenarios for backstage films should bear in mind." Here are some:

—That both members of all mixed two-acts are madly and blindly in love with each other.
—That the male half always gets stewed at the wrong time.
—That the other half is a courageous little wife and trouper.
—That the girl must always be temporarily coaxed away from her partner-husband by a rich and handsome producer who stars her in his new big revue, although she has never been outside of a tab show before.
—That all actors have no other ambition than to play the Palace—"it's the big time, kid."
—That when a small-time act dissolves or gets a booking, *Variety* carries the story with a two-column streamer.
—That one or both members of all mixed two-acts must reach Broadway and stardom at one time or another.[1]

As a group, the backstagers of '30 may not have been much of an improvement over those of the year before, but they did *move* a little better, as developments such as the boom had

begun to improve sound quality by freeing the microphone. Sound-on-film, as opposed to sound-on-disc, became the standard, even at Warners, which ended the old synchronization problems. The camera was still encased in its soundproof booth, and few 1930 pictures had the luxury of prerecording its singers, which meant they still had to vocalize under the hot lights. But the musical was expanding its sights.

LILIES OF THE FIELD
(First National; January 5, 1930)

Director: Alexander Korda. Producer: Walter Morosco. Scenario and Dialogue: John F. Goodrich. Based on the play by William Hurlbut (New York opening, October 4, 1921; 169 performances). Photography: Lee Garmes. Dance Direction: Roy Mack. Running Time: 58 minutes.

Cast: Corinne Griffith (Mildred Harker), Ralph Forbes (Ted Willing), John Loder (Walter Harker), Eve Southern (Pink), Jean Bary (Gertie), Tyler Brooke (Bert Miller), Freeman Wood (Lewis Conroy), Anne Schaefer (first maid), Clarissa Selwynne (second maid), Patsy Page (baby), André Beranger (barber), Douglas Gerrard (headwaiter), Rita Le Roy (Florette), Betty Boyd (Joyce), May Boley (Maizie), Virginia Bruce (Doris), Charles Hill Mailes (judge), Ray Largay (Walter's lawyer), Joe Bernard (Mildred's lawyer), Tenen Holtz (paymaster), Wilfred Noy (butler), Alice Moe (maid).

Songs/Musical Numbers: "Am I Blue?" (Grant Clarke, Harry Akst); "I'd Like to Be a Gypsy" (Ned Washington, Michael H. Cleary);

Fading stars Corinne Griffith and Ralph Forbes hear some bad news in the First National weepie *Lilies of the Field*.

"Speed" [mechanical ballet] (Herb Magidson, Ned Washington, Michael H. Cleary).

William Hurlbut's backstage melodrama *Lilies of the Field* began life as a play, then in 1924 became a silent film for the beautiful star Corinne Griffith (1896–1979), whose own company produced for First National release. Shortly after First National was merged into Warner Bros., the studio tried again. Griffith reprised her role as Mildred Harker, the socialite whose messy divorce leads to heartbreak and destitution. A couple of production numbers were inserted, including a noteworthy "modern" ballet sequence that earns the film (now apparently lost) an entry in this book.

To break up the mournful story, there were two songs, including the newly written "I'd Like to Be a Gypsy," plus a tap dance by Griffith atop a grand piano and the mechanical ballet "Speed," written by Herb Magidson, Ned Washington and Michael H. Cleary. Surviving stills show Griffith, whose character has been reduced to a showgirl's lot, in tights and dressed as a human radiator cap on the hood of a gigantic automobile. Forty seconds of the ballet was reused in the 1932 First National comedy *The Tenderfoot,* for a scene in which a New York rube played by Joe E. Brown attends the Follies and is wowed by the scantily clad dancers.

Lilies of the Field, directed by the young Alexander Korda near the end of his unsuccessful initial stint in Hollywood, was intended to establish Griffith as a talking star. It was her first all-talkie, after *The Divine Lady,* an otherwise silent 1929 film in which songs sung by Griffith's character were dubbed, and two '29 part-dialogue films, *Prisoners* and *Saturday's Children.* The last two revealed her unsuitable voice, which prompted a scribe from *Time* magazine to complain about *Lilies of the Field,* that Griffith "talks through her nose ... it is obvious at times that she is uneasy, too, especially ... when she has to drop her habitual air of dignified seductiveness to dance a tap routine on top of a piano."[2]

Audiences stayed away, and Griffith retired not long after, presumably sensing that her best days as a movie star had passed.

LOVE COMES ALONG
(RKO; January 5, 1930)

Director: Rupert Julian. Producer: Henry Hobart. Screenplay: Wallace Smith. Based on the play *Conchita* by Edward Knoblock (1924). Photography: J. Roy Hunt. Editor: Archie Marshek. Sound: John Tribby. Art Director: Max Rée. Costumes: Max Rée. Musical Director: Victor Baravalle. Orchestrations: Roy Webb. Dance Direction: Pearl Eaton. Running Time: 74 minutes (sound version; also released as silent).

Cast: Bebe Daniels (Peggy), Lloyd Hughes (Johnny), Montagu Love (Sangredo), Ned Sparks (Happy), Lionel Belmore (Brownie), Alma Tell (Carlotta), Evelyn Selbie (Bianca), Sam Appel (Gomez).

Songs: "I Am a Simple Maid" [Daniels], "Night Winds" [Daniels], "A Sailor's Life" [Hughes, chorus; reprised by Daniels, Hughes], "Until Love Comes Along" [Daniels, three times] (Sidney Clare, Oscar Levant).

Disc: RCA Victor 22283 (Daniels/"Until Love Comes Along"/"Night Winds"/78).

It's a stretch to call *Love Comes Along* a backstager, but it does offer Bebe Daniels as a stage actress marooned on a Caribbean island after the failure of a show there. In this adaptation of the Edward Knoblock romantic drama *Conchita*, RKO's surprise diva sings a quartet of songs by Oscar Levant and Sidney Clare, among them the lovely "Until Love Comes Along."

The unlucky singer, Peggy, has a chance to leave her temporary home when she meets and falls for Johnny, a swaggering American sailor distressingly overacted by Lloyd Hughes (1896–1958). Hughes' tough-guy rendition of "A Sailor's Life" appears to be dubbed. The lovers are parted after the swabbie smarts over the attention paid to Peg by the isle's powerful potentate (Montagu Love). Only after the sailor hears Peggy sing "Until Love Comes Along" for the third time—in scarcely over an hour of running time—does he rescue her from the clutches of the heavy.

Between Daniels' triumph in *Rio Rita* and the equivalently budgeted *Dixiana* (both in Chapter 7), RKO used its biggest name in routine programmers like this and two other lackluster '30 releases, *Alias French Gertie* and *Lawful Larceny*. Save for the musical interludes, nobody had much to say about *Love Comes Along*. Declared *The New York Times*: "Miss Daniels sings pleasantly enough in this photoplay, the only evident reason for its being."[3]

CHASING RAINBOWS
(MGM; January 10, 1930)

Director: Charles F. Reisner. Adaptation: Wells Root. Story and Continuity: Bess Meredyth. Dialogue: Charles F. Reisner, Robert E. Hopkins, Kenyon Nicholson, Al Boasberg. Photography: Ira Morgan. Editor: George Hively. Sound: Douglas Shearer, Russell Franks. Art Director: Cedric Gibbons. Costumes: David Cox. Running Time: 100 minutes (sound version; also released as silent). Technicolor sequences.

Cast: Bessie Love (Carlie Seymour), Charles King (Terry Fay), Jack Benny (Eddie Rock), George K. Arthur (Lester), Polly Moran (Polly), Gwen Lee (Peggy), Nita Martan (Daphne Wayne), Marie Dressler (Bonnie), Eddie Phillips (Don Cordova), Youcca Troubetzkoy (Lanning), The Biltmore Trio.

Songs: "Do I Know What I'm Doing?" [Martan; reprised by Dressler, Moran], "Everybody Tap" [Love, chorus], "Happy Days Are Here Again" [chorus; reprised by King, chorus], "Lucky Me—Lovable You" [King, Biltmore Trio; reprised by King] (Milton Ager, Jack Yellen); "Love Ain't Nothin' but the Blues" [King] (Joe Goodwin, Louis Alter); "(My) Dynamic Personality" [Dressler] (Fred Fisher, George Ward, Reggie Montgomery); "Poor but Honest" [Dressler] (John T. Murray, Gus Edwards).

Also Known As: *The Road Show.*

Disc: Brunswick 4615 (King/"Happy Days Are Here Again"/"Love Ain't Nothin' but the Blues"/78); Brunswick 4616 (King/"Everybody Tap"/"Lucky Me—Lovable You"/78).

Video: MGM-UA (laserdisc; excerpts only).

Nearly one year after the release of *The Broadway Melody*, MGM finally unveiled the

Broadway Melody stars Bessie Love and Charles King were reunited for MGM's much less successful backstager *Chasing Rainbows*.

second pairing of that picture's romantic duo. That Bessie Love, and not Anita Page, was teamed with Charles King in *Chasing Rainbows* indicated that the studio was no more accepting of the ending to *The Broadway Melody* than was the clamoring public. The supporting cast hired for this backstage comedy-drama included Jack Benny (in his first feature-film role), Marie Dressler, Polly Moran and, his career as a comic lead now stalled by his English accent, George K. Arthur.

Chasing Rainbows, which was also advertised and reviewed under its working title of *The Road Show*, tells of a traveling musical show managed by Eddie Rock (Benny). The troupe includes a vaudeville two-act, Carlie Seymour (Love) and Terry Fay (King), whose professional and personal relationship is frequently jeopardized by Terry's failed crushes on his various leading ladies. Each crush results in a half-hearted suicide attempt by the love-spurned fellow. This time the show is "Good-Bye

Broadway," and Terry's target is Daphne Wayne (Rita Martan). Terry's quickie marriage to Daphne prompts a hysterical laughing jag from the lovesick little Carlie. Carlie knows that Daphne is only using Terry to further her career, that the vamp is playing around with hack actor Don Cordova (Eddie Phillips). When Terry learns that Daphne is planning to give him "more air than Lindbergh needed to fly to Paris," he again threatens to kill himself. Instead, he decides on contentment with Carlie. In the pull-out-all-the-stops Technicolor finale, against a Great War Armistice show-within-a-show backdrop, Terry sings "Happy Days Are Here Again."

With a domestic gross of $700,000, *Chasing Rainbows* turned a modest profit for MGM. The studio filmed it in 32 days between July 20 and August 27, 1929, then put it on the shelf. The delay kept the company from capitalizing fully upon the initial success of the famous song "Happy Days Are Here Again," by Milton Ager

(1893–1979) and Jack Yellen (1892–1991). According to David Ewen's book *American Songwriters*, Ager and Yellen, who already had written most of the score for *Chasing Rainbows*, received a hurried call from MGM to prepare a choral number to be sung by a group of World War I soldiers. During the time the film was shelved, the composers' own company published the sheet music to the song. George Olsen, the popular bandleader, got a copy of the music and played it at the Hotel Pennsylvania in Manhattan. This was in October of 1929, in the same week as the stock-market crash that brought on the Great Depression. The upbeat "Happy Days Are Here Again" soon became an anthem of hope to those affected by the crisis.[4]

Irving Thalberg heard Olsen and band perform the song during a visit to Hollywood, and thereupon asked why the tune was not being employed in an MGM picture. After being told that it was in the unreleased *Chasing Rainbows*, the production chief ordered that its finale be entirely reshot to punch up the original perfunctory presentation of the song. "Happy Days Are Here Again" became a hit—best-selling covers were done by the Leo Reisman and Ben Selvin orchestras—and its fame was boosted even more when Franklin D. Roosevelt used it as the theme song for his successful 1932 presidential campaign.

Chasing Rainbows has lately been telecast—without its two lost Technicolor production-number sequences—on the Turner Classic Movies channel. About 12 minutes of the film is on laserdisc as part of MGM-UA's "The Dawn of Sound" series. There are a 20-second rendition of "Happy Days Are Here Again" (a black-and-white number joined in progress as the film opens); comic verse by Benny; the comic "Poor but Honest," sung by Dressler; the ballad "Lucky Me—Lovable You," sung by King and the Biltmore Trio; Martan's rendition of "Do I Know What I'm Doing?"; and a burlesque of same by Dressler and Moran. The lost color footage encompasses four numbers. Halfway through the film, there are the Love-led "Everybody Tap" dance number and King's singing of "Love Ain't Nothin' but the Blues." The finale features Dressler's tongue-in-cheek delivery of "(My) Dynamic Personality" preceding "Happy Days Are Here Again." Dressler and Moran, frequently paired in films, play the road show's battling, hard-drinking comedienne and wardrobe mistress, respectively. Marie gets on Polly for her bad breath and lack of marital prospects; Polly chides Marie for her ample poundage and graceless singing voice.

Despite its advantages in improved cast and sound quality, *Chasing Rainbows* could not hope to match the hit status of *Broadway Melody*. Many reviewers were rankled (as was this one) by *Chasing Rainbows'* obvious attempts to mimic the earlier film, right down to Love's dressing-room histrionics. King, earnest but no finesse actor, is painful at times for his insufferable Terry, who actually blames the unbelievably patient Carlie for allowing him to fall in love with his newest unfaithful floozie. *The New York Times* called *Chasing Rainbows* "hapless ... so utterly nonsensical that it become tedious before it is halfway over."[5] In his posthumously released autobiography, Jack Benny (1894–1974) quipped, inaccurately, that the film "was such a box-office flop that the exhibitors renamed it *Chasing Customers*."[6] But the delay in releasing *Chasing Rainbows* slowed the momentum of King's film career, and the decision by MGM not to release *Five O'Clock Girl*, a musical comedy (see Chapter 11) in which he was paired with Marion Davies, represented another lost opportunity. By the cruel autumn of 1930, both he and Love had been dropped by Metro.

Love moved to England to make yet another comeback; she appeared in small roles in films and on the stage there until the early 1980s. King returned to the stage, but his career would not regain its former heights. In 1944, he sailed for England to entertain troops, but he became ill aboard ship and died of pneumonia in a London hospital. Anita Page, whose Navy admiral husband was highly decorated for World War II service, calls King "just as much a hero as the boys who went over there. What more could he give?"[7]

LOVE AT FIRST SIGHT
(Chesterfield; January 28, 1930)

Director: Edgar Lewis. Story and Dialogue: Lester Lee, Charles Levison. Photography: Dal Clawson. Editor: Russell Shields. Sound: George Oschman. Running Time: 65 minutes.

Cast: Norman Foster (Richard Norton), Suzanne Keener (June Vernon), Doris Rankin (Mrs. Vernon), Lester Cole (Paul Russell), Abe Reynolds (Abe Feinstein), Hooper Atchley (Frank Belmont), Burt Mathews (master of ceremonies), Dorothee Adam ("Jig-a-Boo" singer), Jim Harkins, Paul Specht and His Orchestra, Tracy and Elwood, Chester Hale Girls.

Songs: "Jig-a-Boo Jig," "Love at First Sight," "Sunshine," "What Is Living Without You?" (Lester Lee, Charles Levison).

If the few available reviews of this independent production are to be believed, *Love at First Sight* was one unsightly backstager. The musical comedy-drama, produced by the Chesterfield Motion Picture Corp., was a mishmash about a leading lady (Suzanne Keener) forced to choose between the Broadway musical penned by her boyfriend (Norman Foster) and the revue preferred by her ambitious mother (Doris Rankin). Two of the major players were better known for marital associations: Foster was married to Claudette Colbert at the time, and Rankin was the former Mrs. Lionel Barrymore.

Variety's verdict: "Doubtful entry, because the prima can't sing, the customers giggled and [for] bad casting."[8]

THE GRAND PARADE

(Pathé; January 31, 1930)

Director: Fred Newmeyer. Dialogue Director: Frank Reicher. Producer: Edmund Goulding. Screenplay: Edmund Goulding. Photography: David Abel. Sound: George Ellis, Cliff Stein. Art Direction: Edward Jewell, Ted Dickson. Costumes: Gwen Wakeling. Dance Direction: Richard Boleslawsky. Running Time: 81 minutes.

Cast: Helen Twelvetrees (Molly), Fred Scott (Kelly), Richard Carle (Rand), Marie Astaire (Polly), Russell Powell (Calamity Johnson), Bud Jamison (Honey Sullivan), Jimmie Adams (Jones), Lillian Leighton (Madam Stitch), Spec O'Donnell (call boy), Sam Blum (Sam), Tom Malone (Dougherty), Jimmy Aubrey (drunk).

Songs: "Alone in the Rain," "The Grand Parade," "Moanin' for You," "Molly," "Sweethearts" (Dan Dougherty, Edmund Goulding).

Pathé chose *The Grand Parade*, a musical drama about an alcoholic minstrel singer and his ever-loyal wife, to introduce two of the more promising young actors on its slim roster of talent. Helen Twelvetrees (1908–1958) had just finished a semi-conspicuous term as a Fox contractee; she was elected as one of the Wampas Baby Stars of 1929. Her demure beauty and penchant for tragic roles brought her frequent comparisons with Lillian Gish. Fred Scott (1902–1991) was a classically trained tenor who had appeared with the San Francisco Opera and had played bit parts in a handful of films, including *Rio Rita*.

Edmund Goulding's story had Scott playing singer Jack "Come-Back" Kelly, so nicknamed because of his frequent liquor-induced career peaks and valleys. His attachment to Polly (Marie Astaire), a tawdry burlesque actress, is a big part of his problem. Jack ends up in a cheap boarding house where the gentle Molly (Twelvetrees) nurses him back to sobriety. Jack returns to minstrelsy, and when he changes the title of a song he's written from "Polly" to "Molly," he turns it into a hit. He marries Molly, but soon weakens and returns to his old ways with Polly. Meanwhile, Molly has become pregnant, and her determination to keep the family together wins out.

Twelvetrees earned some good notices for her stint in this minor yarn, but not so with the inexperienced Scott. But Pathé (which was soon to merge into RKO) thought enough of the youngsters to give each a five-year contract—and at least one more assignment together.

Fred Newmeyer, a journeyman director, helmed *The Grand Parade*, but two of his behind-the-camera subordinates are better remembered. German import Frank Reicher, the dialogue director, was a well-known director of silents who would make a more lasting career as a character actor. His most famous role was as Captain Engelhorn in *King Kong* (1933). Richard Boleslawsky, who staged the musical numbers, was a Polish-born veteran of the Moscow and Broadway stages who would direct such stylish Hollywood product as *Les Misérables* (1935), *Theodora Goes Wild* (1936), *The Garden of Allah* (1936) and the Lawrence Tibbett musical *Metropolitan* (1935). He died unexpectedly in 1937 at age 48 during the filming of *The Last of Mrs. Cheyney* for MGM.

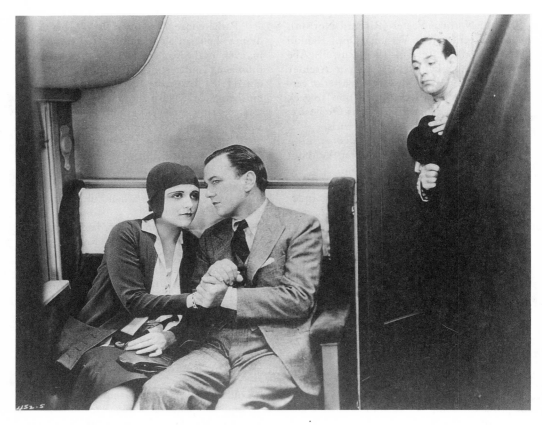

In the baseball backstager *They Learned About Women*, Mary Doran vamps Joe Schenck as Gus Van watches disapprovingly.

THEY LEARNED ABOUT WOMEN

(MGM; January 31, 1930)

Directors: Jack Conway, Sam Wood. Scenario: Sarah Y. Mason. Dialogue: Arthur "Bugs" Baer. Story: A. P. Younger. Titles: Alfred Block. Photography: Leonard Smith. Editors: James McKay, Thomas Held. Sound: Douglas Shearer, Robert Shirley. Art Director: Cedric Gibbons. Costumes: David Cox. Dance Direction: Sammy Lee. Running Time: 94 minutes (sound version; also released as silent).

Cast: Joseph T. Schenck (Jack Glennon), Gus Van (Jerry Burke), Bessie Love (Mary Collins), Mary Doran (Daisy Gebhart), J. C. Nugent (Stafford), Benny Rubin (Sam Goldberg), Tom Dugan (Tim O'Connor), Eddie Gribbon (Brennan), Francis X. Bushman, Jr. (Haskins), Nina Mae McKinney ("Harlem Madness" singer), George Chandler (player).

Songs: "Ain't You Baby" [Van], "Does My Baby Love (Nobody but Me)?" [Van, Schenck], "Harlem Madness" [Van, Schenck; reprised by McKinney, chorus], "He's That Kind of a Pal" [Van, Schenck, twice], "A Man of My Own" [Love], "Ten Sweet Mamas" [Van, Schenck, players], "There Will Never Be Another Mary" [Schenck] (Jack Yellen, Milton Ager); "Dougherty Is the Name" [Van, Schenck], "I'm an Old-Fashioned Guy" [Van, Schenck] (Joseph T. Schenck, Gus Van, Jack Yellen, Milton Ager).

Disc: RCA Victor 22352 (Van and Schenck/"Does My Baby Love [Nobody but Me]?"/"Dougherty Is the Name"/78).

Video: MGM-UA (laserdisc).

"The Pennant Winning Battery of Songland" was Gus Van and Joseph T. Schenck, a famous stage team that debuted in feature films with an odd baseball backstager called *They*

Learned About Women. It was the only full-length film for the Brooklyn-born pair, whose 18-year association soon would end abruptly and prematurely.

Van (1888–1968) and Schenck (1891–1930) used a rich baritone-tenor blend and a knack for comedy dialect songs to build a strong following in vaudeville and nightclubs and on Broadway (*The Century Girl, Ziegfeld Follies of 1919*). Van's booming voice was just right for singing the dialects at which he excelled; tenor Schenck (no relation to the producer Joseph M. Schenck) played piano and typically sang harmony.

The two were beckoned by Hollywood at the outset of sound to make shorts for Warner Bros. and MGM. For *They Learned About Women* (originally titled *Take It Big, The Pennant Winning Battery* and *Playing the Field*), MGM backed them with the tried-and-true Bessie Love and two reliable directors, Jack Conway and Sam Wood. New York sportswriter Arthur "Bugs" Baer wrote the dialogue for Sarah Y. Mason's script about two baseball-playing vaudevillians whose teaming is nearly ruined by romance. Van and Schenck were themselves avid baseball fans, and Schenck once captained the vaudeville "All-Stars" team.

In the film, Jack Glennon (Schenck) is a standout pitcher for the Blue Sox of unknown locale, who must constantly play nursemaid for his teammate and offseason stage partner, catcher Jerry Burke (Van), a hard drinker who is preyed upon by gold diggers. "You give the parties and I pay the checks" is Jack's complaint to his friend. Jack's one and only girl is Mary Collins (Love), a secretary for the team, but their relationship is threatened by the conniving Daisy Gebhart (Mary Doran, Love's nemesis from *Broadway Melody*). Although he pines for Mary, Jerry tries to thwart Daisy's vamping of Jack—too late, for Jerry marries the floozie, who convinces her hubby to quit baseball and make her his new showbiz partner.

Halfway through the next baseball season, Jerry and Mary have become an item, but Jack returns to their lives after throttling a heckler who throws a bottle at Jerry from the stands during a game. Jack, jobless and newly divorced, returns to the Blue Sox and helps pitch them to the pennant. Lovesick for Mary, he loses two World Series games and is benched. Jerry realizes why his pal is so glum, and he gallantly relinquishes Mary to him. The revitalized Jack

returns to pitch in relief in the deciding seventh game. With the Sox a run behind with two out in the bottom of the ninth inning, he is hit in the head by a pitched ball. Woozy, he takes first base, and when Jerry hits a long drive deep into the outfield, Jack circles the bases only to fall down between third base and home. Jerry, following right behind, exhorts Jack to get up and run, which he does, collapsing as he crosses the plate. Jerry is able to slide in after him with the winning run, and all ends happily—even if it will take Jerry longer to get over his heartache than it will Jack to recuperate from his headache.

Although it is little more than a standard sports tale—and Schenck, with his puffy face and slight lisp, isn't the most convincing romantic lead—*They Learned About Women* makes good use of its stars' abilities. Between the two Van and Schenck sing six Jack Yellen–Milton Ager songs, plus two of their own compositions, "Dougherty Is the Name" and "I'm an Old-Fashioned Guy." A ninth selection, Yellen and Ager's "A Man of My Own," is sung by Love to her own ukelele. "Ten Sweet Mamas," led by Van and backed by the other Blue Sox as they shower in their locker room after a game, is an entertaining blues variation on "Ten Little Indians." "Does My Baby Love?" allows the two stars to engage in comic byplay about a fictional lover they unwittingly share. None of these tunes became hits, however. Nina Mae McKinney, inexplicably unbilled after her attention-getting appearance in *Hallelujah!* (see Chapter 9), leads the film's obligatory "hot" dance number, "Harlem Madness."

Benny Rubin and the tongue-tied Tom Dugan stop the story in its tracks with some forgettable low comedy as two bickering Sox who aspire to form their own stage team. (Dugan: "W-W-What's the d-d-difference between a traffic pol-pol- ... cop and a flapper?" Rubin: "When a traffic cop says 'Stop!' he means it!") Dugan's presence here and in MGM's *Take Me Out to the Ball Game* (1949) has given credence to the claim that *They Learned About Women* was partly the basis for the later film, which also tells of two stage-struck ballplayers (played by Gene Kelly and Frank Sinatra).

They Learned About Women was not a big draw, possibly because MGM seems not to have done much with its distribution. It went unreviewed by both *Variety* and *The New York Times*, and *Photoplay* gave it only a middling write-up. *The Film Daily*, however, lauded the film: "The baseball stuff is good and will certainly please the fans. ... A peppy number that should please."[9]

During the film's general release, Van and Schenck resumed touring, but their association came to a sudden end on June 28, 1930, at the Book Cadillac Hotel in Detroit. The morning after a date at the nearby Fisher Theatre, Schenck died of a heart attack in the arms of his partner, whom he had known since they were schoolboys. He was 39. Van continued as a solo for many years, although without the attention that marked his teaming with Schenck. In a brief bit in the 1944 musical *Atlantic City*, Van appeared as himself and Charles Marsh played Schenck.

Although some of Van and Schenck's short subjects survive, *They Learned About Women* is the fullest extant memento of their partnership.

LET'S GO PLACES
(Fox; February 1, 1930)

Director: Frank Schayer. Scenario and Dialogue: William K. Wells. Story: Andrew Bennison. Photography: Conrad Wells. Editor: Al De Gaetano. Sound: Frank MacKenzie. Assistant Director: William Tummell. Dance Direction: Danny Dare. Running Time: 70 minutes.

Cast: Joseph Wagstaff (Paul Adams), Lola Lane (Marjorie Lorraine), Sharon Lynn (Virginia Gordon), Frank Richardson (J. Speed Quinn), Walter Catlett (Rex Wardell), Dixie Lee (Dixie), Charles Judels (Paul Du Bonnet), Larry Steers (Ben King), Eddie Kane, Betty Grable.

Songs: "Hollywood Nights," "Out in the Cold," "Parade of the Blues," "Reach Out for a Rainbow," "Um-Um in the Moonlight" (Sidney Mitchell, Archie Gottler, Con Conrad); "The Boop-Boop-a-Doopa-Doo Trot" (George A. Little, Johnny Burke); "Fascinatin' Devil with Those Angel Eyes" (Joseph McCarthy, James V. Monaco); "Let's Go Places" (Cliff Friend, James V. Monaco); "The Snowball Man" (James Brockman, James V. Monaco).

Even before the release of Joseph Wagstaff's first movie, *A Song of Kentucky* (see Chapter 5), Fox was putting the Broadway song-and-dance man into a second programmer, *Let's Go Places*, which was a more musical musical than *A Song of Kentucky*.

Let's Go Places, a mistaken-identity comedy, found Wagstaff playing an obscure singer who impersonates a famous, although somewhat older, opera tenor. En route to the Coast to forge a Hollywood career, Paul Adams—posing as the esteemed Paul Du Bonnet—takes up with a movie actress named Marjorie Lorraine (Lola Lane). Fortunately for Adams, she wouldn't know Paul Du Bonnet from Paul Bunyan. Adams, accompanied by his instigating chum J. Speed Quinn (Frank Richardson), is able to launch a movie career and occupy Du Bonnet's mansion. Then the real singer (Charles Judels) and his wife (Ilka Chase) show up. Marjorie is none too happy at this revelation, but all ends happily—although implausibly—when Adams is found to be Du Bonnet's long-lost nephew!

The reception to *Let's Go Places* (working title: *Hollywood Nights*) was poor. Fox publicity boasted of "intimate scenes of the real Hollywood," but little was shown beyond a party sequence and some filmed-within-a-film musical numbers led by Sharon Lynn and Dixie Lee. The comedy of Richardson and Walter Catlett, as a temperamental movie director, was judged better than the emoting of Wagstaff, who could sing well enough but came up short in the looks and charisma departments. Opined *Variety*: "[He] looks like several different fellows in as many different sequences, and his niche in the picture ranks is still undefined."[10] Fox would shortly define said niche by sending Wagstaff packing.

BE YOURSELF!
(Art Cinema/United Artists; February 8, 1930)

Director: Thornton Freeland. Producers: Joseph M. Schenck, John W. Considine, Jr. Adaptation: Max Marcin, Thornton Freeland. Story: Joseph Jackson. Photography: Carl Struss, Robert H. Planck. Editor: Robert J. Kern. Sound: Harold Witt. Assistant Director: Roger H. Heman. Art Direction: William Cameron Menzies, Park French, Robert Usher. Costumes: Alice O'Neill. Musical Arrangements: Hugo Riesenfeld. Dance Direction:

Maurice L. Kusell. Running Time: 65 minutes.

Cast: Fanny Brice (Fannie Field), Robert Armstrong (Jerry Moore), Harry Green (Harry Field), G. Pat Collins (McCloskey), Gertrude Astor (Lillian), Budd Fine (Step), Marjorie "Babe" Kane (Lola), Rita Flynn (Jessica), Jimmy Tolson (himself).

Songs: "Kickin' a Hole in the Sky" [Brice, chorus], "Sasha, the Passion of the Pasha" [Brice] (Billy Rose, Ballard MacDonald, Jesse Greer); "Cooking Breakfast for the One I Love" [Brice, Armstrong; reprised by Tolson] (Billy Rose, Henry Tobias); "It's Gorgeous to Be Graceful" [Brice] (Billy Rose); "When a Woman Loves a Man" [Brice, Kane, Astor, chorus; reprised by Brice] (Billy Rose, Ralph Rainger); "A Heart That's Free" [Brice] (Alfred G. Robyn, Thomas T. Railey).

Disc: RCA Victor 22310 (Brice/"Cooking Breakfast for the One I Love"/"When a Woman Loves a Man"/78); Fanett 146 (bootleg LP; ST).

Less than a year after the disappointing *My Man* (see Chapter 2), Fanny Brice was back in the movies with a two-picture contract from Joseph M. Schenck's Art Cinema company. The first (and only) of these was *Be Yourself!*—a less ambitious project than the earlier Warner Bros. part-talkie. In a run-of-the-mill boxing tale that lasted scarcely over an hour, Brice (billed in the opening credits as "Fannie") played another no-nonsense nightclub entertainer.

One night while singing "When a Woman Loves a Man," Fannie Field gets to flirting with punch-drunk prizefighter Jerry Moore (Robert Armstrong, 1890–1973). This irks the bruiser sitting nearby, McCloskey (G. Pat Collins), who happens to be the heavyweight champion. When the drunken Jerry makes the mistake of bad-mouthing the champ, he gets into a brawl that leaves him face down on the cabaret floor. Still, Fannie likes Jerry's punch almost as much as his smile, and she hires herself as his manager, guessing that Jerry can end his bad habit of claiming fouls when he should be fighting to win legitimately. Jerry goes on the wagon, and a string of real victories vaults him into title contention.

Fannie's litigious lawyer brother (Harry Green, 1892–1958) uses the nightclub clash as an excuse to attach McCloskey's earnings, and

the champ is forced to agree to fight Jerry so that the action will be dropped. Jerry wins in an upset, but his victory attracts McCloskey's ex, Lil (Gertrude Astor). The gold digging blonde encourages Jerry to get his crooked nose fixed, and she turns his affections away from the saddened Fannie. But Fannie, who is still Jerry's manager, arranges a rematch with McCloskey. Hoping that Jerry will be beaten, and thus brought back to his senses, Fannie exhorts his foe to strike Jerry in the nose, which he does— with winning results. In the dressing room afterward, Jerry sees that the fickle Lil has returned to McCloskey, and he floors the champ again. Says Fanny: "I knew you could do it. You can lick any guy in the world." Jerry's reply: "You mean, *we* can!"

After the comments on Brice's ethnicity that followed *My Man*, Schenck might have thought to soften Brice's image. Fortunately for us, he didn't. Cast as her regulation-spouting brother was the very Jewish comic Harry Green, and Brice, costumed as a swan, does a Yiddish dialect number, "It's Gorgeous to Be Graceful." It's a variation on one of her *Ziegfeld Follies* routines in which she pranced around in a tu-tu and then was shot with an arrow by a dwarf dressed in a Tyrolian hunter costume. More interesting is the opera spoof in which Brice, dressed in tiara and tight-fitting gown, massacres a soprano solo of "A Heart That's Free" with screechy trilling, garbled diction and rubbery facial contortions. Brice's distinctive singing and clowning were hardly deserving of the lackluster story, but this time she could not even attract urban audiences in significant numbers, despite reviews like *Variety*'s, which called the film "good Brice stuff for the masses."[11]

Too bad, for the holdouts missed one of her most memorable songs, "Cooking Breakfast for the One I Love," with music by Harry Tobias and lyrics by Brice's then-husband, Billy Rose. Its use in the film is unusual for musical numbers of the era in that it contains almost constant movement without resorting to dance. As Armstrong reads a newspaper on the couch of the flat they share with Green, Brice stares at him affectionately and begins to sing as she sets the table for their morning meal. She acts out the lyrics of the song as she moves around the kitchen preparing the various courses— steaming coffee, bacon her baby likes, oatmeal sprinkled with lox, and biscuits she's willing to risk—while worrying that she can cook them right. Brice biographer Herbert G. Goldman has written that the song "contrasts a woman's love for the sweet 'married' life with the comedienne's self-parodying, divorced perspective, echoing the two Brice viewpoints—Fanny the romantic and Fanny the cynic."[12]

The good will generated then is almost negated by the film's major production number, "Kicking a Hole in the Sky," a variation on Dante's *Inferno*. The poorly photographed sequence—in which Brice, perched atop an ersatz Tower of Babel, drives the big bad Devil away from the tempting chorines—reminds us how foolish moviemakers were to think that, in musical terms, bigger was automatically better. The attractive art direction featured giant, urn-shaped pedestals towering above a double staircase.

"When a Woman Loves a Man," sung twice by Brice, was a springboard to the Hollywood career of its composer, Ralph Rainger (1901–1942). Rainger, who had written the hit song "Moanin' Low" for Libby Holman in the Broadway revue *Three's a Crowd*, was asked by Brice to compose a similar torch song for her in *Be Yourself!* Rainger wrote "When a Woman Loves a Man" to the lyrics of Billy Rose, and although the song failed to make much of an impression, it got Rainger a job on the writing staff at Paramount. There, he would team with Leo Robin to write songs for many musicals of the '30s.[13]

But Brice fared less well. After *Be Yourself!* Schenck didn't even bother to cast her in another musical. Instead, he dropped her from his star roster. Brice and Rose sued for breach of contract, but the sad truth was that, although her career would be significantly revived via radio, Fanny Brice would not star in another motion picture.

PUTTIN' ON THE RITZ

(Art Cinema/United Artists; February 14, 1930)

Director: Edward Sloman. Producers: Joseph M. Schenck, John W. Considine, Jr. Scenario: John W. Considine, Jr. Dialogue: William K. Wells, James Gleason. Photography: Ray June. Editor: Hal Kern. Sound: Oscar Lagerstrom. Assistant Director: Jack Mintz. Art Direction: William Cameron Menzies,

Park French, Robert Usher. Costumes: Alice O'Neill. Musical Arrangements: Hugo Riesenfeld. Dance Direction: Maurice L. Kusell. Running Time: 70 minutes. Technicolor sequence.

Cast: Harry Richman (Harry Raymond), Joan Bennett (Delores Fenton), James Gleason (James Tierney), Aileen Pringle (Mrs. Teddy Van Rennsler), Lilyan Tashman (Goldie De-Vere), Purnell B. Pratt (George Barnes), Richard Tucker (Fenway Brooks), Eddie Kane (Bob Wagner), George Irving (Dr. Blair), Sidney Franklin (Schmidt), James Bradbury, Jr. (subway guard), Oscar Apfel (theater manager), Budd Fine (heckler).

Songs: "Alice in Wonderland" ("Come Along with Alice") [Bennett, chorus], "Puttin' on the Ritz" [Richman, chorus; reprised by Richman], "With You" [Richman; reprised by Richman, Bennett, then by Richman, then by Bennett, Richman] (Irving Berlin); "I'll Get By" [Richman, Bennett, Gleason, Tashman] (Roy Turk, Fred E. Ahlert); "Singing a Vagabond Song" [Richman, twice] (Sam Messenheimer, Val Burton); "There's Danger in Your Eyes, Cherie" [Richman] (Jack Meskill, Pete Wendling, Harry Richman).

Disc: Brunswick 4677 (Richman/"Puttin' on the Ritz"/"There's Danger in Your Eyes, Cherie"/78); Brunswick 4678 (Richman/ "Singing a Vagabond Song"/"With You"/78); Meet Patti 1930 (bootleg LP; ST); Music Masters JJA-19744 (bootleg LP; ST); Take Two 104 (bootleg LP; ST).

Jerome Kern once said, "Irving Berlin has no place in American music. He *is* American music." But in 1929, there were some who wondered if Irving Berlin even had a place in American music. His songwriting talents, honed in the ragtime era, were no longer considered cutting-edge in a Broadway milieu in which standards were constantly changing. Berlin's writing supposedly lacked the sophistication and subtlety of works by newer composers. He still had a knack of adding the right song to someone else's score, as with "Blue Skies" in Rodgers and Hart's *Betsy* (1926), but his own creations of the mid- to late '20s (*The Cocoanuts, Ziegfeld Follies of 1927*) were not so highly regarded. Since Hollywood was eager to employ composers of any sort, Berlin hoped he could end his creative slump there.

Despite misgivings over the drawn-out

Lilyan Tashman clowns for Joan Bennett, James Gleason and Harry Richman in a lighter moment from United Artists' *Puttin' on the Ritz*.

process of moviemaking and the effects of recording technology on his music, Berlin (1888–1989) contributed new songs to a handful of early sound films. "Where Is the Song of Songs for Me?" from the D. W. Griffith part-talkie *Lady of the Pavements*, was good enough to nab a record contract for weak-voiced Lupe Velez, and "When My Dreams Come True" was well received in *The Cocoanuts*. But "Coquette," a waltz written for the Mary Pickford drama of the same name, failed as badly as the film did. Berlin also wrote two tunes for *Hallelujah!* (see Chapter 9). However, the first musical in which he took a fully active role was *Puttin' on the Ritz,* initially announced in early 1929 as *The Song of Broadway.*

The song for which the film was named turned out to be one of Berlin's more durable hits. Berlin biographer Laurence Bergreen has noted that "Puttin' on the Ritz" was not intended to be the glamorous evocation of high society that modern listeners believe it to be, that new lyrics added by Berlin in the 1950s

have masked its origin as a mildly condescending "coon" song designed to mock the stepping-out customs of well-dressed Harlem blacks.[14] The sanitized song was revived many times, perhaps most notably by Fred Astaire in *Blue Skies* (1946) and most oddly in a campy disco version that the Dutch-Indonesian entertainer Taco took to the Top 5 of the Billboard magazine pop chart in 1983.

The man who made the first hit of "Puttin' on the Ritz," both on celluloid and on a chart-topping record, was newer to the movies than its composer. Harry Richman (1895–1972) interrupted a busy career in clubs, vaudeville and Broadway revues to come West to star in his first film. The flamboyant Richman was regarded in some quarters as a swarmy, strutting jerk. His autobiography, immodestly titled *A Hell of a Life,* boasts incessantly, especially about its author's sexual conquests. But he had a powerful, sensuous voice often compared to that of Al Jolson, of whom Richman had been a protégé. He was linked to such standards as "On the Sunny Side of the Street," "This Is My Lucky Day" and "Walking My Baby Back Home." Richman wasn't terribly well known outside the big cities when he made *Puttin' on the Ritz*, but he figured to benefit from the publicity gained from a torrid, ongoing affair with Clara Bow.

In the script by John W. Considine, Jr. (dialogue by William K. Wells and actor James Gleason), Richman played a performer, Harry Raymond, who was not unlike himself, a conceited song-and-dance man who runs a popular New York nightclub on the side. Harry starts out as a mere song plugger with big dreams. When showgirl Delores Fenton (Joan Bennett) comes to the publishing office carrying "With You," a tune she's written, Harry's over-enthusiasm in hawking it to his boss (Eddie Kane) gets him fired, and his best pal Jimmy (Gleason) follows him out the door. Harry, Jim, Delores and her friend Goldie (Lilyan Tashman) decide to create a vaudeville act, despite Goldie's observation that Harry is "so big, he needs an 18-day diet for his head."

Sure enough, Harry's arrogance causes trouble one night in the sticks. After performing "Singing a Vagabond Song," he calls the hecklers in the mining-town audience "bohunks" and challenges them to a fight. The foursome is canned, but Harry and Delores receive an offer from Broadway producer George Barnes (Purnell B. Pratt) to join the cast of his new revue. Jim and Goldie must stay behind. "With You," the number that Harry has rewritten into a hit duet, brings him and Delores a huge following in New York. They become engaged, and Harry opens the swank Club Raymond.

But Harry is overextending himself. His drinking and partying are putting his voice at risk, and his cavorting with a dizzy socialite (Aileen Pringle) threatens his relationship with Delores. Jimmy and Goldie, now married, wire Harry about their intended Christmas visit to New York, but Harry is too busy to open the telegram. Thus, his old friends are practically ignored when they show up at a Christmas Eve party Harry gives for his new moneyed pals at his posh digs. But when Harry goes blind after drinking tainted liquor during the party, it is Jimmy who stays around to take care of him. Harry, now estranged from Delores, refuses to allow Jimmy to tell her about his condition. "I

was too good for her when I was a success," he says. "Well, she's too good for me now—and what's more, I know it!"

Months later, Delores opens as a single in a Barnes show, and she leads an "Alice in Wonderland" number that brings a tremendous ovation from the first-nighters. Some of them call out for Delores to sing "With You," but she can't bring herself to do it without Harry. She tentatively begins the song, then falters, but Harry picks up the tune from his seat in the balcony. Delores dashes off the stage to find him, which she does just as he is about to sneak away from the theater. As they tearfully embrace, Harry acknowledges how selfish he has been and how happy he and Delores can be together.

As was too often the case in early musicals, the songs in *Puttin' on the Ritz* far outshine the routine direction (by Edward Sloman, an able silent-film director who didn't make it in talkies) and trite story. At least the scripters saw fit not to contrive a miraculous regaining of Harry's sight, but they practically lifted the climax from one of the most famous incidents in American musical theater. On June 2, 1929, at the Broadway premiere of Florenz Ziegfeld's *Show Girl*, Ruby Keeler's tap dance to "Liza" was supplemented by the voice of her then-husband, Al Jolson, who rose from his seat near the front of the Ziegfeld Theatre and picked up the refrain at the top of his lungs.[15] Some say the "duet" was planned as a publicity ploy by Ziegfeld and Jolson without Keeler's knowledge, and it worked well enough for Jolson to continue it for a week after the opening.

Producer Joseph M. Schenck spent a good deal of money on *Puttin' on the Ritz*, which shows in two excellent production numbers—the title tune and "Alice in Wonderland," two of the three songs written by Berlin. The gaudy sets—credited to William Cameron Menzies but actually designed by Robert Usher—also contribute immeasurably. "Puttin' on the Ritz," performed by Richman and an interracial dance chorus in the context of a Barnes revue, offers silhouetted, rhythmically swaying skyscrapers and a fiendishly grinning giant billboard that add nicely to the song's vaguely macabre feel. "Alice in Wonderland," which takes up most of the closing Technicolor reel, makes good use of the non-singing Bennett. As the little girl propelled into dreamland, she merely has to react to the various literary characters, including an amorous White Rabbit and a line of chorus girl–sized playing cards. This was not a new song; it had been used under the title "Come Along with Alice" in the 1924 *Music Box Revue.*

The third Berlin selection, "With You," is heard four times, but is held back by the shaky contralto of Bennett, who was only 19. Berlin, who was on the set daily, was "very sweet to me," Bennett (1910–1990) told author Bergreen,

> I sang a duet with Harry Richman, and I'm not a singer. When Richman started to blow his top at me for the way I was singing the duet with him, Mr. Berlin stepped in and put him in his place. He said to Richman, "What do you mean by picking on her?"[16]

The other songs in *Puttin' on the Ritz* were among Richman's personal favorites and are put over with gusto, especially the jaunty "Singing a Vagabond Song," cowritten by the entertainer as a signature song of sorts. He also sings "There's Danger in Your Eyes, Cherie" and "I'll Get By." The reviews were generally favorable, although not glowing—for example, *Variety* noted that the film "transcends the triteness of its situations."[17] Broadway know-it-alls predicted a flop; more countrified viewers, turned off by the star's abrasiveness, had no good word of mouth. The picture ended up losing tons of money. Berlin was unhappy with the finished product, and Richman must have been, too, for he barely mentioned the film in *A Hell of a Life.* "*Puttin' on the Ritz* was not the smash that Joe Schenck had expected," he wrote with uncharacteristic understatement.[18]

The numbers are memorable and Bennett's acting (as opposed to her singing) is pretty good, but the primary enjoyment derived from this film is in the rare glimpse of Richman, who made only two other feature films. Despite his wooden acting in it, *Puttin' on the Ritz* verifies Richman's undeniable talent as a master song stylist.

SHE COULDN'T SAY NO
(Warner Bros.; February 14, 1930)

Director: Lloyd Bacon. Scenario and Dialogue: Robert Lord, Arthur Caesar. Based on the play by Benjamin M. Kaye (New York opening, August 31, 1926; 71 performances).

Photography: James Van Trees. Sound: David Forrest. Running Time: 73 minutes (sound version; also released as silent).

Cast: Winnie Lightner (Winnie Harper), Chester Morris (Jerry Casey), Louise Beavers (Cora), Sally Eilers (Iris), Johnny Arthur (Tommy), Tully Marshall (Big John), Gordon [William "Wild Bill"] Elliott.

Songs [all by Lightner]: "Bouncing the Baby Around," "A Darn Fool Woman Like Me," "Ping Pongo," "The Poison Kiss of That Spaniard," "Watching My Dreams Go By" (Al Dubin, Joe Burke).

Warner Bros. still couldn't go wrong with Winnie (*Gold Diggers of Broadway*) Lightner, so it gave the boisterous comedienne top billing for the first time in *She Couldn't Say No.* For this gangster melodrama with a handful of Al Dubin–Joe Burke songs, she was handed jut-jawed tough guy Chester Morris (1901–1970) as a leading man. Morris was being typecast as a crook—he was Oscar-nominated for best actor as one in *Alibi* (1929)—but was just about to go over to MGM. There, he would do some of his best work, in *The Big House* (1930) and *The Divorcee* (1930) before slowly descending permanently into "B" movies.

In *She Couldn't Say No,* Lightner played Winnie Harper, a jokey blues singer who falls for her ex-racketeer manager, Jerry Casey (Morris). But Jerry becomes enamored with a socialite (Sally Eilers), and to raise the money required to squire the rich woman—and also to back Winnie's nightclub revue—he returns to crime. He is mortally wounded and dies in Winnie's arms. With the help of her loyal pianist (Johnny Arthur), Winnie musters up the strength to continue in the show that is Jerry's secret gift to her. The hit song from *She Couldn't Say No* was "Watching My Dreams Go By," performed by Lightner.

Despite having to play it straight for an inordinate amount of screen time, Lightner drew solid reviews for both her dramatic and comedic work. But the picture contained nothing that anyone hadn't seen before—and often. Declared *Photoplay*: "Winnie Lightner *should* have said NO when Warners tried to star her as a dramatic actress."[19]

ROADHOUSE NIGHTS

(Paramount; February 21, 1930)

Director: Hobart Henley. Scenario and Dialogue: Garrett Fort. Story: Ben Hecht (or Dashiell Hammett; see below). Photography: William Steiner. Editor: Helene Turner. Sound: Edwin Schabbehar. Running Time: 69 minutes.

Cast: Helen Morgan (Lola Fagan), Charles Ruggles (Willie Bindbugel), Fred Kohler (Sam Horner), Jimmy Durante (Daffy), Eddie Jackson (Moe), Lou Clayton (Joe), Joe King (John Hanson), Fuller Mellish, Jr. (Hogan), Leo Donnelly (Keeley), Tammany Young (Jerry), Harry C. Bradley (desk clerk), The Durante Orchestra.

Songs: "Everything Is on the Up and Up" [Clayton, Jackson, Durante], "Hello, Everybody, Folks" [Clayton, Jackson, Durante] (Eddie Jackson, Lou Clayton, Jimmy Durante); "It Can't Go On Like This" [Morgan, twice] (E. Y. Harburg, Jay Gorney).

Disc: Trisklog 4 (bootleg LP; ST).

If not for the presence of two legendary entertainers, *Roadhouse Nights* would have been no different than the scores of routine crime melodramas that became so faddish in the early talkie era. But one can hardly dismiss a film with both Helen Morgan and Jimmy Durante in the cast.

Roadhouse Nights may have originated with another famous name, the mystery author Dashiell Hammett. Some sources indicate the film was based—very loosely—on Hammett's first full-length novel, *Red Harvest*, the rights to which Paramount purchased shortly after its publication in 1929. The transaction enabled Hammett to gain a job as a scenarist for the studio—his first original screenplay was *City Streets* (1931). However, the credits on *Roadhouse Nights* itself make no mention of Hammett, citing Ben Hecht for its story and Garrett Fort for its screenplay.

Hammett, Hecht, Fort or whoever centered their tale around Lola Fagan (Morgan), the chanteuse in a seedy nightclub owned by her bootlegger boyfriend, Sam Horner (Fred Kohler), in the sleepy Lake Michigan town of Moran. When a snoopy reporter (Joe King) from the *Chicago Times* disappears while investigating Horner's rackets, the drunken Willie Bindbugel (Charles Ruggles) is assigned by the

Times as a replacement. When Lola, who knows that Sam has murdered the first reporter, discovers that Willie is her long-lost old flame from Kenosha, she attempts to save him by arranging to have him fired. Later, she and Willie decide to elope, but they are waylaid by Horner. His execution of Willie is prevented by the reporter's frantic telegraphic message back to Chicago to summon the Coast Guard.

There are four musical interludes to break up the monotony. Morgan twice sings a torch song, "It Can't Go On Like This," and the other two numbers are provided by the raucous team of Lou Clayton, Eddie Jackson and Jimmy Durante, appearing as comic entertainers at Kohler's joint, The River Inn. Clayton, Jackson and Durante had headlined in vaudeville—they broke box-office records at the Palace in their first stint there—and debuted on Broadway to raves in *Show Girl* (1929). For a month's work on their first film, at Paramount's facility in Astoria, Long Island, "The Three Sawdust Bums" were paid a total of $50,000. But it was a trying month, for although *Show Girl* had closed, the boys still had to squeeze in gigs at the Palace (two shows a day) and the Silver Slipper club in New York.[20]

Durante was clearly the major attraction of the act; he got all the punch lines and song solos. The "Everything Is on the Up and Up" routine that introduces the trio in *Roadhouse Nights* is an indication of what their club act must have been like, and shows how much the two straight men were mere appendages. Jackson, stationed to Durante's right, is frequently out of camera range; Clayton, to Durante's left, has more to do but merely sets up the gags.

Durante: "Say, who do ya think I ran inta yesterday?"

Clayton and Jackson bark out intelligible names.

Durante: "George! And I asked 'im for a loan of 25,000 dollars, and he turned me down."

Clayton: "Refused ya?"

Durante: "Yeah, and he wound up offerin' me two dollars!"

Clayton: "From 25,000 to two dollars? Daffy, did you take it?"

Durante: "Well, yes. I was in no mood to dicker with 'im!"

By himself, Durante (1893–1980) plays a substantial supporting role in *Roadhouse Nights*. As Morgan's crying-towel buddy, he is frequently encouraging her to get out of Horner's clutches; otherwise ... "It's the gallows!" He even helps hero Ruggles (1886–1970), whose performance carries a little more oomph than his usual namby-pamby roles, to thwart the strongly overacting Kohler. The film and its players earned good reviews—*Photoplay* warned its readers to "watch for this Durante!"[21]—but Schnozzola and his pals considered it a one-shot deal. They and Morgan returned to Broadway, she for *Sweet Adeline* and the trio in *The New Yorkers*. When Durante returned to movies in 1931, it would be as a solo act.

LORD BYRON OF BROADWAY

(MGM; February 28, 1930)

Directors: William Nigh, Harry Beaumont. Continuity and Dialogue: Crane Wilbur, Willard Mack. Based on the novel by Nell Martin (1928). Photography: Henry Sharp. Editor: Anne Bauchens. Sound: Douglas Shearer. Art Director: Cedric Gibbons. Costumes: David Cox. Dance Direction: Sammy Lee, Albertina Rasch. Running Time: 66 minutes (sound version; also released as silent). Technicolor sequences.

Cast: Charles Kaley (Roy Erskine), Ethelind Terry (Ardis Trevelyan), Marion Shilling (Nancy Clover), Cliff Edwards (Joe Lundeen), Gwen Lee (Bessie), Benny Rubin (Phil), Drew Demarest (Edwards), John Byron (Mr. Millaire), Rita Flynn (Redhead), Hazel Craven (Blondie), Gino Corrado (Riccardi), Paulette Paquet (Marie), James Burroughs, Albertina Rasch Ballet.

Songs: "A Bundle of Old Love Letters" [Edwards; reprised by Kaley, Edwards], "Old Pal, Why Did You Leave Me?" [Kaley, Rubin], "Only Love Is Real" [Edwards; reprised by Terry], "Should I?" [Kaley; reprised by Terry], "The Woman in the Shoe" [Terry, offscreen male singer, chorus; reprised by male trio], "You're the Bride and I'm the Groom" [Kaley] (Arthur Freed, Nacio Herb Brown); "Blue Daughter of Heaven" [Burroughs, Rasch girls] (Raymond B. Egan, Dimitri Tiomkin); "The Doll Dance" [danced by Flynn, Craven] (Nacio Herb Brown); "The Japanese Sandman" [Edwards] (Raymond B. Egan, Richard A. Whiting).

Disc: Music Masters JJA-19802 (bootleg LP; ST).

With a starring duo lacking even a second of film experience, Metro was taking quite a gamble when it produced the part–Technicolor *Lord Byron of Broadway*. Charles Kaley (1902–1965) and Ethelind Terry (1899–1984) were better known in other realms of show business. He, a Richard Arlen look-alike, was "The Singing Band Leader" of vaudeville, clubs and the recording studio. She was a legitimate stage actress best known for originating the title role in *Rio Rita*. Marion Shilling (b. 1910), who filled out the romantic triangle in the adaptation of Nell Martin's backstage novel, had made only one previous film, the MGM comedy *Wise Girls* (1929). She had toured in stock since girlhood and appeared with Bela Lugosi in the Los Angeles stage production of *Dracula*. To compensate for the lack of star power, the Nacio Herb Brown–Arthur Freed songs in *Lord Byron* would have to be darned good.

The score, which included the hits "Should I (Reveal)?" "A Bundle of Old Love Letters" and "The Woman in the Shoe," turned out fine, but almost nothing else did. In letters to the author in 1993, Marion Shilling Cook, widowed but happily retired in the San Francisco area, remembered the making of the film with some amusement:

> *Lord Byron of Broadway* and *The Road Show* [which was retitled *Chasing Rainbows*] were intended by MGM to be their two musical blockbusters for 1929, following in the wake of the highly successful *Broadway Melody*. But, alas, both of these movies were indeed "busts." During the making of *Lord Byron of Broadway*, the stock market took its notorious plunge, and even more pertinently this film proved the truth of Shakespeare's comment, "The play's the thing."[22]

The banal story centered on a conceited song-and-dance man, Roy Erskine (Kaley), who has a strange mode of gaining inspiration. Whenever something happens to someone he knows, Roy exploits the situation by penning a song about it. For example, when a girlfriend (Gwen Lee) shows him a stack of love letters an old flame has written to her, the result is "A Bundle of Old Love Letters." Roy finds more permanent romance with pretty Nancy Clover (Shilling), whom he plucks out of a music store

The love triangle of the MGM flop *Lord Byron of Broadway*: **Charles Kaley, Marion Shilling and, at right, Ethelind Terry.**

to be a piano accompanist for him and his vaudeville partner, Joe Lundeen (Cliff Edwards, 1895–1971). Predictably, Roy makes it big in New York, and just as predictably—especially if you've seen *Be Yourself!* and *Puttin' on the Ritz*— he strays from ever-faithful Nancy. The temptress is a revue star, Ardis Trevelyan (Terry). Joe is killed in an accident, which prompts Roy to write a song, "Old Pal, Why Did You Leave Me?" about losing his best buddy. Nancy berates Roy for his tactlessness. Recalled Shilling: "Roy finally sees the light, and he and Nancy melt into each other's arms. … Do you wonder why the picture bombed?

Lord Byron of Broadway was in production during the latter half of 1929. The market had just crashed when the film's producer, Harry Rapf, returned from New York having lost a fortune in a few days. You can imagine his mood when he looked at the first rough cut in the projection room. He ordered an almost

complete remake. William Nigh was replaced as director by Harry Beaumont. All of Nigh's cronies in the cast were replaced, and Benny Rubin was recruited to lighten the film's mood. My wardrobe was entirely remade, as skirts had taken a plunge along with the stocks.[23]

Although she portrayed a professional musician, Shilling didn't actually play or sing at all. "I actually played the piano on the stage and in films on occasion, but for *Lord Byron* I learned every note of each selection and performed on a silenced keyboard," she said. "Dave Snell, one of MGM's top musicians, produced the music, sitting at a piano just off camera.

Charles Kaley and Ethelind Terry couldn't have been more pleasant to work with. Cliff Edwards was the life of the set. A wit, a wag, preoccupied with sex, he made racy comments at every opportunity. I was the special object of his jokes, his ideal foil. Having had a shielded rearing by a strict mother, I was naive even by the standards of that innocent era. Benny Rubin was a dear—intelligent, clean-cut.[24]

As Shilling indicated, *Lord Byron of Broadway* did indeed bomb—a $25,000 loss for MGM—despite the late makeover. The inexperienced cast was part of the problem. "You don't feel racked with the proper amount of anguish and irony," remarked the perplexed critic from *Motion Picture* magazine.[25] Said *The New York Times*: "It is another case of a good title going to waste, another test of patience."[26] A scan of other descriptions offered by reviewers revealed descriptions such as "slipshod," "completely lacking" and "a capital offense." Neither Kaley nor Terry received any more film offers, and after a year or two of good featured roles, Shilling found herself mired in shorts and low-budget feature quickies.

Lord Byron of Broadway has languished in the MGM vaults since its release, but its two Technicolor sequences were recycled in the early '30s as material for the studio's short subjects.[27] Both numbers are of substantial interest. "Blue Daughter of Heaven," a "Chinese" floor-show ballet, is partially revealed in lingering, pre–Berkeley overhead camera shots. Its music was cowritten by the young Dimitri Tiomkin, danced by his wife's Albertina Rasch Girls, and sung off-camera by James Burroughs, the tenor from *Broadway Melody*.

The other piece, "The Woman in the Shoe," is a pleasing little fantasy number. Of course, in 1929 it was a *big* fantasy number, with aspirations of topping Brown and Freed's "Wedding of the Painted Doll" from *Broadway Melody*. The two "story" songs sound a good deal alike. Ethelind Terry, dressed as the matron in the "Old Woman in the Shoe" verse, sings about her familiar plight of too many children and too little food. A fairy prince intervenes and, with a wave of his magic wand, transforms the woman's tattered boot into a sleek, modern high-heeled shoe that is perched atop a stairway of gold.

Various nursery rhyme characters—butchers and bakers (bearing gastronomic gifts), a gingerbread man, Jack and Jill (fetching a pail of candy), a ballerina, and a dancing row of four-and-twenty female blackbirds—prance in and out. A now-gowned Terry and an off-cam-

era singer (Burroughs, maybe?) continue the song to its finish in one of the trickier displays of Sammy Lee's choreography.

FREE AND EASY
(MGM; March 22, 1930)

Director: Edward Sedgwick. Scenario: Richard Schayer. Adaptation: Paul Dickey. Dialogue: Al Boasberg. Photography: Leonard Smith. Editor: William Le Vanway, George Todd. Sound: Douglas Shearer, Karl E. Zint. Art Director: Cedric Gibbons. Costumes: David Cox. Dance Direction: Sammy Lee. Running Time: 92 minutes.

Cast: Buster Keaton (Elmer J. Butts), Anita Page (Elvira Plunkett), Trixie Friganza (Mrs. Plunkett), Robert Montgomery (Larry Mitchell), Fred Niblo (himself), Estelle Moran (Mimi), Edgar Dearing (officer), Lottice Howell (singer), Richard Carle (actor), Louise Carver (actress), Ann Dvorak. As Themselves: Lionel Barrymore, Gwen Lee, John Miljan [bedroom scene], Karl Dane, Dorothy Sebastian, David Burton [cave scene], William Collier, Sr., Jackie Coogan, William Haines [premiere], Cecil B. De Mille, Arthur Lange, Joseph Farnham [studio conference].

Songs: "The Free-and-Easy" [Keaton, Moran, chorus; reprised by company], "It Must Be You" [Montgomery, Howell; reprised by Montgomery, company], "Land of Mystery" [chorus], "Oh! King, Oh! Queen" [Keaton, Friganza] (Roy Turk, Fred E. Ahlert).

Video: MGM-UA (cassette/laserdisc).

After years of producing his own pictures independently, Buster Keaton in 1928 made what he later admitted was "the worst mistake of my career."[28] He allowed his wife's brother-in-law, producer Joseph M. Schenck, to talk him into making movies for Metro-Goldwyn-Mayer. The thriving MGM was fast on its way to becoming the industry's leading studio, but its alliance with Keaton (1895–1966) was a curious one from the start. Keaton's highly individual style of comedy—and of comedy picture-making—were bound to be adversely affected by the company's impersonal atmosphere. Keaton was forced to forsake his usual coterie of collaborators to work with directors, producers and writers who had little feel for what worked for him.

Keaton's first two films for MGM—the silents *The Cameraman* (1928) and *Spite Marriage* (1929)—were solid hits, if a shade conventional for their star. More indicative of the impending decline of Keaton's career—although no one had an inkling about it at the time—was his first starring talkie, *Free and Easy*.[29] The film—a hodgepodge of musical comedy, operetta, slapstick and sentimental drama—made a lot of money and was considered quite funny in its day, and it proved that Keaton's flat speaking voice was no obstacle. "His audible performance is just as funny as his antics in mute offerings," wrote Mordaunt Hall in *The New York Times*.[30] Keaton sang "The Free-and-Easy" (with Estelle Moran) and "Oh! King, Oh! Queen" (with Trixie Friganza), two of the four Roy Turk–Fred E. Ahlert songs in the picture. According to the pressbook for the film, part of Metro's publicity campaign was to ask exhibitors to encourage fans to "write a comedy song for Buster."

Keaton played Elmer J. Butts, the nondescript manager of small-town beauty queen Elvira Plunkett (Anita Page), whose contest reward is a trip to Hollywood. On the train West, Elmer, Elvira and her battleaxe mother (former vaudeville star Friganza, 1870–1955) meet young movie star Larry Mitchell (Robert Montgomery), who is returning to his job after a visit to his hometown in Kansas. Larry, who is attracted to Elvira, promises the trio a visit to his studio. Although Elmer wreaks havoc at a movie premiere and then later on the MGM lot, Larry talks director Fred Niblo (played by director Fred Niblo) into casting the rube as an extra in his new film, a musical comedy called *Free and Easy*. Ma Plunkett gets a part, too. Elvira and Larry fall in love, and although Elmer is promoted to the comedy lead in the picture, he is saddened by the loss of his girl.

After a promising start, *Free and Easy* becomes tedious and overlong, and Keaton, who was always the leading man in his pictures, is forced to play character comic to Robert Montgomery's straight man. The director was Edward Sedgwick, whom Keaton worked with well, but the story by MGM contract writers has Keaton unwisely playing for pathos. The music—including "It Must Be You," a theme song of sorts—isn't very good, either. However, much of the first half is quite watchable for its amusing look at Hollywood life, in which some MGM personalities appear as themselves.

At a premiere at Grauman's Chinese Theatre, Jackie Coogan appears to give a short speech, William Haines is upstaged by an unwitting Elmer, and the buffoon is himself made sport of by wily emcee William Collier, Sr. The next morning, Elmer is turned back at the MGM front gate but manages to sneak into the studio anyway, despite the pursuit by an embarrassed security guard (Edgar Dearing). He tries to horn in on a conversation between Cecil B. DeMille, writer Joseph Farnham and musical director Arthur Lange about the leading lady in DeMille's next project, only to be ignored. He causes a premature explosion on a Western set where actors Karl Dane and Dorothy Sebastian are being directed by David Burton; Dane is the befuddled victim.

The funniest gag comes as Lionel Barrymore is directing John Miljan and Gwen Lee in a tense romantic drama. Miljan, in Lee's boudoir, aims a gun at a prop door and dares her off-screen husband to show his face. Elmer, thinking the dialogue is genuine, walks in with his hands raised. "Where on EARTH did you come from?!" thunders Barrymore. "Gopher City, Kansas," counters Elmer. Again Elmer escapes, only to show up as a soldier in the chorus of a stock musical number from the Niblo-Mitchell film, and from there the plot—unfortunately—gets moving again. (In the pressbook, MGM played up Barrymore's brief appearance before the camera, since the member of the famed acting clan supposedly had retired from that end of the business to concentrate solely on directing.)

"He was just a doll, so kind, and we had so much fun" was how Anita Page recalled Keaton to the author.[31] Besides this film, she also worked with him in *Sidewalks of New York* (1931). By this time, Keaton had become quite frustrated over the decreasing quality of his films and was beginning to drink heavily. Two years later, the comic was fired by MGM, and the professional acclaim that Keaton cherished would have to wait until his "rediscovery" in the twilight of his life.

Le Metteur en Scène, a French-language version of *Free and Easy*, was directed by Claude Autant-Lara, who would become a distinguished director of serious dramas in his native France. The Spanish version was titled

Estrellados. Keaton starred in both films; he learned the dialogue phonetically.

MAMMY

(Warner Bros.; March 26, 1930)

Director: Michael Curtiz. Producer: Walter Morosco. Screenplay: Gordon Rigby, Joseph Jackson. Based on the unpublished musical play *Mr. Bones* by Irving Berlin and James Gleason. Photography: Barney McGill. Editor: Owen Marks. Sound: George R. Groves. Musical Director: Louis Silvers. Running Time: 84 minutes (sound version; also released as silent).

Cast: Al Jolson (Al Fuller), Lois Moran (Nora Meadows), Louise Dresser (Mrs. Fuller), Lowell Sherman (Billy "Westy" West), Hobart Bosworth (Meadows), Tully Marshall (Slats), Mitchell Lewis (Hank "Tambo" Smith), Jack Curtis (sheriff), Ray Cooke (Props).

Songs: "Across the Breakfast Table Looking at You" [Jolson], "The Call of the South" [Jolson], "Here We Are" [minstrel band and chorus, numerous times], "In the Morning" [minstrel chorus], "Knights of the Road" [Jolson, hobo chorus], "Let Me Sing and I'm Happy" [Jolson, three times], "To My Mammy" [Jolson] (Irving Berlin); "My Mammy" [Jolson] (Joe Young, Sam M. Lewis, Walter Donaldson); "Oh, Dem Golden Slippers" [minstrel chorus] (James A. Bland); "Old Folks at Home" [minstrel chorus] (Stephen Foster); "When You and I Were Young, Maggie" [male quartet] (J. A. Butterfield, George W. Johnson); "Who Paid the Rent for Mrs. Rip Van Winkle?" [Jolson] (Alfred Bryan, Fred Fisher); "Why Do They All Take the Night Boat to Albany?" [Jolson] (Joe Young, Sam M. Lewis, Jean Schwartz); "Yes! We Have No Bananas" [Jolson, minstrel chorus] (Frank Silver, Irving Cohn; performed as operatic parody to several famous arias).

Disc: Brunswick 4721 (Jolson/"Let Me Sing and I'm Happy"/"Across the Breakfast Table Looking at You"/78); Brunswick 4722 (Jolson/"To My Mammy"/78); Milloball 34031 (bootleg LP; ST); Music Masters JJA-19744 (bootleg LP; ST).

Video: MGM-UA (laserdisc).

After the unexpected failure of *Say It with Songs* (see Chapter 4), Warner Bros. placed the high-priced Al Jolson into something with a stronger pedigree. *Mammy* was based on *Mr. Bones,* an unproduced stage musical cowritten by Irving Berlin, with songs added by the esteemed, if slumping, composer. The film was given one of Warners' best contract directors, Michael Curtiz, and a top leading lady, Lois Moran, on loan from Fox. (Ruby Keeler, then married to Jolson, was supposedly considered for the role.) The result was a better film than *Say It with Songs,* although almost as heavy in melodramatics and mother love but without Davey Lee.

Jolson seemed tailor-made for the role of Al Fuller, the star of one of those traveling minstrel shows that were rapidly going out of fashion even then. This struggling fictional troupe is Meadows' Merry Minstrels, with the alcoholic Hank "Tambo" Smith (Mitchell Lewis) joining Al as an endman and the renowned Billy "Westy" West (Lowell Sherman) as interlocutor. Westy, Al's best friend, is engaged to the boss's daughter, Nora (Moran), for whom Al carries a sizable torch. Al convinces the girl, who is dejected over Westy's wanderlust, to pretend to cozy up to him to make Westy jealous, but the ploy backfires and Nora is humiliated. Upset, Al gets drunk and is cheated out of all his money at cards by Tambo. Westy chews out Tambo, who loads Al's prop pistol with real bullets. That night, during a routine in which Al is to "shoot" Westy, the interlocutor is seriously wounded by his unwitting pal.

Al is immediately accused of loading the gun because of the affair with Nora, and even the bedridden Westy condemns him with "Don't you think you've got a hell of a nerve?" Al is arrested, but escapes when a police wagon overturns. He becomes a vagrant who travels by hopping trains. One day, Al returns to his hometown to see his mother (the misused Louise Dresser, only eight years older than Jolson) and sing "To My Mammy." She convinces him that he must "take the heat" and turn himself in. Just as he is doing so, Al is spotted by the arriving Meadows troupe, and he is told by his welcoming friends, including Nora and the recovered Westy, that Tambo has confessed to the shooting and gone to prison. Once again, Al can deliver his favorite melody, the triumphant "Let Me Sing and I'm Happy."

Warners publicized the New York premiere of *Mammy* with a lengthy minstrel parade led by its star, but the film garnered mixed reviews and lackluster box office. The review from *The New York Times'* Mordaunt Hall was typical: "By the time it switches off into melodramatic lanes, with a strenuous attempt to draw tears, the audience has at least the satisfaction of having enjoyed a period of cleverly pictured good humor."[32] Jolson offered to return the $50,000 the studio had advanced him on his next film, *Big Boy* (Chapter 4).[33]

Mammy deserves to be remembered, however, if only for its presumably accurate depiction of the lost art of minstrelsy. The on-stage sequences, one of which was filmed in Technicolor, of the company are very good, including an amusing operatic parody of "Yes! We Have No Bananas," in which the music from several well-known arias is matched with the lyrics of the '20s pop standard. This number, adapted by Berlin from the pop song written by Frank Silver and Irving Cohn, was originally performed in the *Music Box Revue* of 1923. Jolson punches across the two showcase Berlin tunes, "Let Me Sing and I'm Happy" and "To My Mammy," with more ability than is displayed in his non-singing performance. *Mammy* would be much more favorably remembered in retrospect.

Two numbers that were included in the original release of *Mammy*, Jolson's renditions of Berlin's "The Call of the South" and "Knights of the Road," are absent from existing prints. Noah Beery, Stanley Fields and Lee Moran, listed among the cast of minstrels in some contemporary and modern sources, are absent from the film, at least as it exists today.

SHOW GIRL IN HOLLYWOOD

(First National; April 20, 1930)

Director: Mervyn LeRoy. Producer: Robert North. Adaptation: Harvey Thew, James A. Starr. Dialogue: Harvey Thew. Based on the novel *Hollywood Girl* by J. P. McEvoy (1929). Photography: Sol Polito. Editor: Peter Fritch. Assistant Director: Al Alborn. Art Director: Jack Okey. Musical Director: Leo Forbstein. Dance Direction: Jack Haskell. Running Time: 77 minutes. Technicolor sequence.

Cast: Alice White (Dixie Dugan), Jack Mulhall (Jimmy Doyle), Blanche Sweet (Dottie Harris), Ford Sterling (Sam Otis), John Miljan (Frank Buelow), Virginia Sale (secretary for

Otis), Lee Shumway (Kramer), Herman Bing (Bing), Spec O'Donnell (office boy), Rolfe Sedan (head waiter). As Themselves: Noah Beery, Noah Beery, Jr., Al Jolson, Ruby Keeler, Walter Pidgeon, Loretta Young.

Songs: "Hang Onto a Rainbow" [White, chorus], "I've Got My Eye on You" [White; reprised by White, chorus], "There's a Tear for Every Smile in Hollywood" [Sweet] (Bud Green, Sam H. Stept).

Joining *Let's Go Places* and *Free and Easy* as entries in the Hollywood-insider musical sweepstakes was *Show Girl in Hollywood*, which was actually a semi-sequel to a First National part-sound film of 1928, *Show Girl*. In that comedy-drama based on the J. P. McEvoy novel of the same name (which also adapted into a 1929 Broadway musical), Alice White made good as Dixie Dugan, a petite blonde who parlays a "kidnapping" stunt into stardom in a Broadway show written by erstwhile newshound Jimmy Doyle (Charles Delaney). The couple wed at the climax.

The follow-up, derived from another McEvoy story and sprinkled with three Bud Green–Sammy Stept songs, employed the same characters but didn't continue the storyline. Here, Dixie and Jimmy (Jack Mulhall this time) are merely sweethearts, and she is only the understudy to the star in his show *Rainbow Girl*, which has just flopped. The couple go to the nightclub where Dixie once entertained, and when called upon to sing "I've Got My Eye on You," she is noticed by a Hollywood director, Frank Buelow (John Miljan). Buelow is out East on one of his periodic "talent" hunts; actually, he's seeking casting-couch fodder and stories he can steal. Buelow convinces Dixie to come West to his studio, Superb Productions, where, he says, she can practically walk in and become a star. Jimmy glowers.

Superb's production head, Sam Otis (Ford Sterling), lets Dixie down easy, but her spirits are raised after she meets one of her idols, faded actress Dottie Harris (Blanche Sweet). At age 32, Dottie is "as old as the hills" by Hollywood standards—she lives alone in a half-empty mansion she can't afford to maintain—but pride keeps her from admitting her financial reverses. In the song "There's a Tear for Every Smile in Hollywood," she warns Dixie of the fickle nature of filmland life:

It doesn't look good for the suicidal Dottie Harris (Blanche Sweet), but she, Jack Mulhall and Alice White will enjoy a happy ending in *Show Girl in Hollywood*.

There's a tear for every smile in Hollywood,
Every mile's a weary mile in Hollywood,
A million dreams are born with each day,
A million dreams keep fading away.

Dixie gets her big break soon after. When Jimmy is hired by Otis to adapt *Rainbow Girl* for the screen, she is hired as the star. Dottie gets a part, too. But—egged on by Buelow, who has been fired by Otis—Dixie lets her ego get the better of her. She demands that changes be made in Jimmy's story, and that the director be replaced. Jimmy punches out Buelow, who is revealed to be Dottie's estranged husband. But Otis has canned his temperamental leading lady and shut down production, leaving many jobless, including Dottie. On a lonely evening alone in her mansion, she takes poison and is saved only because she makes a last phone call to Dixie, who rushes over with Jimmy and summons a doctor. The incident startles Dixie into changing her attitude, and the picture that re-sults is a big hit on opening night. In front of the star-studded premiere audience, Dixie and Jimmy announce their impending wedding and two-week honeymoon. "Dixie, make it one week!" cries a mildly disapproving Otis from his seat.

Show Girl in Hollywood suffers from a clichéd story and half-baked wit. (Dixie: "Mr. Buelow only wants to help me, and you know what great pictures he's always made." Jimmy: "And it isn't pictures he's thinking about making now.") And with only four song presentations, the music doesn't make much of an impact, save for the poignant "There's a Tear for Every Smile in Hollywood," delivered by Sweet (1895–1986) with just the right sense of melancholy. Sweet had more in common with the fictional actress than you'd think. A protégé of D. W. Griffith, she had been on screen as early as 1909 and had starred for him in the early feature-length film *Judith of Bethulia* (1913). Even before sound arrived, her roles were becoming fewer and fewer. She made only three talkies, all in 1930, but they failed to rejuvenate her career, and except for a bit part in *The Five Pennies* (1959), she was off the screen for good thereafter. However, she did carry on for a time in vaudeville and settled down to a happy marriage with stage and film actor Raymond Hackett. Her touching performance in this film is easily its best asset.

Like *Free and Easy, Show Girl in Hollywood* offers some intriguing glimpses into the filmmaking process. As the production number for "I've Got My Eye on You" is being staged for the fictional camera, the real lens focuses on various behind-the-scenes technicians, including the camera operator (still working from a soundproof booth), the sound engineer, the lighting coordinator, and the director who barks out commands to them. The number itself has White and chorus dancing around an enormous eye-rolling and teeth-chomping "monkey" set piece. The climax of the film takes place at a Warner Bros. "premiere" of *Rainbow Girl,* where Loretta Young, Noah Beery and future character actor Noah Beery, Jr., give brief speeches before the radio microphone. There is a brief shot of Al Jolson and Ruby Keeler exiting from their limousine, and the handsome fellow who introduces Dixie to the first-nighters is Walter Pidgeon. The closing song, "Hang Onto a Rainbow," from the film within a film, was photographed in Technicolor.

Show Girl in Hollywood was considered strictly routine by most critics and the general public, and it didn't help that White and Mulhall (1887–1979) were losing their popularity, the latter mainly because of advancing age. "Only occasionally funny ... performances are hardly conspicuous," was *Variety*'s judgment.[34] However, *Photoplay* saw it as "Alice White's best talkie, without a quibble ... first-rate entertainment, in spite of a soggy spot or two."[35]

CHILDREN OF PLEASURE

(MGM; April 26, 1930)

Director: Harry Beaumont. Scenario: Richard Schayer. Dialogue: Crane Wilbur. Based on the play *The Song Writer* by Crane Wilbur (New York opening, August 13, 1928; 56 performances). Photography: Percy Hilburn.

Editors: Blanche Sewell, George Todd. Sound: Douglas Shearer. Art Director: Cedric Gibbons. Costumes: David Cox. Dance Direction: Sammy Lee. Running Time: 69 minutes.

Cast: Lawrence Gray (Danny Regan), Wynne Gibson (Emma Gray), Helen Johnson (Pat Thayer), Kenneth Thomson (Rod Peck), Benny Rubin (Andy Little), Lee Kohlmar (Bernie), May Boley (Fanny Kaye), Edward Martindel (Mr. Thayer), Sidney Bracey (Myles), Biltmore Trio, Jack Benny, Cliff Edwards, Ann Dvorak.

Songs: "The Better Things in Life" [Gray], "Girl Trouble" [Gray; reprised by Rubin, Gibson] (Fred Fisher); "Dust" [Gray, Gibson; reprised by Boley, chorus], "Leave It That Way" [Gray, twice] (Andy Rice, Fred Fisher); "A Couple of Birds with the Same Thing in Mind" [Boley, chorus] (Howard Johnson, George Ward, Reggie Montgomery); "The Whole Darned Thing's for You" [Gray, Biltmore Trio] (Roy Turk, Fred E. Ahlert).

Disc: Brunswick 4775 (Gray/"Leave It That Way"/"The Whole Darned Thing's for You"/78).

After playing second (and third) fiddle to Marion Davies, Alexander Gray and Bernice Claire, and the Duncan Sisters, Lawrence Gray (1898–1970) was finally given top billing in a musical. The actor's singing talents were modest, but the genre had revived his flagging career, which had begun promisingly in the mid 1920s when he was "promoted" from unit production manager to leading man at Paramount. MGM took a look at the good notices Gray earned for its *Marianne* and handed him the lead in *Children of Pleasure,* a brisk but modest quickie that dashed in and out of theaters.

The Song Writer, a play by Crane Wilbur, formed the basis for Richard Schayer's scenario about a young composer-publisher and his two very different women. Pat Thayer (Helen Johnson) is an heiress who considers her impending marriage to Danny Regan as merely a trial—and no reason to end her affair with an actor (Kenneth Thomson). Emma Gray (Wynne Gibson), Danny's former vaudeville partner and now his coworker in a Tin Pan Alley publishing house, loves him unrequitedly. On the night before their wedding, Danny learns of Pat's true feelings and goes on a drinking binge. Under the influence, he asks Emma to marry him instead. Danny wakes up the next morning thinking he has married Emma but still wanting Pat. Emma had been smart enough not to go through with the impromptu ceremony, but when Danny calms down, he decides that he truly does love the good girl. At the fadeout, he is running after Emma—and the audience is left to assume that he will catch her.

Variety praised Benny Rubin's comedy but little else: "The others work along vaudeville lines—mostly talk and no acting."[36] "Dust," sung by hefty contralto May Boley and danced by Ann Dvorak and other chorines, is the big production number. Jack Benny and Cliff Edwards play themselves in first-reel cameos.

Gray's film career already had peaked, and after the mid '30s he moved to Mexico with his wife, actress Mary Louise Figueroa, to become a movie executive. Gibson (1899–1987) and Johnson went on to better acting days, the former as a character star and the latter after changing her name to the sleeker Judith Wood.

MOVIETONE FOLLIES OF 1930

(Fox; May 4, 1930)

Director: Benjamin Stoloff. Associate Producer: Al Rockett. Screenplay: William K. Wells. Photography: L. William O'Connell. Editor: Clyde Carruth. Sound: Joseph E. Aiken. Assistant Director: Lew Breslow. Art Director: Stephen Goosson. Costumes: Sophie Wachner. Musical Director: Arthur Kay. Dance Direction: Danny Dare, Maurice L. Kusell, Max Scheck. Running Time: 70 minutes.

Cast: El Brendel (Axel Svenson), Marjorie White (Vera Fontaine), Frank Richardson (George Randall), Noel Francis (Gloria DeWitt), William Collier, Jr. (Conrad Sterling), Miriam Seegar (Mary Mason), Huntly Gordon (Marvin Kingsley), Paul Nicholson (Bill Hubert), Yola D'Avril (Babette), Betty Grable.

Songs: "Cheer Up and Smile" [Francis, chorus], "Doing the Derby" [chorus], "Here Comes Emily Brown" [Richardson, White, chorus] (Jack Meskill, Con Conrad); "Bashful" [Brendel, White], "I Feel That Certain Feeling Coming On" [Brendel, Francis] (Cliff Friend, James V. Monaco); "Having a Ball" [chorus], "I'd Love to Be a Talking Picture Queen" [White] (Joseph McCarthy, James Brockman, James F. Hanley); "You'll Give In" [Brendel, White] (Joseph McCarthy, James F. Hanley).

Also Known As: *Fox Movietone Follies of 1930* and *New Movietone Follies of 1930*.

In the first full year of sound, *William Fox Movietone Follies of 1929* was a big deal. But the bloom clearly had come off the rose by the time the follow-up, copyrighted as *Movietone Follies of 1930*, came around. It, declared *Photoplay*, was "just another revue."[37] There was also no William Fox in the title. The studio czar had overextended himself in a buy-up of theater chains—and in an intended takeover of Metro-Goldwyn-Mayer. Bankrupted by the stock market crash, Fox had relinquished control of his studio to a group of bankers.

Unlike Fox Film's much starrier *Happy Days*, all *Movietone Follies of 1930* had going for it were three of the studio's busiest musical-comedy players—El Brendel, Marjorie White and Frank Richardson. But although it's a bit too routine (little more than an hour, no color, no widescreen treatment) to justify the importance of its title, this is a fun little film with some pleasant surprises.

The dually unimpressive William Collier, Jr. (1900–1987) and Miriam Seegar shoulder the major romantic duty as, respectively, a misbehaving playboy and the virtuous showgirl he loves over the objections of his stuffy uncle (Huntly Gordon). After a falling-out between the lovers, the playboy arranges for the girl's entire stage production to be moved into the estate of his absent uncle as a benefit for war veterans. He's doing this to return to his honey's good graces, a goal that is satisfied through the intervention of the girl's wisecracking chorus chum (Noel Francis). Meanwhile, the playboy's Swedish valet (Brendel) attempts to impersonate a lumber king to impress the two actresses (Francis, White) whose attentions he has captured. Collier, Richardson, Gordon and Brendel end up with, respectively, Seegar, White, Francis and, playing a predictably tempestuous French maid, Yola D'Avril.

Movietone Follies of 1930 is a straight comedy for half of its length, at which point the action stops almost dead for the enactment of the transplanted revue. There are seven numbers: four in the revue, three that occur backstage. Among them are White's charming, name-

Noel Francis (left) and Marjorie White tussle over El Brendel (!) in Fox's *Movietone Follies of 1930*.

dropping rendition of "I'd Love to Be a Talking Picture Queen," in which she describes her intended alliances with the likes of Warner Baxter and Charles Farrell; White's blackface duet with Richardson for "Here Comes Emily Brown"; and Brendel and Francis' comical presentations of "I Feel That Certain Feeling Coming On," first as she seduces him, than later on when the roles are reversed.

The screenplay is pretty standard stuff, but a couple of actors really stand out. For once, Brendel is playing a character with an IQ; his romantic maneuverings show that he has a libido, too. Francis makes a charming partner for him, especially when she comes on to him on a couch while he's trying to cope with the jug of ice cubes he's just sat on. "Something tells me that, deep down in your heart, your love is growing cold," she predicts. "Deeper down than that" is the poor fellow's reply. Francis (1911–1959), a former Ziegfeld girl, was stuck in the floozie/gun moll mold for most of her career

(*Smart Money, I Am a Fugitive from a Chain Gang*), but the tall Texan displays a pleasing contralto on the closing "Cheer Up and Smile" number, in which she taunts a chorus of Gordon's prehistoric servants into getting a life.

Movietone Follies of 1930 was feared lost for many years, but it has survived in an archival 35mm print at UCLA. In trade ads during the summer of 1930, Fox announced a *New Movietone Follies of 1931*, but the industry-wide discord over musicals put an end to that plan.

SWING HIGH
(Pathé; May 18, 1930)

Director: Joseph Santley. Producer: E. B. Derr. Adaptation and Dialogue: James Seymour. Continuity: Ray McCarey. Story: Joseph Santley, James Seymour. Photography: David Abel. Editor: Daniel Mandell. Sound: Homer

Ackerman, Charles O'Laughlin, Ben Winkler. Assistant Directors: Ray McCarey, Bert Gilroy. Art Direction: Carroll Clark. Set Direction: Ted Dickson. Costumes: Gwen Wakeling. Musical Director: Joshua Zuro. Running Time: 75 minutes.

Cast: Helen Twelvetrees (Maryan), Fred Scott (Garry), Dorothy Burgess (Trixie), John Sheehan (Doc May), Daphne Pollard (Mrs. May), George Fawcett (Pop Garner), Bryant Washburn (Ringmaster Joe), Nick Stuart (Billy), Sally Starr (Ruth), Little Billy (Major Tiny), William Langan (Babe), Stepin Fetchit (Sam), Chester Conklin (sheriff), Ben Turpin (bartender), Robert Edeson (doctor), Mickey Bennett (Mickey), Clarence Muse (singer), Rolfe Sedan (trouper).

Songs: "Do You Think That I Could Grow on You?" [Little Billy, Burgess], "It Must Be Love" [Scott] (Mack Gordon, Abner Silver); "Shoo the Hoodoo Away" [Muse, chorus, twice] (Mort Harris, Ted Snyder); "There's Happiness Over the Hill" [Scott] (Raymond B. Egan, Henry Sullivan); "With My Guitar and You" [Scott, twice] (Mort Harris, Edward Heyman, Ted Snyder).

A few months after *The Grand Parade*, Pathé reteamed Helen Twelvetrees and Fred Scott in another showbiz-themed melodrama with songs, *Swing High*. The dull story about a traveling circus of 1880 was enacted by a curious supporting cast of fading juveniles (Nick Stuart and Sally Starr), out-of-style comics (Chester Conklin and Ben Turpin), renowned black performers (Stepin Fetchit and Clarence Muse)—and a midget named Little Billy. Studio ads unabashedly, if not accurately, boasted the "greatest cast ever assembled on the audible screen."

Twelvetrees played an aerialist for "Garner's Circus Supreme"; Scott was the medicine-show singer whose rendition of "My Guitar and You" indirectly causes the merger of the two companies. Maryan and Garry fall in love, although Maryan's new high-wire partner, Trixie (Dorothy Burgess), makes eyes at the young tenor. Trixie, we learn, is a con artist in league with the troupe's shady ringmaster (Bryant Washburn). Garry celebrates his engagement with Maryan by entering a high-stakes poker game, only the game is strip poker and Trixie is a willing participant. Maryan, erroneously be-

lieving that Garry is cheating on her, becomes so distraught that she falls during her act and is seriously injured. With Maryan out of the way, the crooks frame Garry for the theft of circus receipts, but Maryan, returning to the act despite an unhealed shoulder, forces a high-altitude confession from Trixie by threatening to drop her during a stunt. Garry is freed from jail and returns to the show.

Scott sings well—three tunes, including the theme song "There's Happiness Over the Hill"—but he shows no pizzazz as an actor. He would forge a more lasting career in the late '30s as a singing "B" cowboy star. "Shoo the Hoodoo Away," a spiritual of sorts, is sung twice by an uncredited Clarence Muse, and the tastelessly comic "Do You Think That I Could Grow on You?" is crooned by Little Billy to an uninterested Burgess. Their strange relationship—circus midget has crush on beautiful but money-mad aerialist—is reminiscent of the more sinister Harry Earles–Olga Baclanova pairing in the horror classic *Freaks* (1932).

Observed *Variety*: "So many copies of it have been filmed, it's outlived."[38]

THE FLORODORA GIRL
(Cosmopolitan Productions/MGM; May 30, 1930)

Director: Harry Beaumont. Scenario and Dialogue: Gene Markey. Additional Dialogue: Ralph Spence, Al Boasberg, Robert E. Hopkins. Photography: Oliver T. Marsh. Editor: Carl L. Pierson. Sound: Douglas Shearer, Paul Neal. Art Director: Cedric Gibbons. Costumes: Adrian. Running Time: 73 minutes. Technicolor sequence.

Cast: Marion Davies (Daisy Dell), Lawrence Gray (Jack Vibart), Walter Catlett (DeBoer), Louis John Bartels (Hemingway), Ilka Chase (Fanny), Vivien Oakland (Maud), Jed Prouty (Old Man Dell), Claud Allister (Rumblesham), Sam Hardy (Fontaine), Nance O'Neil (Mrs. Vibart), George Chandler (Georgie Smith), Robert Bolder (Commodore), Jane Keithly (Constance), Maude Turner Gordon (Mrs. Caraway), Anita Louise, Mary Jane Irving (Vibart children), Eddie Dillon (stage manager).

Songs: "My Kind of a Man" [male trio], "Pass the Beer and Pretzels" [Davies, chorus, in

Marion Davies dances in the Florodora septet in MGM's breezy turn-of-the-century comedy *The Florodora Girl*.

sing-along] (Clifford Grey, Andy Rice, Herbert Stothart); "Mother Was a Lady" [bartender] (Edward B. Marks, Joseph W. Stern); "Tell Me, Pretty Maiden" [Davies, Gray, Florodora chorus] (Owen Hall, Thomas A. Barrett). Sing-along Medley [Davies, chorus]: "Break the News to Mother" (Charles K. Harris); "In the Good Old Summertime" (Ren Shields, George Evans); "Little Annie Rooney" (Michael Nolan); "Say 'Au Revoir' but Not 'Goodbye'" (Harry Kennedy); "Swing Me Higher, Obediah" (Alf E. Rick, Maurice Scott); "(There'll Be) A Hot Time in the Old Town Tonight" (Joseph Hayden, Theodore M. Metz).

After making a talkie splash in *Marianne* (see Chapter 5), Marion Davies starred in a straight comedy, *Not So Dumb* (1930), a King Vidor-directed adaptation of the play *Dulcy*. Then she returned to musical comedy in the lightly satirical *The Florodora Girl*, an unpretentious and charming bit of Gay Nineties nos-

talgia that evoked a period fondly remembered by Depression-beset audiences. Moreover, it offered another role that was well suited for the comic flair of Davies.

The real Florodora girls were part of a double (female and male) sextette that popularized the song "Tell Me, Pretty Maiden" in *Florodora*, the smash-hit London and Broadway musical of the turn of the century. In the film, Davies plays Daisy Dell, the last remaining active member of the original female sextette; the others have all left the stage to marry into money. But good-hearted Daisy's man is an unexciting cigar salesman, Georgie Smith (George Chandler). "I wouldn't want to marry a man just for his money," she tells a chorus chum (Ilka Chase), who replies, "Can you think of a better reason?" Daisy finds one in Jack Vibart (Lawrence Gray), a handsome but allegedly dishonorable young millionaire. She plays hard to get at first, but succumbs after letting Jack "rescue" her after a feigned drowning.

When Jack proposes that Daisy take an apartment, she is insulted enough to break off the relationship, which drives Jack into the arms of the wealthy Constance (Jane Keithly). They announce their engagement at the prestigious Commodore's Ball, but Daisy, there as the escort of a moneyed friend (Claud Allister), turns out to be the main attraction. Jack realizes his mistake and proposes to Daisy, but then loses the family fortune betting on horses to a disreputable gambler (moustache-twirling Sam Hardy). Jack's mother (Nance O'Neil) asks Daisy to relinquish Jack to Constance in order to restore the family name. She agrees, but Jack, who has started a thriving horseless-carriage business, crashes one of Daisy's shows (photographed in Technicolor) to plead for her hand. The impromptu Florodora boy carries her out of the theater to a waiting auto, where Mrs. Vibart—comprehending the depth of Jack and Daisy's love—happily gives her blessing.

The Florodora Girl is an amusing, if romanticized, reminder of a "simpler" period, of campfire sing-alongs, helmet-less football games, modest-looking bathing suits and bicycles built for two. The score combines newly composed but vintage-sounding songs with listenable standards. The stable of character actors—Walter Catlett, Jed Prouty, Louis John Bartels, Allister, Hardy and Chandler—is an appealing collection of comic buffoons.

Also in the cast was Ilka Chase, the writer and occasional actress, who recalled that some of the film's beach sequence was photographed at Davies' oceanside home in Santa Monica, California. There, the star treated the cast and crew to a sumptuous buffet and tours of the house. In her autobiography *Past Imperfect*, Chase also remembered how director Harry Beaumont kept Davies' paramour (and the film's *de facto* producer), William Randolph Hearst, off the studio set:

> Beaumont ... devised a simple and ingenious trick for keeping the boss from underfoot. When the red light is on outside the door of a sound stage it means a scene is shooting, and God Himself can't come in. Harry posted scouts at all the approaches to the stage, and as Mr. Hearst advanced upon it, he would promptly order the doors closed and would then rehearse his scene in peace while the mighty one cooled his heels. There was one sequence, however, where this ruse failed.

The "Tell Me, Pretty Maiden" scene was shot in *glorious* Technicolor, and because of the blazing lights the stage got so hell-hot the doors couldn't be kept closed longer than five minutes at a time....[39]

The film's appeal was not lost on commentators of 1930. *Time* magazine called *The Florodora Girl* "a brilliant, animated cartoon of the fashions of the Mauve Decade—a cartoon brought to life by the comic playing of Marion Davies and built around an effervescing, satirical story."[40] *The New York Times* considered it "virtually a travesty, but one that is shrewdly directed with a good sense of humor. ... Marion Davies, the stellar performer, is seen to excellent advantage."[41]

For MGM and Davies' production company, Cosmopolitan, the release of *The Florodora Girl* was spoiled by three plagiarism lawsuits filed against them over the dramatic and musical content. The estate of Leslie Stuart, the composer of the song "Tell Me, Pretty Maiden," sued, as did parties representing the rights holders to the play *Florodora* and the publisher of its songs. The first two actions were dismissed; the latter was settled out of court in 1933 for an undisclosed sum.

SAFETY IN NUMBERS
(Paramount; May 30, 1930)

Director: Victor Schertzinger. Screenplay: George Marion, Jr., Percy Heath. Story: Marion Dix. Photography: Henry Gerrard. Editor: Robert Bassler. Sound: Eugene Merritt. Dance Direction: David Bennett. Running Time: 80 minutes.

Cast: Charles "Buddy" Rogers (William Butler Reynolds), Kathryn Crawford (Jacqueline), Josephine Dunn (Maxine), Carole Lombard (Pauline), Geneva Mitchell (Cleo Carewe), Roscoe Karns (Bertram Shipiro), Francis McDonald (Phil Kempton), Virginia Bruce (Alma McGregor), Richard Tucker (F. Carstairs Reynolds), Raoul Paoli (Jules), Lawrence Grant (Commodore Brinker), Louise Beavers (Messaline).

Songs: "Business Girl" [Rogers], "Do You Play, Madame?" [Rogers, Crawford; reprised by Rogers], "I'd Like to Be a Bee in Your Boudoir" [Rogers, Dunn; reprised by Rogers], "My Future Just Passed" [Rogers, Crawford], "Pepola"

In Paramount's *Safety in Numbers*, Buddy Rogers has his pick of (from left) Josephine Dunn, Carol Lombard, Kathryn Crawford and Virginia Bruce.

[chorus], "The Pick-Up" [Rogers, Crawford, Beavers, chorus], "You Appeal to Me" [Rogers, Lombard; reprised by Rogers] (George Marion, Jr., Richard A. Whiting).

Disc: Columbia 2183-D (Rogers/"I'd Like to Be a Bee in Your Boudoir"/"My Future Just Passed"/78); Music Masters JJA-19806 (bootleg LP; ST).

Buddy Rogers' tenor (or was it a high baritone?) may have been shaky, but Paramount was not reluctant to hand over fresh song material to a still-profitable star. Hence, *Safety in Numbers,* in which the leading man sang six of the seven tunes by Richard Whiting and George Marion, Jr. One, "My Future Just Passed," became a minor hit.

Rogers introduces that song three-quarters into the picture, in which he plays William Butler Reynolds, an import-export heir who wants to be a composer. He is dispatched to New York

by his guardian uncle (Richard Tucker) to get a social "education" from a trio of worldly Follies girls played by Kathryn Crawford (1908–1980), Josephine Dunn (1906–1983) and Carole Lombard (1908–1942). Even now, Lombard was getting most of the juicy dialogue.

Bill is to inherit $25 million within months, so the gals have been asked by uncle to protect him from potential gold diggers. This turns out to include themselves, for Bill and the good-hearted Jacqueline (Crawford) fall in love. When Bill sings "My Future Just Passed" to her, Jacqueline realizes the depth of the affections of her young man. Caring about him enough to not want to see him lose his fortune, she prepares to escape to Mexico with a previous admirer (Francis McDonald). But the split is only temporary.

Each of the lady leads gets a duet with Rogers. Dunn and Lombard (reciting) struggle through "I'd Like to Be a Bee in Your Boudoir" and "You Appeal to Me," respectively. But the best song in this minor entry is the sly "Do You Play, Madame?" a Rogers-Crawford love match with a golfing metaphor. There is also a very cinematic dance number—the snazzy "The Pick-Up," in which David Bennett's choreography and Henry Gerrard's photography present the performers attractively silhouetted against the New York skyline.

"Should be good box office stuff and pleasingly tuneful," commented *Variety*.[42] Indeed, *Safety in Numbers* proved quite profitable, although to many in the moviegoing audience, it should have been Lombard, not Crawford, who got her Buddy. Paramount took note of this sentiment by inking Lombard to a seven-year contract. A star was in the making.

MAN TROUBLE

(Fox; August 24, 1930)

Director: Berthold Viertel. Adaptation: George Manker Watters, Marion Orth. Dialogue: George Manker Watters, Edwin Burke. Based on the magazine story "A Very Practical Joke" by Ben Ames Williams (1925). Photography: Joseph August. Editor: J. Edwin Robbins. Sound: Donald Flick. Assistant Director: J. Edmund Grainger. Art Director: William S. Darling. Costumes: Sophie Wachner. Running Time: 87 minutes.

Cast: Milton Sills (Mac), Dorothy Mackaill (Joan), Kenneth MacKenna (Graham), Sharon Lynn (Trixie), Roscoe Karns (Scott), Oscar Apfel (Eddie), James Bradbury, Jr. (Goofy), Harvey Clark (Uncle Joe), Edythe Chapman (Aunt Maggie), Lew Harvey (Chris).

Songs: "Now I Ask You," "Pick Yourself Up, Brush Yourself Off," "What's the Use of Living Without Love?" "You Do, Don't You?" "You Got Nobody to Love" [Mackaill] (Joseph McCarthy, James F. Hanley).

Another gangster story with songs, *Man Trouble* gained some attention as the last movie released prior to the death of its male lead. Ten days after the film's New York opening, 48-year-old Milton Sills dropped dead of a heart attack during a game of tennis at his home in Santa Monica, California. Sills had made two films after a year's absence from the screen due to a nervous breakdown. His final picture, the

Jack London adventure *The Sea Wolf*, was released by Fox in October of 1930.

Sills also died in *Man Trouble*. His character, a New York bootlegger and cabaret owner, gives his life in a gunfight to save the singer (Dorothy Mackaill) he loves and the newspaper reporter (Kenneth MacKenna) *she* loves. James F. Hanley and Joseph McCarthy contributed five songs. One was "You Got Nobody to Love," in which Mackaill, an English-accented actress on loan from Warner Bros., showed off her singing voice for the first time. Sharon Lynn was around to do most of the singing, however.

Another selection in the long-forgotten picture was "Pick Yourself Up, Brush Yourself Off," which is not to be confused with the Jerome Kern–Dorothy Fields tune "Pick Yourself Up," from the Astaire-Rogers musical *Swing Time*.

BRIGHT LIGHTS

(First National; September 21, 1930)

Director: Michael Curtiz. Associate Producer: Robert North. Adaptation and Dialogue: Humphrey Pearson, Henry McCarty. Story: Humphrey Pearson. Photography: Lee Garmes, Charles Schoenbaum. Editor: Harold Young. Sound: George R. Groves. Art Director: Anton Grot. Costumes: Edward M. Stevenson. Musical Director: Leo Forbstein. Dance Direction: Larry Ceballos. Running Time: 73 minutes. Technicolor.

Cast: Dorothy Mackaill (Louanne), Frank Fay (Wally Dean), Noah Beery (Miguel Parada), Daphne Pollard (Mame Avery), James Murray (Connie Lamont), Tom Dugan (Tom Avery), Inez Courtney (Peggy North), Frank McHugh (Fish), Edmund Breese (Franklyn Harris), Eddie Nugent (Windy Jones), Philip Strenge (Emerson Fairchild), Jean Bary (Violet Madison), Edwin Lynch (Dave Porter), Virginia Sale ("Sob Sister"), John Peter Richmond [John Carradine] (photographer).

Songs: "All the Pretty Girls I Know" [Fay], "I've Got a Masculine Complex" (Al Dubin, Joe Burke); "Every Little Girl He Sees" [Courtney, chorus, danced by Dugan, Pollard], "Nobody Cares If I'm Blue" [Fay] (Grant Clarke, Harry Akst); "A Man About Town" [Mackaill, chorus], "Wall Street" [Fay, chorus] (Herb Magidson, Ned Washington, Michael H.

Nasty Miguel Parada (Noah Beery) reintroduces himself—and his scar—to actress Louanne (Dorothy Mackaill) in *Bright Lights*. Philip Strenge (left) and Frank Fay watch.

Cleary); "Collegiate Sam" [chorus] (Benny Davis, J. Fred Coots); "I'm Crazy for Cannibal Love" [Mackaill, chorus] (Al Bryan, Eddie Ward); "I'm Sitting Pretty in a Pretty Little City" [female singer] (Lou Davis, Henry Santly, Abel Baer); "Rubberneckin' Around" [Fay, chorus] (Grant Clarke, Herb Magidson, Ned Washington, Harry Akst, Ray Perkins); "Song of the Congo" [Mackaill, chorus; reprised by Mackaill] (Herb Magidson, Ned Washington, Ray Perkins).

From Humphrey Pearson, author of the 1929 all–Technicolor backstage musical drama *On with the Show!* (see Chapter 3), came *Bright Lights*, a similarly plotted (and plotty) 1930 color backstager also for Warners. Like the earlier film, *Bright Lights* covers a night in the lives of the participants in a stage musical, with their behind-the-scenes stories taking shape as the show progresses in real time. First National

touted the film as the musical debut of its English contract star Dorothy Mackaill, disregarding her one song in Fox's *Man Trouble*.

Mackaill (1903–1990) played a Broadway star singularly named Louanne, who is appearing for the last time in her hit revue, *Bright Lights*, before her retirement to marry the wealthy Emerson Fairchild (Philip Strenge). The master of ceremonies of *Bright Lights* is Wally Dean (Frank Fay), Louanne's longtime friend, protector and former lover. Louanne is prompted by Wally to tell her life's story to a group of newspaper reporters, but her fibs about a pristine "life on the farm in England" hide the reality, shown in flashback, of her stint as an exotic dancer in Africa. There, with Wally's help, she had fended off the sexual advances of Miguel Parada (Noah Beery), a seedy Portuguese smuggler.

The scene shifts back to the present, where the business partner of Wally's friend Connie

Lamont turns out to be the unrepentant Miguel, bearing the scar caused by a lamp thrown at his face by Louanne back in Africa. Miguel is shocked to see Louanne on stage, but he decides that he has "some unfinished business" with her. Connie, realizing Miguel's true nature, gets into a skirmish with the foreigner that leaves the villain dead. Connie's chorister girlfriend (Inez Courtney) and Wally both attempt to provide alibis for the very guilty Connie to the police, but it is the bogus "eyewitness" testimony of a newshound named Fish (Frank McHugh, inebriated again) that clears the young man. Louanne comes to her senses and realizes that Wally is the man for her.

Expectedly, the song numbers in *Bright Lights* are totally unrelated to the action. Mackaill, showing off a mediocre voice, sings three tunes. The saucy "Song of the Congo" presents her in a skimpy hula get-up, in both past and present. For "A Man About Town," she comes onstage in top hat and tails, then disappears behind a huddle of male dancers to ditch the manly digs for a dress. (A double appears to be doing the more complicated dance moves.) Fay's numbers include the introductory "Wall Street," in which he plays a New York tour guide surrounded by dancers in "bull" and "bear" masks. A "collegiate" number, "Every Little Girl He Sees," is sung by Courtney and danced by Tom Dugan and Daphne Pollard. Dugan and Pollard provide alleged comedy as a husband-and-wife team who spend their off-stage moments attempting to do each other in.

Bright Lights was filmed during December 1929 and January 1930, but it was given only a meager release by First National in the fall of 1930, and it didn't show up in New York until February 1931. There, it was reviewed adversely by *The Times*, which cited an "inept story which never rises above dime-store level" and color photography that was "none too good ... out of focus."[43]

Mackaill, miscast in this uninspired picture, broke a rib during the filming of *Bright Lights*. And not long after the film came out, Fay was dropped from the Warners roster and returned to the stage, thereafter to reappear only sporadically in movies such as *They Knew What They Wanted* (1940) and *Love Nest* (1951). A much brighter Hollywood future would be had by a bit player, John Carradine. In his second film, he can be spotted as a newspaper pho-

tographer who appears for the unwinding of Mackaill's tall tale. Long John's powerful voice is heard only in one line: "Hold still, please!"

OH, FOR A MAN!
(Fox; November 29, 1930)

Director-Producer: Hamilton MacFadden. Screenplay and Dialogue: Philip Klein, Lynn Starling. Based on the magazine story "Stolen Thunder" by Mary T. Watkins (1930). Photography: Charles Clarke. Editor: Al De Gaetano. Sound: E. Clayton Ward. Art Director: Stephen Goosson. Costumes: Sophie Wachner. Musical Director: Arthur Kay. Running Time: 78 minutes.

Cast: Jeanette MacDonald (Carlotta Manson), Reginald Denny (Barney McGann), Warren Hymer (Pug Morini), Marjorie White (Totsy Franklin), Alison Skipworth (Laura), Albert Conti (Peck), Bela Lugosi (Frescatti), André Cheron (Costello), William B. Davidson (Kerry Stokes), Bodil Rosing (masseuse), Donald Hall, Evelyn Hall, Althea Henly.

Songs: "I'm Just Nuts About You" [White], "On a Summer Night" [MacDonald] (William Kernell); "Anathema" [Denny] (Alexander von Fielitz); "Believe Me If All Those Endearing Young Charms" [Denny] (Matthew Locke, Thomas Moore). Operatic Excerpt: "The Liebestod," from *Tristan and Isolde* [MacDonald] (Richard Wagner).

The public turnabout against musicals was bound to affect the careers of those stars who had been brought to Hollywood because they could sing as well as talk. Many were forced to return to the legitimate stage or vaudeville or radio or whatever they were doing before, but for players like Jeanette MacDonald, who were deemed too valuable to leave idle, it meant an alteration of image. In the fall of 1930, after being dropped by Paramount, MacDonald was signed to a two-year contract by Fox with the intention of placing her in straight dramatic roles. *Variety* reported that the studio was declaring itself "off" musicals other than its current "Janet Gaynor–George Gershwin project."[44] That was *Delicious*, which was not released until the end of 1931 (see Chapter 11).

The first film of the three MacDonald made for Fox—all little more than program pictures—was *Oh, for a Man!*[45] Its *Pygmalion*-like story, about an opera singer who gives the Eliza Doolittle treatment to a burglar she catches in her apartment, provided an excuse for some music—four songs, plus the *Tristan und Isolde* excerpt that opens the film. But this was a light comedy, not a full-fledged musical.

MacDonald's romantic counterpart was the Englishman Reginald Denny, who, as an unconvincing Irishman named Barney Mc-Gann, catches the fancy of temperamental diva Carlotta Manson when he admits to her that good opera inspires him to do his best work. He also happens to own an impressive profile and a muscular build. "I can just see you now in tights," says Carlotta, dressed in the fetching negligee the intrusive gent has discovered her wearing. She submits the wary burglar to an audition. During his off-key rendering of a Germanic melody, she beams proudly—but the judges (one of whom is the then-obscure Bela Lugosi) are dumbfounded at the stranger's lack of vocal ability. However, to keep Carlotta happy, Barney is signed to a minor contract and told he can work his way up from the chorus.

After a few voice lessons, paid for by Carlotta, Barney declares that he doesn't want to be a singer. He's about to walk out when Carlotta desperately proposes marriage. Barney doesn't want to be referred to as "Mr. Carlotta Manson," so Carlotta vows to quit the opera. The now-married couple head off to Italy for their honeymoon. But there, the relationship sours, as Barney is annoyed by Carlotta's fans and she can't abide two of his old friends, nightclub singer Totsy Franklin (Marjorie White) and boxer Pug "The Walloping Wop" Morini (Warren Hymer), who are also honeymooning. Barney leaves his wife after a quarrel, and she returns to the States for the new opera season, but on the night after the opening performance, a shadowy figure sneaks into Carlotta's boudoir…

Oh, for a Man! didn't make much of an impact at the box office, but both *Variety* and *Pho-*toplay gave it glowing reviews for its freshness and good humor as well as Hamilton MacFadden's accomplished direction. Viewed today, the film seems a little too pat and talky, although the leads are well paired and MacDonald is photographed to great advantage, no matter the degree to which she's clothed. She sings only twice, William Kernell's romantic ballad "On a Summer Night" as well as the Wagner excerpt. (White's lone number, Kernell's "I'm Just Nuts About You," was missing from the archival print watched by the author.) Alison Skipworth is amusing as Carlotta's battleaxe maid and traveling companion. Early in the film, Carlotta is heard emitting moans of pleasure as a group of suitors awaits in the adjacent drawing room. "How much longer is this going to last?" complains a fidgety beau (William B. Davidson). "It won't be long now," replies the maid. "She always cries out like that at the end." Seconds later, Carlotta emerges—with a masseuse in tow.

As *Oh, for a Man!* was being filmed, an incident occurred in Europe that prompted the circulation of strange rumors which hounded MacDonald for nearly a year. In August 1930, Humbert, the crown prince of Italy, was injured in an auto accident in Belgium while on a clandestine ride with an American woman. The woman, who disappeared after the mishap, was alleged to be MacDonald. The story overseas was that the actress had been blinded in the crash, or been killed, or had committed suicide afterward. Confronted with the evidence of *Oh, for a Man!*, some in the European press insisted that a double must have been employed on screen. There was even a book written about the scandal, complete with MacDonald's photo on the cover. In the summer of 1931, MacDonald traveled to Europe for a personal-appearance tour to dispel the rumors herself. She even posed for photos that showed her reading the book, her mouth opened wide in mock astonishment. In time, everyone agreed that the actress had been a victim of mistaken identity.

CHAPTER 9

1929–1930: *A King and Two Aces*

The sameness of look and style that so hindered the first wave of the movie musical was periodically interrupted by films that overcame the dearth of creative and technical resources imposed by sound. That these films succeeded as they did was mainly a function of the creativity and power of their directors. Without the usual degree of interference by studio managers, and aided by the lax censorship of the period (even after the institution of the Production Code in 1930 by morality czar Will Hays), three men created works that had little or none of the trite plotting, cardboard characters and predictable bursts into song of their musical contemporaries. Ernst Lubitsch turned the limited operetta subgenre on its head with the sophisticated, continental *The Love Parade* (1929) and *Monte Carlo* (1930). With the darkly realistic *Applause* (1929), Rouben Mamoulian found new uses for sound and camera within a talkie format. And, in a rare examination of an ignored racial subculture, King Vidor ambitiously melded the themes of sexual and religious fervor to create *Hallelujah!* (1929).

Not coincidentally, the three worked at the industry's two leading companies—Lubitsch and Mamoulian for Paramount and Vidor for Metro-Goldwyn-Mayer. Since the days when Cecil B. DeMille began to flourish there, Paramount had been known as a "director's studio." Like DeMille, Lubitsch and Mamoulian were allowed to function as the producers of their films. B. P. Schulberg, the head of production, monitored the studio's "prestige" movies but did not participate as actively with them as with the bread-and-butter commercial projects. This European-style philosophy, noted author Thomas Schatz in his valuable behind-the-scenes study, *The Genius of the System*, was in direct opposition to the policies at other, more pinch-penny studios, where the size of the budget for a production was matched by the amount of front-office intervention in its making.[1]

At MGM, Vidor also was allowed unusual creative freedom, not because of any house style but because he had made a ton of money for his company. His epic war drama *The Big Parade* (1925), produced for about $250,000, grossed $3.5 million. Thereafter, Vidor was able to alternate conventional assignments (such as *Bardelys the Magnificent,* a swashbuckler with *Big Parade* star John Gilbert) with self-generated "prestige" projects (*La Bohème,* which teamed Gilbert with a chaste Lillian Gish). His most artistic silent was *The Crowd* (1928), an intimate, starkly realistic study of an anonymous big-city office worker. In this semi-documentary peopled with non-"names," the leads were an unknown, James Murray, and Vidor's actress wife, Eleanor Boardman. With production costs twice that of *The Big Parade, The Crowd* got made because Irving Thalberg and Louis B. Mayer thought it gave their studio a dollop of class. That it did, but the film also proved entertaining enough to the masses to turn a small profit.

With its expressionistic look and populist feel, *The Crowd* was influenced heavily by the European directors who brought their enlightening artistry to Hollywood during the 1920s. They emerged from various nations and influences, but they expressed themselves most uniformly through their free-wheeling cameras, inventive light-and-shadow effects and emphasis on realism in acting and theme. Paul Fejos and Victor Seastrom had cut their teeth in Hungary and Sweden, respectively, but most of the others either had been born in Germany or had migrated there to work in its flourishing postwar film industry. There were Josef von Sternberg, F. W. Murnau, Benjamin Christensen, Paul Leni—and Lubitsch, who was a top director-producer for the highly influential UFA studio. Lubitsch was brought to the United States by Mary Pickford, whom he directed, rather unhappily for both, in *Rosita* (1923). But his next project, Warner Bros.' *The Marriage Circle* (1924), began a very successful string of sophisticated domestic comedies that perfectly dissected the American psychology regarding two of its greatest preoccupations—sex and money. For MGM in 1927, he made *The Student Prince in Old Heidelberg*, a money-losing silent version of the hit operetta, which foreshadowed his interest in the future film musical genre. So did the striking ballroom sequence that climaxed his Warners feature *So This Is Paris* (1926); through elaborate multiple superimpositions, it presented Monte Blue, Patsy Ruth Miller, a jazz band, and dozens of extras dancing to music that could not be heard directly—but didn't need to be. As Lubitsch's silent films often communicated through a sort of rhythmic storytelling, one can easily understand his desire to orchestrate more explicit melodies.

Mamoulian, unlike Lubitsch, spent his formative years in the theater—in Moscow and London, although it was as one of Broadway's most inventive directors that he was summoned to Hollywood by Paramount in 1929. When he arrived in New York in 1926 and applied for work at the Theatre Guild, he was told he was "not the type" to direct an American play. Whereupon he helmed one of the most "American" of works: *Porgy*, the stylized dramatization of the DuBose Hayward novel that later would be adapted into *Porgy and Bess*. The success of that revolutionary play, in which Mamoulian employed sound to sometimes dazzling effect, brought him a contract from Paramount. Although all-black musicals had for years been part of the Broadway menu, the impact of the non-singing *Porgy* in 1927 may have influenced two major Hollywood studios to commence the filming of musical features with black casts in 1928 for release the following year. Besides *Hallelujah!* there was Fox's *Hearts in Dixie*, which is also included in this chapter to provide a more conventional comparison to Vidor's examination of African-American life.

No one in the cast of *Hallelujah!* had acted

in a film before. The French Maurice Chevalier, top-billed in *The Love Parade*, and the nightclub chanteuse Helen Morgan, the headliner of *Applause*, were hardly cut from the usual Hollywood-star cloth. But Vidor, Lubitsch and Mamoulian were willing to take chances across the board, and they helped bring definition to a musical genre that sorely needed some direction.

HEARTS IN DIXIE
(Fox; February 26, 1929)

and HALLELUJAH!
(MGM; August 20, 1929)

Hearts in Dixie

Director-Producer: Paul Sloane. Additional Direction: A. H. Van Buren. Story and Screenplay: Walter Weems. Photography: Glen MacWilliams. Editor: Alexander Troffey. Sound: Arthur L. von Kirbach. Assistant Director: Sam Wertzel. Dance Direction: Fanchon and Marco. Running Time: 71 minutes.

Cast: Clarence Muse (Nappus), Stepin Fetchit (Gummy), Eugene Jackson (Chiquapin), Bernice Pilot (Chloe), Clifford Ingram (Rammey), Mildred Washington (Trailia), Zack Williams (Deacon), Gertrude Howard (Emmy), Dorothy Morrison (Melia), Vivian Smith (Violet), Robert Brooks (True Love), A. C. H. Billbrew (voodoo woman), Richard Carlyle (white doctor), Billbrew Chorus.

Songs: "Hearts in Dixie" [offscreen singer over credits], "Here Comes the Bride" [wedding guests], "Jubilatin'" [wedding guests], "Lazy Song" [Fetchit] (Walter Weems, Howard Jackson); "Massa's in de Cold Ground" [danced by Fetchit, others], "Nelly Bly" [chorus], "Old Folks at Home" [Howard], "Ring, Ring de Banjo" [chorus] (Stephen Foster); "Carry Me Back to Old Virginny" [male chorus] (James A. Bland); "Mammy's Gone" [Muse] (B. G. De Sylva, Lew Brown, Ray Henderson); "All God's Chillin Got Shoes," "By and By," "Cat Song," "Cotton Dance Song," "Cotton Pickin' Song," "Every Time I Feel de Spirit," "Liza Jane," "Oh, Peter, Go Ring Dem Bells," "Steal Away," "Way Down in the Cotton Field" (trad.).

Hallelujah!

Director: King Vidor. Scenario: Wanda Tuchock. Dialogue: Ransom Rideout. Treatment:

Richard Schayer. Story: King Vidor. Titles: Marian Ainslee. Photography: Gordon Avil. Editors: Hugh Wynn, Anson Stevenson. Sound: Douglas Shearer. Assistant Director: Robert A. Golden. Art Director: Cedric Gibbons. Costumes: Henrietta Fraser. Musical Director: Eva Jessye. Running Time: 109 minutes (sound version; also released as silent).

Cast: Daniel L. Haynes (Zeke), Nina Mae McKinney (Chick), William E. Fountaine (Hot Shot), Harry Gray (Parson), Fannie Belle de Knight (Mammy), Everett McGarrity (Spunk), Victoria Spivey (Missy Rose), Milton Dickerson, Robert Couch, WalterTait (Johnson kids), Evelyn Pope Burwell, Eddie Connors (singers), Dixie Jubilee Singers.

Songs: "Swanee Shuffle" [McKinney], "Waiting at the End of the Road" [Haynes, Dixie Jubilee Singers] (Irving Berlin); "Dinah" [band in saloon] (Sam M. Lewis, Joe Young, Harry Akst); "Goin' Home" [Haynes] (William Arms Fisher, adapted from Antonin Dvořák's "New World" Symphony); "Old Folks at Home" [chorus] (Stephen Foster); "St. Louis Blues" [McKinney] (W. C. Handy); "Carry Me to the Water" [congregation], "E. I. O." [Spivey, children], "Give Me That Old Time Religion" [congregation; reprised by McKinney], "Go Down, Moses" [offscreen chorus], "Great Day" [children's chorus], "I Belong to Dat Band" [Spivey, Haynes, congregation], "Oh Cotton Hey Cotton" [Haynes, family], "Swing Low, Sweet Chariot" [Haynes, mourners] (trad.).

Academy Award Nomination: Best Director (King Vidor, 1929-30).

Disc: RCA Victor 22097 (Haines/"Waiting at the End of the Road"/78); Music Masters JJA-19744 (bootleg LP; ST).

Video: MGM-UA (cassette/laserdisc).

Of the two African-American musicals of 1929, *Hearts in Dixie* and *Hallelujah!*, the former made it to theaters first.[2] It was advertised as "the first authentic screen record of the Old South. ... All the happy-go-lucky joy of living, laughter and all-embracing gusto of plantation life." Comedy and tragedy were mixed in the slight, episodic story of a poor farmer (Clarence Muse) of the 1870s who endures the deaths of his daughter and granddaughter to send his remaining grandchild (Eugene "Pineapple" Jackson) up North to school so the youth doesn't turn out like his layabout father (Stepin Fetchit).

MGM's *Hallelujah!* was the first film with an all-black cast to be produced by a major Hollywood studio.

Fetchit (1892–1985), who played a drawling, woman-crazy fool, held up the comedy end and attracted most of the critical attention. Fetchit had appeared in a few silents and made a stir in a featured role in the early Fox all-talkie *The Ghost Talks*, but this film made him the first real African-American movie celebrity. *Hearts in Dixie* initially was intended as a short subject, but Fox so liked Fetchit's performance that it expanded the Paul Sloane–directed picture to feature length, with traditional spirituals and other period songs comprising most of the musical content. (MGM's announcement that it was to make its own all-black film may have prompted Fox as well.)

Viewed today, *Hearts in Dixie* engenders predictably ambivalent feelings. Muse (1889–1979) delivers a positive, affecting performance as the self-sacrificing patriarch, and there is a quite powerful scene in which he sings a lullaby, "Mammy's Gone," as he gently rocks his grandson and granddaughter to sleep. Muse's exchanges with the young Jackson convey a remarkable tenderness. But Fetchit's portrayal of the good-for-nothing Gummy is difficult to endure. "Sure does hurt me seeing you do all the work," he says from his over-familiar front-porch chair as his new wife, Violet (Vivian Smith), chops wood. Her reply: "The only time you ever work is when you're watching me!" Gummy forgets his shiftless routine to do a hot dance, as a witnessing chorus races through "Massa's in de Cold Ground," and to mumble through the comical "Lazy Song" while actually chopping wood himself. As with all very early talkies, the dialogue is delivered deliberately, but the pace seems doubly slow in *Hearts in Dixie,* possibly to confirm the opinion that black people talked sort of funny. As if to compensate, there is some surprisingly fluid cinematography, made possible through Fox's sound-on-film Movietone format, especially during a lengthy tracking shot in which Violet walks her errant husband home from one of his outdoor sleeping spells.

The studio chose to begin *Hearts in Dixie* with a prologue, spoken on a proscenium stage by Richard Carlyle, who plays the only white character in the movie, a physician. In attempting to explain the purpose of the film, he calls it "a slice of life … about a race of humans. … Our skins vary in color, but we all laugh when we're happy, we sing, dance, work—we love." This at least seems to indicate that the filmmakers' collective heart was in the right place. Indeed, the African-American film historian Donald Bogle, in his encyclopedia *Blacks in American Film and Television* (1988), credits *Hearts in Dixie* with an attempt, rare for the period, to depict the everyday life of black people. However, Bogle also criticizes the movie: "Throughout, the black characters are almost mindlessly placid, so much that the whole film looks like a parody."[3]

The press reaction to *Hearts in Dixie* was mainly favorable, in part because its fictional populace conformed to the prevailing stereotypes of blacks as childlike, unambitious and perpetually happy. (The actors are constantly breaking into song, although the story limits the length of most of the tunes to mere seconds.) Mordaunt Hall of *The New York Times* called the film "restful … gentle in its mood and truthful in its reflection of the black men of those days down yonder in the cornfields."[4] Richard Watts, Jr., of the *New York Herald Tribune* cheered it as "immensely affecting and honestly amusing."[5] *Hearts in Dixie* found a sizable, and generally respectful, audience (black and white) in the public sector.

Six months after the debut of *Hearts in Dixie* came *Hallelujah!,* the realization of a personal dream for King Vidor (1894–1982), a native Texan who had been a movie director since 1914. He had long wanted to make a film that, cast only with blacks, would combine, as he recalled in his autobiography, the "sincerity and fervor of their religious expression" and "the honest simplicity of their sexual drives.

> In many instances, the intermingling of these two activities seemed to offer strikingly dramatic content. The environment of my youth … had left many indelible memories of the colored man; and I had heard my sister rocked to sleep each night to one of the best repertoires of Negro spirituals in the South.[6]

To interest MGM, which was not about to make a movie that probably would be barred from the all-white theaters of the South, Vidor pledged to sink his own salary into the project as long as the company matched that contribution. The reply from Metro major-domo Nicholas Schenck: "If that's the way you feel about it, I'll let you make a picture about whores."[7] Vidor wrote the story himself, with Paul Robeson and Ethel Waters in mind for the young cotton worker and the hussy who leads him astray romantically and spiritually. Instead, he got Daniel L. Haynes (1894–1954), an understudy in the New York cast of *Show Boat* (and, according to the film's pressbook, an ordained Baptist minister), and Nina Mae McKinney (1913–1967), a teenage chorine from the Broadway musical *Blackbirds of 1928.* McKinney was a last-minute replacement for Honey Brown, a Harlem cabaret singer who had to drop out of the project because of illness. Also in the cast of film neophytes was Harry Gray, an 86-year-old ex-slave lately a porter for the *Amsterdam News*, a black newspaper in New York. He was to play the male lead's father, a rural preacher and tenant farmer. Cast as his mother was Fannie Belle de Knight, who had played in "colored" stock for decades. Victoria Spivey (1908–1976), a real-life blues singer who would get to sing only briefly in the film, was signed to play the moral counterpart to McKinney's character.

Haynes, interviewed for a fan magazine during filming, was quoted as being optimistic about the effect *Hallelujah!* would have upon the public perception of blacks:

> I think and hope this picture will do much for my people. Mr. Vidor has written a story that will be a classic of the Southern Negro. He seems to know us as few white men have bothered to know us. Our race is rich with talents that have gone unrecognized for centuries. This may be our opportunity to prove ourselves.[8]

As hopeful as these comments sound, the tenor of the time was such that Haynes and McKinney received threats of violence against them, and Vidor would not allow them to go anywhere without a guard.[9]

The story, outlined by Vidor and fleshed out by his frequent collaborator, scenarist Wanda Tuchock, and others, concerned a strapping young man named Zeke, who works on his father's farm somewhere in the Deep South in the present day. Part of his large, loving family is Missy Rose (Spivey), who had been adopted into the clan at some point. She and Zeke share an unusual but undefined affection, which is probably romantic. Accompanied by his younger brother Spunk (Everett McGarrity), Zeke takes the family's cotton crop to market to a mill adjoining what looks to be the Mississippi River; there he joins in the singing of "Waiting at the End of the Road," a pseudo gospel tune written for the film by Irving Berlin. Two songs by Berlin were added to the film by MGM; this was against Vidor's wishes and was done because Irving Thalberg wanted material in *Hallelujah!* that could sell records.[10] Most of the remaining music consists of traditional black spirituals presented not as conventional "numbers" but as spontaneous outpourings of the characters' religiousity.

The other Berlin song, "Swanee Shuffle," is sung by McKinney as Chick, a dancer of ill repute who comes on to Zeke after noticing his possession of the $100 bounty from the sold cotton. Accompanied by a jazz band and a group of singing waiters, she performs in a smoky saloon where she has lured Zeke to a crooked crap game run by her con-artist accomplice, Hot Shot (William E. Fountaine). Zeke loses all of his money, then demands to see Hot Shot's dice. The two men get into a fight, and as they grapple for Big Shot's gun, it goes off. Zeke grabs the gun and disperses the crowd by firing some wild shots into the air, then he turns around to look at the moaning victim of the first shot. It is Spunk, who had just walked into the joint to find his brother. Zeke carries him to their wagon, and the young man dies on the journey home. A grief-stricken Zeke repents by deciding to turn his life over to God. He becomes Brother Zekiel, a revivalist preacher.

A while later, Zeke rides into a small town by train, where the crowd gathered to see him includes Chick and Hot Shot. They taunt their old acquaintance, who rebukes them "for making fun of the Lord." But at a rally enhanced by the singing of "Give Me That Old Time Religion," Chick is so affected by Zeke's sermon comparing a train ride to a journey to Hell that she breaks down sobbing and renouncing her evil ways. Her emotions run just as high during a ceremony of mass baptism ("Carry Me to the Water"). After ritualistically immersing her in the lake, Zeke carries the screaming woman to his tent where he is compelled to make love to her. Only the intervention of his Mammy, who believes that Chick is a hypocrite, keeps the two apart.

Chick ends her relationship with Hot Shot, who belittles her conversion: "You ain't never gonna quit sinnin', gal—it's right there in your blood." She responds by knocking him to the floor with a poker. Meanwhile, Zeke, bothered by his desire for Chick, proposes marriage to a receptive Missy Rose. But at the next revival meeting, as the congregation emotionally sings, dances and waves hands to "I Belong to Dat Band," Chick maneuvers her way to the front of the church, where Zeke sees her. Entranced, he robotically follows her through the crowd and out of the building, then carries her off into the night. Missy Rose runs outside, calling "Brother Zeke, where are you?" She re-enters the church, moaning "Zeke's gone!" as her sobs bring the parishioners to their knees in prayer.

Months later, Zeke and Chick are living in a modest rural dwelling as he holds a job in a sawmill. Hot Shot has returned, however, and Chick carries on with him while Zeke is at work. One day, Zeke comes home early to find Hot Shot's carriage next to the house, but the hustler flees out the back door as Chick convinces Zeke that he is mistaken. Chick gives Zeke dinner, then sings him to sleep—her lullaby is "St. Louis Blues"—and is driven away by Hot Shot. Zeke, who was feigning sleep, runs after the two into a swamp. The carriage crashes, mortally injuring Chick. "Before I let you get away from me like that, I'll break you in two!" Zeke warns the moaning woman. "I'se broke in two already, Zeke," replies Chick, seconds before her final breath. In the film's most famous sequence, Zeke pursues Hot Shot, who had paused a few yards away to see if Chick was all right. The younger man easily outraces the stout gambler, whom Zeke catches and then strangles to death.

Zeke is sent to prison for murder; he is briefly shown working on a chain gang. (Vidor filmed, then deleted, a sequence in which Zeke saves his fellow convicts from a flood.) He gains probation after several years and is shown strumming "Goin' Home" on a guitar while on the train home. In the end, he is welcomed back by his forgiving family—including Missy Rose, who has never stopped loving him. Zeke's redemption is complete.

In 1929, *Hallelujah!* could not garner more than a handful of bookings south of the Mason-Dixon Line and was seen infrequently outside of major Northern markets.[11] It cost $320,000 to produce; it lost that, plus $120,000. But it has rightly been acclaimed as one of the best films of its era, and a milestone in its honest, if stereotypical, dramatization of African-American life. Its melodramatic morality-play story—saved vs. unsaved, country vs. city—is nothing new, although it is refreshing in its simplicity. The most powerful scenes are the most elemental: the soothing lullaby with which Mammy rocks her children to sleep, the emotional riverside mass baptism, Zeke's furtive hunt through the swamp. On the other hand, we must wince through the moments in which

the stimulating of Zeke's hormones turns him into a sex-crazed zombie, such as when he goes wide-eyed over Missy Rose as she plays "The Wedding March" on the piano. Commentators of the day, who were mainly respectful (if a little suspicious) of the picture, probably loved scenes like those because they validated their views of black males as undisciplined fools. Their remarks were often condescending, as was *Variety's* "Mark," in a mostly complimentary review, when discussing the ensemble scenes: "Apparently ... Vidor had a mighty tough job holding that bunch back, yet he held them under remarkable restraint and still brought out the effects desired."[12] Indeed, the performances by the cast of unknowns are impressive, especially McKinney's, but none of the actors went on to mainstream success in the white-dominated world of entertainment.[13]

In a time in which even a well-meaning film such as this could not generate a racially integrated New York opening (dual premieres were held downtown and in Harlem), comments like Richard Watts, Jr.'s, were remarkable.

> *Hallelujah!* is one of the great motion pictures, a work to be compared, with unabashed enthusiasm, to such a foreign classic as the mighty *Potemkin.* It is poetry, drama and pictorial magnificence, combined in one stalwart whole. ... It is the talking picture made into a distinctive American dramatic form.[14]

Unrestrained praise for an all-black film was unusual in a racial climate filled with attitudes like that of the English critic James Agate. "Personally I don't care if it took Mr. Vidor 10 years to train these niggers," sneered Agate. "All I know is that 10 minutes is all I can stand of nigger ecstasy."[15]

Its dramatic power aside, the most astounding achievement of *Hallelujah!* is Vidor's use of sound, both as a planned technique and as an aversion of disaster. Vidor had no portable sound recording equipment when he began six weeks of location filming in Tennessee and Arkansas in the fall of 1928. He had figured that MGM would dispatch a sound truck his way, but the company was still constructing the first sound stage on its West Coast lot. Thus, the decision was made to shoot *Hallelujah!* as a silent. This freed the camera to a pleasing extent for the outdoor scenes—e.g., the sermons and baptisms—but made it necessary to add the dialogue later in the studio. The chore of matching the sound and picture was left to film editor Hugh Wynn, who, before the advent of the Moviola, had great difficulty identifying the words that were mouthed on the silent footage. Practically as it ran through the projector, the film had to be marked with a grease pencil in spots to ease the synchronization process. The laborious task soon sent the cutter into an emotional breakdown, which kept him from the production for a week.

Sound effects had to be added to certain scenes, which included the climax in the swamp, which had been filmed back in Arkansas. Vidor, in watching his aides create their own sounds before a studio microphone, was inspired to express the swamp scene in an impressionistic manner. The sense of dread created was thus heightened by the characters' movements. "When someone stepped on a broken branch," recalled the director, "we made it sound as if bones were breaking. As the pursued victim withdrew his foot from the stickiness of the mud, we made the vacuum sound strong enough to pull him down into hell."[16]

Touches such as those are what have made *Hallelujah!* an unforgettable moviegoing experience, and what Donald Bogle has called "the first of Hollywood's attempts to deal with the black family ... directly related to subsequent black family dramas such as *The Learning Tree* (1969) and *Sounder* (1972)."[17]

APPLAUSE
(Paramount; October 9, 1929)

Director: Rouben Mamoulian. Producers: Jesse L. Lasky, Walter Wanger. Associate Producer: Monta Bell. Adaptation and Dialogue: Garrett Fort. Based on the novel by Beth Brown (1928). Photography: George Folsey. Editor: John Bassler. Sound: Ernest F. Zatorsky. Running Time: 78 minutes (sound version; also released as silent).

Cast: Helen Morgan (Kitty Darling), Joan Peers (April Darling), Fuller Mellish, Jr. (Hitch Nelson), Jack Cameron (Joe King), Henry Wadsworth (Tony), Dorothy Cumming (Mother Superior), Jack Singer (producer), Paul Barrett (Slim Lamont).

Songs: "Ave Maria" [nuns at convent] (words, trad.; music, Franz Schubert); "Doin' the Raccoon" [Morgan, Mellish, chorus] (Raymond Klages, J. Fred Coots); "Everybody's Doing It" [chorister] (Irving Berlin); "Everything I Do—I Do for You" [offcamera singer] (Al Lewis, Al Sherman, Abner Silver); "Give Your Little Baby Lots of Lovin'" [Morgan, chorus; reprised by Morgan, then by Peers, chorus] (Dolly Morse, Joe Burke); "The Oceana Roll" [Morgan, Cameron, chorus] (Roger Lewis, Lucien Denni); "Pretty Baby" [Morgan] (Gus Kahn, Tony Jackson, Egbert Van Alstyne); "San" [chorus] (Lindsay McPhail, Walter Michels); "Waiting for the Robert E. Lee" [Cameron, chorus] (L. Wolfe Gilbert, Lewis F. Muir); "What Wouldn't I Do for That Man?" [Morgan] (E. Y. Harburg, Jay Gorney); "Yaaka Hula Hickey Dula" [danced by chorister] (E. Ray Goetz, Joe Young, Pete Wendling).

Disc: RCA Victor 22149 (Morgan/"What Wouldn't I Do for That Man?"/78).

"Everything I saw was wrong, and I decided to do the exact opposite," Rouben Mamoulian recalled decades after his first lesson in filmmaking technique.[18] After signing a one-year contract with Paramount in 1929, he had been given full rein by the studio to walk around and acquaint himself with How Things Were Done. But the visually minded director (1897–1987) was hardly daunted at the prospect of working with unyielding cameras and balky microphones. If cinematic fluidity could be achieved only with an effort that would be as taxing as moving a house, then, he decided, "We'll just move the house, that's all!"[19] He did. Although the same claim could be made for *Hallelujah!* Mamoulian's *Applause* can probably be called the first artistically successful American talking film.

Historians have long cited *Applause's* innovations in cinematography and sound; in fact, the advances were noted by practically every pseudo-expert who saw the film upon its initial release. But also ahead of its time was the grim, unsparing realism that permeated the 78-minute adaptation of Beth Brown's novel about a fading burlesque queen and her virtuous daughter. In 1929 and '30, there wasn't much of an audience for that brand of entertainment, and the film—meekly advertised by Paramount as just another mother-love story—was considered an interesting misfire. Jack Alicoate, editor and publisher of *The Film Daily*, thought *Applause* important enough to explain this paradox in a front-page column on the eve of the New York premiere:

> Here's one … that will probably cause more argument than any picture of the current season. … The Ayes will tell you that from a technical standpoint it is the most artistic and progressive production since *Variety*. That the director Rouben Mamoulian, who came to pictures from the Theatre Guild, brings with him a new definite and sparkling directorial touch. That Helen Morgan … gives one of the finest character studies of the year. That the story by Beth Brown is one of ruthless, virile, naked passions. … [But] the equally vehement Noes will tell you that the story is sordid, oppressive and without entertainment value … that it borders entirely too near the line to be played in anything but those houses catering to sophisticated audiences and, that this type of story should never be placed upon the screen. … No exhibitor should play it without first seeing it.[20]

It's difficult to imagine anyone but Helen Morgan (1900–1941) as the self-destructive Kitty Darling, although Paramount reportedly negotiated with Mae West for the starring role before deciding on a woman whose own life was nearly as tragic as that of the character she played.[21] The plump but fragile Morgan was not yet 30 years old but had done enough living—as a club singer, stage actress (*Show Boat*), New York speakeasy manager, and budding alcoholic—to pass for the dissipated, fortyish Kitty. Morgan's preparation for the film was serious, if we are to believe the report from *Photoplay* that she "bought cheap and inferior scents in keeping with her role."[22] Mamoulian told Charles Higham and Joel Greenberg that Morgan was "one of the most wonderful people I have ever known. Very talented, very sensitive, with an intuitive flair for acting, totally dedicated to her art."[23] *Applause* was filmed at Paramount's Astoria facility on Long Island, and on location in New York City.

Miles Kreuger calls *Applause* an "antimusical," and a case could be made for its exclusion from a book such as this. The film is filled with music, but it carries little primacy. Songs are mostly heard as part of stage performances that do little more than suggest the atmosphere of the burlesque house; they aren't meant to advance the plot or provide some kind

of fantasy element. The titles and lyrics hardly matter.[24] Mamoulian further shows his indifference to this aspect of his film by allowing only a couple of songs to be heard distinctly all the way through; the others fade into the background of dialogue scenes or are halted entirely. Only two songs fit neatly into the story. "Give Your Little Baby Lots of Lovin'" is repeated often as a reminder of the affection Kitty has for her only child, April (Joan Peers, 1911–1975). "What Wouldn't I Do for That Man?" sung *a cappella* by Kitty as she admires a photograph of her boyfriend, Hitch Nelson, explains her dedication to their relationship. But Mamoulian undercuts the romantic effect by splitting the screen diagonally, as Kitty continues humming her song, to reveal the homely, skeletal Hitch (Fuller Mellish, Jr., who gives the one bad performance in the cast) kissing a younger, more beautiful woman in a room across the hall.

The sound of music is used memorably in the opening sequence. Newspapers are blown by the wind down a deserted main street in a hick town; a faded handbill announcing the coming of Kitty Darling and her burlesque show is snatched by a dog, who runs down the street as a bass drum begins to be heard from a distance. Hearing the building music, the townspeople rush out of their buildings to get a look and listen. The song, "There'll Be a Hot Time in the Old Town Tonight," grows louder until the troupe, led by the blonde Kitty blowing kisses aboard a barouche, rides in as the excited onlookers chatter. Mamoulian cuts directly to that night's performance at the town's dingy burlesque house, and he glides his camera across the chubby legs and aging faces of chorus girls singing "The Oceana Roll" while backing Kitty and the troupe's clown, Joe King (Jack Cameron). Kitty moves uncertainly, and Joe whispers to her his concern for her health. At the intermission, Kitty rushes backstage to read a telegram—then faints. The stage manager summons a doctor, who emerges from a balcony fling with a dame to go backstage to tend to Kitty. Joe and the chorus return to the footlights to perform "Waiting for the Robert E. Lee," but soon the news travels up and down the line: "Kitty's got a baby!" King and the girls wander tentatively into the dressing room where Kitty lies; they circle the bed as an overhead camera reveals Kitty's subjective view of the hovering heads. For now, she has forgotten

"Mummy, take me with you. Please" is the caption to this still from *Applause* with Joan Peers and the motherly Helen Morgan.

the news she had read in the telegram: Her husband is about to be put to death for murder.

Five years later, Kitty is teaching little April to dance to the tune of "Pretty Baby." Joe enters her apartment with a necklace that's a gift for the girl. He wants to marry Kitty and make a good home for her and April, but the career-minded Kitty declines. "I'm headed straight to Broadway and the big time!" she assures him. Joe insists that the show-business life is harmful to April, and he suggests that Kitty send the girl to convent school for a proper upbringing. A shot of April with her necklace fades into her holding a set of rosary beads as the Mother Superior introduces her to the convent.

Twelve more years pass. The alcoholic Kitty has little to enjoy but the companionship of the unfaithful Hitch, her new stage comic. He's upset that April, now 17, remains at the expensive convent, and he threatens Kitty that he

will leave her unless April is withdrawn so she can join their act. "We'll just be one big, happy family!" he says, but his silhouetted image against the wall represents the darker side of his nature. As April says goodbye to her Mother Superior, Mamoulian uses a lengthy tracking shot (to the strains of "Ave Maria," sung by a group of nuns in prayer) through the halls and grounds of the convent to contrast its serene, morally upright sterility with the big-city hustle and cacophony of noise into which the girl is now thrust. April, directed to the New York burlesque theater where her mom is performing, is overwhelmed at the sight of Kitty's suggestive dance (to "Give Your Little Baby Lots of Lovin'") and the leering, grotesque faces of the audience shouting insults at the stage. She also doesn't care for her mother's relationship with Hitch.

Kitty promises that if April joins the act, after a fashion the three of them will quit show business and settle down. She sings a "lullaby" to the girl, but all she thinks of is "Give Your Little Baby Lots of Lovin'." April, meanwhile, says a prayer to herself. Mamoulian allows us to hear both. April's dreams are represented by a montage of images from the "clean" convent and the "dirty" city. Shortly thereafter, Kitty and Hitch are married, but he makes sexual advances to the girl. She flees to the streets and is rescued from a masher by Tony (Henry Wadsworth), a gentle sailor who is as unspoiled as she. The kindred souls fall instantly in love, and after a late dinner, greet the sunrise from the top of the Brooklyn Bridge. A few days later, as they sit atop a skyscraper, Tony proposes marriage. Because his hitch is about to end, they can wed the next day and move to his farm in Wisconsin. April happily accepts, and Kitty gives her blessing.

Hitch is angry about April's impending exit and, lashing out at her mother, pronounces the older woman out of the act. He tells Kitty she has little prospects of solo work ("You're a joke! You're a fat old woman!"), then walks out. Not wanting to leave her mother by herself, April changes her mind about the wedding. She gives Tony the news in a restaurant; she wants to stay in showbiz, she claims. He replies that he'll re-enlist and sail to the West Indies. As April picks up a water glass, the scene shifts to Kitty setting hers down in her flat. Only she has just taken poison, for her dreams of Broadway are gone and she cannot bear to impede her daughter's future. After a few minutes of waiting for the poison to take effect, she changes her mind and cries, "April! April!" She struggles to get to the theater, where her show is to close that evening. Hitch and the stage manager think she's drunk. As April and Hitch bicker over Kitty's condition, the dying Kitty writhes on a cot.

April goes on in place of her mother, reprising "Give Your Little Baby Lots of Lovin'." She's a smash hit, but she runs offstage in hysterics. Tony is there, having apparently had second thoughts about the West Indies, and she rushes into his arms. April begs him to take her away from this tawdry life, but explains that she cannot leave Kitty. "Let her come with us," he eagerly replies. They can't wait to tell Kitty the happy news, but the film fades out on a shot of her face smiling from a poster not unlike the handbill shown in the opening scene. They will be too late.

Applause is a triumph of style over substance, as Brown's sobby story is given new life by Mamoulian's celebrated effects. He could make the camera more flexible by filming some shots silent—for example, those in which he pans the burlesque house or in footage of the young lovers walking on the real Brooklyn Bridge—and then wild-tracking sound in later, as King Vidor did in *Hallelujah!* However, enabling us to hear Morgan's lullaby and Peers' prayer at once took more ingenuity. Why not two microphones instead of one? Because it can't be done, said the sound men. And why not shoot the scene all the way through, without one cut? Impossible, said the cameraman, George Folsey. "Luckily the bosses told them they'd have to do the picture my way," said Mamoulian.

> It was five thirty before we had taken two takes of the scene. I had to tell Folsey where to put the lights; he wouldn't even put them up himself. I went home discouraged, worn out. Next morning when I arrived at the studio, the enormous Irish doorman, in a most resplendent uniform—he always reminded me of Emil Jannings in *The Last Laugh*—took his hat off and performed a deep oriental kind of bow, saying, "A happy good morning to you, Mr. Mamoulian," and he opened the door wide. He'd always looked down to me up to then. I was so young, so new. ...[25]

Mamoulian learned that Adolph Zukor, Jesse Lasky and all the big shots at Paramount had looked at the hastily developed footage of the two-channel take, and were raving about it. Their order was to give the director anything he wanted. Mamoulian walked on the set, to a reception more favorable than that of the day before. Folsey, who had questioned Mamoulian's ability, had only to ask where the director wanted the camera.

For Mamoulian—whose emphasis on visuals stemmed from his belief that film was "closer as a medium to painting than to the stage"[26]—*Applause* marked an impressive beginning to an accomplished, if unprolific (16 films in 28 years), career as a Hollywood director. It proved that the sound cinema had the potential to match the artistic beauty lost in the hasty transition from golden silence to often-cheapening talk.

THE LOVE PARADE
(Paramount, November 19, 1929)

Director-Producer: Ernst Lubitsch. Dialogue Director: Perry Ivins. Screenplay: Guy Bolton. Story: Ernest Vajda. Based on the play *Le Prince Consort* by Léon Xanrof and Jules Chancel. Photography: Victor Milner. Editor: Merrill White. Sound: Franklin Hansen. Art Director: Hans Dreier. Costumes: Travis Banton. Musical Director: Victor Schertzinger. Running Time: 110 minutes (sound version; also released as silent).

Cast: Maurice Chevalier (Count Alfred Renard), Jeanette MacDonald (Queen Louise), Lupino Lane (Jacques), Lillian Roth (Lulu), Edgar Norton (Master of Ceremonies), Lionel Belmore (Prime Minister), Albert Roccardi (Foreign Minister), Carl Stockdale (Admiral), Eugene Pallette (Minister of War), Russell Powell (Afghan Ambassador), E. H. Calvert (Ambassador), André Cheron (Le Mari), Yola D'Avril (Paulette), Winter Hall (priest), Ben Turpin (cross-eyed lackey), Anton Vaverka, Albert De Winton, William von Hardenburg (cabinet ministers), Margaret Fealy, Virginia Bruce, Josephine Hall, Rosalind Charles, Hélène Friend (ladies-in-waiting), Jean Harlow.

Songs: "Anything to Please the Queen" [Chevalier, MacDonald], "Champagne" [Lane], "Dream Lover" [MacDonald, Fealy, Bruce, Hall, Charles, Friend], "Let's Be Common" [Lane, Roth], "March of the Grenadiers" [MacDonald, chorus], "My Love Parade" [Chevalier, MacDonald, twice], "Nobody's Using It Now" [Chevalier], "The Queen Is Always Right" [Lane, Roth, servants], "Paris, Stay the Same" [Chevalier, Lane], "Sylvania's Queen" [chorus] (Clifford Grey, Victor Schertzinger); "Valse Tatjana" [ballet] (O. Potoker).

Academy Award Nominations (all for 1929-30): Best Picture, Best Director (Ernst Lubitsch), Best Actor (Maurice Chevalier), Best Cinematography (Victor Milner), Best Interior Decoration (Hans Dreier), Best Sound Recording (Franklin Hansen).

Disc: RCA Victor 22247 (MacDonald/"Dream Lover"/"March of the Grenadiers"/78); RCA Victor 22285 (Chevalier/"My Love Parade"/"Nobody's Using It Now"/78); RCA Victor 22368 (Chevalier/preceding songs in French/78); RCA Victor 22294 (Chevalier/"Paris, Stay the Same"/78); La Nadine 260 (bootleg LP; ST); WRC SH 156 (bootleg LP; ST).

Ernst Lubitsch, usually one of the wiliest filmmakers in Hollywood, was frantic. His first talking picture was at hand, and although he had no less than Maurice Chevalier—fresh from his smash debut in *Innocents of Paris*—at his disposal, he was at wit's end in finding a leading lady. He required someone who was young, could sing and dance, and look regal enough to be a queen but ravishing enough to fill out a skimpy nightgown. Lubitsch (1892–1947) tested several actresses for the role. He liked Bebe Daniels the most and would have signed her—a move which would have left *Rio Rita* without its best asset and might have brought a premature end to RKO. But then he watched a screen test that Paramount had shelved the previous year, 1928. Jeanette MacDonald had made the test in hopes of being cast with Richard Dix in a talkie comedy called *Nothing but the Truth*. Instead, she was hired for what would be perceived as the finest musical film of the 1929-30 period.

MacDonald (1903–1965), a former chorus girl, had lately been playing ingénues in lackluster Broadway productions—*Boom Boom; Yes, Yes, Yvette;* and *Angela*, the show in which her performance prompted Dix to commission her screen test. But with Lubitsch, she had first-rate material: the 1919 source play *The Prince Consort* by Léon Xanrof and Jules Chancel transformed into a light operetta by Guy Bolton and Ernest Vajda's sparkling dialogue and Victor Schertzinger and Clifford Grey's intoxicating music and lyrics. Like many a Lubitsch film, *The Love Parade* was set in a mythical European locale, which somehow enabled puritanism-tinged American audiences to eavesdrop on its adult situations without feeling guilty. Whether they would like it or not—and virtually everybody did—all could agree that they had never seen a talkie quite like this one.

The memorable first few minutes of the battle-of-the-sexes story skillfully tell us all we need to know about the personality of Count Alfred Renard, the dashing rogue played by Chevalier. After an attractive opening title in which the vision of champagne bottles, the Eiffel Tower and the legs of showgirls set the scene in Paris, we move to the suite of Alfred,

Maurice Chevalier and Jeanette MacDonald fight a royal battle of the sexes in Ernst Lubitsch's wonderful *The Love Parade*.

the military attaché to Paris for the tiny kingdom of Sylvania. His efficient butler, Jacques (Lupino Lane), sings "Champagne" as he prepares a dinner for two, then, for effect, yanks the tablecloth out from under the place setting. The voices of a man and a woman are heard arguing from the bedroom. Alfred emerges. "She's terribly jealous," he says in a typically Chevalierian aside to the audience. A young woman (Yola D'Avril) enters, brandishing a garter. We see by her legs that it is not hers. She pulls out a small revolver. There is a commotion at the door; her husband (André Cheron) storms in. Caught in an adulterous transgression, the woman shoots herself. The grieving husband picks up the handgun and shoots Alfred point-blank in the chest. Alfred, prepared for the worst, feels for the blood that isn't running down his shirt. The men examine the gun—blanks. The woman arises, unhurt. Alfred tosses the weapon in a nearby drawer that is full of re-

volvers. Not content to end our introduction there, Lubitsch has the cuckold unsuccessfully attempt to zip up the back of his wife's dress. Alfred, with much more practice at this kind of thing, accomplishes the task in one jerk of his arm: "Voilà!" When the Sylvanian ambassador to France (E. H. Calvert) confronts Alfred, we know what for. "This scandal will be your last," says the perturbed diplomat, "at least your last in Paris." Alfred withdraws to the balcony, where he looks out over the skyline and sings the wistful "Paris, Stay the Same," as scores of his female admirers toast him from their balconies and opened windows.

Alfred is ordered to report to MacDonald's Queen Louise, whose introduction to us is as remarkable as his. Her ladies-in-waiting (including the young Virginia Bruce) enter her bedchamber as she stirs. "Why am I always awakened from my dreams?" she complains. Of what did she dream? Her "Dream Lover," she sings as she rises from her bed to show off her lilting soprano and see-through negligee. In her bath, Louise gets more to the point: "Marriage, marriage ... in all my country, nothing else is ever spoken of ... morning, noon, and night." No kidding, for the cabinet ministers are already outside pacing with concern. The queen has rejected all of her prospective suitors, who are hard enough to find, for as beautiful as the young monarch is, her husband will be merely a prince consort, with "a thousand duties and no rights." Nonsense, Louise tells her cabinet during their daily confab, some man can be found who will love her in spite of her station. She bares her left leg: "There's only one other leg like that in the whole of Sylvania." She reveals her other limb: "And that's it!"

So there they are, two beautiful people who are destined to come together, although not in the most conventional fashion. Alfred is made to explain his trespasses to the queen, and Louise clearly becomes aroused as she reads the report of his noctural pursuits. Alfred is oddly delighted that their much-scrutinized first dinner date cannot become an all-nighter—but the reality of their relationship sets in as soon as they come to the altar. Alfred must pledge to fulfill the queen's every command, and to be "an obedient and docile husband," then she gets to slip the ring onto *his* finger as the priest declares them "wife and man." The visiting Afghan ambassador gets a look at the ceremony and makes a telling comment: "Man is man and woman is woman, and if you change that, there will be trouble."

And how ... at least in Lubitsch's traditionalist view. As Louise goes about her queenly duties, Alfred is left to pass the time with tennis and bridge. When Jacques and his new friend, the lusty maid Lulu (Lillian Roth), sing the comic duet "Let's Be Common," it seems exactly like the thing to do. Alfred is alone to lament, to the audience, the loss of his potent sexuality in "Nobody's Using It Now." The prince consort uses his free time to draft a plan to repair the national budget, but the cabinet members remind him that he is not allowed to participate in affairs of state.

This is the final straw for Alfred, who plans to leave his wife. But as Sylvania requires a foreign loan to prop itself up, he tells Louise that, after their evening at the opera, he will leave for Paris and, after the loan is made, will file for di-

vorce. He walks in late to the performance, upstaging the queen before the inquisitive gallery (which includes the young extra Jean Harlow). Now it is Louise's turn to feel unwanted. As Alfred packs his bags the following morning, she promises that she will follow him to Paris or wherever he goes. He decides that if this is so, he has no need to leave. When they first met, Alfred had acknowledged to the queen that he needed to be punished for improper behavior; now, she makes the same suggestion.

Contrite, she announces that he will take command as a king, not only in affairs of state—but also, here mimicking him, "at home. ... You shall stay here, attached to me, from morning til ... uh, from night until morning." During their courtship, Alfred had compared Louise, in the song "My Love Parade," to the great ladies of Paris. Now, their reprise caps the film, but not before Alfred walks to the bedroom window, nods slightly, grins to the audience, and closes the curtains. Sylvania shall have her king, for this is a man's world.

For 1929, *The Love Parade* was a nearly perfect blending of satirical romantic comedy and music, and it remains a fine example of song expressed in purely cinematic terms. The first great film operetta was nominated for six Academy Awards, and it earned rapturous notices from an artistically starved reviewing press. *The New York Times'* Mordaunt Hall called it "a delightful entertainment, one that makes the spectator hopeful that the silly diatribes that have so recently been seen on the screen will be cast in the background...."[27] He placed *The Love Parade* atop his year's "best of" list. *Variety's* "Char" saw "an outstanding talker production ... . [Lubitsch] has worked [the songs] into the action with the least obtrusiveness yet noticed in pictures requiring as much music."[28]

Indeed, removed from the accompanying dialogue, the songs in *The Love Parade* could practically tell the story on their own. ("Dream Lover" and "My Love Parade" were the biggest hits initially, and "March of the Grenadiers" has proven as sturdy.) Lubitsch was well aware of the European tradition of operetta, in which actors could break into song for no reason, so he had none of the typically Hollywood inhibitions about this use of music, much less anything else. This is not to say that the film is free of the drawbacks of early sound cinema. All but one of the songs ("March of the Grenadiers") was recorded live on the set. Although Victor Milner takes his camera over the top during the elaborate wedding and ballet sequences, the general pictoral rigidity is apparent in comparison to the work of the same man in *Monte Carlo* a year later. The sound recording is not always clean, the pacing a bit slower than desired.

Another drawback was the inability to mix sounds together in the editing process. In *Applause*, Rouben Mamoulian overcame this obstacle by recording Helen Morgan's lullaby and Joan Peers' prayer on two microphones at once. Lubitsch did much the same thing, although his task was tougher—to shoot two musical numbers, with Chevalier and MacDonald paired in the royal bedchamber and Lane and Roth carrying on in the garden. So he had two sets built side by side, each with its own camera and crew. Then, with the orchestra nearby to play live, he directed both scenes at once. Joked *Photoplay*, which published a revealing photograph of the process: "Our hard-working directors may soon be expected to direct three scenes, juggle four pool balls, eat a bacon and tomato sandwich and sing 'Mammy' simultaneously."[29]

But *The Love Parade* is less an achievement of technology than of taste. One can still marvel at its audacities of charm and subtlety with the knowledge that it was made in an industry that thrived on slapstick comedy and sentimentalized romance. Lubitsch's film, which instead makes fun of traditional marital relationships, is full of unexpected touches. After Chevalier's Alfred sings his part of "Paris, Stay the Same," Lane's Jacques picks up the refrain to draw his paramours to their opened windows, and when the servant's dog joins in, his barking attracts a group of female canines. As Alfred nervously prepares for his wedding, he is told that the face of a past monarch shown on one of his medals appears to be cross-eyed. Alfred replies that it has always been bad luck for him whenever he's seen a cross-eyed man, whereupon their next visitor is a lackey played by Ben Turpin! The humor even targets its typical domestic audience. As a bus carrying a load of tourists (read: Americans) pulls up to the royal palace, the occupants read their newspapers and ignore the guide's spiel about the history of the place—until the narrator mentions that its value is "110 million dollars!"—which

motivates the suddenly impressed Babbitts to sit up and take notice. We can see the nosy government officials and palace servants who eavesdrop on the royal couple's every move as reminders of our own repressed voyeurism.

To bolster Chevalier's initial reservations about his role—at 40, he considered himself too old to play it, especially opposite the 26-year-old MacDonald—Lubitsch allowed the actor to sit in on all pre-production story conferences; the result was a zesty, and typically self-assured, performance. But MacDonald, caressed by the camera, matches him throughout. "She photographs beautifully, speaks with a clarity and softness altogether pleasing, and in some numbers is always equal to the occasion," commented *Variety*.[30] The actress is more sensual here than ever, the result, perhaps, of Lubitsch's insistence that she scarf down a few milkshakes to take on the few extra pounds needed to give her a more European beauty. The on-screen chemistry between the two stars is remarkable considering that their relationship was strained. By the time they made the last of their four films together, *The Merry Widow* (1934), it had grown into hatred. He considered her a prude who was unprofessional on the set; she would call him "the biggest bottom-pincher I have ever come across."[31]

Lane and Roth are a splendidly earthy secondary couple. Lane (1892–1959), a rubber-faced member of the famed British show-business family, had been making shorts and occasional features in Hollywood since 1922, but never before had his quirky acting and singing abilities and his acrobatic dancing (for "Let's Be Common") been so well used. Roth, the renowned New York nightclub singer, entered the production thinking she had been cast to romance Chevalier, but swallowed her pride. Her Brooklyn accent may be out of character for a middle European maiden, but Roth is so irresistible—like the rest of *The Love Parade*—that we don't mind it at all.

MONTE CARLO
(Paramount; August 27, 1930)

Director-Producer: Ernst Lubitsch. Screenplay: Ernest Vajda. Additional Dialogue: Vincent Lawrence. Based on the play *Die Blaue Kuste* [The Blue Coast] by Hans Müller.

Jack Buchanan, portraying a count masquerading as a barber, wins Jeanette MacDonald in Paramount's *Monte Carlo.*

Photography: Victor Milner. Editor: Merrill White. Art Director: Hans Dreier. Musical Director: W. Franke Harling. Running Time: 93 minutes.

Cast: Jack Buchanan (Count Rudolph Farriére), Jeanette MacDonald (Countess Hélène Mara), ZaSu Pitts (Berthe), Claud Allister (Duke Otto von Liebenheim), Tyler Brooke (Armand), Lionel Belmore (Duke Gustave von Liebenheim), John Roche (Paul), Albert Conti (Master of Ceremonies), Helen Garden ("Lady Mary"), Donald Novis ("Monsieur Beaucaire"), David Percy ("herald"), Erik Bey ("Lord Winterset"), Sidney Bracey (hunchback), Billy Bevan (conductor), Rolfe Sedan (hairdresser), Edgar Norton, Geraldine Dvorak, Frances Dee.

Songs: "Always in All Ways" [Buchanan, MacDonald, twice], "Beyond the Blue Horizon" [MacDonald, peasants; reprised by MacDonald, Buchanan], "Give Me a Moment, Please" [Buchanan, MacDonald; reprised by Buchanan], "She'll Love Me and Like It" [Allister, chorus; reprised by Allister, MacDonald], "Trimmin' the Women" [Buchanan, Brooke, Roche], "Whatever It Is, It's Grand" [Buchanan, MacDonald] (Leo Robin, Richard A. Whiting, W. Franke Harling); "Day of Days" [crowd at wedding] (W. Franke Harling); music from created-for-film opera *Monsieur Beaucaire* [Percy, Garden, Bey, Novis, chorus] (Robin, Whiting, Harling).

Disc: RCA Victor 22514 (MacDonald/"Always in All Ways"/"Beyond the Blue Horizon"/78); Music Masters JJA-19806 (bootleg LP; ST).

Ernst Lubitsch's second light operetta, *Monte Carlo,* was considered by many to be an improvement on *The Love Parade.* It was again graced by Jeanette MacDonald, noticeably slimmer and without Lillian Roth to divert attention.[32] The Leo Robin–Richard Whiting–

W. Franke Harling score included the stirring "Beyond the Blue Horizon" and the ultra-romantic "Always in All Ways." The plot, about a count who poses as a hairdresser to win the love of an impoverished countess, was, as one of its characters would say, "a silly story, only possible with music." But it was told with a seamlessness made possible by the increased freedom of the camera and Lubitsch's added assurance with sound. A nameless British commentator of the day was tickled enough to announce (with some exaggeration, we presume): "Now they can preserve all the reels of *The Love Parade* and *Monte Carlo* and burn all the rest, and nobody will notice the loss."[33]

Monte Carlo comes up short only in the leading-man dapartment, where Jack Buchanan reigns uneasily in Maurice Chevalier's stead. While Buchanan isn't so bad to deserve Ethan Mordden's pungent description of him as "a swarmy British wimp … [with] a voice like tapioca pudding on a high speed,"[34] he does spend much of the picture giggling and fussing as if in a state of non-romantic intoxication, and we sometimes wonder what the lovely Jeanette sees in him. It is, as the late Gerald Mast asserted, "impossible to admire and enjoy the conceptual cleverness of *Monte Carlo* without excusing Jack Buchanan."[35] So we will pardon him, for the film is too good not to admire and enjoy, and because the poor fellow doesn't *have* to be Chevalier … he's a different actor in a different role in a different story.

Buchanan is nowhere to be found as *Monte Carlo* begins; neither is his leading lady, but her absence sets the story in motion. As a crowd waits (and sings "Day of Days") outside the church for the impending wedding of Duke Otto von Liebenheim (Claud Allister) and Countess Hélène Mara (MacDonald), a storm begins to rage overhead. The foppish, horse-faced Otto finds the intended bridal gown draped over a chair, then we see the legs of a woman running to catch a train. Otto is berated by his father (Lionel Belmore) after Hélène has walked out on him for the third time, but he greets the anxious peasants and informs them that he "will find her if I have to search the whole world." He sings "She'll Love Me and Like It," in which his contentions about his simple heart and nasty temper are repeated by the chorus as snide insults.

Hélène and her maid, Berthe (ZaSu Pitts),

have just made the train, where the conductor tells them they are bound for Monte Carlo, the gambler's paradise of Europe. The countess is delighted, for she can use her last 10,000 francs "to win my freedom." (And maybe this time, she can find a man who can provide sexual stimulation as well as financial security.) The music swells in perfect time to the urgent rhythms of the wheels and whistle of the moving train, and in one of the most imaginatively photographed sequences of the early sound era, MacDonald looks out her window and introduces "Beyond the Blue Horizon":

> Beyond the blue horizon waits a beautiful day.
> Goodbye to things that bore me,
> Joy is waiting for me.
> I see a blue horizon, my life has only begun.
> Beyond the blue horizon lies a rising star.

For the second chorus, MacDonald sticks her head outside to see bands of peasants working in fields; they join in the singing as the storm we had seen a couple of minutes earlier is replaced by the more optimistic sunshine.[36] The sequence remains one of the most exhilarating in the history of the American film musical.[37]

Count Rudolph Farriére (Buchanan) takes sight of Hélène shortly after she arrives in Monte Carlo, and after a couple of false starts, he finally gets to meet her—but not in his correct guise. He and his friend Armand (Tyler Brooke) chanced to meet Hélène's hairdresser (John Roche)—the three had sung of the hidden joys of the stylist's trade in the sly "Trimmin' the Women"—and now the count disguises himself as a hairdresser to gain entry to the countess's suite. He can't bluff his way through a snipping of her hair, but he does give a great head massage. "You must have electricity in your hands!" Hélène coos as the maid snoops at the door and thinks the worst. The countess decides that this man, whom she calls Paul, will stay, for "Whatever It Is, It's Grand."

Paul becomes a one-man staff, and as the countess runs low of money and sexual discipline, she fires the rest of her servants—except Berthe, of course. She faces eviction by the hotel, just as Otto finds her and proposes marriage again. She accepts, again, because she needs his money to subsist. But Paul/Rudy has an idea: He's a whiz at the gaming tables, so why not let him play her last thousand-franc note and turn it into a small fortune? Now bedecked in evening clothes for a night at the casino, the couple pledge loyalty and unspoken love in "Always in All Ways." They end up not playing the tables, but Hélène thinks he has been when the disguised count rewards her with 200,000 francs from his private stash.

Comes the dawn. Hélène, no longer intoxicated by the moment and embarrassed at being assisted by a man of such lowly station, gives him his money back. "We were carried away ... let's forget it!" she says. Angry, he responds, "I have *already* forgotten!" as he embraces her, then flings her on top of her settee. Once his ire has passed, however, Rudy comes up with an ingenious idea. Days later, when the countess needs a hairdresser to prepare her for a night at the opera, he answers the call. She wants a reconciliation, but he's not biting. "I have the greatest interest that you see this opera tonight," he tells her. The opera is *Monsieur Beaucaire*—in which a nobleman poses as a barber and falls in love with a princess. From her box, Hélène is stunned to see her hairdresser dressed in a tux on an adjoining balcony and motioning for her to pay close attention to the story. As the barber is exposed on stage, the truth comes to her. Noticing that Otto has dozed off in the adjoining chair, she dashes over to the count's box. In *Monsieur Beaucaire*, the barber spurns his lover. But "I like happy endings," says Rudy, and at the fade, he and Hélène are on another train, singing "Beyond the Blue Horizon" and looking ahead to their "beautiful day" together.

Monte Carlo was received nearly as well as *The Love Parade*, although the expectations were certainly higher this time. *Variety*'s "Sime" seemed especially hard to please; he called Lubitsch's direction "disappointing" and "matter of fact," was unimpressed by the "Blue Horizon" number, and pinned down Buchanan as "just the usual sort of juv."[38] *The New York Times* correctly noted that the film showed "Mr. Lubitsch at his best after he has had experience with the microphone and now learned to manipulate it as he has done a camera for several years."[39] Reviewers were mainly happy with the fine supporting work by Pitts (1898–1963) and Allister (1891–1970), and were won over by MacDonald. "Jeanette is in particularly lovely voice and her part allows her her best acting opportunities to date," opined *Motion Picture* magazine. "Stardom, I should say, is just around the corner."[40]

MacDonald made four films with Lubitsch; the last two were *One Hour with You* (1932; see Chapter 12) and MGM's *The Merry Widow* (1934), both also with Chevalier. Afterward, he never found a leading lady who was as suitable, and she, locked into her stifling, Nelson Eddy–era Iron Butterfly image, was never as potent without him. She seemed to understand his style of humor better than any woman, and he brought out the best of her charming, vulnerable personality. Long after they stopped working together, MacDonald remained fond of Lubitsch—and his "Lubitsch touch." Said she: "He could suggest more with a closed door than all the hayrolling you see openly on the screen nowadays."[41]

CHAPTER 10

1929–1930: *More Stars Than There Are in Heaven*

When Florenz Ziegfeld wanted to put on one of his eye-popping revues, he knew he had some of the world's greatest singing, dancing and joking talent at his disposal. When movie studio chiefs like Irving Thalberg, B. P. Schulberg and Winnie Sheehan decided to emulate the master, they could aim for "names," too, but primarily they had to choose from their available contract talent, regardless of whether they could sing or dance or quip. Such was a subgenre of widely varying quality: five all-star revues turned out by each of the majors between the middle of 1929 and mid–1930.

Metro-Goldwyn-Mayer titled the first of them *The Hollywood Revue of 1929*; the date probably was used to mimic Ziegfeld but also may have carried an assumption that the screen novelty would spawn a series. Warner Bros. responded with *The Show of Shows*, and a curious public made both films commercial successes. Early in 1930, Fox—having tested the revue market with its backstager *William Fox Movietone Follies of 1929*—put all of its resources, and the few gems in its talent mine, into *Happy Days*. Paramount and Universal premiered *Paramount on Parade* and *King of Jazz*, respectively, on opposite coasts on the same day in April 1930.

The all-star films were glorified promotional devices, ways to make viewers believe they were privy to little-known abilities of a performer (Clara Bow's way with a song, or Marion Davies' yen for dance), or to introduce unfamiliar screen faces (if you liked Irene Bordoni's song in *The Show of Shows*, you'd love her in her own feature, *Paris*). The revues were also screen tests for the sound medium. Thrust before the uncompromising hot lights with little guidance were dramatic actors who struggled to sing or wisecrack, silents-minded comics

who had no sense of verbal humor, and legit or vaude stars who became transfixed by the stubborn camera. In 1929, moviegoers saw what were crucial opportunities for eager but uncertain actors; now, we know their outcomes. John Gilbert's forced smile during his Shakespeare parody in *Hollywood Revue* seems to portend his professional disgrace and personal degradation. Chester Morris and Jack Mulhall earnestly exchanged comic insults in *The Show of Shows*; within a year, Morris would become a first-rank star, but Mulhall would be financially bankrupt, shorn of his studio tie, and beginning a decade-long journey to the dead end of Poverty Row.

Certainly there were stars who welcomed the chance to prove their versatility, but most were not inclined to risk their popularity by looking silly. For a distinctive personality like Clara Bow, whose jaunty confidence had already been shattered by the talkie boom, an assignment to sing in *Paramount on Parade* presented a nerve-wracking challenge. The all-star film was to be produced on the studio's enormous new soundstage, on which four talkies could be shot simultaneously. But not long after it was raised, the facility caught fire (see Chapter 3). Roused from her dressing room during the ensuing ruckus, Bow watched the flames from afar. Ernst Lubitsch rushed past her. "I hope t' Christ it's the soundstage," he heard Bow mutter in her unmistakable Brooklyn accent.[1]

Had the market for them held up, there would have been even more starry extravaganzas. *Radio Revels* was announced by RKO, and even little Pathé made plans for an *International Television Revue*. But these were the first kind of musicals to lose favor with the public. As early as the spring of 1930, the industry was pretty much "declared through with revues," reported *Variety*. "Any kind of a picture, whether musical or not, that does not have a strong story basis, is taking big chances in the opinion of film showmen. Public must have their stories and plots, they say."[2]

What might have been the biggest revue of them all, MGM's *The March of Time*, was the most conspicuous casualty among early sound musicals. The brainchild of producer Harry Rapf, it was to be a part–Technicolor music-through-the-decades epic in three distinct sections. The first was to showcase the great stage names of the past—the comic duo of Joe Weber and Lew Fields (doing their famous pool hall routine), De Wolf Hopper, Louis Mann, Marie Dressler, Fay Templeton, William Collier, Sr., Barney Fagan and Josephine Sabel—in the songs and gags that had made them famous. The other two sections were to spotlight artists of the present and future; the Duncan Sisters (singing "Graduation Days"), Cliff Edwards, Benny Rubin, Gus Shy, Lottice Howell, Polly Moran, Raquel Torres and David Percy were among the performers intended for these. Some of the titles of songs copyrighted for the picture hint strongly at their visuals: "All Gawd's Chillun Got Blues" (George Waggner, J. Russel Robinson); "Dance of the Robots" (Felix Feist, Louis Alter); "The Fan Episode" and "Steel" (Clifford Grey, Herbert Stothart); "Here Comes the Sun" (Arthur Freed, Harry Woods); "The Lock Step" (Roy Turk, Fred E. Ahlert); and "The Merry-Go-Round" (Freed, Nacio Herb Brown).[3] As late as June 1930, MGM was publicizing the coming of *The March of Time*, but by summer's end the uncompleted film was shelved, after an expense of some $750,000.

The money already spent was a prime motivator in MGM's attempts to save a film it considered to be unmarketable. One odd proposal was to split *The March of Time* into six separate shorts designed for various foreign markets. In September 1930, the studio engaged the writer Edgar Allen Woolf to structure a connecting story for the revue footage, but nothing came of it. At the end of 1931, MGM announced in the trades a plan to salvage some of the footage into a feature called *It's Got to Be Good*, with Jimmy Durante as a possible headliner. Finally, Woolf did share story credit two years later on *Broadway to Hollywood* (September 15, 1933), a backstage musical about a trouping showbiz clan (headed by Frank Morgan and Alice Brady) that included four music sequences filmed for *The March of Time*. There were two ballets choreographed by Albertina Rasch, a snippet involving comic hansom cabbies, and, most notably, part of a massive "March of Time" production number. Presented in the newer film as the finale to a Weber and Fields show, it revealed solos by Templeton ("Ma Blushin' Rosie") and Sabel ("Bedelia," "There'll Be a Hot Time in the Old Town Tonight").

Other numbers from *The March of Time* were used in MGM short subjects. For example, a Technicolor ballet by the Albertina Rasch Girls was placed in the 1931 Eddie Buzzell two-reeler *The Devil's Cabaret* (see Appendix II). This short, recently rediscovered, was to be shown at the 1996 Cinecon in Los Angeles. "The Fan Episode" became part of the 1933 Ted Healy and His (Three) Stooges short *Nertsery Rhymes*. The 1994 MGM compilation film *That's Entertainment! III* includes the unearthed "Lock Step" number, in which the Dodge Twins lead a chorus of "guards" and "convicts" in multi-celled rows reminiscent of those in the title number from *Jailhouse Rock* (1957). But, having never been seen as a whole, *The March of Time* remains one of the most tantalizing of "never were" movies.

THE HOLLYWOOD REVUE OF 1929
(June 20, 1929)

Director: Charles F. Reisner. Producer: Harry Rapf. Dialogue: Al Boasberg, Robert E. Hopkins, Joe Farnham. Photography: John Arnold, Irving Ries, Maximilian Fabian, John M. Nickolaus. Editors: William S. Gray, Cameron K. Wood. Sound: Douglas Shearer, Russell Franks, William Clark, Wesley Miller, A. T. Taylor. Assistant Directors: Jack Cummings, Sandy Roth, Al Shenberg. Art Direction: Cedric Gibbons, Richard Day. Costumes: David Cox, Henrietta Fraser, Joe Rapf. Musical Arrangements: Arthur Lange, Ernest Klapholtz, Ray Heindorf. Dance Direction: Sammy Lee, George Cunningham. Running Time: 130 minutes. Technicolor sequences.

Cast: Conrad Nagel, Jack Benny (masters of ceremonies), John Gilbert, Norma Shearer, Joan Crawford, Bessie Love, Lionel Barrymore, Cliff Edwards, Stan Laurel, Oliver Hardy, Anita Page, Nils Asther, Marion Davies,

William Haines, Buster Keaton, Marie Dressler, Charles King, Polly Moran, Gus Edwards, Karl Dane, George K. Arthur, The Brox Sisters, Gwen Lee, James Burroughs, Paul Gibbons, Jane Purcell, Natacha Natova and Company, Albertina Rasch Ballet, The Rounders, The Biltmore Quartet, Belcher Child Dancers, MGM Chorus, Ann Dvorak.

Songs: "I Never Knew I Could Do a Thing Like That" [Love], "Marie, Polly and Bess" [Dressler, Love, Moran, King, Cliff Edwards, Gus Edwards], "Minstrel Days" [Gus Edwards, chorus], "Nobody but You" [Cliff Edwards], "Orange Blossom Time" [King; danced by Rasch Ballet, Belcher Child Dancers], "Your Mother and Mine" [King; reprised by Benny, Dane, Arthur] (Joe Goodwin, Gus Edwards); "Singin' in the Rain" [Cliff Edwards, Brox Sisters, Rounders; danced by MGM Chorus], "Tommy Atkins on Parade" [Davies], "You Were Meant for Me" [King, Nagel] (Nacio Herb Brown, Arthur Freed); "Bones and Tambourines" [chorus], "Strike Up the Band" [Brox Sisters, dancers], "Tableaux of Jewels" [Burroughs, dancers] (Fred Fisher); "For I'm the Queen" [Dressler] (Andy Rice, Martin Broones); "Gotta Feelin' for You" [Crawford, Gibbons, Biltmore Quartet] (Jo Trent, Louis Alter); "Lon Chaney's Going to Get You, If You Don't Watch Out" [Gus Edwards, dancers] (John T. Murray, Gus Edwards); "Low Down Rhythm" [Purcell, dancers] (Raymond Klages, Jesse Greer); "While Strolling Through the Park One Day" [Dressler, Love, Moran, King, Cliff Edwards, Gus Edwards] (Ed Haley, Robert A. King).

Non-Singing Comedy Sketches: "Dance of the Sea" [Keaton]; "Magicians" [Laurel, Hardy]; "Romeo and Juliet by Comparison" [Gilbert, Shearer, Barrymore].

Academy Award Nominations (both 1928-29): Best Picture, Best Interior Decoration (Cedric Gibbons).

Disc: Columbia 1869-D (Cliff Edwards/"Singin' in the Rain"/"Orange Blossom Time"/78); Music Masters JJA-19802 (bootleg LP; ST).

Video: MGM-UA (laserdisc).

In its day, *The Hollywood Revue of 1929* was considered important enough to be nominated for an Academy Award for Best Picture. (It lost to another MGM musical, *The Broadway Melody*.) Filmed in only 25 days for $426,000, it profited to the tune of $1.1 million, as the public thrilled to see so many big names in one sitting. Filmed almost entirely with a head-on camera aimed at a proscenium stage set, *Hollywood Revue* is slow going for even a rabid movie buff. But it remains a fascinating historical document of the stable of talent on display in the world's most successful movie studio during the first full year of sound. "Every one of its sketches … leave [*sic*] one hungry for more," praised Mordaunt Hall of *The New York Times* in a typical response for the time.[4]

Hollywood Revue began production as a two-reel talkie called *The Minstrel Man*. The immediate sensation of *The Broadway Melody* convinced MGM to add more names and expand the short to feature length. The minstrel-show aspect remained, though largely confined to the first hour. Supervised by Harry Rapf and directed by Charles F. Reisner, *Hollywood Revue* was filmed between February 4 and June 11, 1929—mainly, contrary to legend, in daylight hours and some evenings. However, some of the sequences—the one featuring Marion Davies, for example—were shot on the midnight-to-7 a.m. shift so as not to disrupt the schedules of the personnel making other films on the lot. All of Metro's key performers were included, with the minor exception of Ramon Novarro and the major ones of Greta Garbo and Lon Chaney. The studio was not ready to unveil Garbo in a dialogue film; the slinky Swede would not speak until *Anna Christie* (1930). Uncertain of how to integrate speech into his mystery-man persona, Chaney relented only for a sound remake of *The Unholy Three* (1930), which was released shortly before his death of lung cancer.

Hosts Jack Benny, in his film debut, and Conrad Nagel (1896–1970) introduce the cast of 30 acts, which range from low comedy (Laurel and Hardy, Dane and Arthur) to middlebrow crooning (Cliff "Ukelele Ike" Edwards, Charles King, The Brox Sisters) to high "culture" (Norma Shearer and John Gilbert in the balcony scene from *Romeo and Juliet*). Joan Crawford, a doe caught in the headlights as Our Darling Daughter doing Helen Morgan, stands next to a piano and sings "Gotta Feelin' for You" with the Biltmore Quartet before launching into an uncomfortable Charleston-type dance. A mute Buster Keaton appears in ersatz Egyptian drag—his "breasts" look like coffee cups—as a Neptune's Daughter in a ludicrous "Dance of the Sea." Marie Dressler, continuing her career comeback, pleased reviewers as a destitute monarch singing "For I'm the Queen."

Given the asset of trick photography, the film makes redundant use of it in no fewer than three numbers. Bessie Love turns up in Benny's pocket, then grows to human size for a charming comedy song, "I Never Thought I Could Do a Thing Like That," the "thing" being her singing and dancing in *The Broadway Melody*. A smartly uniformed Marion Davies also starts as a miniature, gliding through the widened legs of a guardsman's chorus in an energetic "Tommy Atkins on Parade." The Love and Davies numbers even end the same way, with each wo-

Marion Davies leads the "Tommy Atkins on Parade" number from MGM's *Hollywood Revue of 1929*.

man being thrown around by the male dancers before being dragged offstage in exhaustion. The other "midget" is Charlie King, who gets small from the embarrassment of hearing Conrad Nagel woo Anita Page by borrowing his song "You Were Meant for Me." King (the Charlie of this movie, as opposed to the real guy) had foolishly chided non-singer Nagel for not updating his love-making technique to "words and music."

The Love solo was one of seven songs cowritten for the film by the vaudeville impresario Gus Edwards, who also took a turn before the camera in his only substantial Hollywood credit. (He originally was announced in the trades as the director of *Hollywood Revue*.) A shrewd judge of new talent, Edwards (1879–

1945) helped the likes of Eddie Cantor, George Jessel, Ray Bolger, the Duncan Sisters and Eleanor Powell break into the business through his various kiddie stage acts. For this film, he penned the climactic "Orange Blossom Time," sung by King in a sumptuous orchard decorated by two-color Technicolor, the shapliness of the Albertina Rasch Ballet and, in selected theaters, the emitted aroma of oranges. Even more interesting is a novelty song Edwards performs himself, "Lon Chaney's Going to Get You, If You Don't Watch Out," which was a clever device to capitalize on the name of the holdout star. Benny introduces the number as a gruesomely made-up fellow (not Chaney, but intended to fool people into thinking he is) intrudes with an underpowered "Boo!" The impressed host wants a handshake; the bogey-man gives him a disembodied arm. Edwards, invading an elaborate girls' dormitory set, chills the entranced residents with his foreboding message. A ghoulish gallery of masked Chaney characters enters for a brief "hot" dance, shown partly in a fleeting overhead shot, then all are enveloped in a cloud of steam as the shrieking young women disappear through a large trap door.

A couple of non-musical moments are worth mentioning. The Laurel and Hardy magic-act sketch, possibly written by Laurel himself, was added to the film at the end of May—less than three weeks before the pre-miere—because Harry Rapf wanted a stronger comedy presence. In the skit, the boys' fictional feats of legerdemain are botched repeatedly by Stan. Ollie falls face-first into a well-placed oversized cake, then hurls it offstage; Benny emerges to introduce the next act while covered with frosting. The Gilbert-Shearer pairing, the first of the film's two Technicolor sections, is a typical parody of Hollywood's trivializing of classic literature. The stars do the balcony scene straight, then are told by their director, Lionel Barrymore, that the unnamed studio wants to update the material and call it *The Neckers*. The scene is then repeated with hip slang: "Julie, baby, I'm ga-ga about you … you're the cream in my mocha java, the berries in my pie." Gilbert's voice seems the adequate tenor that it always was, and reviews of the skit in 1929 re-veal no antipathy to it. But the disaster of his first starring sound feature, *His Glorious Night*, was only a few months away.

The "plug" song of *Hollywood Revue* is its most endearing melody, Freed and Brown's "Singin' in the Rain," which was written and first performed for the *Hollywood Music Box Revue*. It is heard instrumentally over the open-ing credits, then performed two-thirds through the film by a rained-on Cliff Edwards, the Brox Sisters and a chorus of singing dancers, whose female figures are briefly shown in silhouette through their transparent rubber coats. The Broxes' rendition is later spoofed by Dressler, Love and Polly Moran, then the song is re-peated at the Technicolor close by the entire company, which stands wearing slickers next to a huge replica of Noah's ark.[5] This presentation of "Singin' in the Rain" is dwarfed in reputation to Gene Kelly's electrifying rendition in the

1952 movie of the same name, but the earlier staging drew a lot of attention at the time. Disc versions by Cliff Edwards and the Earl Burtnett and Gus Arnheim orchestras catapulted the song into the hit parade. The "Singin' in the Rain" and Noah's ark numbers were among the last to be filmed, on May 29 and June 10–11, re-spectively. According to studio records, pro-duction wrapped after what must have been an exhausting 7 p.m. to 12:30 a.m. session that ex-tended into June 11.

To ballyhoo *The Hollywood Revue of 1929*, MGM employed a sensational, if potentially hazardous, publicity stunt. For the June 20 world premiere at Grauman's Chinese Theatre in Hollywood, a billboard on Wilshire Boule-vard boldly came to life as 18 leggy girls in tights sat and stood in tableau on the huge, pro-jected block letters that spelled out "Hollywood Revue." The sight caused traffic to back up for miles, and those who wished an extended gan-der showed up with lunches and camp chairs. There was an even more elaborate "Human Billboard" for the New York opening on August 14 at the Astor Theatre at the predictably grid-locked 46th Street and Broadway. Twenty-six of Chester Hale's dancers danced and sang "Sin-gin' in the Rain" from their lettered perches, harnesses around their waists for security. Only one chorus was sung before it really did begin to sprinkle. The same site was used by the pro-ducers of *The Great Gabbo* for their own living billboard a month later; by then, a New York Supreme Court judge had cleverly ruled that the police could not prevent the exhibition as long as the girls did not move their legs.[6] Smart alecks noticed with some amusement the ciga-rette factory ad sign immediately below the bill-board and just to the upper left of the Astor doorway: "See Them Made Below."

THE SHOW OF SHOWS
(Warner Bros.; November 20, 1929)

Director: John G. Adolfi. Executive Pro-ducers: Jack L. Warner, John B. Adolfi. Pro-ducer: Darryl F. Zanuck. Special Material: Frank Fay, J. Keirn Brennan (and William Shakespeare). Photography: Bernard McGill. Sound: George R. Groves. Art Director: Es-dras Hartley, Max Parker. Costumes: Earl Luick. Musical Director: Louis Silvers. Dance

Direction: Larry Ceballos, Jack Haskell. Running Time: 128 minutes. Technicolor.

Cast: Frank Fay (master of ceremonies), Armida, Johnny Arthur, William Bakewell, John Barrymore, Richard Barthelmess, Noah Beery, Sally Blane, Monte Blue, Irene Bordoni, Hobart Bosworth, Anthony Bushell, Marion Byron, Georges Carpentier, Ethlyne Clair, James Clemmons, Ruth Clifford, William Collier, Jr., Betty Compson, Chester Conklin, Heinie Conklin, Delores Costello, Helene Costello, William Courtenay, Jack Curtis, Viola Dana, Alice Day, Marceline Day, Sally Eilers, Douglas Fairbanks, Jr., Louise Fazenda, Pauline Garon, Albert Gran, Alexander Gray, Lloyd Hamilton, Julanne Johnston, Harriette Lake [Ann Sothern], Lupino Lane, Frances Lee, Lila Lee, Ted Lewis, Winnie Lightner, Beatrice Lillie, Jacqueline Logan, Myrna Loy, Nick Lucas, Philo McCullough, J. Farrell MacDonald, Marcelle, Tully Marshall, Shirley Mason, Otto Matiesen, Patsy Ruth Miller, Bull Montana, Lee Moran, Chester Morris, Jack Mulhall, Edna Murphy, Carmel Myers, Marian Nixon, Wheeler Oakman, Molly O'Day, Gertrude Olmstead, Sally O'Neil, Kalla Pasha, Anders Randolph, E. J. Ratcliffe, Rin Tin Tin, Bert Roach, Reginald Sharland, Sid Silvers, Sojin, Ben Turpin, Ada Mae Vaughn, Alberta Vaughn, Lola Vendrill, H. B. Warner, Alice White, Lois Wilson, Grant Withers, Loretta Young, Jack Haskell Girls, Larry Ceballos Black and White Girls, Pasadena's American Legion Fife and Drum Corps, Ted Williams Adagio Dancers, Harry Akst, Eddie Ward.

Songs/Musical Numbers: "Just an Hour of Love" [Bordoni, with Ward at piano], "Li-Po-Li" ["Chinese Fantasy" number: Loy, Lucas; danced by Haskell Girls; introduced by Rin Tin Tin], "Military March" ["Military Parade" number: marched by Blue, Pasadena corps, dancing girls] (Al Bryan, Eddie Ward); "Dear Little Pup" [Fay], "My Sister" ["Sisters" number: Delores and Helene Costello, Alice and Marceline Day, Ada Mae and Alberta Vaughn, Armida and Lola Vendrill, Blane and Young, Byron and Lake, Dana and Mason, O'Day and O'Neil; introduced by Barthelmess], "The Only Song I Know" [Lucas, with Rin Tin Tin] (J. Keirn Brennan, Ray Perkins); "If Your Best Friend Won't Tell You" [Fay, Silvers], "Ping Pongo" [Lightner] (Al Dubin, Joe Burke); "Lady Luck" [Lewis, band; reprised by Lucas,

then by Gray, choruses], "What's Become of the Florodora Boys?" ["Florodora" number: Heinie Conklin, Hamilton, Lane, Moran, Roach, Turpin, Alice Day, Lila Lee, Loy, Miller, Nixon, O'Neil] (Ray Perkins); "A Bicycle Built for Two" [Bakewell, Collier, Fairbanks, Morris, Mulhall, Withers, Garon, Eilers, Logan, Murphy, Olmstead, Wilson] (Harry Dacre); "If I Could Learn to Love as Well as I Fight" ["Eiffel Tower" number: Carpentier, Miller, White, dancers] (Herman Ruby, M. K. Jerome); "Jumping Jack" ["Black and White" number: Fay, Fazenda, Ceballos Girls] (Bernie Seaman, Herman Ruby, Marvin Smolev, Rube Bloom); "Motion Picture Pirates" ["Skull and Crossbones" number: Arthur, Beery, Curtis, Marshall, Matiesen, McCullough, MacDonald, Montana, Oakman, Pasha, Randolph, Clair, Clifford, Dana, Eilers, Johnston, Frances Lee, Marcelle, Mason, Myers, Lewis and band, Williams dancers; introduced by Fay, Morris, Mulhall, Sojin] (J. Keirn Brennan, M. K. Jerome); "Rock-a-Bye Your Baby with a Dixie Melody" [Silvers] (Joe Young, Sam M. Lewis, Jean Schwartz); "Singin' in the Bathtub" [Lightner, dancers] (Herb Magidson, Ned Washington, Michael H. Cleary); "You Were Meant for Me" ["Singin' in the Bathtub" number: Lightner, Montana] (Arthur Freed, Nacio Herb Brown); "Your Love Is All I Crave" [Fay, with Akst at piano] (Al Dubin, Perry Bradford, Jimmy Johnson); "Your Mother and Mine" ["Recitations" sketch: Fay, Fazenda, Hamilton, Lillie] (Joe Goodwin, Gus Edwards).

Non-Musical Comedy Sketches: "Prologue" [Bosworth, Courtenay, Warner]; "King Richard III" [Barrymore, Bushell, Ratcliffe, Sharland]; "Mexican Moonshine" [Beery, Blue, Fay, Gran, Hamilton, Marshall, Moran, Pasha].

Disc: Columbia 1999 (Lewis/"Lady Luck"/78); Columbia 2027-D (Bordoni/"Just an Hour of Love"/78).

Video: MGM-UA (laserdisc).

Only days after the auspicuous West Coast debut of *The Hollywood Revue of 1929*, Warner Bros. decided it must follow suit with its own all-star picture. An announcement in *Variety* during the first week in July listed Al Jolson, John Charles Thomas, John Barrymore, Elsie Janis, Ed Wynn and W. C. Fields for *The Show of Shows*, although of that group only Barrymore ended up in the movie. Jolson would be conspicuously absent—already bound for United Artists after two upcoming final films for Warners, he unsuccessfully demanded $200,000 to appear in the revue. Even without him, the show included "77 of the brightest stars in Hollywood's heaven," or so boasted the ads, which meant every major player under contract to Warners or First National excepting Marilyn Miller, Corinne Griffith, George Arliss and Dorothy Mackaill.[7] There would be no mere splashes of Technicolor, either, for 107 of the 128 minutes were filmed in the two-strip process.[8]

The musical and comedy numbers in *The Show of Shows* are more elaborate than its predecessor—which made it possible to include many names from the character-actor ranks—but the film is practically as static. Again, there was no story, just a stage set and the comic monologues of Frank Fay to link the acts together. Fay (1894–1961) was a big name in vaudeville, especially as a master of ceremonies, but in films his arrogance got the better of him, and he is quite annoying in *The Show of Shows*. A running gag concerns Fay's failure to convince the studio that he should be allowed to sing a solo; he gets his wish, with "Your Love Is All That I Crave," three-quarters through the film. By now, the host has acquired a "sidekick" in Sid Silvers, who exasperates Fay (and us) for two songs. In "Rock-a-Bye Your Baby with a Dixie Melody," Silvers tries to imitate Jolson. The film reaches its nadir with his second, an ode to bad breath called "If Your Best Friend Won't Tell You (Why Should I?)"

The lengthy patterned dances (a military march led by Monte Blue, a Parisian tap chorus headed by ex-boxer Georges Carpentier) were well received at the time, but now they're the dullest moments. The endless finale, "Lady Luck," is beyond dull: It crawls through no fewer than 10 specialty dancing teams, plus Alexander Gray and, as the "Queen of the Revels," a silent Betty Compson.[9] The hit-and-miss comedy sketches become intriguing as one strains to identify each semi-familiar face. In a number titled "Skull and Crossbones," a pirate-costumed group of character villains cheerfully menaces Ted Lewis and his boys; its leader, Noah Beery, exposes the thundering bass that launched him into operettas. Six lovely actresses and six homely comic actors team for an amusing "What's Become of the Florodora Boys?"

sketch, the idea being that the males have hit hard times (Lupino Lane is a street sweeper, Ben Turpin a waiter, and so on). Beatrice Lillie, Louise Fazenda and Lloyd Hamilton join an inexplicably moustached Fay for a round of comic recitations that, when mixed together, tell a completely different story than when spoken separately.

An interesting novelty is a Larry Ceballos-directed song-and-dance number called "Sisters," in which eight sets of (mostly) real-life siblings represent various global ancestries. The "American" pair, Delores and Helene Costello, lead off the song and almost look as if they're enjoying it. Helene, her career wilted by awful performances in the likes of *Lights of New York*, was already a casualty of sound. Delores, who didn't have much better of a voice, was about to become pregnant and retire from the screen. The presence in "Sisters" of Viola Dana, Molly O'Day and Shirley Mason suggests Warners' intent merely to fill out its familial lineup as opposed to resuming the steady employment of those declining players. A "Sister" with a happier future was Harriette Lake, who in time would blossom into Ann Sothern.

Delores Costello's husband, John Barrymore, would become the hit of this show with his reading of the Duke of Gloucester's soliloquy from *Henry VI*—the first hearing of his authoritative tones in a motion picture. Before the premiere of *The Show of Shows* in New York on November 20, 1929, fans were so eager to see this performance that the city police had to take their horses onto the sidewalk of the Winter Garden just to keep the rush for tickets in check. "Persons who were waiting for friends who held their tickets were ordered away from the theater two and three times, which was naturally far from pleasant at an opening where the guests expected a dignified reception," sniffed *The New York Times*.[10] Almost as thrilling for that crowd, and the throngs that followed, was Barrymore's brief introduction of himself. In street clothes, he related that in the play, the Duke would go on to dispatch his elder relatives "with the graceful impartiality of Al Capone." For these few minutes, Barrymore (1882–1942) was paid a cool $25,000 by Warners, which spent double ($850,000) on *Show of Shows* than MGM spent on *Hollywood Revue*. (Only *Noah's Ark* had cost the studio more.)

But what lingers from *The Show of Shows*

is not Warner Bros.' obvious attempt to make John Gilbert and Norma Shearer look like Fay and Silvers in contrast, but those uncontrived moments propelled by unconventional personalities. True, the short, unphotogenic Nick Lucas is party to an unbearably campy "Chinese Fantasy" production number in which he sings "Li-Po-Li" to Myrna Loy, but his solo of "The Only Song I Know" recalls the relaxed vocal style and straight-ahead guitar that made him one of the biggest record-sellers of the '20s. Even better are the too-chubby Winnie Lightner and the too-suggestive Irene Bordoni, both of whom would be termed too "different" for long-term movie stardom. Bordoni's simple delivery of the torchy "Just an Hour of Love" while standing next to a piano is one of the most affecting events in the early sound cinema.

Lightner punches through two comedy songs, "Ping Pongo" and the satirical "Singin' in the Bathtub." On the huge bathroom set that complements the latter, she is abetted by a chorus of male dancers in old-fashioned women's bathing suits. The Brown-Freed spoof premise is then reinforced by the unlikely Bull Montana, who appears in top hat and tails to sing to Lightner a heavily accented chorus of "You Were Meant for Me." Nineteen twenty-nine is not a memory yet, but one can already see the natural-selection process at work: Winnie would be good enough to stick around, but Bull would not be long for the talkies.

HAPPY DAYS
(Fox; February 14, 1930)

Director: Benjamin Stoloff. Stage Director: Walter Catlett. Dialogue: Edwin Burke. Story: Sidney Lanfield. Photography: Lucien Andriot, John Schmitz. Grandeur Camera: J. O. Taylor. Editor: Clyde Carruth. Sound: Samuel Waite. Assistant Directors: Ad Schaumer, Michael Farley, Lew Breslow. Art Director: Jack Schulze. Costumes: Sophie Wachner. Dance Direction: Earl Lindsay. Running Time: 86 minutes.

Cast: Marjorie White (Margie), Richard Keene (Dick), Charles E. Evans (Colonel Billy Batcher), Stuart Erwin (Jig), Martha Lee Sparks (Nancy Lee), Clifford Dempsey (Sheriff Benton), Tom Kennedy (doorman). As Them-

selves: George MacFarlane (master of ceremonies), Warner Baxter, Rex Bell, El Brendel, Lew Brice, Walter Catlett, William Collier, Sr., James J. Corbett, Charles Farrell, Janet Gaynor, George Jessel, Dixie Lee, Lucien Littlefield, Edmund Lowe, Sharon Lynn, J. Farrell Mac-Donald, Victor McLaglen, J. Harold Murray, Paul Page, Tom Patricola, Ann Pennington, Frank Richardson, Will Rogers, David Rollins, "Whispering" Jack Smith, Nick Stuart, Flo Bert, George Olsen and His Orchestra, The Slate Brothers, Betty Grable (chorine).

Songs: "Crazy Feet" [Lee, Richardson; danced by Patricola, chorus], "Mona" [Richardson], "Snake Hips (Do the Wiggle Waggle Woo)" [Lynn; danced by Pennington, chorus] (Sidney Mitchell, Archie Gottler, Con Conrad); "A Toast to the Girl I Love" [Murray], "We'll Build a Little World of Our Own" [Farrell, Gaynor, Catlett, Littlefield, chorus] (James Brockman, James F. Hanley); "Happy Days" [Smith, company] (James McCarthy, James F. Hanley); "I'm on a Diet of Love" [White, Keene], "Minstrel Memories" [minstrel band; reprised by MacFarlane, chorus] (L. Wolfe Gilbert, Abel Baer); "Vic and Eddie" [Lowe, McLaglen] (Harry Stoddard, Marcy Klauber); "Dixie" (Daniel Decatur Emmett); "Las Golondrinas" (Narsico Serradell); "William Tell" Overture (Gioacchino Rossini); "Zampa" Overture (Louis Joseph Ferdinand Herald).

William Fox and his minions didn't need color to support their entry in the Battle of the Stars. They had "Grandeur," the widescreen (70mm) process that they figured would catch on once enough theaters were equipped for it. This film would mark the first real showcase for the format, as *William Fox Movietone Follies of 1929* had only been previewed in 70mm. Fox started out calling its entry *New Orleans Frolic*, intending a sizable cast but not a full roster of first-rank players. But soon, Fox emptied out its piggybank, adding Janet Gaynor and Charles Farrell, Will Rogers, Victor McLaglen, Edmund Lowe and Warner Baxter—all of whom had been missing from *Movietone Follies*, the earlier revue wrapped-in-a-backstager.

Like *Movietone Follies*, *Happy Days* had a framing story, slight as it was. Here, Captain Billy Batcher (Charles E. Evans), the proud owner of what once was the greatest showboat on the Mississippi, is faced with ruin unless he can find some way to lure prospective customers away from their radios and talking pictures. Margie (Marjorie White), the go-getting fiancée of Billy's unimpressive grandson (Richard Keene), leaves the boat for New York to ask for help from some of the famous actors the captain had once helped along. She dresses as a man to gain admittance to the exclusive Stage and Screen Club, and although her ruse is exposed, the celebs—curiously, all Fox contractees who knew and loved Old Cap—vow to go West and put on a smashing minstrel show for the benefit of their old pal.

Now, one-third of the way into the 86-minute film, the story gives way so completely to the revue that we never do learn if Uncle Billy will escape the poorhouse. The numbers, introduced by the baritone George MacFarlane (1871–1932) with help from former boxing champion James J. Corbett, are predictably a mixed bag, some of them serving to lampoon the screen reputation of the artist(s) featured. In minstrel outfits and Marine caps, McLaglen and Lowe attempt to upstage each other during "Vic and Eddie," an overlong musical denial of the "feud" assumed by watchers of the pair's contentious comedies *What Price Glory?* and *The Cock-Eyed World.* Gaynor and Farrell coo as young marrieds in "We'll Build a Little World of Our Own," then are seen playing their own children, dressed in bonnets and fighting over a bottle in a baby carriage. The comedy worsens as Walter Catlett (in drag) and Lucien Littlefield reprise the song while pushing a giant carriage filled with authentic screaming infants. Of Tom Patricola's Irish jig to a deflating balloon and El Brendel's name-that-odor sideshow ... the less said, the better.

The closest *Happy Days* comes to High Class is J. Harold Murray's distinguished delivery of "A Toast to the Girl I Love," complete with a multiple-screen effect that tells the song's story in vignettes. At least the pretense of a proscenium stage is gone halfway through the revue, and the old-groaner humor gives way to more contemporary (and more cinematic) entertainment. Sharon Lynn sings and Ann Pennington wriggles through a snappy production number called "Snake Hips," which comes with overhead shots. The effective "Crazy Feet" number develops on a huge reproduction of pants legs from which emerges lead singer Dixie Lee and a girly chorus, who move down

stairways masquerading as shoelaces; Tom Patricola chips in with an eccentric dance. "Whispering" Jack Smith cheers up quarreling lovers White and Keene with the climactic title song, which manages to sound just like "Sunnyside Up" even though it was not written by De Sylva, Brown or Henderson. Everybody dances to the fadeout—including the headline players, who take one last bow by excerpting their own songs. Unfortunately, the great Will Rogers appears only in the New York sequence, thus depriving the revue of one performer many viewers would have liked to see.[11]

Happy Days did its best business in houses where the widescreen process could showcase it to best effect. The screen at the Roxy Theatre in New York, site of the film's premiere, was expanded to an unheard-of 42 feet wide and 20 feet high, compared to its usual 24 by 18 dimensions. Although they noted difficulties in the sound reproduction, reviewers mainly praised the visual effect of the twice-as-large screen, and if theater owners hadn't already been asked to bear the cost of revamping their houses to sound, more of them might have installed the necessary features (special projection machines, screens with ground-glass surfaces) to accomodate "Grandeur." Only a few more films were released by Fox in 70mm, among them the early John Wayne Western *The Big Trail* (1930).

Declared *The New York Times*: "*Happy Days* may not be highly exciting, but through the medium of its presentation it affords a really ... impressive entertainment."[12]

PARAMOUNT ON PARADE
(Paramount; April 19, 1930)

Directors: Dorothy Arzner, Otto Brower, Edmund Goulding, Victor Heerman, Edwin H. Knopf, Rowland V. Lee, Ernst Lubitsch, Lothar Mendes, Victor Schertzinger, A. Edward Sutherland, Frank Tuttle. Producer: Albert S. Kaufman. Supervisor: Elsie Janis. Photography: Harry Fischbeck, Victor Milner. Art Director: John Wenger. Dance Direction: David Bennett. Running Time: 128 minutes. Technicolor sequences.

Cast: Leon Errol, Skeets Gallagher, Jack Oakie (masters of ceremonies), Richard Arlen, Jean Arthur, Mischa Auer, William Austin,

George Bancroft, Clara Bow, Evelyn Brent, Mary Brian, Clive Brook, Nancy Carroll, Ruth Chatterton, Maurice Chevalier, Gary Cooper, Stuart Erwin, Kay Francis, Harry Green, Mitzi Green, James Hall, Phillips Holmes, Helen Kane, Dennis King, Fredric March, Nino Martini, Mitzi Mayfair, David Newell, Warner Oland, Zelma O'Neal, Eugene Pallette, Joan Peers, William Powell, Charles "Buddy" Rogers, Lillian Roth, Stanley Smith, Fay Wray, Iris Adrian, Virginia Bruce, Cecil Cunningham, Henry Fink, Edmund Goulding, Robert Greig, Jack Luden, Al Norman, Jack Pennick, Rolfe Sedan, Abe Lyman and His Orchestra, Marion Morgan Dancers, Paramount Publix Ushers.

Songs: "Any Time's the Time to Fall in Love" [Rogers, Roth, chorus], "Helen Kane's Schoolroom" ("What Did Cleopatra Say?") [Kane, Mitzi Green, children], "I'm True to the Navy Now" [Bow, chorus], "Paramount on Parade" [Morgan dancers, ushers, Mayfair] (Elsie Janis, Jack King); "Dancing to Save Your Sole" [Carroll, Lyman and band, danced by Norman], "I'm in Training for You" [Oakie, O'Neal, danced by Mayfair, chorus], "Let Us Drink to the Girl of My Dreams" [Arlen, Arthur, Brian, Bruce, Cooper, Hall, Holmes, Newell, Peers, Wray; introduced by Goulding] (L. Wolfe Gilbert, Abel Baer); "All I Want Is Just One Girl" [Chevalier in "A Park in Paris" sketch; reprised by Mitzi Green] (Leo Robin, Richard A. Whiting); "Come Back to Sorrento" [Martini] (Ernesto de Curtis, Leo Robin); "I'm Isadore, the Toreador" [Harry Green, Francis, Morgan dancers] (Dave Franklin); "Keep Your Head Down, 'Fritzie Boy'" ["Montmartre Girl" sketch: March, Erwin, Smith, Pennick] (Gitz Rice); "Masters of Ceremonies (We're the Masters of Ceremony)" [Errol, Gallagher, Oakie] (Ballard MacDonald, Dave Dreyer); "My Marine" ["Montmartre Girl" sketch: Chatterton] (Raymond B. Egan, Richard A. Whiting); "Nichavo!" [King] (Mana-Zucca, Helen Jerome); "Sweepin' the Clouds Away" [Chevalier, chorus] (Sam Coslow).

Non-Musical Comedy Sketches: "Impulses" [Bancroft, Auer, Austin, Cunningham, Fink, Francis, others]; "In a Hospital" [Arthur, Errol, Holmes, Newell]; "Murder Will Out" [Brook, Oakie, Oland, Pallette, Powell]; "Origin of the Apache" [Brent, Chevalier].

Disc: Columbia 2143 (Rogers/"Any Time's the Time to Fall in Love"/78); RCA Victor 22263 (King/"Nichavo!"/78); RCA Victor 22378 (Chevalier/"All I Want Is Just One Girl"/"Sweepin' the Clouds Away"/78); Caliban 6044 (bootleg LP; ST); Music Masters JJA-19806 (bootleg LP; ST); WRC SH 156 (bootleg LP; ST).

The fourth of the all-star revues—it premiered in New York on the same night that *King of Jazz* debuted in Los Angeles, but entered general release first—*Paramount on Parade* was a definite step up from what had gone before. In keeping with Paramount's reputation for director-driven pictures, this film employed no fewer than 11, and one of them, the estimable Ernst Lubitsch, actually seemed to know what he was doing. Another asset was the general supervisory position of the great vaudeville star and songwriter Elsie Janis. More importantly, there is none of the "big event" pretention of the earlier revues. There is no attempt to make *Paramount on Parade* a visual replica of a Ziegfeld show from curtain to curtain; instead, the presentation of the 20 sequences resembles an informal tour of the studio backlot. Clara Bow, who feared doing the picture but would benefit as much from the picture as any of its 40-odd principals, recalled that she filmed her scene during a break from another movie, with a minimum of rehearsal and no one but herself to do her hair.[13] Clearly, Paramount did not consider this a make-or-break production.

There were three masters of ceremonies—Jack Oakie, Skeets Gallagher and Leon Errol (1881–1951)—but the star among all the stars was Maurice Chevalier. Under the supervision of Lubitsch, Chevalier charmed his way through three scenes, the first two elevated by the director's risqué sense of humor. In "The Origin of the Apache," which purported to describe the beginning of the trendy French dance, Chevalier and wife Evelyn Brent bicker in their boudoir over his wandering eye. In rhythm to the orchestral accompaniment, their "No, dear—yes, dear" assertions turn into excited slaps and pushes. Then they begin to tear off their clothes, but after we have anxiously watched the last article thrown on the floor, the two walk out, arm in arm … in evening wear.

Sometime later, Chevalier turns up as a gendarme patrolling a quiet park in Paris. He admonishes a necking young couple, asking the woman for her address and phone number; her

Evelyn Brent and Maurice Chevalier tangle in the "Origin of the Apache" sequence in *Paramount on Parade*.

sight of Helen Kane let loose in a classroom to teach kids how to boop-boop-a-doop ("What Did Cleopatra Say?') and the transplanting of Harry Green from Noo Yawk into a *Carmen* burlesque, "I'm Isadore, the Toreador." He-man George Bancroft looks uncomfortable in a semi-clever comedy sketch called "Impulses," in which party guests (Kay Francis, William Austin, Mischa Auer) drop their facades to vent their socially unacceptable feelings. Better is the non-musical "Murder Will Out" sketch, in which William Powell, Warner Oland and Clive Brook make fun of their respective mystery-movie roles as Philo Vance, Dr. Fu Manchu and Sherlock Holmes. Fu's victim is the ever-present Oakie, who provides the requisite twist of plot by turning out not to be murdered at all.

partner's vitals will be unnecessary. A frumpy matron points out her straying husband, who is benched with a much younger woman; the cop promptly kayoes the wife with his club, much to the relief of the thankful husband. Chevalier caps the scene by singing Richard Whiting and Leo Robin's "All I Want Is Just One Girl." The Frenchman reappears as a chimney sweep for the Technicolor finale, Sam Coslow's "Sweepin' the Clouds Away," for which he is accompanied by a womanly chorus that dances on artificial rooftops and then underneath a closing "rainbow."

The rest of *Paramount on Parade* isn't nearly as inventive, which accounts for the unnerving

But as different as *Paramount on Parade* purported to be, it retained many of the by-now conventional aspects of the filmed revue. The John Barrymore of this film is Ruth Chatterton, who is first seen lounging in her dressing room—and, to identify with plebian moviegoers—tossing off a slangy "Beat it, kid!" in reply to Gallagher's reminder that time's a-wasting. Her showy number calls for her to sing Whiting's "My Marine," as a French prostitute reminded of her lost wartime love by a quartet of slumming American soldiers, Fredric March among them. "Miss Chatterton does a nice piece of emotionalism, but the song is insignificant," countered *Variety*.[14] There's also another copycat trick with miniatures, as Nancy Carroll and the Abe Lyman band emerge from shoe and shoebox, respectively, for "Dancing to Save Your Sole." Little Mitzi Green recalls, then surpasses, *Show of Shows'* Sid Silvers with her impressions of Chevalier and Charles Mack (of Mack and Moran) doing "All I Want Is Just One Girl."

The Lubitsch Touch aside, the only really memorable part of *Paramount on Parade* is Bow's singing of Janis and Jack King's "I'm True to the Navy Now." Bow, decked out in sailor garb on a swabbie-filled quarterdeck, seems not to be able to decide between her contralto and soprano, but her agreeably self-kidding performance turned into a professional triumph. Her weight down after bouts of whispers over her talkie unsuitability and bad publicity over her affair with Harry Richman (see *Puttin' on the Ritz*, Chapter 8), Bow got a lift from comments like Mordaunt Hall's: "She is vivacious and her voice registers better than in any of her own films."[15] Paramount was so elated by the strong reception to Bow that the song was expanded into a story that became the basis for her next film, *True to the Navy*. She also would get a full-length musical of her own, *Love Among the Millionaires* (see Chapter 5).

Television viewers who saw the 80-minute version of *Paramount on Parade* that made the rounds on cable in the late 1980s missed five of the six performance segments filmed in Technicolor. The only survivor, shown in black-and-white, was the "Sweepin' the Clouds Away" finale. Chevalier's brief color introduction of the imported Italian singer Nino Martini also remained, also in B&W. Absent were: the "Paramount on Parade" opening, with Mitzi Mayfair's toe-dancing followed by a bevy of showgirls; Martini's song, "Come Back to Sorrento"; the Harry Green *Carmen*/"I'm Isadore" sequence; Dennis King's forceful singing of "Nichavo!" ["Nothing Matters"] while he waits to be hanged; and "Let Me Drink to the Girl of My Dreams," for which 10 of Paramount's rising young stars appeared in a Civil War–era waltz parody that began and ended in a gold picture-frame effect.[16] The introduction to this number was included on the TV print, but director Edmund Goulding's speech was chopped off in mid-sentence.

There's some good news, however: The missing sequences have been preserved by the UCLA Film and Television Archive from a faded, deteriorating work print—but unfortunately without a soundtrack. The footage was included in a showing of *Paramount on Parade* during UCLA's annual Festival of Preservation in the spring of 1995.

KING OF JAZZ
(Universal; April 19, 1930)

"Devised and Directed" by: John Murray Anderson. Producer: Carl Laemmle, Jr. Screenplay: Edward T. Lowe, Jr. Comedy Sketches: Harry Ruskin, William Griffith. Dialogue: Charles MacArthur. Animation: Walter Lantz, Bill Nolan. Photography: Hal Mohr, Jerome Ash, Ray Rennahan. Editors: Maurice Pivar, Robert Carlisle. Sound: C. Roy Hunter. Assistant Director: Robert Ross. Art Director: Herman Rosse. Costumes: Herman Rosse. Musical Director: Ferde Grofé. Musical Arrangements: James Dietrich. Dance Direction: Russell Markert. Running Time: 98 minutes. Technicolor.

Cast: Paul Whiteman and His Orchestra, Laura La Plante, John Boles, Jeanette Loff, Stanley Smith, Glenn Tryon, William Kent, Merna Kennedy, Grace Hayes, Kathryn Crawford, Slim Summerville, Otis Harlan, Jeanie Lang, The Rhythm Boys [Bing Crosby, Al Rinker, Harry Barris], Sisters "G," The Brox Sisters, Jack White, George Chiles, Jacques Cartier, Yola D'Avril, Frank Leslie, Charles Irwin, Al Norman, Grace Hayes, Paul Howard, Marion Stattler, Don Rose, Nancy Torres, Russell Markert Girls, Tommy Atkins Sextette, Nell O'Day, Wilbur Hall, Jack Fulton, Beth Laemmle, Walter Brennan, Churchill Ross, Johnson Arledge, Roy Bargy, Paul Small (dance double for Whiteman).

Songs/Musical Numbers: "A Bench in the Park" [Loff, Smith, Brox Sisters, Rhythm Boys, Chiles, Fulton, Whiteman and orchestra], "Happy Feet" [Rhythm Boys, Sisters "G," Whiteman and orchestra, danced by Norman, Markert Girls, Small], "Has Anybody Seen Our Nellie?" [Arledge, Brennan, Ross, unidentified baritone], "I Like to Do Things for You" [Lang, Hayes, Kent, O'Day, Atkins Sextette, Whiteman], "Music Hath Charms" [Crosby], "My Bridal Veil" [Loff, Smith, chorus], "Oh Happy Bride" [bridal chorus], "The Song of the Dawn"

[Boles, chorus] (Jack Yellen, Milton Ager); "It Happened in Monterey" [Boles, Loff, danced by Sisters "G," Chiles, Markert Girls] (Mabel Wayne, Billy Rose); "La Paloma" [Torres in "Monterey" number] (Sebastian Yradier); "Long, Long Ago" [bridal chorus] (Thomas Haynes Bayly); "Mississippi Mud" [Rhythm Boys] (James Cavanaugh, Harry Barris); "Oh! How I'd Like to Own a Fish Store" [White, Rhythm Boys, band members] (Alfred B. Koppell, Billy Stone); "Ragamuffin Romeo" [Lang, Chiles, chorus, danced by Rose, Stattler] (Mabel Wayne, Harry De Costa); "Rhapsody in Blue" [Whiteman Orchestra, Cartier, Bargy] (George Gershwin); "So the Bluebirds and the Blackbirds Got Together" [Rhythm Boys] (Billy Moll, Harry Barris); "Stars and Stripes Forever" [Hall] (John Philip Sousa); "Pop Goes the Weasel" [Hall] (trad.); "Music Hath Charms," "I Like to Do Things for You" [danced by Markert Girls].

"Meet the Band" Medley: "Hot Lips" [trumpet: Harry Goldfield] (Henry Busse, Henry Lange, Lou Davis); "Mexican Trio" [violin: Joe Venuti; guitar: Eddie Lang] (Joe Venuti); "Piccolo Pete" [piccolo: Izzy Friedman] (Phil Baxter); "Caprice Viennois," "Tambourin Chinois" [violins: John Bowman, Kurt Dieterle, Otto Landau, Matt Malneck, Mischa Russell, Joe Venuti] (Fritz Kreisler); "Nola" [saxophone: Chester Hazlett; piano: Roy Bargy; trombone: Wilbur Hall] (Felix Arndt); "Linger Awhile" [banjo: Mike Pingitore] (Vincent Rose, Harry Owens).

"The Melting Pot of Music" Medley: "Rule, Britannia," "Hunt in the Black Forest," "John Peel," "Santa Lucia," "Funiculi-Finicula," "Comin' Thru the Rye," "Money Musk," "Die Wacht am Rhein," "Die Lorelei," "Spring, Beautiful Spring," "The Wearing of the Green," "Killarney," "The Irish Washerwoman," "Royal March of Spain," "Ay-yi Ay-yi-yi," "Hymn of Free Russia," "Song of the Volga Boatmen," "Otchitchornya" ("Dark Eyes"), "La Marseillaise," "Three Captains," "Hold Me," plus reprises of "The Song of the Dawn," "A Bench in the Park," "I Like to Do Things for You," "It Happened in Monterey," "Stars and Stripes Forever," "Happy Feet," "Rhapsody in Blue."

Non-Musical Comedy Sketches: "All Noisy on the Eastern Front" [Brennan, D'Avril, Kent, Whiteman, unidentified actor, men]; "In Conference" [Kennedy, La Plante, Tryon];

"Ladies of the Press" [Crawford, Hayes, Kennedy, Lang, La Plante]; "Oh! Forevermore" [Kent, Brennan]; "Springtime" [Brennan, D'Avril, Summerville]; "baby" sketch [Kennedy, Kent, Tryon]; "horse" sketch [Brennan, Summerville]; "lucky" sketch [Harlan, Summerville].

Academy Award: Best Interior Decoration (Herman Rosse, 1929-30).

Disc: Columbia 2163-D (Whiteman and Orchestra/"It Happened in Monterey"/"The Song of the Dawn"/78); Columbia 2164-D (Whiteman and Orchestra/"A Bench in the Park"/"Happy Feet"/78); Columbia 2170-D (Whiteman and Orchestra/"I Like to Do Things for You"/"Ragamuffin Romeo"/78); Columbia 2223-D (Rhythm Boys/"A Bench in the Park"/78); RCA Victor 22372 (Boles/"It Happened in Monterey"/"The Song of the Dawn"/78); Caliban 6025 (bootleg LP; ST).

Video: MCA-Universal (cassette/laserdisc).

Paul Whiteman (1890–1967) was a big man—and not only because he was the most popular bandleader of the 1920s. Whiteman, tall and portly, was a man of expansive tastes as well as appetites. He lived high and spent as freely as could a man who was pulling in a $1-million income by 1922. At his peak, he controlled nearly 30 bands, in New York and on the road, dispatching them to various locales under the label "Paul Whiteman's Orchestra" while the more authentically billed "Paul Whiteman and His Orchestra" got the classiest gigs. Among the latter was a historic date at the Aeolian Hall in New York, where on February 12, 1924, Whiteman and his Palais Royal unit gave a concert that introduced George Gershwin's symphonic "Rhapsody in Blue," which gave jazz-styled pop music a much-needed boost in prestige. The unveiling of what would become one of the century's greatest musical compositions was auspicious enough that Whiteman's agent bestowed upon his client the title "King of Jazz." The moniker may have been an exaggeration, but Whiteman's unit did include, at one time or another, such names as Bix Beiderbecke, Joe Venuti, Lennie Hayton, Eddie Lang, the Dorsey brothers—and Harry Lillis "Bing" Crosby.

In 1929, Whiteman was still going strong, with a lucrative Columbia record contract and a successful radio show sponsored by Old Gold cigarettes. Universal chief Carl Laemmle, seeking a headliner for a big-budget musical picture to be directed by Paul (*Broadway*) Fejos, enticed Whiteman to come West from New York with his 40 musicians. The ensuing train trip aboard "The Whiteman Special" in May and June of '29 was highly publicized; it lasted 13 days instead of the usual four or five because band and conductor made public appearances at virtually every stop. In Hollywood, Universal housed the band in a specially built lodge on its backlot, complete with rehearsal rooms and recreational facilities.

But the band sat idle for months, for the studio could not find a story for its new act. One false start turned up in a trade ad announcing *King of Jazz* in the summer of 1929. Whiteman, it said, would star in a "magnificent Movietone romance ... in which young love, under the guiding hand of the master of jazz, blossoms to a glorious triumph." Soon, the frustrated "master" and his musicians would temporarily return to the East.[17] After some time, Universal decided to make the Whiteman movie a revue—and its first all–Technicolor film to boot. Since Flo Ziegfeld, Universal's first choice, was unavailable to oversee it, Whiteman suggested the hiring of John Murray Anderson, whose own New York revues made him Ziegfeld's closest competitor in taste and competence.

Universal spent a heady $50,000 to get Anderson (1886–1954), whose influence would show in every minute of *King of Jazz*, an astounding film that is one of the most inventive of early talkies. He brought in his own set designer, Herman Rosse, and dance director, Russell Markert. Markert came from New York's Roxy Theatre, later to be renamed Radio City Music Hall, where he would choreograph the Rockettes' famed routines for years. Universal supplied its best cameraman—Hal Mohr, who for *King of Jazz* would employ the same probing crane he had used for Fejos in *Broadway*—and its contract talent (Laura La Plante, Glenn Tryon, Slim Summerville, Merna Kennedy). Possibly because the studio had no major musical stars (and few notable names, period), Anderson imported performers trained in the East and elsewhere: William Kent, Grace Hayes, The Brox Sisters (who had appeared in *Hollywood Revue*), Jeanie Lang, George Chiles, host

Charles Irwin and a Berlin dancing duo called The Sisters "G."

"The theater is fading into insignificance," declared Hollywood's newest "hot" director,

> When we get stereoscopic film, together with the improved sound that is coming, and the new color achievements that are inevitable, things will be possible to the camera that the stage could never hope to aspire. The man who doesn't realize the importance of the screen now is just a fool. The theater man who comes to the screen and tries to bring the limited teachings of the stage with him is also foolish. A new type of entertainment is springing up. The actor or actress trained in stage artificiality is doomed. Singers will arise who could never get anywhere on the stage....[18]

Anderson wanted to mount an elaborate number around "Rhapsody in Blue," which presented an obvious logistical problem because Technicolor did not photograph blue. To simulate blue, he used a background of gray and silver with a touch of green shading.[19] To enhance the red and green that did exist in Technicolor, he utilized lamps with colored projection. Anderson and Whiteman decided to pre-record all of the music, which ensured a better balance between the band and the vocalists. Laemmle commissioned the making of a cartoon short animated by Walter Lantz, the future creator of Woody Woodpecker who was then under contract to Universal as the maker of animated stories starring the ex–Walt Disney character Oswald the Lucky Rabbit. In all, the production of *King of Jazz* would cost about $2 million, which made its profitability questionable even before its world premiere at the Fox Wilshire Theatre in Los Angeles on April 19, 1930.

Aesthetically, the price was worth it, for almost everything in *King of Jazz* screamed of innovation and spectacle. The sequences, tied together as "pages" of "Paul Whiteman's Scrap Book," begin with the amusing Lantz cartoon, which purports to explain how the bandleader got to be "King of Jazz." In the African jungle, the animated Whiteman soothes the savage beasts (Oswald the Rabbit strangely among them) with "Music Hath Charms," then is plunked on the noggin by an errant coconut that raises a bump that takes the shape of a crown. Back in live-action, Whiteman introduces his "boys" by releasing them, in

Chorines dance upon a giant piano in the overproduced "Rhapsody in Blue" number from *King of Jazz*.

miniature form, from a satchel into a mini-bandstand, which expands to normal size. This Tom Thumb–type gimmick had been done in other film revues, but Anderson enhances the sequence by having Whiteman present each section of the orchestra separately, in shadow or silhouette, with blended backgrounds or overhead camera. In the most interesting effect, banjo player Mike Pingitore performs "Linger Awhile" alone against a back-projected, violet-speckled setting, then the camera slides diagonally upward to reveal him in a huge shadow.

There are other uniquely cinematic moments. One of the brief comedy sketches, this one set in a newspaper editor's office, is prefaced as each component of the set, including actresses La Plante and Lang, appears one after the other in stop-action. For a number called "Happy Feet," stop-action photography is used again as a pair of disembodied shoes emerges from a gift-wrapped box and taps on top of a

platform superimposed on a shot of the orchestra as it begins to play the song. In the same number, the faces of the dancing Sisters "G" are shown in close-up, but in reflection against the surface below, creating an illusion of four disembodied faces. Whiteman's vocal trio, The Rhythm Boys, are part of that number, one of four in which Crosby, Harry Barris and Al Rinker made their film debut. For their first appearance, Anderson begins with the threesome in silhouette, singing their hit "Mississippi Mud." After a few seconds of minor bantering, Crosby turns on a lamp and they light up for "So the Bluebirds and the Blackbirds Got Together." As the song ends, they blend back into the darkness.

The Rhythm Boys occasionally recorded without the Whiteman unit and were fast gaining a reputation of their own. Crosby in particular wanted the chance to come out from under the boss's large shadow; he would, of course, and very soon. Whiteman tabbed Crosby to sing "Music Hath Charms" over the opening credits and also planned for him to solo as the lead of a major production number, "The Song of the Dawn." Crosby supposedly rehearsed the song and was all ready to go until a drunken-driving arrest set him back. Whiteman arranged for Crosby to perform with Barris and Rinker while on daytime furlough from what would be 40 days of a 60-day jail sentence, but John Boles—stylistically a better choice anyway—got "The Song of the Dawn." He sang it dynamically, with the backing of a cowboy chorus, against the breathtaking backdrop of a morning sunrise.

"The Song of the Dawn" was one of eight songs written for *King of Jazz* by Jack Yellen and Milton Ager. Among their other contributions were "A Bench in the Park," the staging and theme of which interestingly predate Busby Berkeley's "Pettin' in the Park" number from *Gold Diggers of 1933*, and "My Bridal Veil," in which a beautiful parade of wedding gowns back vocals by Jeanette Loff and Stanley Smith. But the biggest immediate hit to emerge from *King of Jazz* was not a Yellen-Ager tune but Mabel Wayne and Harry De Costa's "It Happened in Monterey." Boles again does the honors, amid a flashback set in old Mexico in which he wins and then forsakes the love of his life (Loff). Again, Whiteman wanted one of his men, vocalist Jack Fulton, to lead the number, but Universal prevailed with its contractee. The song was well covered by disc artists, among them Ruth Etting, George Olsen and His Orchestra and, of course, the Whiteman band.

The overproduced "Rhapsody in Blue" number shows a caped, high-hatted clarinetist (Jacques Cartier) gliding along a huge piano set with the entire Whiteman unit tucked inside. This time, however, the gaudy sets and scores of dancers needlessly detract from the impact of the music. Memorable still, though, is the introduction to the piece, in which a "native" dancer (also Cartier) gyrates atop a huge African drum that is intended to represent the "jungle" origins of the syncopated rhythms that will follow. Despite assertions to the contrary over the years, the soloist for "Rhapsody in Blue" here is not George Gershwin, but Whiteman's regular pianist, Roy Bargy.[20] The hoary comedy blackouts, some of which were reused from Anderson's most recent Broadway show, *Murray Anderson's Al-*

manac, represent the film's biggest weakness. An example has Walter Brennan complaining about playing the front end of a horse's costume ("I feel like a horse's neck!"), then Slim Summerville popping his head from the back ("Horse's neck? How do you suppose I feel?"). But the concept of *King of Jazz* was to present a potpourri of entertainment. There is also an amusing parody of turn-of-the-century music ("Has Anybody Seen Our Nellie?") and a corny novelty in which Whiteman associate Willie Hall plays the likes of "Stars and Stripes Forever" with a bicycle pump.

Perhaps no musical film includes a wider range of styles, even if some of the samples are heard for only a few seconds. The "meet the band" medley alone varies from Felix Arndt's "Nola" to Fritz Kreisler's "Caprice Viennois" and "Tambourin Chinois" to "Mexican Trio," a Latin-tinged guitar-and-violin duet performed by Eddie Lang and Joe Venuti. The height of diversity is the finale, "The Melting Pot of Music," in which various choruses present an international medley of song spanning the 18th century to the present. Among the selections are "Rule, Britannia," "John Peel," "Santa Lucia," "The Wearing of the Green," "La Marseillaise," "Die Lorelei" and "Otchitchornya" ("Dark Eyes"). Aided by special effects, Whiteman, looking like some kind of mad scientist, stirs the contents of a pot into the intoxicating mix that will become jazz. Unfortunately, the only ethnic contribution to jazz not represented here was the most important one: the African-American influence, although Anderson may have felt the nod to blacks at the outset of "Rhapsody in Blue" was sufficient.

King of Jazz earned many favorable reviews, among them the description by *The New York Times*' Mordaunt Hall of "a marvel of camera wizardry, joyous color schemes, charming costumes and seductive lighting effects."

> The only adverse criticism is that some of the sequences are a little somber, but even in these stretches Mr. Anderson's highly artistic and imaginative mind is constantly apparent. ... It is one of the very few pictures in which there is no catering to the unsophisticated mentality, for all the widely different features are of a high order and yet one can readily presume that they will appeal to all types of audiences.[21]

Less-impressed commentators criticized the movie for its weak comedy and overextravagance. "There are neat camera and other tricks in it," griped "Sime" Silverman in *Variety*, "but … they don't count at the gate."[22] Rosse's sets won an Academy Award. But Universal had entered the revue sweepstakes too late: The earlier, inferior examples had soaked up whatever public interest there had been. *King of Jazz* returned less than $900,000 in grosses during its U.S. release, although the foreign grosses enabled it to turn a small profit.[23] Trade ads in June 1930 announced two productions to be directed by Anderson, but by mid-1931 the studio had let him go. He had been under contract for 18 months at $3,500 weekly and had only *King of Jazz* to show for it. Universal didn't produce another musical until 1933 (*Moonlight and Pretzels*), and it waited until 1942 before it made another color feature (*Arabian Nights*).

Whiteman, like so many other musical performers, became unwanted in Hollywood. The Depression hit him hard enough that he had to reduce his payroll substantially, and the general slump in record sales contributed to his losing his contract with Columbia. Whiteman did recover, financially and professionally, although he had passed his peak. He made only a handful of film appearances, but none were as substantial or as important as *King of Jazz*.[24]

King of Jazz was recut for a fleeting re-release in 1933. Like so many other early musicals, it became practically forgotten, but like too few, it gained new life. A 16mm print was shown archivally on both coasts in the mid-1970s, but in the early 1980s, a more valuable 35mm print was located by a Universal researcher in a vault at the British Broadcasting Company. The patched-together result was considered marketable by Universal because of its Crosby connection, and it debuted on cable television in 1983. A videocassette release followed, and *King of Jazz* has remained available to those who want to see Paul Whiteman wave his baton and Bing Crosby endure his baptism in film.

CHAPTER 11

1931: *Without a Song*

Russ Brown, manager of the Fox Rex Theatre in Eugene, Oregon, just knew he had a clinker. Brown's current attraction was *Movietone Follies of 1930*, and he figured that he knew his audience's tastes well enough to know that they wouldn't endure another musical revue, not even a revue with a framing plot like this one. Short of options, Brown decided to build his entire hometown advertising campaign around the film's top-billed player, comedian El Brendel. In the Northwest, as everywhere, Brendel had an appreciable following, and Brown gambled that his name alone would support a picture. Thus, practically every newspaper and herald ad that emitted from the Rex carried Brendel's name alone. Not once was there a mention of the eight songs, or the singing of Marjorie White and Frank Richardson, or of Fox's shapely dancing girls. But the strong turnout to Russ Brown's house—*even for a musical*—let the manager know that he'd made the right call.

It now seems amazing that anyone would want to recommend a film by invoking the name of El Brendel, but Brown's little ad campaign was deemed inventive enough to earn the top billing in the national "Exploitettes" column in *The Film Daily* of August 13, 1930. It also spoke volumes about the declining stature of the musical film. The plotless revue was the first sub-genre to find disfavor among the public, but soon all manner of music would be frowned upon. Exhibitors didn't want any more musical pictures, and even after the studios decided to stop making them, they were stuck with the ones already in the can.

Although the completed but unreleased *The March of Time* (see Chapter 10) was the most notable of musicals that never were, there were three other major casualties at MGM alone. *Five O'Clock Girl*, a Marion Davies–Charles King starrer with a score by Bert Kalmar and Harry Ruby, had been abandoned back in 1929, maybe less for economic reasons than for a tiff over story content between Irving Thalberg and William Randolph Hearst.[1] *Rosalie*, which would have brought to the screen the 1928 Ziegfeld production with or without its George Gershwin–Sigmund Romberg music, also was intended for Davies. At least 16 of Metro's staff writers tried to come up with a suitable adaptation, and the studio even considered drafting P. G. Wodehouse, who wrote lyrics for some of the source music, to novelize the material so MGM could take a cut of the royalties and then make its film from the book.[2] In the end, Davies' reported indifference to the project may have sunk it.[3]

A bigger loss may have been *Great Day*, an adaptation of a 1929 Broadway flop into which Metro had sunk a good deal of money. The film, with a cast headed by Joan Crawford and a Vincent Youmans score that included "Without a Song," was in production less than two weeks before being halted for a story revision that was never made.

The pages of trade magazines in early to mid–1930 were filled with announcements of musicals for the 1930-31 season that were never filmed. Among them: *The Merry Widow* (MGM, with Lawrence Tibbett); *Maytime* and *Danube Love Song* (Warner Bros.); *Heart of the Rockies* (RKO, with Bebe Daniels and Everett Marshall); *Babes in Toyland* (RKO, with Wheeler and Woolsey); *The Love Cavalier* (Universal, with John Boles, Lupe Velez and Jeanette Loff); *New Movietone Follies of 1931* (Fox; with Claire Luce, Dixie Lee, Marie Saxon, El Brendel and many others). The June 15 *Film Daily* noted that at least 50 musical films were being planned for release by 1931, but nowhere near that number were made.

Some films were planned as musicals but then, as the market began to fall off, were released after being shorn of all or most of their scores. Fox dropped three of six numbers from its Bea Lillie comedy *Are You There?* (see Chapter 5). First National used only three of five copyrighted songs for its football entry *Maybe It's Love* (see Chapter 6), but the film retained enough music to qualify as a musical. Not so with Warner Bros.' *The Life of the Party* (November 7, 1930), which lost five of six tunes sung by comic gold diggers Winnie Lightner and Irene Delroy and their unwitting target, Jack Whiting. Irving Berlin was an unwilling victim with *Reaching for the Moon* (December 30, 1930), a United Artists release starring Douglas Fairbanks, Sr., and Bebe Daniels. Berlin's comic story, about a Wall Street financier who follows an aviatrix to Europe on a luxury liner, was filmed for nearly $1 million and infused with five of his songs, among them the title tune. But director Edmund Goulding, who feuded with Berlin throughout the shooting, ordered the deletion of four numbers a few weeks before release. All that survived was a spirited number called "When the Folks High Up Do the Mean Low Down," sung on William Cameron Menzies' expansive ship's-bar-and-ballroom set by Daniels and, in his first solo film stint, ninth-billed Bing Crosby.

The simplest explanation for the backlash is that Hollywood blunted the public demand for musicals by glutting the market with too many cookie-cutter plots, uncatchy tunes and interchangeable personalities. In the rush for quick profits, too many movies had been made with too little thought, with actors who couldn't sing and singers who couldn't act, and with songs by composers who were overworked, undertalented or both. Any mogul who thought he was fooling the public needed only to read the comment by Miss J. Wright of Dallas, Texas, in the fan magazine *Motion Picture*:

> Please cut out the theme songs. They usually come at the wrong time, anyhow. Can't the hero or heroine rave and curse for a change instead of warbling a song? Can you imagine Will Rogers or George Bancroft crooning a disappointed love song? Awk!!!![4]

A common complaint had to do with the way music was used. Unlike the big-city stage-going public, movie fans in the hinterlands seemed to require a reason for a performer entering into song. The concept of fantasy would not suffice. There seemed to be emerging two distinct schools of thought regarding the employment of music in a film. One held that the music had to be woven so skillfully into the story content of the picture that it would become impossible to separate it from the other essentials. The opposing theory was that the plausibility of music was no more necessary in a movie than in a live stage show such as *Whoopee!* or *The Cocoanuts*. The majority of the public seemed to prefer the first theory—which, in time, would become key to the development of the filmed musical—but moviemakers hoped they would agree with the second.

Chester Bann, writing for the *Syracuse Herald*, contributed a particularly astute commentary along these lines that was reprinted in *The Film Daily*:

> Because one, two, six or 20 filmusicals flop at the box office does not imply that John Public is ag'in them as a form of cinematic entertainment. A more correct interpretation would be that music has been sadly misused in them. Which is to say that composers have been forced to turn out tunes like Armour does sausages—so many feet per hour; that theme songs have been subjected to maddening repetition; that pretentious numbers have been entrusted to fifth-rate singers; and that a tune frequently has been expected to save the day for a trashy story.[5]

Instead of taking advice like this to heart, the panicky studios decided to cut their losses. Already faced with Depression-created financial reverses that would make extravagant productions seem frivolous (movie attendance dropped 40 percent in 1930), they jettisoned most of their musical specialists. Scores of composers and dance directors returned to the East, and those who didn't suffered from disuse. After his *Whoopee!* splash, Busby Berkeley was signed to a $1,000-a-week, one-year contract by Paramount, which then allowed him to sit in his office for months without a minute of work. Later, he was reduced to directing stage prologues for the Fanchon and Marco unit in Los Angeles. Broadway also was besieged by out-of-work movie stars, musical or not. "Why I'm on the Outside Lookin' In," a late–1930 feature article in *Photoplay*, alone mentioned Bernice

Claire, Alexander Gray, Dennis King, Vilma Banky, Tom Patricola, Paul Muni, Lillian Roth, Colleen Moore and that still-young actress who had started in pictures before there was a real Hollywood, Lillian Gish. Some had made their names on the stage; some had thrived exclusively in movies. "They all harbor a little secret yen to try a comeback as they peep wistfully over the studio fence," commented the author, Paul Jarvis. "One day many of them will jump over again. But not just now."[6]

In 1929, more than 60 musicals had emerged from Hollywood; for 1930, there were more than 80. But only 11 premiered during 1931, and one of those was *Kiss Me Again,* the long-delayed First National operetta (see Chapter 7) that opened in New York a scant seven days into the year. Others—*Bright Lights, Oh, for a Man!, New Moon, One Heavenly Night, Under Suspicion, Are You There?*—played briefly near the end of 1930 and gained a wider release in 1931. The year was filled with straight comedies that would have been filled with songs had they been made a few months earlier. Among these was *Fifty Million Frenchmen* (March 25, 1931), which had been one of the most popular musical comedies of the 1929-30 New York season. Warner Bros. figured the Herbert Fields–Cole Porter creation was such a natural for the screen that it financed the Broadway production entirely and, with the film rights thus gained, planned to produce it in Technicolor for its 1930-31 schedule.[7] But when the movie was made, with William Gaxton and Helen Broderick reprising their stage roles, Porter's music was heard only in underscoring. It failed anyway.

Of the crop of genuine musicals in general release during 1931, only two, *The Smiling Lieutenant* and *Palmy Days,* could claim to be financially successful. In too many, the musical content was limited or underpublicized. Dances were rarely seen. This was a year for the inauguration of two great genre cycles: the horror film (with *Dracula* and *Frankenstein*) and the gangster movie (the landmark trio of *Little Caesar, The Public Enemy* and, in early 1932, *Scarface*). The same filmgoers who were being thrilled by monsters and mobsters were being scared off by a mere song or two.

THE HOT HEIRESS
(First National; March 13, 1931)

Director: Clarence Badger. Screenplay: Herbert Fields. Photography: Sol Polito. Editor: Thomas Pratt. Art Director: Jack Okey. Musical Director: Erno Rapée. Running Time: 81 minutes.

Cast: Ben Lyon (Hap Harrigan), Ona Munson (Juliette Hunter), Walter Pidgeon (Clay), Tom Dugan (Bill Dugan), Holmes Herbert (Mr. Hunter), Inez Courtney (Margie), Thelma Todd (Lola), Nella Walker (Mrs. Hunter), George Irving (physician), Joe Bernard, Elise Bartlett.

Songs: "Like Ordinary People Do" [Lyon, Munson, Courtney], "Nobody Loves a Riveter" [Lyon, Dugan], "You're the Cats" [Lyon, Munson] (Lorenz Hart, Richard Rodgers); "Twelfth Street Rag" [band at club] (Euday L. Bowman).

Disc: Music Masters JJA-19766 (bootleg LP; ST).

The Hot Heiress is best known as the film that marked the official Hollywood debut of the great songwriting team of Richard Rodgers (1902–1979) and Lorenz Hart (1895–1943). Composer Rodgers and lyricist Hart had been creating hit musicals on Broadway for five years; their songs were heard in the film adaptations of *Spring Is Here, Heads Up* and *Present Arms* (released by RKO as *Leathernecking*). But *The Hot Heiress* was not their first stab at writing music expressly for the movies. They penned four songs for *Follow Thru* (see Chapter 4), Paramount's version of the De Sylva–Brown–Henderson stage hit, but none made it into the film. Also, Rodgers and Hart appeared in a 1929 Paramount two-reeler, *Makers of Melody,* in which their songs "Here in My Arms," "Manhattan," "The Blue Room" and "The Girl Friend" were performed by various singers (including Inez Courtney, later of *The Hot Heiress*).

In the summer of 1930, Rodgers and Hart were enticed to come West with a contract that paid them $50,000 each to write the scores for three original Warner Bros.–First National musicals. For the first, *The Hot Heiress,* the team quickly came up with five songs. The routine story, scripted by their frequent collaborator Herbert Fields, concerned a common riveter (Ben Lyon) who falls for a society miss (Ona Munson, in a role intended for Marilyn Miller) after one of his hot bolts is accidentally tossed into her penthouse boudoir. She tries to pass him off to her family as an architect, but his lack of pretention betrays him. Embarrassed, he breaks up with her for a time, but she wins him back by setting up shop right next to his latest construction site.

By the time *The Hot Heiress* was ready for release, the prevailing attitude toward musicals motivated the studio to drop two of its songs, "He Looks So Good to Me" and "How About It?" and to publicize the film as a straight comedy.[8] In the entire pressbook for *The Hot Heiress*, Rodgers and Hart were mentioned in two paragraphs. None of the ads for the film referred to its music; instead, there were silly—and, as it turned out, inaccurate—come-ons like "This jane with lots of jack—and lots of johns—will give you a million dollars of laughs!"

In fact, the three songs are hardly Rodgers and Hart's best, but they are practically all that recommend *The Hot Heiress*. Munson (1906–1955) and Lyon (1901–1979) have some appeal as a couple—she's definitely the aggressor in the relationship—but they are held back by the predictable script, which comes complete with a snobby rival for Munson's hand (Walter Pidgeon, for whose baritone Warners now had no use), and plodding direction by Clarence Badger. The best tune of the three, "Nobody Loves a Riveter," starts the picture off with a bang. Lyon and chum Tommy Dugan (1889–1955) are making all manner of on-the-job racket too early in the morning for the apartment dwellers who surround their skyscraper site. A man holding a crying baby yells for mercy from his window. A frustrated violinist smashes his instrument to bits. Out of vignettes such as this grow Lyon's sung declaration that nobody loves a riveter but his mother. Richard Rodgers wrote that he and Hart liked the idea that songs like this were a natural extention of the spoken dialogue, and "not for spectacle."[9] Lyon and Munson, neither impressively voiced, duet on "You're the Cats" over their characters' first breakfast. "Like Ordinary People Do," sung as the Lyon-Munson and Dugan-Courtney pairs enjoy a cozy evening together, is a double duet of sorts, only Dugan doesn't sing.

Lyon told John Kobal of his experience with Rodgers and Hart:

> I remember being very pleased when they wanted me, because these boys ... came with

a terrific reputation, having all those Broadway hits. They were always on the set. I don't remember Fields all that well, but Hart was brilliant. ... He changed styles in lyrics like Gershwin did rhythms. None of this rhyming "moon-swoon" thing for him. At times, when he wasn't satisfied with the way we did a number, he'd leave the set, and come back ten minutes later with lyrics that fit what we had to do like a glove.[10]

Rodgers and Hart's next Hollywood project was to be a Ben Lyon picture called *Love of Michael*, but *The Hot Heiress* fared so poorly that the studio released Rodgers and Hart from their contract with the remaining two movies unmade. But before the end of the year, the ambitious duo would be elsewhere in Hollywood—and making better musicals.

THE SMILING LIEUTENANT
(Paramount; May 22, 1931)

Director-Producer: Ernst Lubitsch. Screenplay: Ernest Vajda, Samson Raphaelson, Ernst Lubitsch. Based on the operetta *Ein Walzertraum* [*A Waltz Dream*] by Leopold Jacobson, Felix Doermann and Oscar Straus (1907), and the novel *Nux der Prinzgemahl* by Hans Müller. Photography: George Folsey. Editor: Merrill White. Sound: Ernest F. Zatorsky, C. A. Tuthill. Art Director: Hans Dreier. Musical Director: Adolph Deutsch. Musical Arrangements: John W. Green, Conrad Salinger. Running Time: 88 minutes.

Cast: Maurice Chevalier (Niki), Claudette Colbert (Franzi), Miriam Hopkins (Princess Anna), George Barbier (King Adolf), Charles Ruggles (Max), Con MacSunday (emperor), Hugh O'Connell (orderly), Robert Strange (Adjutant von Rockoff), Janet Reade (Lily), Elizabeth Patterson (Baroness von Schwedel), Harry C. Bradley (Count von Halden), Werner Saxtorph (Josef), Karl Stall (master of ceremonies), Granville Bates (bill collector), Charles Wagenheim (officer), Maude Allen (woman).

Songs: "Breakfast Table Love" [Chevalier, Colbert], "Jazz Up Your Lingerie" [Colbert, Hopkins; reprised by Hopkins at piano], "One More Hour of Love" [Chevalier, Colbert, Hopkins], "Toujours l'Amour in the Army"

As *The Smiling Lieutenant* (both photos), Maurice Chevalier encounters a feisty bandleader (Claudette Colbert) (top) and a demure princess (Miriam Hopkins) (bottom).

[Chevalier, twice], "While Hearts Are Singing, Live for Today" [Colbert, band; reprised by Colbert] (Clifford Grey, Oscar Straus).

Academy Award Nomination: Best Picture, 1931-32.

Fortunately for those fans who still had patience enough to appreciate first-rate musical films, the man who in 1929 and 1930 had made them better than anyone was still doing so. Paramount wanted Ernst Lubitsch to make movies like *The Smiling Lieutenant* because of his canny sense for comedy, not because his pictures had great music, but for now the songs were still part of the package.

The Smiling Lieutenant was adapted from the Oscar Straus operetta *A Waltz Dream*, which had been produced as a German silent with that title in 1926. The filming, at Paramount's Long Island studio in early 1931, reunited Lubitsch with Maurice Chevalier, whose usually high spirits were blunted by the recent death of his mother. His movie career also needed a nudge after the mediocre *The Big Pond* and *Playboy of Paris*. For both Claudette Colbert and Miriam Hopkins, this marked a first—but not last—association with Lubitsch, who decided to get the best out of his leading ladies by encouraging their tense competitiveness over matters such as their profiles. This became an issue because both women preferred their faces to be photographed on the right side.[11] Hopkins (1902–1972), an established Broadway actress in only her second film, also despaired over her perceived unattractiveness and her finishing-school French accent. But she reluctantly put the latter to good use next to the native tongues of Chevalier and Colbert in *Le Lieutenant Souriant*, a French-language version.

With *The Smiling Lieutenant*, Lubitsch continued his good-natured jabbing at the pomposity and ritual of royalty, although his disrespect for the ruling class didn't extend to permitting the right woman to get her man. Chevalier's Niki, an oversexed Austrian officer of the guards, ends up not with Franzi (Colbert), the worldly violinist and women's orchestra leader he falls for at the outset, but with Anna (Hopkins), the prim, dowdy visiting princess whom he meets by happenstance. Franzi can blame herself partly for the loss, for she is carelessly flirting with the on-duty Niki at the exact moment the carriage bearing Anna and her monarch father (George Barbier) passes between the lovers on a Vienna street. Anna thinks Niki's mischievous smile and wink is intended for her, and she is insulted by the "gesture."

Hauled before the king, Niki cannot reveal the real reason for his flattery, but he is so extravagant in his praise for the princess that she talks her father into permitting a wedding. Trapped, Niki goes through with the nuptials and becomes prince consort of the postage-stamp kingdom of Flausenthurm, but he continues his affair with Franzi. Anna finds out about the extra-curriculars and confronts Franzi, who is so amazed by the princess's lack of guile that she takes pity on her and, before returning to Vienna for good, advises her in song to "Jazz Up Your Lingerie" and transforms her into a ravishing beauty. After being seduced by his sexy "new" wife, Niki decides that life with Anna won't be so dull, after all.

The screenplay by Ernest Vajda and Samson Raphaelson (with uncredited help from Lubitsch) sparkles with typically risqué dialogue, as when Niki, who has brought Franzi to his apartment for the first time, tries to talk her out of packing up her violin to leave.

"You want to go?"

She pauses. "Yes."

"Why?"

A long pause. "I like you too much."

"Shall I see you again?"

"Oh, I hope so."

"When?"

"Well, perhaps tomorrow night we could have dinner together."

"Oh, don't make me wait 24 hours. I'm so *hungry!*"

"Well, perhaps we could have tea tomorrow afternoon."

"Why not breakfast tomorrow morning?"

"No. No. First tea … and then dinner … and then … maybe … maybe breakfast."

She walks to his door, but he takes her in his arms. Fade out to a shot of Niki's orderly frying eggs. It's time for some "Breakfast Table Love."

This sequence provides meaning to Franzi's closing line to the made-over Anna: "Girls who start with breakfast don't usually stay for supper." It is the capper to a memorable performance by Colbert, cast against type. Franzi's favorite song, which she plays and sings for Niki, is "While Hearts Are Singing, Live for Today," but Colbert complements her hard-boiled facade with an unusual vulnerability and sadness. Colbert doesn't have much of a voice (it wavers between soprano and contralto), but she's a superior actress to any real singer (say, Jeanette MacDonald) who could have been cast in the role. Lubitsch continually points out the differences in the personalities of Franzi and Anna, most notably during the "One More Hour of Love" number, in which shots of Niki and Franzi, dancing in a nightclub as he brags of the dynamite in her kisses, are alternated with those of Anna, singing to the palace dowagers of her new sweetheart's modesty and gentleness.

But in *The Smiling Lieutenant,* more than in any of his talkies, Lubitsch eschews dialogue and song and permits the action to speak for itself. This is most apparent at the climax, which begins when Niki trudges home to be greeted by his orderly bearing Franzi's farewell note. He sits down for a drink, then hears music coming from the royal couple's bedchamber. He finds Anna sitting at the piano plunking out "Jazz Up Your Lingerie" while wearing a slinky nightgown and smoking a cigarette. Stunned, Niki runs back to the kitchen for another drink, then quickly returns to see his wife taking off her nightgown to reveal a sexy negligee. Now, he dashes back for an even bigger swig, and fortified, speeds up the stairs to the bedroom. She is at a mirror wearing an expensive fur. "Anna! Is this you?" he cries. "No," she replies, "this is Mandelbaum and Gruenstein," meaning the furriers. She throws off the fur. "This is me!" she cries as she kisses him passionately. "And this is me again!" More passion. Anna picks up the same checkerboard on which Niki had wasted away their wedding night playing with the king. He tosses the board away, but she keeps returning it to him. Finally, to her approval, he throws the board on the bed, where, it's clear, the real games will begin. Niki emerges from the lovemaking for a triumphant final chorus of "Toujours l'Amour in the Army." From his arrival at the palace to his final toss of the checkerboard, seven minutes of screen time has elapsed—with exactly 16 words of dialogue. Wrote William Boehnel of *The New York Telegram*: "Here, Lubitsch has done what René Clair did in *Le Million.* ... It is an excellent example of the use of silent-picture technique and talking and sound-picture methods."[12]

As with *Monte Carlo,* critics fell over each other trying to find new platitudes for *The Smiling Lieutenant.* "Once more the combination of Maurice Chevalier and Ernst Lubitsch results in a piece of artistry, this one ... flawless in its manipulation and not far from perfect in performance. ... Oscar Straus' music needs no commendation," wrote Marguerite Tazelaar in the *New York Herald Tribune.*[13] Said *Photoplay's* anonymous commentator: "With Herr Lubitsch leading him by the hand, back comes Chevalier in one of the breeziest and most tuneful pieces of entertainment that we have seen in a long time. ... If we must have man-and-woman and triangle stories in films, please let Mr. Lubitsch do them."[14] *The Smiling Lieutenant* was nominated—as was Lubitsch's *One Hour with You*—for the 1931-32 Academy Award for Best Picture.

Lubitsch's third talking hit in as many tries, *The Smiling Lieutenant* ranks with the director's greatest films, although recognition for it among historians came a little late. This had mostly to do with the film's unavailability. Paramount somehow lost whatever prints it had, and it wasn't until the late 1960s that one, with subtitles, turned up in the Danish Film Archives. A non-subtitled print was eventually located. Now, those who are lucky enough to see *The Smiling Lieutenant* archivally or at the occasional film convention can marvel at this nearly extinct musical gem.

THE PRODIGAL
(MGM; June 26, 1931)

Director: Harry Pollard. Supervisor: Paul Bern. Continuity and Dialogue: Bess Meredyth, Wells Root. Based on the story "The Southerner" by Bess Meredyth and Wells Root. Photography: Harold Rosson. Editor: Margaret Booth. Sound: Douglas Shearer. Art Director: Cedric Gibbons. Costumes: René Hubert. Running Time: 76 minutes.

Cast: Lawrence Tibbett (Jeffry Farraday), Esther Ralston (Antonia Farraday), Roland Young (Doc Greene), Cliff Edwards (Snipe), Purnell B. Pratt (Rodman Farraday), Hedda Hopper (Christine), Emma Dunn (Cynthia Farraday), Stepin Fetchit (Hokey), Louis John Bartels (George), Theodore von Eltz (Carter Jerome), Wally Albright (Peter), Suzanne

Lawrence Tibbett (with Hedda Hopper and a young Wally Albright and Suzanne Ransom) took on an unconventional role—for him—as *The Prodigal*.

Ransom (Elsbeth), Gertrude Howard (Naomi), John Larkin (Jackson).

Songs: "Chidlins" [Tibbett], "A Child Is Born" [Tibbett], "Looks Like Pappy" [Tibbett, Edwards, Young] (Howard Johnson, Herbert Stothart); "The Glory Road" [Tibbett] (Clement Wood, Jacques Wolfe); "Home Sweet Home" [Tibbett] (John Howard Payne, Sir Henry Bishop); "Life Is a Dream" [Tibbett] (Arthur Freed, Oscar Straus); "Without a Song" [Tibbett] (Edward Eliscu, Billy Rose, Vincent Youmans); "Song of the Gambolier" [Tibbett, chorus] (trad.).

Disc: RCA Victor 1507 (Tibbett/"Life Is a Dream"/"Without a Song"/78).

Alternate Title: *The Southerner*.

Although most of grand opera's contributions to early movie musicals (Grace Moore, Everett Marshall, Alice Gentle) were by now out of the picture for stardom, MGM still had

Lawrence Tibbett and was determined to make him click. *The Prodigal*, the first of Tibbett's two musicals in 1931, was no more than a routine romantic melodrama that cast its star in a non-operetta mold. But Tibbett did get to sing Vincent Youmans' splendid "Without a Song," rescued from the aborted *Great Day*.

The Prodigal (copyrighted and sometimes reviewed as *The Southerner*) matched Tibbett with Esther Ralston (1902–1994), the gorgeous blonde star formerly of Paramount. He is Jeffry Ferraday, a hobo who has returned to his family's Kentucky plantation after five years as the clan's nomadic black sheep. She is his sister-in-law Antonia, trapped in a loveless marriage to his stuffy brother (Purnell B. Pratt). Jeff rescues Toni from a potentially damaging tryst with the brother's best friend (slick Theodore von Eltz) with this explanation: "A man can be a tramp and get away with it, but a woman never can." They fall in love, but Jeff hasn't cured himself of his wanderlust, and he returns to the freight-train circuit with his two grimy pals (Cliff Edwards, cast as a kleptomaniac, and Roland Young). He has been advised by his wise old mother (Emma Dunn) to wait out Toni's impending divorce.

The time alloted to music-making was far less in *The Prodigal* than in Tibbett's previous movies, and the *Variety* reviewer "Char" sensed that some pre-release cutting had taken place.[15] The star's vocals of "Life Is a Dream" and his trademark spiritual, "The Glory Road," were removed by MGM early in the film's release. But, besides "Without a Song," we do see Tibbett singing the standard "Home Sweet Home," and, during a sequence set at a black-folks' Thanksgiving barbecue, the dialect songs "Chidlins" and "A Child Is Born." In addition, Tibbett, Edwards, and Young get in a few bars of a comedy song called "Looks Like Pappy," which is repeated in longer form as background.

The Prodigal was clearly an attempt by MGM to extend Tibbett's popularity beyond the longhair crowd, but it didn't work. The studio would give its pricey star one more try.

MEN OF THE SKY
(First National; June 26, 1931)

Director: Alfred E. Green. Screenplay: Otto Harbach, Jerome Kern. Photography: John Seitz. Editor: Desmond O'Brien. Musical Director: Erno Rapée. Running Time: 71 minutes.

Cast: Irene Delroy (Madeleine Aubert), Jack Whiting (Jack Ames), Bramwell Fletcher (Eric von Coburg), John Sainpolis (Madeleine's father), Edwin Maxwell (Count von Amburg), Otto Harbach (French major), Armand Kaliz (Señor Mendoca), Frank McHugh (Oscar), Lotti Loder (Madeleine's maid), Otto Matiesen (Major Janifer), Mireille (Gabrielle).

Songs: "All's Well with the World" [chorus], "Boys March," "Every Little While" [Whiting, Delroy], "Stolen Dreams" [Delroy, several times], "You Ought to Meet Sweet Marguerite" [male quartet] (Otto Harbach, Jerome Kern).

During the early talkie period, Warner Bros.–First National had under contract some of the best songwriting teams of the era— Rodgers and Hart, Hammerstein and Romberg

… and now, but no more happily, the less prolific but potent pair of Jerome Kern and Otto Harbach. The duo behind *Sunny* was signed in June 1930 to create a Great War-themed musical to be named *Call of the East.* With Jack Whiting and Irene Delroy (b. 1898) in the leads, filming began in July and concluded in mid–September; by then the film had gone through two more titles, *Stolen Dreams* and *The Man in the Sky.*

The picture would be released as *Men of the Sky,* but not widely and not for long. Not even *The New York Times* got to dig its critical claws into the film, which was sneaked into the Strand Theatre in Brooklyn instead of debuting in the more prestigious Manhattan houses. Its status as an "official" movie musical has been long in question, for the score was severely truncated by Warners to make it more palatable to the public. At least two Kern biographers have written that *Men of the Sky* was released as a songless drama, but the film has been lost for decades and it is likely neither writer saw it. The few contemporary reviews available indicated that there was some musical atmosphere, but "very slight and only an incident in the plot," wrote *The Film Daily.*[16] However, the surviving Vitaphone discs are said to reveal a conspicuous amount of music.

Music or no music, *Men of the Sky* was a downbeat little spy drama that the studio hoped might draw the same audience that fortified its recent World War I actioners *The Dawn Patrol* and *The Last Flight.* It hinged upon a young French woman, Madeleine Aubert (Delroy), who leaves her American flier boyfriend, Jack Ames (Whiting), to join her father (John Sainpolis) as a spy for France at an estate in Germany. She is supposed to get cozy with a German officer (Bramwell Fletcher) in order to gain information on a set of secret plans that another spy will steal after landing on the grounds. That spy turns out to be Jack. Madeleine is supposed to signal her compatriot to advance by playing a certain style of song on the piano, but the Germans have found out about the scheme, and Jack is exposed. In a tragic ending, the sweethearts are led out to a firing squad although, noted *Variety,* "both … are treated more as guests in church than enemies."[17] Harbach acted in the film as a French major, and Kern appeared as an extra during an opening scene set at a tennis match.

American flier Jack Whiting (at bar, fourth from left) enjoys a respite from the Great War in First National's ill-fated *Men of the Sky*.

Two notable songs in *Men of the Sky* were "Stolen Dreams," a ballad performed by Delroy several times, and "Every Little While," a gentle love duet for Whiting and Delroy. "Every Little While" was revived from obscurity in 1993 for a compact disc collection, "The Jerome Kern Treasury" (Angel-EMI), on which it was sung by George Dvorsky and Jeanne Lehman, backed by the London Sinfonietta Chorus under the direction of John McGlinn. Miles Kreuger provided liner notes for the collection.

CHILDREN OF DREAMS
(Warner Bros.; July 18, 1931)

Director: Alan Crosland. Screenplay: Oscar Hammerstein II, Sigmund Romberg. Photography: James Van Trees. Editor: Harold McLernon. Running Time: 78 minutes. Technicolor.

Cast: Margaret Schilling (Molly Standing), Paul Gregory (Tommy Melville), Tom Patricola (Gus Schultz), Bruce Winston (Hubert Standing), Charles Winninger (Dr. Joe Thompson), Marion Byron (Gertie), Luis Alberni, Paul Porcasi.

Songs: "Children of Dreams," "Fruit Picker's Song," "Goodbye, My Love, Goodbye," "Her Professor," "If I Had a Girl Like You," "Oh, Couldn't I Love That Girl," "Sleeping Beauty," "That Rare Romance," "Yes, Sir" (Oscar Hammerstein II, Sigmund Romberg).

Children of Dreams was the second original Oscar Hammerstein II–Sigmund Romberg operetta for Warners. An old-fashioned romance, it came and went with scarcely a whimper, although not without regret from *The New York Times*: "It crept into the Beacon (Theatre) without ostentation (but) turned out to be something of a surprise. For the ... audience greeted it with a great deal of applause, more than they have shown for other recent pictures there."[18] *Photoplay*'s opinion was, like the majority, far less open-minded: "Another reason why the box office turned thumbs-down on musicals."[19]

The film—now believed lost, but said to be in private hands in soundtrack form—starred Margaret Schilling (1907?–1976), the leading lady of the Gershwin stage musical *Strike Up the Band*, and Paul Gregory (1904–1942), from the stage and film versions of *Whoopee!* They portrayed two young people who fall in love as apple-pickers in the orchards of California. To save her thieving father from jail, she is forced to take up an operatic career that will estrange her from her beau, who is now her fiancé. As in most operettas (although not with *Men of the Sky* or Hammerstein and Romberg's earlier *Viennese Nights*), a happy ending was inevitable. The girl loses her singing voice but gets back her man.

Not only was *Children of Dreams* hampered by the ill will toward films of its kind, but it also had no star power, neither with the primary pair nor with second leads Marion Byron and Tom Patricola. As explained in the entry for the failing *Viennese Nights* (see Chapter 7), Hammerstein and Romberg's contract was bought out by Warner Bros. even before *Children of Dreams* was released. Nothing in the response to the newer film caused the studio to regret its decision.

PALMY DAYS
(Samuel Goldwyn/United Artists; September 23, 1931)

Director: A. Edward Sutherland. Producer: Samuel Goldwyn. Story and Dialogue: Eddie Cantor, Morrie Ryskind, David Freedman. Continuity: Kenne Thompson. Photography: Gregg Toland. Editors: Sherman Todd, Stuart Heisler. Sound: Vinton Vernon. Art Direction: Richard Day, Willy Pogany. Costumes: Alice O'Neill, Gabrielle Chanel. Music Director: Alfred Newman. Dance Direction: Busby Berkeley. Running Time: 77 minutes.

Cast: Eddie Cantor (Eddie Simpson), Charlotte Greenwood (Helen Martin), Spencer Charters (A. B. Clark), Barbara Weeks (Joan Clark), Charles B. Middleton (Yolando), Paul Page (Stephen Clayton), George Raft (Joe the Frog), Harry Woods (Plug Moynihan), Arthur Hoyt (man in séance), The Goldwyn Girls [including Betty Grable, Virginia Grey].

Songs: "Bend Down, Sister" [Greenwood, girls] (Ballard MacDonald, Dave Silverstein, Con Conrad); "Dunk! Dunk! Dunk! Dunking Song" [orchestra] (Morrie Ryskind, Alfred Newman); "There's Nothing Too Good for My Baby" [Cantor] (Eddie Cantor, Benny Davis, Harry Akst); "Yes, Yes!" [Cantor, girls; reprised by Cantor, Greenwood] (Cliff Friend, Con Conrad).

Disc: RCA Victor 22851 (Cantor/"There's Nothing Too Good for My Baby"/78); Pelican 134 (Cantor/LP; ST).

With *Whoopee!* down in the books as one of Sam Goldwyn's biggest moneymakers, the encore for Eddie Cantor, Busby Berkeley and the Goldwyn Girls didn't need to be much different. *Palmy Days* was filmed in black-and-white instead of color, and its 77-minute length was short for a first-rank production. But there were again the eye-catching opening production number by the girls; Cantor and a love-starved counterpart (Charlotte Greenwood, in for Ethel Shutta); and the forgettable secondary romance filled by two forgettable young actors. Short of Lubitsch, this was practically the only musical comedy formula that was a sure thing in 1931: *Palmy Days* grossed more than $1 million. Did I mention that there were only three song numbers?[20]

This time, Cantor was an inept assistant to a fortune teller (Charles B. Middleton). Eddie Simpson has the unfortunate habit of singing whenever he gets nervous. The phony medium, in order to place undue influence on a baked-goods company and its séance-crazy owner (Spencer Charters), has Eddie installed as— snicker—the factory's efficiency expert. There he meets the boss's daughter (Barbara Weeks), who loves the handsome Steve Clayton (Paul Page), and a much less comely physical culturist (Greenwood)—whom the fearful Eddie calls a "physical torturist." She demonstrates why.

Eddie double-crosses the swami by liking his job enough to stay in it permanently, but he becomes an easy target when the crook learns of a $25,000 stash Eddie has secured in the company's safe. Eddie initially evades the swami's minions by posing as a woman—which creates its own set of problems in the company's girls locker room. Then he protects the money by hiding it in a loaf of bread. Now accused of theft, Eddie has to clear himself by finding the loaf before the crooks get to it. This he does, but only after narrowly avoiding the path of an automated bread-slicer. Mission accomplished, Greenwood can drag out a judge to lasso Cantor as they reprise the upbeat Cliff Friend–Con Conrad tune "Yes, Yes!"

Palmy Days initially was intended as a straight comedy with only one song, "Yes, Yes!" But after a preview, Goldwyn ordered the insertion of more music, including what turned out to be the film's biggest seller, Conrad's "Bend Down, Sister." It's performed by Greenwood and the girls as she reminds them that if they want to keep thin, the likes of ham and eggs, pastry and French dressing should be on the outside looking in. The shapely assembly-line workers continue the number by becoming one of Berkeley's human kaleidoscopes, with exercise sticks as handy props.

The other major dance number, which introduces "Yes, Yes!" has the dancers holding up cards to resemble a cardboard train as the heads of Cantor and Greenwood's peer out the back of the caboose through life-sized cutouts. Truth be told, moviegoers liked better Cantor's silly antics with lips and tongue, a weird quacking sound that catches on with almost every other major character in the story. The comedian's requisite blackface number is performed to "There's Nothing Too Good for My Baby," presented as entertainment in the baking company's fancy eatery. "If they can make musicals like this," beamed *Photoplay*, "then there's no reason at all why they shouldn't come back."[21]

When Goldwyn re-released *Palmy Days* during the 1940s, Greenwood's name was dislodged from second billing by the previously seventh-billed George Raft, who before becoming a major star appeared as the swami's thug "Joe the Frog." Raft fans attracted to their hero's "latest" film must have come away disappointed with dialogue no better than "What's up, boss?"

HER MAJESTY, LOVE
(First National; November 25, 1931)

Director: William Dieterle. Adaptation: Robert Lord, Arthur Caesar. Dialogue: Henry

Blanke, Joseph Jackson. Based on the German film *Ihre Majestät die Liebe,* written by Rudolf Bernauer and Rudolph Öesterreicher (1931). Photography: Robert Kurrle. Editor: Ralph Dawson. Sound: C. Dave Forrest. Art Director: Jack Okey. Running Time: 75 minutes.

Cast: Marilyn Miller (Lia Toerrek), Ben Lyon (Fred von Wellingen), W. C. Fields (Bela Toerrek), Ford Sterling (Otmar von Wellingen), Leon Errol (Baron von Schwarzdorf), Chester Conklin (Emil), Harry Stubbs (Hanneman), Maude Eburne (Aunt Harriette von Wellingen), Harry Holman (Dr. Reisenfeld), Ruth Hall (factory secretary), William Irving (the "third" man), Mae Madison (Elli), Clarence Wilson (Cousin Cornelius), Virginia Sale (Laura), Donald Novis (singer), Gus Arnheim and His Cocoanut Grove Orchestra, Ravero's South American Tango Band.

Songs: "Because of You" [Lyon, Novis; reprised by Miller], "Don't Ever Be Blue" [Novis], "Though You're Not the First One" [Novis; reprised by Lyon, then by Novis], "You're Baby-Minded Now" [Errol, Stubbs, Irving, Miller] (Al Dubin, Walter Jurmann).

Disc: Pelican 102 (Miller/LP; ST).

Although she probably didn't know it at the time, *Her Majesty, Love* was Marilyn Miller's last chance for movie stardom. A breezy musical comedy with flourishes of Germanic operetta, it seemed to misuse Miller's talents badly. Miscast as a Berlin barmaid who has a rocky romance with a handsome ball-bearings millionaire, Miller had no solo dances, only an extended tango with costar Ben Lyon, and she sang only one of the film's four songs by herself. If *Her Majesty, Love* has any reputation now, it is because of the presence of W. C. Fields, who, in his first feature-length talkie, plays Miller's comically unsophisticated father.

It was Miller who asked Fields (1879–1946) to appear in her third film for First National, if one can believe a syndicated newspaper interview with the comedian published in 1934. Fields had appeared in 11 mainly unsuccessful silent films and in a talkie short, *The Golf Specialist*, produced by RKO in New York in 1930. In the early summer of 1931, with Broadway in the dumps, he moved back to Hollywood, where, he recalled, he ran into Miller in a hotel lobby. They talked over old times—they had appeared in the *Ziegfeld Follies* together—

In her final film, *Her Majesty, Love,* **Marilyn Miller was ably supported by old pros W. C. Fields (left) and Leon Errol.**

then she asked if he would play her father in her next picture. Fields' alleged reply: "Yes, dear, beautiful girl, and your grandfather as well!"[22]

Fields, still wearing the clip-on moustache that marked his days in vaudeville and the silents, wasn't allowed full rein over his comedic abilities, but he was allowed to reproduce a bit of the juggling act that helped make his name decades before. He earned the best notices of the cast, although critics were less inclined to fault *Her Majesty, Love* for any acting deficiencies than for its slight story, adapted by a quartet of Warner Bros. writers from a German film. Lia Toerrek (Miller) and Fred von Wellingen (Lyon, a former paramour of Miller's) meet in the cabaret—he is trying to pick up the working girl on a bet. They fall in love so quickly that his stunned brood—especially his domineering older brother, Otmar (Ford Sterling)—decides to put a stop to the perceived mismatch. Otmar offers Fred a long-sought pay raise and promo-

tion within the ball-bearings firm, but only if he promises not to marry Lia.

Lia, giddy over her impending marriage, joyously sings "Because of You" to the accompaniment of the phonograph player in her apartment. A subdued Fred shows up, but he can't bring himself to tell the girl they're through. Later, she sees through his duplicity and tells the whole clan off, toppling the head table at a prestigious dinner. Baron von Schwarzdorf (Leon Errol), who has witnessed this tirade, sees in Lia the strong possibility of a *seventh* wife. She finally gives in to the older man, but on the evening after they are wed, they go to dinner at the cabaret, for old times' sake. There sits a sulking Fred, whose eyes meet Lia's with the same old sparkle. The baron, sadly watching the lovers, realizes that the seventh time is no charm. Lia reminds Fred that his family cannot possibly reject her now that she's a countess.

Director William (né Wilhelm) Dieterle (1893–1972) enjoyed a competent Hollywood career after this, his second English-language film. He went on to helm the likes of *The Hunchback of Notre Dame* (the 1939 version with Charles Laughton), the Oscar-winning *The Life of Emile Zola* and the delightful *The Devil and Daniel Webster* (a.k.a. *All That Money Can Buy*). His attempts at Lubitsch-like style in *Her Majesty, Love* are evident, especially as the film begins amid popping balloons and abrupt, snide close-ups of the bar's aging-and-ogling male habitués. "Mr. Dieterle ... shows himself to be quite a wizard with the microphone," wrote *The New York Times*, "and it is really astounding how he keeps his camera going from place to place."[23] There is also the occasional gem of repartee, as when Errol tells a waiter at the cabaret that he has no "appetite for eating."

"Oysters," replies the waiter, "are excellent for raising an appetite."

"You recommend them?"

"They breed in some of the world's finest beds, sir."

Dieterle keeps the pace lively and handles his actors well, with the exception of Miller, who seems vaguely uncomfortable in a role written partly as a hard-bitten babe and partly as a goody-two-shoes. She deserves credit for trying, but this is the kind of character someone like Marlene Dietrich would have given a lot more zing. Miller injured a knee during a rehearsal early in production, so this might account for her lack of dancing in *Her Majesty, Love*.[24] Lyon is competent enough, but the old-pro supporting trio of Fields, Errol and Sterling makes the film worth watching. Donald Novis, the radio crooner, appears as the cabaret's featured singer for three Walter Jurmann–Al Dubin songs: "Because of You," "Don't Ever Be Blue" and "Though You're Not the First One."

In January 1932, Miller and Warner Bros. announced a parting of the ways. Published reports indicated that Miller, with offers from Broadway in hand, asked to be released from her contract. Shortly before her sudden death of toxic poisoning (from complications of a sinus infection) in 1936, Miller was offered the chance to return to movies by playing herself in MGM's biographical epic *The Great Ziegfeld*. She not only refused to appear (because of a squabble over billing), but also would not allow even the use of her name in the picture. Thus,

Her Majesty, Love marked the end of her highly publicized but ultimately frustrating quest for big-screen fame.

FLYING HIGH
(MGM; November 14, 1931)

Director: Charles F. Reisner. Producer: George White. Adaptation: Charles F. Reisner. Screenplay and Dialogue: A. P. Younger. Additional Dialogue: Robert E. Hopkins. Based on the musical play, book by John McGowan, B. G. De Sylva and Lew Brown, lyrics by De Sylva and Brown, music by Ray Henderson (New York opening, March 3, 1930; 357 performances). Photography: Merritt B. Gerstad. Editor: William S. Gray. Sound: Douglas Shearer, Ralph Shugart. Assistant Director: Sandy Roth. Art Director: Cedric Gibbons. Costumes: Adrian. Dance Direction: Busby Berkeley. Running Time: 78 minutes.

Cast: Bert Lahr (Rusty Krouse), Charlotte Greenwood (Pansy Potts), Pat O'Brien (Sport Wardell), Kathryn Crawford (Eileen Smith), Charles Winninger (Dr. Brown), Hedda Hopper (Mrs. Smith), Guy Kibbee (Mr. Smith), Herbert Braggiotti (Gordon), Eddie Dillon (Watkins), Tom Kennedy (bullying aviator), Richard Carle (hotel manager), Clarence H. Wilson (café patron), Gus Arnheim and His Orchestra.

Songs/Musical Numbers: "Examination" [Winninger, girls], "I'll Make a Happy Landing the Lucky Day I Land You" [Crawford, chorus; reprised by chorus], "We'll Dance Til the Dawn" [Crawford, chorus] (Dorothy Fields, Jimmy McHugh); "It'll Be the First Time for Me" [Greenwood, Lahr] (B. G. De Sylva, Lew Brown, Ray Henderson).

Disc: Music Masters JJA-19765 (bootleg LP; ST).

Also Known As: *George White's Flying High*.

George White's *Flying High*, Broadway's last De Sylva–Brown–Henderson show, was the biggest musical comedy success of the 1929-30 season. Metro-Goldwyn-Mayer hoped it could make a hit out of the film version by acquiring Bert Lahr (1895–1967) to reprise his starring role, but the air-minded story that might have landed a profit in 1929 or '30 flew in and out of theaters in 1931-32.

Daffy pilot Rusty Krouse (Bert Lahr) has just set an altitude record in *Flying High*; his new wife (Charlotte Greenwood) makes sure he's all right.

Unlike most movie musicals of this "moratorium" period, *Flying High* went all out with musical comedy conventions and elaborately staged dance numbers supervised by Busby Berkeley. But it was nothing that anybody hadn't seen before. "A lavish musical comedy, so much so it doesn't look as if Metro can ever get out of the box on it even if [it] were a smash," reported "Sid," *Variety*'s pessimistic critic, after the New York opening. "The picture has been playing around the country now for some time and has been having its troubles."[25] Indeed, MGM seemed hesitant to give *Flying High* a lofty sendoff, for it appeared in mid-sized markets like Providence and Kansas City before New Yorkers got a glimpse in mid–December of 1931.

In his first feature film, Lahr portrayed Rusty Krouse ("Krause" in the stage show), an airplane mechanic and aspiring flier who has invented an "aerocopter," a contraption that can travel the skies vertically as well as horizontally. He is befriended by Sport Wardell (Pat O'Brien, 1899–1983), a newspaperman who looks at the gizmo and thinks "profit." (On the stage, this character was a mail pilot named Tod Addison, played by Oscar Shaw.) But the cash-short partners plummet toward bankruptcy—until Sport decides that Rusty must marry airport café hostess Pansy Potts (Charlotte Greenwood, in a role originated by Kate Smith as Pansy Sparks). This is because Pansy is offering $500 to anyone who is willing to lead her to the altar. "How do you know she'll marry me?" asks Rusty. "She won't when she sees you," Sport replies, "but I'll get the money first."

Actually, the desperate Pansy is quite happy with Rusty, and she reminds him of the novelty of their romance ("It'll Be the First Time for Me"). Rusty passes his aviator's medical examination, despite the challenges provided by the grumpy test administrator

(Charles Winninger, 1884–1969). Meanwhile, Sport has taken up with Eileen Smith (an inadequate Kathryn Crawford), the daughter of an investor (Guy Kibbee) who runs an aviation school. When Sport and Mr. Smith are arrested for selling stocks without a license, Rusty summons up the courage to marry Pansy for her dowry. However, he spends their wedding night sleeping in a bathtub. He enters his aerocopter in a flying contest, and with unwanted help from Pansy, inadvertently sets the world air altitude record after the temporary loss of the throttle sends the craft hurtling into the stratosphere. Rusty, having peaked at 53,000 feet, is able to reverse direction and ease to earth. Pansy exits via parachute. "I fell behind a barn in something soft," she informs a concerned onlooker upon reaching safety.

With the exception of "It'll Be the First Time for Me," Metro relegated the stage music to underscoring, mostly to an instrumental medley played by Gus Arnheim and His Orchestra in an opening airport scene. The compositions heard are "Air Minded," "I'm Flying High," "Mrs. Krause's Blue-Eyed Baby Boy," "Thank Your Father," "Wasn't It Beautiful While It Lasted?" and "Without Love." Three new songs, two performed by Crawford, were provided for the film by Dorothy Fields and Jimmy McHugh for use in dance numbers. "I'll Make a Happy Landing the Lucky Day I Land You" has Berkeley's uniformed choristers forming a giant plane, then spelling out "BYRD" and "LINDY" for the overhead camera. For "We'll Dance Til the Dawn," his glittery girls descend from an art-deco ballroom staircase, form patterns with propellers in hands, then mold themselves into a gigantic prop. The less gaudy "Examination" number is half-sung, half-declaimed by Winninger and then danced to by a female chorus. This kind of extravagance would have to wait to have its day again in Hollywood. "There are too many chorus dances interfering with the Lahr explosions," sniped Julia Shawell of the *New York Graphic*.[26]

The medical exam scene with Lahr and Winninger caused more of an uproar than anything else in *Flying High*. It drew many laughs during previews, which caused the Hays Office to chafe, especially over reported footage of Lahr pouring liquor into a test tube. Having paid $100,000 for the rights to the stage play, MGM fought to keep the scene intact. But a legal fiasco after the film release, in which the manager of the MGM theater in Portland, Oregon, filed suit against local censors for rejecting the film, prompted the studio to delete the most objectionable material from all prints. In the print viewed by the author, Lahr/Rusty does pour a drink from his flask into a glass that the doctor presumably has given him for a urine test. Then he hands it back, telling the doctor, "That's all I could spare." With that, the scene ends abruptly. Also in the print was the doc's earlier question "Do you use narcotics?" to which Rusty replies, after much hemming and hawing, "Ex-Lax!"

As with dance sequences from *It's a Great Life*, *Lord Byron of Broadway* and the unreleased *The March of Time*, some of *Flying High* was reused in a Ted Healy and His (Three) Stooges short subject. The "We'll Dance Til the Dawn" number provided the excuse for the title of *Plane Crazy* (1933), in which Healy and cronies reproduced their nightclub act on a stage nowhere near an airport. The number was also excerpted in the 1986 MGM compilation film *That's Dancing!*

THE CUBAN LOVE SONG
(MGM; December 4, 1931)

Director: W. S. Van Dyke. Producer: Albert Lewin. Screenplay: G. Gardiner Sullivan, Bess Meredyth. Adaptation: John Lynch. Dialogue: John Colton, Gilbert Emery, Robert E. Hopkins, Paul Hervey Fox. Photography: Harold Rosson. Editor: Margaret Booth. Sound: Douglas Shearer, Paul Neal. Assistant Director: Jack Mintz. Art Director: Cedric Gibbons. Costumes: Adrian. Running Time: 86 minutes.

Cast: Lawrence Tibbett (Terry Burke), Lupe Velez (Nenita Lopez), Ernest Torrence (Romance), Jimmy Durante (O. O. Jones), Karen Morley (Crystal McDougal), Louise Fazenda (Elvira), Hale Hamilton (John Burke), Mathilda Comont (Aunt Rosa), Phillip Cooper (Terry, Jr.), Clarence Geldert (officer), George Kuma (tattoo artist), Ernesto Lecuona and the Palau Brothers Cuban Orchestra.

Songs: "The Cuban Love Song" [Tibbett, three times], "Tramps at Sea" [Tibbett] (Dorothy Fields, Jimmy McHugh, Herbert Stothart); "Buche y Pluma n Ma" [Velez, orchestra] (Rafael Hernandez); "The Peanut

Vendor" [Velez; reprised by Tibbett, then by orchestra] (Marion Sunshine, L. Wolfe Gilbert, Moises Simons). World War I Montage [Tibbett, soldiers]: "K-K-K-Katy" (Geoffrey O'Hara); "The Marine's Hymn" (Henry C. Davis; based on music by Jacques Offenbach); "We're in the Army Now" (Tell Taylor, Ole Olsen, Isham Jones).

Disc: RCA Victor 1550 (Tibbett/"The Cuban Love Song"/"Tramps at Sea"/78); Empire 804 (bootleg LP; ST).

"The authors are doing their best to kill my [movie] career. I haven't had a good story yet," a plain-speaking Lawrence Tibbett told *Variety* in an interview on the eve of the release of his fourth picture, *The Cuban Love Song*.[27] Despite his understandable assertion, Tibbett's movies were usually reviewed favorably; even cynical critics were inclined to give special respect to an artist of his stature. With the exception of *The Rogue Song,* which had the allure of the Laurel and Hardy team, the audience response was not as welcoming. But *The Cuban Love Song,* the singer's final musical for MGM, deserved better than the verdict of "uninspired" from the usually Tibbett-friendly *New York Times*[28] and the public apathy that followed. A *Madama Butterfly*–type romance set in the tropics, it sensitively portrayed a doomed relationship between a playful Marine and a fiery peanut seller, played by Lupe Velez (1908–1944). The music was pretty good, too.

The soldier, Terry Burke, is dispatched to Cuba on the eve of America's entry into the Great War. He and two buddies, O. O. (Jimmy Durante) and Romance (a miscast Ernest Torrence), meet the lovely Nenita Lopez after Terry's jeep mashes the back of her cart. Despite the touchy first encounter, Terry and Nenita fall so deeply in love (to "The Cuban Love Song") that he has only minor guilt over Crystal (Karen Morley), the socialite waiting patiently back home. But the war intervenes, and Terry is called to duty elsewhere. Ten years later, a song played at an anniversary party reminds Terry, now married to Crystal, of the true love he had lost in the tropics. Terry and O. O. impulsively board a freighter bound for Havana. There, Terry learns that Nenita had died years before, but he finds the son—their son—he didn't know he had. He brings Terry, Jr., home to the accepting Crystal.

According to his autobiography, Tibbett complained to the MGM brass about his odd pairing with the "Mexican wildcat" Velez for the hot love scenes required in the script.

"That," I said, "is out. I'm no great lover. I'm just an opera singer trying to get along in the movies." We compromised. The great-lover publicity thereupon died unborn, but, if she chose, the dynamic Lupe was to go boiling through the story like Mt. Etna on a rampage. I went around asking everybody, "What's the best way to get along with Lupe Velez?"[29]

Tibbett was inspired simply to compliment Miss Velez for her singing voice. The success of this strategy allowed him to recall that "I have never worked more peacefully with a leading woman."[30]

The Cuban Love Song relies on some incredible story contrivances—for example, Terry's happenstance reunion with O. O. and Romance a decade after their parting, and his finding of Terry, Jr., only because the youngster is singing a chorus of a familiar song. But Tibbett and Velez make a pleasing couple—Hollywood morality of 1931 dictated their characters' permanent parting—and Durante is much less annoying than he is in many of his early comedies for MGM. Louise Fazenda scores in a bit as Durante's impatient wife. And in a nice touch, Tibbett briefly sings simultaneously as a baritone and tenor. As the older Terry ponders his future as the Havana-bound ship prepares to leave a New York pier, his younger, uniformed self appears in split screen and encourages him to find Nenita. Both images sing "The Cuban Love Song" in harmony, then the "ghostly" self disappears as the matured Terry is convinced he must follow his heart.

The Cuban Love Song is built around two songs: the lovely title tune and "The Peanut Vendor." Terry teaches the latter to Nenita to better hustle her wares, and its playing by a Cuban orchestra in a New York nightclub jogs his memory 10 years after. Finally, it enables Terry to identify his son, who has become a peanut vendor himself. "The Peanut Vendor," which had originated as a Spanish tune called "El Manisero," was a major hit for Don Azpiazu and His Havana Casino Orchestra in the early months of 1931. As the movie opened, "The Cuban Love Song" was being covered by

Charles Farrell and Janet Gaynor play a Long Island socialite and a Scottish immigrant, respectively, in Fox's ambitious *Delicious*.

Ruth Etting and the Paul Whiteman and Jacques Renard orchestras.

In 1933, MGM announced Tibbett for the cast of its *Hollywood Revue of 1933*, which was filmed—without him—as *Hollywood Party*. Tibbett returned to films in the mid '30s for two outings with the newly merged 20th Century–Fox. But the big-budget *Metropolitan* (1935) and the programmer *Under Your Spell* (1936) both flopped. Those who have not had the chance to enjoy Lawrence Tibbett's movies or his many concert or radio appearances—or who viewed him inaccurately depicted as an obese, effeminate boob, as he was in the 1991 film *Bugsy*—have missed seeing one of American opera's most versatile and dynamic talents.

DELICIOUS
(Fox; December 25, 1931)

Director: David Butler. Adaptation: Guy Bolton, Sonya Levien. Story: Guy Bolton. Photography: Ernest Palmer. Editor: Irene Morra. Sound: Joseph E. Aiken. Assistant Director: Ad Schaumer. Art Director: Joseph Wright. Costumes: Guy Duty. Running Time: 106 minutes.

Cast: Janet Gaynor (Heather Gordon), Charles Farrell (Lawrence Beaumont), El Brendel (Chris Jensen), Raul Roulien (Sascha), Lawrence O'Sullivan (Inspector O'Flynn), Manya Roberti (Olga), Virginia Cherrill (Diana Van Bergh), Olive Tell (Mrs. Van Bergh), Mischa Auer (Mischa), Marvine Maazel (Toscha), Jeanette Gegna (Momotschka), Crawfurd Kent (purser), Edward J. Le Saint (judge).

Songs/Musical Numbers: "Blah-Blah-Blah" [Brendel], "Delishious" [Roulien],

"Katinkitschka" [Roberti, Auer; danced by Gaynor], "Somebody from Somewhere" [Gaynor; reprised by trio on radio], "Welcome to the Melting Pot" [singers in dream sequence] (Ira Gershwin, George Gershwin); "New York Rhapsody" ("Second Rhapsody") [Roulien at piano, dubbed by Marvine Maazel; played during dream sequence] (George Gershwin).

Disc: Music Masters JJA-19773 (bootleg LP; ST).

Although it boasted Janet Gaynor, Charles Farrell and the inevitable El Brendel, *Delicious* is better known as the first movie musical with a complete score by the great George Gershwin (1898–1937). This was not the first experience in movies for Gershwin and his lyricist brother Ira (1896–1983), for in 1923 they had written a song to accompany a silent Western, *The Sunshine Trail*. In addition, George's music from *Song of the Flame* had been heard in the screen version of that play, and his "Rhapsody in Blue" was featured in *King of Jazz*. In April 1930, the Gershwins signed a lucrative contract with Fox that guaranteed George $70,000 and Ira $30,000 for a score to be written that fall for an upcoming Gaynor-Farrell film.[31] By January 1931, the Gershwins' work was finished, and they returned to New York to begin work on the stage musical *Of Thee I Sing*—which, by coincidence, would open the day of the New York premiere of *Delicious*.

George Gershwin enjoyed his initial stay in Hollywood—he played golf and tennis avidly and played the ponies at Agua Caliente—so much that he might not have put his usual effort into the *Delicious* score. "Delishious," a lively mimickry of the accented speech of the leading lady's character, had been composed some months before. "Blah-Blah-Blah," a parody of the vacuous lyrics of Tin Pan Alley pop, was reworked from "Lady of the Moon," a song originally written for the unproduced stage musical *East Is West*.[32] Two new pieces were striking, particularly for their unusually inventive on-screen presentation: a composition to accompany a dream sequence called "Welcome to the Melting Pot" and an orchestral work initially titled "New York Rhapsody" that became, in extended form, "Second Rhapsody."

They spiced up a tedious, lackluster romance that only Gaynor-and-Farrell fans—all the millions of them—could have loved. The screenplay by Guy Bolton and Sonya Levien found Gaynor playing Heather Gordon, a lowly Scottish immigrant on a ship bound for America. For a predictable contrast, Farrell is Larry Beaumont, a wealthy polo enthusiast from Long Island. From the start, as in *Sunnyside Up* (also directed by David Butler), the message is that poor people have more fun. As Heather and her new Russian musician friends joyously sing and dance in the steerage section, the camera moves upward to catch Larry and his nose-in-the-air girlfriend Diana (Virginia Cherrill) watching the proceedings. "They look awfully happy," says Larry with a touch of wistfulness. "The poor things don't know any better," sneers Diana. Heather, oblivious to the conversation above, teaches the Russians the lyrics to the National Anthem. Diana chides Larry: "I bet you don't remember the words of 'The Star-Spangled Banner.'" He smiles: "I don't even remember what show it was in."

Heather and Larry meet by chance on the boat, and after her attempt to enter the United States is rejected on a technicality, Heather escapes deportation by hiding in the van carrying Larry's pet horse. Larry's valet (Brendel) helps Heather find refuge in the spacious Beaumont mansion, and when the smitten young swain finds out about his new tenant, he wants to help, too. But Heather doesn't want Larry to get in trouble, so she goes to live with the Russians, among whom is an aspiring composer (Raul Roulien) whose love for the Scotch miss is unrequited. Heather, passing as a Russian, performs in a cabaret with the troupe, but she is found out by a dogged immigration official (Lawrence O'Sullivan). Larry is seriously injured on the polo field, and after Heather rushes to his bedside, she is finked on by the jealous Diana. Heather eludes capture by wandering the streets of Manhattan, but she turns herself in at last. She is put on a ship for Scotland, but Larry books passage at the last minute and proposes a shipboard wedding that will resolve everything. Heather agrees, and not just because she wants to be an American.

Gaynor sings only once ("Somebody from Somewhere," which is what Heather wants to be); Farrell, not at all, fortunately. Supporting players handle "Delishious" (Roulien), "Blah-Blah-Blah" (Brendel) and the folky "Katinkitschka" (Manya Roberti, as a Russian dame hot for El, and Mischa Auer). "You Started It," also written for the film, is heard in underscoring. All of these pale compared to the two lengthy production numbers. In "Welcome to the Melting Pot," presented as Heather's shipboard dream, she emerges from the boat to a cadre of shutterbugs snapping from atop the Statue of Liberty, and a quartet of singing newspaper reporters ("We're from *The Journal, The Wahrheit, The Telegram, The Times*") seeking her views on the American woman. A row of Uncle Sams greets Heather with exhausting handshakes, "Mr. Ellis" steps off his "island" to say hello, and dignitaries show up with the Key to the City. Miss Liberty does a climactic snake-hips dance and throws money at her newest subject.

Roulien's character foreshadows the "New York Rhapsody" sequence by playing portions of "his" composition on the piano to impress Heather. (The piano work was dubbed by Marvine Maazel.) Each motif, Roulien says, represents a part of the city—the skyline of "great towers, almost in the clouds" and the teeming "human seeds trying to grow to the light." The seven-minute piece that begins shortly thereafter uses Heather's distraught flight from Larry's home into the unfamiliar urban milieu to present a series of disconcerting, sometimes terrifying, images that illustrate her paranoia. David Butler's direction and Ernest Palmer's restless camera capably complement the pulsating, riveting music. As the piece begins, Gaynor walks along a bustling, noisy street and is accosted by a masher type. "Where ya goin', baby?" he asks; she runs away. She starts to walk down some stairs into a subway, but a mass of emerging riders comes at her. A close-up of her face reveals her emotional pain. She leans on a gate, which swings open and shuts behind her like a prison. A skyscraper dwarfs her. Now, as she leans against a post like a common street-

walker, a passer-by inquires, "Little girl, are you lost?" "What's over there?" Gaynor asks. "The river," she is told. She walks to the shore, stares in the water and sees Farrell's bandaged face. A derelict old woman is watching. "Don't do it, dear," she advises, "I tried it once." The music swells as Gaynor hallucinates that giant hands are clawing at her. She walks to a police station and turns herself in.

The complete "Second Rhapsody" was premiered on January 20, 1932, by Serge Koussevitzky and the Boston Symphony. A reflection of varied musical influences, it has been hailed as a strong statement of Gershwin's ongoing desire to be equated with the period's so-called "serious" composers. The composer's motives, stated in a 1931 letter to a friend, seemed to hint in that direction:

> I wrote it mainly because I wanted to write a serious composition and found the opportunity in California. Nearly everybody comes back from California with a western tan and a pocketful of motion picture money. I decided to come back with both of these things and a serious composition—if the climate would let me. I was under no obligation to the Fox Company to write this. But, you know, the old artistic soul must be appeased every so often.[33]

The reviews of *Delicious* respectfully cited the contribution of George Gershwin. Leo Meehan of the *Motion Picture Herald*, for example, called the "Rhapsody" "one of the finest, if not the finest, musical compositions originally conceived for motion pictures."[34] But the film's ranking among the top grossers of 1932 had, unfairly, much more to do with the never-fail pairing of Gaynor and Farrell than with the man whose music gave important distinction to what could have been a mediocre product.

CHAPTER 12

1932: *On the Way to* 42nd Street

The anti-musical trend continued through 1932, when only 11 "official" singing features were released in the United States. *Crooner,* the lone entry from Warner Bros., and *The Girl from Calgary,* a rare song-and-dance film by the independent studio Monogram, were mere time-fillers with second-rank stars. *Girl Crazy* from RKO and Samuel Goldwyn's *The Kid from Spain* strongly emphasized comedy over music; both starred comedians who could sing, not singers who could quip. Universal, MGM and Fox ignored the genre altogether, in terms of full-length films, although Fox announced for the 1932-33 season a production of Noël Coward's *Bitter Sweet* that was never made.

It was left to Paramount to keep the musical afloat. The company released seven of them, although two (*Horse Feathers* and *Dancers in the Dark*) were borderline as musicals. Still, there was another pleasing effort from Ernst Lubitsch, *Our Hour with You,* and one of the most sublime of all films, Rouben Mamoulian's *Love Me Tonight.* Both were distinguished by the coupling of Maurice Chevalier and Jeanette MacDonald. Besides those two films and *The Kid from Spain* (which boasted Eddie Cantor), the year's only other solid musical hit was Paramount's *The Big Broadcast,* which had the novelty of an all-star radio lineup headed by Bing Crosby.

However, in October of 1932, production began on the movie that would spectacularly rejuvenate the Hollywood musical.[1] The inspiration for making *42nd Street* (February 23, 1933) came from Darryl F. Zanuck, the tough-minded production chief at Warner Bros. Zanuck bought for the studio the same-titled source work, a gritty backstage novel by Bradford Ropes.[2] He saw a freshness in the property that inspired him to take the chance of pro-

ducing it with song numbers, in hopes that audiences would be impressed enough to reconsider their emnity toward full-scale musicals. That Warner Bros. was in severe financial trouble—the company would lose $14 million in 1932—may have bolstered Zanuck's willingness to gamble. But he had to convince Jack and Harry Warner that the project would work, and Harry had forbidden the studio from making any more singing-and-dancing movies.

Zanuck ordered the writing of two scripts for *42nd Street,* one with musical numbers and one without. He showed the draft without music to Jack Warner to gain his approval. Then he had Lloyd Bacon direct the film, sans numbers, on the Warners' main lot. The musical sequences were filmed by Busby Berkeley apart from the rest, on the studio's old Vitagraph lot on Sunset Boulevard, away from the attention of the bosses. After both parts were finished, they were melded together. Now the film was ready to be screened for Jack Warner. Recalled Zanuck:

> Jack went out of his mind. He never knew until it was screened that it was a musical. Only one thing, he loved it! He said, "But what am I going to tell Harry? Have you got another version?" But he sent the musical version to Harry in New York and Harry wired back, "This is the greatest picture you've sent me in five years."[3]

The "greatest picture" cost a not-too-miserly $379,000 to make,[4] but it became the third-biggest moneymaker of 1933 and lifted Warners out of its severe financial difficulties. There was nothing intrinsically special about its putting-on-a-show plot, in which a Broadway director (Warner Baxter) has to replace his star (Bebe Daniels) with a fresh-faced newcomer (Ruby Keeler) to save his musical on opening night. (Remember *On with the Show?*) But there were all of the right ingredients — Bacon's economical direction, Rian James and James Seymour's tangy dialogue, Al Dubin and Harry Warren's catchy lyrics and music, Dick Powell's tenor, Baxter's intensity, Daniels' professionalism, Ginger Rogers' cheek and Keeler's spunky charm. Like the gangster films that had been so lucrative for Warners, *42nd Street* had an edge, apart from its musical content. But the film's greatest assets were Berkeley's jaw-dropping production numbers, which gave *42nd Street* a finishing kick that left audiences ready to spread the favorable word of mouth that a musical—any musical—so sorely needed. Even before they could gauge audience response, critics knew that *42nd Street* was something new and different.

"That enterprising Warners organization … delivers again," wrote *The Film Daily*'s Don Carle Gillettee in a commentary a month before the release of *42nd Street.*

> The pioneers in talking pictures, first to smash box offices with a screen musical comedy, first to set the crowds agog with gangster films, and first in many other production innovations, now lead the way again in the return of musical pictures; and the way they have done it is big news. … Dance formations, ensemble routines and trick photography of marvelous cleverness are packed in the last half hour, and the culmination of the heart interest carries a strong punch. Dialogue sometimes is pretty rough, but it's all in fun. In addition to the wreath that is due the Warners for their courage in producing this lavish entertainment, credit goes to Lloyd Bacon for a grand job of directing; to Warner Baxter for a swell performance … to Ruby Keeler, as the newcomer who makes good. … The success of *42nd Street* will probably bring a new avalanche of musicals.[5]

The Lubitsch and Mamoulian musicals of 1931-32 may have been better films in a purely artistic sense, but they hadn't been accessible enough to reverse the negative trend. Backstage stories were easier to duplicate than boudoir comedy operettas. Just as it took a backstager, *The Broadway Melody,* to begin the first wave of musical films, it took another to launch the second wave. *42nd Street* was one of the first films to recognize that a Depression was going on, even if the references were mainly hidden behind the game smiles of the *Pretty Lady* cho-

risters who were a paycheck away from destitution. People could identify with them. Given the cyclical nature of public opinion, it was time for audiences to be receptive to good musicals — in the collective mind, films that presented music with some degree of logic, instead of conjuring it from thin air or slapping it around haphazardly. Moreover, the technology had by now caught up to inspiration. Camera and sound innovation hardly dreamed of in 1929 was now possible, which made Berkeley's gymnastics all the more impressive.

Although more than 30 musicals of every stripe were released in 1933, backstagers were at the vanguard of the revival. Warners produced *Gold Diggers of 1933* and *Footlight Parade,* both with Keeler, Powell, Berkeley, the Dubin-Warren duo and the studio's trademark grit. Not to be outdone, MGM responded with the somewhat sunnier *Dancing Lady,* with the potent team of Clark Gable and Joan Crawford (and a little bit of Fred Astaire). Mae West's starring comedy-musical debut, *She Done Him Wrong,* and her even more successful follow-up, *I'm No Angel,* found her slaving on the outskirts of showbiz—as a saloon singer and sideshow vamp, respectively. She kept Paramount from going broke. To cap the busy year, Fred Astaire and Ginger Rogers linked up as members of Gene Raymond's band in RKO's *Flying Down to Rio,* which spawned the greatest series of dance musicals in history.

But we are getting ahead of ourselves. Before there was 1933, there was 1932 …

DANCERS IN THE DARK
(Paramount; March 18, 1932)

Director: David Burton. Screenplay: Herman J. Mankiewicz. Adaptation: Brian Marlow, Howard Emmett Rogers. Based on the play *Jazz King* by James Ashmore Creelman (1928). Photography: Karl Struss. Sound: J. A. Goodrich. Running Time: 71 minutes.

Cast: Miriam Hopkins (Gloria Bishop), Jack Oakie (Duke Taylor), William Collier, Jr. (Floyd Stevens), Eugene Pallette (Gus), Lyda Roberti (Fanny Zabowolski), George Raft (Louie Brooks), Maurice Black (Max), DeWitt Jennings (McGroady), Paul Fix (Benny), Walter Hiers (Ollie), Frances Moffatt (Ruby), Alberta Vaughn (Marie), George Bickel (Spiegel),

Mary Gordon (cleaning woman), James Bradbury, Jr., Al Hill, Kent Taylor, Fred Warren, William Halligan, Claire Dodd, Marty Brill, Jack Elder.

Songs: "I'm in Love with a Tune" [Roberti] (Ralph Rainger); "It's the Darndest Thing" [Oakie, band] (Dorothy Fields, Jimmy McHugh); "St. Louis Blues" [Hopkins, twice] (W. C. Handy).

A dance-hall melodrama with three songs, the programmer *Dancers in the Dark* did little for the careers of its actors ... save one. George Raft, who played a murderous gangster with his sights set on taxi dancer Miriam Hopkins, exuded enough menace to be noticed. "A fascinating new type of villain" was *Photoplay*'s description of him.[6] A key loan-out to Howard Hughes for his role as the coin-flipping hit man in *Scarface*, released later in 1932, built Raft up even more. By year's end, Paramount had promoted him to the star ranks.

In *Dancers in the Dark,* Raft is a tangential character in a story that centers on a romantic triangle: a jaded New York bandleader (Jack Oakie, surprisingly unsympathetic), his young sax player Floyd Stevens (William Collier, Jr., in a role originally slated for Buddy Rogers) and the saxman's fiancée (top-billed Hopkins). The bandleader, Duke Taylor, convinces his charge to take a job in another city, for he secretly wants blonde beauty Gloria Bishop all to himself. This scheme fails, however, and in a taut climax, Duke is shot by the gangster for signaling the police about his whereabouts in the club. Duke had just instructed his boys to play "St. Louis Blues," which is the crook's favorite tune because Gloria always sings it. But as Duke reminds the reunited Gloria and Floyd, "You can't kill a bandleader with one shot."

Hopkins appears to be dubbed for her two renditions of "St. Louis Blues," and Oakie's megaphone delivery of "It's the Darndest Thing" is certainly not the voice heard in his previous Paramount musicals. Lyda Roberti, in her feature-film debut, lends her own voice to a comic number, "I'm in Love with a Tune."

ONE HOUR WITH YOU
(Paramount; March 23, 1932)

Director-Producer: Ernst Lubitsch. Additional Direction: George Cukor. Screenplay:

Samson Raphaelson. Based on the play *Nur ein Traum* [Only a Dream] by Lothar Schmidt (1909). Photography: Victor Milner. Editor: William Shea. Sound: M. M. Paggi. Art Director: Hans Dreier. Costumes: Travis Banton. Musical Director: Nathaniel Finston. Running Time: 80 minutes.

Cast: Maurice Chevalier (Dr. André Bertier), Jeanette MacDonald (Colette Bertier), Genevieve Tobin (Mitzi Olivier), Charles Ruggles (Adolph), Roland Young (Professor Olivier), George Barbier (police commissioner), Josephine Dunn (Mademoiselle Martel), Richard Carle (detective), Charles Judels (policeman), Barbara Leonard (Mitzi's maid), Sheila Mannors (Colette's downstairs maid), Leonie Pray (Colette's upstairs maid), George Davis (taxi driver), Donald Novis (orchestra vocalist), Eric Wilton (André's butler), Charles Coleman (Marcel, Adolph's butler), Florine McKinney (girl).

Songs/Musical Numbers: "It Was Only a Dream Kiss" [MacDonald, Chevalier], "Mitzi-Colette Talk Song" [MacDonald, Tobin], "Oh! That Mitzi" [Chevalier], "We Will Always Be Sweethearts" [MacDonald; reprised by MacDonald, Chevalier], "What a Little Thing Like a Wedding Ring Can Do" [Chevalier, MacDonald] (Leo Robin, Oscar Straus); "One Hour with You" [Novis, Tobin, Chevalier, Ruggles, MacDonald], "Three Times a Day" [Chevalier, Tobin], "What Would You Do?" [Chevalier] (Leo Robin, Richard A. Whiting); "Police Number" [Barbier, chorus] (John Leipold).

Academy Award Nominations: Best Picture, 1931-32.

Disc: RCA Victor 22941 (Chevalier/"Oh! That Mitzi"/"What Would You Do?"/78); RCA Victor 22944 (Chevalier/preceding songs in French/78); RCA Victor 24013 (MacDonald/"One Hour with You"/"We Will Always Be Sweethearts"/78); RCA Victor 24019 (MacDonald/preceding songs in French/78); Ariel CMF-23 (bootleg LP; ST); Caliban 6011 (bootleg LP; ST); Music Masters JJA-19806 (bootleg LP; ST); WRC SH 156 (bootleg LP; ST).

Ernst Lubitsch's remake of his 1924 silent comedy *The Marriage Circle, One Hour with You* received the requisite kudos from critics and public, and was nominated for the Best Picture Academy Award of 1931-32. Viewed as part of the whole of its director's work, it falls just short of *The Love Parade* and *The Smiling Lieutenant*, or the later *Trouble in Paradise* and *To Be or Not to Be*. Although *One Hour with You* may not quite deserve its description by Lubitsch biographer Scott Eyman as "a soufflé that obstinately refuses to rise,"[7] it is slow to jell and plays a shade too conventionally. Even its score, composed by Oscar Straus and Richard Whiting, is no better than one would expect. But the film is highly entertaining, certainly better (and still more risque) than most romances and musical comedies of its day. Given its troubled genesis, it could been a disaster.

One Hour with You was really not to be a Lubitsch picture, at least not from a directorial standpoint. Lubitsch, who was his own producer, became tied up in the making of *The Man I Killed* (1932), a downbeat World War I drama that was to be his first "serious" sound film. So when the *Marriage Circle* remake was slated by Paramount, Lubitsch the producer hired George Cukor to direct it. Cukor, a young man who had shown a flair for directing comedy on Broadway and in a handful of films for Paramount in 1930-31, began to shoot *One Hour with You* in November 1931 from a script prepared by Samson Raphaelson and (uncredited) Lubitsch. However, after only two days, Lubitsch looked at the rushes and decided they lacked the continental flavor he required, that the actors were overplaying. Within days, he assumed almost all directorial aspects of the $1.1-million production, which was rushed to completion by the first week of January 1932.[8]

On February 9, 1932, *One Hour with You* was shown in a preview in Los Angeles; as per the original agreement, the credits read: "An Ernst Lubitsch Production ... Directed by George Cukor." However, a very complimentary review that subsequently appeared in *The Hollywood Reporter* gave all the praise to Cukor. This insensed Lubitsch, who went to Paramount production head B. P. Schulberg and asked that his name be taken off the picture if he could not receive full credit. Schulberg, eager to placate Lubitsch, who had indeed directed all but a few incidental scenes, ordered that Cukor's name be removed. Cukor then sued the studio and threatened to file an injunction against the exhibition of the film unless his credit was restored. The film opened in New York on March 23, but only after a compromise

was made. Cukor settled for secondary credit on *One Hour with You* but was permitted to go to RKO to direct a film with Constance Bennett for his friend David O. Selznick. That film, *What Price Hollywood?*, proved to be the first major success in a memorable directorial career. The final credits for *One Hour with You* read: "An Ernst Lubitsch Production," then "Directed by Ernst Lubitsch," and below that in smaller letters, "Assisted by George Cukor."

However their contributions were recognized, Lubitsch and Cukor had at their disposal a fine cast headed by Maurice Chevalier and Jeanette MacDonald (in their first pairing since *The Love Parade*), with Genevieve Tobin (1901–1995) as a saucy third component of a romantic triangle and Charlie Ruggles and Roland Young on hand for stalwart support. Kay Francis and Carole Lombard originally were cast in the key female roles, but Chevalier, who was romantically involved with both, balked at the prospect. As a change of pace, the Chevalier and MacDonald characters were married—and happily—from the start. Paris physician André Bertier and his wife Colette, make sport of their "lawful ... and awful nice" situation with the Straus song "What a Little Thing Like a Wedding Ring Can Do."

Mitzi Olivier (Tobin), an old friend of Colette's married to a stuffy college professor (Young), sets her sights on a resistant André. Meanwhile, the romantically inept Adolph (Ruggles) covets Colette. On the eve of a lavish dinner party given by the Bertiers, Colette catches André attempting to switch the table placements of Mitzi and Mademoiselle Martel (Josephine Dunn), and she automatically assumes he is carrying on with the latter. When Mitzi becomes André's partner on the dance floor, Colette is falsely relieved, for the flirt lures him outside to seduce him. Colette, blaming Martel for her husband's absence, is too distraught to take seriously the feeble post-party overtures of poor Adolph.

He: "Any man who leaves a woman like you on a night like this with a man like me deserves it."

She (sobbing): "But it was my fault! I was wrong!"

He: "You have a right to be wrong. You're a woman. Women are born to be wrong. (He leans closer to her in a flash of passion.) ... I like my women wrong!"

André jubilantly shows off his affections in the picture's best song, Straus' "Oh, That Mitzi," but he loves Colette too much to stray further. Still, he has been found out by the detective (Richard Carle) hired by the professor, and is called as a witness in a divorce suit brought against Mitzi. As he has at times throughout the film, Chevalier turns to the audience for an aside, this time asking in song, "What Would You Do?" He decides to admit his brief indiscretion. Colette responds by saving face—that may be so, but she has had a fling with Adolph, whom Colette forces to confess their "sins." "An eye for an eye ... an Adolph for a Mitzi," she explains. The film ends with Colette and André reciting to the audience:

She: "Ladies—"
He: "And gentlemen—"
She: "If he were your husband—"
He: "And she were your wife—"
She: "And he is a Don Juan—"
He: "And she has dreams."
She: "And he confesses."
He: "And she admits—"
She: "But you like him."
He: "And you love her."
She: "And you adore him."
He: "And you're crazy about her."
She: "What would you do?"
He: "What *could* you do?" (Then, a kiss.)

This conclusion might have pleased 1932 audiences expecting an upbeat finish, but today it seems almost a copout. A more interesting finish might have been the ending that was filmed, and then deleted, in which André—because "there must be no understanding between us"—begins to explain to the audience exactly what did happen between he and Mitzi after the party. But the fadeout comes just as he is getting to the part where "we went into her apartment and we sat down in the living room."[9] The implication is clearly that André has been sexually unfaithful.

Chevalier and MacDonald aren't as effective together here as in their other film pairings; there is too little spark to their relationship and they don't seem to be enjoying themselves. Instead, they are upstaged by players of lesser stature. Tobin, who spent too much of her Hollywood career in unsatisfying assignments for Universal and Warner Bros., all but steals the picture from MacDonald, and Ruggles is a stitch in one of his better timid-

bachelor roles. But it's easy to speak after the fact. All that mattered to Paramount were the box-office returns and pronouncements like that of *The New York Times*: "*One Hour with You* is an excellent production, with Lubitsch and Chevalier at the top of their form."[10]

One Hour with You was produced in a French-language version, *Une Heure Pres de Toi*. Chevalier and MacDonald reprised their roles, but Lily Damita supplanted Tobin as "the other woman."

GIRL CRAZY
(RKO; March 24, 1932)

Director: William A. Seiter. Additional Direction: Norman Taurog. Executive Producer: David O. Selznick. Producer: William LeBaron. Screenplay: Tim Whelan. Adaptation: Herman J. Mankiewicz. Dialogue: Eddie Welch, Walter de Leon. Based on the musical play, book by Guy Bolton and John McGowan, lyrics by Ira Gershwin, music by George Gershwin (New York opening, October 14, 1930; 272 performances). Photography: J. Roy Hunt, Edward Cronjager. Editor: Arthur Roberts. Sound: Hugh McDowell. Art Director: Max Rée. Costumes: Max Rée. Musical Director: Max Steiner. Running Time: 75 minutes.

Cast: Bert Wheeler (Jimmy Deegan), Robert Woolsey (Slick Foster), Eddie Quillan (Danny Churchill), Dorothy Lee (Patsy), Mitzi Green (Tessie Deegan), Kitty Kelly (Kate Foster), Arline Judge (Molly Gray), Stanley Fields (Lank Sanders), Lita Chevret (Mary), Chris-Pin Martin (Pete), Brooks Benedict (George Mason), Nat Pendleton (motorcycle cop), Monty Collins, Alfred Cooke (bartenders), Josephine Ramos, Esther Garcia (señoritas), High Eagle (Eagle Rock), Max Steiner (orchestra leader), Creighton Chaney [Lon Chaney, Jr.].

Songs: "Bidin' My Time" [cowboy chorus], "But Not for Me" [Quillan, Judge, Green], "I Got Rhythm" [Kelly, chorus], "You've Got What Gets Me" [Wheeler, Lee, danced by Green] (Ira Gershwin, George Gershwin).

Disc: Music Masters JJA-19773 (bootleg LP; ST).

One of the more glaring stage-to-film misfires of the pre–*42nd Street* period, RKO's

Bert Wheeler and Dorothy Lee get serious for a moment in RKO's version of *Girl Crazy*.

Girl Crazy bore little resemblance to the same-named Broadway hit of 1930. The studio, intent upon turning the property into a Wheeler and Woolsey vehicle, jettisoned most of George Gershwin's score. And what charm the film might have retained was apparently erased in post-production editing.

The snappy little comedy programmer that resulted failed to do justice to the source material. Bert Wheeler inherited Willie Howard's popular comic role as the New York taxi driver who becomes sheriff of the town of Custerville, Arizona, but the very ethnic character name of Gieber Goldberg was homogenized into Jimmy Deegan. Bob Woolsey became Slick Foster, a con man whom the playboy Danny Churchill (Eddie Quillan, 1907–1992) summons from the East to Custerville to run the gambling aspect of his new dude ranch. Arline Judge took Ginger Rogers' Broadway role of Molly Gray, the peppery postmistress whose big song in the stage show was "But Not for Me."

Kitty Kelly and Dorothy Lee were on hand as, respectively, Woolsey's wife and Wheeler's girlfriend. Nowhere to be found was Frisco Kate Fothergill, the barroom toughie played so memorably in New York by Ethel Merman. The story, as on stage, saw the inexperienced

lawman menaced by the town's resident sheriff-killer (hulking Stanley Fields), who thinks he has been had by Danny's lucrative new venture. Three songs remained from the Broadway show ("Embraceable You" was filmed but then removed), although one "new" George and Ira Gershwin tune was added. Most of the music in the underscoring was from the stage version, but some was written for the film—apparently with the Gershwins' permission—by Max Steiner, RKO's general musical director.[11]

Girl Crazy was the last RKO project headed by its founding head of production, William LeBaron, who was replaced at the financially foundering studio by the estimable David O. Selznick. Selznick, who didn't care for Wheeler and Woolsey, ordered that $200,000 in retakes be added to the $300,000-plus already spent. The retakes, mainly of the final reel, were directed not by William A. Seiter, who had made the picture, but by Norman Taurog. "None of us," Eddie Quillan told Wheeler-Woolsey historian Edward Watz years later, "really cared about *Girl Crazy* anymore when we saw David … replacing perfectly good scenes with pointless ones."[12]

The emphasis was strictly on comedy, which was fine for Wheeler and Woolsey fans. "The picture bunch wants its plots, menaces and romances straight, sans any Gershwinesque fol-de-rol," wrote *Variety*'s Abel Green.[13] But for those who happened to like the "fol-de-rol," the picture was a mess. The Gershwin standards are either unwisely staged or thrown away. Kelly's underpowered rendition of "I Got Rhythm" at least gets a production number, but one with a silly montage that includes dancing cacti and, on the wall of Danny's jumpin' nightclub, swaying moose heads. The new Gershwin tune, "You've Got What Gets Me," makes for a forgettable light romantic duet by Woolsey and Lee. The brothers created this song by adding a verse and chorus to the middle section of their song "Your Eyes, Your Smile," which was written for, but not used in, the 1927 Broadway musical *Funny Face*.[14]

The most awful treatment is accorded the wistful "But Not for Me," which is insistently played for laughs. The weak-voiced Quillan and Judge, who are supposed to be bickering lovers, alternate verses with Mitzi Green, who is supposed to be Woolsey's pesky sister. Worse yet, Miss Green is then handed her usual "impressions" speciality, with Bing Crosby, Roscoe Ates, George Arliss and Edna May Oliver as *they* would have sung "But Not for Me." Actually this was not as bizarre as it sounded, for in the original, Willie Howard had reprised "But Not for Me" with his own mimicry of Maurice Chevalier and Rudy Vallee. Who could ask for anything more from little Mitzi? We could ... for Ginger Rogers as *she* would have sung it.

Even with the retooling—or because of it—*Girl Crazy* was a financial and critical flop. A more faithful rendering of the stage show would have to wait for MGM's Judy Garland-Mickey Rooney–Busby Berkeley spectacular of 1943.[15] We leave the last word on the first *Girl Crazy* film with an unsympathetic Dorothy Lee, whose Girl of the Golden West was practically ignored in the scenario—thanks, she says, to Selznick's revisions. "I tried to get out of that one," she told the author,

> Bert Wheeler said, "You're crazy, you're getting $1,000 a week, so what do you care what you do?" So I did it. I don't think the film was well done at all. ... I saw it once, and that was enough. I couldn't look at it again. And all my fans who know me well, they say, "Oh, Dottie, let's look at *Girl Crazy* where they photograph you behind the post." So it was badly photographed and the whole thing was lousy, as far as I can remember.[16]

THIS IS THE NIGHT
(Paramount; April 15, 1932)

Director: Frank Tuttle. Associate Producer: Benjamin Glazer. Screenplay: George Marion, Jr., Benjamin Glazer. Based on the musical play *Naughty Cinderella*, book by Avery Hopwood, lyrics and music by E. Ray Goetz and others (New York opening, November 9, 1925; 121 performances), adapted from *Pouche* by René Peter and Henri Falk (1923). Photography: Victor Milner. Sound: J. A. Goodrich. Running Time: 78 minutes.

Cast: Lily Damita (Germaine/Chou-Chou), Charles Ruggles (Bunny West), Roland Young (Gerald Grey), Thelma Todd (Claire Mathewson), Cary Grant (Stephen Mathewson), Irving Bacon (Sparks), Claire Dodd (the real Chou-Chou), Davison Clark (studio official), Donald Novis (singing gondolier).

Songs: "This Is the Night" [Novis; reprised by Young, then by offscreen chorus], "Tonight Is All a Dream" [Novis] (Sam Coslow, Ralph Rainger); "Madame Has Lost Her Dress" [Parisians] (George Marion, Jr., Ralph Rainger); "One Venetian Night" [Novis; reprised by Damita] (Ralph Rainger).

Who in America besides Ernst Lubitsch could master the kind of frothy, continental farce that René Clair and Wilhelm Thiele were making over in France and Germany? At least once, it was Frank Tuttle, a better-than-competent Paramount contract director whose *This Is the Night* was a rare delight for moviegoers of 1932. Bolstered by an alluring Ralph Rainger score, this romantic tale was taken from the Avery Hopwood play with music *Naughty Cinderella*, a 1925 Broadway vehicle for Irene Bordoni which was itself based on the French comedy *Pouche*. A Pola Negri–headlined Paramount comedy of 1926, *Good and Naughty* (see Appendix I), was a more immediate derivative of Hopwood's play.

In *This Is the Night*, the saucy Lily Damita (1901–1994) had the Bordoni role, that of a Paris actress named Chou-Chou who is hired by playboy Gerald Grey (Roland Young) to portray his non-existent wife for a trip to Venice with his lover, Claire Mathewson (Thelma Todd, 1905–1935), and her champion javelin-thrower husband, Stephen (Cary Grant, in his first feature film). The ruse is necessary to avert the suspicions of Stephen, who is pretty sure what's going on. Along for the ride is Gerald's sidekick (Charlie Ruggles), who falls for Chou-Chou. The athlete's eyes start to wander, too, which makes Claire suddenly envious. But Chou-Chou's heart belongs to her "husband"—if only he will take notice.

Attractively photographed by Victor Milner, *This Is the Night* is full of the sly sexual satire that inevitably brought comparsions to Lubitsch's "touch," and not just because Young (1887–1953) and Ruggles were Lubitsch alumni. The opening sequence, in which Rainger's underscoring is tied to movement and sound effects substituted for dialogue, shows the gaiety and casual salaciousness of Paree. A sleazy street-corner chap sells a packet of postcards with "10 Beauties de Paris" to an older American man, who opens the package and is enraged to find a drawing of Uncle Sam

Cary Grant made his movie debut opposite Lily Damita in Paramount's delectable *This Is the Night*.

grinning back at him. He throws the cards on the street, and a car runs over them. Against a silhouette of the marquee for the Folies de Paris, a man accosts a woman and offers her a flower; she stamps her feet in displeasure but the two go off together. Now a car, the one we have just seen, pulls up in front of the theater. Gerald gets out first, then his "date," Claire. The chauffeur (Irving Bacon), distracted by a gendarme's demands that the car be moved, slams the door on Claire's gown as she walks toward the theater, and the ensuing sight prompts the onlookers (whose voices we can now hear) to chant and sing "Madame Has Lost Her Dress." As Claire stews, the news is bandied about the city, from the sewers to the high-rises and from atop the Eiffel Tower.

The title song is also introduced attractively, though with a quite different mood. Saddened by Gerald's indifference toward her in Venice, Chou-Chou stands on their hotel balcony and stares down at a gondolier (Donald

Novis) singing in Italian. Gerald walks outside to join her during the song. Caught up in the moment, he looks adoringly into her eyes and, speaking the song's lyrics in English, tells her that this is the night he has waited for. He takes her in his arms, and they kiss. She will win him for good, but not until after he learns that she is not the worldly actress he thought he had hired, but a virtuous extra named Germaine who had taken the job because she was starving.

The debut for Grant (1904–1986) in a Hollywood musical was not as odd as it might seem, for although the handsome stage import couldn't sing, his New York credits included a small role in the original *Golden Dawn* (1927) and featured parts in two ill-fated Shubert musicals of 1929, *Boom Boom* (with Jeanette MacDonald) and *Wonderful Night*. None of these assignments taxed his shaky vocals, and neither did his first film appearance: a small part as a sailor in a 1931 New York–made Paramount musical short, *Singapore Sue.* Shortly thereafter, he would make his way West, to a Paramount contract.

In *This Is the Night,* Grant has the least screen time of the five principals. His first moment in the movies is, oddly, a musical one, as he walks up the stairs to the Mathewson flat singing a few bars of something called "My Girl Is Named Yvonne" with a bagful of javelins on his back. Grant made enough of an impression to be called "efficient" by *The New York Times*[17] and "a potential femme rave" by *Variety.*[18] The actor, watching himself for the first time on screen, supposedly was so appalled by his performance that he sneaked out of the theater before the preview was over and planned a return to New York for the stage before friends talked him out of it.

Grant's self-perceived ham acting might have upset him, but even his uncharacteristically feeble attempts at light comedy don't dampen the spirit of *This Is the Night.*

HORSE FEATHERS
(Paramount; August 10, 1932)

Director: Norman Z. McLeod. Screenplay: Bert Kalmar, Harry Ruby, S. J. Perelman, Will B. Johnstone. Photography: Ray June. Sound: Eugene Merritt. Assistant Director: Charles Barton. Running Time: 70 minutes.

Cast: Groucho Marx (Professor Quincy Adams Wagstaff), Harpo Marx (Pinky), Chico Marx (Baravelli), Zeppo Marx (Frank Wagstaff), Thelma Todd (Connie Bailey), David Landau (Jennings), Florine McKinney (Peggy Carrington), James Pierce (Mullen), Nat Pendleton (McCarthy), Reginald Barlow (college president), Robert Greig (Professor Hornsvogel), Edward J. Le Saint, E. H. Calvert (professors), Vince Barnett (speakeasy patron), Edgar Dearing (bartender), Ben Taggart (policeman).

Songs: "Everyone Says 'I Love You'" [Zeppo; reprised by Chico, then by Harpo on harp, then by Groucho], "Whatever It Is, I'm Against It"/"I Always Get My Man" [Groucho, Zeppo, chorus] (Bert Kalmar, Harry Ruby).

Disc: Decca 79168 (Marx Brothers/LP; ST); MCA MUP-395 (Marx Brothers/LP; ST); Pelican 130 (Marx Brothers/LP; ST).

Video: MCA-Universal (cassette/laser-disc).

After scoring in the screen versions of their musical comedies *The Cocoanuts* and *Animal Crackers* (both Chapter 4), the Marx Brothers made their first written-for-the-screen romp, *Monkey Business* (September 19, 1931). It was a story set aboard an ocean liner with music as mere incidentals, although there is a hilarious sequence in which all four brothers attempt to pass through U. S. customs by pretending to be Maurice Chevalier singing "You Brought a New Kind of Love to Me."

Their fourth film, the collegiate comedy *Horse Feathers,* was an original script that was also light on music. But it did have two (or three) Bert Kalmar–Harry Ruby songs and, unlike *Monkey Business,* a handful of song numbers to go with the requisite instrumentals by Harpo and Chico.

As the madcap Professor Quincy Adams Wagstaff, Groucho kicks off the rally that introduces him as president of little Huxley College by singing about his personal credo, "Whatever It Is, I'm Against It." This segues into what appears to be a different song, "I Always Get My Man," as Zeppo and a chorus of faculty and students join in. The theme song of *Horse Feathers* is "Everyone Says 'I Love You'," performed by each of the brothers separately as a serenade to the "College Widow" (Thelma Todd). Zeppo sings, Harpo harps, Chico plunks his piano and Groucho strums a ukelele. The widow is so impressed that she ends up taking all four to the altar. The romance, such as it is, is secondary to the main plot, in which Wagstaff and cohorts plan for Huxley's big football game against hated rival Darwin.

Considered by some to be the brothers' funniest film, *Horse Feathers* earned this strange but somehow appropriate compliment from *Photoplay*: "You won't know at all what it's all about. But then neither do the Marx Brothers. It's that funny."[19]

LOVE ME TONIGHT
(Paramount; August 17, 1932)

Director-Producer: Rouben Mamoulian. Screenplay: Samuel Hoffenstein, Waldemar Young, George Marion, Jr. Based on the play *Le Tailleur au Château* [The Tailor in the Château] by Leopold Marchand and Paul Armont (1924). Photography: Victor Milner. Editor: William Shea. Sound: M. M. Paggi. Art Director: Hans Dreier. Costumes: Travis Banton. Musical Director: Nathaniel Finston. Running Time: 90 minutes.

Cast: Maurice Chevalier (Maurice Courtelin), Jeanette MacDonald (Princess Jeanette), Charlie Ruggles (Vicomte Gilbert de Vareze), Charles Butterworth (Count de Savignac), Myrna Loy (Countess Valentine), C. Aubrey Smith (Duke d'Artelines), Elizabeth Patterson, Ethel Griffies, Blanche Frederici (three aunts), Joseph Cawthorn (Doctor Armand de Pontignac), Robert Greig (Major-Domo Flammond), Bert Roach (Emile), Herbert Mundin (groom), Ethel Wales (dressmaker), Marion Byron (bakery girl), Mary Doran (Madame Dupont), Cecil Cunningham (laundress), Tyler Brooke (composer), Edgar Norton (valet), Rita Owin (chambermaid), Clarence Wilson (shirtmaker), Gordon Westcott (collector), George Davis (Pierre), Rolfe Sedan (taxi driver), Tony Merlo (hatmaker), William H. Turner (bootmaker), George "Gabby" Hayes (grocer), George Humbert (chef).

Songs: "Isn't It Romantic?" [Chevalier, Roach, Sedan, Brooke, soldiers, gypsy violinist, MacDonald], "Love Me Tonight" [MacDonald, Chevalier], "Lover" [MacDonald], "Mimi" [Chevalier; reprised by Smith, Ruggles, Griffies, Patterson, Butterworth], "The Poor Apache" [Chevalier], "The Son of a Gun Is Nothing but a Tailor" [Smith, Patterson, Griffies, Frederici, Loy, Greig, Norton, Cunningham, Orwin, Humbert, MacDonald], "(That's) The Song of Paree" [Chevalier, Byron, Hayes, Parisians], "A Woman Needs Something Like That" [MacDonald, Cawthorn] (Lorenz Hart, Richard Rodgers).

Disc: RCA Victor 24063 (Chevalier/ "Mimi"/"The Poor Apache"/78); RCA Victor 24066 (Chevalier/preceding songs in French/ 78); RCA Victor 24067 (MacDonald/"Love Me Tonight"/"Isn't It Romantic?"/78); RCA Victor 24068 (MacDonald/preceding songs in French/78); Box Office (number undetermined; bootleg LP; ST); Caliban 6047 (bootleg LP; ST); Music Masters JJA-19766 (bootleg LP; ST); WRC SH 156 (bootleg LP; ST).

If Rouben Mamoulian had had his way, he wouldn't have had anything to do with *Love Me*

Tonight. Having followed his critically acclaimed *Applause* (see Chapter 9) with two more stylish melodramas, *City Streets* (1931) and the box-office hit *Dr. Jekyll and Mr. Hyde* (1932), he didn't see a light musical as a logical next step. But Paramount wanted him to produce and direct a film with Maurice Chevalier and Jeanette MacDonald, two highly priced stars who needed a solid vehicle to follow Ernst Lubitsch's *One Hour with You*. Mamoulian balked a little, then proceeded to make a movie that out-Lubitsched Lubitsch. *Love Me Tonight*, blessed with a beautiful Rodgers and Hart score, closely integrated picture, dialogue and song for one of the most cohesive, adventurous musicals of all time. It lost nothing in terms of entertainment value, for its innovation was complemented by a charming, mildly risqué romantic story. *Love Me Tonight* proved, once and for all, that the musical film could succeed on its own terms and not as some poor stepchild of the legitimate stage show.

Love Me Tonight was based on *Le Tailleur au Château*, a French play about a common tailor who poses as a nobleman. One of the playwrights, Leopold Marchand, suggested to Mamoulian that the work be adapted for his musical project. Mamoulian thought the story "had a kind of fairy tale romantic magic," he recalled to authors Gene Ringgold and DeWitt Bodeen years later, and he asked Paramount to buy it.

> I then got Richard Rodgers and Lorenz Hart to develop the songs for the film. You understand, all the songs were carefully planned, with the lyrics to advance the story line, and their place in the story itself designed before the writers of the screenplay were engaged. ... When the screenwriters—[Samuel] Hoffenstein, [George] Marion, Jr. and [Waldemar] Young—came on the picture it was their job to construct the scenes and bridge the dialog between the song numbers, so that the songs flowed from the action sequences and the actors didn't stop and sing a song. It worked perfectly.[20]

In its most audacious foray into perfection, *Love Me Tonight* ingeniously uses its first 16 minutes to link the two primary players by foreshadowing their interaction. Included in this "symphony" is two complete songs as well as Rodgers and Hart's rhythmic dialogue (speech delivered in verse against a musical background).

Maurice Chevalier charms man-hungry Myrna Loy and others in a scene from Rouben Mamoulian's sublime *Love Me Tonight*.

To begin the film, Mamoulian achieved a look reminiscent of the opening of his landmark stage drama of 1927, *Porgy*. At the outset of that DuBose Hayward play (later adapted into the operetta *Porgy and Bess*), Mamoulian had created a slowly building syncopated rhythm of common sounds to depict the awakening of a tenement village at sunrise. Now, a shot of the Eiffel Tower and the surrounding housetops reveals the setting as Paris, its streets deserted as day breaks. A road worker wields his pick on cobblestone, a church bell rings, a woman sweeps her doorstep, a baby is heard crying from above. A blacksmith and bootmaker commence to work side by side, their hammering of tacks perfectly complementing each other. The noise builds to a cacaphony. The camera peers into a window where a straw hat is hung on a wall; we know who we'll see next.

It's Chevalier, who, as the tailor Maurice Courtelin, pulls on his shirt and greets the morning ("You are much too loud for me!") by closing his bedroom window and singing "The Song of Paree." He leaves his flat and walks down a street toward his shop, greeting friends and acquaintances, some of whom tell us something about Maurice's personality. We know he is a playboy, for two women argue over "their" night for him. We know he has had to pinch pennies, for a grocer complains about his late bill. Maurice arrives at his shop. One of his few regular customers, Emile (Bert Roach) comes in to pick up a tuxedo for his upcoming marriage. Maurice brags that the rest of his rack holds 16 suits for the wealthy Vicomte Gilbert de Vareze. Just then the vicomte (Charlie Ruggles) enters in top hat and underwear. "The girl's husband ... he came home unexpectedly ..." is his explanation for abruptly joining in the road race that has just passed. The vicomte dons one of the suits Maurice has for him, then surprises the tailor by asking for a sizable loan. However, he promises to pay the 40,000 francs he owes by the next day, after he receives his allowance from his uncle, the Duke d'Artelines.

After the vicomte leaves, Emile compliments Maurice on his fine work. In turn, Maurice expresses his gladness that Emile is to be wed. The tailor begins to sing "Isn't It Romantic?" and Emile departs with the "very catchy strain" on his lips. As he hums, he greets a taxi driver waiting for a fare. The driver (Rolfe Sedan) takes up the melody, and his next customer, a composer, decides to jot down the notes. On a train, as the composer (Tyler Brooke) sings the words he has just penned for the tune, a troop of soldiers within earshot joins in. As the soldiers march in the countryside, a gypsy violinist hears their song and plays it at his camp. His performance is heard by the lovely Princess Jeanette (Jeanette MacDonald) as she walks onto the balcony of her family's impressive château. She finishes the song almost as if it were an aria. "Isn't It Romantic?" You bet.[21]

Jeanette, widowed three years before by her much-older husband, is bored of life in the staid family home and wishes for some excitement—specifically, a man. The persistent Count de Savignac (Charles Butterworth), a colorless fuddy-duddy whose idea of fun is playing his flute off-key, will not do. Also residing in the Château d'Artelines are Jeanette's stuffed-shirt father, the duke (C. Aubrey Smith); the irresponsible vicomte; his cousin, the nymphomaniac Countess Valentine (Myrna Loy); and, recalling the witches in *Macbeth*, three spinster aunts (Elizabeth Patterson, Ethel Griffies, Blanche Frederici), who chant spells in hopes that the princess will regain her vitality. The duke entertains his guests with endless rounds of bridge. The countess complains about the age of the fossilized hired help: "Can't you even get a footman under 40 in this place?"

Back in Paris, Maurice learns that the vicomte owes money to tailors all over Paris. Determined to recover the 63,000 francs due to him and his colleagues, he sets out for the château. On a country road nearby, his car is disabled with a flat tire, and while the driver is repairing it the princess rides by in a carriage singing "Lover" (her words are interrupted periodically by commands to her horse). Trying to avoid Maurice's car, she veers off the side of the road and her carriage topples. Maurice is auto-

matically smitten; he wants this beautiful woman to sit for a while and rest her sore foot. He sings to Jeanette the jubilant love song "Mimi." "I've known you for a hundred years … a thousand years!" he cries. Intimidated, she rides away to the castle, then faints once she is inside. A physician (Joseph Cawthorn) is summoned to diagnose Jeanette's malaise. He goes to her bedside to have a look. In an insinuating recitative of rhyming dialogue ("A Woman Needs Something Like That"), she declares that she is wasting away. You're not wasted away, the doctor replies, "you're just wasted." He tells the duke that Jeanette's "cure" will be a marriage to a man of her own age. "Exercise, exercise—and exercise!" is his prescription.

Maurice now arrives, but the nervous vicomte conceals the visitor's reason for coming. The tailor, he claims, is "Baron Courtelin," from the south of France. Not only does the princess perk up, but Maurice's enthusiasm is infectious to all. The next morning, the duke, the vicomte, the count and the aunts awake to sing their own verses of "Mimi." But the jealous count is suspicious of the newcomer, and while the rest of the principals embark on a stag hunt, he plans to research all of the family trees in France. To test the "baron," Jeanette assigns to him a bucking bronc named "Solitude," so named because he always returns home alone. But Maurice mounts the steed and is able to ride off on it. Later, at a small cottage in the woods, Jeanette finds Maurice feeding oats to the stag ("a happy ending of which we both approve"). She declares that he is no gentleman, and he replies that she knows nothing about style, charm or love. Her appearance, he says, is too severe to be womanly. When the rest of the hunting party appear, Maurice tells them that the stag is asleep and that they should all go home on tiptoe. The count is now certain that there is no Baron Courtelin in the blueblood listings, but the vicomte hints that Maurice is a member of a royal family traveling under a *nom de plume*.

At the ensuing Hunt Ball, Maurice regales the audience with a song about the miserable life of a tough Parisian, "The Poor Apache." Still attempting to reign in her feelings for Maurice, the princess runs out into the garden and faints. Maurice follows, and revives his intended with a kiss. She slaps him, but now finally admits that she is in love, too. Maurice is suddenly saddened, for the truth must be told. "You don't know who I am ... if I were not what you think ..." he says. She responds that it doesn't matter, that she will love him "whoever you are, whatever you are, wherever you are." "Whatever happens tomorrow," he implores, "love me tonight!" That night, Maurice dreams that the princess is accepting of his true station in life. The two are heard singing "Love Me Tonight," as the screen divides to show them both sleeping—and dreaming.

The next morning, Jeanette shows off her new riding habit, for which Maurice has some helpful—too helpful—fitting suggestions. He insults the seamstress, who storms out. The principals enter to find Maurice measuring Jeanette's waist. Upset, the duke requires Maurice to prove that he is a tailor, and the visitor is ordered to fashion a correct habit within two hours. Maurice joyfully completes his measurements with a reprise of "Isn't It Romantic?" Soon, the job is finished.

"It's too perfect. ... How were you able to make it at all?" wonders the confused princess.

"Because ... I am a tailor," replies her beau.

"Maurice, you're joking."

"No, I am not a baron. I am a tailor."

"Ohhhhh ..." (Jeanette backs away.)

"Does that make so much difference?" Maurice asks hopefully, but he knows the answer, for Jeanette dashes out of the room.

"The Son of a Gun Is Nothing but a Tailor" is the sung revelation of the entire household, from the duke, to the aunts, to the countess, the count, the majordomo and various other servants (valet, chambermaid, chef, laundress). Humiliated, Maurice leaves, but Jeanette, watching him walk away from her upstairs window, recalls the promise she had made to him in the garden. As she agonizes over what to do, her image is superimposed on footage of Maurice boarding a train. On horseback, the princess follows in desperate pursuit. The action cuts back and forth between the two travelers, then between the horse's galloping feet and the train's spinning wheels. Miraculously, Jeanette catches up. "I love you!" she cries as he peers out his window, "I can't live without you!" "I love you," he yells in response, "but you can't be a tailor's wife! ... You belong in the château!" As the train approaches a bend, Jeanette rides straight ahead so she will beat the train to a spot. She stands on the tracks, daring to be run over. The train stops at her feet, and the lovers embrace.

Cut to the three aunts sitting on a sofa. "Once upon a time," says one, "there was a princess and a Prince Charming ..."

" ...Who was not a prince ..." says the second.

" ...But who was charming!" says the third.

" ...And they lived happily ever after," says the first aunt.

They reveal the finished needlepoint they have been sewing throughout the film. It's a tableau of a gallant knight on a horse, a princess and a castle. A cinematic fairy tale is over.

With *Love Me Tonight*, Mamoulian took the screen musical to a level of artistry that has rarely been surpassed. Musicals became "bigger," more colorful (figuratively and literally) and more technically elaborate as the years passed, but few were as seamless in exposition and the dialogue-to-music transition as this one. In some of the numbers—for example, the Paris street opening and "A Woman Needs Something Like That"—the rhythmic dialogue blends so well with song that it is difficult to determine which is which. This shows Rodgers and Hart's close collaboration with Mamoulian, who asked Rodgers to compose the incidental score as well as the songs.[22] There are no dance numbers to break the rhythm of the film, but dance never made much sense in a Chevalier-MacDonald musical anyway. "Lover," "Isn't It Romantic" and "Mimi" became Rodgers and Hart's first song hits to be introduced in a motion picture, although the pair had some anxious moments upon meeting the exacting Chevalier.

In their tiny cubicle at Paramount, the songwriters played some of the music slated for *Love Me Tonight* for the star. Chevalier sat silent and expressionless the whole time, then rose and left without a word. According to Rodgers in *Musical Stages: An Autobiography:*

We were stunned. The only conclusion we could reach was that he didn't like what he'd heard. Now what? ... Would the studio replace us with another team? And what about our reputation ... ? The next morning we tried to sneak into our little room without anyone seeing us ... we couldn't do any work. After a couple of hours the door burst open and there again stood our smiling ... boy. "Boys," Chevalier said, throwing one arm around Larry and the other around me, "I just had to come back to tell you. I couldn't sleep a wink last night because I was so excited about your wonderful songs!" … It was a tough job for Larry and me to conceal our feeling of relief.[23]

Mamoulian, ever the experimenter, complements the songs and story with some nifty directorial tricks. When Maurice rides off on the devil horse at the hunt, Victor Milner's camera speeds up the movement to illustrate the tailor's rough trip. After he asks the hunters to return home on tiptoe, they appear to do just that, as we see them move in slow motion. At the moment the maiden aunts tell the duke that Maurice is only a tailor, a vase falls from its stand; the spill is accompanied by an effect that sounds like a bomb exploding. For the "Love Me Tonight" number, Mamoulian combines the off-camera voices of MacDonald and Chevalier with a split-screen effect to present a captivating duet of two people sleeping.

Oddly enough, the stars are called by their real first names, although this does not mar the timelessness of the story. In Chevalier's case, the script has some fun with his star persona. After Jeanette's horse runs over his trademark straw hat during the lovers' introduction, the tailor's driver (George Davis), who is changing a flat tire, exclaims, "What will you do without your straw hat, Maurice? And where is that smile of yours? No straw hat, no smile. It's all over, Maurice, you can't go on!" To which Maurice reaches for a box in the back seat and pulls out a spare hat. Unlike *One Hour with You,* in which both actors seem vaguely uneasy with their characters, MacDonald and Chevalier are in full control, confident of themselves. Neither would make a better movie, together or apart.

Film buffs commit to memory Loy's famous line early in the film. After Jeanette has fainted, Ruggles asks the countess, "Valentine, can you go for a doctor?" and she replies, suddenly alert and primping her hair, "Certainly, bring him right in!" Before filming began, the studio wanted to eliminate the countess from the screenplay, probably because she was considered extraneous. But Mamoulian, a good friend of Loy's, had plans for Valentine, and for the actress. Loy recalled in her memoirs that the director told her

"I know what I plan to do with her, but she won't be in the script. I'll send you your lines separately until they see it my way." Well, I

had confidence in Rouben: "Sure, I'll try anything!" Every few days, he'd send little pieces of blue interoffice-memo paper with four or five lines typed on them. This was my part. I don't know how Rouben managed it, but when the men in the front office saw my first scenes, they said, "Oh, yes, keep her."[24]

Loy's deadpan performance is terrific, and in her evening gowns emerges as even more beautiful than MacDonald. American audiences were deprived of her rendition, while wearing a skimpy negligee, of "Mimi" during the song's reprise at the castle. The sequence was considered too racy, although it was seen in Europe. (Dropped prior to the release of the film were two Chevalier-MacDonald duets: "The Man for Me" and "Give Me Just a Moment.") All of the supporting actors, many of whom came from Ernst Lubitsch's informal stock company, are appealing, from Ruggles, Butterworth and Smith down to the bit actor/singers who populate the streets of Paris and the halls of Château d'Artelines.

Although the reviews of it were uniformly complimentary, *Love Me Tonight* was considered something of a knock-off of Lubitsch or René Clair when it was released. Note that, for example, *The New York Times'* Mordaunt Hall left *Love Me Tonight* off his 10-best list for 1932 in favor of Lubitsch's *One Hour with You* and *Trouble in Paradise* and Mamoulian's *Dr. Jekyll and Mr. Hyde.* The motion-picture academy ignored the film altogether, nominating Lubitsch's *One Hour with You* and *The Smiling Lieutenant* as Best Picture for 1931-32 and the musical *42nd Street* and Paramount's musical comedy *She Done Him Wrong* for 1932-33. *The Times'* Hall noted that although Mamoulian "may not reveal Ernst Lubitsch's satire and keen wit or René Clair's clever irony, he, in a somewhat precise and often theatric fashion, gives to his scenes a charming poetic suggestion."[25] *Time* magazine's critic wrote that *Love Me Tonight* "has that air of light poetry as well as farce that the French comedies of René Clair contributed to cinema technique. … The only illogicality is Chevalier's preferring Jeanette MacDonald to Myrna Loy…."[26]

Love Me Tonight is the rare film with a reputation that has deservedly grown with the passage of time. Interviewed by Kevin Thomas of the *Los Angeles Times* in 1982, for the 50th anniversary of the premiere of *Love Me Tonight,*

Mamoulian admitted that it was one of his favorites among his 16 films. And he was still amused about the reaction to some of his unconventional methods of filmmaking:

> At the time people said you couldn't do such things. But of course you can. Your brain tells you you're crazy, your assistant tells you you're crazy. I say to myself, "I know that, but I've got to do it anyway." I always follow my instincts.[27]

CROONER

(First National; August 18, 1932)

Director: Lloyd Bacon. Screenplay: Charles Kenyon. Story: Rian James. Photography: Robert Kurrle. Editor: Howard Bretherton. Art Director: Robert Haas. Costumes: Orry-Kelly. Running Time: 67 minutes.

Cast: David Manners (Teddy Taylor), Ann Dvorak (Judy Mason), Ken Murray (Peter Sturgis), William Janney (Pat), Eddie Nugent (Henry), J. Carrol Naish (Nick Meyer), Claire Dodd (Mrs. Brown), Teddy Joyce (Mack), Clarence Nordstrom (Tom), Allen Vincent (Ralph), Guy Kibbee (Mike), William Halligan (theater manager), William Ricciardi (head waiter), Sheila Terry (hat check girl), Betty Gillette (Meyer's secretary), Sumner Getchell, John Harron, William Morgan (band members), Luis Alberni (voice teacher), Hattie McDaniel (nightclub attendant), Herman Bing.

Songs: "I Send My Love with the Roses" [Manners, band, vocals dubbed by Brick Holton] (Al Dubin, Joe Burke); "In a Shanty in Old Shanty Town" [Joyce, band] (Joe Young, Little Jack Little, John Siras); "Sweethearts Forever" [Manners, band, twice, vocals dubbed by Holton] (Cliff Friend, Irving Caesar); "Three's a Crowd" [Manners, band, three times, vocals dubbed by Holton] (Al Dubin, Irving Kahal, Harry Warren).

A satirical joust at the Crosby-Columbo-Vallee school of pop music idolatry, *Crooner* told the tale of a handsome young bandleader who, through a fluke, rises to stardom and thereby becomes insufferable. The title role went to a non-singer, David Manners (b. 1901), who (dubbed by Brick Holton) performed three songs as the headliner of "Teddy Taylor and His Collegians."

At the outset of this cynical programmer, the struggling Teddy and boys are on the verge of disbanding when they gain a tryout at the Silver Slipper Club, owned by Nick Meyer (J. Carrol Naish). But on the eve of their performance, their vocalist (Teddy Joyce) comes down with a sore throat. Teddy, forced to sing as well as conduct, is almost laughed off the dais for his light tones before an amiable inebriate (Guy Kibbee) sarcastically hands him a megaphone à la Rudy Vallee. The resulting amplification enables Teddy to send the girls swooning and drive their unimpressed dates to sanctuary in the restroom. Press agent Peter Sturgis (Ken Murray)—who happens to be in love with Teddy's girl, Judy Mason (Ann Dvorak, the former MGM chorine turned leading lady)—promises to make Teddy a star within six months.

The acerbic Sturgis thinks radio is "Marconi's gift to the morons," but he puts Teddy and the band over the airwaves without hesitation. Soon, the Collegians' fan mail is up to 2,000 letters a week, and Teddy is self-impressed enough to hire a valet, take a suite at the Waldorf, lunch at the Ritz, show off his French, and hobnob with society matrons. One of them (Claire Dodd) becomes his lover. Judy drops Teddy for Sturgis, and so does all of showbiz after he punches out a crippled heckler who had berated the band for its now-draggy repertoire. But Teddy, reduced to playing sax in a small dance club, is reunited with Jane by the suddenly gallant Sturgis. Contrite, he is headed back toward the top.

Manners—a "tennis, anyone" type of leading man best known for his battles with monsters in Universal horror films (*Dracula, The Mummy, The Black Cat*)—is lightweight enough to be the most believable in the scenes in which he has gone uptown. But no one could see him as a bandleader, much less a crooner, and this role was his finale as a decreasingly successful Warners–First National contractee. Dvorak and Murray are much more able. Incidentally, it's sad to see John Harron, the male lead as a band musician in *Street Girl* (see Chapter 3), reduced to a non-speaking role as one of the least conspicuous Collegians.

THE GIRL FROM CALGARY
(Monogram; September 24, 1932)

Director: Phil Whitman. Dialogue Director: Leon D'Usseau. Producer: I. E. Chadwick. Supervisor: Trem Carr. Screenplay: Lee Chadwick. Story: Sig Schlager, Leon D'Usseau. Photography: Harry Neumann. Editor: Carl L. Pierson. Sound: David Stoner. Art Director: Hickson. Running Time: 59 minutes. Color sequence.

Cast: Fifi D'Orsay (Fifi Follette), Paul Kelly (Larry Boyd), Robert Warwick (Bill Webster), Edwin Maxwell (Earl Darrell), Astrid Allwyn (Mazie Williams), Eddie Featherstone (Monte Cooper).

Songs [all by D'Orsay]: "Comme Ça Va," "Maybe, Perhaps," "Misbehavin' (Dancing) Feet" (Albert Hay Malotte).

Video: Video Yesteryear (cassette).

Monogram, a Poverty Row studio, was more accustomed to making Westerns than backstagers in 1932, so *The Girl from Calgary* gave viewers a little of the first genre to go with the second. Fifi D'Orsay, the erstwhile vaudeville headliner, brought her Gallic charm to the role of Fifi Follette, a zesty singer and bronco buster imported to New York from the wilds of Canada by an enterprising press agent. The PR man, Larry Boyd (Paul Kelly), lands Fifi a featured song-and-dance job in a Broadway revue produced by Earl Darrell (Edwin Maxwell), but the show's powerful backer (Robert Warwick) falls in love with her. When Larry punches him out in disgust, the big shot arranges to have the young man gunned down. But the wound turns out not to be fatal, and Fifi and Larry make plans to desert the bright lights for a less distracting life together.

Both D'Orsay (1904–1983) and Kelly (1899–1956) were attempting comebacks of sorts in *The Girl from Calgary*. She recently had walked out on her seven-year contract with Fox, where her credits had included *They Had to See Paris* (1929; Will Rogers' first talkie), *Hot for Paris* (see Chapter 5), and *Women Everywhere* (see Chapter 7). D'Orsay was upset that Fox was paying her only $400 a week while cashing in on her loan-outs to other studios. Kelly's story was much different. He had served two years in prison for manslaughter in the beating

death of actor-producer Ray Raymond in 1927. The much-publicized incident stemmed from a fistfight over Raymond's wife, actress Dorothy Mackaye, who was sent to prison for compounding the felony. She would later become Mrs. Kelly. After his release in 1929, Kelly embarked on a successful stage career before taking time off for this Monogram quickie.

Kelly—and D'Orsay, too, for that matter—would go on to make better movies than *The Girl from Calgary*. It suffers from poor direction, lackluster plotting and dialogue, and cramped, chintzy-looking sets. Even the opening color sequence, set at the famed Calgary Stampede rodeo, was dismissed by *Variety* as "out of focus."[28] This sequence survives in black-and-white only.

THE PHANTOM PRESIDENT
(Paramount; September 25, 1932)

Director: Norman Taurog. Screenplay: Walter de Leon, Harlan Thompson. Based on the novel by George M. Worts (1931). Photography: David Abel. Sound: Eugene Merritt. Running Time: 77 minutes.

Cast: George M. Cohan (Theodore K. Blair/Peter "Doc" Varney), Claudette Colbert (Felicia Hammond), Jimmy Durante (Curly Cooney), George Barbier (Jim Ronkton), Sidney Toler (Professor Aikenhead), Louise Mackintosh (Senator Sarah Scranton), Jameson Thomas (Jerrido), Julius McVicker (Senator Melrose), Paul Hurst, Ed Brady (sailors), Hooper Atchley (announcer), Charles Middleton (Abraham Lincoln), Alan Mowbray (George Washington).

Songs/Musical Numbers: "The Convention" [Cohan, Durante, chorus], "The Country Needs a Man" [company], "Give Her a Kiss" ["animals and birds"; reprised by radio vocalists], "The Medicine Show" [Cohan, Durante, Barbier, MacIntosh, McVicker, chorus], "Somebody Ought to Wave a Flag" [Cohan, Durante, chorus] (Lorenz Hart, Richard Rodgers); "Schnozzola" [Durante] (Lorenz Hart, Arthur Johnston, Jimmy Durante); "Sick" [Durante] (Lorenz Hart, Jimmy Durante).

Disc: Box Office (number undetermined; bootleg LP; ST); Folk RFS-604 (bootleg LP; ST); Music Masters JJA-19766 (bootleg

George M. Cohan made his talkie debut (with Jimmy Durante) in Paramount's *The Phantom President*.

LP; ST); Old Shep GMC-1000 (bootleg LP; ST).

He was once the toast of Broadway, but in 1932 success was not coming so easily for George M. Cohan (1878–1942). His jaunty, optimistic musical comedies seemed out of place in the Jazz Age, and after *Billie* (1928) he would debut no more of them in New York. In 1930, he revived his plays *The Tavern* and *The Song and Dance Man* for a short Broadway run before touring the country, to favorable reviews, with both in repertory. But Cohan could not fall back on the past forever, and soon he was semi-retired (read: idle) again. When Paramount chief Jesse Lasky asked him to star in *The Phantom President,* Cohan had no alternative, although his only previous stint in pictures (three films in 1917-18) had been unhappy. "I am stage-minded, not motion-picture minded," he said.[29]

Still, *The Phantom President* would be a presidential satire for a presidential election year, and the fabulously successful stage musical comedy *Of Thee I Sing* had proven there was an audience for that kind of thing. Moreover, Paramount offered Richard Rodgers and Lorenz Hart, lately of *Love Me Tonight,* to create the score, and there were assurances from Paramount that Cohan would have a hand in writing the script. Unfortunately for Cohan, nothing went right. The studio did not allow him to do anything but act, and he felt mistreated and ignored. He did not get along with Rodgers and Hart, who thought his attitude condescending. "There was never anything overt," wrote Rodgers in his autobiography, "simply a curtness and disdain that he displayed not only to us, but also … to anyone who had anything to do with the picture.

One just knew he could direct better than the director, write a script better than the scriptwriters, and write music and lyrics better than Rodgers and Hart. During the shooting he never remained on the set when he wasn't required in front of the cameras, but always returned directly to the seclusion of his dressing room. I don't recall that he ever deigned to grant interviews, sign autographs or speak a civil word to anyone. It was obvious that he felt miserable about making the picture and wanted us all to know it.[30]

The dual role Cohan played in *The Phantom President* was similar to the real man of 1932: one side stern and complaining, the other a still-eager old trouper. That Cohan gets to troupe a little in this otherwise mediocre film is enough to make it an invaluable historical record of an American original. In the adaptation of George F. Worts' novel, Cohan is both a cold, humorless financier named Theodore K. Blair and a lively, charismatic medicine-show performer named Peter "Doc" Varney. A coterie of powerful politicians and business types wants to get Blair elected to the U. S. presidency, but his drab personality is a drawback. "Chivalry is all right, but a little Chevalier wouldn't hurt," jokes one of the kingmakers, slyly played by Sidney Toler. "You know, in this day and age, America can stand a president who's just a little bit naughty."

While watching a medicine show one day, the bigwigs find their man in look-alike Varney, who is brought in to "stand in" for Blair during the campaign. Not only does he win over the American people, he steals the heart of Blair's girlfriend, Felicia Hammond (Claudette Colbert), who doesn't know of the switch. With the help of his old partner, Curly Cooney (Jimmy Durante), Varney dazzles the delegates at his party's convention by employing a simple variation on his snake-oil spiel ("every plank's a drug to cure your ills"). The jealous Blair, by now practically a hostage in his own mansion, conspires with his butler (Jameson Thomas) to hire thugs to kidnap Varney and dispatch him to the Arctic Circle. But Felicia, who now realizes that it's Varney she loves, outsmarts the crooks and Blair is the one sent away. On the eve of the election, Varney reveals the duplicity, but a forgiving public elects him anyhow. Felicia will be the new First Lady.

There are only three Rodgers and Hart songs, if one does not include the extended convention sequence set to some of the same music and more of the pair's rhyming dialogue. (Two songs with lyrics by Hart and music by Durante

are sung by Durante during the medicine show sequence, and one Rodgers-Hart piece, "There He Is—Theodore K. Blair," was not used.) "The Country Needs a Man" is inventively presented at the outset of the film by Capitol wall "portraits" of George Washington, Thomas Jefferson, Abraham Lincoln and Theodore Roosevelt, who come to life to pass the leadership buck.[31] "Somebody Ought to Wave a Flag," performed by Cohan in blackface as part of his medicine-show act, is a weak tribute to the star's "Grand Old Flag"–type material (a few bars of the original are interpolated). But it is a treat to watch him do some of his famous eccentric dancing.

"Give Her a Kiss" is incongruously "introduced" by various birds, bees and frogs alongside the open-top auto in which Cohan courts Colbert. (Awkwardly, the music begins when Colbert turns on the car radio.) As offscreen vocalists croon blandly, the two actors look bored and uncomfortable. The convention sequence, which aptly begins as a horse's rear fades into the talking head of a dull keynote speaker, livens up the proceedings some. However, Durante's incessant mugging becomes tiresome. "He's a Harvard man, he's conservative, and he's against liquor!" the Schnozz exhorts about his pal, winking broadly on the last assertion. Fittingly, somehow, the number ends when Durante is hit on the head with a piano tossed into the air by celebrating delegates.

But the upbeat denouement is unconvincing, even for a musical comedy, and when he is not singing or dancing, Cohan shows little of the spark that had made him one of the world's most colorful performers. He's just grumpy. And Cohan is too old to be romancing Claudette Colbert, to whom he groused during a break in production, "I can make more money at the race track in one afternoon than I can for this whole movie."[32]

The Phantom President, released little more than a month before the real presidential election, earned some good reviews as "just the sort of thing to give you one swell evening's entertainment," according to *Photoplay*.[33] But the mixed critical and commercial response to it did nothing to make Cohan change his mind about motion pictures, nor Paramount to want him back. Cohan made one more film, a little-seen independent production of his play *Gambling* (1934). He would even be teamed with Rodgers and Hart again, on stage in *I'd Rather Be Right* (1937), this time playing a real president, Franklin D. Roosevelt. But *The Phantom President* would remain a sore spot. Shortly after Cohan's stint out West, he was asked during a radio interview about the movie business. "If I had my choice between Hollywood and Atlanta," he offered, "I'd take Leavenworth." Makes you wonder what he had against Atlanta.

THE BIG BROADCAST
(Paramount; October 14, 1932)

Director: Frank Tuttle. Associate Producer: Benjamin Glazer. Screenplay: George Marion, Jr. Based on the play *Wild Waves* by William Ford Manley (New York opening, February 19, 1932; 25 performances). Photography: George Folsey. Sound: J. A. Goodrich. Running Time: 97 minutes.

Cast: Stuart Erwin (Leslie McWhinney), Bing Crosby (Bing Crosby), Leila Hyams (Anita Rogers), Sharon Lynne (Mona Lowe), George N. Burns (Mr. Burns), Grace [Gracie] Allen (Miss Allen), George Barbier (Mr. Clapsaddle), Spec O'Donnell (office boy), Ralph Robertson (announcer), Tom Carrigan (sheriff's officer), Ernie Adams (crook), Frederick Sullivan (attorney), Major, Sharp and Minor (telephone operators). As Themselves: Kate Smith, The Mills Brothers, The Boswell Sisters, Arthur Tracy, Donald Novis, Cab Calloway and His Orchestra, Vincent Lopez and His Orchestra, Eddie Lang, Don Ball, James Wallington, Norman Brokenshire, William Brenton.

Songs (*medley in opening credits; **"Big Broadcast" finale): "The Boswell Weeps" [Major, Sharp and Minor], "Here Lies Love" [Tracy; reprised by Lopez orchestra, then by Crosby], "Please" [Crosby and Lang; reprised by Erwin, Lang, Crosby**] (Leo Robin, Ralph Rainger); "Dinah" [Crosby] (Sam M. Lewis, Joe Young, Harry Akst); "Where the Blue of the Night Meets the Gold of the Day" [Crosby*] (Roy Turk, Bing Crosby, Fred E. Ahlert); "It Was So Beautiful" [Smith**] (Arthur Freed, Harry Barris); "When the Moon Comes Over the Mountain" [Smith*] (Harry Woods, Howard Johnson); "Crazy People" [Boswell Sisters**] (Edgar Leslie, James V. Monaco); "Shout, Sister, Shout" [Boswell Sis-

ters*] (Clarence Williams, Tim Bryan, Alexander Hill); "Drummer Man" [Lopez orchestra**] (Vincent Lopez); "Nola" [Lopez orchestra*] (Felix Arndt); "Hot Toddy" [Calloway orchestra] (Benny Carter); "Kickin' the Gong Around" [Calloway orchestra**] (Ted Koehler, Harold Arlen); "Minnie the Moocher" [Calloway orchestra*] (Cab Calloway, Irving Mills); "Goodbye Blues" [Mills Brothers*] (Arnold Johnson, Dorothy Fields, Jimmy McHugh); "Tiger Rag" [Mills Brothers**] (The Original Dixieland Band); "Marta" [Tracy*] (L. Wolfe Gilbert, Moises Simons); "Trees" [Novis**] (Joyce Kilmer, Oscar Rasbach).

Disc: Brunswick 6394 (Crosby/ "Please"/78); Brunswick 6406 (Crosby/"Here Lies Love"/78); Brunswick 6538 (Novis/ "Trees"/78); Brunswick 6847 (Boswell Sisters/ "Crazy People"/78); Decca F-3495 (Tracy/ "Here Lies Love"/78); Sountrak STK-101 (bootleg LP; ST).

If the public's interest in the physicality of its radio favorites could be satisfied by the feeble likes of *Check and Double Check* (Amos 'n' Andy) or *Mother's Boy* (Morton Downey), then an assemblage of voices with faces to match figured to pack a wallop. Hence, *The Big Broadcast*, an instant hit for Paramount that would spawn three similar revue-style films.

The studio was so certain about the filmability of William Ford Manley's play *Wild Waves* that it financed the short-lived Broadway production to gain the screen rights. Into the sparse source story of a struggling radio station and its unreliable headline crooner, director Frank Tuttle invested the breezy comic style and visual gimmickry that had made his *This Is the Night* so watchable earlier in the year.[34] But the hook, of course, was the starring lineup: George Burns and Gracie Allen (billed as "George N. Burns" and "Grace Allen"), Kate Smith, Arthur Tracy (The Street Singer), The Boswell Sisters, The Mills Brothers, the Cab Calloway and Vincent Lopez orchestras—and, more or less playing himself, Bing Crosby, billed second in his first major role in a feature.

Story, gags and lotsa music are shoehorned into 97 minutes, but what *The Big Broadcast* lacks in sense it compensates for in novelty. The dizzy, surrealistic opening evokes René Clair in its rhythmic timing of sound with action. New York radio station WADX is gripped by si-

READ THIS GREAT LIST OF RADIO CELEBRITIES!

STUART ERWIN
BING CROSBY
LEILA HYAMS
BURNS & ALLEN

THE BIG BROADCAST

KATE SMITH
BOSWELL SISTERS
MILLS BROTHERS
ARTHUR TRACY
(THE STREET SINGER)
VINCENT LOPEZ
AND HIS ORCHESTRA
CAB CALLOWAY
AND HIS ORCHESTRA

Everyone famous...the most astonishing array of talent ever gathered in one production. Appearing together in a drama of Radio Land... of its trials...its struggles... its loves...its hates...the real story of the men and women of the air.

a Paramount Picture

Paramount's *The Big Broadcast* boasted an impressive roster of radio personalities.

trick photography—by a shushing office boy. A note slipped to the announcer reveals bad news: "Bing ... isn't ... here ... yet." Crosby, the show's popular star, is late again. The hour begins anyway, as Cab Calloway's band plays "Hot Toddy." The enraged sponsor, Mr. Clapsaddle (George Barbier) stalks in, ready to take no prisoners. In response, the hands of the wall clock animate into an alarmed face, and the black cat dashes for safety underneath a door. Clapsaddle goes to Burns, the station manager, and demands Crosby's firing. He pounds the table in disgust, and Tuttle cuts to a driver pounding his horn in Manhattan traffic. The cab stops in front of the station building—but with Bing driving, for the cabbie is sitting in the back seat. Bing emerges, but he drops his glove on the sidewalk, and as he bends to pick it up he is mobbed by an adoring group of lady fans, one of whom climbs from a wheelchair at the sight of her idol. The crush carries the singer into the lobby and up the elevator to the studio. Lipstick smeared over his face, Bing finally staggers to the mike and begins to sing "I Surrender Dear," but now he is cut short by the show's signoff.

lence—only the ominous ticking of a clock is heard—in the final seconds before its "Grip Tight Girdle Hour" goes on the air. A black cat roaming the halls is stopped in its tracks—thanks to one of the film's frequent examples of

Crosby's frequent tardiness—art imitating

life—is caused by his new girlfriend, Mona Lowe (Sharon Lynne, the former Fox starlet now billed with an "e"), a party dame who has been keeping him out nights. Her sudden elopement with a millionaire leaves a disconsolate Bing to get drunk with his new friend Leslie McWhinney (top-billed Stuart Erwin), a Texas oilman himself recently jilted. Leslie has returned to New York to see a long-lost sweetheart, Anita (Leila Hyams), who just happens to be a WADX secretary with a crush on Crosby. In a nightclub, Bing and Leslie hear Arthur Tracy sing the mournful "Here Lies Love." Then Bing, having returned to his apartment with Leslie, takes up the tune with suicide on his mind. He turns on the gas to his stove, then he and Leslie hallucinate over a spectral form (Tracy, again) that continues the dirge.

The boys survive this unholy night, which leaves the rest of the movie for the planning of a "Big Broadcast" for WADX, which has been saved from ruin by Leslie's sizable bank account. Crosby is to sing his newest smash, "Please," but Mona reappears (to the strains of "Moanin' Low") and threatens to keep Bing away. Actually, Bing is acting carelessly on purpose so Anita will stop pining for him and return to Leslie. The film's final minutes shift back and forth between the radio performances and Leslie's frantic attempt to find a phonograph record of Crosby singing "Please" to use in his stead. The record warps, and Leslie's twang makes for a poor on-air imitation, but Crosby walks in at the last possible minute to grab the mike away and save the day.

Crosby's career was already busting out all over, and *The Big Broadcast* made him a permanent star in the big-screen galaxy. (A series of two-reel shorts made for Mack Sennett already had been making the singer a reputation in the movies.) "Please" and "Here Lies Love," both concoctions of lyricist Leo Robin and composer Ralph Rainger, would be added to his hit list. Crosby (1901–1977) would introduce many other Rainger tunes in Paramount musicals during the '30s, among them "Love in Bloom" (*She Loves Me Not*), "June in January" (*Here Is My Heart*) and "Blue Hawaii" (*Waikiki Wedding*). During the opening credits of *The Big Broadcast*, each airwave act comes to life from a lobby ad photo and sings a few bars of a tune with which it is identified closely. Burns and Allen do comedy in their bit.

The Big Broadcast marked the first feature film for Burns (b. 1896) and Allen (1902–1964), who—before disappearing halfway through—exchange typical banter as the harried station manager and his Dumb Dora stenographer:

Burns (attempting to dictate a letter): "Regarding Bing Crosby…"

Allen (interrupting): "You know, my whole family is named after flowers. I have a brother named Bob."

Burns (sarcastically): "Bob. That's my favorite flower."

Allen: "Don't be silly. We just call him Bob for short. His whole name is Rhubarb."

Burns (flustered): "Rhubarb … (dictating again) "My dear Mr. Clapsaddle…"

Allen: "And I have a sister named Rose and I have a brother … not my brother, my uncle. He's named after a flower you put on the lapel of your coat. What do you call that flower?"

Burns: "It couldn't be a carnation?"

Allen: "That's right … reincarnation."

Burns: "Listen, Gracie, reincarnation is not a flower. Reincarnation means that when you leave this earth you come back in some other form. Like *you* might come back with a little intellect."

Allen: "Oh, Mr. Burns, don't be silly! I'm not even married!"

Except for those by Crosby, Burns and Allen, the radio specialties were filmed on the East Coast and cut into the remainder of the made-in-Hollywood film. During a newspaper interview with the author in 1992, Burns, still wisecracking at age 96, recalled working with Bing Crosby in this movie and others:

> I loved him. We both sang in the same key. He was nice to work with. … Everybody who was in radio was in those movies. … Movies are very easy to do, because you could do most of them sitting down. Now at my age, it's better to do something when I'm sitting down. I pay somebody to sit down for me.[35]

Despite the public affinity for *The Big Broadcast*, Paramount did not produce a follow-up right away. Burns and Allen would headline the first two, *The Big Broadcast of 1936* (produced in 1935) and *The Big Broadcast of 1937* (1936). W. C. Fields gained top billing in the finale, *The Big Broadcast of 1938* (1938), which introduced Crosby's future partner, Bob Hope, to feature films.

THE KID FROM SPAIN

(Samuel Goldwyn/United Artists, November 17, 1932)

Director: Leo McCarey. Producer: Samuel Goldwyn. Production Executive: Arthur Hornblow, Jr. Screenplay: William Anthony McGuire, Bert Kalmar, Harry Ruby. Photography: Gregg Toland. Editor: Stuart Heisler. Sound: Vinton Vernon. Art Director: Richard Day. Costumes: Milo Anderson. Musical Director: Alfred Newman. Dance Direction: Busby Berkeley. Running Time: 98 minutes.

Cast: Eddie Cantor (Eddie Williams), Lyda Roberti (Rosalie), Robert Young (Ricardo), Ruth Hall (Anita Gomez), John Miljan (Pancho), Noah Beery (Alonzo Gomez), J. Carrol Naish (Pedro), Robert Emmett O'Connor (Detective Crawford), Stanley Fields (José), Paul Porcasi (Gonzales), Sidney Franklin (himself), Julian Rivero (Dalmores), Theresa Maxwell Conover (Martha Oliver), Walter Walker (dean), Ben Hendricks, Jr. (Red), Grace Poggi (specialty dancer), Edgar Connor (bull handler), Leo Willis (thief), Harry Gribbon (traffic cop), Eddie Foster (patron), Harry C. Bradley (man in line at border), The Goldwyn Girls [including Dorothy Coonan, Paulette Goddard, Betty Grable, Toby Wing].

Songs/Musical Numbers: "In the Moonlight" [Cantor, girls], "Look What You've Done" [Cantor, Roberti], "Opening Chorus" (college number) [chorus] (Bert Kalmar, Harry Ruby); "What a Perfect Combination" [Cantor, girls] (Bert Kalmar, Irving Caesar, Harry Ruby, Harry Akst); "College March" [college band] (Harry Ruby).

Disc: Columbia 2723-D (Cantor/"Look What You've Done"/"What a Perfect Combination"/78); Epic 1128 (Cantor/LP; ST); Pelican 134 (Cantor/LP; ST).

Sumptuously produced for $1.4 million, *The Kid from Spain* gave Samuel Goldwyn, Eddie Cantor, Busby Berkeley and their Girls a third straight musical comedy hit, not to mention one of the year's biggest box-office draws of any stripe.

In a plot supplied by Bert Kalmar, Harry Ruby and William Anthony McGuire, Eddie Williams (Cantor) is forced to pass himself off as a master matador in Mexico to evade capture on a bogus bank-robbery charge by a border-crossing detective (Robert Emmett O'Connor). Actually, Eddie is merely a college man just tossed from school in the United States after being caught inside the women's dormitory with his Mexican roommate (Robert Young). But a chance encounter with a real gang has him on the run, pretending to be one Don Sebastian the Second, son of Mexico's late, great bullfighter. After some run-ins with Mexican toughs, Eddie himself ends up in the ring—but with a wild bull substituted for the tame animal he had thought he would be able to halt on command. ("Popocatepetl," the word Eddie is supposed to say that will tame the trained bull, is actually the name of a volcano in Mexico.) The result was a comic triumph, anyway. "Here is the season's opportunity to laugh your head off," commented *Photoplay*.[36]

Young and Ruth Hall make a run-of-the-mill romantic couple for director Leo McCarey, and Cantor is aided more memorably by the exuberant, platinum-blonde comedienne Lyda Roberti, cast as Hall's sidekick. This was the kind of man-hungry role in which the Polish-born and -accented Roberti (1906–1938) specialized on Broadway and in Hollywood before her sudden death from a heart attack. Here, she asks her temporarily reluctant lover to "kees me like a hawk—like a heagle" before they settle down a little for a musical duet, "Look What You've Done."

As he had in *Whoopee!* and *Palmy Days*, Berkeley put the Goldwyn Girls through their paces. The untitled opening number begins as the maidens (among them Betty Grable, Paulette Goddard and Toby Wing) awaken in their uncommonly luxurious dormitory. They all take a dip in their handy mansion-sized swimming pool, then emerge to undress in silhouette behind skimpy screens. The girls assist Cantor in two other songs, "In the Moonlight" and, for his usual blackface showcase, the future standard "What a Perfect Combination." In the latter, set on the dance floor of a nightclub, they are seen forming a giant tortilla and, finally, the head of a bull as seen from the overhead camera.

The Kid from Spain began life as an idea for a story Cantor devised with a childhood friend, American bullfighter Sidney Franklin. Goldwyn passed on the story, preferring to commit to *Palmy Days* instead, but then revived his interest when a premise for their next picture was needed. The mogul sent Cantor and his musical staff to the Fox Theatre in San Francisco, where they polished their material before the public for weeks, much as the Marx Brothers would do when making films for Irving Thalberg. Only after this did Goldwyn give his approval for filming.[37] Franklin, billed professionally as "The Bullfighter from Brooklyn" (he was not related to the film director of the same name), appeared briefly as himself in the climactic sequence.

The next Goldwyn-Cantor-Berkeley extravaganza—*Roman Scandals,* released in December 1933—did not exist in the vacuum that *The Kid from Spain* had. In the 13 months that separated the two films, the Hollywood musical changed forever.

APPENDIX I

1914–1928: *Silent Feature Films Inspired by Broadway Musicals*

Had the talking movie arrived earlier than it did, some of the following titles might have been the first Hollywood musicals. Instead, they retained the plotlines, to varying degrees, of their stage predecessors without the musical scores—except, in some cases, for instrumental accompaniment played by movie-house musicians. Although not all of these films are directly derived from Broadway shows—sometimes they merely share the same source material—the popularity of the stage versions likely influenced their making. An asterisk (*) by a star's name indicates that he or she was reprising a Broadway role.

1914

America (November 12; All-Star Feature Corp.) Cast: Bert Shepherd, The Australian Wood Choppers. Director: Lawrence McGill. Based on the musical drama of the same name (Broadway debut: August 30, 1913).

Tillie's Punctured Romance (December 21; Keystone Film Co.) Cast: Marie Dressler*, Charles Chaplin, Mabel Normand. Director: Mack Sennett. Based on the musical comedy *Tillie's Nightmare* (Broadway debut: May 5, 1910).

1915

The Chocolate Soldier (January; Daisy Feature Film Co./Alliance Films Corp.) Cast: Alice Yorke, Tom Richards. Directors: Walter Morton, Stanislaus Stange. Based on the operetta (Broadway debut: September 13, 1909).

Old Dutch (February 8; Shubert Film Corp./World Film Corp.) Cast: Lew Fields*, Vivian Martin, Charles Judels. Director: Frank Crane. Based on the musical comedy (Broadway debut: December 22, 1909).

Pretty Mrs. Smith (March 29; Oliver Morosco Photoplays/Bosworth Co./Paramount) Cast: Fritzi Scheff*, Louis Bennison, Owen Moore. Director: Hobart Bosworth. Based on the musical comedy (Broadway debut: September 21, 1914).

The Slim Princess (May 24; Essanay Film Co.) Cast: Francis X. Bushman, Ruth Stonehouse, Wallace Beery. Director: E. H. Calvert. Based on the musical comedy (Broadway debut: January 2, 1911).

My Best Girl (June 14; Rolfe Photoplays/Metro Pictures Corp.) Cast: Max Figman, Lois Meredith, Lawrence Peyton. Director undetermined. Based on the musical comedy (Broadway debut: September 12, 1912).

A Black Sheep (October 18; Selig Polyscope Co.) Cast: Otis Harlan*, Rita Gould, Grace Darmond. Director: Thomas N. Heffron. Based on the musical comedy (Broadway debut: January 6, 1896).

1916

The Black Crook (January 10; Kalem Co./General Film Co.) Cast: E. P. Sullivan, Gladys Coburn, Roland Bottomley. Director: Robert G. Vignola. Based on the musical comedy (Broadway debut: September 12, 1866).

The Red Widow (April; Paramount–Famous Players) Cast: John Barrymore, Flora Zabelle, John Hendricks. Director: James Durkin. Based on the musical comedy (Broadway debut: November 6, 1911).

1917

Alma, Where Do You Live? (July; Newfields Producing Corp.) Cast: Ruth MacTammany,

George Larkin, Jack Newton. Director: Hal Clarendon. Based on the musical comedy (Broadway debut: September 26, 1910).

Madame Sherry (September 1; Authors' Film Co./M. H. Hoffman Inc.) Cast: Gertrude McCoy, Frank L. A. O'Connor. Director: Ralph Dean. Based on the musical comedy (Broadway debut: August 30, 1910).

1918

Good Night, Paul (June 20; Select Pictures Corp.) Cast: Constance Talmadge, Norman Kerry, Harrison Ford. Director: Walter Edwards. Based on the musical comedy (Broadway debut: September 3, 1917).

Fan Fan (November 17; Fox) Cast: Virginia Lee Corbin, Francis Carpenter. Directors: Sidney A. Franklin, Chester M. Franklin. Based on the operetta *The Mikado* (Broadway debut: July 20, 1885).

The Girl of My Dreams (December 15; National Film Corp./Exhibitors Mutual Distributing Corp./Robertson Cole Co.) Cast: Billie Rhodes, Jack MacDonald. Director: Louis William Chaudet. Based on the musical comedy (Broadway debut: August 7, 1911).

1919

The Belle of New York (February; Marion Davies Film Corp./Select Pictures Corp.) Cast: Marion Davies, Etienne Girardot, Rogers Lytton. Director: Julius Steger. Based on the musical comedy (Broadway debut: September 28, 1897).

Oh, Boy! (June 22; Albert Capellani Productions/Pathé) Cast: June Caprice, Creighton Hale, Flora Finch. Director: Albert Capellani. Based on the musical comedy (Broadway debut: February 20, 1917).

Strictly Confidential (October 11; Goldwyn) Cast: Madge Kennedy, John Bowers, Robert Bolder. Director: Clarence Badger. Based on the musical comedy *The Rainbow Girl* (Broadway debut: April 1, 1918).

1920

La La Lucille (July 19; Universal) Cast: Eddie Lyons, Anne Cornwall, Lee Moran. Director: Eddie Lyons, Lee Moran. Based on the musical comedy (Broadway debut: May 26, 1919).

The Slim Princess (July; Goldwyn) Cast: Mabel Normand, Hugh Thompson. Director: Victor Schertzinger. Based on the musical comedy (Broadway debut: January 2, 1911).

Forty-Five Minutes from Broadway (August 30;

Charles Ray Productions/Arthur S. Kane Pictures) Cast: Charles Ray, Dorothy Devore, Eugenie Besserer. Director: Joseph DeGrasse. Based on the musical comedy (Broadway debut: January 1, 1906).

So Long Letty (October 17; Christie Film Co./Robertson-Cole Co.) Cast: Colleen Moore, T. Roy Barnes, Walter Hiers, Grace Darmond. Director: Al Christie. Based on the musical comedy *So Long, Letty* (Broadway debut: October 23, 1916).

Youth's Desire (October; Alkire Productions/Forward Film Distributors) Cast: Joseph Bennett, Doris Baker. Director undetermined. Based on the musical comedy *Going Up* (Broadway debut: December 25, 1917).

Oh, Lady Lady (November or December; Paramount) Cast: Bebe Daniels, Harrison Ford, Walter Hiers. Director: Major Maurice Campbell. Based on the musical comedy *Oh, Lady! Lady!!* (Broadway debut: February 1, 1918).

1922

The Beauty Shop (May 14; Cosmopolitian Productions/Paramount) Cast: Raymond Hitchcock*, Billy B. Van, Louise Fazenda, James J. Corbett. Director: Edward Dillon. Based on the musical comedy (Broadway debut: April 13, 1914).

Queen of the Moulin Rouge (September 2; Pyramid Pictures/American Releasing Corp.) Cast: Martha Mansfield, Joseph Striker. Director: Ray C. Smallwood. Based on the musical comedy *The Queen of the Moulin Rouge* (Broadway debut: December 7, 1908).

1923

Little Johnny Jones (August 19; Warner Bros.) Cast: Johnny Hines, Wyndham Standing, Molly Malone, Mervyn LeRoy. Directors: Arthur Rosson, Johnny Hines. Based on the musical comedy (Broadway debut: November 7, 1904).

Going Up (September 20; Douglas MacLean Productions/Associated Exhibitors) Cast: Douglas MacLean, Hallam Cooley, Marjorie Daw. Director: Lloyd Ingraham. Based on the musical comedy (Broadway debut: December 25, 1917).

Maytime (November 16; B. P. Schulberg Productions/Preferred Pictures) Cast: Ethel Shannon, Harrison Ford, Clara Bow. Director: Louis Gasnier. Based on the operetta (Broadway debut: August 16, 1917).

1924

George Washington Jr. (February 2; Warner Bros.) Cast: Wesley Barry, Gertrude Olmstead, Otis Harlan. Director: Mal St. Clair. Based on the musical comedy (Broadway debut: February 12, 1906).

The Yankee Consul (February 10; Douglas MacLean Productions/Associated Exhibitors) Cast: Douglas MacLean, Arthur Stuart Hull, Patsy Ruth Miller. Director: James W. Horne. Based on the musical comedy (Broadway debut: February 22, 1904).

Listen Lester (May 20; Sacramento Pictures) Cast: Louise Fazenda, Harry Myers, Eva Novak. Director: William A. Seiter. Based on the musical comedy (Broadway debut: December 23, 1918).

1925

Miss Bluebeard (January 26; Paramount) Cast: Bebe Daniels, Robert Frazer, Raymond Griffith. Director: Frank Tuttle. Based on the musical comedy (Broadway debut: August 28, 1923).

Sally (March 29; First National) Cast: Colleen Moore, Lloyd Hughes, Leon Errol*. Director: Alfred E. Green. Based on the musical comedy (Broadway debut: December 21, 1920).

Sally of the Sawdust (August 2; D. W. Griffith/United Artists) Cast: Carol Dempster, W. C. Fields*, Alfred Lunt. Director: D. W. Griffith. Based on the musical comedy *Poppy* (Broadway debut: September 3, 1923).

The Merry Widow (August 26; MGM) Cast: Mae Murray, John Gilbert. Director: Erich von Stroheim. Based on the operetta (Broadway debut: December 30, 1905).

Sally, Irene and Mary (December 27; MGM) Cast: Constance Bennett, Joan Crawford, Sally O'Neil. Director: Edmund Goulding. Based on the musical comedy (Broadway debut: September 4, 1922).

1926

Stop, Look, and Listen (January 1; Larry Semon Productions/Pathé) Cast: Larry Semon, Dorothy Dwan, Mary Carr. Director: Larry Semon. Based on the musical comedy (Broadway debut: December 25, 1915).

Irene (February 21; First National) Cast: Colleen Moore, Lloyd Hughes, George K. Arthur. Director: Alfred E. Green. Based on the musical comedy (Broadway debut: November 18, 1919).

Mademoiselle Modiste (March 21; Corinne Griffith Productions/First National) Cast: Corinne Griffith, Norman Kerry, Willard Louis. Director: Robert Z. Leonard. Based on the operetta *Mlle. Modiste* (Broadway debut: December 25, 1905).

The Prince of Pilsen (May 2; Belasco Productions/Producers Distributing Corp.) Cast: George Sidney, Anita Stewart, Allan Forrest. Director: Paul Powell. Based on the musical comedy (Broadway debut: March 17, 1903).

Good and Naughty (June 7; Paramount) Cast: Pola Negri, Tom Moore, Ford Sterling. Director: Mal St. Clair. Based on the musical comedy *Naughty Cinderella* (Broadway opening: November 9, 1925).

Battling Butler (August 22; Buster Keaton Productions/MGM) Cast: Buster Keaton, Sally O'Neil, Francis MacDonald. Director: Buster Keaton. Based on the musical comedy (Broadway debut: October 8, 1923).

Kid Boots (October 4; Paramount) Cast: Eddie Cantor*, Clara Bow, Billie Dove, Lawrence Gray. Director: Frank Tuttle. Based on the musical comedy (Broadway debut: December 31, 1923).

The Clinging Vine (October 6; De Mille Pictures/Producers Distributing Corp.) Cast: Leatrice Joy, Tom Moore, Robert Edeson. Director: Paul Sloane. Based on the musical comedy (Broadway debut: December 25, 1922).

The Better 'Ole (October 7; Warner Bros.) Cast: Sydney Chaplin, Doris Hill, Edgar Kennedy. Director: Charles Reisner. Based on the musical comedy (Broadway debut: October 19, 1918).

Take It from Me (October 10; Universal) Cast: Reginald Denny, Blanche Mehaffey. Director: William A. Seiter. Based on the musical comedy (Broadway debut: March 31, 1919).

1927

The Red Mill (January 29; Cosmopolitan Productions/MGM) Cast: Marion Davies, Owen Moore, Louise Fazenda. Director: William Goodrich [Fatty Arbuckle]. Based on the operetta (Broadway debut: September 24, 1906).

The Gingham Girl (July 16; R-C Pictures/Film Booking Offices) Cast: Lois Wilson, George K. Arthur, Charles Crockett. Director: David Kirkland. Based on the musical comedy (Broadway debut: August 28, 1922).

The Student Prince in Old Heidelberg (September 21; MGM) Cast: Ramon Novarro, Norma Shearer, Jean Hersholt. Director: Ernst Lubitsch. Based on the operetta (Broadway debut: December 2, 1924).

1928

Rose-Marie (February 11; MGM) Cast: Joan Crawford, James Murray, House Peters. Director: Lucien Hubbard. Based on the operetta *The Student Prince* (Broadway debut: September 2, 1924).

Lady Be Good (May 6; First National) Cast: Jack Mulhall, Dorothy Mackaill, John Miljan. Director: Richard Wallace. Based on the musical comedy (Broadway debut: December 1, 1924).

Oh, Kay! (August 26; First National) Cast: Colleen Moore, Lawrence Gray, Alan Hale. Director: Mervyn LeRoy. Based on the musical comedy (Broadway debut: November 8, 1926).

APPENDIX II

1928–1932: *Selected Short Subjects*

The following is a list of American-made, English-language sound shorts (four reels or less) featuring musical acts or significant musical content that were reviewed in the trade publication *Variety* before January 1, 1933. Animated shorts, newsreels and shorts produced for foreign audiences are not included. This is not intended to be a definitive compilation of shorts, for many more than these were produced in the early sound era. Rather, it is a survey of the spectrum of acts—famous and obscure—and subjects dealt with in short films. Note that many future stars—among them Humphrey Bogart, Ethel Merman, Judy Garland and Ginger Rogers—made early appearances in productions listed here.

Variety began its weekly "Talking Shorts" reviews section on May 23, 1928. Before then, the influential show-business publication only occasionally analyzed short subjects—mainly some of the important early Vitaphone and Fox Movietone entries. The date listed in each entry is the edition in which the review appeared; however, many of the shorts were older. For example, the Beniamino Gigli–Marion Talley short reviewed in May of 1928 was produced and initially shown in 1927. It is likely that, as more theaters were being wired for sound, some of the early shorts were reissued. The number of reels per short is in parentheses. Musical content is listed if known, although the wording of some song titles may not be precise as they are listed as they appeared in the review or in other sources. Shorts known to be in color are noted with an asterisk (*).

Trend seekers will note that the performance-only shorts of the very early talkie era were gradually superseded by plotted shorts—mini-musicals—in which the title gained prominence (at least in *Variety*'s collective eye) over the performers' names. Note also that the decline in the market for feature-length musicals after 1930 seems to have extended to song shorts, as many fewer of the latter were reviewed after the summer of '30 than previously. However, the number of all shorts designated for review declined starting in 1931, and for a handful of weeks in the latter half of 1932 there were no shorts reviewed at all.

Special thanks go to Ron Hutchinson of the Vitaphone Project for supplying in-depth information on the Warner Bros. shorts. Some details on operatic entries came from William Shaman's excellent article "The Operatic Vitaphone Shorts" in the Spring 1991 *ARSC Journal*.

1928

MAY

Earl Burtnett and His Los Angeles Biltmore Hotel Orchestra, Vitaphone Varieties No. 2295 (Warner Bros.), May 23 (1) ["I Fell Head Over Heels in Love"/"An Old Guitar and an Old Refrain"/"Blue River"].

The Florentine Choir, Vitaphone 2282, May 23 (1) ["Ninna Nanna"/"Santa Lucia Luntana"].

Beniamino Gigli (tenor) and Marion Talley (soprano), Vitaphone 499, May 23 (1) ["Ver-

ranno a te sull'aura" from *Lucia di Lammermoor*].

Beatrice Lillie (comedy, songs), Fox Movietone 15, May 23 (1) ["The Roses Have Made Me Remember"].

Georgie Lyons (harpist), Vocafilm, May 30 (1).

Will Mahoney (comedy songs), Fox Movietone, May 30 (1).

Eddie Peabody in *Banjoland*, with Jimmy Maisel, Vitaphone 2560, May 23 (1) ["Barcarolle"/"Ramona"/"Diane"/"Together"/"Dream Kisses"].

The Radio Franks (song and piano), Vocafilm, May 30 (1).

[Pat] Rooney and [Marion] Bent, with Pat Rooney III (song and dance), Fox Movietone 17, May 23 (1) ["Sweet Rosie O'Grady"].

John Vincent (vocalist) with an "Illustrated Song," Fox Movietone, May 23 (1) ["When You and I Were Young, Maggie"].

JUNE

The Arnaut Brothers (pantomime, whistling), Vitaphone 571, June 27 (1) ["Pop Goes the Weasel"/"Two Little Love Birds"].

Gus Arnheim and His Cocoanut Grove Ambassadors (band), Vitaphone 2585, June 6 (1) ["I Ain't Got Nobody"/"If I Can't Have You (I Want to Be Lonesome, I Want to Be Blue)"/"Mighty Lak' a Rose"/"There's Something About a Rose (That Reminds Me of You)"/"Tiger Rag"].

The Brox Sisters (vocal trio), Vitaphone 2571, June 13 (1) ["Back in Your Own Back Yard"/ "Kentucky Babe"/"Call of the South"].

By the Campfire, with the Xavier Cugat Orchestra, Vitaphone 2540, June 20 (1) ["Celito Lindo"/ "Morenita Mia"/"Elito Lindo"/ Gypsy dance/ "The Old Refrain"].

Anna Case (soprano) in *La Fiesta*, with the Flying Cansinos, the Metropolitan Opera Chorus and the Vitaphone Symphony Orchestra, Vitaphone 294, June 20 (1) [this short was in the first Vitaphone program from 1926].

Bernardo de Pace (comedy, mandolin), Vitaphone 443, June 13 (1) ["Morning, Noon and Night in Vienna"/"That's Why I Love You"/"Tarentella"/ medley of "Souvenir," *Tales of Hoffmann* and "Humoresque"].

The Fashion Plates of Harmony (vocal trio), Vitaphone 2283, June 13 (1) ["My Wild Irish Rose"/"The Wild Man of Borneo"/"El Palmar"/"The Noble Duke of York"].

The Four Aristocrats (guitars, piano), Vitaphone 545, June 6 (1) ["Hello! Swanee, Hello!"/"Don't Sing Aloha When I Go"/"I Never See Maggie Alone"/"Me Too"].

Venita Gould ("Famous Star Impersonations"), Vitaphone 562, June 20 (1) ["Way Down Yonder in New Orleans" (Blossom Seeley)/"Blame It on the Waltz" (Grace LaRue)/"I'm Tellin' the Birds, Tellin' the Bees (How Much I Love You)" (Ted Lewis)/"There Ain't No 'Maybe' in My Baby's Eyes" (Karyl Norman)].

Hearst Newspaper Radio Kids, Vitaphone 512, June 27 (1) ["That Night in Araby"/"That's What I Call a Pal"/"My Hour"/"Let the End of the World Come"/"It All Depends on You"].

Willie and Eugene Howard (comedy, songs), Vitaphone 572, June 20 (1) ["Oh How I Love My Boatman"/"Lay Me Down to Sleep in Carolina"].

In a Monastery Cellar, with The Monastery Quartet, Vitaphone 2142, June 13 (1) ["The Rosary"/ "Im Tiefen Keller"/"Love's Own Sweet Song"/ "Drink to Me Only with Thine Eyes"/"Drinking Song"].

In a Music Shoppe, Fox Movietone 16, June 20 (2) ["My Old Kentucky Home"].

Ruby Keeler ("a short but nifty tap dance"), company not listed, June 6 (1).

The Kentucky Jubilee Singers, Fox Movietone, June 20 (1).

Nellie and Sara Kouns ("The Mirror Voiced Sopranos"), Vitaphone 515, June 27 (1) ["Just an Echo in the Valley"/"La Paloma"].

Abe Lyman and His Orchestra, Vitaphone 2274, June 13 (1) ["Among My Souvenirs"/"The Varsity Drag"/"Twelfth Street Rag"].

Giovanni Martinelli (tenor), Vitaphone 510, June 20 (1) ["Va prononcer la mort" from *La Juive*].

Requel Meller (vocalist), Fox Movietone 6, June 13 (1) ["Flor del Mal"].

Florence Moore (comedienne), with Lieutenant Gitz Rice (composer-pianist), Vitaphone 519, June 20 (1) ["And He Never Said That to Me"/"You'll Be Sorry That You Made Me Cry"].

Meyers and Hanford (comedy, songs, dance), Vitaphone 2593, June 20 (1) ["Down in Arkansas"/"In the Shade of the Old Apple Tree"/"I Ain't That Kind of Baby"/"Old Black Joe"/ "Dawn of Tomorrow"].

Billy and Elsa Newell (comedy, songs), Vitaphone 2296, June 6 (1) ["Bum Ta Rum Tum Tum"/ "L'Estudiantina"/"Gypsy Love Song"/ "Ain't That Too Bad"/"Giannini Mia"].

Rosa Raisa (soprano), Vitaphone 2545, June 20 (1) ["Good-bye"/"Eili! Eili!"].

Val and Ernie Stanton (comic songs in "English as She Is Not Spoken"), Vitaphone 2587, June 20 (1) ["Let a Smile Be Your Umbrella (On a Rainy Day)"/"Horsie, Keep Your Tail Up"/ "'Cause It Ain't That Kind of Cow"/"The Little Pig Moved Right Away"/"Alice, Where Art Thou Going?"].

Those Pullman Porters, with The Kings of Harmony ("colored quartet"), Vitaphone 2101, June 27 (1) ["Those Pullman Porters on Parade"/"Casey Jones"/"Calliope Song"/"Little David, Play on Your Harp"/"Ain't It a Shame?"/"Good Night, Ladies"/"Hear That Whistle Blow"].

JULY

Gus Arnheim and His Cocoanut Grove Orchestra, Vitaphone 2584, July 18 (1) ["I'll Be Loving

You Always"/"I Can Do Without You"/"La Rosita"/"Stay Out of the South (If You Want to Miss a Heaven on Earth)"].

Ben Bernie and His Orchestra, Fox Movietone 9, July 4 (1) ["My Castle in Spain Is a Shack in the Lane"].

The Larry Ceballos Revue, with the Vitaphone Girls, the Owen Fallon Orchestra and Al Herman (master of ceremonies), Vitaphone 2562, July 18 (1) ["Dream Kisses"/"Annabel Lee"/"At Dawning"/"Muddy Water"/"Mississippi Mud"/ "Let a Smile Be Your Umbrella (On a Rainy Day)"/"Wob-a-ly Walk"/"Smile"].

Lynn Cowan's "Community Sing," Vitaphone 2288, July 11 (1) ["The Sidewalks of New York"/"After the Ball"/"Take Me Out to the Ball Game"/"My Gal Sal"/"Alexander's Ragtime Band"].

Jay C. Flippen (comedy, songs) in *The Ham What Am*, Vitaphone 2581, July 18 (1) ["Keep Sweeping the Cobwebs Off the Moon"/"Magnolia"].

The Foy Family (six children of vaudevillian Eddie Foy) in *Foys for Joys*, Vitaphone 2879, July 18 (1) ["My Gal Sal"/"My Blue Heaven"].

Friedland's Ritz Review, with Al Wohlman, Anatole Friedland, Peaches Browning, Lou Holtz, Harry Rose and Friedland Review Girls, Fox Movietone 12, July 18 (1) ["Lindy Hop"].

Hoot Gibson Trio ("three Hawaiian musicians" signed to play at ranch of cowboy star), Vitaphone 2132, July 11 (1) ["Dreaming a Waltz Away"/"Alabamy Bound"/"Chimes"/ "Aloha Blues"].

Beniamino Gigli in *A Program of Concert Favorites*, Vitaphone 498, July 11 (1) ["Bergère légère"/ "Mirame asi"/"Come, Love with Me"/"O sole mio"].

The Happiness Boys [Billy Jones and Earnest Hare] (comic songs), Vitaphone 536, July 11 (1) ["How Do You Do, Everybody"/"That's My Hap-Hap-Happiness"/"I Would Rather Be Alone in the South"/"Good-Bye, Everybody"].

Willie and Eugene Howard in *Between the Acts of the Opera*, Vitaphone 349, July 4 (1) [imitations of grand opera stars].

Imperial Russian Cossacks (band), Vitaphone 2280, July 4 (1) ["Katinka"/"Ak Rasposhol"/ "Song of the Volga Boatmen"/"Second Cossack Regiment March"/"Stars and Stripes Forever"].

Irving and Jack Kaufman (tenor-baritone duo), Vitaphone 560, July 25 (1) ["High, High, High Up in the Hills"/ Russian lullaby/"Deedle Deedle Dum"].

Ed Lowry (master of ceremonies, vocalist) and Orchestra, Vitaphone 2565, July 4 (1) ["When You're in Love with Somebody Else"/"Mama's Gone Young"/"Laugh! Clown, Laugh"].

Ed Lowry and Orchestra, Vitaphone 2561, July 18

(1) ["Coming Home"/"I, Myself and Me"/ "Poet and Peasant Overture"/"You Gonna Be Home Tonight"/"Voice of the Southland"].

Giovanni Martinelli, Vitaphone 204, July 11 (1) ["Se queli guerrier ... Celeste Aida," from *Aida*].

A Night at Coffee Dan's, with William Demarest (master of ceremonies), Miss Gogo (vocalist), Nita Martan (vocalist), and Hutchings and Hallaway (harmonica players), Vitaphone 2562, July 18 (1) ["Hail, Hail, the Gang's All Here"/"Let's Go Down to Coffee Dan's"/"We Know It Just the Same"/ harmonica medley/"Blue Skies"].

Police Quartet (harmony vocals), Vitaphone 2320, July 11 (1) ["Skinna-Ma, Rink-a-Dink"/ Mother Goose medley/"Cluckin'"/"Waddle"].

"Jolly" Fanny Rice (vocals) in *Types*, Vitaphone 2243, July 18 (1) ["Nobody Seems to Care"/ "Isle d'Amour"].

Adele Rowland in *Stories in Song*, Vitaphone 2348, July 25 (1) ["White Wings"/"High, High, High Up in the Hills"/"Little Tu Shi"/"There Must Be Somebody Else"/"Swanee Shore"].

[Blossom] Seeley and [Benny] Fields (vocals), Vitaphone 548, July 4 (1) ["All the Stars Are Shining"/"Hello, Bluebird"/"Call of the South"/"In a Little Spanish Town"].

Reb Spikes and His Follies Entertainers ("Premiere Colored Orchestra"), Vitaphone 2123, July 11 (1) ["Clarinet Marmalade"/"Lonesome and Sorry"/"Red Lips (Kiss My Blues Away)"].

[Georgie] Stoll, [Edythe] Flynn and Co. (violinist and vocalist), Vitaphone 2349, July 25 (1) ["Beautiful"/"Ain't She Sweet?"/"Sing Me a Baby Song"/"What'll You Do?"/ "Nobody's Baby"/"After I Say I'm Sorry"/"Is She My Girl Friend?"/"I Ain't Got Nobody"].

J. & J. Trigg (The Trigg Brothers) and [John] Maxwell (novelty singer), Vitaphone 2105, July 18 (1) ["Real Estate Papa"/"Take In the Sun, Hang Out the Moon"/"Melody in F"/ "Giannina Mia"/"Miserere"].

AUGUST

Bailey and Barnum (blackface vocal-and-banjo duo) in *Two White Elephants*, Vitaphone 2558, August 1 (1) ["Back in Your Own Back Yard"/"I'm Walkin' on Air"/"No Wonder I'm Happy"].

Richard Bonelli (baritone), Fox Movietone, August 8 (1) [excerpt from *The Barber of Seville*].

The Brox Sisters in *Glorifying the American Girl*, Vitaphone 2570, August 1 (1) ["I Just Roll Along"/"Together"/"Sunshine"].

Eddie Conrad (comedy, songs), with Marion Eddy, Vitaphone 563, August 29 (1) ["So Far,

So Good"/"O sole mio"/"What Does It Matter?"/"Give Me Rain"].

Lynn Cowan (piano, songs), Vitaphone 2245, August 1 (1) ["Cross Roads"/"I'm Down in Buenos Aires"/"Way Out West in Hollywood"].

Evening on the Don (Russian songs), Vitaphone 183, August 22 (1).

The Foy Family in *Chips Off the Old Block,* Vitaphone 2580, August 15 (1) ["I Just Roll Along"/"Bye-Bye Pretty Baby"/"Smile"].

French Leave (musical comedy playlet), Vitaphone 2149, August 22 (2) [parodies of "Hinky Dinky Parlay Voo" and "You're in the Army Now"/ "Come On, Papa"].

Master Gilbert ("Sensational Child Artist"), Vitaphone 2260, August 29 (1) ["Just Once Again"/ "No Wonder I'm Happy"/"He's the Last Word"].

The Harrington Sisters (vocal duo) in *A Garden of Songs,* Vitaphone 2262, August 22 (1) ["My Sweetie Turned Me Down"/"Gosh but We're Gonna Be Wild"/"Wait Till We're Married"].

Al Herman (comedy songs in blackface), Vitaphone 2578, August 15 (1) ["Don't Lean on the Bell"/"Ida! Sweet as Apple Cider"].

Winnie Lightner ("Broadway's Favorite"; comedy, songs), Vitaphone 2592, August 15 (1) ["That Brand New Model of Mine"/"You've Got a Lot to Learn"/"Lala Pa Looza"].

Will Mahoney, Fox Movietone 25, August 1 (1).

Giovanni Martinelli, Vitaphone 198, August 29 (1) ["Vesti la giubba" from *I Pagliacci;* this short was in the first Vitaphone program from 1926].

[Ray] Mayer ("cowboy piano player") and [Edith] Evans (vocalist), Vitaphone 2339, August 29 (1) ["He's Mine, All Mine"/"There's a Trick in Pickin' a Chick-Chick-Chicken"/ "Sing Me a Baby Song"].

Miller and Farrell (vocals, guitars), Fox Movietone 24, August 8 (1).

Cliff Nazarro (piano, dance) and The Two Marjories (vocals), Vitaphone 2116, August 22 (1) ["Me and My Shadow"/"Dance of Pep"/"Lay Down My Life for My Lord"/"I'm on the Right Side"/"I'm Going to Sing My Troubles Away"].

Karyl Norman (female impersonator, "The Creole Fashion Plate") in *Types,* Vitaphone 2662, August 22 (1) ["Valse Modern"/"Georgianna"/ "Daisy Days"/"Five Foot Two, Eyes of Blue"].

[Rosa] Raisa and Giacomo Rimini (baritone), Vitaphone 524, August 29 (1) [excerpt from Act IV of *Il Trovatore*].

Dick Rich and Band (comedy, songs), with The Dean Sisters, Vitaphone 2594, August 29 (1) ["Chloe"/"Lovely Little Silhouette"/"St. Louis Blues"].

Dick Rich and Band, Vitaphone 2595, August 22 (1) ["Ramona"/"There Must Be a Silver Lining"/"Sunshine"].

Mme. [Ernestine] Schumann-Heink (contralto), Vitaphone 379, August 29 (1) ["Danny Boy"/ "The Rosary"/"Stille Nacht"].

Dixie Days (spirituals), Vitaphone 2566, August 29 (1) ["All Along the Mississippi River"/ "All God's Children Got Shoes"/"The Old Ark's a-Movin'"/"Hallelujah to the Lamb"].

[Gus] Van and [Joe] Schenck (vocals), Vitaphone 395, August 1 (1) ["Me Too"/"Hard-to-Get Gertie"/"Because I Love You"/"She Knows Her Onions"].

Albert Spalding (violinist), Vitaphone 439, August 22 (1) [Gypsy airs/"Souvenir"].

Frances Williams ("Broadway's Queen of Jazz"), with the Vitaphone Symphony Orchestra, Vitaphone 573, August 15 (1) ["I'm the Only Boy in the World"/"If It Takes Two Hours to Make Philadelphia"/"It Goes on Like That"/"Oh Baby, Don't We Get Along?"].

SEPTEMBER

Earl Burtnett and His Los Angeles Biltmore Hotel Orchestra, Vitaphone 2294, September 26 (1) ["What'll You Do?"/"The Song Is Ended (but the Memory Lingers On)"/"Tiger Rag"].

Dolly Connolly (vocals) and Percy Wenrich (composer-pianist), Vitaphone 2583, September 5 (1) ["I Told Them All About You"/"I'm Tellin' the Birds, Tellin' the Bees (How I Love You)"/"They Didn't Believe Me"/"My Pretty Rainbow"/"Put on Your Old Gray Bonnet"/"Moonlight Bay"/"Sweet Cider Time"/ "When You Wore a Tulip and I Wore a Big Red Rose"/"Where Do We Go from Here?"/"Lindy Lady"].

[Bud] Cooper and [Sammy] Stept in *Song Hit Writers* ("pianolog"), Vitaphone 2159, September 12 (1) ["Beside a Lazy Stream"/"High Life Made a Low Life Out of Me"/"No One but My Tootsie"].

Kitty Doner (male impersonator) in *A Bit of Scotch,* Vitaphone 2668, September 19 (1) ["Bertie"/ "Griffith Ripples"/"The Campbells Are Coming"/"Sally"/"Annie Laurie"/ "Auld Lang Syne"].

Sally Fields (vocals) in *The Hostess,* Vitaphone 2147, September 5 (1) ["The Hostess"/ "Hello, Bluebird"].

Hazel Green and Company, with John Lucuria and jazz orchestra, and the Vitaphone Symphony Orchestra, Vitaphone 2112, September 12 (1) ["I've Grown So Lonely"/ "Ain't She Sweet?"/"A Bird's-Eye View of My Old Kentucky Home"/"That's Why I Love You"].

Ann Grey (vocals) and Don Warner and His KFWB Orchestra, Vitaphone 2600, September 19 (1) ["Sweet Sue"/"The Lonesome Road"/

"Hollywood Rhythm"/"Red Hot Henry Brown"/"Down by the Delta"].

Charles Hackett (tenor), Vitaphone 2379, September 5 (1) ["Who Is Sylvia?"/ Schubert's "Serenade"].

Hawaiian Nights (steel guitars, dance), Vitaphone 422, September 5 (1) ["Honolulu Dance"/ "Honolulu Tomboy"/"On the Beach at Waikiki"/"Hula Girl"].

Joseph E. Howard ("America's Popular Composer"), Vitaphone 2596, September 12 (1) ["Good-Bye, My Lady Love"/"What's the Use of Dreaming?"/"Oh Gee, Be Sweet to Me, Kid"/"I Wonder Who's Kissing Her Now"].

Adele La Narr (songs, dance), Vitaphone 611, September 5 (1) ["Road to Fame"/"Red Lips (Kiss My Blues Away)"/"Roll Dem Roly Boly Eyes"/"Slow River"].

Mischa Levitzki (pianist), Fox Movietone, September 19 (1) [Liszt's Sixth Rhapsody].

Winnie Lightner ("The Song-a-Minute Girl"), Vitaphone 2591, September 12 (1) ["Heaven Help a Sailor on a Night Like This"/"Raise Myself a Papa"/"We Love It"].

Abe Lyman and His Orchestra, Vitaphone 2338, September 12 (1) ["Waters of Perkiomen"/ "Did You Mean It?"/"The Varsity Drag"].

Karyl Norman in *Silks and Satins*, Vitaphone 2663, September 26 (1) ["When You're with Somebody Else"/"Chloe"/"Daddy Come Home"].

Vincent Rose, Jackie Taylor and Their Orchestra, with B.B.B. [Bobby Bernan], Vitaphone 2292, September 26 (1) ["My Little Dream Home on the Hill"/"Beneath Venetian Skies"/ "Just Once Again"].

Marion Talley, Giuseppe De Luca (baritone), Beniamino Gigli and Jeanne Gordon (contralto), Vitaphone 415, September 26 (1) [Quartet from Act III of *Rigoletto*].

Pat West and His Musical Middies ("Syncopated Blues Players"), Vitaphone 2189, September 19 (1) ["Following You Around"/"Baby, Baby and Me"/"Mine"].

OCTOBER

The Brox Sisters, Universal, October 3 (1).

Chief Caupolican ("The Indian Baritone"), Vitaphone 2598, October 31 (1) ["Bedouin Love Song"/"After Long Absence"/"Pale Moon"].

Harry and Dan Downing (songs, female impersonation) in *High Up and Low Down*, Vitaphone 2127, October 24 (1) ["Lay Me Down to Sleep in Carolina"/"Because I Love You"].

Marion Harris (vocalist), Metro Movietone, October 24 (1) ["I Wonder"/"More Than Satisfied"].

Hurley, Putnam & Snell (piano and vocals), Vitaphone 2180, October 3 (1) ["One Summer Night"/"I Wonder What Will William Tell"/ "Parade of the Ivories"/"Pasta Fa Zooli"].

The Ingenues (all-girl band), Vitaphone 2573, October 17 (1) ["Sunshine"/"Let a Smile Be Your Umbrella (On a Rainy Day)"/ Spanish dance/"St. Louis Blues"].

Roger Wolfe Kahn and His Orchestra, with Henri Garden (tenor) and The Williams Sisters, Vitaphone 468, October 31 (1) ["Indian Butterfly"/"My Heart Is Calling"/"Thinking of You"/"Yankee Rose"].

[Florrie] Le Vere and [Lou] Handman (piano, vocals), Vitaphone 2131, October 24 (1) ["Alabammy Twilight"/"Little Old New York"/"I'm Gonna Clap Hands Until Papa Comes Home"/"Irish Reel"].

Eddie Peabody in *Banjomania*, with Jimmy Maisel, Vitaphone 2103, October 10 (1) ["Poet and Peasant Overture"/"Sailing On"/"St. Louis Blues"/"Sad and Blue"/"Ida! Sweet as Apple Cider"].

The Revelers (piano and vocals; Franklyn Baur, tenor; Lewis James, tenor; Elliott Shaw, baritone; Wilfred Glenn, bass; with Frank Black at piano), Vitaphone 482, October 24 (1) ["Sing"/ "Just Around the Corner"/"Oh! Miss Hannah"].

Frank Richardson ("The Joy Boy of Song"), Vitaphone 2329, October 31 (1) ["Red Lips (Kiss My Blues Away)"/"Sing Me a Baby Song"/"My Blue Heaven"].

Shaw and Lee (comedy, songs), Vitaphone 2686, October 3 (1) ["While Strolling Through the Park One Day"/"Don't Forget to Breathe or Else You'll Die"].

Carolynne Snowden Co. (band, vocals), Vitaphone 2109, October 31 (1) ["St. Louis Blues"/ "Just Another Day Wasted Away"/"San"/"Every Tub"/"Learn to Do the Charleston"].

The Six Original Brown Brothers (comic saxophonists), Vitaphone 549, October 17 (1) ["In a Little Spanish Town"/"The Bull Frog and the Coon"/"Yankee Rose"/"Deed I Do"/ medley of bridal hits/ *I Pagliacci* excerpt/"Rosy Cheeks"/ "There's Something Nice About Everyone, but There's Everything Nice About You"].

Jesse Stafford and His Orchestra, Vitaphone 2730, October 31 (1) ["Shine"/"Wob-a-ly Walk"/ "Yankee Rose"].

John Charles Thomas (baritone), Vitaphone 481, October 31 (1) [Prologue from *I Pagliacci*].

Undersea Revue, with the Larry Ceballos Girls, James Clemmons, Lyda Roberti and the Vitaphone Symphony Orchestra, Vitaphone 2661, October 17 (1).

[Gus] Van and [Joe] Schenck, Metro Movietone, October 10 (1).

Fred Waring's Pennsylvanians (band), Vitaphone 428, October 31 (1) ["Collegiate"/"In a Little White House"/"Where Do You Work-a, John?"].

Reinald Werrenrath (baritone), Vitaphone 361, October 3 (1) ["On the Road to Mandalay"/ "Duna"].

Dorothy Whitmore (vocals), Vitaphone 2538, October 31 (1) ["For Old Time's Sake"/ "Mammy Is Gone"/"Trees"/"I'm Walking Between the Raindrops"].

NOVEMBER

Richard Bonelli, Fox Movietone, November 7 (1) [Prologue from *I Pagliacci*].

Florence Brady (blues singer) in *A Cycle of Songs*, Vitaphone 2699, November 28 (1) ["Sunshine"/"I Can't Get Him Off My Mind"/"Here Comes the Showboat"].

Burns and Kissen (comedy, songs), Vitaphone 2679, November 28 (1) ["Yes, We Have No Bananas"/"Strawberry Pie"/"Mary Lou"/"It All Depends on You"].

Eddie Cantor (comedy, songs) in *That Certain Party*, with Bobbe Arnst, Paramount Movietone, November 14 (1) ["Hungry Woman"/ "That Certain Party"].

Lynn Cowan's "Community Sing," Vitaphone 2547, November 21 (1) ["In the Shade of the Old Apple Tree"/"Sweet Rosie O'Grady"/ "Down Among the Sheltering Palms"].

The Croonaders (vocal-ukelele trio) in *Melodious Moments*, Vitaphone 2736, November 14 (1) ["Blue Grass"/"Twelfth Street Rag"/"What Is It Like to Be Loved?"/"From Monday On"].

Crystal Cave Revue, with the Larry Ceballos Girls, Vitaphone 2693, November 14 (1) ["I'm Afraid of You"/"Lullaby Lane"/"Over Here"].

Doris Duncan, Herring and Zeh (vocals), Vitaphone 2115, November 7 (1) ["Mine"/"Come to Me Tonight"/"Side by Side"/"From Now On"].

Ruth Etting (vocalist), Paramount Movietone, November 21 (1) ["Because My Baby Don't Mean 'Maybe' Now"/"Roses of Yesterday"].

The Fashion Plates of Harmony, Vitaphone 2283, November 7 (1) ["My Wild Irish Rose"/ "The Wild Man of Borneo"/"El Palmar"/"The Noble Duke of York"].

Neville Fleeson (piano) and Gladys Baxter (vocals), Vitaphone 434, November 28 (1) [musical satire of *Rain*].

The Happiness Boys, Vitaphone 537, November 21 (1) ["How Do You Do, Everybody"/"Pardon Me While I Laugh"/"An Operatic Syncopation"/"Good-Bye, Everybody"].

Marion Harris, Metro Movietone, November 21 (1) ["Afraid of You"/"We Love It"].

In a Persian Garden ("sound effects with song"), Tiffany-Stahl, November 14 (1).*

Johnny Marvin (vocalist), Metro Movietone, November 7 (1).

Johnny Marvin, Vitaphone 492, November 21 (1) ["Strum My Blues Away"/"A Little Music in the Moonlight"/"Moonlight and Roses"/"Deed I Do"].

Odette Myrtil (violin, song), Metro Movietone, November 7 (1).

The Ponce Sisters (vocal duo), Metro Movietone, November 7 (1) ["Too Busy"].

Sandra Ratti (soprano), RCA Phonophone, November 21 (1) ["My Man"].

Joseph Regan ("America's Foremost Irish Tenor"), Vitaphone 2628, November 21 (1) ["Mary Ann"/"I'll Take You Home Again, Kathleen"/"Jo-Anne"].

John Charles Thomas, Vitaphone 493, November 21 (1) ["Danny Deever"/"In the Gloaming"].

[Gus] Van and [Joe] Schenck, Metro Movietone, November 21 (1) ["Cohen's Living Life of Reilly"/"I Gotta Have an Italian Girl"/"Away Down South in Heaven"].

Visions of Spain, with Lina Basquette and Sam Ash (tenor), Vitaphone 2104, November 7 (1) ["Capriccio Espagnola"/"Sanctus"/"Dance Boheme"/"Serenade"/"March of the Toreadors"].

Jack Waldron (song and dance) in *A Little Breath of Broadway*, Vitaphone 2691, November 21 (1) ["Back in Your Own Back Yard"/"Goody, Goody"/"Black Maria"].

George Dewey Washington (blues singer), Metro Movietone, November 21 (1).

DECEMBER

[Irving] Aaronson and His Commanders (band), Metro Movietone, December 5 (1).

Leo Beers (piano, vocals), Metro Movietone, December 12 (1) ["Arabella"/"In the Usual Way"].

[Frank] Browne and [Kay] La Velle (comedy, songs) in *Don't Handle the Goods*, Vitaphone 2589, December 12 (1) ["Mary Ann"/"Why Is a Popular Song?"/"Beautiful"].

James Clemmons (eccentric dance, vocals) in *Dream Café*, Vitaphone 2242, December 12 (1) ["Hearts and Flowers"/"Valse Bleue"/ "The Wedding March" from *Lohengrin*].

Cliff Edwards ("Ukelele Ike"), Metro Movietone, December 5 (1).

Irene Franklin (comedy, songs), Vitaphone 2705, December 26 (1) ["Red Head! Red Head!"/ "Be Your Age"/"Help! Help! Help!"].

[Steve] Freda and [Johnny] Palace (comedy, songs), Vitaphone 2271, December 5 (1) ["Bartch-A-Kalloop"/"Talking to the Moon"].

Beniamino Gigli, Vitaphone 517, December 5 (1) ["Cielo e mar" from *La Gioconda*].

George Givot (comedy, songs) and Leonard and Hinds (vocal duo), Vitaphone 2107, December 5 (1) ["Why Should I Marry?"/"I Wish't I Was in Peoria"/"Dixie"/"Cuddle Up a Little Closer"].

Fuzzy Knight (… "and His Little Piano"), Metro Movietone, December 26 (1).

Henri Le Bel (organist), Vitaphone (number not shown), December 12 (1) ["Angela Mia"].

Polly Moran (comedy, songs) in *The Movie Chatterbox*, Vitaphone 2297, December 26 (1) ["Polly with a Fractured Past"/"Sleepy Piano"/ "Any Place That I Make Money Is Home Sweet Home"].

Gene Morgan Orchestra, Vitaphone 2266, December 12 (1) ["Pale Moon"/"Oh for the Life of an Osteopath"/"Haunting Blues"].

Harry Wayman's Debutantes ("Premiere Feminine Jazz Band"), Vitaphone 2261, December 26 (1) ["Over Moonlit Waters"/"The Doll Dance"/ "What Do We Do on a Dew-Dew-Dewy Day?"].

Eddie White (comedy, songs) in *I Thank You*, Vitaphone 2689, December 5 (1) ["Let a Smile Be Your Umbrella"/"Get Out and Get Under the Moon"/"That's My Mammy"].

Frances White (comic vocalist), Metro Movietone, December 26 (1).

Russ Wildey and Billy Sheehan ("pianolog duo"), Vitaphone 2113, December 5 (1) ["Don't Sing Aloha"/"A Trip to the Circus"/"Side by Side"].

Britt Wood ("The Boob and His Harmonica"), Vitaphone 2129, December 5 (1) ["The Last Rose of Summer"/"Lost John"/"Old Folks at Home"].

Zimmerman and Grandville in *An Alpine Romance*, Universal Movietone, December 19 (1) ["Home Sweet Home"/"Sleep, Baby, Sleep"].

1929

JANUARY

"Aunt Jemima" [Tess Gardella] (vocals), with Art Sorenson (piano), Vitaphone 566, January 9 (1) ["Dixie"/"One Sweet Letter from You"/"My Idea of Heaven"/"Everybody Stomp"].

Trixie Friganza (comedy, songs) in *My Bag o' Trix*, Vitaphone 2791, January 30 (1) ["John! Leave the Room"/"The Peevish Widow"].

The Freeman Sisters (piano-ukelele duo), Vitaphone 625, January 30 (1) ["Wild Flower"/ "Dewy Dew"/"I Gotta Get Myself Someone to Love"/ ukelele medley].

Frank Gaby (ventriloquist) in *The Tout*, Vitaphone 2188, January 9 (1) ["I'm the Son of a Horse Thief"/"Hearts and Flowers"/"Elegie"].

The Gale Brothers (singing tap dancers), Vitaphone 610, January 16 (1) ["Ain't She Sweet?"/ "Mary Lou"/"Hello Cutie"].

Gertrude Lawrence (vocals), Fox Movietone, January 9 (1) ["I Don't Know How It Happened"].

Mary Lewis (soprano) in *Way Down South*, Vitaphone 383, January 23 (1) ["Swing Along Sue"/"Dixie"/"Carry Me Back to Old Virginny"].

Vincent Lopez and His Orchestra, Vitaphone 390, January 23 (1) ["Hello, Bluebird"/ "California Sunshine"/"Bing, Bing"/"Trail of Dreams"].

Dora Maughan (comedienne) in *Song Impressions*, with Walter Fehl (tenor), Vitaphone 2732, January 16 (1) ["My Heart Keeps Speaking of Love"/"Divorced and Married"/"I Can't Do Without You"].

Borrah Minevitch and His Harmonica Rascals in *Boyhood Days*, Paramount Movietone, January 16 (2).

Jack North (banjo, vocals), Vitaphone 2756, January 16 (1) ["Back in Love Again"/"Oh Baby Don't We Get Along"/"When Banana Skins Are Falling"].

The Record Boys [Al Bernard, Frank Kamplain, Sammy Stept], Vitaphone 530, January 30 (1) ["Oo-Long's in Hong Kong"/"I'm Looking for a Girl Named Mary"/"Twenty Five Years from Now"/"Yeedle Deedle Lena"].

The Revelers, Metro Movietone, January 30 (1).

The Rollickers (vocal quartet), Vitaphone 420, January 16 (1) ["Barcelona"/"Jersey Walk"/ "Mary Lou"].

Cantor Josef Rosenblatt, with Machtenberg's Male Choir, Vitaphone 2203, January 16 (1) ["Hallelujah"].

[Noble] Sissle and [Eubie] Blake (composer-singers), Vitaphone 463, January 9 (1) ["I Wonder Where My Sweetie Can Be"/"You Can Bet You're in Love"/"High, High, High Up in the Hills"].

Phil Spitalny and His Pennsylvania Hotel Orchestra, with Al Wohlman (master of ceremonies), and the Paul Sisters, Penn Trio, Chester Hale Girls, Metro Movietone, January 30 (2) ["There's a Rainbow 'Round My Shoulder"].

Irene Stone (vocalist) in *Songs as You Like Them*, Vitaphone 2783, January 16 (1) ["I Got a Big Date with a Little Man"/"Tom-Cattin' Papa"/"I'm a Goil of Very Few Woids"/"I Ate the Bologney"].

Nina Tarasova (vocalist) in *The Hut*, Fox Movietone, January 9 (2) ["There Were Once Happy Days"].

Ulis and Clark (comedy songs) in *In Dutch*, Vitaphone 2758, January 16 (1) ["O, Katharina"/
"Ten Little Miles from Town"/"Mammy
o' Mine"].

FEBRUARY

Al Abbott (songs "in character") in *Small Town
Rambles*, Vitaphone 2703, February 6 (1) ["Chi-
nese Love Song"/"My Gal Irene"/"Please Let
Me Go Home"].
Donald Brian (tenor), Vitaphone 2733, February
6 (1) ["Mary (What Are You Waiting
For?)"/"Over There"/"There's a Long, Long
Trail"/"You're a Real Sweetheart"].
Carl Emmy and Pals (dogs), Metro Movietone,
February 20 (1).
Ruth Etting, Paramount Movietone, February 27
(1) ["My Mother's Eyes"/"That's Him Now"].
Bobby Folsom ("narrative song"), Vitaphone 2839,
February 20 (1) ["Priscilla of the Puritan
Days"].
Jane Green (vocalist), Vitaphone 2750, February
13 (1) ["Ten Little Miles from Town"/ "There's
Somebody New"/"Anything You Say"].
Mal Hallett and His Entertaining Orchestra, Vi-
taphone 729, February 20 (1) ["Doin' the Rac-
coon"/"Tin Pan Parade"/"Bugle Call Rag"/
"Yankee Doodle"/"Harvardiana"/ "Come, Let's
Take a Stroll"/"We Love the College Girls"].
Lipton (imitations of musical instruments) and
Terrell (hula dancer), Vitaphone 2310, February
27 (1) ["Oo-La-La"/"Sleep, Baby, Sleep"/
"Tamiami Trail"/"Aloha Oe" and "Waikiki"
medley].
Georgie Lyons, Metro Movietone, February 6 (1).
Giovanni Martinelli, with Louis D'Angelo (bass),
Vitaphone 509, February 13 (1) [duet from Act
IV of *La Juive*].
Murray and Lavere (accordionist and singer), with
De Sues, Furney and Johnson (vocal trio), Vi-
taphone 2108, February 13 (1) ["Sunday"/"My
Sunday Girl"/"There Ain't No 'Maybe' in My
Baby's Eyes"/"When Honey Sings an Old-
Time Song"/"Baby Face"].
The Neal Sisters (vocal trio), Vitaphone 719, Feb-
ruary 20 (1) ["Gentlemen Prefer Blondes"/
"Doin' the Raccoon"/"Boola Boola"].
The Paragons (vocal quartet) in *In the Tropics*, Vi-
taphone 2883, February 20 (1) ["Kentucky
Babe"/"The Winter Songs"].
Jan Rubini (violinist), with Vernon Rickard
(tenor) and Mona Content, Vitaphone 2790,
February 6 (1) ["Zigeunerweisen"/"I Love You
Truly"/"I Hear You Calling Me"].

MARCH

Phil Baker ("A Bad Boy from a Good Family";
talk, song, accordion), Vitaphone 724, March
13 (1) ["Baker Blues"/"Big Butter and Egg
Man"/"How About Me?"/"I'll Get By"].
Eddie Cantor in *Midnite Frolics*, Paramount
Movietone, March 13 (2).
Sam Coslow (composer-singer) in *The Broadway
Minstrel*, with June Clyde (singer), Vitaphone
2659, March 27 (1) ["The Show Is Over"/"I
Can't Get Enough of You"/ "Don't Be Like
That"].
Bernie Cummins and His New York Biltmore Or-
chestra, Vitaphone 752, March 20 (1) ["Come
On, Baby"/"If I Had You"/"Here Comes My
Ball and Chain"].
Hope Hampton (soprano), Vitaphone 740, March
20 (1) [Act II from *Manon*].
Willie and Eugene Howard in *The Music Makers*,
Vitaphone 722-3, March 20 (1) ["Mister Gal-
lagher and Mister Shean"/"It's Ray-Ray-Rain-
ing"/"Baby Curls"].
Walter Huston (actor) in *Carnival Man*, Para-
mount Movietone, March 13 (2) ["Why Speak
of That?"].
Leon Navarra (pianist), Vitaphone 2190, March 6
(1) ["Prelude in C Sharp Minor"].
Bob Nelson ("Broadway's Popular Singing Co-
median"), Metro Movietone, March 27 (1).
Newsboys Harmonica Band, Vitaphone 2300,
March 20 (1) ["March of the High Sierras"/
medley of old-time airs].
Eleanor Painter (soprano), Vitaphone 746, March
13 (1) ["Love Is Best of All," from *The Princess
Pat* /"L'Amour est un oiseau rebelle," from *Car-
men* /"How About Me?"].
Julia Sanderson and Frank Crumit (vocal duo) in
Words of Love, Vitaphone 733, March 20 (1)
["No Wonder You're a Beautiful Girl"/"I Can
Live Without You"/"A Precious Little Thing
Called Love"].
Dr. Sigmund Spaeth ("comedy pianolog"), Fox
Movietone, March 6 (1) ["Yes! We Have No
Bananas"].
The Sunshine Boys [Dave Ringle, Eddie Roth,
Billy Sharkey] (vocals), Vitaphone 540, March
6 (1) ["Sunshine"/"No One but You"/"Muddy
Waters"/"In 1932"].
Rudy Vallee and His Connecticut Yankees (band),
Vitaphone 771, March 27 (1) ["Down the
Field"/"Deep Night"/"Outside"].
Fannie Ward (62-year-old "Miracle Woman of
the Century"), Vitaphone 721, March 20 (1)
["Flapper Fannie"/"Radio Widow"].
Gil Wells (clarinet, dance, vocals) in *A Breeze from
the South*, Vitaphone 2735, March 20 (1) ["Trust-
ful Joe"/"International Dan"/"Jubilee Blues"].

Frank Whitman (trick violin), Vitaphone 703, March 27 (1) ["The Irish Washerwoman"/"O, Katharina"/"We Won't Get Home Until Morning"/"I'd Love to Live in Loveland with a Girl Like You"].

APRIL

Janet Adair (vocals) in *Here Comes the Bridesmaid*, Vitaphone 2629, April 17 (1) ["Bridesmaid"/"No One's Fool"/"It's Right Here for You"].

The Capitolians and Walt Roesner (band), Metro Movietone, April 17 (1) ["Angela Mia"/"O sole mio"].

Bobby Clark and Paul McCullough with Lois Moran in *Belle of Samoa* (comedy, songs), Fox Movietone, April 24 (2) ["Samoa"].

Frank Crumit (tenor-composer; "The One Man Glee Club"), Vitaphone 727, April 10 (1) ["The Song of the Prune"/"I Miss You, Lize"/"Little Annie Rooney"/"In the Shade of the Old Apple Tree"/"A Bird in a Gilded Cage"/"Bedelia"/"She Was Happy Till She Met You"/"The Preacher and the Bear"].

Xavier Cugat and His Gigolos (band), Vitaphone 2299, April 10 (1) ["El Relicario"/ "Estrellita"/"Mighty Lak' a Rose"/"Y ... como lo va"].

Gus Edwards Revue, *Song of the Roses*, Metro Movietone, April 3 (1) ["Mighty Lak' a Rose"/"My Wild Irish Rose"/"Rose of Washington Square"/"Rosey"].*

Bobby Gillette (banjo) in *Syncopated Breezes*, with Doris Walker (soprano), Vitaphone 2838, April 17 (1) ["Happy Days and Lonely Nights"/"The Rosary"/"St. Louis Blues"/"Ida! Sweet as Apple Cider"].

Green's 20th Century Faydetts (band), Vitaphone 710, April 17 (1) ["Because My Baby Don't Mean 'Maybe' Now"/"Ah! Sweet Mystery of Life"/"Changes"].

The Happiness Boys, Metro Movietone, April 10 (1).

Harry Horlick and His A & P Gypsies (band), Vitaphone 763, April 10 (1) ["Two Guitars"/ "Dark Eyes"/"Chiquita"/"The March of the Toys"/"Gypsy Love Song"].

Madame [Maria] Kurenko (soprano), Metro Movietone, April 10 (1) [excerpt from *Faust* / 'The Last Rose of Summer," from *Martha*].

The Locust Sisters (vocal quartet), Metro Movietone, April 10 (1).

Tim McCoy ("screen cowboy here revealed as a singer of range songs ... in a light but melodious voice"), Fox Movietone, April 10 (1).

"Sunshine Sammy" [Morrison] (song and dance), Metro Movietone, April 3 (1) ["Steppin' Along"/"Swanee"].

William O'Neal (tenor), Metro Movietone, April 3 (1).

Frances Shelley (guitar, vocals), Vitaphone 713, April 10 (1) ["She's Funny That Way"/"I'll Get By"].

Val and Ernie Stanton in *Cut Yourself a Piece of Cake*, Vitaphone 2586, April 10 (1) ["Beautiful"/"Raymond" Overture/"original blue song"].

Jay Velie (tenor), Vitaphone 2784, April 3 (1) ["Because I Love You"/"A Little Bit of Heaven"/"The Americans Come"].

Jay Velie in *Songs of Love*, Vitaphone 718, April 3 (1) ["You Gave Your Heart to Me"/ "Tommy, Lad!"/"Mother Machree"].

Fred Waring's Pennsylvanians, Vitaphone 427, April 17 (1) ["Sleep"/"Breezin' Along with the Breeze"/"Me Too"].

MAY

James Barton (song and dance) in *After Seven*, Paramount Movietone, May 29 (2) ["Waiting for the Evening Mail"].

Dave Bernie Orchestra in *Here Comes the Showboat*, Vitaphone 2796, May 8 (1) ["Here Comes the Showboat"/"Oh, You Have No Idea"/"High Up on a Hill Top"/ "C-O-N-S-T-A-N-T-I-N-O-P-L-E"].

Bernardo de Pace, Metro Movietone, May 22 (1) ["Morning, Noon and Night"].

Gus Edwards Revue featuring Charles King (vocalist) in *Climbing the Golden Stairs*, with Sidney Jarvis, The Pearl Twins, The Aber Twins, The Bo Twins and The Clute Twins, Metro Movietone, May 1 (2) ["Climb the Golden Stairs"/"Heart of Broadway"/"Hello Melody—Goodbye Jazz"/"It Takes a Cop to Cop a Girl"].*

Irene Franklin, Vitaphone 777, May 22 (1) ["The Waitress"/"The Flapper Mammy's Lullaby"].

Vincent Lopez (piano), Metro Movietone, May 15 (1) ["Canadian Capers"/"Twelfth Street Rag"].

Metro Movietone Revue (Jack Pepper, Frances White, Ponce Sisters, Reynolds Sisters, Joseph Regan), Metro Movietone, May 15 (2) ["Blue Skies"/"I'd Like to Be a Monkey in a Zoo"/"Girl of My Dreams"/"Sweet Sue"/"Ten Little Miles from Town"/"When Irish Eyes Are Smiling"].

The Palm Beach Four (guitar, vocals), Vitaphone 794, May 29 (1) ["Nobody's Fault but Your Own"/"Some Sweet Day"/"Poo-Poo-Paroop"].

Roof Garden Revue, with the Larry Ceballos Girls, Vitaphone 2627, May 8 (1) ["Over the Garden Wall"].

Lillian Roth (vocalist) and The Piano Boys, Paramount Movietone, May 29 (1) ["Walking with My Sweetness"/"Watch My Baby Walk"].

Tito Schipa (tenor), Paramount Movietone, May 8 (1).

Roy Sedley and His Night Club Revue (band revue), with Beth Miller (vocalist) and Billy Smith (dancer), Vitaphone 796, May 15 (1) ["Blue Grass"/"I Ain't Takin' Orders from No One"/"Sonny Boy"].

Clarence Tisdale ("Southland's Spiritual Tenor"), Vitaphone 766, May 22 (1) ["The Sweetness of Your Song"/"In the Sweet Bye and Bye"/"Oh! Didn't It Rain"].

[Gus] Van and [Joe] Schenck, Metro Movietone, May 15 (1) ["Chloe"/"Don't Blame It All on Broadway"].

JUNE

The All-Girl Revue, with Lillian Price, Betty Lou Webb, Ellen Bunting with De Paco and Kazvlki, and Jean Rankin's Bluebells Orchestra, Vitaphone 818, June 12 (1) ["That's Her Now"/"I'm an Indian"/"Chrysanthemums"/"My Pet"].

Baby Rose Marie ("The Child Wonder" vocalist), Vitaphone 809, June 5 (1) ["Heigh-Ho! Everybody, Heigh-Ho!"/"Who Wouldn't Be Jealous of You?"/"Don't Be Like That"].

Jules Bledsoe (baritone), Columbia, June 5 (1) ["Old Man Trouble"/"Wadin' in the Water"].

Alice Boulden (vocalist), Paramount, June 12 (1) ["Easy Come, Easy Go"/"One I Love"].

Guido Deiro (piano, accordion), Vitaphone 2968, June 12 (1) [Tchaikovsky's "Romeo and Juliet"/ Drigo's "Serenade"].

Gus Edwards "Song Revue," Metro Movietone, June 26 (1) ["By the Light of the Silvery Moon"/"If I Were a Millionaire"/"Jimmy Valentine"/"School Days"/"Sunbonnet Sue"].*

Segar Ellis and His Embassy Club Orchestra, Vitaphone 822, June 26 (1).

Harry Fox and His Six American Beauties (comedy, songs), Vitaphone 828, June 26 (1) ["Halfway to Heaven"/"Belles of Hotels"].

The Gay Caballero, with Frank Crumit and Doris Abeles, Columbia, June 12 (1).

Arthur and Morton Havel in Playmates (comedy, songs), Vitaphone 769, June 12 (1) ["I Want to Be with My Mammy Down in Miami"/"Heigh Ho, Cheerio"].

Lambert and Hillpot ("The Harmony Boys"), Paramount Movietone, June 26 (1).

Memories (song vignettes), Columbia, June 5 (1) ["The Sidewalks of New York"/"Sweet Rosie O'Grady"].

Mexican Tipica Orchestra, Vitaphone 707, June 12 (1) ["Mexican Rhapsody"/"La Paloma"/ "Jarabe Tapatio"].

Leo Reisman and Hotel Brunswick Orchestra in

Rhythms, Vitaphone 770, June 5 (1) ["Mooche"/ "Waters of Perkiomen"/"If I Had You"/"Hijo Mio"/"Milenberg Joys"/ "Lonely"/"Some of These Days"].

Guy Robertson (tenor) in High Water, Vitaphone 813, June 12 (1) ["High Water"].

Richard Rodgers [spelled "Rogers"] and Lorenz Hart in Makers of Melody, Paramount Movietone, June 19 (2) ["The Blue Room"/"The Girl Friend"/"Here in My Arms"/"Manhattan"; sung by Robert Cloy, Inez Courtney, Allan Gould, Kathryn Reece, Ruth Tester and uncredited male trio].

Norman Thomas Quintette (vocals) in Harlem Mania, Vitaphone 827, June 26 (1) ["Sleep, Baby, Sleep"/"Listen to the Mocking Bird"/ "Melody in F"].

Rudy Vallee and His Connecticut Yankees, Paramount Movietone, June 19 (1).

Jack White and the Montrealers (band with comedy), Vitaphone 791, June 12 (1) ["I'm Ka-razy for You"/"Mean to Me"/"Goodbye Broadway, Hello France"/"Finiculi-Finicula"/"Laugh, Clown, Laugh"/ I Pagliacci excerpt/"Over There"/"Anvil Chorus"/"The Rose of No Man's Land"].

JULY

"Oklahoma" Bob Albright and Rodeo Do Flappers (song, dance), Vitaphone 810, July 3 (1) ["My Pony Boy"/"Chloe"/"Yodel"/"Salter Dog"].

James Barton in It Happened to Him, Paramount Movietone, July 10 (1) ["Miss Annabelle Lee"].

Bobby Folsom, Vitaphone 788, July 3 (1) ["Two Little Maids"/"Tess"/"I Lost My Stockings"].

Jan Garber Orchestra, Metro Movietone, July 10 (1) ["Blue Shadows"/"Memories of France"/ "Tiger Rag"].

June (vocalist), with John Hundley, Vitaphone 735, July 10 (1) ["Me and the Man in the Moon"/"My Troubles Are Over"].

Mal Hallett and His Way Down East Orchestra, Vitaphone 730, July 24 (1) ["Lots of Mama"/ "Mother Machree"/"war medley"].

Keller Sisters and Lynch (vocal trio), Metro Movietone, July 10 (1) ["Doin' the Raccoon"/ "What a Night for Spooning"/"Where'd You Get Those Eyes?"].

Johnny Marvin, Metro Movietone, July 17 (1) ["Heartbroken and Lonely"/"Old Man Sunshine"].

Georgie Price in Don't Get Nervous (comedy, songs), Vitaphone 841, July 31 (1) ["Hello, Sunshine, Hello"/"Sweetheart's Holiday"] (same short reviewed September 11 as Don't Get Excited).

Lillian Roth and Alan K. Foster Girls in *Raising the Roof*, Paramount Movietone, July 3 (1).

Frances Shelley and the Four Eton Boys, Vitaphone 846, July 31 (1) ["Finding the Long Way Home"/"If I Were You, I'd Fall in Love with Me"/"Am I Blue?"].

AUGUST

Dave Apollon and His Russian Stars (band of "Phillipinos in Scotch kilties playing American jazz"), Vitaphone 875, August 21 (1) ["If I Had You"/"Louise"/"Mean to Me"/"Boo Boo Blues"].

The Big Paraders ("Six Heavyweight Boys and Girls in a Song and Dance Revue"), Vitaphone 840, August 28 (1) ["Broken Hearted Blackbird"/"Prelude in C Sharp Minor"/"Doin' the Raccoon"].

Edison and Gregory (novelty instrumentalists), Vitaphone 868, August 14 (1).

George Givot, De Forest Phonofilm, August 21 (1).

Cora Green ("The Famous Creole Singer"), Vitaphone 825, August 28 (1) ["Brother-in-Law Dan"/"Travelin' All Alone"/"I'll Tell the World"].

[Grace] Hayes and [Neville] Fleeson in *Diamond Till* (Mae West parody), Vitaphone 871, August 21 (1).

Willie and Eugene Howard in *My People*, Vitaphone 750-1, August 28 (2) ["Song of the Volga Boatmen"/"Blue Grass"/"My People"].

Godfrey Ludlow (violin) with NBC concert orchestra, Radio, August 7 (1) ["Symphonie Espagnole"].

New York Philharmonic Orchestra, conducted by Henry Hadley, Vitaphone 314, August 28 (1) [Overture from *Tannhäuser*] [this short was in initial Vitaphone program of 1926].

Douglas Stanbury (baritone) and His Veterans in *Marchin' Home*, Vitaphone 861, August 28 (1) ["I'm Marching Home to You"].

[Gus] Van and [Joe] Schenck, Metro Movietone, August 28 (1) ["Ain't Got Nothin' Now"/"Everything's Gonna Be All Right"/"St. Louis Blues"].

SEPTEMBER

Booklovers, with Joseph Santley and Ivy Sawyer, Paramount Movietone, September 18 (2).

Emil Boreo (tenor), Metro Movietone, September 18 (1) ["Dance of the Wooden Soldiers"/ "La Marseillaise"].

Ted Brown Band, De Forest Phonofilm, September 11 (1) ["Humoresque"].

Stewart Brady ("boy soprano"), Vitaphone 2745, September 11 (1) ["At Dawning"/ Paderewski's "Minuet"/"Giannina Mia"].

Segar Ellis and His Embassy Club Orchestra, Vitaphone 823, September 18 (1) ["How Can I Love Again?"/"Am I Blue?"/"I've Got a Feeling I'm Falling"].

[Harry] Fox and [Bea] Curtis (vocals) in *The Fox and the Bee*, Vitaphone 829, September 11 (1) ["Underneath the Wabash Moon"/"Love Baby"].

Ben Pollack and His Park Central Orchestra, Vitaphone 872, September 11 (1) ["Memories"/ "My Kinda Love"/"Song of the Islands"].

St. Louis Blues, with Bessie Smith, Radio, September 4 (2) ["St. Louis Blues"].

Stanley and Ginger ("songs and talk") in *A Few Absurd Moments*, Vitaphone 714, September 18 (1) ["That's My Weakness Now"/"Just Like a Melody Out of the Sky"].

Jack White and His Chateau Madrid Club Entertainers, Vitaphone 844, September 11 (1) ["Am I Blue?"/"Kansas City Kitty"/"Then We Canoe-dle Oodle"/"Senorita"].

OCTOBER

Will Aubrey (vocalist) and Company in *A Night on the Bowery*, Vitaphone 896, October 2 (1) ["My Gal Sal"/"Roll On, Silver Moon"/"Caroline"/"Daddy, Won't You Please Come Home?"/ "Ida! Sweet as Apple Cider" /"Some of These Days"].

The Biltmore Trio, Metro Movietone, October 9 (1).

Robert Chisholm (baritone), Metro Movietone, October 9 (1).

Ruth Etting, with Phil Ohman and Victor Arden (pianists), Vitaphone 886, October 9 (1).

Jan Garber Orchestra, Metro Movietone, October 16 (1) ["Oh Baby"/"That's My Weakness Now"].

The Gotham Rhythm Boys (vocal, guitar trio), Vitaphone 832, October 9 (1) ["Kansas City Kitty"/"Building a Nest for Mary"/"My Wild Irish Rose"/"Alabamy Snow"].

Charles Hackett in *Faust* (Act I), with Cosmo Baromeo (bass), Vitaphone 899-900, October 9 (1).

Charles K. Harris, Paramount Movietone, October 16 (1) ["After the Ball," sung by its composer].

Horace Heidt and His Orchestra, Vitaphone 892, October 9 (1).

Grace Johnston (vocals) and the Indiana Five (band), Vitaphone 869, October 2 (1) ["Bashful Baby"/"Clarinet Marmalade"/"Glad Rag Doll"].

The Kentucky Jubilee Singers in *The Water Boy*,

Fox Movietone, October 16 (1) ["Daniel"/"Good News"/"Water Boy"].

Bob Nelson, Metro Movietone, October 23 (1).

Night Club, Paramount Movietone, October 30 (3) (performances by Fanny Brice ["Sasha, the Passion of the Pasha"], Bobbe Arnst, Jimmy Carr and His Orchestra, Tamara Geva, Vivienne Osborne, Ann Pennington, Pat Rooney, Pat Rooney III, others).

Titta Ruffo (baritone), Metro Movietone, October 9 (1) ["Largo al factotum" from *The Barber of Seville*].

Yvette Rugel (soprano), Metro Movietone, October 23 (1) ["Roses of Yesterday"/"Old Folks at Home"].

Tito Schipa, RCA Photophone, October 16 (1) ["El Gaucho"/"I Shall Return"/ aria from *L'Elisir d'Amour*].

Syncopated Trial ("jazz musical"), with Lew Spencer and Morgan Morley, Pathé–RCA Photophone, October 2 (2).

Tchaikovsky's [1812] Overture, Hugo Riesenfeld and orchestra, United Artists, October 2 (1).

Al Wohlman ("songs and talk"), Metro Movietone, October 16 (1) ["Pullman Porter's Parade"/"Spell of the Blues"].

NOVEMBER

The Barber Shop Chord (song and dance), Vitaphone 3640, November 13 (1) ["The Barber Shop Chord"/"Oh! What I Know About Love"/"It's a Fast Life and a Hot One"].

Bits of Broadway, with Earl and Bell (comedy singer-guitarists), Titta Ruffo, Keller Sisters and Lynch (vocal trio) and Phil Spitalny Orchestra, Metro Movietone, November 6 (1).

Black and Tan, with Duke Ellington and His Cotton Club Orchestra, and Fredi Washington, Radio, November 6 (2) ["Black and Tan Fantasy"/"Black Beauty"].

Dance of the Paper Dolls ("kid revue"), Vitaphone 3669, November 13 (1) ["Dance of the Paper Dolls"/"You Can't Believe My Naughty Eyes"/"Loose Ankles"/"All I Want to Do-Do-Do Is Dance"].*

Earl and Bell, Metro Movietone, November 20 (1) ["Blue Hawaii"/"Just a Melody, Wish I Could Hear It Again"/"K-K-Kiss Me Again"].

Elba Ersi (vocals) and Nat Ayres (piano), Metro Movietone, November 27 (1) ["The Merry Widow Waltz"].

Roy Evans and Al Belasco (song and dance), Metro Movietone, November 20 (1).

Flinging Feet (international dancing), Castle Color Novelty, November 13 (1).*

Eddie Miller ("the one man quartet"), Vitaphone

881, November 13 (1) ["Heart of My Hearts"/"In the Garden of My Heart"].

The Opry House, with Lew Hearn (comedian), the Mound City Blue Blowers (instrumental quartet) and Mabel Walker (vocals), Vitaphone 834, November 13 (1) ["I Ain't Got Nobody"/"Let Me Call You Sweetheart"/"My Gal Sal"].

Zelda Santley ("song imitations" of Ted Lewis, Fanny Brice, Mae West, Maurice Chevalier) in *Little Miss Everybody,* Vitaphone 919, November 13 (1) ["Me and My Shadow"/ "When My Baby Smiles at Me"/"My Man"/"Frankie and Johnny"/"Too Busy"/ "Louise"].

DECEMBER

[Irving] Aaronson and His Commanders, Metro Movietone, December 18 (1) ["I'll Get By"/"Nobody's Sweetheart"].

Buck and Bubbles in *In and Out* (comedy, dancing), Pathé, December 4 (1).

Clyde Doerr and His Orchestra, Metro Movietone, December 11 (1) ["If I Had You"/"The Wedding of the Painted Doll"].

The Doll Shop, Metro Colortone Revue, December 18 (2).*

Cliff Edwards ("Ukelele Ike"), Metro Movietone, December 11 (1) ["Good Little Baby"/"Halfway to Heaven"].

Gilbert and Sullivan Ensemble, Metro Movietone, December 18 (1).

Ann Greenway (vocalist) in *And How,* Vitaphone 3719, December 11 (1) ["Memories"/"Peter Minuet"].*

Giovanni Martinelli, with Livia Marracci (soprano), Vitaphone 932, December 11 (1) ["M'appari" from *Martha*].

Giovanni Martinelli, with Livia Marracci, Vitaphone 944, December 25 (1) ["Ah, si ben mio" and "Di quella pira" from *Il Trovatore*].

Metro Movietone Revue No. 12, with Locust Sisters, Johnny Marvin, Miss Rose Marie Sinnott, George Dewey Washington, Harry Rose, Metro Movietone, December 11 (2) ["If You Don't Love Me"/"I'm Walkin' on Air"/"On the Road to Mandalay"/"Sunshine"/"That's My Mammy"].

Ed and Lou Miller (vocals), Metro Movietone, December 18 (1) ["Auf Wiedersehen"/"High Up on a Hill Top"].

The Music Shop, with Dick Henderson, Vitaphone 3413, December 25 (2) ["Good Night, God Bless"/"Da-Da, Da-Da, Look What Charlie's Doing"].

Red Nichols and His Five Pennies (band), Vitaphone 870, December 25 (1) ["Ida! Sweet as Apple Cider"/"Who Cares?"/"China Boy"].

Georgie Price, Columbia, December 18 (1) ["Station B. U. N. K."].

Georgie Price in *What Price Georgie?*, Metro Movietone, December 25 (1) ["I'm Marching Home to You"/"The One That Loves You"].

Titta Ruffo, Metro Movietone, December 11 (1) ["Adamastor" from *L'Africaine*].

Titta Ruffo, Metro Movietone, December 18 (1) ["Iago's Credo" from *Otello*].

James Stanley (baritone) in *Mandalay*, Pathé, December 11 (1).

Vitaphone Symphony Orchestra, conducted by Herman Heller, Vitaphone 447, December 18 (1) ["Poet and Peasant Overture"].

Frances Williams and Yacht Club Boys in *On the High C's*, Paramount Movietone, December 25 (1) ["Nasty Nancy"/"True Blue"].

1930

JANUARY

After the Show, with Jack Pepper ("comedy, songs, dances"), Pathé–RCA Photophone, January 1 (2).

Mme. Frances Alda (soprano), Vitaphone 943, January 1 (1) ["Ave Maria" from Verdi's *Otello*].

The Biltmore Trio in *College Romeos*, Metro Movietone, January 29 (1) ["On the Old Ohio"].

Cow Camp Ballads (comedy, songs), Paramount, January 15 (1) ["Bu-l-oo-o-d"].

Crosby's Corners ("song, dance, comedy"), Pathé, January 29 (1).

Georges Bizet ("musical novelty"), FitzPatrick Pictures, January 29 (1).

Herschel Henlere ("Madcap Musician" with piano and "one-piece jazz band"), Vitaphone 933 (1) ["Sonny Boy"/"I Lift My Finger and Go Tweet Tweet"].

A Night in a Dormitory, with Ginger Rogers ("who drops two songs in her usual cute personality way"), Thelma White, Si Wills [Morgan Morley], Ruth Hamilton, Thelma White and Eddie Elkins and His Orchestra, Pathé, January 1 (2) ["Dormitory Number"/"I Love a Man in Uniform"/"Song of the Volga Boatmen"/"Stay with It"/"Where the Sweet Forget-Me-Nots Remember"/"Why Can't You Love That Way?"].

The Revelers, Metro Movietone, January 29 (1).

The Song Writers' Revue, with Jack Benny (master of ceremonies), Gus Edwards, Dave Dreyer, Fred E. Ahlert, Roy Turk, Ray Heindorf, Nacio Herb Brown, Arthur Freed, Ray Egan, Fred Fisher and Dave Snell, Metro Movietone, January 8 (2) ["Dardanella," played by Fisher/"The Japanese Sandman," played by Egan/"School Days," played and sung by Edwards/"Me and My Shadow," played by Dreyer/"Mean to Me," played by Ahlert/ "The Wedding of the Painted Doll," played by Brown and sung by Freed].

Douglas Stanbury with the Lyric Quartette in *Pack Up Your Troubles*, Vitaphone 918, January 1 (1) ["Take Me Back to Dear Old Blighty"/"Keep the Home Fires Burning"/"Keep Your Head Down, 'Fritzie Boy'"/"Fuzzy Wuzzy"/"On the Road to Mandalay"].

The Trumpeter ["war novelty" by baritone], Pathé, January 1 (1).

United States Indian Band in *Moonbeam's Bride*, Paramount, January 1 (1) ["Pale Moon"].

The Voice of Hollywood (radio revue), with Reginald Denny (master of ceremonies), Julian Eltinge, Paul Whiteman, Anita Page, Julia Faye and Bobby Vernon, Tiffany, January 15 (1).

FEBRUARY

Mme. Frances Alda, Vitaphone 805, February 12 (1) ["The Last Rose of Summer," from *Martha*/ "Birth of Morn"].

Buck and Bubbles in *Darktown Follies*, Pathé, February 19 (2).

Eddie Cantor in *Getting a Ticket*, Paramount, February 5 (1) ["My Wife Is on a Diet"].

Georges Carpentier (boxer-singer-dancer) in *Naughty, but Nice*, Vitaphone 3761, February 26 (1) ["I Love to Walk, She Loves to Walk"].

Guido Ciccolini (tenor) and Eric Zardo (pianist), Vitaphone 876, February 19 (1) ["Elegie"/ Rachmaninoff's "Prelude in C Sharp Minor"/ "Serenade"].

Clark and Bergman (comedy, songs) in *Do It Now*, Columbia, February 26 (1).

The Cossack's Bride ("romantic sketch"), Tiffany, February 19 (1).*

Evolution of Dance ("revuette") with Lupino Lane, Vitaphone 3895-96 (1).

Alice Gentle (soprano), Vitaphone 3336, February 19 (1) ["Habanera" from *Carmen*].*

Horace Heidt and His Californians, Vitaphone 908, February 12 (1) ["I'm Ka-razy for You"/ "Rose of the Rio Grande"/"Old Man River"/ "Sleep"].

Low Down (revue; "A Bird's Eye View of Harlem"), with Monette Moore, Gertie Chambers and Mary Barnes, Vitaphone 914, February 26 (1) ["Dynamite"/"Weary River"/"Georgia"/ "That Thing Called Love"/"San."

Joseph Regan, Metro Movietone, February 12 (1).

Herman Timberg (comedy, dance) in *I Came First*, Paramount, February 26 (1).

Wanderlust ("scenic with songs"), Paramount, February 5 (1).

MARCH

Bobbe Arnst and Peggy Ellis (songs and piano), Vitaphone 913, March 5 (1) ["The Album of

My Dreams"/"The Doll Dance"/"There Was Nothing Else to Do"].

Busy Fingers, with Leon Navarra, Columbia, March 5 (1).

The Dresden Doll (song "novelty"), Paramount, March 26 (1).

Ruth Etting in *Broadway's Like That,* with Humphrey Bogart (his first film appearance), Mary Philips (Bogart's wife at the time) and Joan Blondell, Vitaphone 960, March 5 (1) ["The Right Kind of Man"/"From the Bottom of My Heart"] .

The Fair Deceiver ("song comedy"), Radio, March 26 (1).

50 Miles from Broadway, with Harry B. Watson, Pathé, March 12 (2).

Fisher and Hurst (comedy, songs) in *Apartment Hunting,* Vitaphone 920, March 5 (1) ["You Want Lovin' and I Want Love"/"All I Need Is You"].

Mountain Melodies ("musical scenic"), Paramount, March 19 (1).

Molly Picon (songs), Vitaphone 917, March 5 (1).

16 Sweeties (revue), with Eddie Elkins Orchestra and Thelma White, Pathé, March 12 (2).

Al Trahan with Lady Yukona Cameron in *The Musicale* ("comedy pianolog"), Vitaphone 936, March 19 (1).

APRIL

Ben Bernie and His Orchestra, Vitaphone 958, April 9 (1) ["Sweeter Than Sweet"/"Have a Little Faith in Me"/"Hello Baby"/"Lady Luck"].

[Guiseppe] Creatore and His Band, Tiffany, April 16 (1).

A Day of a Man of Affairs, with Maurice Holland, Ginger Rogers ("showing plenty … as the night club girl") and Mell Ray, Columbia, April 16 (1).

Duci de Kerekjarto (violinist), Metro Movietone, April 9 (1).

Eventually but Not Now, with Alberta Vaughn, Kit Guard and others, Radio, April 16 (2).

Footnotes (dance novelty), with Oscar Grogan (vocals) and Polly and Peggy Paige, Vitaphone 985, April 2 (1) ["Only the Girl"/"Hello Baby"].

Fowler's Studio Varieties (singing, dancing), with Mlle. Jazzelle, Four Harmony Boys and Charlie Wellman with band, Ted Toddy, April 9 (1).

Glorious Vamps (song and dance novelty), United Artists, April 2 (1).

Hello Baby (revue), with Ann Pennington, Norman Selby, James Clemmons, Phyllis Crane, Adrienne Dore and the Larry Ceballos Boys and Girls, Vitaphone 3641-42, April 30 (2) ["Hello Baby"/"Believe Me"/"I Gotta Have You"/"Dance of the Wooden Shoes"/"Huddlin'"].*

A Holiday in Storyland, with the Vitaphone Kiddies, Vitaphone 3824, April 2 (1) ["When the Butterflies Kiss the Buttercups Goodnight," performed by Gumm Sisters as a trio/"Blue Butterfly," performed by 7-year-old Frances "Baby" Gumm, the future Judy Garland/"Storyland Holiday"/"And Still They Fall in Love"/"Go to Bed"].*

Kiddie Kabaret, with Ethel Meglin's Famous Hollywood Wonder Kiddies, Mayfair, April 16 (2).

Fay Marbe (vocalist) in *A Continental Evening,* Columbia, April 23 (1) ["What Do We Do on a Dew-Dew-Dewy Day?"].

Giovanni Martinelli, with Yvonne Cecile Benson (soprano) and Louis D'Angelo, Vitaphone 974, April 2 (1) ["Prison Scene" from *Faust*].

Giovanni Martinelli, Vitaphone 953, April 30 (1) ["Celeste Aida"].

The Ormond Sisters in *Toys* (singing, dancing), Paramount, April 9 (1).

Spanish Fiesta, with Roberto Guzman (tenor), Vitaphone 3279, April 2 (1) ["La Paloma"/"Te Quiere"].*

Spike Speaks, with Frank Moulan (comedy, songs), Columbia, April 16 (1) ["Under the Wiaduct"].

Buddy Traps (Buddy Rich, as a teen-age trick drummer), Vitaphone 949, April 30 (1) ["That Wonderful Boy Friend of Mine"/"Am I Blue?"/"If You Were Mine"/"Bashful Baby"/"Stars and Stripes Forever"].

The Voice of Hollywood (radio revue), with Bert Wheeler (master of ceremonies), Ken Maynard, Marceline Day, Wesley Barry and Marjorie "Babe" Kane, Tiffany, April 16 (1) ["Must Be Love"].

Yamekrow, with Louise Cook and Margaret Sims, Vitaphone 1009, April 30 (1).

Ye Heart Shoppe, with Kathryn Reece and Jerry Norris, Columbia, April 23 (1).*

MAY

The Cave Club, with Marjorie Leach, Frank Tinney, Ted Lewis, Harriette Harbaugh and ("for a capital comedy number, 'Sockety-Sock'") Ethel Merman, Vitaphone 999, May 14 (1).

Chinatown Fantasy (song and dance revue), Paramount, May 21 (1) ["What's the Use of Dreaming?"].

Felix Ferdinando Orchestra, William H. Bristol/Educational, May 21 (1).

Hawaiian Romance, with Holous Hawaiians, Columbia, May 28 (1).

Holland (songs, dance), Vitaphone 3897, May 28 (1) ["In Sweet Tulip Time"].*

Waite Hoyt ("The Boy Wonder of Baseball") and J. Fred Coots (composer-pianist) in *A Battery of Songs,* with Mae Questel (future voice of Betty

Boop), Vitaphone 972, May 14 (1) ["Back in Your Own Back Yard"/"I'm Only Making Believe"/"Do Something"].

The Jazz Rehearsal ("a Hollywood talking picture stage during the rehearsal of a singing and dancing film"), Vitaphone 3760, May 7 (1) ["Loose Ankles"/"That's the Low Down on the Low Down"/"Wouldn't It Be Wonderful?"/"He's a Good Man to Have Around"].*

The Military Post, with Roberto Guzman, Vitaphone 3278, May 7 (1) ["La Golondrina"/"La Luz de la Luna"].*

Office Steps, with Harry McNaughton, Jack Thompson, Reed and Duthers, Gertrude McDonald and The Phelps Twins, Vitaphone 1002, May 28 (1) ["Office Steps"/"Painting the Clouds with Sunshine"/"Singin' in the Bathtub"/"Miss Wonderful"].

Princess Lady Bug, with Kathryn Reece, Columbia, May 7 (1).*

Ranch House Blues, with Don Douglas and Mildred Harris, Pathé, May 14 (2).

Red Heads, with Nat Carr, Charles Kaley and Joan Gaylord, Pathé, May 7 (2).

Songs of Mother, with Francis Luther and Elizabeth Lennox, Pathé, May 14 (1).

The South Sea Pearl, with Gaston Glass, Vitaphone 3829, May 7 (1).*

The Voice of Hollywood (radio revue), with Johnny Mack Brown (master of ceremonies), Jack Duffy, Lillian Rich, Dorothy Gulliver, George Lewis, the Duncan Sisters, Mack Sennett, Antonio Moreno, and Mr. and Mrs. Calvin Coolidge, Tiffany, May 21 (1).

Voice of the Sea ("song sketch"), Pathé, May 28 (1) ["When the Bells in the Lighthouse Ring"].

The Wedding of Jack and Jill, with the Vitaphone Kiddies, Vitaphone 3826, May 7 (1) ["Hang on to the Rainbow," performed by Frances "Baby" Gumm (Judy Garland) of the Gumm Sisters/"The Wedding of Jack and Jill"/"Bad Babies"/"Allana"].

The Window Cleaners, with Neely Edwards and Lew Brice (comedy, songs), Vitaphone 3668, May 7 (1).

JUNE

Chills and Fever, with Al Shean, Mary Clark and Evalyn Knapp, Pathé, June 25 (2).

Contrary Mary, with Bobby Watson and B.B.B., Vitaphone 3753, June 4 (1) ["My Mary Dear"/"That's How Much I Need You"/"Dream Boat"].*

The Devil's Parade, with Sidney Toler, Joan Blondell, Gerald Oliver Smith, Harry Clarke, Blanche Bow, Jessie Busley, Eddie Green and the "Fifty Million Frenchmen" Chorus, Vita-

phone 992, June 11 (1) ["Harlem's Hotter Than Hades"/"He's Such an Adorable Liar"].

Felix Ferdinando Orchestra, Spizzi, June 11 (1).

Japanese Bowl, Vitaphone 3899, June 11 (1).*

Jazz Preferred, with Zelaya (pianist) and band, Paramount, June 11 (1).

Kandy Kabaret, with students of the Merrial School of Dancing, Paramount, June 25 (2).

Billy Lytell and Tom Fant in *Two of a Kind,* Vitaphone 945, June 4 (1) ["Snap Steps"/"Kansas City Kitty"/"Crazy Words, Crazy Tune"/"Mine All Mine"].

The Stage Door Pest, with Boyce Coombs, Columbia, June 25 (1).

The Voice of Hollywood (radio revue), with Lloyd Hamilton (master of ceremonies), Ernest Hilliard, Walter Hiers, Leatrice Joy, Dorothy Burgess, Donald Kerr, Carlotta King and Ruth Hiatt, Tiffany, June 4 (1) ["The Song of Siberia"].

What a Life (prison comedy with music), Vitaphone 3849, June 11 (1) ["Chicago Rhythm"/"Carrissima"/"Hello Baby"].

JULY

The Artist's Reverie, Paramount, July 23 (1).

Audio Review No. 20 (novelty, music), Pathé, July 2 (1) ["Anchors Aweigh"/"Frogs"/ "Havana"].

Don Azpiazu and His Havana Casino Orchestra, Paramount, July 30 (1).

Eddie Buzzell in *The Royal Fourflusher,* Vitaphone 975-6, July 2 (1) ["Here We Are"/"My Senorita"].

Desert Thrills, with Edwin Bartlett, Vitaphone 989, July 23 (1) ["Don Juan's Serenade"/"Memories of France"/"All on Account of You"/"Le Temple d'Isis"].

Hello Sunshine, with Ethel Meglin's Famous Hollywood Wonder Kids, Capital, July 30 (2).

Humanettes (novelty revue) with Benny Rubin, Radio, July 30 (1) ["Baby Buggy Blues"].

Hungarian Rhapsodie (musical drama), United Artists, July 16 (1).

Jim McWilliams in *Grand Uproar* (pianolog), Vitaphone 1000, July 16 (1) ["Toreador Song"/"In the Lauterbach I Lost My Stocking"/"Ach Du Liebe Augustin"/"The Farmer in the Dell"/"Hail, Hail, the Gang's All Here"].

Manhattan Serenade, with Raymond Hackett, Mary Doran, The Brox Sisters and others, Metro Colortone Revue, July 9 (2) ["Manhattan Serenade"].*

Lee Morse (vocalist), Paramount, July 30 (1).

Ann Seymour (comedy, songs) in *Song Paintings,* Vitaphone 1011, July 16 (1) ["My First Rendezvous"/"The Best of Them Are None Too Good"].

The Sultan's Jester, with Edward Lankow (bass) and Joyzelle (dancer), Vitaphone 3850, July 23 (1) ["Persian Rug"/"Here's to the Sultan"].*

The Voice of Hollywood (radio revue), with Ruth Roland (master of ceremonies), George E. Stone, Charles King, Davey Lee, Estelle Taylor, Charles Irwin and Jack Benny, Tiffany, July 9 (1).

AUGUST

Betty Compton in *The Legacy*, with John Hundley and Jack White, Vitaphone 4270-71, August 27 (2) ["When We Are Millionaires"/"When Little Red Roses Get the Blues for You"/"Stairway to Happiness"/"That Thing"].

Old Seidelburg (operetta), with Elsa Peterson, Orville Rennie, Gus Reed and Janet Gilmore, Vitaphone 4169, August 27 (1) ["Here Is My Heart"/"Drinking Song"].

Road Knights, with Georges Railly and Eddie Davis, Vitaphone 4122, August 13 (1).

School Daze, with Jack White, Vitaphone (number not shown), August 27 (1).

Tre-Ki (flutist), Paramount, August 20 (1).

Two Plus Fours, with Nat Carr, Thelma Hill and The Rhythm Boys (Bing Crosby, Harry Barris, Al Rinker), Pathé, August 20 (1).

SEPTEMBER

Lionel "Mike" Ames (female impersonator) in *The Varsity Vamp*, Vitaphone 977, September 10 (1) ["Lena"/"I Don't Want Nobody but You"].

Conchita (vocalist), International Photoplay, September 17 (1).

[Guiseppe] Creatore and His Band in *Fire Worshippers*, Tiffany, September 24 (1).

[Charles] Derickson (tenor) and [Burton] Brown (pianist) in *A Song Drama*, Vitaphone 912, September 17 (1) ["The Song of Siberia"/"She's Funny That Way"].

Ruth Etting in *Roseland*, with Donn Cook, Vitaphone 1041-42, September 17 (1) ["Let Me Sing and I'm Happy"/"Dancing with Tears in My Eyes"].

Gates of Happiness, with Arthur Pat West (master of ceremonies), Norman Spencer Singers, 20th Century Steppers and The Murray Sisters, Vitaphone 4149, September 24 (1) ["Stairway to Happiness"/"Get Busy and Save Your Soul"].

Johannes Brahms ("Music Master" series), Fitzpatrick, September 17 (1).

Pirates, with Benny Rubin, Connor Sisters and Jack Randall and Co., Metro Colortone Revue, September 3 (2) ["Love Pirates"].*

Eva Puck and Sammy White in *Sing, You Dancers*, Paramount, September 10 (1).

OCTOBER

Dogway Melody (novelty with dogs), Metro Movietone, October 29 (1) ["Singin' in the Rain"].

Fashion's Mirror (revue), with Jack Thompson, Barbara Newberry and the "Fifty Million Frenchmen" Chorus, Vitaphone 1045, October 15 (1) ["You Can Tell a Lady by the Way She Wears Her Clothes"/"My Man Was on the Make, but He Wasn't on the Make for Me"/"My Organdie Gown"].

The Flower Garden, with Cliff Edwards, The Locust Sisters, Lottice Howell and others, Metro Colortone Revue, October 15 (2).*

A Night at the Shooting Gallery, with the Albertina Rasch Ballet, Metro Colortone Revue, October 1 (1).*

Shakespeare Was Right ("musical playlet"), Vitaphone 3989, October 1 (1) ["If I Can't Have You"/"Help Yourself to My Love"/"Brand New Rhythm"].*

Douglas Stanbury in *The Wanderer*, Vitaphone 1050, October 8 (1) ["A Cottage for Sale"/"Just a Wanderer"].

Tapping Toes, company not listed, October 29 (2).

Varsity Show (football musical comedy), Vitaphone 1032-33, October 29 (1).

The Yacht Club Boys in *A Private Engagement*, Vitaphone 1043, October 8 (1).

NOVEMBER

All for Mabel, with Sally Starr, Pathé, November 26 (2).

Armida in *While the Captain Waits*, Paramount, November 5 (1).

Clock Shop, with Cliff Edwards, Jackie Heller and Betty and Ramon, Metro Colortone Revue, November 12 (2).*

College Capers, with Baron and Janet Gilmore, Parvis and Crowell, and Ken and DeBard Brothers, Vitaphone 2124, November 5 (1).*

Hall Johnson Choir in *A Syncopated Sermon*, Vitaphone 1080, November 12 (1).

Romeo and Juliet (death scene from the opera), with Charles Hackett (tenor) and Rosa Low (soprano), Vitaphone 1143, November 5 (1).

DECEMBER

Ruth Etting in *One Good Turn—*, with Jay Velie, Vitaphone 1122-23, December 10 (1) ["If I Could Be with You"/"The Kiss Waltz"].

A Hollywood Theme Song, with Harry Gribbon and Yola D'Avril, Mack Sennett, December 3 (2).

Johnny Perkins in *Lady, You Slay Me*, Paramount, December 3 (1).

Douglas Stanbury in *Alpine Echoes*, Vitaphone

1087, December 10 (1) ["Across the River"/"There's a Sunny Smile Waiting for Me"].

1931

JANUARY

Father's Advice, with Will King, Lester Cole, B.B.B. [Bobby Bernan] and Earl Burtnett Orchestra, Franklyn Warner, January 7 (2).

Marion Harris in *Two's Company,* Paramount, January 7 (1) ["I'm Yours"/"If I Could Be with You"].

Handel ("sketch with music"), with Nat Shilkret Orchestra, Educational, January 28 (2).

Penthouse Blues, with [Muriel] D'Or and Hoyt, Paramount, January 14 (1).

Ginger Rogers in *Office Blues,* with Clayborne Bryson and E. R. Rogers, Paramount, January 21 (1) ["Dear Miss"/"Dear Sir"/"We Can't Get Along"].

Service Stripes, with Joe Penner "and Co.," Vitaphone 1124, January 14 (1).

FEBRUARY

Around the Samovar ("commercial"/"music novelty"), Paramount, February 18 (1).

The Happiness Melody, with Ted Lewis and His Band, Paramount, February 11 (1).

George Jessel and His Russian Art Choir, Vitaphone 1176, February 25 (1) ["Nightingale"/"Cossack Farewell Song"/"Down by the Neva River"/"Schilnichky"/"All God's Children Got Shoes"].

Let's Stay Single, with Frances Williams, Paramount, February 4 (1) ["I Can't Make a Man"/"Wait Till the Summer's Over"].

Pathé Audio Review, Pathé, February 25 (1) ["Sunrise and You"].*

Henry Santrey and His Soldiers of Fortune (band), Vitaphone 1128, February 25 (1).

MARCH

Angel Cake, with the Albertina Rasch Girls, Cy Landry, Jimmy Ray, The Foursome and The Paige Sisters, Vitaphone 1179-80, March 4 (2) ["Here Comes the Sun"/"Baby's Birthday Party"/"I've Got a Feeling I'm Falling"/"Walking My Baby Home"/"The Glad Girl"/"Soul"/"Black Maria"/"Angel Cake"/"Barcarolle"].

The Brittons [Frank and Milt] (comedy band) in *Hitting the High C's,* Vitaphone 1196, March 25 (1) ["O.K., Baby!"/"So Beats My Heart for You"/"Bye Bye Blues"/"Anchors Aweigh"/"When You're Smiling"/"Danse Macabre"/"How Dry I Am"/"Danse Trivani"].

Eddie Buzzell in *The Devil's Cabaret,* with Albertina Rasch Girls [in ballet excerpt from unreleased MGM revue *The March of Time*], Metro Colortone Revue, March 11 (2).*

The French Line, with Gina Malo, Paramount, March 11 (1).

Dolly Gilbert in *With Pleasure,* with Billy Wayne, The Collette Sisters, The Corbett Sisters and The Pearl Twins, Vitaphone 1155-56, March 11 (2).

Sky High, with Janet Reade, Dudley Clements, Larry Adler and The Lovey Twins, Vitaphone 1200, March 25 (1) ["Puttin' It on for Baby"/"I'm One of God's Children"/"St. Louis Blues"/"I've Got a Feeling I'm Fallin'"/"Hungarian Rhapsody No. 2"/"Black Maria"/"Cheerful Little Earful"/"You're Driving Me Crazy"].

Verdi ("sketch with music"), James J. FitzPatrick, March 4 (1) [excerpt from *Aida*].

APRIL

The Beauties, Pathé, April 1 (2).

Crazy House, with Benny Rubin, Vernon Dent, Polly Moran and Karl Dane, Metro Colortone Revue, April 15 (2).*

Ruth Etting in *Freshman Love,* with Jeanie Lang, Don Tomkins and Max Hoffman, Jr., Vitaphone 1204-05, April 15 (2) ["She's Funny That Way"/"Love Is Like That"].

Humanettes ("musical novelty"), with Charles Judels, The Rhythm Boys [with Bing Crosby?] and Gus Arnheim and His Orchestra, Radio, April 29 (1) ["another of the series built on the Bert Levy creation of life size human heads over the bodies of Punch and Judy dolls"].

June MacCloy in *Laugh It Off,* Paramount, April 29 (2).

Giovanni Martinelli, Vitaphone 1213, April 15 (1) ["Come Back to Sorrento"/"Nina"].

Walter O'Keefe in *Night Club Revels,* with The Collette Sisters and Muriel Abbott Dancers, Vitaphone 1193 (1) ["I Love Love"/"Doin' the Sigma Chi"/"When You Were the Blossom"/"He Is Not Worth Your Tears"/"I'm Alone Because I Love You"].

MAY

Giovanni Martinelli in *The Troubador,* with Fowler and Tamara (dance team), Vitaphone 1226, May 6 (1) ["Estrellita"/"Pavo real"].

JUNE

Franz Liszt ("Music Master" series), Paramount, June 2 (1) ["Hungarian Rhapsody No. 2"].

Helen Morgan in *The Gigolo Racket,* with Joseph

Striker and Reed Brown, Jr., Vitaphone 1255-6, June 16 (2) ["I Know He's Mine"/"Nobody Breaks My Heart"].

Just a Gigolo ("organ novelty"), Vitaphone 4817, June 2 (1).

Eddie Miller in *Fair and Square Ways*, Paramount, June 16 (1) ["Sing You Sinners"].

Dr. Sigmund Spaeth ("The Tune Detective" in "skit with music"), Paramount, June 2 (1).

JULY

Don Azpiazu and His Havana Casino Orchestra, Paramount, July 7 (1).

Little Prayer for Me ("organlog"), Vitaphone (no number listed), July 28 (1).

AUGUST

Joe Penner in *Gangway*, with Polly Walters, Vitaphone 1198-9, August 11 (2) ["And Then Came the War"].

SEPTEMBER

Big House Party ("band novelty"), Vitaphone 1268, September 22 (1).

Jack Hazzard in *Playing with Fire*, with Bob DuPont and Mason & Sands, Vitaphone 1188, September 1 (1) ["mock ballad"/"Cheerful Little Earful"/"Oh for the Life of a Fireman"/"The Kiss Waltz"/"Senora Waltz"/"Anitra's Dance"/"Morgenstimmung"/"Spring Song"].

Helen Kane in *A Lesson in Love*, Paramount, September 1 (1).

When Your Lover Has Gone ("organlog"), with Harry Q. Mills and Dorothy Vogel, Vitaphone 4648, September 15 (1).

OCTOBER

Ruth Etting in *Old Lace*, Vitaphone 1238-9, October 27 (2) ["Let Me Call You Sweetheart"/"Pretty Baby"/"In the Good Old Summertime"/"Kommt ein Vogel"/"A Bird in a Gilded Cage"].

Havana Cocktail ("orchestra novelty"), with The Cordoba Sisters, Vitaphone 1279, October 6 (1).

Giovanni Martinelli in *Gypsy Caravan*, Vitaphone 1245, October 27 (1) ["The Life of a Gypsy"/"Otchichornya"/"The Old Gypsy"/"The Only Girl"].

Musical Mystery, with Albertina Rasch Girls, Vitaphone 6305, October 27 (2).

No More Hookey ("schoolroom musical"), with children from Merriel Abbott School, Paramount, October 13 (1).

NOVEMBER

Ruth Etting in *Words and Music*, Vitaphone 1288-89, November 10 (2) ["I'm Falling in Love"/"Now That You're Gone"].

I Surrender Dear, with Bing Crosby, Sennett/Paramount, November 10 (2) ["I Surrender Dear"].

Jazz Reporters, with Charles Davis and Band, Paramount, November 24 (1).

Puff Your Blues Away, with Lillian Roth, Paramount, November 24 (1).

DECEMBER

Bing Crosby in *Just One More Chance*, Sennett/Paramount, December 22 (2) ["Just One More Chance"].

Footlights, with Barbara Newberry, Russ Brown, Sisters "G", Dorothea Jones and Albertina Rasch Girls, Vitaphone 1299-1300, December 29 (2).

Horace Heidt and His Orchestra, Vitaphone 1308, December 1 (1).

Hal LeRoy in *High School Hoofer*, with Eleanor King, Vitaphone 1312, December 8 (1).

Out West Where the North Begins ("musical poem"), Picture Classics, December 29 (1).

The Tamale Vendor, with Tom Patricola and Charles Judels, Educational, December 8 (2).

Rudy Wiedoeft (saxophonist) in *Darn Tootin'*, with Dixie Lee and Lucille Page, Vitaphone 1293, December 8 (1).

1932

JANUARY

Close Harmony, with the Boswell Sisters, Paramount, January 12 (1).

The Voice of Hollywood (radio revue), with Leon Janney and Helen Chandler, Tiffany, January 5 (1).

George Dewey Washington in *Rhythm of the River*, Paramount, January 26 (1).

FEBRUARY

Bing Crosby in *Dream House*, Sennett/Educational, February 16 (2) ["Dream House"].

Hello Good Times, with Major, Sharp and Minor and Albertina Rasch Girls, Vitaphone (number not listed), February 2 (2).

MARCH

Henry Santrey and His Soldiers of Fortune in *Spreading Sunshine*, Vitaphone 1367, March 29 (1).

Sea Legs, Vitaphone 1355-56, March 29 (2).

Subway Symphony (revue), with Charles Benning-ton Harmonica Band, Frances Langford, Joan Abbott, Frank Hazzard, Dave Gould Dancers and Five Rhythm Boys, Vitaphone 6309, March 8 (2).

$10 or 10 Days, with Eddie Younger's Moun-taineers, Paramount, March 8 (1).

The Voice of Hollywood (radio revue), with Franklin Pangborn and Anita Louise (in a harp solo), Tiffany, March 15 (1).

APRIL

Beyond the Blue Horizon, with Vincent Lopez Or-chestra, Paramount, April 26 (1) ["Beyond the Blue Horizon"].

Niagara Falls, with June MacCloy, Marion Shilling, Gertrude Short and Eddie Nugent, Radio, April 12 (2).

A Trip Through the Old Family Album, Supercolor Picture, April 5 (1).*

MAY

Ruth Etting in *A 'Mail' Bride,* Vitaphone 6303, May 24 (1) ["Auf Wiedersehen"/"Penthouse Serenade"/"Talk It Over"].

Vincent Lopez Orchestra, Paramount, May 10 (1).

Nina Mae McKinney in *Pie, Pie Blackbird,* Vita-phone 1391, May 31 (2) ["I Belong to You"].

JUNE

Knowmore College, with Rudy Vallee, Paramount, June 28 (1) ["You Can Find a Rhyme for Every-thing but Orange"].

Ethel Merman in *Ireno,* Paramount, June 7 (1).

Arthur Tracy ("The Street Singer"), with Norman Brokenshire, Radio, June 14 (1).

What an Idea, with Harriet Hilliard [the future Harriet Nelson], Armand Cortes, Danny Dare Girls, Lucille Page, Three Harmony Misses, and Karry, Mooney and Noyes, Vitaphone 1395, June 14 (2) ["Dracula, Frankenstein and Hyde"].

JULY

C'est Paree, Vitaphone 1415-16, July 26 (2).

Ruth Etting in *Artistic Temper,* Vitaphone 1403-04, July 19 (2).

Rambling 'Round Radio Row, with Jerry Wald (host), The Boswell Sisters, Kate Smith, Colonel Stoopnagle and Budd, and Abe Lyman and His Band, Vitaphone 1408, July 26 (1).

Lillian Roth in *Puff Your Blues Away,* Paramount, July 12 (1) ["Puff Your Blues Away"].

Switzerland, with Lester Allen, Paramount, July 19 (1).

AUGUST

Coffee and Love, with Jesse Crawford and Charles Carlile ("organlog"), Master Art, August 16 (1).

Hollywood on Parade (revue), with Stuart Erwin (master of ceremonies), Bing Crosby, Gary Cooper, [George] Burns and [Gracie] Allen, and [Ole] Olsen and [Chic] Johnson, August 2 (1).

I Love a Parade, with Harry Richman, Stanley Distributing Corp., August 2 (1) ["I Love a Pa-rade"].

Old Songs for New ("songlog"), with the Georgie Stoll Orchestra, Paramount, August 9 (1).*

Tee for Two, with Franklin Pangborn, Esther Howard, Helen Lynd, Marjorie "Babe" Kane and Dave Morris, Vitaphone 1417-18, August 30 (2).

SEPTEMBER

Campus Spirit, with Douglas Stanbury and New York University Glee Club, Vitaphone 1350, September 6 (1) ["I Love a Parade"].

The Musical Doctor, with Rudy Vallee and Mae Questel, Paramount, September 20 (1) ["Keep a Little Song Handy"].

OCTOBER

Northern Exposure, with John Sheehan, Snub Pol-lard, Sheila Terry, Gogo DeLys, Sally Sweet and Tut Mace, Vitaphone 1413-14, October 18 (2).

Roger Wolfe Kahn and His Orchestra in *The Yacht Party,* with Gertrude Niesen and Melissa Mason, Vitaphone 1457, October 18 (1).

Rambling 'Round Radio Row, with Jay C. Flippen (master of ceremonies), the Four Lombardo Brothers [Guy, Victor, Liebert, Carmen], Aunt Jemima [Tess Gardella], William Hall, Baby Rose Marie, Johnny Marvin and the Lester Lanin Orchestra, Vitaphone 6911, October 25 (2).

Tip, Tap, Toe, with Hal LeRoy and Mitzi Mayfair, Vitaphone (number not listed), October 25 (1).

NOVEMBER

The Lease Breakers, with Aunt Jemima [Tess Gardella], Vitaphone 1468, November 8 (1).

Smash Your Baggage, with "colored talent," Vita-phone 1387, November 15 (1).

DECEMBER

"America's Greatest Composer" series, starring Morton Downey and featuring the music of Lew Brown and Ray Henderson, with Stepin Fetchit and Nick Kenny, Universal, December 13 (2).

Melody Makers, with Sammy Fain, Evelyn Hoey, The Eton Boys and Norman Brokenshire, Master Art, December 6 (1).

NOTES

CHAPTER 1

1. Max Wilk, *The Wit and Wisdom of Hollywood* (New York: Atheneum, 1971), p. 3.
2. Miles Kreuger, *The Movie Musical from Vitaphone to 42nd Street, as Reported in a Great Fan Magazine* (New York: Dover, 1975), ix.
3. *Ibid.*
4. *Moving Picture World*, January 16, 1909.
5. Miles Kreuger, "The Birth of the American Film Musical," *High Fidelity* magazine, July 1972, p. 43.
6. Jack L. Warner and Dean Jennings, *My First Hundred Years in Hollywood* (New York: Random House, 1964), p. 168.
7. *Photoplay*, August 1926.
8. *The New York Times*, August 7, 1926.
9. *Ibid.*, October 8, 1926. The one-reel *Al Jolson in a Plantation Act* short was thought to be lost until recently, when a silent version was discovered in a mislabeled film can at the Library of Congress. It had been identified as the trailer to *The Jazz Singer*. Then, some time later, the accompanying sound disc was located by the Vitaphone Project, a society of dedicated early-talkie preservationists. Full restoration by the UCLA Film and Television Archive followed, and the short was to be re-premiered at the 1995 UCLA Festival of Preservation with the rest of the original second Vitaphone program and *The Better 'Ole.*
10. *Variety*, June 29, 1927.
11. Bob Thomas, *Clown Prince of Hollywood: The Antic Life and Times of Jack L. Warner* (New York: McGraw-Hill, 1990), p. 59.
12. Walter Wagner, *You Must Remember This* (New York: Putnam, 1975), pp. 89–90.
13. Robert L. Carringer, ed., *The Jazz Singer* (Madison: University of Wisconsin Press, 1979), pp. 18–19.
14. *Ibid.*, pp. 11–12.
15. Harry M. Geduld, *The Birth of the Talkies* (Bloomington: Indiana University Press, 1975), p. 145.
16. *Variety*, October 12, 1927.
17. Carringer, *The Jazz Singer*, pp. 27–28. Carringer cited a feature article written on the film by Edwin Schallert for *Motion Picture News*. The article of July 8, 1927, is reprinted in its entirety in Carringer's book.
18. The theater sequences for *The Singing Fool* were, according to the film's pressbook, filmed at the new, $3 million Warners Theatre in Hollywood. Shooting had to be done on the night shift, so as not to interrupt the facility's busy screening schedule.
19. Merson, an English music-hall comedian, brought suit because he believed he, and not the publisher of "The Spaniard That Blighted My Life," was entitled to the rights to the song because its publishing (in 1910) preceded the 1911 English Copyright Law. Warner Bros. won the case on appeal, but the music was never restored to *The Singing Fool.*
20. *Motion Picture*, December 1928.
21. *Judge*, October 20, 1928.
22. *Harrison's Reports*, October 25, 1928.
23. Geduld, *Birth of the Talkies*, p. 195.

CHAPTER 2

1. *The New York Times*, November 16, 1928.
2. William Bakewell interview with author, July 27, 1992.
3. John Kobal, *People Will Talk* (New York: Knopf, 1986), p. 116.
4. Anita Page interview with author, February 19, 1993.
5. *Variety*, January 2, 1929.
6. *The New York Times*, May 12, 1929.
7. *Variety*, July 25, 1928.
8. *Motion Picture*, September 1929.
9. *Photoplay*, September 1929.
10. *Variety*, December 26, 1928.
11. Herbert G. Goldman, *Fanny Brice: The Original Funny Girl* (New York: Oxford University Press, 1992), p. 139.
12. Norman Katkov, *The Fabulous Fanny: The Story of Fanny Brice* (New York: Knopf, 1952), pp. 207–208.
13. Charles Higham, *Merchant of Dreams: Louis B. Mayer, MGM, and the Secret Hollywood* (New York: Donald I. Fine, 1993), pp. 140–141.
14. Samuel Marx, *Mayer and Thalberg: The Make-Believe Saints* (New York: Random House, 1975), p. 111.
15. *The New York Times*, February 9, 1929.
16. *Variety*, December 12, 1928.
17. Anita Page interview.
18. John Kobal, *Gotta Sing Gotta Dance: A Pictorial History of Film Musicals* (London: Hamlyn, 1971), pp. 38–39.
19. Anita Page interview.
20. *Ibid.*
21. *Ibid.*
22. *Photoplay*, April 1929.
23. *Variety*, February 13, 1929.
24. Anita Page interview.
25. "You Were Meant for Me" is said to have been dedicated to Anita Page by Nacio Herb Brown. The two were married briefly in 1934. Page told the author that she didn't recall that it was written with her in mind, but it became closely identified with her, as well as with Charles King. In 1992, Anita Page was honored for her work in *The Broadway Melody* by the Southern California Motion Picture Council.
26. Anita Page interview.
27. Gary Carey, *All the Stars in Heaven: Louis B. Mayer's MGM* (New York: Dutton, 1981), p. 129.
28. Anita Page interview.
29. *Variety*, February 13, 1929.

CHAPTER 3

1. *Variety*, January 2, 1929.
2. Tom Shales et al., *The American Film Heritage: Impressions from the American Film Institute Archives* (Washington, D. C.: Acropolis, 1972), p. 151.
3. Some of the information in this entry is taken from the notes prepared by Eric Aijala for the screening of the restored *Lucky Boy* at the UCLA Film and Television Archives Festival of Preservation on April 12, 1994. The 86-minute print was restored by UCLA from two tinted nitrate prints, in cooperation with the National Film and Television (New Zealand) and the New Zealand Film Archive.
4. *Variety*, November 14, 1928.
5. *Time*, March 11, 1929.
6. *Variety*, January 9, 1929.
7. *Ibid.*, March 20, 1929.
8. *The New York Times*, March 18, 1929.
9. The characters played by Oakie, Gallagher and Harry Green in *Close Harmony* popped up again, more or less, in the 1933 Paramount Bing Crosby musical *Too Much Harmony*. In the latter film, based

on a story by Joseph L. Mankiewicz, Oakie and Gallagher appeared as singing songwriters named Benny Day and Johnny Dixon—their names were Ben Barney and Johnny Bay in *Close Harmony*. Green's stage-producer character, called Max Mindil in the '29 movie, became Max Merlin. Plot similarities also suggest that the '33 musical was a remake of sorts. In *Too Much Harmony*, the male half of a romantic duo (Crosby, cast as a Broadway crooner) helps a female newcomer (Judith Allen) to the top.

10. Dorothy Lee interview with author, March 5, 1993.
11. *The New York Times*, April 8, 1929.
12. *Ibid.*, May 8, 1929.
13. *New York Post*, May 8, 1929.
14. *Variety*, April 24, 1929.
15. Gene Ringgold and DeWitt Bodeen, *Chevalier: The Films and Career of Maurice Chevalier* (Secaucus, N. J.: Citadel, 1973), p. 73.
16. Maurice Chevalier, *The Man in the Straw Hat: My Story* (New York: Crowell, 1949), pp. 197–198.
17. *Ibid.*, p. 198.
18. The print of *Innocents of Paris* viewed by the author at the Library of Congress was missing the first two reels and part of a third.
19. *Variety*, May 1, 1929.
20. *The New York Times*, April 27, 1929.
21. William Bakewell interview with author, July 27, 1992.
22. *The Film Daily*, May 29, 1929.
23. *The New York Times*, May 29, 1929.
24. Bakewell interview.
25. *Variety*, March 6, 1929.
26. Irene Kahn Atkins, interviewer, *David Butler: A Directors Guild of America Oral History* (Metuchen, N. J.: Directors Guild of America and Scarecrow Press, 1993), pp. 65–66.
27. *Los Angeles Times*, 1929, date unknown; quoted in *The Film Daily*, June 11, 1929.
28. Jackie Cooper, *Please Don't Shoot My Dog* (New York: Morrow, 1981), pp. 31–32.
29. *The Film Daily*, May 26, 1929.
30. *The New York Times*, May 28, 1929.
31. *Motion Picture* Classic, August 1929.
32. Sophie Tucker, *Some of These Days* (Garden City, N. Y.: Doubleday, 1945), p. 290.
33. *Ibid.*, pp. 291–292.
34. *Variety*, March 27, 1929.
35. *The Film Daily*, June 30, 1929.
36. *Motion Picture*, August 1929.
37. *Photoplay*, October 1929.
38. Colleen Moore, *Silent Star* (Garden City, N. Y.: Doubleday, 1968), p. 199.
39. *The Film Daily*, July 24, 1929.
40. *Motion Picture*, November 1929.
41. *The New York Times*, August 7, 1929.
42. Gates script, undated (United Artists/Warner Bros. collection, University of Wisconsin–Madison.
43. Oscar Levant, *The Memoirs of an Amnesiac* (New York: Putnam, 1965), p. 83.
44. *New York American*, August 19, 1929.
45. *New York Herald Tribune*, August 19, 1929.
46. *The New York Times*, August 16, 1929.
47. *Photoplay*, November 1929.
48. Anthony Slide, *The Vaudevillians: A Dictionary of Vaudeville Performers* (New York: Arlington House, 1981), p. 96.
49. *Variety*, September 4, 1929.
50. William Bakewell interview with author, October 23, 1992.
51. Joe Kennedy borrowed Vincent Youmans from RKO to write songs for the operetta overhaul of *Queen Kelly*. But the production was shut down after only a few days of filming in December 1929. Gloria Swanson had a good singing voice, and she was called upon to use it in her first three talkies, all released through United Artists. She sang two songs, including Edmund Goulding's "Love, Your Magic Spell Is Everywhere" in *The Trespasser* (October 5, 1929); three Youmans tunes in *What a Widow!* (September 13, 1930); and, after splitting with Kennedy, two De Sylva–Brown–Henderson compositions in *Indiscreet* (May 7, 1931). *The Trespasser* was a critical and commercial success; the others were neither.
52. *The Film Daily*, September 15, 1929.

53. *Ibid.*, November 10, 1929.

54. *Motion Picture*, January 1930.

55. *Variety*, September 10, 1930.

56. *Photoplay*, January 1930.

57. *The Film Daily*, January 5, 1930.

58. *Variety*, January 8, 1930.

59. *Motion Picture Classic*, March 1930.

60. *The New York Times*, January 18, 1930.

61. *New York Mirror*, January 20, 1930.

62. *Photoplay*, September 1929.

63. Mary Eaton came from a show-business family, and not only she was giving Hollywood a go. Her sister Pearl was the resident dance director at RKO. Another sister, Doris, and a brother, Charles, were also then acting in films.

64. Charles Higham, *Ziegfeld* (Chicago: Regnery, 1972), p. 199.

65. Brian Taves, *Robert Florey: The French Expressionist* (Metuchen, N. J.: Scarecrow, 1987), p. 106.

66. The ballet sequence from *Pointed Heels* is missing from many circulating prints, but it has been restored to the print of the film held by UCLA.

67. Fay Wray, *On the Other Hand: A Life Story* (New York: St. Martin's, 1989), p. 104.

68. *Variety*, January 1, 1930.

69. *Ibid.*, January 15, 1930.

CHAPTER 4

1. *Variety*, September 24, 1930.

2. Groucho Marx, *Groucho and Me* (New York: Random House, 1959), pp. 224–225.

3. Joe Adamson, *Groucho, Harpo, Chico, and Sometimes Zeppo* (New York: Simon & Schuster, 1973), p. 86.

4. *The Cocoanuts*, as filmed, must have contained a lot more music; its original preview length was 2 hours, 20 minutes (Adamson, p. 98).

5. *Time*, June 10, 1929.

6. Groucho Marx and Richard J. Anobile, *The Marx Bros. Scrapbook* (New York: Darien House, 1973), p. 116.

7. *The New York Times*, May 25, 1929.

8. *Time*, September 30, 1929.

9. *The Film Daily*, February 9, 1930.

10. "Let's Misbehave" was also in Porter's score for *Paris* until it was dropped during out-of-town tryouts.

11. Michael Marshall, *Top Hat and Tails: The Story of Jack Buchanan* (London: Elm Tree, 1978), p. 95.

12. *Photoplay*, April 1930.

13. Charles Higham, *Ziegfeld* (Chicago: Regnery, 1972), pp. 141–142.

14. Warren G. Harris, *The Other Marilyn: A Biography of Marilyn Miller* (New York: Arbor House, 1985), p. 159.

15. *The New York Times*, December 24, 1929.

16. *The Film Daily*, December 29, 1930.

17. T. Roy Barnes (1880–1937) was a leading man in silent light comedies, but by 1929 his career was fading. By the mid 1930s, he was reduced to bit parts. Barnes is best known to film buffs as the insurance peddler who acosts an insomniac W. C. Fields in *It's a Gift* (1934). He's the chap looking for "LaFong! Carl LaFong! Large 'C,' small 'a,' small 'r,' small 'l,' large 'F,' small 'o,'" and so on.

18. Jack Oakie, *Jack Oakie's Double Takes* (San Francisco: Strawberry Hill, 1980), p. 103.

19. *Ibid.*, p. 104.

20. *Motion Picture*, March 1930.

21. *Variety*, January 22, 1930.

22. Bernice Claire interview with author, June 13, 1993.

23. *Photoplay*, March 1930.

24. *The New York Times*, May 5, 1930.

25. Warner Bros. inter-office communication, January 4, 1930, United Artists/Warner Bros. collection, University of Wisconsin–Madison.

26. *Variety*, March 26, 1930.

27. *Ibid.*, April 2, 1930.

28. *Photoplay*, July 1930.

29. *Film Pictorial*, March 19, 1932.

30. Sam Coslow, *Cocktails for Two: The Many Lives of Giant Songwriter Sam Coslow* (New Rochelle, N. Y.: Arlington House, 1971), p. 107.

31. *The New York Times*, April 26, 1930. The three Technicolor sequences of *The Cuckoos*—the song numbers "Goodbye" and "Dancing the Devil Away" and the finale—were lacking from many prints aired on television over the years. They were restored when the film first aired in 1994 on the Turner Classic Movies cable channel.

32. Dorothy Lee interview with author.

33. *Ibid.*

34. Edward Watz, *Wheeler & Woolsey: The Vaudeville Comic Duo and Their Films, 1929–1937* (Jefferson, N. C.: McFarland, 1994), p. 77.

35. Diane Jacobs, *Christmas in July: The Life and Art of Preston Sturges* (Berkeley: University of California Press, 1992), p. 118.

36. *Photoplay*, July 1930.

37. *Ibid.*, September 1930.

38. *The New York Times*, May 19, 1930.

39. Lillian Roth, with Mike Connolly and Gerold Frank, *I'll Cry Tomorrow* (New York: Frederick Fell, 1954), p. 84.

40. Adamson, *Groucho, Harpo*, p. 103.

41. Taylor scripts, March 30, 1930, and April 14, 1930, United Artists/Warner Bros. collection, University of Wisconsin–Madison.

42. *Big Boy*'s short run of 48 performances on Broadway is misleading, for the show was very well received and would have enjoyed a long stay had not Al Jolson become ill with bronchitis.

43. *The New York Times*, September 13, 1930.

44. Jack Haley's first featured part in a film was in *Follow Thru*, but it was really his second movie appearance. His debut was in a bit as a radio announcer in *Broadway Madness* (1927).

45. Eight of the actors credited in the film *Whoopee!* were in the original Broadway cast. They were Eddie Cantor, Ethel Shutta, Paul Gregory, John Rutherford, Spencer Charters, Chief Caupolican, Albert Hackett and William H. Philbrick.

46. A. Scott Berg, *Goldwyn: A Biography* (New York: Knopf, 1989), p. 197.

47. Eddie Cantor, *Take My Life* (Garden City, N. Y.: Doubleday, 1957), p. 154.

48. Berg, *Goldwyn*, p. 199.

49. *The New York Times*, October 1, 1930.

50. Higham, *Ziegfeld*, p. 204.

51. Tony Thomas and Jim Terry with Busby Berkeley, *The Busby Berkeley Book* (Greenwich, Conn.: New York Graphic Society, 1973), p. 25.

52. *Variety*, October 15, 1930.

53. James Robert Parish and William T. Leonard, *Hollywood Players: The Thirties* (New Rochelle, N. Y.: Arlington House, 1976), pp. 162, 164.

54. *The Film Daily*, December 28, 1930.

55. Ethan Mordden, *The Hollywood Musical* (New York: St. Martin's, 1981), p. 56.

56. The only other song sung in *Follow the Leader* is "Broadway, the Heart of the World," which is voiced by a male chorus over the opening and closing credits. The song played fragmentally on a piano as Ginger Rogers' character dances in her *Scandals* audition is "Brother, Just Laugh It Off," which had been heard previously in *Queen High*.

57. Anthony Slide, *The Vaudevillians: A Dictionary of Vaudeville Performers* (New York: Arlington House, 1981), p. 74.

58. *Variety*, December 12, 1930.

CHAPTER 5

1. The title of the film has been written as both *Sunnyside Up* or *Sunny Side Up*. The main title on screen reads as two words, but Fox's publicity, as well as all of the reviews we consulted, carried the

Sunny Side Up spelling. Both the photoplay and the title song were copyrighted as *Sunnyside Up,* which accounts for that usage throughout this text. However, the generic spelling is used to convey the broader sentiment of the title of this book.

2. *Variety,* September 4, 1929.

3. Scott Kolk, best known as one of the young soldiers in *All Quiet on the Western Front* (1930), was brought to Hollywood to perform in another Marion Davies musical, the aborted *Five O'Clock Girl.* Kolk, a discovery of Louis B. Mayer, was a drummer for the Meyer Davis Orchestra. However, he neither plays nor sings in *Marianne.*

4. *Marianne* was shot as a silent prior to the production of the talking version. In the silent, Oscar Shaw had the Lawrence Gray role, and Robert Castle and Robert Ames played the characters portrayed in the talkie by George Baxter and Cliff Edwards, respectively. Stage commitments kept Shaw and Ames from appearing in the dialogue film.

5. Fred Lawrence Guiles, *Marion Davies* (New York: McGraw-Hill, 1972), p. 257.

6. *The Film Daily,* October 20, 1929.

7. *Photoplay,* September 1929.

8. *Variety,* April 3, 1929.

9. Stanley Green, *Hollywood Musicals Year by Year* (Milwaukee: Hal Leonard, 1990), p. 8.

10. *Variety,* August 21, 1929.

11. *New York Daily Mirror,* October 4, 1929.

12. *Variety,* October 9, 1929.

13. Irene Kahn Atkins, interviewer, *David Butler: A Directors Guild of America Oral History* (Metuchen, N.J.: Directors Guild of America and Scarecrow Press, 1993), pp. 75, 78.

14. *Cinema,* February 1931.

15. Connie J. Billips, *Janet Gaynor: A Bio-Bibliography* (Westport, Conn.; Greenwood, 1992), p. 19.

16. *New York Herald Tribune,* October 4, 1929.

17. Atkins, *David Butler,* p. 78.

18. *The Film Daily,* December 29, 1929.

19. Sheridan Morley, *Gertrude Lawrence* (New York: McGraw-Hill, 1981), p. 71.

20. Robert Florey, *Hollywood d'hier et d'aujourd'hui* (Paris: Editions Prisma, 1948), pp. 158–159.

21. Brian Taves, *Robert Florey: The French Expressionist* (Metuchen, N.J.: Scarecrow, 1987), p. 106.

22. *Ibid.,* p. 118.

23. *Variety,* February 12, 1930.

24. *The New York Times,* December 2, 1929.

25. *Ibid.,* December 14, 1929.

26. *Variety,* June 5, 1929.

27. *Motion Picture,* February 1930.

28. *Photoplay,* April 1930.

29. Maureen O'Sullivan letter to author, April 17, 1994.

30. Lily McCormack, *I Hear You Calling Me* (Milwaukee: Bruce, 1949), p. 153.

31. *The New York Times,* March 12, 1930.

32. *Motion Picture,* July 1930.

33. McCormack, *Calling Me,* p. 153.

34. *Variety,* September 9, 1930.

35. *The New York Times,* April 19, 1930.

36. *The Film Daily,* June 22, 1930.

37. *Variety,* July 9, 1930.

38. *The New York Times,* August 30, 1930.

39. *Photoplay,* October 1930.

40. *The Film Daily,* October 5, 1930.

41. One of the actors on the dirigible is Katherine DeMille, the director's daughter. She was cast as one of the "wives" of the fellow costumed as King Henry VIII.

42. Lillian Roth, with Mike Connelly and Gerold Frank, *I'll Cry Tomorrow* (New York: Frederick Fell, 1954), p. 82.

43. Charles Higham, *Cecil B. DeMille* (New York: Scribner's, 1973), p. 198.

44. *Motion Picture,* November 1930.

45. Donald Hayne, ed., *The Autobiography of Cecil B. DeMille* (Englewood Cliffs, N. J.: Prentice-Hall, 1959), p. 301.

46. James Lincoln Collier, *Duke Ellington* (New York: Oxford University Press, 1987), p. 99.

47. *Variety*, April 16, 1930. To announce the acquisition of "Amos 'n' Andy," RKO filled up four pages of ads in *Variety*.

48. David Ewen, *American Songwriters* (New York: H. W. Wilson, 1987), p. 343.

49. Fox reportedly sealed a print of *Just Imagine* into an airtight can and placed it in a vault on its lot, where it was to be reopened and shown in 1980 (*Motion Picture Herald*, February 7, 1931). No word can be had about its fate.

50. O'Sullivan letter to author.

51. Atkins, *David Butler*, p. 98.

52. *Time*, December 8, 1930.

53. Beatrice Lillie with James Brough, *Every Other Inch a Lady* (Garden City, N. Y.: Doubleday, 1972), p. 226.

54. *Ibid.*, p. 215.

55. *Ibid.*, pp. 215–216.

56. *Variety*, July 14, 1931.

57. *Exhibitors Herald-World*, December 6, 1930.

CHAPTER 6

1. Roger Dooley, *From Scarface to Scarlett: American Films in the 1930s* (New York: Harcourt Brace Jovanovich, 1979), p. 432.

2. Gerald Bordman, *American Musical Theatre: A Chronicle* (New York: Oxford University Press, 1986), p. 427.

3. Warner Bros.' *The Time, the Place, and the Girl* (July 6, 1929) is often cited as the first college musical, but in fact it is not truly a musical. A hearing of the soundtrack for the 70-minute feature (the visuals are apparently lost) reveals two brief and incidental vocal numbers, not the musical content sufficient for inclusion in this book. Most of the nine songs credited to the film in many sources—"Collegiate," "Jack and Jill," et al.—are heard instrumentally in the background. The film, which starred Grant Withers and Betty Compson, was loosely based on the Frank R. Adams–Joseph E. Howard–Will Hough musical comedy of 1907, but none of the original score is heard in the talkie.

4. Phillips Holmes was originally announced for the cast of *Sweetie*, presumably for the Biff Bentley role. Another early name mentioned was Frank Ross. He was a Long Island real-estate agent discovered by Paramount for his fine baritone voice, but his career never panned out and he became better known in Hollywood as the husband of actress Jean Arthur.

5. *Variety*, October 30, 1929.

6. *Motion Picture News*, October 20, 1929.

7. *Time*, May 3, 1929.

8. *Motion Picture*, January 1930.

9. Douglas Fairbanks, Jr., interview with author, August 28, 1992.

10. *Ibid.*

11. *Ibid.*

12. Douglas Fairbanks, Jr., letter to author, July 14, 1993.

13. *Photoplay*, June 1930.

14. *Exhibitors Herald-World*, March 1, 1930.

15. *The New York Times*, March 30, 1930.

16. *Ibid.*

17. Joe Collura, "Penny Singleton: Not Only Blondie," *Classic Images*, October 1994, p. 22.

18. *Ibid.*, p. 24.

19. *Variety*, September 10, 1930.

20. *Photoplay*, August 1930.

21. Jackson script, undated, United Artists/Warner Bros. collection, University of Wisconsin–Madison.

CHAPTER 7

1. *Variety*, July 23, 1930.

2. Miles Kreuger, *Show Boat: The Story of a Classic American Musical* (New York: Oxford Univer-

sity Press, 1977), p. 76. Kreuger's book is the most complete history of the various incarnations of *Show Boat* through the mid '70s.

3. *Ibid.*, p. 83.

4. *Show Boat* premiered in Palm Beach, Florida, on March 16, 1929. The actual world premiere was to be held the previous evening in Miami, but a break-in at the theater caused the event to be canceled (Kreuger, p. 84). The film did not open in New York until April 17. We have used the Palm Beach date for this book's chronology, which explains why *Show Boat* is listed ahead of *The Desert Song*, which premiered in Los Angeles on April 8 and in New York on May 2.

5. *New York Herald Tribune*, April 18, 1929.

6. *The Film Daily*, April 17, 1929.

7. Souvenir program from the presentation of "The 50th Anniversary of *Show Boat*" by the Institute of the American Musical at the New York Museum of Modern Art, December 27, 1977.

8. In the prologue footage on laserdisc, all that could be used from the Helen Morgan numbers (according to Miles Kreuger, who narrated the disc material) was a frame blow-up from heavily deteriorated footage of "Can't Help Lovin' Dat Man."

9. The contract between Warner Bros. and the creators of *The Desert Song* is on file in the United Artists collection at the University of Wisconsin at Madison.

10. *Variety*, February 6, 1929.

11. James Kotsilibas-Davis and Myrna Loy, *Myrna Loy: Being and Becoming* (New York: Knopf, 1987), pp. 56–57.

12. *Photoplay*, June 1929.

13. *New York Herald Tribune*, May 2, 1929.

14. *Los Angeles Daily News*, February 27, 1951.

15. *The New York Times*, September 23, 1929.

16. John Kobal, *Gotta Sing Gotta Dance: A Pictorial History of Film Musicals* (London: Hamlyn, 1971), pp. 28–29.

17. Betty Lasky, *RKO, the Biggest Little Major of Them All* (Englewood Cliffs, N. J.: Prentice-Hall, 1984), p. 45.

18. Dorothy Lee interview with author.

19. According to Edward Watz's *Wheeler & Woolsey: The Vaudeville Comic Duo and Their Films, 1929–1937, Rio Rita* was abridged by RKO for its 1932 reissue. However, a restored print was to air in 1995 on the Turner Classic Movies cable channel.

20. Kobal, *Gotta Sing*, p. 31.

21. Dorothy Lee interview.

22. *Ibid.*

23. *Photoplay*, November 1929.

24. *Variety*, October 9, 1929.

25. *New York Herald Tribune*, October 7, 1929.

26. *Motion Picture*, February 1930.

27. *Ibid.*

28. *Time*, February 24, 1930.

29. Lawrence Tibbett, *The Glory Road* (privately published, 1933; reprinted by Arno Press, 1977), p. 53.

30. *Variety*, January 29, 1930.

31. William M. Drew, *Speaking of Silents: First Ladies of the Screen* (Vestal, N. Y.: Vestal Press, 1989), p. 207.

32. Randy Skretvedt, *Laurel and Hardy: The Magic Behind the Movies* (Beverly Hills, Calif.: Moonstone, 1987), p. 180.

33. Tibbett, *Glory Road*, p. 60.

34. *The New York Times*, January 29, 1930.

35. *Photoplay*, March 1930.

36. *Variety*, February 5, 1930.

37. Lillian Roth, with Mike Connolly and Gerold Frank, *I'll Cry Tomorrow* (New York: Frederick Fell, 1954), p. 75.

38. *Motion Picture*, April 1930.

39. Sharon Rich, *Sweethearts: The Timeless Love Affair—On-Screen and Off—Between Jeanette MacDonald and Nelson Eddy* (New York: Donald I. Fine, 1994), p. 94.

40. *Photoplay*, May 1930.

41. *The New York Times*, March 30, 1930.
42. *Photoplay*, July 1930.
43. *Time*, May 19, 1930.
44. *The New York Times*, June 7, 1930.
45. *Ibid.*, May 22, 1930.
46. *Variety*, June 25, 1930.
47. *The New York Times*, July 26, 1930.
48. Anthony Slide, "Vivienne Segal," *Film Fan Monthly*, August 1972.
49. *Photoplay*, January 1930.
50. Dorothy Lee interview.
51. Kobal, *Gotta Sing*, p. 33.
52. Dorothy Lee interview.
53. *Ibid.*
54. *Variety*, September 10, 1930.
55. *The New York Times*, September 6, 1930.
56. *Motion Picture*, November 1930.
57. *Variety*, September 10, 1930.
58. Grace Moore, *You're Only Human Once* (Garden City, N. Y.: Doubleday, 1944), p. 168.
59. *The New York Times*, November 8, 1930.
60. *Variety*, November 12, 1930.
61. *New York Graphic*, November 8, 1930.
62. Moore, *You're Only Human Once*, p. 169.
63. *Variety*, February 23, 1932.
64. Hugh Fordin, *Getting to Know Him: A Biography of Oscar Hammerstein II* (New York: Random House, 1977), p. 104.
65. *Variety*, December 3, 1930.
66. Fordin, *Getting to Know Him*, p. 104.
67. MGM initially planned to star Moore and Tibbett in a version of the operetta *Rose-Marie* (*Variety*, February 19, 1930).
68. *The New York Times*, July 27, 1930.
69. Moore, *You're Only Human Once*, p. 172.
70. *Variety*, December 31, 1930.
71. A Scott Berg, *Goldwyn: A Biography* (New York: Knopf, 1989), p. 206.
72. *Variety*, February 18, 1931.
73. *Ibid.*, December 31, 1930.
74. A silent version of *Mlle. Modiste* was produced under that title by First National in 1926. It starred Corinne Griffith and Norman Kerry and was directed by Robert Z. Leonard.
75. *Variety*, January 14, 1931.
76. The one feature film Bernice Claire made for Warner Bros.–First National that is not covered in this book is a non-musical crime melodrama, *Numbered Men* (1930). Her only other recorded credit in a feature is an unbilled cameo in the 1933 Universal musical *Moonlight and Pretzels*.

CHAPTER 8

1. *Variety*, November 13, 1929.
2. *Time*, March 10, 1930.
3. *The New York Times*, February 1, 1930.
4. Ewen, *American Songwriters*, pp. 10–11.
5. *The New York Times*, February 22, 1930.
6. Joan Benny and Jack Benny, *Sunday Nights at Seven: The Jack Benny Story* (New York: Warner Books, 1990), p. 38.
7. Anita Page interview with author.
8. *Variety*, February 5, 1930.
9. *The Film Daily*, July 6, 1930.
10. *Variety*, March 5, 1930.
11. *Ibid.*, March 12, 1930.

12. Herbert G. Goldman, *Fanny Brice: The Original Funny Girl* (New York: Oxford University Press, 1992), p. 143.

13. Roy Hemming, *The Melody Lingers On: The Great Songwriters and Their Movie Musicals* (New York: Newmarket Press, 1986), p. 189.

14. Laurence Bergreen, *As Thousands Cheer: The Life of Irving Berlin* (New York: Viking Penguin, 1990), p. 287.

15. Herbert G. Goldman, *Jolson: The Legend Comes to Life* (New York: Oxford University Press, 1988), p. 191.

16. Bergreen, *As Thousands Cheer*, p. 289.

17. *Variety*, February 19, 1930.

18. Harry Richman with Richard Gehman, *A Hell of a Life* (New York: Duell, Sloan & Pierce, 1966), p. 163.

19. *Variety*, February 19, 1930.

20. Jhan Robbins, *Inka Dinka Doo* (New York: Paragon House, 1991), pp. 89–90.

21. *Photoplay*, March 1930.

22. Marion Shilling Cook letter to author, January 12, 1993.

23. *Ibid.*

24. Marion Shilling Cook letter to author, January 29, 1993.

25. *Motion Picture*, April 1930.

26. *The New York Times*, March 8, 1930.

27. The Technicolor "Woman in the Shoe" number from *Lord Byron of Broadway* is part of the color short *Nertsery Rhymes* (1933), which is framed by newly shot comedy footage with Ted Healy and His Stooges (sans Healy, the "Stooges" later became The Three Stooges). The "Blue Daughter of Heaven" color sequence is included in the 1933 short *Roast Beef and Movies*, which starred George Givot and, in a rare appearance without fellow Stooges Moe Howard and Larry Fine, Jerome "Curly" Howard. If you're alert (because it's not identified as such), you can spot a few seconds of the "Woman in the Shoe" number in the MGM compilation film *That's Entertainment! III*.

28. Buster Keaton, *My Wonderful World of Slapstick* (Garden City, N. Y.: Doubleday, 1960), p. 201.

29. *Free and Easy* marked the first time Keaton's voice was heard on screen, but he was seen in *Hollywood Revue of 1929*, in which he, wordlessly and in drag, appeared in an Egyptian dance sequence (see Chapter 10).

30. *The New York Times*, April 19, 1930.

31. Anita Page interview.

32. *The New York Times*, March 27, 1930.

33. Goldman, *Jolson*, p. 195.

34. *Variety*, May 14, 1930.

35. *Photoplay*, June 1930.

36. *Variety*, August 26, 1930.

37. *Photoplay*, July 1930.

38. *Variety*, June 25, 1930.

39. Ilka Chase, *Past Imperfect* (Garden City, N. Y.: Doubleday, 1942), p. 120.

40. *Time*, June 9, 1930.

41. *The New York Times*, May 31, 1930.

42. *Variety*, June 4, 1930.

43. *The New York Times*, February 10, 1931.

44. *Variety*, October 29, 1930.

45. Before it became attached to the MacDonald comedy, *Oh, for a Man!* was the working title of an otherwise unrelated Janet Gaynor-Charles Farrell musical comedy that was announced in the spring of 1930 but never filmed (*The Film Daily*, May 1930).

CHAPTER 9

1. Thomas Schatz, *The Genius of the System* (New York: Pantheon, 1988), p. 75.

2. Although there were two black-themed musicals of 1929, only *Hallelujah!* is actually an all-black film—the first for Hollywood, in fact. The one white character in *Hearts in Dixie* appears in two scenes and the prologue.

3. Donald Bogle, *Blacks in American Film and Television: An Encyclopedia* (New York: Garland, 1988), p. 105.

4. *The New York Times*, February 28, 1929.

5. *New York Herald Tribune*, February 28, 1929.

6. King Vidor, *A Tree Is a Tree* (New York: Harcourt, Brace, 1952), p. 175.

7. *Ibid.*, p. 176.

8. *Motion Picture Classic*, February 1929.

9. *Ibid.*

10. Nancy Dowd and David Shepard, interviewers, *King Vidor: A Directors Guild of America Oral History* (Metuchen, N. J.: Directors Guild of America and Scarecrow Press, 1988), p. 103. In this oral history, Vidor said he was against the insertion of "Waiting at the End of the Road" because "it seemed to have a Tin Pan Alley popular Broadway sound to it that I didn't want. To this day it disturbs me." Not surprisingly, "Waiting at the End of the Road" became a pop hit as covered by Paul Whiteman and his band.

11. *Hallelujah!* was re-released in 1939, which explains the non-period titles that accompany the version of it that exists today on videotape and laserdisc.

12. *Variety*, August 28, 1929.

13. Daniel Haynes never played anything other than bit parts in his other Hollywood movies. He can be recognized as one of the African laborers in the Boris Karloff–Bela Lugosi horror film *The Invisible Ray* (1936). Nina Mae McKinney sang and danced in shorts, all-black features and occasional Hollywood films through the late 1940s—her last known credit was *Pinky* (1949)—but by the late '50s she was working as a maid. Victoria Spivey never appeared in another feature film, but she made blues records throughout the '30s and '40s as Queen Bee Spivey in a career that lasted well into the 1960s. In 1964, Spivey cut an album with her contemporary Big Joe Williams and the young Bob Dylan.

14. *New York Herald Tribune*, August 21, 1929.

15. Raymond Durgnat and Scott Simmon, *King Vidor, American* (Berkeley: University of California Press, 1988), p. 101.

16. Vidor, *Tree*, p. 183.

17. Donald Bogle, *Toms, Coons, Mulattoes, Mammies, and Bucks: An Interpretive History of Blacks in American Films* (New York: Viking, 1973), p. 30.

18. Charles Higham and Joel Greenberg, *The Celluloid Muse : Hollywood Directors Speak* (London: Argus & Robertson, 1969), p. 130.

19. *Ibid.*

20. *The Film Daily*, October 8, 1929.

21. *Variety*, April 10, 1929.

22. *Photoplay*, April 1930.

23. Higham and Greenberg, *Celluloid Muse*, p. 133.

24. For the record ... in addition to the 11 songs listed at the beginning of the essay on *Applause*, which are those presented vocally or which are played instrumentally to stage dances, these are heard: "Alexander's Ragtime Band" (over the opening credits), "There'll Be a Hot Time in the Old Town Tonight," "Smiles," Handel's "Largo," "That's My Weakness Now," "Sweetheart of All My Dreams," "I've Got a Feeling I'm Falling" and "Heigh-Ho! Everybody, Heigh-Ho!"

25. Higham and Greenberg, *Celluloid Muse*, p. 131.

26. *Ibid.*, p. 129.

27. *The New York Times*, November 20, 1929.

28. *Variety*, November 27, 1929.

29. *Photoplay*, November 1929.

30. *Variety*, November 27, 1929.

31. Edward Behr, *The Good Frenchman: The True Story of the Life and Times of Maurice Chevalier* (New York: Villard, 1993), p. 153.

32. David O. Selznick, who oversaw Paramount's story and writing staff, fought unsuccessfully against the risk of starring MacDonald in a film without a forceful leading man such as Chevalier (James Robert Parish, *The Jeanette MacDonald Story* [New York: Mason/Charter, 1976], p. 47).

33. *Cinema*, December 1930.

34. Ethan Mordden, *The Hollywood Musical* (New York: St. Martin's, 1981), p. 38.

35. Gerald Mast, *Can't Help Singin': The American Musical on Stage and Screen* (New York: Overlook, 1987), pp. 104–105.

36. When *Monte Carlo* was released, there was some talk (see *Variety*, September 10, 1930) that the

"Beyond the Blue Horizon" sequence looked distinctly similar to a portion of a German film, *Melody of the Heart,* released in 1929. In the earlier film, a song was also introduced on a railroad train as a chorus of peasants sang along from nearby fields. Lubitsch said at the time that he had not heard of the German film before the similarity was brought to his attention.

37. MacDonald also sang "Beyond the Blue Horizon" in the Universal wartime revue *Follow the Boys* (1944). Her rendition, during a USO-style show at a military base, takes on a decidedly different (and poignant) context, as the "beautiful day" is an Allied victory—a victory that many of the real soldiers who heard the song died to achieve. Because the lyric "rising star" was considered an indirect reference to the enemy Japanese, the words were changed to "shining star."

38. *Variety,* September 3, 1930.

39. *The New York Times,* August 28, 1930.

40. *Motion Picture,* November 1930.

41. Philip Castanza, *The Films of Jeanette MacDonald and Nelson Eddy* (Secaucus, N. J.: Citadel, 1978), p. 23.

CHAPTER 10

1. David Stenn, *Clara Bow: Runnin' Wild* (New York: Doubleday, 1988), p. 182.

2. *Variety,* May 14, 1930.

3. Besides the titles mentioned in the text, the other songs copyrighted for *The March of Time* were "Goodbye" (George Ward, Reggie Montgomery); "Poor Little G String" (Roy Turk, Fred E. Ahlert); "Meditation Brings Me You" (Howard Johnson, Dimitri Tiomkin); and "There's a Kick in the Old Girl, Yet" (Dorothy Fields, Jimmy McHugh).

4. *The New York Times,* August 15, 1929.

5. The Brox Sisters filmed at least two other songs for *The Hollywood Revue of 1929,* "Just You, Just Me" and "Hang On to Me." Those numbers appeared in *Gems of MGM,* a two-reel short that consisted of sequences cut from the revue. The short, hosted by Benny Rubin, also featured Marion Harris, who sang "She's Funny That Way" as "I'm Funny That Way," and Belcher's Kiddie Ballet. "Just You, Just Me" and "Hang On to Me" were put to better use in the Marion Davies musical *Marianne* (see Chapter 5).

6. *Variety,* September 25, 1929.

7. Another Warners–First National contractee who missed out on *The Show of Shows* was Jack Buchanan, who filmed a comedy sequence that was dropped. "The Glee Quartet" was based on Buchanan's popular number in the London stage version of *Sunny* in which he played the antic last-minute substitute in a glee-club foursome. Warner Bros. released "The Glee Quartet" as a short subject in early 1930.

8. The only surviving color footage from *The Show of Shows* is the "Li-Po-Li" number featuring Nick Lucas, Myrna Loy and the Jack Haskell Girls.

9. In the MGM compilation *That's Dancing* (1985), some of the "Lady Luck" sequence was excerpted to prove the film's broad assertion that all early talkie musical numbers were boring and unimaginative. Unfortunately, this example makes the point well.

10. *The New York Times,* November 21, 1930.

11. *Happy Days* was released at 86 minutes, according to the *Variety* review, but it was advertised shortly before release as "1 hour and 40 minutes of the greatest entertainment you've ever seen or heard." As the actor Gilbert Emery is listed in the cast in those same ads, one might assume that his footage was cut, as could have been an advertised comedy sequence that included "6 minutes of James J. Corbett, William Collier and Walter Catlett trying to find Jim Jeffries' glove." Corbett and Jeffries were both retired heavyweight boxing champions.

12. *The New York Times,* February 14, 1930.

13. Eleanor Knowles, *The Films of Jeanette MacDonald and Nelson Eddy* (New York: A. S. Barnes, 1975), p. 55.

14. *Variety,* April 23, 1930.

15. *The New York Times,* April 21, 1930.

16. Another of Paramount's top young performers, Jeanette MacDonald, was absent from the American release of *Paramount on Parade,* but she did host a Spanish-language version, *Galas de la Paramount,* and sang in it in place of Nino Martini. In a French version, most of the English song sequences were retained (albeit dubbed), but the comedy scenes—including the three by Maurice Chevalier—were refilmed.

17. The filming of *King of Jazz* came too late to include Leon "Bix" Biederbecke, Whiteman's star cornetist. Biederbecke, an alcoholic, became ill during a recording session in the late summer of 1929 and was put by Whiteman on a train for his hometown of Davenport, Iowa, where he was to recuperate on sick leave. Biederbecke never rejoined the band to make the trip to Los Angeles. He died in 1931. Another early death occurred during the Whiteman unit's initial stay in California, when band member Mario Perry was killed in an auto accident.

18. *Photoplay*, June 1930.

19. John Murray Anderson with Hugh A. Anderson, *Out Without My Rubbers: The Memoirs of John Murray Anderson* (New York: Library Publishers, 1954), p. 124.

20. Although Gershwin did not participate on screen in *King of Jazz*, he did appear on stage with Whiteman and orchestra to perform "Rhapsody in Blue" to accompany the film during its first week in New York. *King of Jazz* opened at the Roxy Theatre on May 2, 1930.

21. *The New York Times*, May 3, 1930.

22. *Variety*, May 7, 1930.

23. Thomas A. DeLong, *Pops: Paul Whiteman, King of Jazz* (Piscataway, N. J.: New Century, 1983), p. 149.

24. One of the foreign-language versions of *King of Jazz* was in Hungarian, and featured horrormeister Bela Lugosi as the host.

CHAPTER 11

1. Fred Lawrence Guiles, *Marion Davies* (New York: McGraw-Hill, 1972), p. 250.

2. *Variety*, November 19, 1930.

3. *Ibid.*, October 1, 1930.

4. *Motion Picture*, December 1930.

5. *The Film Daily*, October 5, 1930.

6. *Photoplay*, December 1930.

7. *Variety*, June 25, 1930. *Top Speed* was the other 1929-30 Broadway musical boosted by Warner Bros. money. The studio made it into a musical comedy (see Chapter 4) in 1930.

8. A fragment of "He Looks So Good to Me," a rewrite of Rodgers and Hart's "He Was Too Good to Me" from their Broadway show *Simple Simon,* is heard as background music during a party scene in *The Hot Heiress.* "How About It?" which was copyrighted for use in *Heiress,* turned up instead in Rodgers and Hart's 1931 stage musical *America's Sweetheart.*

9. Richard Rodgers, *Richard Rodgers, Musical Stages: An Autobiography* (New York: Random House, 1975), p. 139.

10. John Kobal, *Gotta Sing Gotta Dance: A Pictorial History of Film Musicals* (London: Hamlyn, 1971), p. 47.

11. Scott Eyman, *Ernst Lubitsch: Laughter in Paradise* (New York: Simon & Schuster, 1993), p. 167.

12. *New York Telegram*, May 24, 1931.

13. *New York Herald Tribune*, May 24, 1931.

14. *Photoplay*, July 1931.

15. *Variety*, June 30, 1931.

16. *The Film Daily*, July 19, 1931.

17. *Variety*, July 21, 1931.

18. *The New York Times*, July 20, 1931.

19. *Photoplay*, April 1931.

20. "Dunk! Dunk! Dunk!" was copyrighted for use in *Palmy Days* but is heard only in the background as Eddie gives a restaurant patron a donut-dunking lesson. The pressbook also lists "Goose Pimples" by Ballard MacDonald, Dave Silverstein and Con Conrad, but there is no song by that name on the cue sheet or in the print of the film watched for this book.

21. *Photoplay*, October 1931.

22. Ronald J. Fields, *W. C. Fields: A Life on Film* (New York: St. Martin's, 1984), p. 79.

23. *The New York Times*, November 26, 1931.

24. Harris, *The Other Marilyn*, p. 185.

25. *Variety*, December 15, 1931.

26. *New York Graphic*, December 12, 1931.

27. *Variety*, November 17, 1931.

28. *The New York Times*, December 5, 1931.
29. Lawrence Tibbett, *The Glory Road* (privately published, 1933; reprinted by Arno Press, 1977), p. 68.
30. *Ibid.*
31. Charles Schwartz, *Gershwin: His Life and Music* (Indianapolis: Bobbs-Merrill, 1973), p. 197.
32. "Lady of the Moon" previously had been reworked by Gershwin as "I Just Looked at You," which was cut from the score of the stage musical *Show Girl.*
33. Schwartz, *Gershwin,* p. 201.
34. *Motion Picture* Herald, December 12, 1931.

CHAPTER 12

1. *42nd Street* was actually the third musical to debut in 1933. The first was *Hallelujah, I'm a Bum* (United Artists; January 27), which featured Al Jolson and a Rodgers and Hart score in a rare Depression-centered tale about a group of hoboes living in Central Park. Lewis Milestone directed with an ear toward experimentation; the talk was in rhyming couplets to ease transitions to the rhythmic dialogue of the song numbers. But the film, which cost a lofty $1.2 million to produce, flopped badly. The last two pictures on Jolson's lucrative $25,000-a-week, three-film United Artists contract were never made. The second musical released in '33 was Paramount's *Hello Everybody* (January 29), the unsuccessful starring debut of singer Kate Smith. Smith played a farm girl whose rise to radio vocal stardom is blunted by her unrequited love for the man (Randolph Scott) who loves her sister (Sally Blane). Smith sang five Arthur Johnston–Sam Coslow songs.
2. *42nd Street* opened in New York at the Strand Theatre on March 8, 1933, but it had already played in other cities around the country as part of a publicity tour by the "42nd Street Special," a train that carried some famous cargo. Among the Warners contractees aboard were Bette Davis, Tom Mix, Joe E. Brown, Preston Foster and Laura La Plante. The tour began in Denver on February 23 before heading East and arriving in New York on March 9.
3. Mel Gussow, *Don't Say "Yes" Until I Finish Talking: A Biography of Darryl F. Zanuck* (Garden City, N. Y.: Doubleday, 1971), p. 56.
4. J. Hoberman, *42nd Street* (London: British Film Institute, 1993), p. 29.
5. *The Film Daily,* February 3, 1933.
6. *Photoplay,* July 1932.
7. Scott Eyman, *Ernst Lubitsch: Laughter in Paradise* (New York: Simon & Schuster, 1993), p. 188.
8. The fullest account of the Lubitsch-Cukor dispute can be found in a 1979 doctoral thesis by historian Barry Sabath, "Ernst Lubitsch and Samson Raphaelson: A Study in Collaboration." Sabath concludes that Lubitsch directed virtually all of the important footage in *One Hour with You.*
9. Original "final" Samson Raphaelson script, Paramount collection, Academy of Motion Picture Arts and Sciences Library.
10. *The New York Times,* March 24, 1932.
11. *The American Film Institute Catalog of Motion Pictures, Feature Films, 1931–40* (New York: Bowker, 1993), p. 758.
12. Edward Watz, *Wheeler & Woolsey: The Vaudeville Comic Duo and Their Films, 1929–1937* (Jefferson, N.C.: McFarland, 1994), p. 159.
13. *Variety,* March 29, 1932.
14. Edward Jablonski, *Gershwin* (New York: Doubleday, 1987), p. 210.
15. The durability of the Gershwins' music was verified impressively when a "new" Gershwin musical comedy, *Crazy for You,* debuted in New York in 1992. It was essentially the book from *Girl Crazy* updated a bit, with the heart of that score combined with other Gershwin standards ("They Can't Take That Away from Me," "Someone to Watch Over Me") and some rarely heard material. But in the idea-starved climate of modern musical theater, *Crazy for You* was a huge hit. At this writing, it is still playing on Broadway and touring to packed houses.
16. Dorothy Lee interview with author.
17. *The New York Times,* April 16, 1932.
18. *Variety,* April 19, 1932.
19. *Photoplay,* October 1932.
20. Gene Ringgold and DeWitt Bodeen, *Chevalier: The Films and Career of Maurice Chevalier* (Secaucus, N.J.: Citadel, 1973), p. 112.

21. Mamoulian told Charles Higham and Joel Greenberg in *The Celluloid Muse* (p. 136) that the idea of a song traveling from Paris through various sources came "from a story my grandmother told me, about a prince who finds a piece of embroidery blown by the wind over seven seas and seven lands, and says that whoever made it must be his wife. Finally he discovers her, and she's a princess."

22. Two Rodgers and Hart songs, "Give Me Just a Moment" and "The Man for Me (The Letter Song)" were dropped from *Love Me Tonight* before its release.

23. Richard Rodgers, *Richard Rogers, Musical Stages: An Autobiography* (New York: Random House, 1975), p. 152.

24. James Kotsilibas-Davis and Myrna Loy, *Myrna Loy: Being and Becoming* (New York: Knopf, 1987), p. 72.

25. *The New York Times*, August 18, 1932.

26. *Time*, August 29, 1932.

27. *Los Angeles Times*, August 14, 1982.

28. *Variety*, November 22, 1932.

29. John McCabe, *George M. Cohan: The Man Who Invented Broadway* (Garden City, N. Y.: Doubleday, 1973), p. 136. Cohan is said to have agreed in 1928 to write the script and songs, as well as produce and direct, an Al Jolson movie for United Artists, but the film was never made.

30. Rodgers, *Musical Stages*, p. 154.

31. A song called "We Need a Man," written by Cohan, is linked with *The Phantom President* in copyright records, but it is not on the ASCAP cue sheet and does not appear to be in the film.

32. Lawrence J. Quirk, *Claudette Colbert: An Illustrated Biography* (New York: Crown, 1985), p. 50. The quote is taken from an interview Colbert gave to William A. Raidy of the Newark Sunday *Star-Ledger* in 1981.

33. *Photoplay*, November 1932.

34. John Beal played the young singer in *Wild Waves* who successfully substitutes for a top radio crooner, gets fired for absenteeism, and then straightens himself out to find happiness.

35. George Burns interview with author, September 29, 1992, for *Flint Journal* article of September 30, 1992.

36. *Photoplay*, January 1933.

37. A Scott Berg, *Goldwyn: A Biography* (New York: Knopf, 1989), p. 226.

BIBLIOGRAPHY

Adamson, Joe. *Groucho, Harpo, Chico, and Sometimes Zeppo.* New York: Simon & Schuster, 1973.

The American Film Institute Catalog of Motion Pictures: Feature Films, 1911–20. New York: Bowker, 1988.

The American Film Institute Catalog of Motion Pictures: Feature Films, 1921–30. New York: Bowker, 1971.

The American Film Institute Catalog of Motion Pictures: Feature Films, 1931–40. New York: Bowker, 1993.

Anderson, John Murray, with Hugh A. Anderson. *Out Without My Rubbers: The Memoirs of John Murray Anderson.* New York: Library Publishers, 1954.

Anobile, Richard J. *Hooray for Captain Spaulding: Verbal and Visual Gems from "Animal Crackers."* New York: Crown, 1974.

Atkins, Irene Kahn, interviewer. *David Butler: A Directors Guild of America Oral History.* Metuchen, N.J.: Directors Guild of America and Scarecrow Press, 1993.

Basten, Fred E. *Glorious Technicolor: The Movies' Magic Rainbow.* New York: A. S. Barnes, 1980.

Behr, Edward. *The Good Frenchman: The True Story of the Life and Times of Maurice Chavalier.* New York: Villard, 1993.

Benjamin, Ruth, and Rosenblatt, Arthur. *Movie Song Catalog: Performers and Supporting Crew for the Songs Sung in 1,460 Musical and Nonmusical Films, 1928–1988.* Jefferson, N.C.: McFarland, 1993.

Benny, Joan, and Benny, Jack. *Sunday Nights at Seven: The Jack Benny Story.* New York: Warner Books, 1990.

Berg, A. Scott. *Goldwyn: A Biography.* New York: Knopf, 1989.

Bergan, Ronald. *The United Artists Story.* New York: Crown, 1986.

Bergreen, Laurence. *As Thousands Cheer: The Life of Irving Berlin.* New York: Viking Penguin, 1990.

Billips, Connie J. *Janet Gaynor: A Bio-Bibliography.* Westport, Conn.: Greenwood, 1992.

_____. *Maureen O'Sullivan: A Bio-Bibliography.* Westport, Conn.: Greenwood, 1990.

Bloom, Ken. *American Song: Vol. 1, Musical Theatre Companion, 1900–1984.* New York: Facts on File, 1985.

Bogle, Donald. *Blacks in American Film and Television: An Encyclopedia.* New York: Garland, 1988.

_____. *Toms, Coons, Mulattoes, Mammies, and Bucks: An Interpretive History of Blacks in American Films.* New York: Viking, 1973.

Bordman, Gerald. *American Musical Theatre: A Chronicle.* New York: Oxford University Press, 1978.

_____. *Days to Be Happy, Years to Be Sad: The Life and Music of Vincent Youmans.* New York: Oxford University Press, 1982.

_____. *Jerome Kern: His Life and Music.* New York: Oxford University Press, 1980.

Burton, Jack. *The Blue Book of Hollywood Musicals.* Watkins Glen, N.Y.: Century House, 1953.

Cantor, Eddie. *Take My Life.* Garden City, N.Y.: Doubleday, 1957.

Carey, Gary. *All the Stars in Heaven: Louis B. Mayer's MGM.* New York: Dutton, 1981.

Carringer, Robert L., ed. *The Jazz Singer.* Madison: University of Wisconsin Press, 1979.

Castanza, Philip. *The Films of Jeanette MacDonald and Nelson Eddy.* Secaucus, N.J.: Citadel, 1978.

Chase, Ilka. *Past Imperfect.* Garden City, N.Y.: Doubleday, 1942.

Chevalier, Maurice. *The Man in the Straw Hat: My Story.* New York: Crowell, 1949.

Collier, James Lincoln. *Duke Ellington.* New York: Oxford University Press, 1987.,

Cooper, Jackie. *Please Don't Shoot My Dog.* New York: Morrow, 1981.

Coslow, Sam. *Cocktails for Two: The Many Lives of Giant Songwriter Sam Coslow.* New Rochelle, N.Y.: Arlington House, 1971.

DeLong, Thomas A. *Pops: Paul Whiteman, King of Jazz.* Piscataway, N.J.: New Century, 1983.

Dickens, Homer. *The Films of Ginger Rogers.* Secaucus, N.J.: Citadel, 1975.

Dooley, Roger. *From Scarface to Scarlett: American Films in the 1930s.* New York: Harcourt Brace Jovanovich, 1979.

Dowd, Nancy, and Shepard, David, interviewers. *King Vidor: A Directors Guild of America Oral History.* Metuchen, N.J.: Directors Guild of America and Scarecrow Press, 1988.

Drew, William M. *Speaking of Silents: First Ladies of the Screen.* Vestal, N.Y.: Vestal Press, 1989.

Durgnat, Raymond, and Simmon, Scott. *King Vidor, American.* Berkeley: University of California Press, 1988.

Eames, John Douglas. *The MGM Story.* New York: Crown, 1975.

_____. *The Paramount Story.* New York: Crown, 1985.

Everson, William K. *American Silent Film.* New York: Oxford University Press, 1978.

Ewen, David. *American Songwriters.* New York: H. W. Wilson, 1987.

_____. *The New Complete Book of the American Musical Theatre.* New York: Holt, Rinehart & Winston, 1970.

Eyman, Scott. *Ernst Lubitsch: Laughter in Paradise.* New York: Simon & Schuster, 1993.

Fairbanks, Douglas, Jr. *The Salad Days.* New York: Doubleday, 1988.

Farkas, Andrew, ed. *Lawrence Tibbett: Singing Actor.* Portland, Ore.: Amadeus Press, 1989.

Fernett, Gene. *Poverty Row.* Satellite Beach, Fla.: Coral Reef Publications, 1973.

Fields, Ronald J. *W. C. Fields: A Life on Film.* New York: St. Martin's, 1984.

Florey, Robert. *Hollywood d'hier et d'aujourd'hui.* Paris: Editions Prisma, 1948.

Fordin, Hugh. *Getting to Know Him: A Biography of Oscar Hammerstein II.* New York: Random House, 1977.

Fumento, Rocco, ed. *42nd Street.* Madison: University of Wisconsin Press, 1980.

Geduld, Harry M. *The Birth of the Talkies.* Bloomington: Indiana University Press, 1975.

Goldman, Herbert G. *Fanny Brice: The Original Funny Girl.* New York: Oxford University Press, 1992.

_____. *Jolson: The Legend Comes to Life.* New York: Oxford University Press, 1988.

Green, Abel, and Laurie, Joe, Jr. *Show Biz: From Vaude to Video.* New York: Henry Holt, 1951.

Green, Stanley. *Encyclopaedia of the Musical Film.* New York: Oxford University Press, 1981.

_____. *Hollywood Musicals Year by Year.* Milwaukee: Hal Leonard, 1990.

_____. *Ring Bells! Sing Songs! Broadway Musicals of the 1930s.* New York: Galahad, 1971.

_____, ed. *Rodgers & Hammerstein Fact Book.* New York: Lynn Farnol, 1980.

Grossman, Barbara W. *Funny Woman: The Life and Times of Fanny Brice.* Bloomington: Indiana University Press, 1991.

Guiles, Fred Lawrence. *Marion Davies.* New York: McGraw-Hill, 1972.

Gussow, Mel. *Don't Say "Yes" Until I Finish Talking: A Biography of Darryl F. Zanuck.* Garden City, N.Y.: Doubleday, 1971.

Harris, Steve. *Film, Television and Stage Music on Phonograph Records: A Discography.* Jefferson, N.C.: McFarland, 1988.

Harris, Warren G. *Cary Grant: A Touch of Elegance.* New York: Doubleday, 1987.

_____. *The Other Marilyn: A Biography of Marilyn Miller.* New York: Arbor House, 1985.

Hart, Dorothy, and Kimball, Robert, eds. *The Complete Lyrics of Lorenz Hart.* New York: Knopf, 1986.

Hayne, Donald, ed. *The Autobiography of C. B. DeMille.* Englewood Cliffs, N.J.: Prentice-Hall, 1959.

Hemming, Roy. *The Melody Lingers On: The Great Songwriters and Their Movie Musicals.* New York: Newmarket Press, 1986.

Higham, Charles. *Cecil B. DeMille.* New York: Scribner's, 1973.

_____. *Merchant of Dreams: Louis B. Mayer, MGM, and the Secret Hollywood.* New York: Donald I. Fine, 1993.

_____. *Ziegfeld.* Chicago: Regnery, 1972.

_____, and Greenberg, Joel. *The Celluloid Muse: Hollywood Directors Speak.* London: Argus & Robertson, 1969.

Hirschhorn, Clive. *The Columbia Story.* New York: Crown, 1989.

_____. *The Hollywood Musical.* New York: Crown, 1980.

_____. *The Universal Story.* New York: Crown, 1983.

_____. *The Warner Bros. Story.* New York: Crown, 1979.

Hoberman, J. *42nd Street.* London: British Film Institute, 1993.

Hummel, David. *The Collector's Guide to the American Musical Theatre, Volume 1, The Shows.* Metuchen, N.J.: Scarecrow, 1984.

Jablonski, Edward. *Gershwin.* New York: Doubleday, 1987.

Jacobs, Diane. *Christmas in July: The Life and Art of Preston Sturges.* Berkeley: University of California Press, 1992.

Jasen, David A. *Tin Pan Alley: The Composers, the Songs, the Performers, and Their Times*. New York: Donald I. Fine, 1988.

Jay, David. *The Irving Berlin Songography*. New Rochelle, N.Y.: Arlington House, 1969.

Jewell, Richard B., with Vernon Harbin. *The RKO Story*. New York: Arlington House, 1982.

Katkov, Norman. *The Fabulous Fanny: The Story of Fanny Brice*. New York: Knopf, 1952.

Keaton, Buster. *My Wonderful World of Slapstick*. Garden City, N.Y.: Doubleday, 1960.

Knowles, Eleanor. *The Films of Jeanette MacDonald and Nelson Eddy*. New York: A. S. Barnes, 1975.

Kobal, John. *Gotta Sing Gotta Dance: A Pictorial History of Film Musicals*. London: Hamlyn, 1971.

_____. *People Will Talk*. New York: Knopf, 1986.

Kotsilibas-Davis, James. *The Barrymores: The Royal Family in Hollywood*. New York: Crown, 1981.

_____, and Loy, Myrna. *Myrna Loy: Being and Becoming*. New York: Knopf, 1987.

Kreuger, Miles. *Show Boat: The Story of a Classic American Musical*. New York: Oxford University Press, 1977.

_____, ed. *The Movie Musical from Vitaphone to 42nd Street, as Reported in a Great Fan Magazine*. New York: Dover, 1975.

Lamparski, Richard. *Whatever Became Of?* (various volumes). New York: Crown.

Lasky, Betty. *RKO, the Biggest Little Major of Them All*. Englewood Cliffs, N.J.: Prentice-Hall, 1984.

Levant, Oscar. *The Memoirs of an Amnesiac*. New York: Putnam, 1965.

Lillie, Beatrice, with James Brough. *Every Other Inch a Lady*. Garden City, N.Y.: Doubleday, 1972.

Lorentz, Pare. *Lorentz on Film: Movies 1927 to 1941*. New York: Hopkinson and Blake, 1975.

McCabe, John. *George M. Cohan: The Man Who Invented Broadway*. Garden City, N.Y.: Doubleday, 1973.

McCormick, Lily. *I Hear You Calling Me*. Milwaukee: Bruce, 1949.

Maltin, Leonard. *The Great Comedy Shorts*. New York: Bonanza, 1972.

_____. *Movie Comedy Teams*. New York: Plume, 1970.

Mantle, Burns. *The Best Plays* (annual editions). New York: Dodd, Mead.

Marshall, Michael. *Top Hat and Tails: The Story of Jack Buchanan*. London: Elm Tree, 1978.

Marx, Groucho. *Groucho and Me*. New York: Random House, 1959.

_____, and Anobile, Richard J. *The Marx Bros. Scrapbook*. New York: Darien House, 1973.

Marx, Samuel. *Meyer and Thalberg: The Make-Believe Saints*. New York: Random House, 1975.

Mast, Gerald. *Can't Help Singin': The American Musical on Stage and Screen*. New York: Overlook, 1987.

Mattfeld, Julius. *Variety Music Cavalcade: Musical Historical Review, 1620–1961*. New York: Prentice-Hall, 1952.

Moore, Colleen. *Silent Star*. Garden City, N.Y.: Doubleday, 1968.

Moore, Grace. *You're Only Human Once*. Garden City, N.Y.: Doubleday, 1944.

Mordden, Ethan. *The Hollywood Musical*. New York: St. Martin's, 1981.

Morley, Sheridan. *Gertrude Lawrence*. New York: McGraw-Hill, 1981.

Mosley, Leonard. *Zanuck: The Rise and Fall of Hollywood's Last Tycoon*. Boston: Little, Brown, 1984.

Nolan, Frederick. *Lorenz Hart: A Poet on Broadway*. New York: Oxford University Press, 1994.

Oakie, Jack. *Jack Oakie's Double Takes*. San Francisco: Strawberry Hill, 1980.

Parish, James Robert. *The Jeanette MacDonald Story*. New York: Mason/Charter, 1976.

_____, and Leonard, William T. *Hollywood Players: The Thirties*. New Rochelle, N.Y.: Arlington House, 1976.

_____, and Pitts, Michael R. *The Great Hollywood Musicals*. Metuchen, N.J.: Scarecrow, 1992.

_____, and _____. *Hollywood Songsters: A Biographical Dictionary*. New York: Garland, 1991.

Quirk, Lawrence J. *Claudette Colbert: An Illustrated Biography*. New York: Crown, 1985.

Rich, Sharon. *Sweethearts: The Timeless Love Affair—On-Screen and Off—Between Jeanette MacDonald and Nelson Eddy*. New York: Donald I. Fine, 1994.

Richman, Harry, with Richard Gehman. *A Hell of a Life*. New York: Duell, Sloan & Pierce, 1966.

Ringgold, Gene, and Bodeen, DeWitt. *Chevalier: The Films and Career of Maurice Chevalier*. Secaucus, N.J.: Citadel, 1973.

Robbins, Jhan. *Inka Dinka Doo*. New York: Paragon House, 1991.

Rodgers, Richard. *Musical Stages: An Autobiography*. New York: Random House, 1975.

Roth, Lillian, with Mike Connolly and Gerold Frank. *I'll Cry Tomorrow*. New York: Frederick Fell, 1954.

Rust, Brian. *The American Dance Band Discography, 1917–1942* (Vols. 1 and 2). New Rochelle, N.Y.: Arlington House, 1975.

_____, with Allen G. Debus. *The Complete Entertainment Discography, from the Mid–1890s to 1942*. New Rochelle, N.Y.: Arlington House, 1973.

Schatz, Thomas. *The Genius of the System*. New York: Pantheon, 1988.

Schwartz, Charles. *Gershwin: His Life and Music*. Indianapolis: Bobbs-Merrill, 1973.

Shales, Tom, et al. *The American Film Heritage: Impressions from the American Film Institute Archives.* Washington, D. C.: Acropolis, 1972.

Skretvedt, Randy. *Laurel and Hardy: The Magic Behind the Movies.* Beverly Hills, Calif.: Moonstone, 1987.

Slide, Anthony. *The Encyclopedia of Vaudeville.* Westport, Conn.: Greenwood, 1994.

_____. *The Vaudevillians: A Dictionary of Vaudeville Performers.* New York: Arlington House, 1981.

Stenn, David. *Clara Bow: Runnin' Wild.* New York: Doubleday, 1988.

Swindell, Larry. *Screwball: The Life of Carole Lombard.* New York: Morrow, 1975.

Taves, Brian. *Robert Florey: The French Expressionist.* Metuchen, N.J.: Scarecrow, 1987.

Thomas, Bob. *Clown Prince of Hollywood: The Antic Life and Times of Jack L. Warner.* New York: McGraw-Hill, 1990.

Thomas, Tony, and Terry, Jim, with Busby Berkeley. *The Busby Berkeley Book.* Greenwich, Conn.: New York Graphic Society, 1973.

_____, and Solomon, Aubrey. *The Films of 20th Century–Fox: A Pictorial History.* Secaucus, N.J.: Citadel, 1979.

Tibbett, Lawrence. *The Glory Road.* Arno Press, 1977 (reprinting of memoirs privately published in 1933).

Truitt, Evelyn Mack. *Who Was Who on Screen.* New York: Bowker, 1974 and 1984.

Tucker, Sophie. *Some of These Days.* Garden City, N.Y.: Doubleday, 1945.

Tuska, Jon. *The Detective in Hollywood.* Garden City, N.Y.: Doubleday, 1978.

Vidor, King. *A Tree Is a Tree.* New York: Harcourt, Brace, 1952.

Wagner, Walter. *You Must Remember This.* New York: Putnam, 1975.

Walker, Alexander. *The Shattered Silents.* London: Elm Tree, 1978.

Warner, Jack L., and Jennings, Dean. *My First Hundred Years in Hollywood.* New York: Random House, 1964.

Waters, Ethel, with Charles Samuels. *His Eye Is on the Sparrow.* New York: Doubleday, 1950.

Watz, Edward. *Wheeler & Woolsey: The Vaudeville Comic Duo and Their Films, 1929–1937.* Jefferson, N.C.: McFarland, 1994.

Weinberg, Herman G. *The Lubitsch Touch: A Critical Study.* New York: Dutton, 1968.

Whitburn, Joel, ed. *Joel Whitburn's Pop Memories: 1890–1954.* Menomonee Falls, Wis.: Record Research Inc., 1986.

Wilk, Max. *The Wit and Wisdom of Hollywood.* New York: Atheneum, 1971.

Wray, Fay. *On the Other Hand: A Life Story.* New York: St. Martin's, 1989.

INDEX

Numbers in **boldface** *refer to pages with photographs.*